The Carnegie Official History of
Yorkshire County Cricket Club

The Carnegie
Official History of
Yorkshire County
Cricket Club

Derek Hodgson

Leeds Met Press

First published 1989 by
The Crowood Press
Ramsbury
Marlborough
Wiltshire SN8 2HE

This edition published 2009 by
Leeds Met Press
Leeds Metropolitan University
Old School Board
Calverley Street
Leeds LS1 3ED

British Library Cataloguing-in-Publication data
A catalogue record for this book is available from the British
Library.

ISBN 978-0-9560099-4-4

Designed and typeset by Collective (UK) Ltd.
Printed in the UK by Collective (UK) Ltd.

'The old Firm'. Holmes (left) and Sutcliffe reunited.
Ron Deaton collection

Contents

Acknowledgements

The major sources for this History are recorded elsewhere. The author is also grateful to the following:

Joe Lister, Charles Burgess, Philip Shaw, Kathleen Rainford, Bill Bridge, David Hopps, John Featherstone, the Reverend Malcolm Lorimer, John Callaghan, David Warner, Anthony Woodhouse, Roy Wilkinson, Richard Streeton, Edward Sheard, J.B. Daffern, Lascelles Hall CC, Paul Dyson, Alan Thompson, Tom Naylor, Jeremy Lonsdale, Prior Timothy Ratcliffe, Andrew Barker, Roger Mann, Peter Pickup, Peter Davy, Henry Norris, Mark Graham, Jack Sokell, A.D. Oates, Mick Pope, N. Pearn, Sir Leonard Hutton, Jean Ough, N.W.D. Yardley, Bill Bowes, David Bairstow, Constance Whitworth, Margaret Thomas, Moira Banks, Graham Hart, Viscount Mountgarret, Sir Lawrence Byford, Keith Moss, Bob Platt, Chris Hassell, Robin Smith, David Hall, Ron Deaton, David Byas, James Greenfield, Stewart Regan, Liz Neto, Tony Collins, Dave Russell, Andrea Rayner, Alex Waring, Jahanara Khatun, Bethan Thomas, Claire Mortimer, Duncan Hamilton, Martyn Moxon, Steve Oldham, Kevin Sharp, Anthony Bradbury, Martin Howe, David Clay, Matt Reeder and Ben Cotton.

DEREK HODGSON
December 2008

The author and publishers are grateful to the following for permission to reproduce photographs:

Yorkshire County Cricket Club, Yorkshire Post Newspapers Ltd, Ron Deaton collection, Mick Pope.

Foreword

Yorkshire County Cricket Club has a long and proud history. Leeds Metropolitan University is delighted both to celebrate that history through the production of this excellent book and to be so involved in the club's exciting plans for the future. As Derek Hodgson makes clear, Yorkshire was at the forefront of the modern game in the Victorian and Edwardian period. At a time when gentleman-amateurs were a powerful force in the game, Yorkshire sides were composed largely of skilled professionals who raised standards within the national game. Social convention, even in Yorkshire, still demanded that the captain be an amateur but the best of them treated the job with intense seriousness. Lord Hawke, despite a birthplace outside Yorkshire, led with great success at the turn of the century. Two social worlds combined in common purpose to build a tradition that led to the club winning 30 County Championships since the 1890s.

The club has long been a focal point within Yorkshire, giving a sense of community and shared interest to people from often quite contrasting backgrounds. In this sense Yorkshire cricket widened fan and player participation across social and more recently cultural backgrounds, which is at the very heart of the value of sport. Yorkshire and Lancashire, fierce rivals, but bound by a similar sense of cricketing values, were united as much as they were divided by the game and often enjoyed a quiet satisfaction when the other vanquished its southern foes in Surrey and Middlesex. That the club has long been a world-class regional institution made it a natural partner for the University, a partnership rooted since its inception in 2006 in the desire of both Yorkshire County Cricket Club and Leeds Metropolitan University to maximise the link between education and sport. Our partnership will shortly take another step forward with the opening of the innovative new pavilion at Headingley Carnegie Stadium, combining a world-class educational environment for students and state-of-the-art facilities for players.

Derek's rich chronicle of cricketing history teaches, entertains and inspires. This is 'official' history in the best sense. His love of the game and expert knowledge of it is always apparent, as is his willingness to confront some of the more problematic aspects of the club's history. May future editions record achievements as impressive and characters as fascinating as those documented here.

Peter Rodgers
Dean of Sporting Partnerships
Leeds Metropolitan University

Foreword

The publication of this outstanding Carnegie Official History of Yorkshire County Cricket Club by Derek Hodgson could not have been more perfectly timed.

The most famous Cricket Club in the world is currently building a new pavilion and media centre which will make Headingley Carnegie Cricket Ground instantly recognisable as a leading state-of-the-art venue for our summer game at both Test and County level.

But if the future is important then the past is equally so for a club with the rich heritage of Yorkshire CCC and as it stands on the threshold of an exciting new era in 2009 it also looks back with nostalgic pride to its golden days.

This year marks the golden anniversary of Yorkshire's great Championship winning season of 1959 when captain Ronnie Burnet's young lions brought to an end Surrey's run of seven consecutive titles. For Yorkshire it was the start of a magical era which saw the club clinch the Championship seven times in ten seasons and once again impose their authority on a competition which they have won on a record 30 occasions.

How appropriate, therefore, that Brian Close, one of that happy band who made Yorkshire a force again, should be Yorkshire's current president, leading from the front – as he always did on the field of play – as his beloved county rebuild and strengthen from the base upwards.

Despite being one of Yorkshire's and England's outstanding captains – and held in great affection by the players of both camps – Brian Close experienced turbulent as well as triumphant times while serving the White Rose with utter dedication until he was sacked after the end of the 1970 season and went on to forge a new career with Somerset. He is, of course, not the only one to have undergone the agony and the ecstasy of playing cricket for Yorkshire; our current Board Director, Geoffrey Boycott, being another who constantly made the headlines, as did another of our greatest sons, Raymond Illingworth. As a leading sports journalist, who later served with distinction as Secretary and then President of the Cricket Writers' Club, Derek Hodgson has known and written about all three of them, as he has done with scores of other Yorkshire first team players. He built his reputation on fine writing allied to fairness and a keen understanding of the game. Perhaps most importantly, however, he is passionate about cricket in general and Yorkshire in particular, which shines out in this splendidly updated history.

Nothing is hidden or swept under the carpet – it would not be a true and reliable history if it were – but whether he's focussed on Lord Hawke or John Hampshire, Ted Lester or Maurice Leyland, Wilfred Rhodes or Emmott Robinson, the writing has as much style as the players under his microscope had on the field of play.

The tapestry of Yorkshire cricket is not woven from dull threads, it is a history that is alive with colour and wonderful stories. It is the same with this book and we are indebted to Leeds Metropolitan University for making its production possible.

Stewart Regan
Chief Executive
Yorkshire County Cricket Club

Introduction: God's Own County

Yorkshiremen are multi-religious, resentful of central authority, lovers of music –particularly choral and brass – disputatious and often simply bloody-minded. Convinced of the justice of a cause they are stubborn last-ditchers, loyal to a fault; wary of hard times, they are careful with their money. They have an innate belief in their own superiority and when they hear the phrase 'God's Own County' it would rarely occur to them that it might carry a derisive implication; to them it is no more than the truth.

When they were known as Brigantes they gave the Romans so much trouble that a fortress city had to be established at Eboracum and a Legion posted. The Emperors Septimus Severus and Constantine were proclaimed in York. Had the Northern earls Edwin and Morcar reached Harold in time there might have been no Norman Conquest. Enraged at the intractability of the men north of the Humber, the Conqueror brought fire and sword and laid the land waste, thus inserting antipathy to London's edicts into the genetic memory.

Richard, Duke of Gloucester was a much admired administrator of the North before he was translated into a wicked uncle and the crook-backed Richard III. His device of the white boar and white rose is still worn proudly by many Yorkshiremen more than 500 years after the Tudors won the last battle and wrote the history. Henry VIII's dissolution of the monasteries, at a time when Yorkshire boasted 28 abbeys and 26 priories, brought the county's last armed rising against central government, the Pilgrimage of Grace. No English king was safe unless his man held York.

The Industrial Revolution brought steel to the South, textiles to the West, shipbuilding to the East and coal just about everywhere through the Ridings. Strong backs, hearty lungs and nimble fingers were needed by the new overlords, the master at the mill or the mine. The chapel took hold on Sundays, proclaiming a simpler, more

fundamental faith whose preachers thundered against sin and strong drink, advocated unity as strength, rehearsed *The Messiah* and formed Sunday-school cricket teams.

The story follows: what needs to be mentioned in this introduction is the line of administrators whose strength of purpose first persuaded the recalcitrant parts to come together in a county club; who ensured, once the Club was founded, there would be no fissures serious enough to bring it down; and whose diligence took the Club prosperously into its second century.

Each of these men appears within the context of this History but deserves further mention, starting with Michael John Ellison, the Sheffielder who could see beyond Hallamshire. As Peter Thomas wrote: 'Each milestone in the early history of Yorkshire county cricket is a milestone in the endeavour and generosity of the white-bearded Ellison.'

He was 44 when he first urged the setting up of the Club's forerunner, the Public Match Fund Committee, and two years older before the Club was actually formed. He took on the arduous role of President-Treasurer, and it is accepted that when the Committee prevailed upon him to accept a refund of some of the money he had spent to keep the Club afloat, the amount (£400, probably worth around £400,000 today) was only a token repayment of the full debt. Another of South Yorkshire's institutions, Sheffield United, also owes Ellison a debt for he guaranteed the rent of Bramall Lane to his employer, the Duke of Norfolk.

Ellison's son Michael succeeded his father as Treasurer in 1894, a post he surrendered to Charles Stokes in 1899. Michael had played full-back for Sheffield United, while Stokes, a dentist and an accomplished violinist, was regarded as the enthusiast who put the United Football Club on its feet. Stokes was a member of the Yorkshire Committee for 36 years.

Joseph Beckett Wostinholm was the Secretary of the Club from 1864 to 1902 and ruled it during the formative years at Ellison's right hand. Originally paid 10% of all subscriptions, he was then paid a fixed £10 from 1870 to 1882, at which point the Committee felt he was worth £25 per annum.

Significantly, when the 'perfect Tartar', as Hawke described him, did retire, the Club was forced to offer the huge salary of £350 in order to replace him, and it was not until he had gone that the Committee felt able to move the Club offices from Sheffield to Leeds, another indication of Wostinholm's influence and prestige. He was as intimately connected with Sheffield United for 40 years. Wostinholm was presented with a portrait in oils, several silver articles and a testimonial of £200 by the Club.

Frederick Toone, Wostinholm's successor, had made his name with Leicestershire where, in five years, he had lifted the membership from 500 to 1,800, and on his arrival in Leeds in 1903 he was equally successful. In his 27 years of office he raised the membership figure by 100% to 6,000, revised many of the Club rules, organised players' benefits and insisted, as the County Secretary, on taking charge of the county's matches wherever they were played in Yorkshire.

His reputation for management won him appointment to England's tours of Australia in 1920, 1924 and 1928, and on his return from the third tour he was knighted for his services to cricket. He was, in Warner's words, 'the perfect manager' and *Wisden* described him as 'the organiser supreme'. It was Toone who revised and edited that other Yorkshire cricket institution, the *Yearbook*, in a style that has not greatly altered to this day. In 1923 he was appointed by the Government to the 'Crowds Committee', set up to enquire into the safety of spectators at sporting events, a sequel to the Bolton-West Ham FA Cup Final when the crowd overflowed on to the pitch and were marshalled to safety by one policeman on a white horse.

Hawke wrote of Toone in 1924: 'It is remarkable that our office is run by one secretary and a boy.'

That boy was for many years John Henry 'Jack'

Nash, appointed Assistant Secretary in 1922, succeeding Toone in 1932 to serve in that office for the next 40 years. Nash had a classical Yorkshire cricket background, born in Farsley and educated at Pudsey Grammar.

Toone's death occurred when Nash was only 25, and several of the Committee, including Hawke, had misgivings about appointing so young a successor, but Nash had been well trained and the office continued smoothly; he was rewarded in 1950-51 when he managed the England tour of Australia.

A church organist, Nash was regarded by some, especially among the enlarged and encroaching media, as a rather distant and aloof man, and it is doubtful if he ever considered what is now called 'public relations' as part of his duties. A small but memorable kindness might be recorded: the author, when a National Serviceman in 1948, wrote to Nash asking if he could be proposed for membership, apologising for the lack of a proposer and seconder, his father having resigned on moving to Bedfordshire in 1932. Strictly against the rules as they were at that time, Nash arranged for the 18-year-old aircraftsman to be elected and took the trouble to write a terse but welcoming note to Royal Air Force Hospital, Ely.

Yorkshire's fifth Secretary, succeeding Nash, Joseph Lister, had another exemplary Yorkshire background. Born in Thirsk and related to George Macaulay, he was educated at Cheltenham, played hockey for Yorkshire and as a right-hand bat played 24 first-class matches between 1951 and 1959, although only twice for Yorkshire.

After becoming secretary of Worcestershire he was the obvious candidate to replace Nash in 1971 and felt the full force of the gale of change that swept through cricket in the ensuing years, a long trial that tested his strength. The County Secretary today has tasks and pressures undreamed of in Wostinholm's time.

In the Treasurer's chair, an honorary position, Stockes was followed by the Heselton father and son who served the club for a total of 49 years, the son Wyndham becoming one of the first honorary life members in 1946. Principals of a firm of Bradford accountants, they gave life service to both Yorkshire and the Bradford club and the father did most to raise the funds necessary to purchase the Park Avenue ground.

Michael Grove Crawford, who succeeded in 1963, was a right-hand bat who was educated at Shrewsbury and Cambridge (a soccer Blue) and a contemporary of Joe Lister's in the Yorkshire second team, making one first-team appearance in 1951. Crawford is the only Treasurer to become Chairman of the General Committee (a post created in 1971 to ease the President's duties), an office he filled capably during a stormy four years until it became clear that as a moderate he was a target for both sides of the then controversy.

David Welch, from Rotherham, Treasurer from 1980-84, was another forced out by the continuing political battles although he returned to serve the General Committee; Peter Townend taking office in 1984 and becoming one of the Club's few officers to command the confidence of all factions at that disputatious time.

Hawke apart – and he was President for 40 years – the holder of the Club's premier office preferred to play the gentle helmsman, and it was not until Sir Keith Parkinson's term (1974-81) that the President became involved in the raging arguments over policy. Sir Keith, who was also chairman of the *Yorkshire Post*, and his successor, the greatly respected Norman Yardley, tried but failed to restore unity, and it was not until the Viscount Mountgarret was elected in October 1984 that a new force appeared.

A descendant of the Butler Earls of Ormonde, whose titles had been won while pacifying Ulster, Mountgarret came into office with a background of the Irish Guards and Eton and no preconceived attitudes nor loyalties. He conceded, from the start, that he would have to learn by trial and error, but he was the fresh new strength the Club needed, and he exercised his influence and power like no one present since Hawke, forcing through a new constitution, strengthening the central government of the Club and rallying support by, in effect, asking one simple question of the members: 'I will always put the good of the Club first. Will you?'

Mountgarret could not be accused of place-seeking, nor social climbing, nor self-glory. The early success he needed came when Philip Carrick's team won the Benson and Hedges Cup in 1987.

Mountgarret's rise inevitably diminished the office of Chairman of General Committee that had been occupied, since 1971, by the able Arthur Connell from Sheffield, by Crawford and then, by the overthrow of the General Committee in March 1984, by Reg Kirk of Hull. Kirk, in his 18 months of office, was able to fulfil one promise in that he did open up his office, and the Committee generally, to the members and the public; and the Club's administration, since Kirk, has been seen to be more immediately accessible.

When Kirk stood down the General Committee turned to Brian Walsh QC, from Leeds, a brilliant speaker who, when allowed by his busy schedule, was able to put the Club's argument forcefully and wittily whether at Lord's or in a working man's club.

For four years in the late 1980s the Club found a relative stability with Mountgarret as President, Walsh as Chairman and the admirable Joe Lister, the true hero of the conflict, effectively a troika system of government. By 1989 the Viscount, impulsive and more suited to wartime than peace, perhaps a little bored, stood down with the applause of appreciative members behind him and the office went, obviously, to Sir Leonard Hutton, Yorkshire's outstanding player and the first former professional to occupy the office of President.

His hopes for the future of the Club, and the part he hoped to play in fulfilling them, were captured in a film made by Mike Burns, to be used in a filmed history of the Club, a sequence lost in the editing but with a clip retained fortunately by the Club. Sadly he died a few months later, the first of three unexpected demises that might have caused a severe disruption. Joe Lister died in 1991, aged 61, departing by simply announcing that he would be away for a while in hospital. The Club, and his many friends, were shaken to hear of his death. A former amateur batsman, the nephew of George Macaulay, he had played for Yorkshire and Worcestershire and been secretary at New Road until, on John Nash's retirement in 1971, he rejoined his native county where his stoicism, dry humour and sense of balance served the Club brilliantly through difficult times.

He was not fond of journalists, disliked intensely the growing hyperbole surrounding the game, yet was held in great affection by those members of the press who had come to know him, and his quirks and foibles, over the years. His career and personality was captured by Robert Mills' excellent essay 'The Headmaster of Headingley', published in the *Yorkshire Post* and reproduced in the 1991 *Yearbook*.

The third blow was the illness that brought the resignation in 1991 and later death of the chairman, Brian Walsh, a distinguished lawyer who gave the Club an impressive profile at Lord's and who might have become an important figure in English cricket. While the General Committee might still be split into what could be called, in shorthand, pro- and anti-Boycott groups, they were both united and responsible enough to resolve what might have been another awkward spell by making two sensible appointments.

Sir Lawrence Byford, a former Chief Inspector of H.M. Constabulary and a lifelong Yorkshire follower, was invited to become President and, by way of ensuring that there would be no repetition of the pull in different directions, was also elected Chairman of the General Committee making him the most powerful individual in the Club since Hawke's time. To replace Lister, Yorkshire appointed Chris Hassell, the Lancashire secretary who had also been secretary to the football clubs of Everton and Crystal Palace.

Hassell's strength lay in his experience of dealing with players' contracts and players' agents, a valuable asset in the new decade that was to see players' wages zoom, bringing increasing mobility and in Yorkshire's case the abandonment of the birthright tradition, signing overseas players in sharp competition from other counties and countries. It is to his credit that Yorkshire, with Byford's close support, began by engaging the world's best young batsman, Sachin Tendulkar. The Cricket committee wanted a fast bowler, and agreement had been reached with Australia's Craig McDermott, but there is no doubt that in the new world where television had supplanted the newspaper as the principal medium, Tendulkar's signing won the most attention.

Members were cheered by the fact that both of the two new leading executives had arrived with no baggage; neither had been involved in the wrangling and arguments of the previous 20 years and both had a refreshing habit of looking only forward. While Sir Lawrence, especially, was deeply aware of the Club's tradition and history, his career had taught him that the past is for the learning of lessons to be applied to the future. Hassell took the title Chief Executive, leaving the finance office in the care of David Ryder, Club cricketer and county stalwart through a long career at Headingley.

When in the late 1990s the rebuilding (and ownership) of the Headingley ground became critical concerns, the Club was fortunate to have a financier/accountant, businessman Keith Moss, as Chairman and he was able to guide through the rebuilding of the West and East stands before the Club was hit, and all but capsized, by the financial hurricane of 1999-2000 that caused the emergency general meetings and the revision of the Club's constitution. Without the skills of Robin Smith, a lawyer, Brian Boutell, a financial expert and Colin Graves, an entrepreneur attuned to the world of new business, Yorkshire County Cricket Club might not have seen the start of the 21st century.

The Beginnings 1750–1880

If Thomas Lord, vintner, speculator and entrepreneur, is the first Yorkshire cricketer known to history, founding as he did the most famous ground in the world, he had a contemporary, who, but for internal circumstances, might have stolen some of his thunder. Francis Godolphin Osborne, fifth Duke of Leeds, was enough of a Yorkshireman to insist upon being buried at Harthill in the old West Riding. He was also Vice-Admiral of Yorkshire and Lord Lieutenant of the East Riding. His Grace's full connections with cricket are undetermined, but he did have the foresight, as Secretary of State for Foreign Affairs, to appoint a cricketing devotee, the Duke of Dorset, as His Majesty's Ambassador to the Court of Louis XVI.

The Times, in its second year of publication, recorded in May 1786 a match played in Paris on 16 April: '…by some English gentlemen, in the Champs Elyses [*sic*]. His Grace of Dorset was, as usual, the most distinguished for skill and activity. The French, however, cannot imitate us in such vigorous exertions of the body; so that we seldom see them enter the lists.'

Dorset, vaguely rumoured to have been a lover of Marie-Antoinette, invited a Surrey team to play an exhibition match in the Bois de Boulogne a little over three years later. The tourists had reached Dover when they were met by the Duke, who had sagely concluded that the storming of the Bastille was not the most propitious of moments for the launching of the game upon the French. Any claim the Duke of Leeds might have presented to have promoted the first Test match therefore went up in smoke and flame. However, Dorset did return to England with one predilection of the Bourbons – an interval for tea – duly adopted at his matches.

After the Napoleonic wars English lacemakers spread the game throughout Northern France, and clubs are mentioned in Paris, Dieppe, Calais and Boulogne. Teams from Nottingham went on tour across the Channel, having the usual impact on Anglo-French relations, according to one verse:

> That England has no rival
> Well know the trembling pack,
> Whom Charley Brown by Calais Town
> Bowled out behind his back.

The French, in turn, obstinately refused to have such wonders thrust upon them. In 1867 a Frenchman observed to a touring Englishman, a member of the Butterflies touring team: 'I cannot understand why you do not engage a servant to field for you.' At about the same time the French made an attempt to describe the game: 'The bowler, grasping the ball in the right hand, watches for a favourable moment when the attention of the batsman is distracted and then launches it at him with incredible force; the batsman, however, is on the alert; he strikes to an enormous height and immediately runs.'

The exiled Napoleon III, watching a match between Bickley Park and Beckenham, was so impressed by the taking of a spectacular catch that he despatched an aide to request that the fielder repeat the feat. The last French Emperor also intervened when the Paris CC was in danger of being suppressed as dangerous, a batsman having tripped and broken his arm during the course of a game.

One reason for this emphasis on cricket's French connection is that the word 'crice' (a 'staff') is one possible etymological source of the name of cricket. The same language also contributes 'criquet', a stick used in bowls. An illustration, depicting two men playing with a bat and a ball, can be seen in a mid-13th-century French book named as *Chronique d'Angleterre*. The Bodleian Library possesses a manuscript showing monks engaged in some sport that involves fieldsmen, and Guildford Corporation records refer to 'crickett' in 1597.

Cricket in Yorkshire probably derived from several different sources. Stool-ball, in which a stool, known in some parts as a 'cricket', was turned on its side and defended like a set of stumps, is one; in a later form the stool is turned upside down and a comb placed across two of the legs – a primitive wicket with a bail. Then, too, there was knurr and spell, a ball or stone being propelled from the ground and hit by a bat or stick while in flight, the hitter scoring 'runs' while the ball was retrieved. A catch was 'out'. Several public schools played variations of bat and ball game; rounders is yet another development, a branch that an American Civil War general, Abner Doubleday, turned into baseball in 1839.

There is historical record of cricket in Yorkshire by 1751 when Sheffield engaged professionals to 'amuse the populace and draw them from cock-fighting'. In the same year the Earl of Northumberland's XI defeated the Duke of Cleveland's XI at Stanwich, near Richmond. Six years later, in Leeds, the Church burgesses paid 14 shillings and sixpence to cricketers to entertain the local population on Shrove Tuesday, 'to prevent the infamous practice of throwing at cocks'. A more refined occasion occurred on Chapeltown Moor in 1776, as the Colonials were revolting in New England, when the Married Men played the Bachelors for five guineas and a dinner, the single men winning by six runs. Another four years and a Leeds theatre was

---

Tom Marsden Sheffield's Pride

The most famous man in the city's history, Marsden had poems written of his prowess, which he regarded highly enough for him to challenge, for a side-stake of £50, any man in England in 1828 to a single-wicket match (with a further £10 offered for travelling expenses). For five years no one was bold enough to take him on until in 1833 Fuller Pilch, who, ironically, had Sheffield connections, routed him by an innings and 70 at Norwich.

Such was Sheffield's faith in her 28-year-old champion that 20,000 crowded the Darnall ground to watch the return, only to see Pilch triumph again, this time by 127 runs. The Sheffielder's reputation was such, however, that Pilch went on to advertise himself as the man who had defeated 'Marsden the Champion'.

Marsden stood 5ft 8in, batted left-handed and bowled fast under-arm, occasionally switching to round-arm medium. His 227 for Sheffield and Leicester against the mighty Nottingham club side of 1826, scored in eight hours, was only the third double-century in history, and the first by a Yorkshireman. He was then 21 and the innings included one hit of more than 130 yards and over a 45 foot-high wall; such was the crowd's enthusiasm that a collection for him, perhaps the first in the coun-

ty, was organised. As he also took six wickets, he clearly deserved his reward.

Marsden may also have been the first Yorkshire cricketer to have had too many hospitable friends. Famous at 21, he had achieved most of his great performances by 25 and was only 38 when he died. Holmes described him as 'a rollicking sort of fellow', citing a match played against a G. Jarvis, Marsden promising to pull down the sign on his inn 'The Cricketers' if he lost; he didn't. The professions of inn-keeping and cricket are ill-suited. There is no direct evidence that Marsden's career was affected by over-indulgence, but such were his popularity and fame that his well-wishers were legion.

Two years after Marsden's death the Treasurer of the Leeds club, a Mr Clarke, was presented with a gold breast-pin, subscribed for by the members, as a token of respect for his two years in office. The pin was composed of a bat, stumps and a ball and, adds Holmes, 'instead of a chain were two links of the late Tom Marsden's hair'. Such a gesture might today smack of voodoo, but in 1845 photography was still rare and any memento of the renowned was treasured. 'At cricket he's nature's perfection,' writes an unknown poet of Marsden's skills, and to him must be given the major credit for advertising the game and its attractions throughout the county.

advertising, on the bill for a night's entertainment, 'a new dance called The Cricketers, or the Sports of Chapel-Town.'

By then cricket was becoming organised. A club was formed in York in 1784. In October 1786 the Gentlemen of York defeated the Gentlemen of Doncaster, reputedly for 100 guineas – a vast sum and one that must be treated with caution, for it was common practice to advertise matches for great prizes when in fact no money was at stake. Wetherby, too, was playing matches as the 19th century neared, meeting Scruton over two days in 1797, and by 1802 there occurred what today might be called a sponsors' match – Smiths and Co. defeating Goodman and Co. in Sheffield.

While Britain fought Napoleon the game of cricket advanced dramatically. Scores, notched on a stick, gave way to the scorebook in which individual accounts were kept, enabling clubs to publish proper records. The strong Ripon club, who played as far afield as Nottingham in 1816, were showing the way towards standardisation by publishing in 1825, the 'Laws of Cricket as Approved by the Mary-le'Bone Club'. The first glimmering of a Yorkshire county identity, certainly unrecognised at the time, came with the opening of a custom-made (to use the modern term) cricket ground at Darnall, Sheffield in 1822, and it was fitting that the southern city

Harry Sampson The Landlord

Even if Harry Sampson had not been a formidable cricketer in his own right, he would have a place in the history if only because he was for 20 years the landlord of the Adelphi Hotel in Sheffield, birthplace of both the Yorkshire County Club and of Sheffield Wednesday Football Club. He was described as a small (5ft 4in), stout man who as a batsman was a back player of very high quality and as a bowler was renowned for his accuracy.

Marsden was the first Yorkshireman to be chosen for the Gentlemen against the Players in 1827, then a fixture bearing much more prestige than a modern Test match, and Sampson was the second, selected in 1841. This followed his appearance for The North against The South at Lord's the previous year, and after his appearance for the Players he was appointed a ground bowler and coach to the MCC, opening his first hostelry in 1842, in Reading. Mr Sampson did not allow the grass to grow under his feet.

It was at about this time, in 1841, that Sampson, a member of the United England XI met the now declining Marsden in a single-wicket match at the Hyde Park ground, Sampson proving his right to the succession with a substantial victory by an innings and 50 runs. Marsden was bowled twice for 19

Harry Sampson 'a lithograph from 1852'
Mick Pope

and nine, and in the second innings of what sounds a very tense affair Sampson bowled 445 consecutive deliveries, conceding more than seven wides.

Harry Sampson was also a fine long-stop, a passionate fisherman, and even today holds one world record: playing for Wednesday against Sheffield Town on 8 February 1841, he scored 162, on ice.

James Dearman Brave Little Jimmy

The last Yorkshireman to challenge the rest of England to a single-wicket match, Dearman came from a cricketing family of many talents. He was a Sheffield filesmith who bowled fast round-arm, and in 1838 he issued his challenge, £100 a side. Fuller Pilch accepted but was pressed to fit the contest into a busy schedule, so Alfred Mynn, the 'Lion of Kent' agreed to deputise, the match being arranged for Town Malling on 2 August 1838.

About 5,000 spectators attended, Mynn appearing, according to a witness, in 'a close fitting jersey bound with red ribbon, a red belt around his waist and a straw hat with a broad red ribbon'. As a study in scarlet it was far too much for little Jimmy, who conceded 34 and 89 runs, scoring only three and eight in reply, but the courage of the diminutive Dearman displayed against the strong 6ft 2in of Mynn won him much praise and applause. It was suggested that the kindly Mynn fed him a few easy deliveries until, near 6 pm, there were shouts of 'Finish him off, Alfred,' the witness adding: 'I have a vision of middle stump flying up in the air and spinning like a wheel.'

The return match was in September in Sheffield where Dearman lost his bails to a ball of 'lightning speed', but there, at least, the margin was only 20 runs. Dearman played regularly for The North against The South and for the infant Yorkshire XI, retiring to take over the inn and ground at Darnall, his wife following as 'mine hostess'. He is known to be buried in the Attercliffe cemetery, but he was never given a tombstone.

---

should have seen the first major establishment, for Sheffield is the true birthplace of Yorkshire county cricket.

Darnall, as represented on a contemporary illustration, consisted of a field in front of a fairly substantial mansion, the balcony apparently providing a view for ladies of quality, with the crowd gathered around a seemingly unmarked boundary upon which were stationed a few tents and at least one hut, where two handsomely dressed ladies and a Regency buck appear to be taking wine or tea. The umpires, in polished knee boots, wine-dark dress coats and top hats, have an air of authority far beyond that possessed by today's more humble arbiters. The players, all in white and tight breeches, wear dark caps; the bats are straight, the stumps are three and the bowler is about to deliver, underarm. The whole ambience is one of enjoyment and not a little wealth, suggesting that our Georgian and Victorian forefathers may have experienced hard times, but never lost their enormous capacity for enjoying themselves.

Darnall opened at a momentous point in the game's history. Since 1750 the under-arm bowler had reigned without challenge to his method, but as pitches improved batsmen began to assert an increasing advantage, leading bowlers, in the natural course of things, to strive to make the method of delivery more potent. In trying to increase the pace without jerking the ball, which was illegal, bowlers began to deliver the ball further away from the body.

There is another theory, adopted by romantics, that round-arm stemmed from the inability of that formidable lady Mrs Grace, the Doctor's mother, to bowl under-arm in a hooped skirt. Whatever the circumstances, the bowling of William Lillywhite and Jem Broadbridge of Sussex was causing concern, and MCC, who had paid their first and only visit to Darnall in 1825, instituted a series of three 'test' matches in 1827 between England and Sussex to judge the new style of bowling, with Darnall, confirming its rank among cricket grounds, being chosen for the first of those trials.

Sussex won that first experiment by seven wickets, and it was the exposure of so many high-class cricketers in the county that fired the imagination of Yorkshiremen with enormous enthusiasm for the game. Over the next 15 years cricket clubs are recorded as Bedale, Dalton, Thirsk, Beverley, Bradford, Otley, Rotherham, Mexborough, Harrogate, Keighley,

Andrew Crossland Exceedingly Well

Crossland was the most famous product of Dalton, another Huddersfield village that, around mid-century, almost rivalled Lascelles Hall for cricketing prowess. Born two years after Waterloo, he was regarded as Yorkshire's best bowler (right arm round) for many years and a batsman of great tenacity, once batting on a Hyde Park flier for 150 minutes to make eight runs.

In one surviving photograph he is seen to be a handsome man wearing a cap not greatly dissimilar in style to the one sported by Geoffrey Boycott a century later. He played for and against the All-England XI, the equivalent of Test-match status today, taking 12 of their wickets at York in 1854 and 4-11 against them at Hull, the city in which he died at the ripe age of 85.

His batting style was much remarked upon, *Scores and Biographies* noting that 'he got much off his ground to play the ball'. What he took as a batsman he could only dish out, once having Julius Caesar caught 'from a ball that rose as high as his head'. He made 24 on his debut at Lord's on a rough pitch against Grundy and Wisden. *Bell's Life* reporting: 'Each day the teams were invited to Mr Dark's house where they partook of old English fare of roast beef and plum pudding, which we imagine many of the visitors would have been glad to get a sight of.'

Crossland's obituary read: 'He could bat, bowl and field exceedingly well.'

George Anderson The Ramrod

'Old Ebor's' affectionate portrait of George Anderson in 1898 begins:

It is a snug room in a comfortable house in Aiskew, Bedale. Two striking portraits assist in embellishing the walls and mark the old cricketer's dwelling; the original of each sits in his cosy armchair and chats pleasantly …The two portraits show George Anderson in two stages of his career; now he has passed into his seventies, no longer perhaps as erect as when he wore the white flannel and red spots of the All-England Eleven but still commanding presence …

The earlier portrait was sketched in 1853 by N.Felix. George Anderson appears as a young man of seven and twenty under Felix's brush and pigments. The other was drawn in Melbourne ten years later and shows the matured cricketer at the height of his career.

The quotation illustrates both the affection and respect with which Anderson was regarded through his 26 years (he died in 1902). He played alongside all the great men: Felix, Pilch, Mynn, Clarke, Parr, Wisden, Box, Caffyn, Sampson, Willsher and Julius Caesar. He played for Yorkshire for 20 years (captain for four) and for All England for 21, and he was the first Yorkshireman to score 1,000 runs in a Summer, in 1862.

His height, over six feet, is often remarked upon, as were his military bearing and hitting power. In 1903 he was judged to have been Yorkshire's hardest hitter, and in the days when all scores had to be run out he hit an eight at The Oval in 1862, declaring afterwards that it would have been nine had not his partner Carpenter, from Cambridgeshire, been 'dead beat'. He must have been a ferocious driver, his style comparing with George Ulyett's:

'We were not in the habit of letting balls go by on the off side. If we had stood at the wicket and allowed balls to go by, as some modern [1898] batsmen do, we should have been hooted, and properly so,' he told 'Old Ebor'.

Anderson was a member of the second England team to tour Australia, under George Parr's leadership, in 1863-64. The voyage out took 61 days, leaving the Mersey on 14 October, and the tour began in Melbourne on New Year's Day before a crowd of 14,000. Sixteen matches were played, all against teams of 22; ten were won, none was lost. Anderson's diary recorded a dreadful trip out, with seasickness day after day, but his Victorian spirit was unflagging.

Despite being a county captain and a prominent player, Yorkshire did not reward this popular man with a benefit until he was in his 69th year, and Anderson himself had no doubt that this was because of his leadership of the 'strike' that stemmed from John Lillywhite's no-balling of Edgar Willsher at The Oval in 1862.

Lillywhite was standing in his first match, Surrey v All England, and warned the Kent bowler Willsher that his arm was getting high. Two overs later Lillywhite called seven balls in succession, and the bowler flung down the ball and walked off the field, followed by the team's nine professionals who included Anderson and three other Yorkshiremen. Anderson said later that the professionals had been convinced that Surrey had prompted Lillywhite to call Willsher, and as a result he declined to play against Surrey again.

That decision – and he was recognised as a stubborn man – cost him good years, and he did not appear for Yorkshire again, until 1867, declining to captain the team in 1865 because it meant he would have to play against Surrey. The controversy grew until it became a rift between the northern and southern professionals that led, in 1865, to the formation of a United South of England XI that competed in touring fixtures with All England and United England.

Anderson scored 114 not out at the age of 50, for Constable Burton against Darlington, and then decided to retire. He remembered as a 16-year-old playing against W.G. Grace in Sheffield and recalled W.G.'s famous mother, the lady it was said who invented round-arm bowling: 'I think the mother was a better player than the father. She was the only lady I ever saw who could throw a ball. She could throw it 60 or 70 yards.'

He was very proud of his north-country origin, nostalgically recalling when there were four Bedale men in the All-England XI. By that Askew fireside he told 'Old Ebor': 'I was born in Bedale, have lived there all my life and hope to die there.'

Scarborough, Redcar and Barnsley.

But it was to Sheffield that all Yorkshire clubs rightly deferred, for cricket was so well established among the grinders that its eventual displacement by football in the city remains to this day something of a mystery. (The Wednesday began as a cricket club, and Sheffield United's title was 'Cricket, Football and Athletic Club', reflecting the enormous interest of much of the population.) There was another reason for Sheffield's status, however: it had pioneered out-of-county games against Nottingham, thus attracting a partisan interest.

Nottingham's lacemakers, like the weavers of Huddersfield and Sheffield's grinders, needed a happy marriage of hands and eye to be successful in their work. They were mostly self-employed on a piece-work basis, and they, too, cheerfully embraced cricket. Between 1771 and

1860 the players of Sheffield and Nottingham met 26 times, Nottingham winning 14 of the matches and being regarded as the superior side, for Sheffield were sometimes offered odds. In 1800 Sheffield played 22 such matches, in 1822 15, in 1857 and 1860 16, and in later matches Sheffield were assisted by Leicester and Durham.

Sheffield, nevertheless, had what would today be called the 'Man of the Series' in the doughty Tom Marsden. Three three-figure scores were recorded in these inter-city contests, Marsden making two of them (227 in 1826 and 125 in 1828), and he was the only player to carry his bat in the series. In this period of the game's formation it should also be remembered that players thought nothing of starting a match at 9 am, nor of playing on into November if weather permitted.

From this Sheffield-Nottingham series came Yorkshire's first county fixture, an all-Sheffield venture on the Hyde Park ground, home of the Wednesday club, in 1833. The origin of the match is not clear, although it may have arisen from the need to raise a team to match the status of the first opponents, Norfolk. Three gentlemen, or amateurs as they were to become known, were in that first Yorkshire team, hinting at a different organisation from that at Darnall, but as the side included two of the city's great professionals, Marsden and Sampson, the result was never in doubt, despite the appearance for Norfolk of three Pilches, including Fuller.

While Fuller Pilch was Norfolk-born, he was a member of the Wednesday club, and had assisted Sheffield against Nottingham and The North against The South. This first county fixture was won by Yorkshire by 120 runs, Marsden and Dearman contributing 93 of the second-innings total of 196 and taking eight of the 20 Norfolk wickets (four batsmen were run out).

Further fixtures between the two counties followed in 1834 and 1836, but as Fuller Pilch had departed to play for Kent, at the enormous annual salary of £100 in the intervening year, Norfolk's strength, and therefore its attraction as an opposition, had declined to such an extent that further meetings could no longer be considered viable. Pilch's aggregate in the five matches was 385 runs at an average of 48, a tremendous contribution.

Having now developed the taste and the organisation for county matches, this Sheffield-based Yorkshire then set about enlarging the fixture list. Sussex were met in 1835 and 1855, Manchester three times in 1844-85, the first Roses match was played in 1849, and Kent also provided the opposition for the first time in that year. Surrey joined the list in 1850. From 1846 William Clarke's famous All-England XI, founded the previous year, began fixtures against various Yorkshire combinations of between 14 and 22 players. Their great rivals, the United All-England XI, played a Yorkshire XIV in 1853.

Yorkshire's fielding, on the rough surfaces of the time, must have been worth watching. In one of the early matches in 1835, six Sussex batsmen were run out in the two innings, Sussex thereupon conceding victory with Yorkshire needing 21 and an innings to play!

The spreading strength of cricket in the county can be judged from a series of fixtures between Sheffield and Yorkshire in 1849-50. The city

---

Isaac Hodgson Ikey

The first of Yorkshire's great slow left-arm spin bowlers, 'Ikey' Hodgson was born in Bradford and with Billy Slinn formed the first of the county's famous bowling partnerships. Both men began their careers playing for travelling teams at fairs and feast days. Hodgson's style was reported to be similar to that of Wilfred Rhodes, although he was also renowned for a variation of pace that suggests he might also have been compared to Derek Underwood.

Hodgson won fame by attaching himself to the various sides of 22 that met the All-England XI, and it was said that when a local club met to organise a side to meet the Englanders then Hodgson's was the first name to be put down, with Slinn's as the second.

In six seasons he took 473 wickets against All England, an astonishing figure, with his greatest feat coming in, of all places, Glasgow. All England, containing Daft, Caesar, Alfred Clarke, Hayward, Anderson, H.H. Stephenson and Tinley, needed 49 to beat a Caledonian XXII. Hodgson, sensing that the 'cracks' would expect him to push the ball through on a pitch deadened by rain, instead, warning the Scots to watch their catching, held it back and took 7-8, All England being dismissed for 20.

He played only 28 matches for Yorkshire, but still managed 139 wickets. He was a cheerful, popular performer, known for his 'good-natured grin', but like many of his generation his health was poor and he died aged only 39.

Roger Iddison First Captain

A jovial Bedale man, also given to flashes of temper, Iddison was one of the early organisers of professional cricket in the North. A shrewd judge of the game, its players and its commercial possibilities, Iddison was the obvious choice to lead Yorkshire into their first county match in 1863.

Typical of the professionals of his day he could both bat and bowl, 'crafty, insidious lobs' according to the Reverend Holmes, and, in the loose affiliations of the time, he played for both Lancashire and Yorkshire and ran what was called a 'cricket depot', in Manchester. As a batsman he was considered to have a curious stance, moving the left leg while awaiting delivery, and he was also famous as a fielder at point.

In fact Lancashire's first century in county cricket was Iddison's 106 against Surrey in 1866, and the following year he played for both the Roses counties. With Ned Stephenson he was the first Yorkshireman to tour Australia where his lobs wreaked havoc, taking 22 wickets against a XXII of Victoria, and he returned with a tour aggregate of 103 at an average of 6.59.

But Iddison had other connections with the game. He was Secretary to the Yorkshire United Club, joint Secretary of North of England United, and regularly organised teams for Lord Londesborough. It was this very partisanship that led him into the North-South schism of 1864 when he failed to arrive to play in a match at Islington, sending his brother, a much lesser player.

Roger Iddison
YCCC

Iddison claimed that he had never agreed to turn out, but ill feeling rumbled on for several years.

Together with Anderson, Atkinson, Slinn and Hodgson, Iddison was the backbone of the first Yorkshire team and his popularity never declined in the North, not even when he grew to 17 stone of ruddy corpulence. He was held in such esteem that the great George Freeman came out of retirement in order to play in Iddison's benefit match. He led Yorkshire for their first ten years.

---

won three of the four matches, but the fact that the rest of the county could even raise a team to match the experts was as remarkable as it was encouraging. Such was the enormous interest in South Yorkshire that by 1855 a third cricket ground had been opened in Sheffield.

Darnall, as mentioned earlier, was regarded as one of England's premier grounds. 'It is much to be regretted that the Darnall Ground is so far from London and other principal places where

the noble game is played, as it may justly be considered the finest in the kingdom,' was the opinion of one southern newspaper.

In fact, there were two Darnall grounds on the Glossop Road. The first, opened on 26 August 1822, saw Sheffield engage Nottingham and during the match a stand gave way, two spectators were killed and more than 50 injured. George Steer, the owner, was undeterred by this tragedy, and set about building a more substantial ground in the same district, which opened in 1824 and passed into the management of William Woolhouse, a noted Sheffield left-handed amateur batsman who married Steer's daughter, Mary. At one end a terrace was built to accommodate 8,000 spectators, and upon that terrace a handsome brick pavilion stood upon stone pillars. It was sad, then, that such a well-appointed ground should house top-class cricket for only five years.

Darnall was three miles from the city centre, so that when the Hyde Park ground opened in 1826, costing £4,000, at only half that distance, the crowd, almost all of whom would be walking, naturally preferred the shorter journey. Darnall passed to James Dearman and then to his wife, who was reported to have promoted rabbit coursing on the 'Old Cricket Ground'. Andrew Crossland was another famous name at Hyde Park.

On high ground, Hyde Park became known for its splendid views and rapid draining and drying, and Woolhouse was astute enough to bring it into his orbit. Hyde Park's five and half acres enabled it to be used for massed cricket, like Parker's Piece or the Maidan in Bombay. In September 1830 Pierce Egan's Book of Sports noted that upwards of 200 cricketers could be seen at work. It was at Hyde Park that Yorkshire played their first match, against Norfolk in 1833, and when All England played Sheffield in 1846 Hyde Park housed an astonishing 16,000. As for Woolhouse, Peter Thomas wrote the perfect epitaph when he described him as 'the Thomas Lord of Sheffield'.

But, as with Darnall, the early promise failed to flourish. The ownership passed to a landlord who thought he might make greater profits from sports other than cricket, making it impossible after a while for the game to be played there. The Hallamshire Volunteers took over Hyde Park as their drill ground, and last century the site was used for high-rise community flats.

The fulcrum of Yorkshire cricket then moved to Bramall Lane, even more central and as handsome a ground, enclosed by a ten-foot wall with 'beautiful stands and refreshment rooms for visitors', according to a Sussex player whose team met Yorkshire in the first principal match on the ground in 1855. The cricketers too had perhaps learned a lesson from their experiences of private management at Darnall and Hyde Park, for Bramall Lane was leased by the Sheffield United club from the Duke of Norfolk for 99 years, provision of the annual rent of £70 being the responsibility of Michael Ellison, the Duke's agent, who became one of the founder members of the County Club. After Ellison's death in 1898 Sheffield United bought the freehold for £10,300, the Duke's stipulation being that it could not be resold for any purpose other than recreation for the next 21 years.

Another £6,000 was spent on rebuilding the pavilion, and throughout Yorkshire's formative years Bramall Lane was the County Club's

---

Billy Slinn

A Sheffielder, Slinn bowled fast right-arm to complement Hodgson in Yorkshire's first county attack. A tall man, he was described as having a classical action in the days when round-arm was still widely practised. His great gift seemed to be his ability to win extra life from any pitch, often with a good length ball, and this, combined with excellent direction, made him a formidable bowler.

Like Hodgson, Slinn earned his money playing for selected teams against the great touring XIs. He took all ten All-England

wickets at Scarborough in 1862 (and 6-23 in the second innings) and did the hat-trick against another All-England XI at Bramall Lane. The great Tom Hayward once faced him for 40 minutes without being able to score.

Slinn was also compared to Hodgson in the mediocrity of his batting, even managing a duck in his benefit match against All England in 1863. The rise of Emmett and Freeman brought his retirement at the age of 38, but in the following decade he was employed by the University of Cambridge as a coach and practice bowler.

Lascelles Hall

While Sheffield provided Yorkshire's earliest cricketers of renown, the village of Lascelles Hall, three miles from Huddersfield, near the Kirkheaton birthplace of Hirst and Rhodes, followed with a record of producing cricketers of high class that can be surpassed in the world only by Hambledon.

Between 1820 and 1860 the club from the village on the hill was strong enough to defeat, among others, All England, Yorkshire, Sheffield, Yorkshire Gentleman, Surrey and any number of clubs and public schools. The village contributed six players to the county XI at one time, and it was said there were up to 23 professional cricketers living there, six in one row of cottages. Certainly a list exists of 21 village cricketers who appeared for Yorkshire.

Alan Thompson, who did much research into the beginnings of the club and published his findings in a booklet (1952), discovered that the village revolved around five families: Lockwood, Pollard, Redfearn, Hill and, most famous of all, Thewlis. Thompson identified 35 Thewlises who played cricket, many of them professionally, and so confusing was their ubiquity in so small an area that identification was reduced to such names as 'young Jack t'youngest'.

Thompson believed that there were two distinct clans of Thewlises, who were cousins to the Lockwoods, who in turn were related to the Eastwoods and the Bateses. The most famous Lockwood, Ephraim, married the niece of the most famous cricketer of his day, Fuller Pilch. In 1866 the Thewlises fielded not only an entire XI against Chickenley at Lascelles Hall, but the gateman, scorer and umpire were all named Thewlis too. The Family were dismissed for 250, Chickenley having made 37-2 when rain ended the match.

So much extraordinary proficiency in one area is explained by Thompson. West Riding villages were all concentrated on cottage industries before the mechanical loom

was invented, the children being trained in hand-loom weaving as soon as they were able. In those days the textile industry was beginning to profit from the inventors, but before the new machinery arrived the men at Lascelles Hall used to throw the shuttle from hand to hand to save their single-width cloth. That needed a very sharp and accurate eye for if the shuttle was dropped the cloth had to be pulled back, a process that lost time and in turn lost money for payment was by the piece; not often, then, was the shuttle dropped.

The loom could be worked in the dark, by the light of a 'farthing dip' during the evenings or in bad weather. When the weather was fine the village lads could turn such co-ordination of hand and eye to the development of other skills, notably cricket. In the mid-19th century there were few other distractions for the poor.

The Lascelles Hall club was founded in 1825 when the village consisted of grey stone cottages around a gentleman's residence and an inn. Several boys were caught playing in the grounds of the Hall and two of them, named by A.A. Thomson as George Jessop and John Hudson, were said to have gone to see the squire, Mr Joseph Walker, to 'beg off'. Mrs Walker is said to have intervened, saying to her husband: 'These lads are fond of cricket. Why not give them a try?'

They practised first in a quarry and then in a small field known as the Croft, which had a stone wall down one side, the reason, it is said, why so many of the Hall's batsmen were fine off-side players. Practice took place in every minute of fine weather, each batsman received 40 balls and no more, and, while awaiting the next man in, the fielders always flicked the ball from man to man, hand to hand.

A permanent ground was opened in 1866 when the club boasted 90 members, each of whom contributed work and money until the ground was completed – this was at a time, after the American Civil War, when many weavers had no work. John

Lockwood, Eph's cousin, was one of the early groundsmen, later taking charge of The Oval.

The full list of players provided to Yorkshire by the club reads: John Thewlis, Luke Greenwood, Ephraim Lockwood, David Eastwood, Andrew Greenwood, Henry Lockwood, Allen Hill (born in Kirkheaton but who moved to the Hall as a boy) and, of course, Billy Bates. Had Hill not had a minor accident in 1874, the Yorkshire team playing Gloucestershire would have contained seven men from the village. Subsequently new technology, in the shape of the power loom, destroyed the village's pre-eminence.

If times were hard and poverty and illness never far away, there were happy times too.

Thompson unearthed a provisions list of 1882 for matches against Harrow Wanderers and Uppingham: 'Half gallon Scotch whisky, gallon brandy, half-gallon rum, nine boxes ginger beer, 30 lbs beef, 2 hams, 12 dozen pies – for the first day'. Their colours rival I Zingari's: purple, cream and black.

No wonder then, that when Sir Stanley Jackson was visiting Huddersfield his first words, on passing through that imposing entrance to the railway station, were the enquiry: 'Which would be the road to Lascelles Hall?'

home. The Reverend Holmes, in 1904, asserted it to be the most attractive of all enclosures, mentioning the Sheffield crowd's reputation for knowledge and fairness: 'The crowds all together there seem to have the genuine sporting instinct – a love of the game for its own sake. Where else in the country is the accommodation so ample? No less than 60,000 persons can see every ball most of them from comfortably-seated terraces.'

For 120 years Bramall Lane was to keep at least some part of that fame and reputation until it, too, was sacrificed for ambitions of a different kind and slipped into football mediocrity.

Cricket was so much a part of the life of Sheffield from 1820 to 1860, and an interest that crossed the divides of a class-ridden society, that it seems in retrospect surprising that it should have taken until 1861 before an attempt was made to establish a county club on a properly representative basis. Nevertheless, on 7 March 1861, a meeting was called at Harry Sampson's hotel, the Adelphi, on the site of what is now the Crucible Theatre famous worldwide as the venue for the World Snooker Championships. The purpose was to set up not a county club, but a 'Public Match Fund Committee', and it was resolved that such a committee should consist of the Bramall Lane Management Committee with the addition of one representative from each club

willing to contribute not less than £1 to the Fund.

The Wednesday club, founded in the same hotel and whose football section was also to be established there six years later, and the clubs of Pitsmoor and Hallam, also from Sheffield, paid up immediately, but a year passed before an outsider, Scarborough, forwarded their money. M.J. Ellison was elected President and Treasurer; W. Whittles was the first Secretary. A match between the first XI and the next XVI was arranged, and the Secretary was instructed to seek home and away games with Surrey. Players were to be sounded out as to their terms for playing against Surrey.

Two dozen 'books' were printed seeking financial support from noblemen and gentlemen of the county, but the Fund was soon in trouble, apparently being unable to convince the rest of the county that it was not merely another Sheffield grouping. Lack of funds prevented matches being played against Lancashire at Manchester in 1862, yet of Yorkshire's cricketing prowess there was no doubt, for although Yorkshire lost to England's strongest county team at The Oval, they were able to take their revenge against Surrey at Bramall Lane.

As a London journalist pointed out, Yorkshire possessed cricketers of the calibre of Atkinson, Hodgson, Slinn, Iddison, Stephenson, Anderson,

Rowbotham and Luke Greenwood, and 'in a year or two Yorkshire could be second to none in England'. So another attempt was made to launch a county club, and on 8 January 1863 it was resolved 'that a county club be formed', the membership to be unlimited, the minimum subscription 10s 6d. The stated object was to provide funds for the playing of first-class matches 'either in Sheffield or in any other towns of the county according as arrangements may be made'.

The mayor of Sheffield, T.R. Barker, was elected the first President, despite his Derbyshire birth, according to the minutes George Padley was first Secretary, and with Ellison as

Joe Rowbotham Old Tarpot

Joe Rowbotham was Yorkshire's second captain, following Roger Iddison to lead the county in 1874 after a long and thoroughly professional career. Born almost next door to Bramall Lane, his home overlooked the Sheffield Milton ground, and as his father was described as 'a bit of a cricketer', the boy was encouraged to practise in the time he had free from his trade as a sawmaker.

'A fine punishing bat in front of the wicket', Rowbotham also attracted attention for his brilliant fielding, especially at long stop, which was regarded as a difficult and dangerous position in the days of unprepared pitches and outfields.

Like Allen Hill, young Rowbotham was taken on the staff at Old Trafford as a 21-year-old, then became a temporary professional with Rochdale and while there was spotted by George Parr, travelling and playing with the All England team for the next decade. Joe was always pleased to recount how he played in the opening match at Bramall Lane in 1855 and in Yorkshire's first match in 1863, but he was 38 before he reached real renown, scoring 101 against Surrey at The Oval in 1869 and 100 against Nottinghamshire at Bramall Lane, the first Yorkshireman to score two centuries in one season – an indication of how valued was a three-figure score at that time.

Rowbotham toured America with Edgar Willsher's team in 1868, only he, the captain and George Griffith of Surrey not being ill on the voyage. Indeed, Joe's ability to eat a meal whatever the weather, no matter how rough the sea, led Ted Pooley of Surrey to say that he 'stuck to everything he ate so well we nicknamed him "Old Tarpot"'.

Rowbotham's own account of that voyage concerned the death of an old lady and the birth of a boy 'to a female steerage passenger. We collected about £5 for her and gave her also the proceeds of a concert which we got up on board. The ship was the City of Baltimore and the mother said she would christen the child "Baltimore".'

He was an abstemious man, as his financial accounting of that tour reveals. The players were given £50 as travelling expenses and seven and a half dollars a day once in American waters, and Rowbotham proudly reported that he had 'made' £100 on the trip.

His captaincy coincided with George Freeman's virtual retirement, Rowbotham himself giving way at the age of 44 'as I had got too stout and could not run'. In fact he did make two further appearances for the county, one as late as 1883, by which time he had become a first-class umpire and had clashed with the great Doctor. He gave Grace out caught at the wicket at Trent Bridge. W.G. asked the umpire what he thought he was doing, scratching his forearm. Joe replied: 'I've given you out and I shall do it again if it happens.'

There was no ill-will. Rowbotham's benefit in 1873 was against Gloucestershire at Bramall Lane. Nottinghamshire wanted Grace at Trent Bridge, and Rowbotham travelled up to London to ask the 'Champion' what he would do. 'Joe, I will play for you and no one else on that day as I promised.'

Joe Rowbotham also kept the New Inn in Eccleshall Road, Sheffield for more than 30 years.

Edwin Stephenson Merry Ned

From Hallam, Sheffield, Ned Stephenson was Yorkshire's first wicket-keeper/batsman who could also bowl useful round-arm when allowed. He played 36 matches for Yorkshire and, mostly to the bowling of Slinn and Hodgson, collected 57 victims, 27 stumped and 30 caught.

One of his stumpings, against Surrey in 1864, was off fast bowler Slinn, and against Nottinghamshire that same season he stumped five, four off Iddison's lobs. As a batsman he was renowned for his tenacity, and it was this all-round ability that undoubtedly won him a place on the first tour of Australia.

Stephenson was, in William Caffyn's words, 'quite a character, always saying something to put a roomful into a roar of laughter'. He was a notorious prankster and enjoyed jokes played upon him, and it was possibly his joviality and sense of companionship that brought him troubles in later life, when he was said to be 'heard of at the Plough Inn, Hallam, any night'. According to *Wisden*, 'in his later days he unfortunately fell into very poor circumstances'. He died at the age of 66.

George Freeman Meteor

Although he played county cricket for only five years, Freeman in action was a meteor, acknowledged by all his contemporaries as the best fast bowler of this time and, indeed, up until the advent of Trueman, accepted as Yorkshire's greatest fast bowler. Born in Boroughbridge and coached assiduously through boyhood by a cricket-mad clergyman (who would keep wicket and discreetly signal to the boy as to which delivery he should next bowl), Freeman had a dazzling career ended only by his opening of a successful business as an auctioneer in Thirsk.

At his peak Freeman stood a handsome 5ft 10_ in, weighed 14 stone and wore a rich black beard. Handsome is as handsome does, and while he was regarded as a highly intelligent and affable man, he was always a formidable prospect on the field. A natural bowler, he took a run of only a few steps with a long delivery stride, virtually round-arm, but according to Eph Lockwood 'he used to make the ball come back six inches, whipping like lightning from the pitch. It was all done with a remarkable whip of the wrist.'

He was also credited with being able to bowl a shooter at will, and, if this seems hardly credible, it was J.M. Kilburn who

George Freeman
Ron Deaton collection

pointed out that Freeman, on poorly prepared pitches, would deliver the ball with an action that would appear low today, but was then regarded as suspiciously high. W.G. and Richard Daft both regarded him as the best bowler they had faced, and Grace considered a hit on the leg from a delivery by Freeman as 'being cut with a knife'. Daft said the insides of his legs were often black and blue after facing Freeman. One of Freeman's deliveries once uprooted all three stumps of a Gloucestershire batsman.

Freeman made his debut for Yorkshire in 1865, on Billy Slinn's retirement, taking 4-29 against Cambridgeshire at Bradford, and was joined in attack the following season by Emmett; Yorkshire not surprisingly won all their seven matches, Freeman taking 51 wickets at an average of 7.4, Surrey and Lancashire were both beaten by an innings.

Freeman took 209 wickets for Yorkshire in only 32 matches, and his early retirement might have been hastened by a muscle strain in his elbow that must have affected the famous 'whip'. It was never more deadly than in Yorkshire's first match against MCC at Lord's in 1870 when, on a poor pitch, Freeman and Emmett made the ball fly dangerously, taking 19 wickets between them. Grace made 66, an innings regarded as marvellous by everyone who saw it, the Yorkshire pair reporting afterwards that 'it was a marvel that the doctor was not either maimed nor unnerved for the rest of his days or killed outright'. Grace's partner, the Essex amateur C.E. Green, was supposed to have carried a livid bruise over his heart, caused by Freeman, for the rest of his days.

So accurate was Freeman that batsmen felt

that if he did not hit their legs he would certainly hit the stumps, and he terrorised local XXIIs when playing for the United North – as, for instance, when a Tadcaster XXII lost seven wickets to his first nine deliveries. As Peter Thomas pointed out, bowlers of that era aimed at the stumps because they could not trust the judgement of many umpires, especially the local ones.

As one of Willsher's American tourists in 1868, Freeman took 104 wickets, bowling 74 of his victims. From New York he wrote home: 'Today we played a match at baseball and were again defeated. It is a fool to cricket, still the Yankees think otherwise.'

Freeman's career was unusual for another reason. He might have been the first professional to be invited to become a 'Gentleman'. Four years after his retirement he was invited by MCC to appear against the Players at Lord's but, according to 'Old Ebor', had to decline for an undisclosed reason, possibly business. 'Old Ebor' is certain that Freeman was asked to play for the Gentlemen of England against the Australians at The Oval in 1882, the year after he finished with Yorkshire, and would have played had he not been a witness in a criminal trial at the Old Bailey. His wife would jokingly assert afterwards that George was afraid of what the Colonials might do to his bowling.

A successful life came to a sadly premature end, for George Freeman died at the age of 51 after two years of suffering with Bright's disease.

Treasurer, Joseph Wostinholm became Secretary after the first year. No record, according to the Reverend Holmes, was ever made of Mr Barker's attending a meeting, and no minute has been found of Ellison's translation to the presidency, but according to official accounts Michael Joseph Ellison was President from the foundation meeting until 1898, and to him must go the major credit for steering the Club through some difficult formative years.

Ellison was, in fact, the first of the benevolent

dictators who have built Yorkshire cricket, Lord Hawke, hardly a populist himself, described Ellison as 'a jolly old autocrat', adding later that Ellison and Wostinholm 'ran it for years'. What will never be known is how much of the fledgling club's financial burdens were borne by the President. As mentioned earlier, Ellison guaranteed the rent of the Bramall Lane ground to his employer, the Duke of Norfolk. In 1884, 21 years after foundation, the Committee voted to refund to the President 'the money expended by him from his private purse in supporting first-

John Thewlis 'Think dead; if not, Manchester'

Those five words, in reply to an enquiry from A.W. Pullin ('Old Ebor' of the *Yorkshire Evening Post*) as to the whereabouts of Thewlis, aged 70, are as meaningful as any ever uttered in the cricketing world. So stirred was Pullin at the old cricketer's plight that he straight away pitched into Yorkshire and cricket administration generally, his message winning great public sympathy and bringing into being such unheard-of reforms as Winter pay. That estimable body, the Professional Cricketers' Association, might one day think of honouring 'Old Ebor'.

Pullin had started to write a series of Winter articles on old Yorkshire cricketers for the *Evening Post* in 1898, in the course of which he not only produced one of the most valuable source books on Victorian cricket, but also discovered how desperate were the circumstances in which some of these old heroes lived – none more so than Thewlis, the most distinguished cricketer of all that great Lascelles Hall clan.

Thewlis was yet another born in Kirkheaton (along with Hill, Hirst, Rhodes) who, like Hill, went into hand-loom weaving at the Hall. He never attended school, being sensitive about his shock of white hair, but he taught himself to read and write and was playing cricket with his pals as soon as he was able. Before he reached the Lascelles Hall XI he was practising on the ground one day when the visiting team arrived. Asked if he was to play against them, the lad replied that he wasn't good enough. The visitors' reaction is recorded: 'They thought the others must be very good for they declined to play'.

When young John did join the first team, his hair turning light brown then black as he grew older, he wore a coat when batting in his first away match. The crowd called for him to take it off but the boy refused, being too ashamed to show the holes in his shirt.

He was 32 before he broke out of local cricket, Luke Greenwood recommending him to George Parr as a batsman of redoubtable defence on the rough tracks of the day, who could also hit fiercely when required. At 35 he was opening for Yorkshire and he continued playing until he was 48. He was, of course, responsible for bringing his nephew Ephraim Lockwood into first-class cricket with that marvellous debut at The Oval.

Thewlis' recollection of that famous occasion began when he met his nephew at King's Cross.

> Going on a bus to The Oval I said to him 'If tha does well in this match it'll be a rare good thing for thee.' I can remember hearing people around asking 'Who's yon farmer that Thewlis has brought?' Ephraim must have made his mark in due time but it was just a toss up whether or no he should have his chance at the time he did.

John Thewlis was a good enough player to have once taken on Eleven Landlords of Chickenley, all runs to be scored in front of the wicket, at Dewsbury Savile. The Landlords dismissed Thewlis for one in the first innings but couldn't get him out on the second, so the match was left drawn.

Lascelles Hall could in time field a whole team of Thewlises, and the fact that they were related to the Lockwoods and Greenwoods makes Thewlis' later misfortunes somewhat mysterious. He received about £350 from his benefit in 1875, and might have expected the support of such a large family. However, when Pullin set off for Manchester to find the old man, he discovered that he was living in Failsworth, making a meagre living carrying baskets of laundry the four miles into Manchester.

When Pullin found him he was anxious to get back to earn a few more coppers carrying coal. The old man said he was well and could still managed his 20 miles a day: 'I have had to cease going to matches because I could not see what was taking place at the wicket. I have lost my teeth but perhaps it is as well for there hasn't been much for them to do lately.' Pullin commented:

> The moral responsibilities of cricket managers, so far as a player is concerned, should surely not end with the termination of his active career. He ought not to be cast aside like an old shoe…

> It is necessary therefore to protest strongly and publicly against the way in which a few old Yorkshire cricketers have been allowed to sink into oblivion and even into poverty. One would have thought that the kindly remembrance of past services would at least have enabled the Yorkshire County Club to know whatever old players were under the sod or above it.

The story had a happier ending. Pullin's bitter words stirred consciences and old John Thewlis got a job that following Summer (1898) as groundsman at the Greenfield Club. Yorkshire, in turn stirred by Lord Hawke, gave the old man a 'Winter allowance'.

A year later in December 1899, old John went home to Lascelles Hall to spend Christmas with his clan. He had a jolly night or two with old friends and players in the Tandem Inn, but was then taken ill and died on 29 December. Billy Bates struggled out of a sick bed to attend the funeral on an icy day, caught a chill and died himself ten days later.

John Thewlis junior, who played for Yorkshire in three matches as a batsman in 1879, was a nephew and not, as *Wisden* reported at the time, old John's son.

---

class and county cricket during the years preceding the founding of the county club in 1863'. The sum granted was £400, and the suspicion is that this was only a fraction of the money spent on Yorkshire cricket during Ellison's 35 years in office.

In his youth Ellison was a useful enough batsman to open the innings for Sheffield against Leeds at the latter's Victoria ground, and it was said that for 70 years he never failed to shoot his grouse on 12 August (he died at the age of 81). In an undated photograph he is shown as a man of sturdy build, balding, with a long white beard, steady of eye, wearing a thick tweed suit, with watch chain, and assuming a pensive pose leaning upon a mantelpiece.

Ellison may have been a difficult man to cross, but he was also an able administrator and rock-like in his principles. It was he who laid down that only Yorkshire-born players should be selected, yet when it was pointed out that the young Martin Bladen Hawke, of an old Yorkshire family, had actually been born in Lincolnshire, he took a Nelsonian attitude: 'Don't tell me then, and let me have a convenient memory.'

It was also Ellison, supported by C.W. Alcock of

Surrey, who campaigned for the admission of Derbyshire, Essex, Leicestershire, Warwickshire and Hampshire to the first-class list in 1894-95. *Wisden* attacked him for over-extending his players with the additional fixtures, but Ellison believed the game had to be expanded to a national basis. He also insisted, at Lord's meetings, that umpires 'should not be allowed to stand for the counties for whom they had played'.

Ellison and Wostinholm, when they began, were among friends and colleagues, for the first County Committee consisted of 12 Sheffield men who decided, among other resolutions of those early days, that 'a central or any fixed ground shall not be considered requisite'; recommendation of young players was 'earnestly invited', while clubs were asked to apply for county fixtures.

The response was disheartening. York, as the county capital, were willing to bid to share fixtures with Sheffield but could rely on only a £50 attendance. Bradford were interested but independent, and in the end Yorkshire county cricket settled into Sheffield for 30 years. Bradford, in fact, tried to go it alone, arranging matches against Nottinghamshire, while York still felt they had rights, too. A mystified Kent cancelled

George Atkinson Windmill

George Atkinson was the first of Yorkshire's line of deadly accurate right-arm medium to fast bowlers. When the mayor of Keighley, in an excess of pride, said that Ripon's Atkinson could pitch on a sixpence, the bowler commented, with straight face: 'That statement is not far wrong.'

He had an unusual approach and action, as an amateur of his time described:

As he delivered the ball with his right hand his left arm swung round with similar action. You thus might have thought he was going to deliver the ball with his left hand. He came sailing up to the pitch with both arms swinging like a windmill.

Odd he might have been, but there were plenty to testify to his accuracy and efficacy. On his first visit to Lord's in 1859, playing against the mighty All Englanders for the United XI, he took 5-17 in 36 overs, four years later he took 6-18 for The North against Surrey at The Oval. His own preferred performance was 7-19 against Surrey at The Oval in 1868 (Ephraim Lockwood's debut).

Born in Ripon, he moved to Leeds where his father combined butchery with the management of a public house. Young George was apprenticed to a glass-blower but 'couldn't stand that game so I went and followed cricket'. He was dutiful enough to develop a pleasant tenor voice with the Leeds Parish Church choir and had something of a reputation as a singer, but when the family moved back to Hunslet young George found a much more congenial occupation making cricket bats from old oak barrel staves.

There he could mix with cricketing professionals, becoming one himself in time, travelling all over the North and making one mysterious allusion: 'I wish I had never seen Middlesbrough. The reasons for this statement will be known to some old cricketers.'

He later coached at Marlborough and Rossall and tells of a match between the latter school and Preston Garrison in 1880. The soldiers' side being short, he persuaded a well-known Lancashire bowler to enlist for the day, playing him as Private Jones. The boys, unaware of the ringer, scored 398, one reaching 205 not out, and 'Jones' departed grumbling that he would never soldier again.

Atkinson coached, among others, A.G. Steel and Lord Tennyson, and was proud to have received from his Lordship's grandfather, the Poet Laureate, a book in appreciation. In a happy career Atkinson had only one disappointment, when in 1863 eight Yorkshire players threatened not to turn out against Surrey if Atkinson was chosen. Yorkshire had lost to Nottinghamshire by a narrow margin and blamed Atkinson for not turning up, although he claimed that he had never agreed to play. In the end the other eight did appear against Surrey, Atkinson did not, but the matter was smoothed over.

Like all old cricketers he became very critical of his juniors. 'Old Ephraim Lockwood would have given these modern off-bowlers some pepper,' he declared at the turn of the century. 'Men are now frightened of being caught in the slips.' A final word on his legendary accuracy: he angrily denied that he had once bowled two wides in a match. 'I only remember bowling one wide in my life.'

Luke Greenwood One Wide

Job Greenwood was the first cricket professional to come out of Lascelles Hall. His brother Luke was the first Lascelles Hall professional to play for Yorkshire, and his son played in the first two Test matches for England.

Luke, in fact, opened many gates. At 24, clean-shaven except for a short goatee beard, he was engaged as a bowler (right-arm, medium to fast) by the Duke of Sutherland in Staffordshire, then followed

Roger Iddison to Broughton, Manchester and was there when recruited for George Parr's All-England XI. He made his debut for Yorkshire in 1861 and for the Players (W.G. appearing for the first time for the Gentlemen) in 1865, and a year later added 114 with Alfred Shaw for the Players' ninth wicket, having been chosen for his bowling.

He introduced John Thewlis to the All-England XI and subsequently to Yorkshire. His views on bowling remain fascinating:

> There is nothing that beats a batsman better than a good length straight ball. There is a length which the batsman cannot play and it is the business of a good bowler to find that length. Modern bowlers [he told 'Old Ebor' in 1898] have an advantage compared with those of our day. If we bowled above our shoulder we were no-balled. Now they can bowl as high as a mill chimney and they ought to come down much straighter than from a round-arm delivery.

He was with Alf Shaw one day at Nottingham, when they were both asked how many wides they had bowled for their counties. 'One,' replied Greenwood, explaining apologetically that it had happened in a thunderstorm at The Oval. 'None,' replied Shaw.

After serving Yorkshire as an all-rounder for their first 13 years, he became an umpire – 'the Australians always behaved like gentlemen to me' – and then, like many of his old comrades, fell upon hard times. As an umpire, Luke Greenwood was perhaps not enamoured of the great Doctor.

In the Oval Test of 1882, Spofforth told how he deliberately 'drew' W.G.'s front leg down the pitch and then sent him a perfectly straight ball on the leg stump. 'Howzat?' he asked umpire Greenwood. As the finger went up and W.G. departed grumbling and growling, Greenwood told him: 'I can't help it, no, not if you was the Prince of Wales himself.'

In the Australian second innings, Murdoch and Jones took a quick single while Lyttleton, keeping wicket, fielded the ball down the leg side and threw it to Peate, described as short-slip. The batsmen were home and Peate made no attempt to throw the ball, whereupon Jones left his crease to pat the pitch. According to Greenwood, at the bowler's end, Grace then walked across, collected the ball and broke the wicket, appealing to umpire Bob Thoms at square, who agreed that Jones was out. Murdoch snapped, 'That's a very sharp practice, W.G.' and Greenwood concurred, commenting that he would not have allowed the appeal, believing the ball to be dead.

As an older man Greenwood was poor, but loved his cricket enough to walk from his Ossett home to watch Yorkshire at Leeds, Bradford and Huddersfield. He set out one Sunday night to walk to Sheffield where Sussex were playing, but on hearing that Ranji was not included he turned back. For all his penury, he never complained: 'They [Yorkshire] always behave to me like a gentleman and send me a card every year.'

---

fixtures in 1864, the Secretary declaring he had doubts as to 'who were the proper parties to get up Yorkshire matches'. Yorkshire (Sheffield) wrote to explain, but Kent changed their minds only so far as to play Yorkshire at Bradford.

In 1886 *The Cricketers' Companion* summed up the claimants, describing York as 'the gentleman's club', and Bradford as boasting 'a most energetic Committee and a liberal subscription list'. But Horton Lane was described as 'too confined' for first-class cricket, while the *Companion* asserted that Bramall Lane was '…a splendid area. Except Nottingham there is no town in England where the spectators are so numerous or enter so thoroughly into the spirit of the game.'

Modern histories tend to regard Sheffield's supremacy in Yorkshire county matters as unchallenged, whereas there were at least two major attempts to unseat what many, especially in the North Riding, regarded as dictatorship. As early as November 1863, ten months after the

Sheffield launch, a meeting was called at Harker's Hotel, York for the purpose, said *Bell's Life*, of 'forming a cricket club for the county of Yorkshire.'.

The Hon G.E. Lascelles took the chair over representatives of Bradford, Leeds, Huddersfield, Wakefield, York, Middlesbrough, Doncaster, Sheffield, Hull, the Vale of Derwent, Harewood, Boroughbridge, Bedale and Redcar. Earl Fitzwilliam was named President and the Lords Londesborough, Feversham and Wenlock agreed to join, which made for an impressive start. However, the structure had no sooner been assembled than it fell apart. Not one but two clubs emerged from the meeting: one for amateurs, the Gentlemen of York, which survived, and a county club, which didn't. Sheffield, of course, had the best ground by far and, at that time, almost all the players, and thus the public appeal.

Eleven years later after the first season of Championship cricket, another rebellion flickered again centring on York. This time the meeting, 28 January 1874, was called at Abbott's Railway Hotel with Lord Londesborough in the chair, and was more overtly North Riding with representatives of Malton, York, Leeds, Scarborough, Bedale, Hull, Hornsea and Middlesbrough. Among the delegates were, interestingly, two great names – Roger Iddison and George Anderson. It seems that Nottinghamshire were not above stirring this

Tom Emmett Sostenutor

Emmett was the best-loved cricketer of his day and, after W.G., the most famous. He was a splendid left-arm fast bowler, a punishing left-hand batsman, a tireless fielder, a player alert to every nuance of the game, and a spontaneous wit who remained cheerful to the last ball of the longest, hottest day.

Many of cricket's hoariest old jokes originated with Emmett. It was Tom who first said: 'There's an epidemic here today and it ain't catching.' A bad sailor, he observed on crossing the Bay of Biscay that they had forgotten the heavy roller. Emmett was so natural a fulcrum of the team that once, when bowling from the start until lunch, he completely forgot who was in charge, muttering 'Why doesn't the old fool take me off?' He himself was that 'old fool'.

On one occasion, after suffering all day at the hands of W.G., who served up 318 – a not uncommon occurrence for Yorkshire – Emmett summed it up by saying: 'It was Grace before men, after meat and all day.' Another time he growled that Grace should be made to play with 'a littler bat'.

Emmett was born in Crib Lane, Halifax in September 1841, learning his cricket at the

Tom Emmett
Ron Deaton collection

entrance to the driveway leading to the house of a local luminary, Henry Ambler. The stone gateposts served as stumps, and it was here that young Emmett first learned to hit the post, round-arm. 'I have never been so big since as I used to be then.'

Between dodging the constabulary, Mr Ambler frowning upon such goings-on in his drive and local residents fearing for their windows, young Emmett learned to be quick. He began, as a boy, bowling for the Illingworth club, learned to break back the ball and was eventually invited to play for Halifax – 'for five shillings, or two and six, I don't know which. My cricket bag, I do know, consisted of the *Halifax Courier* or the *Halifax Guardian* and I invariably went in clogs.'

For three years he played professionally for Keighley, being lured away by the promise of a Winter job, and by 1866 was on the road followed by so many of his contemporaries, hired by local XXIIs to take on All England, winning attention in a match for Keighley against Todmorden in which he scored 119 not out and 'took six or seven wickets'. In August of that year Yorkshire met his terms – £5 to play at Nottingham (this fee included travel and keep).

The following year Emmett had little opportunity to progress until, against Surrey at Bramall Lane in late June, after Freeman and Luke Greenwood had been frustrated by a stand between Stephenson and Tom Humphrey, he was called upon to bowl, with sensational results: six wickets for seven runs in 12 overs. Emmett, when 40 and close to retirement, was leading Yorkshire at The Oval when, in similar circumstances, he put himself on to take 8-22, including a spell of five wickets for no runs in three overs.

Emmett was called the 'Wicket and Wide Man', and was probably the first top-class bowler to appreciate the advantage to be gained by the full use of the bowling crease in altering the angle of attack. He would also alter his length by delivering the ball from behind the crease, and was also perhaps the first to bowl deliberately wide of the off stump in the hope of inducing an edge. There seems little doubt that at least some of his many wayward balls were despatched quite deliberately to affect the batsman's concentration; one ball in any over was liable to be quick and dead on middle stump.

Then there was his 'sostenutor' ('What else would you call it?' he asked) that was acknowledged as being one of the marvels of the age. Said W.G.: 'I have had occasional balls from him that would have beaten any batsman; his best was one pitching between the legs and wicket with sufficient break and rise to hit the off bail.' Richard Daft described him as 'all wire and whipcord: one of the very best bits of stuff a cricketer was ever made of'.

Emmett's 1216 wickets for Yorkshire were taken at an average of 12.71. He also scored 6315 runs at an average of 15.10, his solitary first-class century coming against the premier power, Gloucestershire. Tom Emmett was also the fifth and last of Yorkshire's professional captains until the election of Vic Wilson in 1960. Tom was not, according to his contemporaries, an ideal leader, being over-modest with his own bowling and taking a liberal view of Yorkshire's fielding, which was regarded as something of a joke among the counties, it being said that Emmett's team was too polite to run out an opponent.

County committees in the 1880s were veering strongly towards the view that professionals were ill-suited to leadership. The Reverend Holmes wrote in 1904:

> Without the smallest grain of snobbishness of all men like to be commanded by their social superior. One can with confidence point to Yorkshire cricket, for confirmation during the last decade. That the County Committee were of the same opinion the following minute in 1878 shows: 'That T. Emmett be made captain in the absence of a gentleman'.

The Reverend adds: 'Perhaps the word "amateur" is less open to criticism.'

If Emmett was aware of this attitude within the Committee, he never allowed such thoughts to spoil his delightful attitude to the game. After a stirring victory over Nottinghamshire, the Yorkshire captain was recorded as having turned a somersault in the middle of the pitch by way of celebration. Hawke called him 'the greatest character that ever stepped on a cricket field, a merry wag who could never lose heart or temper'. Another peer, Lord Harris of Kent: 'I have never known a keener or merrier [cricketer] than dear old Tom. He was as hard as a board and as active as a cat.'

Emmett's ability to laugh at himself endeared him to the dressing rooms. His huge nose was described by Hawke as 'if not so obtrusive as that of Cyrano de Bergerac yet it was as highly coloured'. He must have laughed as much as anyone after the famous pitch invasion at Sydney when a crowd of 2,000 in ugly mood swept up Lord Harris, A.N. Hornby and George Ulyett. A 'larrikin' struck at Harris, Ulyett prepared to hit back with a stump, but 'Monkey' seized the lad and used him as a battering ram to clear a patch to a policeman. 'Where was Tom?' Ulyett was asked. Emmett had, in fact, returned to the pavilion to change his socks, but according to his fellow Yorkshireman 'the crowd gave him such a fright he was seen running like a madman towards the harbour'.

Emmett was 47 when he retired, and even then many Yorkshiremen felt he should have been retained a little longer, although the parting was not entirely happy: 'When I finished a remark was made to the effect that they didn't want to see me any more. It may have been meant as a joke but it was not well put; indeed, after my long service on the county it seemed in bad taste and I felt it.'

His benefit match raised £620 and he played briefly as a professional with both Bradford and Leicester clubs, but his later days were remembered by pupils at Rugby where be became coach in March 1889 and sought to have the church bells silenced during practice and for some elms to be cut down to improve the ground. Sir Pelham Warner wrote: 'Every Rugby boy knew him and loved him. I can see him…striding across the Close with his grey and well-shaped head crowned by a Yorkshire cap held high and his body as straight as the most ramrod sergeant.'

His closing days, according to *Wisden*, were 'unhappily clouded', but he lived to 63 to see in the new century and the Golden Age.

---

particular pot, their Secretary writing to advise the meeting that 'for a successful county policy one ground only be used and that be York'. From this meeting emerged Yorkshire United Club, which, under Londesborough's leadership, regularly called upon leading Yorkshire players to play a fixture list that never attained first-class recognition.

Londesborough tried once again, in 1884. After the demise of the United club, he formed the North Riding of Yorkshire XI, a team that were totally crushed when they met the full power of the county XI, scoring 162 and 41-3 in reply to 530. Another four years and Londesborough became President of the North and East Ridings XI, Lord Derwent succeeding him the following year, but that, too, failed to capture public interest.

All this would seem to make William Henry Forester Denison, Earl of Londesborough, a malcontent, when in fact he was a great benefactor to the early game. His enthusiasm and support brought into being the Scarborough Festival; he greatly assisted the foundation of Hampshire cricket by taking teams to Lyndhurst; and his generosity to old professionals was legendary. He offered to pay for specialist treatment for Harry Dewse's battered hands. Said Dewse: 'When I found it would cost him £50, and as I had no pain, I declined to go.'

Londesborough became President of the MCC in 1876 when his carriage became a familiar sight at both Lord's and Scarborough, where his wife would also attend, showing equal enthusiasm for the game. The Countess, in fact, loved listening to the repartee and broad accents of the old cricketers. One Yorkshireman, angry at being caught in the deep at Lord's by the Gentlemen, brought a peal of laughter with his irate explanation of how he came to be out to such a ball: 'Ah meant to put t'bugger over t'pavilion.'

Somehow, Yorkshire did manage to take the field with a fully representative XI in that Summer of 1863. Captained by Iddison (Bedale), the team read: Thewlis (Lascelles Hall), Berry and Dawson (Dalton), Iddison and Anderson (Bedale), Atkinson (Ripon), Hodgson (Bradford), Rowbotham, Stephenson and Slinn (Sheffield). At The Oval on 5 and 6 June Surrey raised a then huge 315, to which Yorkshire replied with 257 and then bowled out Surrey in

The Halifax Connection

Halifax has minimal claim to fame in relation to Yorkshire cricket. However, one player alone guarantees the town's place in the annals of the YCCC. That man was Thomas Emmett, born precisely 98 years before the outbreak of the Hitler War, on 3 September 1841. He was one of the five Yorkshiremen who represented England in the very first Test, at Melbourne, in 1877 and he captained the county from 1878 to 1882. Maybe equally importantly, he dismissed the great 'W.G.' before the Victorian legend had troubled the scorers. Tom's fame also extends to his regular journeys down Crib Lane, Halifax, with his cricket gear wrapped in a copy of the local 'Courier'. This humorous, left-arm fast bowler, who died on 30 June 1904, with an average of 13.36, heads the list of White Rose bowlers who have taken over 1,000 wickets.

Thrum Hall ground, Halifax, enjoys an elevated position, rather more than two miles from the town centre. One must go back to the last two decades of the century for the connection with the County Cricket Club. First-class matches were played in the West Riding wool town between 1888 and 1897, but the previous year's (1887) fixture list involved a second-class encounter with Cheshire, where Yorkshire were defeated by an innings and 235 runs. Fred Lee from Basildon scored 206. Louis Hall of Batley was his partner in a stand of 175.

In 1888 Halifax was favourite with yet another minor engagement, this time with Warwickshire, and the initial first-class match, against Gloucestershire. I understand the ground was not surprisingly packed by virtue of the presence of Dr W.G. Grace himself. The 40-year-old cricketing giant disappointed. He fell to the England left-arm bowler, Bobby Peel, in each innings. The Morley born all-rounder took

13 wickets for a mere 84 runs, to ensure victory.

Middlesex provided the first-class opposition in 1890. Thrum Hall did not stage a match in 1889. However, the London County's game did not provide the noteworthy feature of the former season. Benjamin Charles Bolton, right-arm pace bowler, from Cottingham, took 8-26 on his Yorkshire debut against Warwickshire. The Midlands County did not attain first-class status until 1894, but it was a sensational entry for a cricketer who played only four matches for the county. Bolton's end was sad; in 1910 he fell from an express train bound for Hull and his death resulted from the subsequent injuries.

The final, victorious 1897 Kent match saw Bobby Peel to the fore once more. He captured eight wickets for 53 runs, including the hat-trick. The 1898 season featured Worcestershire at Thrum Hall, with J.T. Brown of Driffield scoring 104. This was the first engagement between the two counties on Yorkshire soil. It was also the last appearance of a White Rose team at Halifax.

One other Test cricketer first saw light of day on that day. He was the undertaker-wicketkeeper-batsman, Hanson Carter, the only Yorkshireman who played in the Headingley Test of 1921 and he was representing Australia. He emigrated and was a member of the New South Wales team.

Tom Naylor

Tom Naylor was a retired railwayman from Halifax who thought nothing of rising at 3 am to catch his train connections, daily, to watch Yorkshire all over England. He could rarely afford to stay overnight. This contribution remembers a devoted follower of the Club.

their second innings for 60, with Ikey Hodgson taking nine wickets and Billy Slinn six in the match. Those early teams were made up of free-lance professionals usually paid £5 a match from which all living and travelling expenses had to be paid.

By 1865, however, the Club was plunged into its first player crisis by the refusal of five senior players – Anderson, Atkinson, Iddison, Rowbotham and Stephenson – to play against Surrey. The dispute was not of Yorkshire's making but arose from the no-balling of Kent's Edgar Willsher when playing for the All-England XI against Surrey at The Oval in 1862. AEE players suspected that Surrey had put up umpire John Lillywhite to no-ball Willsher and when, in 1864, Iddison failed to appear in a

North v South match at Islington, the Southern players, 13 in all, seceded from the AEE and the United England XI to form the United South of England XI, whose red, white and blue blazer was soon to be worn by a prodigious young player from the West – William Gilbert Grace.

In 1865 Anderson, offered the Yorkshire captaincy, declined saying he would 'not play against those who have combined to sweep us from the cricket field altogether if they could' – in other words, most of the Surrey XI. The Committee thundered that they 'cannot help reminding you that every professional player is bound to play for his county when called upon to do so'.

Anderson had support, however, and with the backbone of the side gone Yorkshire did not win

George Pinder Prince of Keepers

Pinder not only followed Ned Stephenson as Yorkshire's wicket-keeper, he also lived in the same street in Eccleshill, Sheffield. A tall, lean man with curly hair and deep moustache, Pinder had a tremendous reach and fiercely disputed Blackham's claim to be the first keeper to dispense with a long-stop.

According to Pinder it was in a match between The North and The South at Lord's in 1878 when A.N. Hornby, captaining The North, asked if he could do without a long-stop. The bowlers were Morley and Emmett, and Pinder replied truthfully: 'You know, sir, if one passes it means a four.' Hornby took the risk and The North won comfortably. Later, at The Oval, after Ephraim Lockwood had been fielding long-stop he came up to Pinder and said: 'I've been behind thee for 23 overs and have not had to stop a ball. I think I can find a better place.'

So who was the first to keep without a long-stop? G.D. Martineau in *The Valiant Stumper* is unable to give a verdict, although he points out that Australia's Jack Blackham was in England at that time. Blackham made his Test debut two years earlier, so he should have the stronger case

George Pinder
YCCC

in an argument that in no way detracts from Pinder's status as a pioneer of the craft.

Pinder has a good claim to being the first to stand up to all his county bowlers, and as these included George Freeman, the fastest of his time, Allen Hill, almost as fast and deadly accurate, and the eccentric and erratic Tom Emmett, he must have been a sight. His leg-side work was legendary. He once managed to stump Tom Hearne of Middlesex off a shooter down the leg side.

Pinder, aged ten, was apprenticed to a pen and pocket-blade grinder in Sheffield and was almost 18 before he got the chance to play for the St Mary's Club, as a bowler. For a match against the powerful Hallam Club St Mary's were without a keeper and pressed the young Pinder into the job, and so successful was he that his career was made.

He was 24, still bent over the grindstone, when Sheffield Shrewsbury, a club he described as a 'gentleman's organisation', asked him to keep for their XXII against All England. Pinder caught three and stumped two of the all-stars, was invited by Ossett and Worksop to play against them, and finally played with them at Whitehaven.

Then a professional, he took over from Ned Stephenson and three years later, on Harry Sampson's recommendation and on condition that All England's fixtures took priority, replaced Stephenson as Yorkshire's keeper. Of keeping to Freeman, Hill and Emmett, he told 'Old Ebor':

> It was no joke, especially to Tom Emmett, who used to sling in the ball at times in a way that made the stumper keep his eyes wide open and his wits about him. There was a certain ball which appeared to be going to leg but which would whip in on the middle and off stumps. As soon as I saw that ball I gave the batsman up.

To the end of his days Pinder firmly believed he had stumped Arthur Shrewsbury before the great man completed his first century (for Nottinghamshire against All England), but the umpire had favoured the batsman. On W.G. Grace, Pinder commented: 'I got his wicket oftener than anybody and more often than the umpires would give it to me. I think the umpires in those days either favoured or were a bit frightened of W.G. who of course had a tremendous reputa-

tion – and not more than he deserved.'

Pinder collected 246 victims in his 124 matches for Yorkshire, 100 of them stumped, and it is sad that his career with the county should have ended in controversy. In 1880, in a needle match with Nottinghamshire, he missed two catches and was dropped for the next match, although paid as an umpire. Yorkshire also wanted him to umpire in the next match, against Middlesex at Bramall Lane, but Pinder claims he was not told of this: 'It was scarcely likely that I would throw a £5 note away.'

He completed the season, and a benefit match that September raised £300. Pinder then turned down, on the advice of 'one or two Yorkshire committeemen', an invitation to join the staff at Lord's. The following Spring, having heard nothing from Yorkshire, he attended the first match, at Bramall Lane, and was prevented from entering the pavilion by an official who told him: 'You are not a player.' Pinder admits: 'I let my tongue slip more freely than was wise, though I think my provocation was great.' Thereafter the great Pinder had to pay to watch Yorkshire, becoming an innkeeper in Sheffield and in Worksop, where 'Country Vicar' remembered him as 'a big man with grey, curly hair and a genial red face'. His hands were badly distorted after keeping for 20 years on rough surfaces.

Pinder was big enough to praise his successor Joe Hunter as 'a very good man', and in his last days, as groundsman at Hickleton Main Colliery, he felt compelled to compare, in a letter, the lot of professionals at the turn of the century, by which time they received £2 a week Winter pay, with his own remuneration:

> We only got £5 [a match] wherever we went, and the largest number of matches I played in one season was 24. That was £120. Out of that I had to pay my hotel bills, my railway travelling and maintain my home, my wife and four children. We started in May and gave up in September and then had seven months to get over.

a match in 1865 and cancelled fixtures for the following year. The other four strikers did play against Cambridgeshire at Bradford in the year of the strike, and it was in that match that the first of Yorkshire's indisputably great bowlers appeared: George Freeman, taking four wickets for 29 on his debut.

Early in April 1867 the Committee, having had a long Winter to think things over, decided to seek a rapprochement, announcing that they would select those players who had refused the previous Summer 'on their expressing regret for what had happened before'. All five apologised although Anderson, the ringleader, never appeared for Yorkshire again. Writing almost 30 years later, the Reverend Holmes was able to conclude: 'Ever since that year there has reigned the most perfect harmony between the Committee and the cricketers of the Yorkshire County Club.'

Although Yorkshire had no official fixture list in 1866, three matches were played of considerable historical implications, two against Nottinghamshire, one against Cambridgeshire,

all at Bradford. Freeman played in two and sadly surprised his admirers by not taking a wicket; Billy Slinn having retired in 1865, this was Ikey Hodgson's last Summer and there must have been a few Yorkshire cricket followers who could not visualise the team without both Slinn and Hodgson. However, in compensation for Hodgson's departure and Freeman's apparent failure there did arrive from Halifax one Tom Emmett who, against Nottinghamshire, took 6-55.

If the county's first four years had been clouded, 1867 burst through into brilliant sunshine, all seven matches being won, Surrey being beaten twice (once by an innings), Lancashire three times (twice by an innings), and Cambridgeshire twice. The difference was, of course, the arrival in harness of Freeman and Emmett, the former taking 51 wickets at an average of 7.4, the latter 30 at 5.2. Opposing batsmen were simply swept aside and such was Yorkshire's confidence – perhaps almost arrogance – that they accepted challenges to play XIs of Surrey and Nottinghamshire, Middlesex and Cambridgeshire and of Sussex at a stake of

Ephraim Lockwood Old Mary Ann

Eph Lockwood was the first Yorkshire cricketer to enter the county's folklore, a phlegmatic but easy going character who became Yorkshire's fourth captain and their first major batsman, whose cutting off middle stump was regarded as one of the wonders of the age.

He learned the game at Lascelles Hall and then became a 'Saturday man', a professional, for Kirkburton and, in turn, Meltham Mills, Lockwood and Cheetham Hill, Manchester, by then aged 23. His first-class debut is a tale woven into the fabric of the game.

George Freeman and Luke Greenwood were injured in a bus accident at Derby, and Yorkshire arrived in London on the Saturday night knowing they were a man short for the match against Surrey starting on the Monday. The captain, Roger Iddison, wished to send for protégé Milner Gibson,

but John Thewlis, hearing substitutes were being discussed, modestly put forward the name of his nephew. Iddison was unconvinced until Tom Emmett chimed in to say 'Eph's a good 'un'. A wire was sent to Cheetham Hill but Lockwood had already left to play for Lascelles Hall at Yeadon, and it says something for the telegraphic service of 1868 that the message reached him in time for him to present himself in London on Sunday evening.

Surrey made 195 after young Lockwood, his gear wrapped in a paper parcel under his arm, had apparently had some difficulty in winning admission to The Oval. Iddison, perhaps anxious to get over any embarrassment quickly, send in the young man to open with his uncle, Thewlis, saying as they walked out: 'Eph, lad, play thi usual game and tha'll be allreet.' The crowd hooted at the sight of what appeared to be a boy in a green, black and red check shirt, too-tight trousers shortened by washing and borrowed boots that were too big for him. But he and Uncle John batted all through a hot afternoon and evening, Emmett appearing at one point with some drinks from what must have been a jubilant dressing room to tell Lockwood, with a straight face: 'Think on, tha's on thi merits.'

By the close Thewlis was 51, Lockwood 57 and the stand reached 176, a first-wicket record that stood for 18 years, Lockwood making 91 on debut (Thewlis 108). Ned Stephenson, first wicket down, wore his pads through three sessions and got a duck.

Lockwood from that day was considered Yorkshire's premier batsman, the predecessor of a great line that led on to Tunnicliffe, Brown, Holmes, Sutcliffe, Hutton and Boycott. So important was he to the side that when he was out George Pinder would say to the number 11: 'Get thi pads on, Mary Ann's out.' Observers spoke of his broad shoulders and, always, of the power of his cutting. One fast bowler is reported to have posted six slips to him and still they were pierced. He scored regularly with a half-cock shot over mid-off that appeared to be a mis-drive; he would also move out as if to drive on the leg side and then, at the last minute, play a late cut. This shot was known as 'Lockwood's Folly'.

Those were his major strengths, but he could play all round the wicket and in 1878 the Australians regarded Lockwood as second only to Grace for variety of strokes. In 1883 he hit 208 against Kent, an innings probably worth double on today's pitches. Twice invited to tour Australia he turned down a third invitation in order to marry Fuller Pilch's niece, of whom it was said that she was the one lady who knew as much about the game as her husband.

He did, however, tour America in 1879, the scene of the second classic Lockwood story. Taken with George Pinder to Niagara Falls, he is supposed to have observed: 'Ah reckon nowt to it. Ah'd sooner be in Lascelles Hall.' A.A. Thomson thought that this somewhat dour reaction to one of the world's wonders might have been explained by Ephraim's punishment by mosquitoes, which made his face swell 'like a pudding'.

As Yorkshire's captain for two years (1876-77), he was by all contemporary accounts considered far too easy-going, causing even the jovial Emmett to flare up on one occasion when he failed to persuade Allen Hill to bowl again at the 'big un', W.G.: 'Why don't you make him, you're the captain?'

He was known to be careful with his money, once allegedly falling conveniently asleep when the collection plate came round, and when he retired in 1884 he eventually opened a sports shop in Huddersfield. He died as late as December 1921, and thus would have been able to tell a grand tale to modern generations.

£1,000 per match. Perhaps fortunately for Yorkshire pockets, the matches never took place.

That such contests should be contemplated confirms that county cricket was still loosely organised and that such towns as Bradford, especially, and, occasionally, Middlesbrough, Dewsbury and Hunslet continued to promote their own county fixtures for a decade. Not until 1873 was the County Club's authority recognised and accepted.

The following year, too, had its great moments, even if the level of success could not be maintained. In 1868 John Thewlis scored the first century for Yorkshire. 108 at The Oval, the match in which his country cousin Ephraim Lockwood made his famous debut. Freeman and Emmett were again irresistible, bowling unchanged against Lancashire and hitting the stumps 18 times, the Red Rose being humiliated at Holbeck for 30 and 34.

Yet in an incredibly hot Summer (so intense was the heat that play against both Lancashire and Surrey had to be stopped for an hour) Yorkshire won only four of their seven matches. The costume of the time would not have helped: striped or coloured shirts with separate collar and tie, a heavy belt with a metal buckle (braces having been slowly phased out) and brown boots.

In 1869 Rowbotham scored centuries against Surrey and Nottinghamshire, the first Yorkshireman to compile two three-figure scores in one year. Rowbotham was awarded £5 for this innings against Nottinghamshire, Iddison £5 for a 112 against Cambridgeshire, and the latter was also given a silver cup for his batting in that match. Yet there was no doubt that the star of that Summer was Emmett. Against Cambridgeshire, who were dismissed for 40 and 46, he took 16 wickets for 38 runs, nine in the second innings, completing a remarkable match by catching another off Freeman. Such a feat, however, won him no extra rewards for, in the prevailing conditions, it was runs rather than wickets that were valued. As the Reverend Holmes commented: 'No wonder that certain promising young bowlers became batsmen.'

Yorkshire's record in 1869 – won four, lost one – was bettered the following year when six of the seven matches played were won, and although no championship existed there is no doubt that Yorkshire were England's premier county team. Freeman had another Summer of devastation, taking 50 wickets for 327 runs in what, sadly, was his last full season for the county. He and Emmett were aided by the appearance of George Pinder behind the stumps for, valuable as Ned Stephenson had been, Pinder proved to be a brilliant keeper against fast bowling. As the Second Empire fell to the Prussians, the Yorkshire pair were the Lillee and Thomson of their day.

Pinder was the first to stand up to the wicket (with Rowbotham initially behind him at long stop), a move to make any batsman apprehensive facing Freeman's pace and Emmett's movement off the surfaces of those days. Freeman's increasing commitments meant that he played in only three of Yorkshire's seven matches in 1871, but he did leave cricket with an immortal testimonial from W.G: 'the finest fast bowler I ever played against'. Ten years later Freeman was persuaded to return for one match, and at the age of 37 he took nine wickets against Lascelles Hall and was also Yorkshire's top scorer with 60 runs.

Freeman's departure did open a door for another great fast bowler, Allen Hill, whose 12-57, all bowled, against Surrey must have hit county cricket like a thunderclap. The success of these

years began to be reflected in the balance sheet, a healthy profit enabling the Committee to grant Bramall Lane £50 for the repair and improvement of seating.

It was the custom then for the ground authority to award prizes and marks of distinction; a function now taken over by sponsors, and it was Yorkshire who awarded talent money to the Surrey brothers Tom and Richard Humphrey for their 140 out of 165 at Bramall Lane. That particular match ended in some controversy for, with neutral umpires standing for the first time, Surrey walked off the field after one over of the second innings, deciding for themselves that the light was too bad for batting. Then, without waiting to see if there would be any improvement, Surrey dressed and left Sheffield.

That year Yorkshire won only three of their seven matches, also losing three – an indication of changing strengths, for worse was to following in 1872. The programme was increased to ten matches of which no less than seven were lost, the Reverend Holmes adding that the toss was lost in 'nearly every match'.

A new power had arisen in the West: the Gloucester of the Graces. Six years later Francis Thompson captured some of the glitter and splendour of that team when he wrote, of a match at Old Trafford:

> The champion of the centuries, he cometh up
>   against thee,
> With his brethren, every one a famous foe,
> The long-whiskered Doctor, that laugheth
>   rules to scorn
> While the bowler, pitched against him,
> Bans the day that he was born.
> And G.F., with his science,
> Makes the fairest length forlorn,
> They are come up from the West, to work thee
>   Woe.

W.G. Grace had appeared in Sheffield in 1869, scoring 122 out of 173 for The South against The North. He returned for the county fixture in 1872, a match that was also Iddison's benefit, with Freeman also reappearing to mark this special occasion. W.G. and T.G. Matthews batted through the first day and were not separated until

Allen Hill Devastator

Hill, fast right-arm, had the ultimate pedigree for a Yorkshire cricketer: born in Kirkheaton, birthplace of Hirst and Rhodes, he learned his cricket as a hand-loom weaver in Lascelles Hall, and it is the latter village which, quite rightly, claims him. Indeed, according to A.A. Thomson it was a Kirkheaton man who wished, in the 1890s, that Hirst would be as good a player as Hill.

The youngster's bowling prowess soon attracted attention, and at 17 he became another 'Saturday man', playing for Dewsbury Savile and then Mirfield Old for five shillings (25p) a match (including all expenses). He then became coach and groundsman at Stonyhurst, on Luke Greenwood's recommendation, subsequently joined the Lancashire ground staff, and was actually Burnley's professional when he made one of the most sensational starts in cricketing history.

George Freeman had broken down, and Roger Iddison invited the almost unknown Hill to take his place against Surrey at The Oval on 21 August 1871. He was then 26 and unusual in that he struck with a round-arm action even when over-arm bowling was legalised. He took a short run, relying mostly on accuracy, length and sheer pace, bringing the occasional ball back, and his action was described by a contemporary as 'a beautiful delivery'.

Surrey batted first, and Hill opened with Emmett taking 6-33 in 27 overs. When Yorkshire batted, raiding 100 to Surrey's 111, Hill was top scorer with 28 before taking the ball again to improve on his first-innings figures: 6-23 in 23 overs.

Hill had some difficulty in getting his release from Burnley for the rest of that season, but from 1872 he played regularly with Yorkshire for 12 seasons, taking over from Freeman who played only another five matches after that year.

Hill's accuracy and pace can be assessed by his three hat-tricks and by a performance

Allen Hill
Ron Deaton collection

against XXII of Cambridgeshire when, bowling on Parker's Piece, he thrice broke a middle stump in half. Among his hat-trick victims were 'Monkey' Hornby and W.G. Grace.

Emmett rated Hill Yorkshire's best fielder of that era, but it may be that old Tom was biased. At Bramall Lane in July 1876, Lancashire needed only 80 to win and looked like competing an easy victory with Hornby and Barlow at the wicket. 'Never mind about Barlow,' said Emmett. 'We can get him out if he tries to get runs. But we must get rid of the other.' Emmett promptly bowled Hornby with what is remembered as one of the worst ever deliveries seen in a Roses match, a slow half-volley outside the off stump, which Hornby leapt upon and hammered, only for Hill, at point, to take a most astonishing point-blank catch. Emmett promptly put Hill on to bowl at the other end where he took five wickets for three runs, all bowled, and Lancashire were all out for 70.

Hill was one of five Yorkshiremen, with

Ulyett, Emmett, Armitage and Andrew Greenwood, who toured with Lillywhite's team in 1876-77, taking 10-9 against XVI of Adelaide ('we had to leave the match to catch our steamer'). Touring then presented hazards unfamiliar to today's players. Crossing a gorge in New Zealand in two coaches, the party found themselves caught in a sudden flood and had to wade to safety up to their waists: 'We expected to be drowned any moment.'

Hill's benefit match, appropriately against Lancashire, raised £376 in 1884, and when his career ended after he broke his collar bone, he returned to the Red Rose as a coach. Yet although Allen Hill spent five years as a young professional in Lancashire before Yorkshire's call, he was never approached to qualify for them.

the first wicket had raised 238, W.G. contributing 150. Bramall Lane now boasted turnstiles.

The search for greater competition was illustrated by a combined Nottinghamshire-Yorkshire fixture against England and the first realisation in Yorkshire that reserve strength was needed. Two matches, Seniors v Juniors and a Yorkshire XI v a Colts XI, were played this Summer, the Juniors beating the Seniors (including Iddison, Rowbotham, Anderson, Thewlis and Atkinson) by seven wickets, a result that must have heartened a Committee perhaps disappointed by the earlier happenings of the season.

Dissatisfaction with the laxity of the qualification requirements stirred Surrey into calling a meeting of the counties then considered first-class (Surrey, Derbyshire, Gloucestershire, Kent, Lancashire, Middlesex, Sussex and Yorkshire. Nottinghamshire being ranked but not represented), and on 11 December 1872, at 15 Hanover Street, London, a set of regulations was approved that would still be regarded as liberal today. Because there were some discrepancies between these regulations and another draft, prepared earlier by MCC, another meeting was called before the start of the 1873 season, on 15 April, at which a compromise was agreed and the first steps were taken towards the founding of a properly organised county championship competition.

It should be emphasised at this point that the counties did not see themselves as setting up a championship, otherwise some formula for the deciding of such a competition would also have been agreed upon in that Spring. The pressure for an official recognition of merit came from the media. Although the 1860s newspapers had been publishing unofficial tables, based upon results, and this practice was to continue for another 22 years until MCC, again apparently reluctant arbiters, stepped in and decreed: 'After the close of each season the Committee of MCC shall decide the County Championship.'

Well, it wasn't quite as autocratic as it sounds. From 1873, the generally recognised year for the start of the Championship, the 'unofficial' table was determined by the number of defeats. From 1887 for two years, each win brought one point, a half-point being awarded for a draw; from 1890 for four years, defeats were deducted from victories and draws were ignored.

MCC then decided that one point should be awarded for each victory, one point deducted for each defeat, the total to be modified by the number of matches played (the regulations specified a minimum of eight matches but no maximum). This meant that a team playing ten matches, winning six and losing four, would finish with two points, which, when turned into a percentage (2 x 100 ÷10), would be represented in the Championship table by a percentage of 20. Thus was set the pattern for the complicated system of deciding England's premier county.

Over almost 140 years of Championship history, no form of calculation has been proof against some anomaly. The 'least defeats' principle fell in 1886 when Nottinghamshire, having won seven and drawn seven, won the Championship before a Surrey record of 12 won and three lost. The emphasis had to be switched to 'most wins' to maintain a reasonable balance and, in fairness to MCC, their method was successful enough to see the Championship launched successfully.

Yorkshire began their Championship career with what must have been a certain amount of opti-

George Ulyett Happy Jack

Wisden said at Ulyett's death in June 1898: 'A finer cricketer the county has never produced. He was for years the best bat in the team and if he had not been able to get a run he would have been worth his place for his bowling and his fielding.'

Ulyett was born at Pitsmoor, Sheffield, and learned to play with a team of boys in Crabtree Village who would challenge local teams to play for money, matches not always being decided by the 'Laws'. Ulyett remembered one such match in which he had one eye closed by contact with the ball and the other as a result of a difference with an opposing player. The Secretary of the Pitsmoor Club kept a benevolent eye on proceedings, and so impressed was he by the young Ulyett that he persuaded his committee to bend the rules to admit a 16-year-old two years before his eligibility for membership. Mr Pickersgill must soon have won a vote of confidence for his enterprise, for the new member took 12 wickets in his first match, a Whitsuntide two-day fixture against great rivals Staveley.

Young Ulyett was actually working in a rolling mill at this time, and although an enraged employer would frequently sack him for taking time off to play, the man must have been enough of a Yorkshireman to give the lad back his job. In time he became a professional at Bradford and it was there, on the old Horton Road ground, that he bowled for the club against a United South XI and dismissed W.G., Yorkshire showing an interest for the first time.

As a batsman Ulyett, for all he opened the innings, was renowned as a hitter, so it made sense for Yorkshire to install Louis Hall as his partner. A fierce driver, he was credited with clearing the players' seats at Lord's in 1878, dropping the ball into the gravel behind the pavilion, a hit of 109 yards. Said Grace: 'He threw all his gigantic strength into his strokes.' In America, challenged on his opinion that baseball was a child's sport, he hit a famous pitcher for 162 not out.

George Ulyett
Ron Deaton collection

Ulyett bowled fast-medium with a break-back, could make the ball lift and was regarded as a very unpleasant prospect to face on some of the suspect pitches of those days. Tall, he weighed 14 stone and his back was as broad and robust as his humour. He became Hawke's sergeant major, and when Hirst arrived they were known in the team as Old and Young George, Ulyett always referring to Hirst as 'young 'un'.

The first Englishman to score two 50s in a Test match, Ulyett also had some fine bowling performances against Australia, including a 7-36 at Lord's in 1884 – a Test in which he made a catch that is still regarded as one of the most remarkable ever seen to put out George Bonnor, the 6ft 6in Australian who was judged to be close to Jessop in hitting power. Bonnor hit back a half-volley with all his force and power. Ulyett put out a hand and the ball stuck. Grace and Harris both told Ulyett he was foolish for even attempting to catch, asserting that if the ball had hit arm or wrist bones would have been broken. Ulyett said the ball came back to him as if on an elastic string, and it was such a talking point that MCC's oldest member gave him a sovereign (probably worth about £100 today) and said it was the finest catch he had seen in his long life. *Punch* commented that more like Ulyett were needed to go to war, as they would be useful in catching cannonballs.

At has peak 'Happy Jack', a dressing room nickname bestowed by Charlie Ullathorne, was described as tall, broad-shouldered, with a high colour and heavy dark moustache which, in almost every portrait, hides the beginning of a mischievous smile, often betrayed by his eyes. His jokes and humour have remained a legend.

He and Ted Peate once managed to get into a reception held by Mr Gladstone in 10 Downing Street, Ulyett evading queries by pretending to be stone deaf, Peate feigning ignorance as Ulyett's 'keeper'. All went well until one of the guests, a Lancashire amateur, recognised the pair and, recalled Peate, 'you should have seen the look of astonishment on his face'. Pressed for an explanation, Ulyett came up with: 'We thought it was a place of entertainment.'

An innings by Ulyett was recalled by 'Country Vicar', writing in 1930:

He was good to watch; he played the game with such a light heart. No poking about for him. No allowing the ball to hit the bat. He did the hitting and with right good will from the first moment he reach the wicket. And his powerful strokes travelled in every direction; there was no paucity of strokes. Cuts, drives, leg-hits, he kept every shot in his locker…a little reckless perhaps at times and had he played a little more steadily he might have made even more runs. But to play steadily was not Ulyett's game; it was all fire and force but graceful withal. He was the greatest professional batsman of his time and there is no professional batsman now, to my mind, who plays the dashing, dazzling game he did.

Ulyett's benefit match in 1887 lasted only two days, but a subscription list was opened and, in the end, the fund topped £1,000, a very handsome sum for those days and a measure of Yorkshire's regard for 'Happy Jack'. He became landlord of the Vine Hotel in Sheffield, many reporting on the happy times to be had and laughter to be heard 'at the sign of the wicket'.

A golden Autumn was sadly cut short in his 47th year. Despite carrying a cold he insisted on attending Bramall Lane on a chill, damp day in June 1898. According to A.A. Thomson, he met George Hirst on the pavilion steps and said, simply: 'I'm finished, young 'un,' Hirst, alarmed, replied: 'Nay, niver in this world.' But Ulyett's premonition was correct, for he died of pneumonia a few days later.

There was also a Jack Ulyett, George's older brother, who was groundsman at Bramall Lane for many years. George Ulyett also maintained the links between cricket and football in Sheffield in that era, keeping goal for the Wednesday for a spell up until 1883.

---

mism, fielding as they did a team of considerable skill and experience. Freeman had retired, but Emmett and Hill were as formidable a pair of fast bowlers as any, Ephraim Lockwood was regarded as the best professional batsman, Rowbotham and Thewlis were hardened veterans, Andrew Greenwood was entering his third season in third place in the averages; Pinder was supreme as wicket-keeper, while Luke Greenwood, even in his 40th year, remained a powerful all-rounder. Waiting in the Colts were some as yet unfamiliar names such as Alf Smith, Louis Hall and George Ulyett; the Yorkshire fielding won praise everywhere.

Sadly, the expectations were rarely realised. The succession of professional captains was not a success, and the mercurial performances, from the brilliant to the pathetic, suggested that dressing-room discipline hardly existed. The line of captains – Iddison, Rowbotham, Luke Greenwood, Ephraim Lockwood and Emmett –

never managed to take the side beyond third place and by 1877 Yorkshire had dropped to eighth (of nine). 'It may have been a fact,' wrote the Reverend Holmes, 'that some of the playing members were lacking in that self-control which is indispensable to conspicuous success'. A blunter reference to Yorkshire's team of this era was the description 'a team of ale-cans'.

London Life noted in 1863:

'A short life and a merry one' is all the professional can hope as regards his cricketing existence – younger and more brilliant men tread upon his heels. Popular applause is proverbially capricious and the smoking, drinking and good living during the summer, contrasted with the greens and bacon – and not too much of the latter – all through the winter; all this is unfavourable to the preservation of high cricketing condition…for now five and thirty is old for an All-England man whereas Pilch and Lillywhite and their friends were deemed quite young at five and forty…we may add that in those days celebrated players had more of a monopoly….Few of the professionals have been a shilling left when winter has drained their store…these are the ups and downs of a professional that should make us one and all regard them with interest and kindly sympathy.

Keith Sandford, in his paper 'Amateurs and Professionals in Victorian County Cricket', was able to illustrate further the professional cricketer's almost nihilistic approach to life by contrasting the income that could be expected by the working classes with that of the 'gentlemen' at a time when there was no social security net for the handicapped, unhealthy or unemployed:

The best [professional cricketers] could hope for was to be hired on the MCC ground staff at Lord's for £2-3 per week. Most first-class counties also paid a professional £5 for each county game at home and £6 for a match of the road (when he paid for his own travel and accommodation). The social significance of these statistics can perhaps best be understood when compared to Home Gordon's fees as a cricket reporter in the Golden Age. As a writer for the *Daily Express* he received £20 for covering a first-class match in London and £30 when he had to leave the capital. He also boasted that he seldom earned less than 10 guineas for any of the articles he submitted to cricket journals.

Louis Hall The Batley Giant

A strict teetotaller, non-smoker and lay preacher in Methodist chapels, Louis Hall was the Roundhead to George Ulyett's Cavalier in Yorkshire's first regular opening partnership. They became the first pair to make a century stand in each innings, against Sussex at Hove in 1885, and raised a 100 together for the first wicket 12 times.

Hall was renowned for both his defence and slow scoring (12 in 165 minutes against Kent, 40 in 265 minutes against Nottinghamshire). He carried his bat for Yorkshire on 14 occasions, but there were times when he could hit, particularly to leg, once lifting W.G. Grace out of the Batley ground.

Hall made his debut in 1873 against Middlesex, but his 37 in 100 minutes made little impression, for he was allowed to return to local cricket with Batley. In 1878, playing for a Hunslet XVIII, he scored 79 against the Australians, including Spofforth, an innings that brought him a hurried recall to Yorkshire, holding his place until 1894 and often captaining the side.

Apart from his stalwart batting over nine seasons and useful slow round-arm or lob bowling, to the side was his setting of a professional example to younger players who were so easily led down the primrose path. He led, too, in many other ways, accepting deferment of his own benefit so that Billy Bates, who had damaged an eye in Melbourne, could have the first call on public sympathy. He was also able to help returning cricketers, particularly those who had made no provision for old age, through his chairmanship of the Cricketers' Benevolent Fund.

His nickname, the 'Batley Giant', was probably due to his lean stature as much as his height, for he was barely 6ft but was clearly always a commanding, if stooping figure to bowlers. In Heavy Woollen League circles he was known, of course, as 'Lewis', and after he had hit Lancashire for 160 at Bradford, in 1887, Yorkshire totalling 590, a song beginning 'Here's health and wealth to Lewis Hall', written earlier, became popular in his area.

'Country Vicar', writing in 1930, described what might be said to be the definitive Louis Hall scene:

> The smoke of Sheffield drifting slowly across the ground, hanging over the field of play like a filmy curtain through which the flannelled figures of the Surrey players glimmered white. I can see Louis Hall, long and lean, dull to watch, dogged and dour.

A.G. Steel, of Lancashire and England, added: 'Nothing in cricket can be more dull and dismal than bowling to this batsman on a sodden wicket at Bramall Lane in a real "Sheffield fog".' Twelve runs an hour was a fair average for an innings.

On retirement Hall himself was apologetic: 'I cannot tell how I acquired a slow style but I found afterwards that it was of more value to my side than to myself and I don't think I should adopt the same principle again.'

Hall became coach to Uppingham School in 1895, umpiring first-class during the holidays and opening a sports shop in the town. When the giant Australian Bonnor was ribbing that prodigious hitter C.I. Thornton, he joked: 'I've got a sister back home who can hit as well as you.' 'Right', replied 'Buns'. 'Bring her over and we'll marry her to Louis Hall.'

Sandiford adds:

> An equally vital role was played by basic economic realism. The fact is throughout the century the job market for professional cricketers was gutted. In the wake of the great cotton slump of the 1860s (a by-product of the American Civil War) and the prolonged agricultural depression after 1873 there were literally hundreds of competent cricketers, especially in the Northern counties, who were seeking to escape from an abject poverty.

He then remarks on the comparative affluence of the professional cricketer: 'an annual income of £100 in 1875 to about £250 by 1900'. The labourer's wage had risen from £80 to £100 per year over the same period. 'As late as 1904 E.J. Smith ["Tiger" of Warwickshire fame] was glad to escape from a factory job which had brought him only 16 shillings [80p] for 60 hours of hard labour.'

Sandiford also found an illustrative example of the vast gulf that existed between the Victorian notions of gentleman and player. In 1898 Henry Perkins retired after 22 years as Secretary to MCC, during which time he had received £500 a year; he was given life membership and a pension of £400 a year. On the very same day Tom Hearne, who had served the Club as head bowler and chief groundsman and who was forced to retired through ill health, was awarded a pension of £30 a year. There was intense pressure, too, on the professional to keep his place in the side; there were no contracts and a queue of eager and willing young cricketers at the county gate. It is hardly surprising, then, that many a professional made the very most of his good times and convivial evenings, knowing that a dark Winter lay ahead.

Jeremy Lonsdale has been a diligent researcher into the environment of Yorkshire's early professionals and points out that a surfeit of parochial indulgence was sometimes a factor in shortening the careers of local favourites. Morley was happy to fete Bobby Peel (in a banquet at the Brunswick Arms in September 1877, attended by 50 including the Mayor and Council). Billy Bates was presented with a solid silver tankard in 1884, presumably in Huddersfield. When Louis Hall topped Yorkshire's averages in 1883, hundreds waited for him at Batley Station on his return home from the Surrey match; he was escorted by the Temperance Brass Band to the town hall where a 'vast crowd' heard him congratulated by the Mayor. The crowd then massed outside Hall's home, demanding that he appear so that they could be guaranteed that the 'Batley Giant' was not the worse for drink. A lesser man might have succumbed.

That Yorkshire's players did weaken more than occasionally is confirmed by two notices in a Sheffield newspaper, the first a letter from 'An Old Cricketer':

At Dewsbury last year [1880] they stayed up so late on the Friday night that they lost the match against the Australians next day. We regret that occasionally the XI may have erred in not taking sufficient sleep or, owing to the generosity of their friends, they have taken a glass too much, *Lilleywhite's Guide* says that Yorkshire lost the match at Dewsbury by their 'bad fielding' and it is no wonder when I am told that they went to bed at 4 or 5 o'clock.

Even ten years later the *East Riding Chronicle* reported:

The Chairman said that the ill-fortune which had attended the county team during last season was largely due to people who called themselves supporters of cricket who could not see a professional on the ground without wanting to give him a glass of drink.

Jeremy Lonsdale found another reason for the professional need to take sustenance in copious quantities when offered: the time and tedium spent in travelling. The *Leeds Mercury* in 1883 mentioned one itinerary: from Leeds to The Oval, back to Bradford, two days at York and then on to Sheffield – and all this before the age of the motor car. Four years later the team were playing Gloucestershire at Dewsbury until 6 pm and had to start a game in Hastings the following day at 1 pm. All-night journeys were expected and commonplace, but none the less tedious for that.

Any imposition, however, was to be preferred to not being a county cricketer, yet there is no doubt that the constant stress brought some careers, and even some lives, to an early close. Ikey Hodgson, for instance, was already broken in health in 1866 when, at the age of 38, he travelled to Glasgow and back for three games in seven days, and by August he was clearly exhausted but dare not refuse an engagement. On 30-31 July he played at Keighley, 2-3 August at Trent Bridge, 9, 10 and 11 at Stoke (here he bowled 20 consecutive overs for one run), 13, 14 and 15 at Mansfield and 16,17 and 18 at Shrewsbury. He was back home in Bradford on 18 August and was due to play in Tynemouth on 20 August, but Tom Emmett had to deputise.

Hodgson never played cricket again; deteriorating health had forced him to give up a public house several years earlier, and by the Summer of 1867 he knew he could not resume playing. One of the most famous cricketers in England, he nevertheless found himself unable even to support his wife. Fortunately for Ikey, his fellow Bradfordians and Yorkshiremen rallied around him and although he died of consumption in November 1867, a fund of £230 was passed on to his wife. The Bradford club, which 120 years later had to leave Park Avenue because they could no longer afford the ground, gave his widow an annuity and paid the funeral expenses and doctors fees. Hodgson's tragic end would have served as a lesson to every young Yorkshire cricketer.

As a team, Yorkshire's practice was to begin superbly but tail away disastrously. They were probably a popular side, and for all that they were professionals while most southern counties were amateurs, they did not lack sportsmanship. In the very first match in Championship history, which began at Prince's on 22 May 1873, Middlesex defeated Yorkshire by ten wickets – but only after the scorers had declared a Middlesex victory when in fact the contest was tied. Yorkshire could have insisted on leaving the match a tie, but took the field again for Middlesex to score the one run needed.

If Iddison or Emmett had been giving evidence on the performance of the team over its first four years, they would no doubt have pointed out some extenuating circumstances. Pinder often

Billy Bates The Duke

One of the country's great players who is almost forgotten today, Billy Bates won his nickname as much for his style of play as for his sartorial elegance at a time when professional cricketers were not expected to be well dressed. Lord Hawke thought him the finest professional batsman up until Jack Hobbs; W.G. Grace thought he would have been considered the 'greatest all-round player of his time' had his fielding matched his batting and bowling.

William Bates was another product of Lascelles Hall. His father loved the game, two brothers played for the club, and Billy was regarded as a prodigy as a boy. He was such a promising batsman that the village lads were reluctant to give him an innings, knowing that they might not get him out. It was while waiting for them to relent that he took to bowling slow to medium off-breaks, a skill that was curiously to bring him more fame than his batting.

Billy Bates
YCCC

He stood a slender 5ft 10in, and his bowling performances for Yorkshire, often at the other end to the great Peate, suggest that he was a bowler of great accuracy and flight: 5-1 in four overs against Surrey at The Oval in 1878; 8-21, again at The Oval, the following year; 6-11 against Middlesex; 8-45 against Lancashire; 5-15 against Derbyshire. As a batsman he was known in those days as a 'dasher'. He was especially prolific on fast pitches, hence his successes in Australia, and his on-drive was regarded as one of the great strokes of his era. On tour in 1886 he scored the first 46 runs on the board against New South Wales, and in 1884, for Yorkshire against Nottinghamshire, he hit 116 out of 137 scored in 165 minutes.

The pinnacle of his career came when, at the age of 27, he won a Test match virtually on his own, the second of Ivo Bligh's tour, at Melbourne in January 1883. England had been forced to follow on and lost the First Test, also in Melbourne, but in the Second England won the toss, scored 294. Bates scored 55, and then bowled out Australia for 114. Bates taking 7-28 in 26.2 overs, including the first hat-trick.

Australia had reached 78-3 when Percy McDonnell was bowled and George Giffen gave a return catch of the next ball. Next man in was the giant George Bonnor, renowned as hitter and scourge of slow bowlers. After consultation it was agreed that even Bonnor, anxious to avert a hat-trick, would play forward to the first ball. Walter Read agreed to stand in the suicidal position of silly mid-on to Bonnor, and to creep forward if Bates could promise a quickish delivery on the leg stump.

The roar of welcome given Bonnor by the 'larrikins' was stilled as the ploy worked to perfection. Bonnor, astonished at Read's audacity, played slowly forward and guided the ball directly into Read's hands, six feet away. In those days a hat-trick meant exactly that, and Billy won what A.G. Steel described as a 'very smart, tall, silver hat for his pains'.

He was, it seems, generous and charming

to a fault, although it needed both courage and tenacity in those days to tour Australia five times and America once. 'O dashing one', as a lady described him, so impressed the king of the Sandwich Isles with his rendering of 'The Bonny Yorkshire Lass' at a ship's concert that the king insisted on returning to the ship every day of the visit to hear Bates sing the song again.

Billy's midsummer marriage prompted a famous remark from Ted Peate: 'That Bates is a foo-il. He shoulda got married in t'middle o'winter so as to give his undivided attention to it.' Then again, perhaps Peate was deadly serious.

Billy Bates was in his high Summer, at the

age of 33, when in Melbourne in 1887 he was struck in the eye while at net practice. His sight was so impaired that an acute depression followed, and he tried to commit suicide on the voyage home. He recovered sufficiently to be able to coach and to return to league cricket with Leek, full circle to his first professional engagement, as a 17-year-old, at Rochdale.

Although a sick man, and living upon the generosity of friends, Billy insisted upon attending the funeral of John Thewlis on what was described as a bitterly cold day in January 1900. He suffered a severe chill and within ten days was dead himself and buried beside Thewlis in that same graveyard. He was 41.

had to stand down because of damaged hands, the result of his standing up to the fast bowlers on uneven pitches. And Hill had an unfortunate career in the number of injuries he sustained, as a cricketer he seemed accident prone.

In 1874, however, one good authority – W.G. himself – nominated Yorkshire as the true champions. They did win eight of their 12 matches, but Derbyshire won three of their four and were named the 'official' champions, as Yorkshire had also lost three while Derbyshire remained unbeaten.

The Committee took some criticism for a traditional reluctance to replace seasoned performers by untried Colts. The sober, studious Hall, for instance, was allowed to drift back into league cricket in 1873 and was not to reappear for five seasons, while many felt that Ulyett's undoubted promise should have been given greater encouragement.

If the playing results in this first era of professional captaincy were not all that was hoped, the County Club was laying a firm foundation. With perhaps no more than 300 members the accounts showed a regular annual profit, enabling grants for £1,250 to be made to Bramall Lane in the years 1874-83. In 1877 the first travelling expenses were paid, £1 each to those players engaged against Gloucestershire at Clifton; in 1884 came the first regular talent money, for the

hat-trick. In 1892 it was minuted that '£1 be awarded for 50 runs, 30 shillings for 75, £2 for 100', but that, let it be noted, 'the question of talent money for bowling be postponed'.

In 1878 Yorkshire tried to broaden their programme by playing a first match at Wakefield, against Sussex, while York became the venue for Surrey's visit the following year. Those were the days of the patrons, for in 1874 the Earl of Londesborough financed both matches against Middlesex, at Prince's and Scarborough.

There must have been a considerable celebration in 1875 when Gloucestershire were beaten for the first time despite scores of 111 and 43 from W.G.. In that same Summer Lancashire won the Old Trafford Roses match by ten wickets, those favourites of Francis Thompson, Hornby and Barlow, raising 148 in the second innings against Emmett, Hill, Tom Armitage and Ulyett.

There was a row at Sheffield, involving those perennial rivals Nottinghamshire, that would have caused a sensation today. Billy Oscroft of Nottinghamshire was given run out; he disputed the decision on the grounds that when the ball reached Pinder it was dead. Yorkshire argued that Pinder had signalled Hill to throw him the ball in order to run out Oscroft. After half an hour's delay, the batsman gave way.

Two highly commendable bowlers emerged in

these early years: Armitage and Robert Clayton. Armitage was a huge Sheffielder, described by Peter Thomas as a 'Falstaffian figure', who bowled cunning lobs that broke 'twice the width of the wicket' according to a Middlesex captain. Armitage was also a sound batsman. He first appeared in 1872 but was not given a regular place until three Summers later when he routed Nottinghamshire, taking 5-8 in four overs, improving upon that the following season with a match return of 13-46 against Surrey at Sheffield. That particular feat won him a place in the Lillywhite tour of Australasia (1876-87) where, in the famous flood incident near Christchurch, New Zealand, jolly Tom distinguished himself. The two coaches could not cross a flooded gorge, so a horse was unharnessed and a rider put upon his back, with another man taking hold of his coat-tails. In this way a human chain was forged, the line of passengers being taken to safety, and Armitage carrying a young lady upon his back.

Bob Clayton might have been a famous name. A bowler from a village near Otley, he was for nine years among the fastest in England, serving for many years on the Lord's ground staff when not required by Yorkshire. In 1871, playing for Yorkshire against MCC, he had match figures of 10-94, including the wicket of W.G., and when The North required a replacement for the great Freeman, it was Clayton who was called upon.

His county career did not begin until he was 26 and he took 154 wickets for Yorkshire at an average of 16, yet played only once for the county after 1877. When he and Andrew Greenwood were both dropped at the end of that same year there was considerable criticism without any justification being offered. Only in comparatively recent times have county committees felt it necessary to vindicate their decisions, and it was left to Emmett, later, to hint at why Clayton was discarded: 'He was no judge of the game. He never studied the batsman's weak points.' In other words, in a team of professionals Clayton, for all his speed, wasn't considered professional enough.

By 1877, of course, another shooting star had arrived in the form of Billy Bates, spoken of, as a young man, as 'another Alfred Shaw'. Bates took 94 wickets in his second season. Ulyett, too, was developing into a superb batsman who could bowl. It may be that had Clayton been with another county, then more attention might have been paid to his prospects.

The overall results remained disappointing, only two county matches of 12 being won in 1877 and five (of 14) in 1880. Some highly significant happenings passed almost unnoticed. In 1879 Edmund Peate made his first appearance for the county; in 1881 a 21-year-old Old Etonian, Martin Hawke; in 1882 Robert Peel. The team was gathering strength; the captain had arrived.

Lord Hawke and the Golden Age 1880–1914

The Golden Age of cricket is usually regarded as stretching from 1890 until the outbreak of the Great War in 1914, during which years the game was just one manifestation of a seemingly endless Edwardian Summer when the world was at peace, the sun never set, wealthy benefactors abounded, civilisation advanced and all humanity knew that things could only get better. It was the time of Sherlock Holmes and Winnie the Pooh, of *The Wind in the Willows* and Jerome K. Jerome, of the striped blazer, the boater, the parasol, an era of good manners and genteel courtesy, when others really believed that an Englishman's word was his bond and nearly all small boys aspired to be gentlemen.

Nothing happens by chance. Britain was at the zenith of its empire-building, a nation of unbounded confidence drawing upon the planet's resources and bursting with talent. Similarly, cricket had come through its formative period, had climbed the hill and reached that plateau where bat and ball were achieving a graceful balance; both batting and bowling were becoming recognisably modern, and an all-white uniform had evolved. It had not been until 1788 that the rolling, watering, covering and mowing of a pitch had been permitted 'by mutual consent', and not until 1849 could a pitch be swept and rolled before each innings. By 1883, rolling was permitted before the start on each day.

Pads were first advertised in *Wisden* in 1880, 30 years after wicket-keepers had worn the first gauntlets. In 1816 the bowler had had to keep the hand below the elbow, in 1835 below the shoulder, over-arm bowling being legalised only in 1864. It was not until 1889 that a declaration was permitted, and then only on the third day (not until 1957 was a declaration at any time allowed). Boundaries are first mentioned in the 'Laws' in 1884, and in 1910 the six was changed from a hit out of the ground to a hit over the boundary.

Yorkshire entered this halcyon period with no

presentiment of the great times ahead. Eight amateurs, including Hawke, appeared in 1881, and Pinder gave way to Joe Hunter behind the stumps. In 1883 Yorkshire had good cause to claim the Championship by virtue of their nine victories to two defeats, one of which was inflicted by Sussex, by three runs. Consolation was drawn from two defeats of Lancashire. Yet it was Nottinghamshire, the team of the decade, who headed the table with four wins to one loss.

Louis Hall was now Yorkshire's leading bat, although Eph Lockwood was still a batsman to be wondered at, as Kent did at Gravesend that year when 'Old Mary Ann' made 208 out of 297 scored while he was at the wicket. He contributed all but 40 to a partnership of 182 with Edward Lumb, another who is remembered as a batsman of potential greatness. Lumb, an amateur from Dalton, played for Yorkshire Colts at the age of 15 and captained Dalton when he was 20.

On his debut in 1883, Lumb carried his bat against Leicestershire for 82, and then went on to make 70 and 24 not out against Middlesex at Huddersfield. He was patient but stylish, the Reverend Holmes describing him as 'a beautiful batsman', such promise being sadly cut short by illness. He was forced to retire at the age of 33, and he died in 1891. The Lumb Cup, in Huddersfield cricket, commemorated a player who was recalled with great affection.

Yorkshire's recruitment of amateurs was limited but distinguished and despite the flush of 1882, when eight appeared, there were complaints that the Committee preferred professionals, a strange notion in those days. Jeremy Lonsdale uncovered some evidence of a minor but intriguing controversy on this subject. In March 1882 a delegation to the Committee raised this point and were told that the county often lost games in which amateurs were called upon and, secondly, that they often did not or could not turn up at the last minute.

Ted Peate The Immaculate

The reference is, of course, to the length of his slow-left-arm bowling, the wonder of all his contemporaries, and not to his disorderly private life that, under Hawke's rule, caused a magnificent career to come to a premature close. He was, in the opinion of some of those who saw all three, including Yorkshire wicket-keeper David Hunter, superior to Peel and Rhodes, a judgement that never ceased to amaze those who saw the latter pair but not Peate himself.

Born in Holbeck, he began his career as a quick bowler in Yeadon, joining in 1875 a troupe called Treloar's Cricket Clowns which included acrobats. Yorkshire, and Sheffield in particular, took none too kindly to having the game held up to ridicule, and the Clowns were 'mobbed and sodded' by cricket-lovers. Peate then spent a Winter practising in the Yeadon shed where he worked as a warp-twister, realising that by reducing the speed of his round-arm delivery he had much greater control of length and direction.

He was spotted at Scarborough by the Reverend E.S. Carter who, after several recommendations, persuaded Yorkshire to give him a trial with the Colts in 1879. Peate took 17-33 runs in the match and scored 25 not out, and Yorkshire had found their first slow left-arm bowler since Hodgson. He was promoted to the first team, his first two matches being all but washed out, but in his third, against Kent at Sheffield, he achieved match figures of 12-77.

From contemporary accounts it seems that Peate was not a great spinner of the ball, relaying on a teasing length, flight and variations of pace, the amount of turn depending upon conditions. He was blessed, wrote Hawke, 'with the most perfect action of any man I have seen deliver the ball'. He had, it was said, a 'natural break' and there could be no doubt he could be deadly when the pitch offered purchase. Not that he was purely a 'bad-wicket' bowler, as he demonstrated on the 1881-82 tour of Australia with returns of 6-100 against New South

Ted Peate
Ron Deaton collection

Wales, 6-30 against Victoria and 8-57 against Murdoch's XI. When the Australians visited England the following Summer Peate was irresistible, taking 63 Australian wickets in all matches at an average of 12.9, twice as many as any other English bowler.

Peate's part in the Oval Test match that year, the contest won by Australia by seven runs that originated the legend of the Ashes, has often been remarked upon. England needed nine runs to win and Peate, despite being a useful batsman (95 against Surrey in 1884), was last man, joining Charles Studd, the Cambridge all-rounder who that year was to follow W.G. as the second man ever to complete the 'double'. Peate scored two and then, in trying to force, was bowled. The recriminations have never ceased, and Peate is regularly chosen in mock XIs assembled for supposed incompetence and stupidity. The true story is rather different.

Studd, for all his ability, was 22 years old, and undergraduate playing in his first Test match, Peate was a hardened professional four years his senior, who had doubtless been through similar fires successfully. His error was to utter, when taxed afterwards, the famous phrase: 'I couldn't trust Mr Studd.'

According to C.I. Thornton, who spoke about the incident as though he had been in the England dressing room at the time: 'Charlie was walking around with a blanket around him; Steel's teeth were all in a chatter and Barnes' teeth would have been chattering if he had not left them at home.' Peate, renowned for his impassivity, must have concluded that he had to take the responsibility. In that final half-hour, wrote a reporter, one spectator dropped dead and another gnawed through the handle of his umbrella.

Peate's only recorded comment afterwards was to say that he had not been nervous and that if three or four other England batsmen had scored as many runs as he there would have been a victory (Barlow, Steel and Read were all dismissed for nought).

The following year Peate gave his home town figures that astonished the world: eight wickets for five runs against Surrey (all out 31). Peate commented: 'Someone suggested to a Holbeck man that a collection should be made in recognition of my bowling. What do you think was the reply? "Oh, be --, he has ruined the game. I shall object to the hat going round."' In 1884, bowling against Lancashire at Old Trafford on a flat pitch he took 5-28 in 41 overs and 5-23 in 38.

In his eight seasons Peate took 1,033 wickets at 13 runs apiece, his best being 9-21 against Sussex in 1886, the year before Hawke ended his career. At least two contemporary observers used the phrase 'rapid decline' in reference to the years 1886-87. Failing eyesight was one reason, but he may also have fallen foul of his Lordship for his personal habits, for *Wisden* spoke in it obituary of 'his death, ostensibly through pneumonia, but for some time as a result of his way of life he had been in a poor condition'.

Hawke recorded afterwards: 'One of my saddest tasks was to dismiss him from the Yorkshire XI. But he bore no grudge and...invariably...greeted me with the same, slow, spontaneous "Good morning, my lord, I hope you are as well as I am."'

Peate was able to play league cricket for several more years, still able to return figures worthy of red ink in the scorebooks. David Hunter remembered him as 'the finest left-arm slow bowler I ever saw. He had a beautiful action and was extraordinarily accurate, seldom if ever losing his length.'

Peate died at the aged of 45, having spent five of his last seven years playing for Skipton. His memory would have been held all the greater but for his succession by two slow left-arm bowlers who were to become even more famous: Peel and Rhodes. He averaged five wickets a match in his 160 games for Yorkshire.

There was, too, an underlying hint of animosity between the Club and Yorkshire Gentlemen among the new members of the Committee: 'There was no reason to include Yorkshire Gentlemen; they wanted to have all games at York, at the expense of everywhere.'

There is little doubt that some of the amateurs whose names were put forward were simply not first-class players. Lonsdale cites Charles Landon who, despite the misfortune of his being born in Kent, came into the county side with a

fine record for Yorkshire Gentlemen, but made five noughts in nine innings. Dr George Thornton, from Skipton, who went on to play for Middlesex and Transvaal, also appeared for Yorkshire in 1891 when he was described as being 'well out of his depth'.

There were gifted amateurs eligible, but the North-South divide of affluence has existed for much longer than a century and few northerners could afford to play county cricket and neglect careers or business, as could many landed and

George Harrison Shoey

A shoemaker in his native Scarborough, hence his nickname, George Puckrin Harrison was a bowler of genuine pace who had the distinction of appearing for the Players in his first season (1883), the equivalent then of playing for England in a first Summer.

He made a sensational start for the Colts of the North against Colts of the South, not appearing to bowl until the second innings when he took 9-14, taking four wickets with successive balls, then six in seven balls in all, hitting the stumps every time.

Such was the impact of this performance that he was chosen for the Players against the Gentlemen taking place a few days later. W.G. announced that he would open the innings to get a good look at this Colt, and in 15 minutes all but destroyed the 21-year-old. The other Gentlemen followed W.G.'s example, yet Harrison bowled 52 overs in the day (almost as many as some entire teams manage today) for 108 runs and three wickets, those of Lucas, Studd and Lord Harris. The boy, only just a man, admitted afterwards: 'When I got back to the hotel I couldn't eat me dinner. I took off me boots and let me feet cool on the oilcloth. Then I got into bed and cried like a babby."

Harrison still managed to take 88 wickets, 72 of his victims being bowled, in his first season at 11.92, recovering some of his glory before 10,000 at Bramall Lane when he sent back three Lancastrians, including Steel and Royle, for one run. Alas, the following year he put out his arm when fielding substitute for a Gloucestershire player, and was never able to recapture that great pace for long.

He did return to form in the seasons of 1890-91, taking 123 wickets over the two Summers although bowling at reduced speed. This action was thought by some to be doubtful but he was never called, and after leaving Yorkshire he became a highly successful professional with Bowling Old Lane and Idle, and then a first-class umpire of whom Jessop wrote, '"Shoey", whose smile when he dismissed one to the pavilion made one extremely loath to leave'. He lived until he was 78, and for many years was a happy and regular spectator at the Scarborough Festival.

But for those two strokes of fate – meeting W.G. on a flat pitch and dislocating his arm – 'Shoey' might have had a great career, for he came into cricket when English fast bowlers were extremely rare.

---

aristocratic southerners. The *Hull Daily Mail*, in 1904, mentioned two: Charles Gifkins (born in Surrey) and Lamplough Wallgate of Malton. Amateurs were, as we have seen, considered to be unreliable although, Lonsdale suggests, that might merely have meant that the Committee found them less easy to manage. The very brave *Dewsbury Reporter* commented in 1884: 'Hawke and Lumb will play when in humour but they cannot be relied upon.' Tadcaster, Lord Hawke's home was presumably beyond the *Reporter's* circulation area.

One of 1892's flock, Robert Sidgwick of Embsay, was expected to play against the Australians at Dewsbury but did not appear

'because of business'. In 1893 the match against Essex would have caused a furore today: Hawke was unavailable, Arthur Sellers, the nominated deputy, withdrew over the weekend before the Monday start, and the next in line, F.S. Jackson, failed to appear. There had been rumbles three years earlier when Jackson, like many of his peers, wanted to have a choice of the games in which he played for Yorkshire; after considerable argument, during which Hawke threatened resignation, Jackson agreed to make himself available for 1891 without conditions.

A proper gentleman's social obligations were, of course, many and varied, and it was most certainly not the done thing to evade them, not even in the cause of cricket. Robert Frank, of Pickering, objected to being called upon as a late choice (the Committee selected on Tuesday for a Thursday start), which is why he captained the Colts with distinction in the years 1900-14 but was not again invited into the first XI. But Yorkshire's difficulties were no doubt minimal

The Reverend E.S. Carter, a skilled spotter of Yorkshire cricketing talent and probably the man who recommended Lord Hawke to the county.
YCCC

compared with those county clubs who relied much more heavily on the amateur and had few professional resources, such as Essex or Somerset.

If the years 1879 and 1880 were lean ones for Emmett – 76 wickets in two Summers – Yorkshire's left-arm attack had been immeasurably sharpened by the advent of the slow left-arm Peate who, in his first four Summers, 1879-82, collected 75, 139, 139 and 165 wickets respectively, his average cost never exceeding 13 runs. In 1883 he produced a staggering performance at Holbeck, taking 8-5 against Surrey, a performance that was to stand for 67 years until displaced by that of Jim Laker, another Yorkshireman who unfortunately happened to be engaged by Surrey at that time.

George 'Shoey' Harrison also burst upon English cricket in that season of 1883, taking 88 wickets for under 12 runs each. But there is no doubt, in retrospect, what was to be the most important event of that Summer, overshadowed as it may have been by Ulyett's hat-trick against Lancashire at Sheffield. The captaincy was offered to the 23-year-old Cambridge undergraduate, Hawke.

The team continued under Emmett until the end of the University term, whereupon the greatest reign in county cricket history began, a captaincy that was to last 27 years and was to establish Yorkshire supremacy for another half-century. Hawke was shrewd enough to learn slowly, thoroughly and carefully. He noted: 'The senior professional in the Yorkshire team always fielded at point. He was never told to go there but went as a matter of course. It was his right.'

Not that there was an immediate surge to greatness, for 1884 was another disappointment, the high promise of the previous Summer fragmenting. In the Spring, Harrison, the fast-bowling sensation who had appeared for the Players (today's equivalent would be a Test selection) in his first season, dislocated his arm while fielding substitute for a Gloucestershire player in Moreton-in-Marsh, and was never able to bowl really fast again. John 'Turnkeycock' Rawlin won distinction with Middlesex, and George Baker blossomed with Lancashire.

Time overtook the veteran Lockwood, Ulyett appeared to reserve his best performances for the Players, and Bates, apart from a 116 against Nottinghamshire, had a thin season. Over this period younger players – Fred Lee, Irwin Grimshaw and Joe Preston – appeared from the Colts without making the impact of a Harrison or a Lockwood.

Occasionally Yorkshire would flash into form again, as when Gloucestershire were routed for 43 at Moreton-in-Marsh in 1884, Peate taking 6-13. At Brighton in 1885 Ulyett and Hall established a new record by scoring century stands in both innings against Sussex, while the arrival of a new talent from Sheffield, the all-rounder Edward Wainwright, promised stability in the future. The county's income had been increased handsomely by the raising of the subscription, in

Martin Bladen Hawke Warlord

Nearly a century and a half ago one Edward Hawke, Rear-Admiral of the White, achieved so splendid a victory over the French that he presently got command of an expedition fitted out to act against the French coast; and having hoisted his flag aboard the *Royal George*, he led his fleet in pursuit of the enemy, whom he signally defeated off Bellisle, thereby making himself very memorable in our naval annals, and still more so in those of the French. He was the worthy beginning of the Barony to which Martin Bladen Hawke, seventh Baron, succeeded nearly five years ago. He was born two-and-thirty years ago, and in due course went to Eton, where he began to justify himself of his motto – (which is 'Strike') – better and more wholesomely than ever did labour monger; hitting up runs at cricket with increasing vigour. He went on to Magdalen College, Cambridge, and continued to hit them up. He is now Captain of the 3rd Battalion of the Princess of Wales's Own Yorkshire Regiment, as well as Captain of the Yorkshire County Cricket Eleven; for which he has done great things, being the only amateur player who has regularly captained the County Eleven; and this he has done for ten years. And though, owing to an injury to his hand, he did not accomplish much for his county last year, he yet most creditably managed a team in America in the autumn; sparing no trouble to make his own men comfortable nor to teach the Americans cricket. And he is now about to take another team to India; for he is always full of keen love for the game, and though not so sure a run-getter as are some of his fellows, yet his zeal for, and his knowledge of, it make him an excellent and popular captain.

He is a member of the Carlton and of the Bachelors', and a good-looking, pleasant, modest fellow; and though he is not as yet a great statesman he is

Martin Bladen Hawke
Ron Deaton collection

a good Conservative.
He is a light-hearted bachelor.

Vanity Fair, 24 September 1892.

The greatest figure in Yorkshire's cricket history was a contradictory man. Made famous by one remark rejecting a professional captain of England, he advanced the cause of the professional cricketer as no man has before or since. The quintessential Yorkshireman, devising the players' white rose badge, he was actually born in Lincolnshire. A natural autocrat, he was respected and followed by Yorkshire's cricketers and public for almost 70 years, commanding such confidence and authority that he was also regarded as an obvious leader by MCC and the selectors.

A batsman of middling ambitions and ability, he played for England in five Test matches, captaining them in four. He took more teams abroad than any other tourist before or since – Australia, India, Ceylon, Canada,

United States, South Africa and West Indies were all visited one or more times when travelling was an undoubted hardship. Yet when in England nothing would stop him attempting to get home on a Sunday in order to go to church with his mother. He passed on to Pelham Warner what he regarded as the 'two essentials' in choosing an XI: 'good temper and good manners'.

At the close of his playing career, in 1911, Warner described him thus:

It is no secret that when he took over the leadership of that famous county things were not as they should have been. There was little discipline and practically no esprit de corps, but by wise and tactful management he soon altered that and under his guidance the Yorkshire eleven were looked on as the model of what county side should be, well disciplined, well drilled and efficient.

Of course he had cricketers under his command but in the first instance he created the spirit and organisation out of which that splendid team arose. He has been a good friend to the professional.

Hawke was born in 1860 in the Lincolnshire rectory of the old Yorkshire family of the famous Admiral (whence the motto 'Strike'), and the family soon moved up to Tadcaster. His father could recite the whole of 'The Deserted Village' without error, and loved gladioli and hollyhocks. His grandmother danced at the famous ball in Brussels on the eve of Waterloo and the following day rode out to Quatre Bras 'to see what was going on'. While a schoolboy at Eton he began to play for Yorkshire Gentlemen (the successor to Vale of Derwent), with whom he caught the eye of the Reverend E.S. Carter, the founder, with Lord Londesborough, of the Scarborough Carnival (later Festival). Carter had already 'found' Ted Peate for Yorkshire, and his next discovery was invited to Scarborough. Carter it was who always denied that he was the cricketing cleric who announced, one Sunday morning from the pulpit: 'Here

endeth the first innings.'

Hawke appeared twice for Yorkshire in 1881, scoring 46 runs in four innings, but won his Blue at Cambridge the following year, returning to the county at the end of term to extend his career aggregate by another 353 runs in 24 innings. Hawke won further Blues in 1883 and 1885, missing the intervening year 'for military duties', captaining the University in the final year when he led Cambridge to a seven-wicket victory over Oxford.

There seems little doubt that Yorkshire would have named him captain as early as 1882, as a 22-year-old, but he preferred to find his way among a band of hard-bitten, some hard-drinking, professionals under Emmett's relaxed leadership until the official appointment came the following year, Hawke assuming office as soon as he came down. As no one expected immediate improvements, they were not disappointed. Hawke was only nominal captain in 1884-85, playing only seven matches in the late Summer, and the professional aegis continued.

There is an excellent photograph, by E. Hawkins and Co. of Brighton, of Yorkshire in dour mood in 1884, not an amateur in sight, although the Greaseborough left-hander Billy Harris sports a suspiciously ringed cap of some brilliance. In the centre, wearing what appears to be a paisley tie under his Yorkshire cap, is the sternly-moustachioed 'Batley Giant', the caption reading 'Hall (Captain)'.

There seems little doubt that Hawke used his sporadic appearances in his first three Summers to assess his men thoroughly. By 1886 he was in full charge and the Yorkshire renaissance had begun. He was shrewd enough to listen carefully to his senior professionals and, unlike many amateurs of this time, willing to ask their advice publicly and to follow it. Hawke's success – eight Championships in his 27 seasons – was founded upon the assessments of Hall, Emmett, John Tunnicliffe, George Hirst and David Hunter, but it was the captain who made the decisions, and once his mind was made up he acted swiftly and decisively.

One of his first targets was the club's financial structure, particularly the professionals' pay. He abolished the fixed talent payments of £1 for 50 runs or six wickets, preferring to award merit marks for performances according to the conditions, the state of the game, the condition of the pitch, the light and the weather, all being recorded in his notebook. Good fielding, enthusiasm and courage were also noted.

At the end of the season the team were invited to the Hawke seat at Wighill Park, the captain distributing the merit money in packets. The highest amount won in one year was £52.50 by George Hirst, possibly in his golden year of 2,000 runs and 200 wickets in 1906.

His generosity was balanced by his single-minded devotion to the cause, as exemplified by his attitude towards those players that he felt were letting down the side. He dismissed two of the greatest spin bowlers in history, Ted Peate and Bobby Peel, before their time. Three highly promising Colts, all of whom might have reached England status, were despatched. He introduced the Yorkshire cap, borrowing the idea from Lancashire, who wore a red rose on a navy-blue cap, designing his own white rose of petals, 'to be worn only by capped players'. The Hawke colours, Cambridge blue, Oxford blue and gold, became Yorkshire's.

As a right-hand middle-order batsman and deep field, Hawke probably underrated himself, often batting at nine or ten when he would have been five or six in lesser sides. He scored more than 700 runs in 1886-87, and a thousand in 1895, a figure he came close to equalling three times more in his career.

Warner described his play:

He was an uncertain starter as a batsman but he could drive very hard and late cut

well, and when he got runs he got them in such good style that one wondered why he was not more often successful. More than once he pulled Yorkshire out of a tight place.

In 1898 he was directly responsible for a long-needed national reform, publicly criticising the established system of selection of England's teams by the appropriate ground authority. Hawke spoke in May, and by July the selection of England's team was passed to the Committee of MCC.

As Yorkshire's captain he was astonishingly successful. In addition to the eight Championships his reign included the two unbeaten years of 1900 and 1908, a spell of nine years in which only 18 matches were lost. While still captain, he succeeded Michael Ellison as Yorkshire's President in 1898. He delayed his retirement until his 51st year in the hope that T.L. Taylor would become available as captain. He became, in turn, Treasurer and then President of MCC and Chairman of England's selectors.

In 1925 when Cec Parkin, in a newspaper attacked Gilligan's captaincy of England in Australia, Hawke told Yorkshire's AGM: 'Pray God, no professional shall ever captain England. I love and admire them all but we have always had an amateur skipper and when the day comes when we shall have no more amateurs captaining England it will be a thousand pities.' It is perhaps easier to understand, if not agree with, such sentiments now than it was then. Professional captaincy has now ruled long enough for fair comparisons to be made with a system that, while growing rapidly obsolete, was not without its virtues. Hawke knew his Gentlemen and his Players; he also knew his players and his gentlemen. It was at Hawke's insistence, recorded Kilburn, that Yorkshire's cricketers were given entitlements in the society of sport: they ceased to be hired hands, they became associates.

1881, from a half-guinea to a full guinea, but while the team's form remained inconsistent the Club depended more upon the loyalty of the members than on the response from the general public. On Whit Monday 1886 there was, reported Hawke, a 'nasty row' at Sheffield when the match against Kent was not resumed after lunch because of the wet conditions: 'The big holiday crowd tramped on the pitch, tearing up the stumps.'

It was also in 1886 that Hawke's old comrade C.I. 'Buns' Thornton, who always batted without gloves and pads, played his famous innings at Scarborough in which he scored 107 in just over an hour; his hits from the pavilion end including one on a chimney pot on one of the tall houses opposite, another through a window in the same houses and a third through the air into Trafalgar Square. According to Hawke, it was at Harrogate, later that Summer, that a lady approached Thornton to check whether it was true that he had hit a ball into Trafalgar Square. Thornton nodded, whereupon the lady enquired: 'And were you batting at Lord's or The Oval?'

Four years later Thornton, together with Lord Londesborough, launched the famous Festival, 'Buns' going off to Lord's to ask for an MCC side. 'Certainly,' replied the then Secretary R.A. Fitzgerald, 'do as you like. Take any four professors and invite who you like.' Londesborough too gave generous support to cricket's cause; when the county played at Lord's he always arranged for boys from the Yorkshire Orphans' School to be given seats in the Grandstand and to be treated afterwards to a 'blow-out' tea. So taken was Louis Hall with the Londesborough family that he named his son and daughter after the Earl and Countess.

The following year, 1887, saw Peel replace Peate and stride immediately into the Players'

Joe Preston

From all contemporary accounts Joseph Merritt Preston might have been one of Yorkshire's great cricketers. As a bowler, fast to fast-medium and accurate, he was compared in pace and hostility, by 'Old Ebor', to Freeman, Hill and 'Shoey' Harrison. 'He could also bowl off-crease, all with an easy and attractive action, was a batsman who could hit fiercely if rashly but who could also defend, and a fielder of the highest class. Yorkshire fully expected him to become as accomplished an all-rounder as Billy Bates.'

'Country Vicar' (the Reverend R. Hodgson), to whom we owe thanks for his many engaging memories of the University of Cambridge and Yorkshire cricket in the final decade of the last century, has two memories of Preston. He saw him at Bramall Lane – 'a most promising player but he lost his form suddenly and died quite young'. And on another occasion on the same ground: 'They had a companion, a young man who wore a dark blue cap bearing a white rose, a dark blue blazer with a similar badge on the pocket and his flannels were quite beautiful – white as driven snow!'

The young Hodgson was introduced to Preston as 'a cricketer', whereupon Preston

replied: 'That's good; now we're four cricketers together.' Remarked 'Country Vicar': 'The gracefulness of that speech – J.M. Preston, most promising of the young Yorkshiremen, placed us in the same rank with himself.'

Preston was born in Yeadon, and played for that club and Rawdon before joining a touring band of cricket clowns. Professional engagements in Swinton and Farnworth followed and he first appeared for Yorkshire at the age of 19, his promise being confirmed by selection for the Colts of the North at Lord's. He had three splendid years, 1886-88, appearing for the Players, the equivalent today of Test-match selection, in the last-named year, a Summer when he took 102 wickets at 13.05 apiece. His highest score was 93 against Derbyshire in 1887, and in the previous season he raised six scores of more than 50.

Yet by 1889 his career was over, and he had died, at the age of 26, by the following November. Hawke's comment pointed to a contributory factor in the shockingly early death of a personable and talented young man: 'Preston was an irresponsible individual who, had he possessed the least restraint might have become one of the finest cricketers Yorkshire ever produced; he had too many friends.'

team at Lord's and The Oval, the equivalent of instant Test selection. Yet despite Peel's achievements it was the only Summer, said Hawke, 'in my recollection when Yorkshire's batting proved distinctly superior to its bowling'.

Yorkshire touched bottom in 1889, or at least, near enough to cause considerable alarm, losing 12 matches to eight won and finishing last but one in the table. One obvious factor in the decline was the loss, for various reasons, of Emmett, Bates and Peate, while Preston was dropped through loss of form. Less understandable, or forgivable, was the standard of fielding, which the Reverend Holmes dismissed as 'execrable'. It was alleged that no less than 12 catches were missed off Peel at Brighton alone.

Peel, in fact would have been tempted by some of today's newspapers to tell an astonishing story. Personally he had a marvellous season, topping the batting and bowling averages, taking three times as many wickets as any other player and scoring the only century by a Yorkshireman in county matches. But the season's general disappointment was reflected in the financial figures, the club recording a profit of only £79 that was accompanied by a loss of £203 in Colts matches.

Not surprisingly there was a fairly ruthless reappraisal of the team at the end of that 1889 Summer. Fred Lee, the Baildon batsman who had flared and faded for eight Summers, Irwin Grimshaw, a Farsley batsman who had had three brilliant Summers 1884-86, Saul Wade, also from Farsley, a batsman who could bowl huge off-breaks, and fast bowler Joe Preston, all ended their first-call careers. The decision was almost certainly made by Hawke as captain, and the only clue as to the reason for the dismissals came in a comment by President Ellison to the Committee: 'The great difficulty with which they had to contend arose from what I might term the "demon drink". They had to put out of the team one upon whom they relied as a tower of strength for a great many years and at a critical time they had to suspend another.'

That the Committee, no doubt prodded by Hawke, was aware of a crisis in the making is proved by their preparation for that turbulent Summer: several matches were arranged before

the competitive programmes began, and six games were played between the Seniors and the Colts.

From this thorough investigation into playing resources, three new players appeared for the first time; David Hunter, Bobby Moorhouse and J.T. Brown. In the following season, 1890, the University of Cambridge made the giant contributions of F.S. Jackson and Ernest Smith.

It would be wrong to leave 1889 without mention of a curious contest at The Oval, renowned at the time as the 'Gaslight Match'. After a succession of low scores it was agreed that, in order to get a finish on the second day, play would be prolonged for half an hour. At 6.45 pm on 27 August, Surrey needed another eight runs to win, but the light was so poor that it was said that neither stumps nor ball could be seen beyond a few yards. Surrey's batsmen not surprisingly decided to play on, gaslights were lit in surrounding streets and the pavilion, and spectators left their seats to crowd the boundary edge, to see the winning hit made on the stroke of seven.

So to 1890 when Ullyett alone managed a century, Hawke was the most consistent batsman, Hall was his stalwart self, and Peel was magnificent again, taking 91 wickets to Wainwright's 37. Various and many representative matches removed Ulyett, Peel, Hawke and Hunter from time to time and form remained unpredictable, the powerful Surrey being thrashed, but both Warwickshire and Derbyshire beat Yorkshire twice.

Yet 1890, when compared with the following season, was deemed a success. In 1891 twice as many competitive matches were lost as were won, and Yorkshire again finished next to bottom of the table. Peel was probably wearying, Ulyett and Hall had passed 40 and the amateurs were rarely available before mid-Summer. 'Shoey' Harrison, who had made a welcome and promising return in 1890 (51 wickets), reached 72 wickets in this Summer only to fade again and finish. Worse, such players as Jackson, Smith, Moorehouse and Brown were proving to be, according to the Reverend Holmes, 'cricketers of moderate class only'.

Readers of recent Yorkshire history will not be

Ted Wainwright Masterly

Wainwright, like George Ulyett, was a Sheffield man from Tinsley, and he followed 'Happy Jack' into the XI whereupon the mould must have been broken, for Wainright was the last great all-rounder to have produced by the capital city of the county's cricket. In 1913, when Wainwright was 48, he became coach to Shrewsbury when the assistant professional was the young Neville Cardus, who left us an affectionate sketch:

> He was a tall man with a shrewd, lean face who walked as though he didn't care a damn for anybody. There was something sinister about him. Every night he got drunk as a matter of course, quietly and masterfully.

One wet afternoon the coach and assistant were sitting in the dressing room overlooking 'misty green fields':

> Suddenly the Headmaster rode straight across the sacred turf on a bicycle, Wainwright leapt to his feet, flung open the window, stuck out his head, put two fingers into his mouth, emitted a piercing whistle then shouted: 'What the 'ell dost tha think tha's doin'? Get off t'grass, tha bloody lookin' foo-il.'
>
> He waved the Headmaster of Shrewsbury to a by-path and the Reverend Cyril Alington abruptly and docilely veered to it and disappeared round a corner, most humbled. I was horrified.
>
> 'Ah doan't give a bugger who he was. Oought to 'ave more sense. Ridin' 'is bloody bicycle over t'turf on a day like this! T'ell wuth 'im.'
>
> The Reverend Alington admitted the following morning that he was at fault – 'my mind was pre-occupied. I had just come from a Governors' meeting. Wainwright was quite right. But I do think he might have admonished me in language a little, er, less drastic.'

Ted Wainwright
Ron Deaton collection

In his autobiography published in 1947, Cardus described the changing times:

> He belonged to a period that marked a transition in the development of the social life of the English professional cricketer; he was a bridge from the simple and dignified fore-lock touching William [Attewell] to the Hammonds and the Sutcliffes who burnish their hair and go to Savile Row for their clothes.

He was also a masterly cricketer, ranked by Peter Thomas 'among the ten best professionals of his day'. He played his first trial for the Colts at 29, reached the first XI against MCC at Lord's in May 1888, and in June of that year, in misty weather at Park Avenue, he made his name.

The Australians scored 367, to which the giant George Bonnor contributed 115 of which 100 were boundaries. Yorkshire replied with 228 of which Wainwright, batting at number nine, made 20 not out. Following on, Yorkshire sent Wainwright in first and he scored 105 not out, the first of his 21 centuries for Yorkshire.

He went on to score 12,768 runs in the next 14 seasons and to take 1,173 wickets with his right-arm off-spin. He credited Ulyett with teaching him a grip for the off-break, fitting the ball between thumb and first finger with the finger along the seam. His turn, on a sticky pitch, was described by 'Old Ebor' as 'prodigious', but he often rubbed the finger raw and would finish an innings with it bleeding. Early in his career he often had to stand down because he was waiting for his hand to heal up; sometimes he would play with the finger bandaged, accepting a loss of purchase on the ball.

At Dewsbury in June 1894, after finishing with match figures of 13-38 against Sussex, he was presented with a ball that bore this inscription: 'With this ball E. Wainwright clean bowled three men in three consecutive balls and took the last five wickets in seven balls for no runs.'

Wainwright was also the first Yorkshire bowler to take all ten wickets, for 31, against Staffordshire at Sheffield in August 1890. Four years later, also in his own city, he captured nine Middlesex wickets, Jackson depriving him of the tenth.

With Tunnicliffe he formed a deadly slip partnership. 'Long John' at first or 'short', Wainwright at second. He played in five Test matches and hit one double century, against Surrey at The Oval. Six years after Cardus knew him he died, back in Sheffield, after a long illness, at the age of 54. An admirer of Wainwright, unhappy at Cardus' picture of the Shrewsbury coach, wrote to George Hirst in 1948. Hirst replied: 'I am of the opinion that Cardus has overdone that period at Shrewsbury School. Ted Wainwright was one of my friends. We played years together. His cricket was good and clean, and no use of bad language, a bit weak in some things but never a bad sort.'

---

surprised by the reaction at that time of both members and public: 'Sack the Committee' was the prevailing cry. The Committee was alleged to have lost touch with popular feeling; it needed to be selected on a broader basis, it needed greater knowledge of grass-roots cricket.

As the Club and Committee were still Sheffield based, the southern city took much of the blame for the lack of success, just as the supposed 'gin and tonic brigade' were to be castigated almost a century later. The irony, not to be lost on succeeding generations, was that Yorkshire were upon the brink of their first great flowering of the White Rose, a bloom generated by the emergence and development of many truly great cricketers.

As to a broader representation of government, the club had been moving in that direction since 1883 when Bradford, Dewsbury, Halifax, Huddersfield, Hull, Leeds and York were each invited to nominate a Committee member to join the 14 that represented Sheffield. Although the Heavy Woollen Cup Council was refused in 1887 and Wakefield in 1889, Barnsley (1888), Wakefield (1890) and Scarborough (1891) were

admitted in turn, Sheffield's representation being reduced to 13 although all the officers remained south Yorkshiremen.

The Committee undoubtedly heeded the agitation of 1890-91, for two years later a complete reorganisation was voted in that produced a body on recognisably modern lines: Sheffield members were reduced to seven, Bradford and Leeds were given three seats each, and eight other districts were awarded one seat each. Two new Vice-Presidents, Lord Hawke (York) and Major W.H. Shepherd (Bradford), were elected, and after the death of Michael Ellison in 1898 Hawke became the club's first and only captain and President.

When, upon the death of Joseph Wostinholm in 1902 after 38 years as Secretary, the offices were moved from Sheffield to the centre of Leeds (not Headingley), for the simple reason of geographical accessibility, it could be said that Yorkshire had become a proper county club. Reforms had clearly been necessary: in 1891 subscriptions had yielded only £90, and in 1893 the issue of the first Yearbook had revealed a membership

Saul Wade One Famous Over

Wade has a place in history for one famous over bowled to the 1886 Australians. Born in Farnley, he came to Yorkshire's attention while playing as a professional opening batsman and occasional bowler with Saddleworth. However, it was his bowling, slow but formidable off-breaks, that brought him success. His best, among many successes in the four seasons he played with Yorkshire, was 7-10 against Leicestershire, the team against whom he scored his highest innings, 103 not out.

At Sheffield in 1886, the Australians needed 19 off the last over (four balls) with six wickets standing, and Wade was summoned to bowl to the touring captain, Dr H.J.J. 'Tup' Scott, a batsman, according to Ray Robinson, whose 'batting was noted more for solidity than style, for grit rather than gaiety.' However, the doctor could hit, having on that same tour put a ball from A.G. Steel on to the roof of The Oval pavilion. Hawke knew that Yorkshire could not win the match, but clearly hoped to embarrass the tourists with Wade's unusual bowling, while the grinders, noting that Wade had puzzled earlier batsmen, saluted the move with cheers.

Scott leaned back and hoisted the first ball over square leg for six (which, in those days, had to be out of the ground); the second ball went in the same direction for four; the third was again pulled out of the ground. Such hitting had not been seen before, and in all the excitement the umpire miscounted and called 'Over'. Somehow, above all the hubbub, the scorers managed to signal a ball short, the umpires called the fielders back to their places, up rolled Wade again and BANG, the ball flew out of the ground again. Twenty-two runs off a four-ball over was a sensation.

Like several of his contemporaries, Wade's county career was short, the Reverend Holmes commenting that 'he had only himself to blame'. He went off to play for Church in the Lancashire League, and lived to be 73.

list of only 175 names. The success of the team from 1893, and the wider appeal of the club membership, brought startling increases, the membership reaching just under 1,000 by 1897 and more than 3,000 in 1903.

Contemporary historians were gratified by such progress and, indeed, most date the foundation of the club proper from this period. Only in one respect was the Committee found to be too pessimistic and doubtful of the loyalty of Yorkshire's members, for the Reverend Holmes was moved to predict: 'One dreads to anticipate the effect on the county membership of a decade of disasters to Yorkshire in the cricket field.' In fact, although Yorkshire lost their overall lead in the number of county members to Lancashire in the years of turmoil from 1970 onwards, the total never dipped below 7,000, a testimony to the tradition built by Hawke and his committee members at the turn of the century. Indeed, by the mid-1920s Yorkshire boasted a larger membership than MCC.

So, despite the alarms and criticisms, the club was shaping up for the twentieth century by 1893, although no one could have possibly foreseen the golden era about to unfold. Surrey were the giants of that time, as grand and powerful as they were to become again in the 1950s, and, as is the way with sporting teams, subtle shifts in strength can exert enormous influence on the balance of power. Surrey then lost that magnificent bowler George Lohmann through ill health, while Yorkshire were all but bursting with burgeoning talent.

Louis Hall had retired in 1892, but in the previous Summer a lanky young man from Pudsey, John Tunnicliffe, had made his first appearance, reaching 1,000 runs for the season for the first time in 1893. A Keighley amateur, Arthur Sellers, contributed two of the three centuries scored in that year, and while Jackson and J.T. Brown were slow starters, the University of Cambridge found another substantial

Yorkshireman in 1894, Frank Mitchell, while from Wakefield another batsman appeared, David Denton.

Yorkshire's early burst in 1892, unbeaten until the middle of June, had hinted of things to come, but Surrey, with Lohmann in form, won on the new Headingley ground while at Taunton the Somerset array of amateurs helped to build up the astonishing total of 592.

Perhaps the Championship of 1893 was the first confirmation of Hawke's striving for teamwork and discipline. By modern reckoning this was Yorkshire's first undisputed Championship and all contemporary reporters agreed that it was achieved by cumulative effort. Only four batsmen averaged more than 20, the wickets were shared by Wainwright (overtaking Peel) and the fast-emerging Hirst, the last-named also making significant contributions with the bat. This was also the year of what many regard as the greatest Roses match. A.A. Thomson wrote of his Uncle

Walter, who was present at Manchester that Bank Holiday, that 'the excitement of that game remained with him, warmly glowing, for the rest of his life'. Asked what was his chief impression, Uncle Walter replied: 'Funny umpiring.'

There were a record 25,000 present on the first day to see Lancashire make an horrendous start. MacLaren was caught by Hirst at mid-off from a drive the crowd thought was going for four; Sugg became the first of Tunnicliffe's six victims at slip; Briggs was lbw to Hirst, Peel and Ernest Smith then finishing off the innings for only 64. Three Yorkshire wickets then went down for seven to the enormous delight of an incredulous crowd, the innings being stabilised by Tunnicliffe and Brown (in the days before they became a famous opening partnership). Uncle Walter, suffering as any good Yorkshireman would, remembered Briggs bowling with a 'jiggly, bouncing deceptiveness', while Mold hurled them down from the other end. Only Peel made any real resistance and Yorkshire were put out for 58. Lancashire's MacLaren and Ward then

David Hunter Old Ironside

Indisputably the greatest wicket-keeper never to play for England, David Hunter wore Yorkshire's gauntlets for 21 years. Tall for a keeper, a little over 6ft, he refused to wear rubber tips in his gloves yet on his retirement his hands were unmarked. For Yorkshire he caught 952 batsmen and stumped 352, and in other matches his totals were 64 and 45. During his years Yorkshire won eight Championships, one of which, that of 1908, Hunter could claim as his own for he led the side in all but the 11 matches when Hawke was present.

A man who loved his seaside Scarborough home, as a boy playing cricket on the beach Summer and Winter until the tide washed away the stumps, and more than once in a snowstorm, Hunter was a man of many parts: clog dancer, follower on foot of the hunt, weight-lifter, skilled bell-ringer, concertina player and breeder of canaries.

His soft voice kept a gentle commentary of

David Hunter
YCCC

events from behind the stumps, as Pelham Warner recorded. Warner was facing Rhodes at Bradford: 'Ah, Mr Warner, you play Wilfred better than any of the others.' Before Warner could reply there was a sharp 'Howzat?', the bails were shipped off and Hunter continued: 'Good afternoon, Mr Warner. What a pity, when you were playing Wilfred so well.' Then, as the batsman trailed back to the pavilion, Warner heard that same soft voice up the wicket: 'Well bowled, Wilfred, well bowled.'

Hunter followed his brother Joe as Yorkshire's keeper, Joe ironically playing five times for England yet generally regarded as an inferior player to David who, incidentally, thought the younger William, who never played first-class cricket, the one with the most natural ability.

David Hunter at first insisted on standing up to the bowling, yet he kept to the most formidable and versatile trio, Hirst, Haigh and Rhodes, ever to play county cricket. Hirst's swing and break-back were lethal and legendary, Rhodes' fractional variations in length would have tested Job, Haigh was unfathomable, even to himself, yet Summer by Summer Hunter was always there, poised, the batsman knowing he would rarely be allowed even one slight error.

He wore what was known in those days as a cavalry moustache, described by A.A. Thomson as 'rich and hanging'. In his first match, as a Colt, he did not get a chance to keep wicket and in his second, at Bradford, he had to keep to Joe Preston. He told 'Old Ebor':

Preston bowled very fast – and by the way, I thought I had never seen a better all-round cricketer than Merritt Preston – and I didn't know whether I was on my head or my heels, but after an over or two I took him quite easily. I always stood up to fast bowling until the late '90s and was then prevailed upon to stand back, though I did not like to do so.

Twice he took six wickets in an innings, and four times stumped five men in a match; against Surrey at Bradford in 1898 he stumped six and caught two. Such prowess should have made his selection for England mandatory, but his omission can be explained on two counts. He had some formidable rivals, among them Dick Lilley and Gregor McGregor, and, as C.B. Fry put it: 'He is second to none in catching and stumping…the only possible reason for the selectors to have ignored him so often can have been that the others were better batsmen; they were certainly not his superior behind the stumps.' At one point in 1891, when 3,500 runs had been scored at the crease, Hunter had conceded 25 byes.

Hawke thought highly of Hunter's determination and 'grit' as a batsman, and it was with his captain that Hunter put up a last-wicket stand for the county of 148, which stood for 84 years.

When his golden career ended in 1909, Hunter would coach young players on Scarborough afternoons, and Kilburn remembered him at 60: 'His charm was irresistible; he never showed the slightest signs of impatience or disparagement. In ability we juniors were at widely different levels but the best and worst of us received exactly the same courteous attention.'

David Hunter died in January 1927 at the age of 67.

---

made seven without further loss before close of play at 6.30 pm when the triumphant crowd headed back towards the city or out into Cheshire.

Overnight came the rain but in that Summer, as in Camelot, the sun shone each morning, and the

pitch was steaming before another packed ground when Lancashire resumed play, the opening stand raising 22 before MacLaren was given out, caught Hunter, bowled Peel. MacLaren was reported to stand still for a moment, astonished, and then to say, 'Never within an ensanguined mile of it'. That story is almost certainly totally untrue but, as the editors of small-town newspapers in Arizona were wont to say around that time, 'Never let the facts spoil the legend.'

Sugg and Briggs went to the eight-armed Tunnicliffe at slip. Peel, the other England slow left-arm bowler in this match, was as devastating as Briggs, and the upshot was that Yorkshire needed 57 to win, the 25,000 crowd by then reeling with the intoxication of it all – when they were not booing the umpires.

Three innings of the match had then raised a total of 172 runs. Yorkshire sent in two of their amateurs, Jackson and Sellers, who after scoring 20 without great difficulty, appeared to have the match won. But at 24 Briggs hit Jackson on the pad, the ball scurried off down the leg side and the batsmen ran, Jackson pulling up in middle wicket thinking he had been given out left before. The crowd howled, the umpire frantically signalled again to demonstrate a leg bye, by which time the ball was in the keeper's hands. 'Howzat?' he shouted at square leg umpire. The umpire asked what the appeal was for, then refused to give a stumping, but when the keeper appealed for a run-out he raised his finger.

So Jackson went, and Yorkshire descended into a near lunacy. Brown, Tunnicliffe and Wainwright all followed quickly, and Ernest Smith was given out to a low, diving catch off a fierce drive, the amateur clearly believing the catch had not been made cleanly. So indignant was Smith, a schoolmaster, that he had to be ordered to go by the umpire.

At 46-7, from 24-0, Yorkshire should have been beaten, but their last four were Moorhouse, the young Hirst, Ulyett in his last season, and Hunter. It was a simple enough 'get 'em singles' situation. But cool and sensible thinking had long since deserted this particular match. Moorhouse leapt at Briggs and was stumped; Hirst, then 23 and played for his bowling, went for one of his soon to be famous pulls, to be caught in the deep.

When Hunter joined Ulyett, six were still needed. Ulyett said afterwards that he feared for Hunter against Briggs – one explanation for his

attempt to hit Briggs' next, tossed-up delivery, so that the match would be over with one blow. Alas, as Yorkshiremen in the crowd were on their feet and cheering, the ball failed to carry over the boundary and dropped, as if aimed, into the safe hands of Ward on the long-off boundary. That contest is still known as the 'mad' Roses match.

By 1895 the Championship was assuming modern proportions with the admission of five more county clubs, and Yorkshire never recovered from a poor start, losing three of the first eight matches, although winning seven of the next ten was good enough to take them into third place. Brown, after an Australian tour, was less successful but Denton continued to thrive. Jackson burst to the front as an international all-rounder, while Peel and Hirst both topped 130 wickets. For the first time both Yorkshire openers, Tunnicliffe and Brown, the first famous pairing, each passed 1,000 runs.

It was in that Summer, too, that the first hint of discord between Yorkshire and Middlesex appeared, for when the 'Metropolitans' appeared at Bradford in August they were disconcerted to find Wainwright was present to play against them, Yorkshire having refused to release him to play for England, and Middlesex having forgone Stoddart.

Although the useful Sellers retired into business in 1894, Denton's arrival brought a new dimension to the batting, for here was a player who made his runs quickly – too quickly according to some watchers. But the season overall was a disappointment, Yorkshire finishing second as Surrey bounced back to the top. The weather was influential, Yorkshire being denied one, perhaps two victories; however, there were compensations. Somerset, making a first visit to Huddersfield, were beaten in a day, and there were times in a damp Summer when the combination of off-spin and leg-spin purveyed by Wainwright and Peel was almost unplayable.

Hirst, too, was making his presence the more powerful as the months passed, with 56 wickets at an average of 13 and a century at Bristol. What caught the eye that Summer, however, was Yorkshire's fielding, drawing praise wherever they played. The advent of younger, fitter, more

George Hirst Lionheart

Although he is only two-and-thirty, it is not too much to say that he is the best all-round cricketer of this English generation. Born at Kirkheaton, near Huddersfield, he is a Yorkshireman to the backbone; and for Yorks he has played cricket since 1889, having scored a thousand runs or more and having taken a hundred wickets in four separate seasons. Though he is not so good a sailor as he is cricketer, he is willing to risk the voyages to Australia whenever he is wanted there; for he is full of grit. If he is not a great linguist, he is at least a complete master of the West Riding dialect, who has played for England no fewer than ten times. He bowls with a noted 'swerve', he bats with a daring 'pull', he fields with all the virtues, and he will ever be remembered as the hero of the England v Australia match at The Oval last year. His coming 'Benefit' should be a well deserved reward; and he may be summed up as a really fine fellow with the heart of a lion.

He has a good appetite and quite a nice smile.

Vanity Fair, 8 August 1903.

As Emmett's magnificent career ended in 1888 there was room in Yorkshire's ranks for another quick left-arm bowler to complement Peel, and the village of Kirkheaton, near Huddersfield and across the valley from Lascelles Hall, duly obliged, providing Hirst (always George Herbert, never just George), who was almost certainly the greatest county cricketer ever and an all-rounder who, in English conditions, would always be a contender for an all-time England XI.

Six years older than Wilfred Rhodes, he gave his villagers that immortal, boasting question: who is the world's greatest all-rounder? Answer: he bowls left-handed, bats right and comes from Kirkheaton. Hirst, at 5ft 6in, was the smaller of the two

George Hirst
YCCC

Titans, a more open and outgoing man than Wilfred, cheerful, good-humoured and with a smile, said Lord Hawke, that reached round to the back of his neck.

Born in the Brown Cow, a village pub since demolished by the entry of a new road, young Hirst was playing for Kirkheaton at the age of 15 and was winning prizes, offered by a Sunday newspaper, for both batting and bowling. Pancake Tuesday was the recognised starting day for the practice to begin and so seriously was this undertaken on the ground, opened in 1883 when Hirst was 12, that the side nets were taken away to ensure that the fielding was authentic.

By the age of ten Hirst had already left school, working first for a hand-loom weaver in a corner cottage, then in a dye works, and such were his prowess and reputation that he was taking professional engagements as the 'Saturday man' for the clubs of Elland, Mirfield and then Huddersfield. He was also remembered as a more than useful rugby union full-back.

Yorkshire could hardly overlook such a prodigy and he was called upon at the age of 18, proudly attending Bramall Lane with his gear in a canvas bag, although he admitted later than he had worn a sweater over his blue shirt. He bought a white shirt with his first pay.

His introduction to county cricket was gentle, playing in only one match in each of his first three seasons. *Wisden* confused him with one of the Huddersfield brothers, both amateurs, and referred to him as 'E. Hirst'. In those days Hirst bowled a brisk left-arm over attack, and batted at number ten. Lord Hawke thought him a bowler with 'a nice action, straight and quick', while the Reverend Holmes was already warning W.G. Grace that the young man, who could also hit straight and lustily, would develop into a powerful batsman.

The decline of Joe Preston left a gap in the team that Yorkshire had to fill, and 'Young George' as he was known, in contrast to 'Old George' Ulyett, was an obvious candidate. By 1893 Hirst had begun to develop, his striking rate improving as the season ended to finish third behind Peel and Wainwright with 69 wickets at an average of 16.

There was no confusion about his identity the following year, for Hirst strode to the forefront of the all-rounders, taking 125 wickets at 14 apiece and scoring 419 runs, playing a major part, along with Peel, in Yorkshire's first undisputed Championship.

Grace had no further doubts about Hirst in the next season when the Yorkshireman scored 115 against Gloucestershire, including 17 fours, and also took 95 wickets at an average of 15, establishing himself as one of Yorkshire's opening partnership of Hirst (fast left-arm) and Peel (slow left-arm). Hirst also laid the foundation of his reputation as a one-man fire brigade, repeatedly rescuing Yorkshire from a hot spot with bat, ball or some consummate piece of fielding.

By the last decade of the 19th century Hirst was one of the pillars of Lord Hawke's team, a small but powerful man of tireless energy, his face and arms bronzed, a fund of good nature and humour, loved by both Yorkshiremen and the opposition. His bowling, which began with a little hop, step and jump, developed into one of the most potent weapons in cricket history, a prodigious swerve that had Somerset captain Sammy Woods complaining: 'I don't really see how one can be expected to play a ball which when it leaves the bowler's arm appears to be coming straight but when it reaches the wicket is like a very good throw from cover point.'

Hirst's ability to make the ball move in the air made him a terror to batsmen in all conditions, wet or dry. If they managed to keep a delivery out of their stumps they were liable, by a defensive reflex, to steer it into the ranks of leg-side fielders. Hawke said of him in 1901: 'It may be questioned if any other bowler ever swerved in the air, match after match, as Georgie did that Summer – of course, it did not last through a long spell but in conjunction with his great pace it should be memorable as long as cricket is played.' Hirst hit, added Hawke, like a 'kicking horse'.

In 1896 he performed the first of his 14 'doubles', and a second in the Gold Jubilee Summer of 1897 (in all matches) won him a place in A.E. Stoddart's team for Australia, where his bowling proved to be nothing like as forceful as in English conditions although he was hampered by a pulled muscle, an injury that followed him into the following Summer when he began his historic partnership with Wilfred Rhodes.

By 1899 Hirst was as formidable a batsman as he was a bowler, topping 1,500 runs and scoring centuries in succession against Surrey, Hampshire and Nottinghamshire. When he played for England against Australia at Trent Bridge he saw W.G.'s last appearance for England, although Hirst's own contribution to an historic occasion was unimpressive.

The new century brought new and powerful masters to English cricket, Yorkshire winning three successive Championships with Hirst, Rhodes and Schofield Haigh forming a triumvirate that ruled the kingdom and were unchallenged in their supremacy for a half-century until Surrey produced Bedser, Laker and Lock.

However, Hirst's fielding at mid-off was outstanding and it was suggested he was worth his place in the England side for that alone. A contemporary wrote of him: 'You might as well try to drive through a brick wall as try to pass those iron hands.'

By 1901, as Hawke noted, Hirst had fully developed his deadly swerve, a phenomenon that was to reduce the greatest batsmen to outraged exasperation. 'Sometimes it works, sometimes it doesn't' seems to be as near as George ever came to explaining a delivery that was ranked in its time alongside Bosanquet's googly. Hirst needed, for full effectiveness, not a crosswind but a headwind, and the vagaries of the English climate explain in part why he was more successful on some days than others. In 1901 he had a match return of 12-29 against Essex at Leyton on a pitch that would have brought TV crews hurling down today, for Yorkshire, raising only 104 themselves, won by an innings and 33. Congratulated on that performance, Hirst would recall wryly his figures against Somerset: 1-89.

In that year of 1901 Yorkshire won 20 of their 27 matches and lost only to Somerset at Headingley in a game that has excited comment ever since. The following year, 1902, Hirst took his place at Edgbaston in what is still regarded by many historians as England's finest team, to take three Australian wickets for 15 while Wilfred, from the other end, bowled one of the most devastating spells in Test-match history: 11-3-17-7. Australia were all out for 36, Victor Trumper making 19 in poor light. C.B. Fry, as close and clear a witness as might be found, said afterwards that well as Rhodes had bowled it was Hirst who 'caused the debacle'.

A.A. Thomson, visiting Kirkeaton, mentioned this remarkable double perform-

ance, only to be told that the pair had once dismissed rivals Slaithwaite for 9, Hirst taking 5-2, Rhodes 5-3. There were four byes because, said Thomson's informant, 'ower stumper were reight freetened o'George Herbert'.

Although England could not force a victory because of the weather, Australia's escape was only temporary for from Edgbaston they travelled to Headingly to be put on the rack again, this time by Yorkshire, Hirst taking 5-9 and F.S. Jackson 5-12. Trumper again threatened to hold off an English victory until Hirst bowled him with what he afterwards described as 'the best ball of my life'. Yet Hirst admitted to Hawke that he felt he could not do himself justice in Test matches; he never liked them and never wanted to play in them.

A calf muscle injury reduced Hirst's power in 1903, Yorkshire slipping to third, yet an casual reader of the records would wonder at such judgement on a player that still managed to perform the 'double' and top both the batting and bowling averages for his county. Two years later his batting bloomed once again, averaging 61, his scores including a 341 against Leicestershire, still the highest by a Yorkshireman in county games.

That innings was characteristic of Hirst, for his seven hours at the wicket were not a mere orgy of scoring. The pitch must have been good, Leicestershire scoring 419, but Yorkshire were 74-5 when Hirst took charge, his hits (indicative that he was playing for the team) being a six and 53 fours. All this was merely the prologue to 1906, truly an *annus mirabilis* for Hirst managed the unmatched and unparalleled feat of scoring 2,385 runs and taking 208 wickets in a declining team.

In a career of 32 years Hirst scored 60 centuries, 56 for Yorkshire, took 2,569 wickets for Yorkshire, scored a thousand runs in 19 Summers, took a hundred or more wickets in 17 and of his 14 'doubles', 11 were performed in succession. He also took 551 catches. He never once managed all ten wickets, but he did take nine four times. At

Leeds, after dismissing nine Lancashire batsmen, bowling eight of them, he asked for the ball as a memento. 'Nay,' countered Schofield Haigh, who had taken the other wicket. 'We mun cut to'ball in half. We took'em between us, George.'

Hirst's good nature, kindliness, patience and deep knowledge made him a great natural coach, a post he fulfilled for Eton, Scarborough and Yorkshire with enormous distinction. He did much towards making George Macaulay into a fine bowler, and Bill Bowes, another of his pupils, left a memorable epitaph: 'I never met a finer cricketer nor a finer man.' Such was Hirst's popularity that his benefit match, against Lancashire at Headingley in 1904, was attended by 78,792 spectators.

In these days when so much apparent cheating is almost officially sanctioned as 'professionalism', it is warming to hear Hirst's contemporaries, to a man, praise his absolute honesty. The England wicket-keeper Lilley, for instance, commented: 'Scrupulously fair – there has been more than one occasion when he would have been justified in appealing for lbw but he did not do so.'

Small wonder then that Hirst is one of the very few cricketers who have earned poems in their honour, William Kerr describing him thus:

But here in Common sunshine I have seen George Hirst

Not yet a ghost, substantial, his off-drives

Mellow as brown ale,

And crisp Merry cuts and brave Chaucerian pulls.

When war broke out in 1914 Hirst was almost 44 but continued playing league cricket, often, it was said, claiming only his expenses when he knew the club that had engaged him was short of funds. He resumed his cricket with Yorkshire in 1919 as though the Great War had been no more than a troubled weekend, hitting MCC for 180 not out in the opening match. He retired at 50, was talked into playing a Festival match at the age of 58 and, when bowled by Bowes for one, told the bowler: 'That were a grand ball, lad. I couldn't have played that one when I wer good.'

---

disciplined cricketers had produced a class of specialists – Denton in the deep, J.T. Brown (succeeding Ulyett) at point, Hirst at mid-off, Wainwright and Tunnicliffe at slip.

Hunter, too, was in virile form, catching 54 and stumping 18, and 1895 was also the year of one of Jessop's hurricanes against Yorkshire, 63 out of 65 in 30 minutes at Cheltenham. The Committee, perhaps sensitive to comments about Wainwright in 1893, agreed to release any player chosen for the Gentlemen or Players at Lord's.

The Sun in Splendour, the badge of the Plantagenet House of York, might have symbolised Yorkshire's cricket in 1896. The Reverend Holmes rightly described it as 'prodigious': no less than 17 centuries were scored, 12 players topped 20 in the averages, five innings topped

400 runs and four more than 300, and in five matches more than 1,000 runs were scored. Yorkshire's batsmen broke records everywhere: an innings of 887 against Warwickshire; 660 against Leicestershire; 543 against Sussex.

Four Yorkshiremen (Jackson 117, Wainwright 126, Peel 210 and Hawke 166) made centuries in the Birmingham monster, Moorehouse (72) and Hirst (85) being among the failures in an innings of ten hours 50 minutes! It was perhaps from these three days in May 1896 that Edgbaston first won its reputation as a batsman's pitch. A declaration was not permitted, at that time, until the third day, so not surprisingly Warwickshire managed to draw after being bowled out for 203 (Hirst 8-59).

In such a Summer, Wainwright, Peel and Hirst all paid a little more for their wickets, but the

Club found an immense compensation, just when Wainwright's career was past its peak, in the arrival from Huddersfield of Schofield Haigh, another professor of in-swing and off-spin. He won his county cap by taking 14 Durham wickets, and then demonstrated that Hawke had not been impetuous in the award by finishing the season with 71 wickets. Not surprisingly, the advent of a fifth top-class bowler (with Wainwright, Peel, Hirst and Jackson), added to the mighty weight of the batting, secured Yorkshire's second Championship.

Hawke celebrated his 13th year of captaincy, the

Committee voting 100 guineas towards a public testimonial, which was later translated into a presentation of a portrait in oils and 'a handsome service of plate'. This was also the year in which Winter pay for professionals was instituted, £2 a week from 7 September to the start of the following season. This was later amended, the Club keeping half the Winter pay, to which 4% per annum was added, the whole being presented to the player on his retirement. A bonus fund, collected from an additional £2 awarded to each player for every county appearance, was also set up, and in the wondrous seasons of 1900-03 extra monies were added to the bonus fund. Thus

Bobby Peel An Idol

So great was the fame of Peate's successor that the illustrious Edwardian actor-director Henry Ainley always regarded the highlight of his life the time he was allowed to carry Peel's bag from station to ground. If Peate had failed through too much hospitality, then Peel's fall also came about because the little man from Churwell, Morley, was too often the toast of the town.

Peel's career overlapped Peate's by five years, but while the latter was senior bowler Peel seemed content to play the lesser part, not fully blossoming until Peate's departure in 1887, this despite Peel's debut performance taking 9-29 in the match against Surrey at Sheffield in 1882, Peate having sprained his ankle appearing for the Players. Hawke later recalled: 'Even Wilfred Rhodes did not make a more promising appearance.'

While a contemporary of Peate, Peel took 163 wickets in five seasons but his batting and fielding were such that Yorkshire could afford to play both, with the junior slow left-arm bowler in the role of all-rounder. From 1888 to his own departure in 1897 Peel took a further 1,273 wickets. He completed the 'double' in 1887, making 1,000 runs in five of his 15 seasons, and toured Australia no less than four times, an extraordinary accomplishment at that time. He played 20 times for England, worth more than 100 Tests today.

Bobby Peel
Ron Deaton collection

Peel's mastery of length matched Peate's batsmen testifying to his ability to hold back the ball in flight; he used a quicker arm ball and seems to have turned the ball more on a helpful pitch when, all agree, he was virtually unplayable. A.C. MacLaren called Peel 'the cleverest bowler of my time', a handsome tribute from a Lancashire captain who commanded Johnny Briggs. MacLaren added:

No one ever had a better knowledge of the game and he was the quickest I have ever played with or against at spotting the weak point of the batsman against whom he was bowling. I place Peel first on my list of great left-handed bowlers on account of his wonderful judgment, his diabolical cleverness and his great natural ability.

Peel's performance, season after season, brought him fame throughout the Empire. A cheerful, gregarious man, he took to hospitality and entertaining with alacrity and moved in such society, particularly in London, that when one of the foremost journalists of the day asked to see him he was fobbed off by a man who announced himself as 'Peel's secretary', adding: 'He does not like interviews and has little to say. He sent me to take his place.' It is not impossible, of course, that Bobby was either shy or 'indisposed' at that particular moment.

His departure from cricket is one of the saddest on record. The unpleasant story is that Peel arrived drunk on the pitch one morning, urinated publicly and was sacked on the spot. I have never been convinced of this account because it has always seemed to be so much out of character for a cricketer of that time when so much stress was placed upon behaving 'like a gentleman', even in one's cups.

When A.A. Thomson asked George Hirst for his account, a different tale emerged. According to Hirst he was preparing to leave the team's small Chesterfield hotel one morning when Peel appeared in what Hirst described as 'a proper condition'. A horrified Hirst persuaded Peel to return to his bedroom, got him undressed and into bed and then set off for the ground, explaining to Hawke: 'Peel was taken queer in the night, m'lord. He apologises but won't be able to turn out this morning.'

Hawke probably guessed that a cover-up was taking place but accepted the explanation, told the 12th man he would be playing and, on losing the toss, led his men on

to the field. A shaken Hirst then realised that Yorkshire had 12 men on the field, for out in the middle, red-faced and grinning, cap and ball in hand, was Bobby Peel, according to Hirst in 'a properer condition than before'. Hirst added that he dared not even glance at Hawke, but heard him say: 'Leave the field at once, Peel.' To which the euphoric Peel replied: 'Not at all, m'lord. I'm in fine form this morning.' Then, as if to demonstrate the fact, he turned and wheeled his arm over to deliver a cunning ball in the direction of the sight-screen.

Later Hawke reported how he took Peel gently by the arm and led him back to the pavilion. When Hirst returned to the hotel that evening Peel was sleeping it off and then awoke, probably with a hangover, certainly truculent. 'You must write an apology to his lordship, at once,' said Hirst. Replied Peel: 'That I never will.'

'Then you're finished.'

'Niver in this world,' said Peel. 'They can't do wi-art me.'

Peel was, of course, sacked. 'Nothing ever gave me greater pain,' Hawke wrote later. A month earlier Peel had taken 8-53 against Kent, and although aged 40 was at his peak as a player.

For many years afterwards Peel played league cricket, notably for the Lancashire League club Accrington, and was later a hotelier in Leeds. He must have been a tough little man for he did not die until his 84th year, in 1941.

As with Peate, Lord Hawke soon made up with his departed cricketer and Peel never lost contact with Yorkshire. In 1922 he was helping Hirst with scouting and coaching, once asking a tall lad named Hedley Verity, who bowled swingers at the nets, 'Cannot you bowl faster than that?' In his 75th year he and 5,000 other enthusiasts were in Leeds station to see Yorkshire's Australian tourists Sutcliffe, Leyland, Bowes and Verity depart, Bobby presenting each of them with a white rose.

did Yorkshire, much of it at Hawke's suggestion, lead the way in caring for the Club's servants.

Yorkshire have also generously supported the grounds upon which the county have played first-class cricket. By 1902 as much as 35% of the gross takings at the gate were passed on to the local club. Nor was the support confined to Yorkshire grounds: £25 was sent to Leicestershire in 1899 to help develop a head-quarters.
After 1896 the following Summer was certain to be something of an anticlimax, although a fall to fourth place was hardly expected. For various reasons the captain missed several matches, players suffered injury and neither the bowling nor the batting carried the penetration and confi-dence of the previous campaign. By mid-July Yorkshire had been beaten only once, but in high August they were unable to force victory often enough to sustain the expected challenge.

At Sheffield another huge total, 681, was raised against Sussex, Tunnicliffe and Brown setting a new first-wicket record of 378. Schofield Haigh performed the hat-trick against Derbyshire, Essex won by one run at Huddersfield, while Jessop took on Yorkshire again, this time at Harrogate: 101 runs in 40 minutes.

This Summer held a particular sadness in that it saw the end of Bobby Peel's first-class career. He finished with 64 wickets at an average of 19, and his sudden departure must have worried many Yorkshire followers accustomed to the enormous contributions made by the all-rounder to the success of the county. History then records a succession that has to be described, in the words of any era, as sensational, but it was not, in fact, altogether as straightforward as it is sometimes remembered.

When Peel departed there were two candidates for this vacancy: Wilfred Rhodes of Kirkheaton, who had been playing as a professional for Galashiels and in whom Warwickshire were interested, and Albert Cordingley of Eccleshill. Cordingley was in fact given the first trial and played in one match, took 0-35, was never given another chance and went off to play briefly for Sussex and then Lytham. Yorkshire almost cer-tainly planned to give Cordingley a longer trial, one match being a patently unfair test of a young

player, and there is one story that selection for the following match, Cordingley or Rhodes, was decided by the toss of a coin between Hawke and Jackson.

What is certain is that Rhodes appeared for Yorkshire against MCC, 20 years old, and according to the Reverend Hodgson ('Country Vicar'), 'pleasant, ruddy faced with eyes of won-derful blue…with a high easy action'. Rhodes took 2-39 and 4-24, and one of cricket's greatest careers had been launched.

Rhodes' second match was at Bath, where he achieved figures of 13-45, and in a season of mixed weather when batsmen were often caught on drying pitches, the devastation continued until he finished his first season with 142 wick-ets for Yorkshire, at an average of 13.95 (and scored 515 runs).

Rhodes was not the only extraordinary per-former in 1898. Tunnicliffe hit four centuries in an aggregate of 1,713, Jackson five towards 1,442, also taking 91 wickets at an average of 15; perhaps fortunately for the other counties Hirst was less effective, but Haigh also managed 107 wickets and 500 runs. Twenty matches were won and Yorkshire were handsome champions.

This was also the year of the great Tunnicliffe-Brown opening partnership of 554 against Derbyshire at Chesterfield in a benefit match for Walter Sugg at a time when no declarations were allowed. Tunnicliffe contributed 243 and Brown 300 on this famous occasion, the long man from Pudsey batting virtually without nourishment. He and David Hunter had spent the previous night in a Leeds hotel, and in dashing to catch the train Tunnicliffe had been able to seize no more than a biscuit. At lunchtime, such was the size of the crowd, the caterers were unable to satisfy the hungry multitude, and the Yorkshire professionals had to be satisfied with just a sand-wich each. At 5 pm he managed a cup of tea in the interval and then, at the close, with Yorkshire 480-0, he walked back to the team's hotel and before dinner was served fell asleep, not to wake up until breakfast the following morning.

By then Hawke's orders to Tunnicliffe and Brown were to hit out – which they did, 63 com-ing in the first 15 minutes, Tunnicliffe being

David Denton Lucky

Denton was, as Peter Thomas pointed out perceptively, the answer to all those who believed that to be a Yorkshire batsman was to be dull. *Wisden* thought his batting 'a calculated risk', but Denton always resented the nickname 'Lucky', once saying: 'I think a man who has made over 30,000 runs for Yorkshire must have something more than luck at the back of him.'

In another sense Denton was distinctly unlucky, for there is no doubt that had he not been a contemporary of Lancashire's Johnny Tyldesley he would have represented England far more often and won much greater fame for his audacious and entertaining play and brilliant deep fielding.

A glimpse of Denton in his prime came from 'Country Vicar' in 1912:

David Denton
YCCC

He was a positive delight to anyone who likes to see the figures on the scoreboard to move rapidly. There was no waiting to play himself in; he thumped the first ball, if he could. And he hit right merrily as long as he was at the wicket. He had all the strokes, cuts, drives, pulls, leg-hits, but I think his off-side play was his main distinction. A glorious fieldsman too – magnificent in the deep. Very fast on his feet, a fine thrower and a sure catch. It was said on a melancholy occasion, when by some mischance he missed a 'ballooner' one of his colleagues burst into tears. Such an accident was entirely unexpected.

It was while our 'Country Vicar' was musing upon Denton on a sunny day at Southampton that his wife Angela went in search of Yorkshire autographs and came back with, upon one page, 'S. Haigh, W. Rhodes, G.H. Hirst, A. Drake', a page that would cause a few misty eyes among the Cricket Memorabilia Society today.

Another view of Denton in his prime came from Pelham Warner:

...the hardest hitter of his size and weight I have ever seen and no one timed the ball better. He possessed very supple wrists. He was always going at the bowling and being possessed of plenty of strokes generally got his runs at a great pace. He had a lovely stroke over extra cover's head, pushed the good length ball between point and cover and on a slow wicket was a fine puller and hooker. His fielding in the long field and at third man has never been surpassed.

Denton won his place in 1895 behind Tunnicliffe and Brown, and when he retired in 1920 he came in at number three behind Holmes and Sutcliffe; with Hirst and Rhodes he saw the transition from the Golden Age to the Jazz Age. Three times he topped 200 in his 69 centuries, and three times scored two centuries in one match. He played 11 times for England and scored one century, in comparison with Tyldesley's 31 Tests, and it was generally accepted that while there was little between the two, the Lancastrian was the better player of spin on a turning pitch.

Denton came from Thornes, near Wakefield, was originally recommended to the county as a bowler (he once had W.G.

Grace lbw), and would no doubt have continued playing after the age of 46 but for ill health. He was reckoned to be a shrewd man and when he died, aged 74, he left more than £10,000.

caught when the total had reached 554, Brown played on deliberately, when he reached 300. Hirst, ironically, was out for a duck in the match.

'A Country Vicar', trawling his memories in 1946, was unequivocal about the deep disappointment of the following season:

> Which brings me back to the misfortunes of my own county in 1899. They had, I think, more than their share of bad luck but they also showed, at times, some very indifferent form. And the reason for this was at least partly due to a want of self-control on the part of the players – particularly to a desire to quench their thirst with little regard for the after effects of attempting to do so.

The Championship seemed likely to be retained in 1899 until a late defeat by Kent at Tonbridge enabled Surrey to take the lead. Jackson's bowling was severely limited by a damaged shoulder, Brown missed the August fixtures, Tunnicliffe's average dropped by 20, while Hirst, although batting better than ever, suffered a decline as a bowler. The University of Cambridge supplied another cricketer in T.L. Taylor, a future President, while Frank Mitchell recorded the highest aggregate. Rhodes, in his second season and in a batsman's Summer, was even more impressive, taking 150 wickets for 16 runs each.

Another J.T. Brown appeared, this one from Darfield as opposed to Driffield, a fast bowler of a pace not seen since Shoey Harrison's days. He had played twice in 1898 but it was in the following season, against Worcestershire, that he recovered from a foot injury sustained the previous evening to wreck the second innings by taking six wickets for 19 in nine overs; he was so fast, according to A.W. Pullin ('Old Ebor'), that 'the Worcestershire batsman could not or dare not look at him'. Yorkshire thus won a match they had appeared to have lost, by 11 runs.

On another occasion young Brown bowled a Gloucester batsman at Huddersfield with such fury that a bail flew 48 yards. Australia's Joe Darling, bowled first ball by Brown, commented afterwards: 'All I saw was a big fist high in the air, then I heard a thud and found the wicket down. I never saw the ball, it was so fast.'

In more modern times Yorkshire would either have had to give such a talent as Brown's a chance to expand or accept his transfer to another county. Despite his 57 wickets for the county that Summer, Brown was never able to establish a place in the side and, like Harrison, his career ended abruptly, at the age of 29, when he dislocated a shoulder at Taunton in 1903.

Over the next three seasons Yorkshire came to full prosperity, days of sunshine and glory. Only two matches were lost of the 80 played in seasons 1900-02, and the Championship was not so much won as surrendered by a dazed opposition. Yorkshire's pre-eminence was rarely challenged, and the question in both the later years was simply who would be second? This was achieved despite the absence of Jackson, serving his country in South Africa, for two of those years, and the death of that brilliant but erratic all-rounder Frank Milligan, who was killed in the column that relieved Mafeking.

The year 1900 was garlanded in England by the bowling of Rhodes (206 wickets at 12 apiece) and Haigh (145 at 14), so it was not altogether surprising that Yorkshire's batting was less predominant than usual and Hirst's bowling a superfluous luxury. Hirst did average 40, Tunnicliffe was as reliable as ever and another of the Cantabs, T.L. Taylor, made regular contributions with the bat, while David Hunter, in his 12th season, was unmatched.

Only Nottinghamshire and Surrey managed to

top 300 against Yorkshire that season, and such was the prowess of the team that the Reverend Holmes called for a restoration of matches against England:

Let us have such a trial of strength as Surrey, Sussex and Kent did in olden times, in the height of the season and before the Players are getting stale through excess of cricket. Such a team as Yorkshire possessed in those years – a team in which every man could make and save runs and which had in

Rhodes and Hirst a couple of bowlers superior perhaps to those in any other county – would certainly have made a great fight with the most carefully picked England eleven.

The strength and resilience of the sides seemed, to the opposition, beyond measure. In 1901, for example, Haigh had knee trouble so Hirst picked up the ball again to reveal that his swing was deadlier then ever. The batting was led by Frank Mitchell, whose aggregate of 1,674 was a new Yorkshire record, and of the 16 players who

Frank Mitchell Springbok

Frank Mitchell, from Market Weighton, took an almost classical route into Yorkshire's team: St. Peter's, York to the University of Cambridge (Blues at cricket and rugby) and then the Gentlemen. After a distinguished ten years with the county, he broadened his career beyond any other wearer of the white rose, playing for London County, Transvaal, England and finally becoming captain of South Africa.

Mitchell bowled right-arm medium-fast but was renowned for the weight of his driving on the off side: 'There are not many batsmen against whom it is a heavier task to field mid-off,' was *Wisden's* comment in 1902.

Hawke had already spotted him before, as an undergraduate, when he made 75 and 92 against Yorkshire; the following year (1895) he hit two centuries. He became Cambridge captain in 1896 and changed the course of cricket history in the Varsity match of that year. There was a compulsory follow-on at that time for teams more than 120 runs in arrears, but as Mitchell wanted Oxford to bat last, Oxford needing ten runs to clear the deficit, he ordered the bowler to concede extras, the next over costing 12.

Such was the uproar at Lord's with booing and demonstrations – one irate Oxford supporter in the pavilion actually threw a pair of binoculars at the Cambridge captain – that the young Cambridge team made a nervous show of their second innings, scor-

ing 212 and leaving Oxford to march to a triumphant 330-6 and victory.

The debate raged on for three more years before the regulations were altered, the follow-on becoming optional and the margin being raised to 150. Mitchell became a regular in the Yorkshire side after touring South Africa under Hawke in 1899, joining Wainwright in a partnership of 329 against Leicestershire and making two other centuries; in one spell of 12 days that Summer he hit seven scores of more than 50.

His love for South Africa was increased by his Boer War service after which, in 1901, he returned to Yorkshire to score seven centuries, hitting, in another purple match, a sequence of 100, 104 not out, 106 not out and 12, 162 and 52. He opened the innings for England in Johannesburg and Cape Town in 1899, became Sir Abe Bailey's secretary and then led South Africa in the Triangular Tournament of 1912. He returned to England to fight as a Lt-Colonel in a West Riding regiment.

Mitchell also played for England at rugby, kept goal for Sussex FA, and wrote the Badminton book on rugby football. Pictured at the crease in David Frith's *The Golden Age of Cricket*, Mitchell is casually leaning his left hand on his pad, the impression being that the next ball will be hit no matter what the bowler contrives. Slim, dark, determined, he has the air of a man who might have flown a Sopwith Pup or a Spitfire.

appeared that season, three played in only one match each. J.T. Brown's benefit figure was a new record amount, too, of £2,300.

But in a year of glory the rest of England's counties marked that Summer for Somerset's visit to Leeds for what became one of the greatest Championship matches. As Cardus put in *West Country Lads* (1929):

> In one gaudy week in July 1901 piping hot history was written by these West Country gallants. At that time Yorkshire, as ever, were champions. And they were invincible. Leeds, Sheffield and Bradford had watched Yorkshire man and boy for a summer and a half and not once had they seen their darlings beaten.

Somerset batted first on a warm sunny morning at Leeds and were dismissed for 87 (who else but Hirst and Rhodes?), to which Yorkshire replied with 325 (Haigh 96), Somerset making plans to cancel their second night's accommodation. Near teatime on the second afternoon, Cardus, a schoolboy in Manchester, recalled: 'During a change of lessons I was told Somerset was making a fight, that at long last Yorkshire's attack had been tied into strange complicated knots.'

Some fight! Braund and Palairet, opening Somerset's seemingly doomed second innings, hit Yorkshire for 222 in 140 minutes; the innings reached 630, and on a crumbling wicket on the third afternoon Yorkshire were dismissed for 113 and Somerset had won by 279. Again according to Cardus, Yorkshire believed that Braund had been caught at slip by Tunnicliffe when at 55. The umpire had his view impeded by the bowler, the square-leg umpire gave Braund the benefit, and the incident so wounded the chivalrous and scrupulously fair George Hirst that when Somerset passed 500 even he was moved to dissent, saying to umpire Wright: 'Eeh, Walter, tha knaws, thou'rt a reight foo-il.'

The whole point of the story, and of a glorious match, was of course the cracking of Yorkshire's apparent invincibility. A month earlier at Trent Bridge they had dealt the powerful Nottinghamshire team a deadly blow. Yorkshire had scored 204 (Denton 73) and then, to the astonishment of a cricket world accustomed to

extraordinary performances from Lord Hawke's team, they had dismissed Nottinghamshire for 13 in 15.5 overs, Rhodes taking 6-4, Haigh 4-8; A.O. Jones was the Nottingham top scorer with four. A second innings of 173 failed to save Nottinghamshire from an innings defeat.

Somerset were the only team to defeat Yorkshire that Summer, as they were again in 1902 when F.S. Jackson returned to serve both Yorkshire and England. This year, too, saw the emergence of Irving Washington, the first left-hander to be played purely for his batting, 'who promises to be very brilliant' said *Wisden*. It was Washington, with the batsman of the year T.L. Taylor, who saved Yorkshire from the possibility of a rare defeat with a stand of 43 at The Oval.

That those Summers were mostly good is confirmed by the fact that the abandonment of a match (in 1901 at The Oval, in 1902 at Chesterfield) was considered worthy of note. Tunnicliffe became the first Yorkshireman to take 500 catches, while the incredible Rhodes passed 1,000 wickets in his fifth season. Mitchell's emigration to South Africa, which would have been a shattering blow to most teams, was hardly noticed in the results, much though his personality was missed. So devastating were Rhodes and Haigh that Hirst was able to have one of his less strenuous years (by his measure). Particular satisfaction would have been gained by the dismissal of Lancashire for 72 and 54 (an innings defeat), from the fact that Middlesex failed to score 100 in four completed innings, and that in seven successive matches in May and June the various opposition sides failed to reach 130 in an innings.

Apart from lacking a great fast bowler such as Freeman or Trueman (although in English conditions Hirst more than sufficed), Lord Hawke's team of those years could perhaps have been matched only by Yorkshire in 1939, Surrey in the 1950s and Yorkshire again in the 1960s. Most pundits would probably put their money on Hawke. To a string of gifted amateurs – Jackson, Mitchell, Taylor, Sellers, Ernest Smith – Hawke could add the best first three of any county at the time: Tunnicliffe, Brown and Denton, together with astonishing all-round power of Hirst and Rhodes.

John Tunnicliffe
Long John, loyal of the loyal

John Tunnicliffe stands among the first of Yorkshire's cricketers for several reasons. He was a man of iron discipline, an opening batsman who scored more than 20,000 runs in his 17 seasons, and an outstanding lieutenant to Hawke, who nominated him the 'loyal of the loyal' for his service both to his captain and his team, but above all for his astonishing dexterity as a slip catcher.

Tunnicliffe was a long-armed man of 6ft 2in, who was said to know instinctively where to stand for each bowler in whatever condition. He took 691 catches in his career, a total surpassed only by Wilfred Rhodes (794) who, of course, played for 34 years. It was Tunnicliffe's catching off Rhodes' bowling that made him world-renowned; many a batsman is said to have descended the pavilion steps, sniffed the damp, eyed the sunshine and said to himself, 'Ullo, caught Tunnicliffe, bowled Rhodes' – and 100s were in both innings.

John Tunnicliffe
YCCC

As a batsman he was, in his long and famous partnership with J.T. Brown, regarded as the long and dour half of the partnership, the Ironside to Brown's Cavalier, but that was because Tunnicliffe deliberately sublimated himself and his own instincts to the requirements of this career and the team. As a youth in Pudsey he was famous as a hitter – so famous in fact that the Britannia Club called a special general meeting to alter a rule that prevented playing membership until the age of 18. Young John was admitted as a 16-year-old, and two years later was playing for Yorkshire Colts.

His spectacular style of play, however, cannot have endeared him to the county coaches, for another seven years passed before he made his first-class debut. In that year of 1891 he was remembered for a colossal drive off a Nottinghamshire bowler that cleared the old Bramall Lane pavilion, crossed the road and landed in a brewer's yard.

He soon realised that he would have to modify his play and tighten his defence if he were to survive in the professional game, and it took him until 1895, at the age of 29, to pass 1,000 runs for the first time and to score a maiden century. That was the first of 22, his highest coming three years later – 243 of the world record of 554 with J.T. Brown at Chesterfield.

Only briefly did Tunniclife shed his cloak of care and austerity: A.A. Thomson mentions a 'screaming drive' in Ranji's direction at Fenner's; in 1893 he again drove a ball out of the ground at Bramall Lane, and another at Bradford. The Reverend Holmes, writing of him around this time, described his strokes as 'few but mighty'. His limitations may have precluded his playing for England, but he did appear for the Players and was one of *Wisden's* Five Cricketers of the Year in 1901.

Of his fielding it might have been thought, because of his height and the necessity to stoop at slip, that he would have difficulty in moving to either side, but this he overcame by the speed of his reflexes and the distance of his leap, rather like the modern goalkeeper. C.B. Fry saw him thus: 'yards of him wrapped up in the slips – alert to unfold – to shoot out an unerringly prehensile hand followed by an unerring eye'. So safe a catcher was Tunnicliffe that when one of the mighty hitters of his time, say Jessop, appeared, 'Long John' was dispatched to the most likely spot in the deep.

He was regarded as being still in his prime at 41 when, in 1907, having scored 1,195 runs that Summer, he accepted the post of coach at Clifton and also took care of the young Gloucestershire professionals, among them Hammond. A Methodist lay preacher, Tunnicliffe went on to become a member of the Gloucestershire Committee while his son became the county Secretary in 1921. He was 82 when he died in July 1948.

It was with reference to this era that J.M. Kilburn created what might be called the 'Yorkshire syndrome' in county cricket – the feeling in the other shires that Yorkshire's success had bred an arrogance and an insularity that left the team rather less than popular. This was not, of course, always the fault of the players. As we have noted, Middlesex were upset in 1893 when they discovered, after they had released Stoddart to England, that Yorkshire had kept Wainwright back to play against them. In 1901 Yorkshire, at Hawke's instigation, refused to allow Hirst and Rhodes to join A.C. MacLaren's team to tour Australia, at first glance another example of bloody-mindedness. In fact Hawke was making a point of principle, refusing to release players until Test matches were arranged by a properly constituted authority – as they soon were, by a Board of Control at home and MCC abroad.

Kilburn best defined this 'Yorkshireness':

It was recognisable by more than a cap with a white rose. It came to be regarded as the cricket of a close community, cricket expressed in terms of high self-confidence, cricket of technical excellence moulded and devoted to a team purpose. Cricketers from Yorkshire underwent a subtle metamorphosis into Yorkshire cricketers.

It was Hawke, early in his captaincy, who gave Yorkshire their most famous identification, the White Rose badge, borrowing the idea from Lancashire who had already adopted the Red Rose. But while Lancashire's was an easily identifiable floribunda, the Yorkshire rose has never been seen on any tree, nor in any garden. Hawke devised his own version of the hedge rose, bearing 11 petals to denote the first XI, and decreed

that only capped players could wear the device.

His Lordship's wishes, even 50 years after his death, are rarely ignored within the Club, and it took a radical and revolutionary Committee to give consent to the badge's use as a marketing device. Even now traditionalists within the Club would still reserve the badge for players.

Yorkshire's first golden age came to an end in 1903 when Middlesex and Sussex preceded Yorkshire in the table. The reason for the decline was glaringly obvious. One excellent amateur had been lost in Mitchell, while another, Taylor, went into business to re-emerge later as President. Illness deprived Washington of a season and Hawke a part of the Summer, Jackson was rarely available, young fast bowler Brown's career ended at Taunton, and even the mighty Hirst was suddenly struck down with a leg injury that put him out for three weeks. On the positive side, two Colts, fast bowler Billy Ringrose and batsman Jim Rothery, made a promising start.

With such variations in strength it is hardly surprising that Yorkshire's results were inconsistent. By the end of June the once 'Invincibles' had been beaten four times, before eight of the next 11 matches were won and of the three that were drawn the opposition were happy to escape. Yorkshire's hopes of retaining the Championship were finally dashed at Brighton where Sussex completed their second victory of the Summer, Fry having earlier scored 234 at Bradford.

The number of centuries scored declined to seven (as opposed to 13, 17 and 14 in the three previous years). Rhodes, after a poor start, was as penetrative as ever, taking 8-12 against Worcestershire and 13-152 against Lancashire. With so many former regulars missing at one stage or another of the season, it is to be expected that the fielding suffered. In match after match vital catches were missed, not by Hunter, who was as alert and safe as ever, but by the close field. A Middlesex opener at Leeds put three consecutive balls from Hirst into short-leg's hands, and all three were dropped. Hirst, despite his injury, had a phenomenal Summer, hitting four centuries, averaging 44 and taking 118 wickets at 12 apiece. Fully fit he might have achieved his *annus mirabilis* three years earlier.

Among Yorkshire's defeats in 1903 was one by those perennial intractables Somerset, at Taunton in May, their first defeat outside the county since Tonbridge in August 1899. This was the same Taunton match in which Brown of Darfield ended his career, and Hirst took the leg injury that put him out for three weeks while Tunnicliffe injured a finger, so that Yorkshire batted two men short in their second innings.

Yorkshire suffered another severe loss the following season with the departure through ill health of their famous opening batsman J.T. Brown, thus breaking up the renowned record breaking partnership with Tunnicliffe. His characteristically courteous and modest letter of resignation was, as a mark of respect, written into the Club's minutes.

A more joyful occasion was a benefit for Hirst. Lancashire, on request, switched the Whitsun game from Headingley to Old Trafford so that the beneficiary could have the advantage of the August Bank Holiday, and Yorkshiremen showed their appreciation of the great man when, in idyllic weather, crowds of 31,826, 31,579 and 15,387 were recorded over the three days. The final figures brought in a new record of £3,703, 'which in all probability will never be excelled' wrote 'Old Ebor'.

Lancashire arrived in Leeds unbeaten but their bowling was set about merrily, Yorkshire hitting 403 before dismissing MacLaren, Spooner and Johnny Tyldesley for nine. Two more Lancastrians were despatched before the score had reached 50, and although Hornby defended stoutly for 59, Lancashire had to follow on 230

behind. A splendid century by Tyldesley enabled Lancashire to hang on for the draw, still 67 behind at the close with seven wickets standing. They remained undefeated, too, winning the Championship with Yorkshire second.

It was a placing that was perhaps better than expected, for the losses of the two previous Summers had not been made up. Washington had been sent to South Africa in the hope of effecting a cure, and, in all, 25 players were tried including Grimshaw, Rudston, Rothery and Wilkinson; Rudston and Rothery winning further engagements. Yet Jackson, who had appeared in only seven games in 1903, was present on 12 occasions, averaging 43, while Hirst passed yet another record: the first Yorkshireman to get 2,000 runs and 100 wickets in a season. Inexhaustible, inextinguishable.

Denton and Tunnicliffe still contributed their quotas, the massive strength of the all-rounders compensated for any faltering of the middle order, and the bowling remained in such hands as those of Hirst, Haigh and Rhodes, with Jackson and Ringrose awaiting an opportunity. Hawke's field was pre-ordained: Tunnicliffe and Wainwright at slip, Brown and Denton (with Hawke) in the deep, Hirst at mid-off, a key position for the off drive, Rhodes or Mitchell or Taylor in the covers. The player who did take his chance splendidly that season was Hubert Myers from Yeadon, an all-rounder who had appeared fleetingly in 1901 and 1903 and who owed his prolonged examination that following Summer to the intervention of Frank Mitchell.

By then Mitchell was captain of the South African team touring England, but in the free and easy manner of those times he had arranged leave to play for Yorkshire at Oxford where, after a net, he expressed the opinion that Myers was underrated as a bowler and capable of swerving the ball almost as much as Hirst. Given Hawke's blessing, the 26-year-old bowled with zest and confidence and by mid-season was accepted as Hirst's partner on faster pitches. At Dewsbury in July, he shattered Gloucestershire with the best return of the season by a Yorkshireman – 8-31 – following this with 5-77 against Sussex. Myers finished second only to Haigh in the averages, with 78 wickets at 20 apiece, and Yorkshire felt that Brown of

F.S. Jackson Jacker

He is a nice young fellow of two-and-thirty, who may not be obnoxious even to Rudyard Kipling, since he was patriotic enough to give up cricket to serve his country in South Africa; whence he is returned safe and sound and Captain of the 3rd Royal Lancasters, as well as of the Yorkshire Eleven. He is also a director of W.L. Jackson and Sons, Limited; and the son of that Statesman who is just improved by his King into a Peer. Himself was sent to Harrow, where he played cricket; and thence to Trinity, Cambridge, where he played more cricket until he was made Captain of the Light Blue Eleven. Since then he has pretty constantly played for the Gentlemen and for England. He is good at most games, being an excellent shot, a keen man to hounds, and a devoted fisher; but, of course, it is as a cricketer that he has done most for his country. He was first chosen to play for England against Australia in 1893, and he was played in each home match against them since; being, indeed, so capable a player of the game that most people were grieved (and some aggrieved), when, on W.G. Grace's retirement from big matches, he was not called upon to captain the English Eleven. But he still played the game, despite the commiseration of his friends; for, as they say of him, a 'better chap never walked'. He is now about to plunge into matrimony, so that the other day a fellow cricketer asked him if he had congratulated the young lady to whom he was to be sacrificed! Yet is he not at all conceited, for he can tell such a story against himself; and another: as when he overheard one of his brother Officers telling others that they had 'at least succeeded in making a good chap of him'! He has a jaunty step, a lordly manner, and exceeding confidence in himself: which is a very necessary quality at cricket. He has indeed shown himself the man for a big match, and he is probably the finest all-round cricketer of the day.

F.S. Jackson
YCCC

He is said to be full of childish simplicity, and he is quite well known as 'Jacker'.

Vanity Fair, 28 August 1902.

The illustrious magazine was wrong on one point: Jackson was never elected captain of Yorkshire, often though he led the side, a circumstance that led the witty J.L. Carr to comment: 'Despairing of ambition's chiefest prize, the Yorkshire captaincy, he took to politics and was consoled with the Governorship of Burma [sic]. There he escaped an assassin's sword by "the quickest duck I have ever made".'

Mr Carr, too, was wrong, for Jackson became Governor of Bengal in a career so dazzling that only Fry's can compare, at least inasmuch as Fry was offered the kingdom of Albania. Francis Stanley Jackson was an Englishman of Renaissance proportions; businessman, soldier, politician: MP for Howdenshire, Financial Secretary to the War Office, Chairman of the Conservative Party.

Born in Chapel Allerton, the son of Lord Allerton, the boy's prep-schoolmaster in Hemel Hempstead predicted: 'That boy will play for England.' At Harrow his father promised him, in 1888, a shilling for every run he made and a sovereign for every wicket he took against Eton: he scored 80 runs and took 11 wickets. After that, not surprisingly, he went on to win a Blue in all four Summers at Cambridge, captaining the University for two years and appearing for England while an undergraduate, scoring 91 and 103 against Australia in the first innings of each of his first two Test matches. As captain of England, in 1905, he won the toss five times, won the series and topped the batting and bowling averages. He went on to become President of Yorkshire and President of MCC. F.S. Jackson, wrote 'Old Ebor', 'will always appear on the front page'.

Of his 31 centuries, 21 were scored for Yorkshire and no less than five against Australia in England; he played in 18 successive home Tests between 1896 and 1905. Warner described his batting:

> [He] had a beautiful style and, though thoroughly orthodox, possessed all the strokes. He was a fine cutter and on-driver, excelled especially on soft wickets and his supreme confidence was an enormous asset both to himself and to his side. The reputation he gained as 'the man for the big occasion' was indeed thoroughly deserved.

He was fast-medium right-hand bowler of deadly accuracy and puzzling length who could usually do enough off the pitch to worry the best. When Yorkshire played Australia at Leeds in 1902 the tourists collapsed in their second innings, losing six wickets for 23, five of them to Hirst, one to Jackson. Dissatisfied with his county's rate of progress, a voice in the crowd beseeched Hawke to take off Jackson: 'Put Schof [Haigh] on!' Jackson promptly took four wickets in the next over and as he was leaving the field a small man in a bowler hat approached him: 'F.S., it were me who shouted to take thee off.' Jackson, a little embarrassed, stroked his moustache and said: 'Well, I don't think you are a very good judge,' to which the little man replied: 'P'raps, but by gum, they batted bad.'

He played intermittently for Yorkshire over 17 seasons, business or military commitments frequently taking him away, but he still managed more than 10,000 runs and 500 wickets. His golf, too, was remarkable for he played off one and many felt he could have taken the British amateur title had he put his mind to it.

When President of MCC he found a sub-committee in deep discussion about the exact wording to be placed on the Grace Gates. 'Why not "The Great Cricketer?"' he suggested.

In 1900 he was home on leave from the Boer War and was invited to play in the Scarborough Festival. Newspaper placards in the resort announced: 'F.S. JACKSON WILL DEFINITELY PLAY.' He did, and scored 134. Robertson-Glasgow wrote of him: 'He had dignity, not pomp; diplomacy with simplicity. He is a chapter in cricket history.'

Darfield's place had been filled.

Lees Whitehead, the almost regular 12th man for more than a decade, retired in 1904 after a Summer of many draws (16 in 27 matches) and of the 'Harrogate Wicket Incident'. The match with Kent at St George's Road on 7, 8 and 9 July was abandoned on the second day as the pitch was judged to have been worked upon overnight, some spots being filled in with every indication that someone had rolled and watered it. Kent, their captain admitted, were happy to escape, for Yorkshire had batted first and the pitch had showed every sign of breaking up on the evening of the first day.

As a big crowd was waiting expectantly, the two teams played until 5 pm, Haigh performing the hat-trick with some experimental leg-breaks. The news was considered sensational in cricket:

the Harrogate club called for an MCC inquiry, but Lord's sensibly backed the judgement of the umpires and the decision of the captains to abandon the match. Yorkshire concurred, but the controversy raged on in the press, locally and nationally, for some time, the General Committee member for Harrogate receiving a postcard referring him to Genesis: 'But there went up a mist from the earth that watered the whole face of the ground.' No culprit was every discovered, and it is perhaps surprising that a telegram was not despatched to 221B Baker Street, for Holmes was then at the height of his fame, 1904 being the year of *The Missing Three-Quarter*.

In that year, too, Yorkshire and Nottinghamshire experimented with a time-limit match, a forerunner of limited overs. Each innings was to be of no more than four and a quarter hours, boundaries were not to exceed 60 yards and the result would be decided by the number of runs scored. Yorkshire won by lunchtime on the third day, all four innings having been played out thus making the time limit meaningless. MCC ruled firmly and decisively that matches under such conditions were not played according to the 'Laws' and therefore could not be included in the records. Some may feel it to be a tragedy that MCC were unable to make a similar ruling when one-day cricket was first proposed.

Jackson captained England against Australia in 1905 in the first bid to regain the Ashes, and Hawke proclaimed Yorkshire's unflagging loyalty to the cause by declaring it was to be 'England first and the rest nowhere'. This meant a considerable sacrifice on Yorkshire's part for they lost Jackson for five Tests, Rhodes for four, Hirst for three and Denton and Haigh for one each. In three Championship matches they were without all five senior players, yet they still managed to improve upon their third place in 1903 and second in 1904 to win their seventh Championship. It had perhaps been the thought of their handicaps that had precipitated such a poor start, Lancashire, Derbyshire and Kent all recording victories by the end of June. But from July onwards they lost not another match, and they crowned a brilliant Summer with a victory over the Rest of England at The Oval.

Ernest Smith

Smith, of Morley, deserves to be better known, for he was a formidable all-rounder who, had he been a professional, would have been at the forefront of the game at the turn of the century. He was a quick bowler who used his head, a fierce hitter who could defend, and a fast and safe fielder anywhere. In 1890-91, years when he played against Cambridge, he was regarded as one of the best cricketers to appear at Oxford. Each Summer from 1889 to 1907 he would leave his prep school in Eastbourne to ginger up Yorkshire's efforts in the crucial weeks of the Summer.

Hawke was later to admit: 'I let him fall out of the side all too soon for he has retained his skill to an age when others had long lost it, nor has his excellence at golf – he has been captain at Rye – abated his enthusiasm for cricket.'

Smith was a schoolboy prodigy at Clifton: he scored 185 against East Gloucestershire and then 117 for Oxford against the Gentlemen, an innings that won him a Blue and a place against the Players in 1891. Against MCC, for Yorkshire, he shared a stand of 66 in 18 minutes with Jackson, Smith contributing 40: the same pair made 94 in an hour against Middlesex, and for The North against The South, also in 1891, he contributed 154 to a stand of 254 in 105 minutes.

Smith took 284 wickets for Yorkshire at an average of 23, and still holds a place in Yorkshire affections for a massive act of defiance. In 1905 at Leyton Yorkshire needed 408 to win on the final day with nine wickets gone; in a brilliant spell, Douglas had taken five wickets in eight balls, all bowled, and Smith, with an hour to go, had to bat out time to save the game. This he did, finishing on nought not out.

He died at the age of 76 after amputations necessitated by a poisoning of the legs.

Bobby Moorhouse The Man of Bruises

Moorhouse, from Berry Brow, Huddersfield, earned his nickname for his batting on the bumpy pitches in the last decade of the 19th century. The faster the bowling and the more spiteful the pitch, the more rock-like was Moorhouse, bringing to the Yorkshire team a courage and application that were to be handed down to Brian Close in a later era.

Bobby came to Yorkshire's attention when playing with Armitage Bridge, a club that also fostered his brother Fred (Warwickshire), John Beaumont (Surrey), another Warwickshire player in Crowther Charlesworth and, most famous of all, Schofield Haigh. Bobby played for the Colts in 1888 and was drafted straight into the first XI for the match against the University of Cambridge at Fenner's in late May. His ability to shore up an innings made him a fairly regular member of the team for the next 11 years, his value being appreciated more in the dressing room than outside.

Moorhouse himself told 'Old Ebor' in 1904 that his finest performance came at Bramall Lane in June 1893 when Surrey, spearheaded by that magnificent pair of fast bowlers Richardson and Lockwood, dismissed Yorkshire for 98 and 91: 'The wicket was the roughest I have ever played on – I was badly knocked about and finished black and blue all over. I can still feel the blows to this day.' Moorhouse contributed 39 and 38 to Yorkshire's combined total and, due to the bowling of the Middlesbrough all-rounder Tom Wardall, a purveyor of 'donkey drops', Yorkshire won the match, Wardall claiming his moment of fame with a match return of 9-19.

The following year at Huddersfield, against the man reckoned the fastest of his time, Kortright of Essex, Moorhouse made 68 when Yorkshire, needing 299 to win the fourth innings on a broken pitch, lost by one run. Kortright's bowling that day aroused the ire of the Huddersfield spectators and when Frank Milligan was struck the crowd roared 'Tak 'im off!' However, when Milligan, perhaps in desperation, struck Kortright for four fours in one over, they delightedly advised Hugh Owen, the Essex captain: 'Keep Kortright on!'

Moorhouse, a compact right-hander, was also a useful off-spinner and a renowned outfielder, C.B. Fry writing of him '...he might be called quite a sprinter and had a very safe pair of hands for a steeping catch or a hard-hit skimmer'. It was sad, then, that a missed catch should have led to his departure.

Yorkshire were playing Middlesex at Lord's when, according to Frank Mitchell, Albert Trott from the Nursery End lifted the ball as high as the pavilion. Moorhouse, the man in line, let the ball drop about five yards in front of him and then had to explain himself to a very angry Lord Hawke: 'Ah didn't think it were coming that far. And when Ah seed it up there Ah says "Oh, damn it!"' Hawke wasted no more time: 'If you won't try, you'll have to go'. Moorhouse was then 33; he played one more match, for MCC, in 1900 and died at the age of 56, in Berry Brow.

Lancashire's early win was at Old Trafford, Spooner and Johnny Tyldesley raising 223 for the second wicket in a first innings of 399 in excellent weather. The Lancashire pair had their moments, a ball from Jackson hitting Spooner's off stump, failing to dislodge the bail but nevertheless reaching the boundary for four. The partnership had then reached 33 and Tyldesley, when at 14, was dropped at slip. These escapes failed to inhibit the Lancashire pair, even 'Old Ebor' commenting on their 'delightful' stroke-play.

Rain followed and Yorkshire, batting on what was described as a 'bumpy pitch', were dismissed for 133 and 214 and beaten by an innings. A second defeat, by nine wickets, followed in the same week, Derbyshire recording their first victory over Yorkshire for ten years, but this was one of the matches for which Jackson, Hirst, Haigh and Rhodes were absent on duty for England. Kent, on their first visit to Hull, then won through the bowling of Colin

Blythe, whose match return of 12-89 won him a first appearance for England after Rhodes, who could bowl only three overs in the Kent second innings because of a sore finger, had to drop out.

Hirst, almost by habit, broke yet another record in 1905 – a figure that has still not been overtaken more than 100 years later. Leicestershire, batting first on their old Aylestone Road ground, raised 419 and then took Yorkshire's first five wickets, including Tunnicliffe, Denton and Rhodes, for 74. Hirst, entering this battered innings at number four, survived an lbw appeal before he had scored and then remained for seven hours, scoring 341 (a six and 53 fours), the highest individual score by a Yorkshireman in county cricket and one that Sutcliffe, Hutton and Boycott were unable to surpass, although one suspects that Lehmann could have done so had he been so inclined.

Prime place in the county calendar had by this time been taken by Lancashire, and it was the August Bank Holiday fixture at Sheffield that decided the Championship in 1905, a Roses match that had the North agog for three days. On the first day it seemed that Lancashire would repeat their Whitsuntide success. Yorkshire's first innings raised only 76 runs, a total that MacLaren and Spooner passed, the first

Lancashire wicket not falling until the score had reached 90, but the lead by the end of the second day must have disappointed MacLaren. From a position of 152-5 Jackson forced a collapse, taking 4-15 in 56 deliveries, the last five Lancastrians being dismissed for 25.

Again Lancashire made inroads, Tunnicliffe and Rothery falling for 11 before Denton and Jackson raised 143. Rhodes added another 74, he and Denton driving Walter Brearley so fiercely that his first-innings figures of 7-35 were followed by 6-122 in the second. Lancashire thus needed 185 to win in the fourth innings, a difficult target at a time when pitches rarely lasted beyond two days. Lancashire started the third day needing another 135 with MacLaren and Spooner dismissed, and on a helpful surface Rhodes and Haigh were their demonic selves, the last eight wickets falling for 90 runs.

This victory set up Yorkshire for a final run-in to the Championship; Surrey were beaten at Leeds (Rhodes 10-115), Essex at Huddersfield, and rain saved Middlesex at Bradford when Yorkshire needed 33 runs with all second-innings wickets in hand. After the softer turf of the North the return match with Essex, on a hard Leyton pitch, proved a shock, Essex running up 521 and the famous Yorkshire bowlers having

---

Lees Whitehead Twelfth Man

Whitehead, a useful all-rounder from Delph, won his county cap for his cheerful loyalty over 15 Summers when he was almost permanent 12th man in Hawke's powerful sides. Hawke paid him the highest compliment: 'incomparable in that position, always sympathetic, ready to turnout at a moment's notice after being a jolly good practice bowler in the nets and useful in all departments, especially the most important, fielding, when called upon'.

A right arm fast-medium bowler and sound batsman, Whitehead joined Yorkshire from the Lord's ground staff. He scored his runs in half-centuries but in 1900 actually topped the averages, 321 runs at 53, while in 1889 he took 52 wickets at 16 apiece. In 1904 Yorkshire granted him £250, which

was topped up to £400 with which he bought a business in West Hartlepool, having won a professional engagement for the local club in previous years.

In a team photograph of Hawke's XII of 1901, which includes eight Test players, Whitehead is on the left of the back row, alongside Rhodes and behind Tunnicliffe, wearing his white rose cap and blazer proudly, looking very much a member of one of the great cricketing sides – which, no doubt, was always his chief ambition.

He caught a chill at a football match in 1913 and died at the age of 49. Long after he had finished playing, 'Old Ebor' wrote that 'no one could follow the fortunes of his colleagues with greater keenness and enthusiasm'.

J.T. Brown Steathdy John

Brown, from Driffield, was one of those Victorian crickets, like Grace and later Fry, who were better known by their initials. His famous partner might be John Tunnicliffe, but to the public John Thomas Brown was 'J.T.' – 'Jack' to his intimates. His tendency to lisp made his cry of 'Steathdy, John' a feature of one of the most renowned partnerships in county cricket.

Jack Brown was a short, thick-set right hander who excelled at the cut or 'chop', was a prolific scorer just wide of point, rarely drove straight or through mid-off and was a formidable hooker. At 19 he was recommended to Perthshire by Louis Hall who had seen him play for Driffield, and it was the youth's disregard of Scotland's damp Summers, so 'Old Ebor' believed, that caused so much later illness.

The following year, 1889, he made his debut for Yorkshire, against Leicestershire at Bradford. Ill health, notably a chronic rheumatism, delayed his progress but by 1893 he was established, passing 1,000 runs for the first time, and the following season, after Bobby Abel had withdrawn, Brown was chosen for Stoddart's tour of Australia, winning national fame with his performance in the final Test.

The rubber stood at 2-2 and England, at Melbourne in March 1895, needed 297 to win in the last innings and lost their first two wickets for 28. Brown then joined Albert Ward (a Yorkshireman who played for Lancashire) in a stand of 210 of which Brown's share was 140, his first 50 coming in only 28 minutes, the fastest in Test history, as was his 100 (95 minutes). England won by six wickets to win the series and Brown returned a hero, four centuries to his name and top of the averages.

With Tunnicliffe, Brown now formed the first great Yorkshire opening partnership: against Sussex in 1897 they raised 278 (Brown 311); against Derbyshire the following year they cracked all records with 554, Brown breaking his wicket when he

J.T. Brown
YCCC

reached 300. Tunnicliffe was the long, lean and patient one, Brown the compact dasher. He was also a fine off-side fielder at point or cover, and bowled what are described as 'innocent' leg-breaks which were, however, evil enough to take a hat-trick against Derbyshire in 1896. In his 14-year career he took 194 wickets for Yorkshire.

While he was generally a popular player he did, after his Australian success, needle Hawke sufficiently for the captain to say that he had 'more of an eye to his figures than the rest of us'. Another eminent amateur said of Brown that he 'always appeared to have a grouse against life'.

Possibly Brown sensed that his career (and his life) would be a short one; he always wanted to score many runs and to score them quickly. He had a good sense of humour, liked to play a joke and could take one against himself – as, for instance, when the English umpire who traveled with Stoddart's team persuaded the local umpire at Newcastle, NSW that Brown was 'throwing' his leg-breaks. As soon as the local man went to square leg to view Brown's bowling he called 'no-ball' and had the mystified Brown bowling from a good yard behind the crease before he realised, from the suppressed merriment of his colleagues, that he had been set up.

Brown scored 25 centuries for Yorkshire, played eight times for England and attracted 40,000 to his benefit match at Leeds in 1901 for a then record sum of £2,282. Although he turned against alcohol, empty-

ing all the beer in his house down the kitchen sink, he was a heavy smoker, another factor in his increasing asthma.

On the third day of the match against Leicestershire at Bradford in May 1904, he arrived at Leeds station, to catch the train with David Hunter but found himself so unwell, through difficulty with his breathing, that he had to return home. The following 19 July he formally resigned from Yorkshire's team, and he died on 4 November, aged 35.

---

some embarrassing figures – Rhodes 2-107, Hirst 0-111, Haigh 1-53. Yorkshire needed to avoid defeat to clinch the Championship, but it was a task that seemed well beyond them after the disaster of their first innings.

Rothery was bowled for a duck before 'Johnny' Douglas struck with five wickets in 18 balls for three runs, including a hat-trick: coming on as first change he knocked out Tunniclffe's leg stump with his fifth ball, at which point lunch was taken. Resuming, Douglas bowled Hirst with the sixth ball of the uncompleted over, and two overs later he bowled Rhodes, Haigh and Myers with successive deliveries, genuine fast bowling on a pitch yards quicker than the Yorkshiremen had seen for weeks. Denton, who always enjoyed fast bowling, stood firm for 40, Hawke dug in for another 36, and the innings recovered from 42-7 to 98.

Rothery, sadly, failed again on the follow-on and Yorkshire began the third day 408 behind with nine wickets standing and a good Leyton crowd scenting Yorkshire blood. Unable to win, Yorkshire could aim for no more than a draw. Tunnicliffe and Hirst stayed together for 195 minutes and 136 runs for the second wicket, Hirst in all batting for 290 minutes for his 90 runs, but with an hour's play left Yorkshire had lost their sixth wicket. Ernest Smith then batted out time, assisted by Hawke, playing out the final 60 minutes without scoring a run. It was a performance not to the amusement or appreciation of the crowd, but it secured the Championship.

Both Hirst and Denton exceeded 2,000 runs,

Denton hitting eight centuries, seven in the Championship and 153 against the Australians at Bradford. Haigh, Hirst, Rhodes, Myers and Ringrose shared 433 wickets, with the last named being the most expensive – 60 wickets at 20 apiece.

By any reckoning 1906 had to be Hirst's year and yet, perhaps not seeing the wood for the trees, 'Old Ebor' remembered the Summer mainly for the fact that Yorkshire could be said to have missed retaining the Championship by one run. That they came within this tiny margin was due almost entirely to George Hirst for what must still be regarded as the greatest individual performance in the history of county cricket. Asked if he thought anyone would ever match his feat of taking 2385 runs and over 200 wickets in 1906, he replied in a now much copied phrase: 'If he does, he'll be tired.'

Hirst's prodigious talents were needed, for the team was not in a good shape, the school of younger players – Rothery, Grimshaw, Wilkinson, Rudston and Myers – being unable to mount a sustained challenge to the great veterans they were hoping to succeed. Jackson was available for only two matches, but Taylor, having been absent on family business for three Summers, was free for a few fixtures. In all 27 players were called upon, and in a Summer of experiment two newcomers emerged, the Bradford amateur all-rounder Charles Midgley and a fast bowler professional from Littleborough, Herbert Sedgwick.

Midgley, brought into the side as a bowler, distinguished himself with a 59 not out at a critical

Frank Milligan

Milligan loved to hit the ball hard and high, describing it as 'skyscraping', and was for many years the archetypal amateur of the Golden Age. An Etonian, he was actually born near Aldershot and may have owned his Yorkshire elevation to a friendship with Hawke and Jackson, playing first for the county in 1894 at the age of 24.

He bowled fast, hit like a whirlwind, fielded superbly and was as impetuous in business as he was in his cricket. Milligan appeared four times for the Gentlemen, and toured South Africa in 1898-99 with Hawke's team, playing in both Test matches with limited success, although he did put out Sinclair, the noted South African hitter, with a well-remembered catch, nonchalantly leaning over the boundary to take the ball one-handed.

In his four Summers he scored 2,151 runs and took 136 wickets at 23.12, but his career was too short, as Peter Thomas wrote for a full assessment. He was certainly a much-loved character, devoted to children, who volunteered, along with Frank Mitchell and F.S. Jackson, for service in the Boer War.

He was killed in action in the relief of Mafeking on 31 March 1900, and when Lord Hawke unveiled a memorial to him in Bradford in 1902 all Yorkshire's professionals attended. The memorial read: 'To the memory of Lieutenant Frank Milligan of Royds Hall, a member of the Yorkshire County Eleven. He fell bravely defending the position assigned to him under Colonel Plummer with the Rhodesian Frontier Forces in the attempted relief of Mafeking.' He was 29 years old.

---

moment against Derbyshire, while Sedgwick appeared to be a genuine discovery when, in his first match at Hull, he took 5-8 against Worcestershire and did the hat-trick in the second innings. *Wisden* reported a 'startling performance' and, once again, as with Brown of Darfield, Ringrose and Myers, Yorkshire thought they had discovered a partner for Hirst. Alas, the promise faded once more and neither Midgley nor Sedgwick played for Yorkshire again after 1906.

With all these handicaps Yorkshire must have surprised themselves by arriving at their last two matches, away to Gloucestershire and Somerset, needing only draws to retain the Championship. Gloucestershire were dismissed for 164 at Bristol. Rhodes, filling yet another gap as an opening batsman, was dismissed at 11, and five wickets went for 73 before Ernest Smith, captain in Hawke's absence, hit 34 and Haigh was left on 26 not out. Nevertheless Gloucester had won a lead of five, which increased to 233 in their second innings.

Yorkshire thus needed 234 to win and at 185-6 seemed to be in a comfortable position. Rudston, who had hit an encouraging 40, then played on

to Jessop and with two wickets remaining Yorkshire needed 27. Myers and Hunter had reduced the deficit to 11 when last man Ringrose joined Myers, and the all-rounder had knocked off nine of those runs when Ringrose faced the bowling. Jessop, Gloucestershire's captain, put himself back on to bowl and his first delivery was a near wide down the leg side that would have given Yorkshire victory had not John Board, the wicket-keeper, dived, got the tip of his glove to the ball and turned it back to hold it. Two balls later the left-handed Ringrose was leg before, Gloucester had won by one and Yorkshire's Championship chance had gone.

Yorkshire remained the premier attraction on the county circuit, bringing 80,000 to The Oval in three days to watch the benefit of Surrey's Yorkshire-born Walter Lees. This was also the year of the curious but well-remembered appearance of Cecil Parkin, later to become so famous with Lancashire and England.

Parkin was one of the younger players called up in the diligent search for new talent, and he appeared against Gloucestershire at Headingley in the first week in July, taking 2-23 in the first innings. He did not score and bowled only two

Schofield Haigh Sunshine

'For eighteen years the sunshine of the Yorkshire eleven' was 'Old Ebor's' famous summary of Haigh who, from Berry Brow, Huddersfield, joined those two Kirkheaton men Hirst and Rhodes to form the mighty triumvirate of all-rounders that gave Yorkshire cricket so much supremacy in the Golden Age. If Haigh's achievements brought him only third ranking, they were impressive enough by the measurements of any other county: 100 wickets in a season nine times (2,014 wickets at an average of 15.94), ten times top of Yorkshire's averages, three times top of the national averages; 1,000 runs in 1904, four centuries for Yorkshire, and five hat-tricks! In all his career he scored 11,711 runs, and it was said that 'Scof's' off-drive was the finest in the county.

These are the bare bones of a career that is remembered with enormous affection years after his death. 'There is no nicer professional cricketer,' said Pelham Warner.

Haigh began as a quick bowler and as such won a professional engagement in Perth (Scotland) where he first began experimenting in shortening his run, slowing his pace and developing spin. Warner described him 'in his prime as difficult a bowler on a sticky wicket as any left-hander'. He possessed an enormous and very quick off-break and a capital fast yorker, and his flight was very deceptive for he used to 'pull the ball back' in the air without any apparent change of action.

> His run-up to the wicket was very peculiar, for in his final stride his body was very near the ground, his left leg being shot out in front of him with a very long reach. He dragged his right foot along the ground as his arm came up and for this reason wore an armour plate of brass on the toe of his right boot.

C.B. Fry described him as 'a bowler of temperament; one day the subtle spirit is alive within him; another strive he ever so hard

Schofield Haigh
YCCC

and it is dead; but the lively day is often a long one'.

The off-break was perhaps a misnomer, for there was nothing gentle about it – 'like the kick of a horse' according to A.A. Thomson. Often the break was such that he had to bowl round the wicket; his yorker, produced so sparingly that Hawke had to prod him to use it, was a fast and deadly accurate delivery, while the slow ball was also of a disconcertingly full length, described by one victim in the words: 'You think it's coming right on to you, then it hangs, and you have finished your stroke before the ball is on the floor and then you hear a nasty rattle of timber behind you.'

David Hunter, who kept to Haigh for so many year, described him as 'the worst bowler on earth for the batsman and the keeper. His break-backs were tremendous and at all times he could disguise what he was going to do. In Hawke's judgment, 'no bowler of his day could take more advantage of a wicket affected by rain and sun.'

Haigh was not an opening bowler, although England once believed him to be, and against Test match batsmen on flat surfaces he was far less successful, although under Hawke in South Africa in 1905-06 he took 102 wickets at an average of 10.83. He helped Trott to dismiss the South Africans for 35 in 1898-99, taking 6-11.

A modest man, he was always happy to stand a little behind Hirst, his hero, and Rhodes, and whatever his personal feelings, in success or failure he always managed to greet the world with a smile, if not a joke – 'the stranger to despair, the enemy of long-faced misanthropy' according to 'Old Ebor'.

Strangely, hardly ever did Haigh and Hirst enjoy a successful bowling season together; either one or the other was 'pretty expensive' according to Hawke.

Haigh left Yorkshire to coach at Winchester in 1913, and he had been acting as an umpire in the Scarborough Festival of 1920 when he told 'Old Ebor' that he had an 'athletic heart'. He wore such a broad grin that Mr Pullin thought some joking play on heart strain was intended and thought no more of it until he heard, the following February, that Haigh was dead, at 50. 'The news stunned.'

---

overs in the second innings, whereupon it was discovered that he had been born on the wrong (Durham) side of the Tees and was therefore not qualified by birth. An obviously shocked 'Old Ebor' intoned: 'The Yorkshire Committee and Lord Hawke did not require to be told their duty in the matter.'

Parkin, not surprisingly, had a different version of events, as he recorded in his memoirs:

I was born at Eaglescliffe, near Yarm, 20 yards over the Yorkshire border. That season [1906] I played for Yorkshire II in several matches, taking 13 wickets at an average of 14,30 so you can guess that I was delighted when I received the invitation to play with the Yorkshire County Eleven. And my two wickets for a score or so runs delighted me still more.

Imagine my disappointment when, after one match with the White Rose the news reached me that I had been disqualified from playing for Yorkshire because my birthplace was not actually in Yorkshire. But let me say here that Lord Hawke was fully aware, when I first played for Yorkshire, that I was born in Durham. I did not get into the Yorkshire Eleven under false pretences. And it was not, as the story goes, Yorkshire County that got me disqualified. The MCC did the disqualification from information received from some evidently kind friend of mine.

Parkin, a stormy petrel in his career with Lancashire, retained one memory of his Yorkshire match:

I had a severe attack of nerves as I was going on to bowl. As I was rolling up my sleeves, I was only a nipper, with my fingers trembling on the ball, I got a pat on the back. It was George Hirst who, with a kindly glance, said 'Don't worry, just stick at it.' He is a human being in a thousand.

The season of 1907 was that seeming rarity, a damp Summer. The loss of a whole day's play was thought worthy of mention, and May of that year was fairly dreadful even by the standards of the 1980s, not a match being completed for four weeks.

Fry's 85 at Sheffield led to a Sussex victory, but from 13 July to 21 August Yorkshire were unbeaten, Worcestershire then completing a rare double. They had won at Worcester on a fast pitch, and then won again at Bradford when Yorkshire did have an excuse, being without Hirst, Hawke, Rhodes and Rothery for various reasons. Nottinghamshire were the eventual champions, and it was to Yorkshire's abiding regret that the weather prevented the two teams from getting to grips: play was abandoned at Trent Bridge with Yorkshire on 47-1, while not a ball was bowled in the return fixture at Huddersfield.

By calling on another 24 players Yorkshire signalled they were not happy with the composition of the team. Even those stalwarts Tunnicliffe and Hirst were showing signs of the wear and tear of many years of professional cricket, although it was in this Summer that both passed 20,000 runs for the county.

Indeed, it turned out to be Tunnicliffe's last season – his 17th – his retirement being hastened by an excellent offer of the position of cricket coach to Clifton College. His departure must have saddened a few, for it was probably difficult to imagine Yorkshire without his long lean figure emerging to open the innings or taking his customary position at first slip.

That the old order was changing was never more evident. Jackson and Ernest Smith each appeared only once; Rothery was ill from June until August and played only one more innings, for two runs, before being injured; Grimshaw, Myers and Rudston all faded, although the left-handed Wilkinson remained an interesting prospect. W.E., the son of the great Billy Bates, made a first appearance and seemed to be a great outfielder in the making. In the circumstances, Yorkshire finishing joint second with Worcestershire was a minor miracle; perhaps it was that the team was simply carried on to some victories by the sheer momentum gained in the great years.

Hawke celebrated his 25th year as captain in 1908, an extraordinary service in any era, and with a team sadly lacking in great names, nevertheless managed to win an eighth Championship – an achievement, opined 'Old Ebor', 'that created as much surprise in Yorkshire as it did throughout the country'. The team picture of that year, taken at Headingley in July under some blessed foliage, shows six very familiar faces along the front row: Haigh, Hirst, Hawke, Hunter, Denton and Rhodes. Otherwise we are faced with relative 'unknowns'.

Completing the front row is Billy Wilkinson, the left-hander from Thorpe Hesley whose form that year – 1,232 runs at 24 – brought him a county cap. This was his one sound year, however, and he was never able to sustain that form, departing in 1910 after having spent seven years trying to establish himself.

Uncapped players on the back row are Billy (William Edric) Bates junior, mentioned above. Like his famous father he was an elegant dresser, so it was not unnatural that, his father having been nicknamed 'The Duke', Junior should be known in the dressing room as 'The Marquis'. He was always a brilliant fielder but his batting suffered, inevitably, by comparison with his father's, and after six seasons he moved on to Glamorgan where he enjoyed much more success, founding a famous opening partnership with another Yorkshireman, John Bell, leaving a memory of a fine 72 against the Australians when recalled in 1909.

Another contributor to the Championship was Charlie Hardisty from Leeds who played so well in the match against the Rest of England that year (66 and 59) that *Wisden* seriously suggested that Yorkshire had found a successor to J.T. Brown. The following year Hardisty could hardly put an innings together, and dropped out of the side.

Rothery and Myers had both won their caps without achieving a consistency of form, but the tall remaining figure is of considerable interest: Jack Newstead, from Middlesbrough. He stands proudly in what appears to be a new Yorkshire cap, but glowering as if he knew what to expect from a tantalising fate: tried as a batsman in two matches in 1903, he went on to the ground staff at Lord's where Yorkshire refused his request to qualify for Middlesex.

Four years later he was recalled by Yorkshire as a right-arm medium to fast bowler whose repertoire included what was described as a 'fast off-break'. He had an extraordinary spell against Kent of 17-14-3-2 and followed that, at Bradford, by taking seven Worcestershire wickets for ten. His impact on the 1908 season was enormous and there is no doubt that his contribution, supporting the veterans, propelled Yorkshire to the Championship, for Newstead took 131 wickets at 15 and scored 885 runs at 25. 'Had there been a Test match that season,' wrote 'Old Ebor', 'Newstead would have been chosen as leader of the England attack'. His consolation was to be one of *Wisden's* Five Cricketers of the Year.

Wilfred Rhodes Legend

It cannot have been entirely by chance that in his 1929 essay on Rhodes, Cardus described him as 'The Legendary', as if a reference to one of the seven wonders of the ancient world. Born, like Hirst, in Kirkheaton, whose ground can be seen across the dale from Lascelles Hall, Rhodes was a unique cricketer whose career could, in one sense, be summed up by its longevity: he played for Yorkshire for 32 years, from 1898 to 1930; he first played for England in 1899, and played the last of his 58 Tests in 1926, at the age of 49! Cardus could have replaced 'legendary' with 'phenomenal' and been equally accurate.

Rhodes opened both bowling and batting for England, and not as a makeshift; his defensive technique was such that he was regarded as the best man for the job. He began as a Test-match bowler, became a Test-match batsman and then, when the Great War had taken its toll, became a Test-match bowler again. As Peter Thomas wrote, Rhodes was 'having Peel, Sutcliffe and Tunnicliffe in one player'.

Sixteen times he did the 'double' of 100 wickets and 1,000 runs in one Summer; in 29 consecutive seasons he was missing from the top 20 in the bowling averages only four times; in his first five seasons he was twice first and three times second in the national bowling averages. Returning to bowling after the Great War he was four times first and once second in the years 1919-24; five times he reached scores of more than 190, and he twice scored a century in each innings of a match. Rhodes bowled 184,289 balls and took 4,184 wickets at 16 apiece, scored 29,772 runs at 30 and took 708 catches; in his first three seasons he took, respectively, 154, 179 and 261 wickets.

He was a dour, some might say grim man, the introvert to George Hirst's expansive, open fellowship; they both played for Kirkheaton, for Yorkshire and for England, but (remembering that Rhodes was six years the junior, a long time in a cricketing career)

Wilfred Rhodes
Yorkshie Post

he admitted:

> We were never buddies. Perhaps it might have started as professional jealousy. In my early days I had a ball which used to suddenly duck in towards the end of its flight much as Georgie's swerver, but much slower, of course. It was always George that had to have the wind right for his swerver; but I don't think jealousy was the real reason; more likely it was the things he said.

Hirst enjoyed a joke and is often pictured smiling; photographs of a Rhodes smile are very rare, although Harry East was able to persuade Norman Bazell to publish a picture of a beaming Wilfred, with Hawke, in 1908. Perhaps Rhodes was always too conscious that he owed his start to not a little luck and was always wary that that good luck might just as easily desert him – although if there has been any cricketer in the game's existence who left less to chance then it can only be Geoffrey Boycott.

While Peel was the idol of Yorkshire and other parts of England, the young Rhodes was merely a promising trier from Hirst's home village. Rhodes went off to play with Galashiels, a club that to this day claims to have taught him all he knew, and it was while he was waiting to be called up for a trial with Warwickshire that Peel was sacked. Even then Rhodes' path into the first team was far from assured, for he had a rival whose claims, to the Committee, were as valid: Albert Cordingley. The Bradford man came highly recommended from Lytham and in an end-of-season trial he took 8-33 against the Colts and 3-62 against the Seniors. Rhodes, then 19, could manage only 2-99.

Both were included in the party for Lord's for the opening match against MCC in April 1898. There is one tale that Hawke and Jackson could not agree upon which left-hander to play and Rhodes was selected on the toss of a coin. Hawke later denied this: 'I never had any doubts as to choosing Rhodes. I asked Jackson to look at both bowlers in the nets at Lord's and he came back and said Rhodes.' After match figures of 6-33 Rhodes was naturally retained for the next match against Somerset, Cordingley traveling to Bath where, on the first day, he received a telegram informing him of his mother's death. Returning home he would read of Rhodes' match figures of 13-45 and accept that he was unlikely ever to play for Yorkshire on a regular basis.

Cordingley never seemed able to recover from that early but deadly comparison with Rhodes. According to Michael Pulford's profile (*The White Rose*, May 1985), young Albert was well supported in his native Bradford, the *Daily Argus* noting: '...a pleasant, modest young man...a nice over-hand action...varies his pace considerably'. After Rhodes had marched ahead into the Yorkshire team it seems that the Committee still had hopes of Cordingley whom, being nearer medium pace than slow, they might have seen as providing sufficient contrast to Rhodes.

Cordingley, however, felt that Yorkshire's interest was more in seeking a deputy for

Rhodes and turned down the offer of an engagement in 1899 to become a professional with Wiseton Hall, Nottinghamshire. A year later he joined the Sussex of Fry and Ranji and spent 1901-02 qualifying in Brighton club cricket, where he bowled sufficiently well for the *Evening Argus* to claim, at the end of 1901 season: 'We may be champions next year should Cordingley turn out to be a second Rhodes.'

However, Cordingley managed only two worthwhile performances, a 5-22 against Nottinghamshire and a 24 not out in a ninth-wicket stand of 115, with Ranji against Surrey; by 1903, although retained, he was second choice to George Cox. He kept his Sussex connections, becoming player, coach and groundsman to Pease Pottage, near Crawley, and won praise from the *Sussex* and *Surrey Courier* in 1913 for 'doing his utmost to spread cricket among his neighbours'. He died in Crawley, aged 72, in 1945, a few years before Rhodes was to follow him south, to neighbouring Hampshire.

Meanwhile, the 20-year-old Rhodes was one of *Wisden's* 'Five' after taking 141 wickets for Yorkshire and playing for England, in his second year ousting Johnny Briggs from his place. His runs, too, began to increase – 561 in 1900, 841 in 1901 – and in 1902, by then a pillar of the England team, he and Hirst made history at The Oval in the Fifth Test. Needing 263 to beat Australia, England were reduced to 48-5 on a turning pitch, but Jessop hit 104 out of 139 in 75 minutes, and when last man Rhodes joined Hirst, 15 were still needed. 'We'll get 'em in singles,' Hirst is supposed to have told his Kirkheaton junior, but both afterwards denied that any words were spoken: 'who needed words?' They scored the runs in singles.

Rhodes first toured Australia in 1903-04 as a bowler and improving batsman and returned in 1911-12 as Hobbs' opening partner. Hobbs averaged 82 in that series, Rhodes was second with 57 and bowled only 18 overs in the entire series without taking a wicket. Back in England the highly successful opening partnership continued and for Yorkshire, in 1914, he scored 1,325 runs and took 117 wickets: 'He has never enjoyed bowling half so much as batting,' commented Hawke.

It was in 1903, at Sydney, that Rhodes produced what is remembered, by Englishman and Australian alike, as one of the great bowling performances in history. On a pitch described as 'hard and polished', with no possibility of turn, Australia scored almost 500 runs, Trumper making 185, yet Rhodes with only variations of flight and pace to help him, had figures of 5-94 off 48 overs. Trumper, it was said of that innings, had three strokes for every ball, but it is also said that after playing yet another maiden from Rhodes he called down the wicket: 'Please, Wilfred, give me a little peace.'

Rhodes learned to bowl on a patch of grass cut by his father near their cottage. Practice went on Summer and Winter, in a wood-shed, and to measure his power of spin he would coat one side of the ball with chalk. On the lightly prepared uncovered pitches of his youth he could turn the ball wickedly; as pitches improved and covering began, he turned to flight and length with spin a subordinate weapon to use with conditions permitted and as a trap for the unwary batsman. 'If they think it's spinning,' he said more than once, 'then it's spinning'.

For a short spell he worked in the engine sheds at nearby Mirfield, finishing at 2 pm on a Saturday afternoon, which meant that he had virtually to run the three miles to Kirkheaton to begin play at 2.30 pm. His railway service is said to have ended when one Saturday he rang the knocking-off bell at 1.30 pm. A spell of labouring ended when Galashiels made him an offer to become a professional and, as A.A. Thomson pointed out, cricket in the Borders was not greatly different from that in the Pennines. Indeed, added Thomson, a kindly natured Borderer is likely to agree that a Yorkshireman is, after all, a second-class Scot.

As the Galashiels 'pro' he had to open the batting and bowling, at medium-fast pace, hence the legend that he learned to bowl slow in Scotland. After two years on the Borders he was advised to try Yorkshire; by then, as we know, the Peel reign had come to a sad and abrupt end.

It was in the nature of the man that he should have had the most economical of runs, bowling in his cap, a classical wheel of the arm – none of which in itself would have made him exceptional. The secret, say those who watched him bowl regularly, was in the flight. 'Is there anything in cricket, or in any game, more lovely to see?' asked Cardus. 'But the beauty is a skill; the monotonous rhythm of it, as ball after ball comes dropping, dropping on the same spot at the same pace – take heed, batsman, your senses are being numbed.' To the end of his life, at 95, Rhodes would say: 'Ah were never hooked and ah were never cut.'

As a batsman he was no stylist – 'two or three effective strokes but a sound technique' according to Pelham Warner – and in later years was criticised for his square-on stance, perhaps the first indication of deteriorating eyesight. He brought to his batting a keen cricketing brain and as a runner between wickets he was superb; he and Hobbs were reckoned to have a perfect understanding. He made much use of his pads and rarely allowed anything loose on the off side to escape. One of his most famous remarks is supposed to have been addressed to a young batsman making his debut, who hit his first two balls for four. At the end of the over, we are told that Wilfred walked down the pitch: 'Hey, lad, what's tha doing? We don't play cricket in Yorkshire for foon.'

According to A.A. Thomson, when MCC first elected a number of old professionals to life membership, all except Rhodes gave the expected reactions – 'pleased, proud or delighted'. Wilfred said: 'Ah doan't rightly knaw what it means yet.'

As he grew older (Yorkshire's benefit match was awarded before he was half-way though his career) his eyesight deserted him, and he lived with his daughter in Bournemouth in his last years, occasionally appearing at Lord's where one or more of his contemporaries would report the happenings. Cardus met him again in 1950, when he was 73, and was surprised to find that the terse, taciturn player had turned into an old man whose fast-failing sight had been balanced by an apparently inexhaustible flow of conversation – 'history comes from his mouth in rivers'. He had much to tell.

In the period between Hawke's departure and his own retirement (19 years) he, in tandem with Hirst and then, from 1919, Emmott Robinson and Sutcliffe, effectively captained Yorkshire in tactical terms, hence another famous story. Yorkshire had removed three eminent batsmen very cheaply, but their bowling was then set upon by two unknown youngsters who, with luck and bravado, began laying about them with abandon. As the ball flew past, or dropped short of a fielder, or was edged to the boundary, Yorkshire's frustration, with the fiery Macaulay to the fore, was

expressed in ripe and violent terms, bringing an outraged protest from one of the umpires who said it was like trying to 'keep order in a parrot house'. Why didn't the captain stop it? 'Ah,' was the reply, 'Wilfred had sent him into t'deep to save him from the language'.

One of the reasons, it was said, why Sutcliffe rejected the captaincy when it was offered to him in 1929 was because he sensed how much offence and embarrassment this might cause Rhodes who, although in his final two years, was still a very important member of the team. Characteristically there is no record of Rhodes making any comment on a matter that must have been very close to his heart. He went on to coach at Harrow but was not remembered as a success as was Hirst at Eton where, again, the difference in nature between the two men probably provides the explanation.

Newstead owed his advance partly to a damaging injury to Haigh, who suffered a broken finger when batting against Brearley of Lancashire in the Whitsuntide Roses match. Haigh was unable to regain his former grip and power of spin, but he nevertheless managed 97 wickets to supplement Rhodes' 100 while the almighty Hirst, at the age of 37, scored 1,513 runs and took 164 wickets.

As for Newstead, his decline after that one glorious Summer was sad and inexplicable: 89 wickets in 1909, 36 the following year, and only 19 in 1911. The harder he tried, thought 'Old Ebor', the more difficult he found it to regain that perfect length and 'fizz' that had made him such a prodigy in 1908. His batting, too, declined almost as quickly, and it was Hawke, an admirer of his play, who summed up: 'Who would have believed that he was to be virtually a one-season man, being also a careful, capable bat into the bargain?'

More than Newstead had their moments in Yorkshire's Summer without defeat: Wilkinson hit 1,200 runs, Hardisty 733, Rothery 735, the latter pair sharing the job of opening the innings with Rhodes (a sight that must have brought

many a sigh for Tunnicliffe and Brown from the Bramall Lane grinders). Rothery's 161 against Kent at Dover was described as an innings of considerable force and artistry.

'Old Ebor' described 1908's success as the 'clean sheet Championship', and such was the all-round level of bowling and fielding that only twice did the opposition reach more than 300 in an innings – Leicestershire and the Rest of England. Yorkshire-Middlesex rivalry was again keen, Yorkshire winning at Lord's by three wickets after being required to score 127 in the last innings. At Bradford, Yorkshire felt confident enough to declare at 153-1 in the second innings and were a little shaken when Middlesex finished only 36 short of victory with eight wickets standing. In contrast, Northamptonshire were dismissed for 27 and 15 at Northampton.

But many Yorkshiremen will have noted the year for the celebration of Hawke's 25 years of captaincy. The club raised a fund of £1,000 and the *Yorkshire Evening Post* another £824 through their 'Tyke Fund', the 'Tyke' being a creation of that newspaper's cartoonist, J.A. Dodgson. Hawke, in selecting his gifts, chose six heirlooms. The crowd watched and applauded the presentation, at Headingley in July, and went off in high good humour, Nottinghamshire having been beaten by 140 runs. 'Cricket in Edwardian times' wrote Kilburn, 'was an institution, like the Royal Navy, the gold sovereign, the Empire'.

The following Summer the expected decline in the team's performance occurred, a year later than expected, perhaps, but none the less disappointing. Hardisty, Bates and Newstead slipped backward, Rothery stood still, Wilkinson was less successful (but a thumb injury removed him from several matches and must have affected his form). More trials were needed and two more promising newcomers were found: a stubborn and useful batsman in Benny Wilson, who actually reached 1,000 runs in his first full season, and a player whose actual entry was that of a left-handed batman, the piratically named Alonzo Drake.

An invaluable account of cricket at all levels in this period comes from the memoirs of E.J., later Sir Everard, Radcliffe who occasionally deputised for Hawke as captain and eventually succeeded to that position, once half-humorously described by J.L. Carr as 'the greatest honour an Englishman can aspire to'. He arrived at Downside in May 1894.

There was one ground on the site of the present one, but only about half of its present size. Except on 1st XI match days, when the whole ground was reserved for the XI, the 1st and 3rd games played there, the 2nd on a pitch between the school buildings and big chestnut tree, and the 4th between the Old house and the new swimming baths. It was to the 4th game I was allocated, and I gradually crept up until 1898 I played twice for the 1st XI. In 1896 a match was played between Mr Roper's school, then at Bournemouth, and an under-14 XI of Downside, in which I distinguished myself by taking seven wickets for seven runs. I daresay I was perhaps unusually promising as a slow leg break bowler as the ball turned sharply without any great effort on my behalf. Unfortunately in November 1897 I had to have an operation for hernia, and the surgeon forbad me to bowl the following season, with the result that I found I had entirely lost my natural leg break, indeed I

have never been able to bowl from the same finger since then.

Except for Bruno Hicks, Charlie Nevile, and perhaps Thaedie Ryan, there were few cricketers of any note amongst the boys during my time, but Sebastian Cave, an outstanding athlete in every department, Joe McEvoy and one or two others were good players amongst the Masters, though how they managed to play any game with efficiency is difficult to fathom, as the Monks always had to be attired in black trousers and unsuitable kit all round.

There was little coaching in my time, in the first place few knew sufficient about he game, and the few professionals were poor coaches. If only I had been taught the real rudiments of the game I might have been a fifty per cent better player than I was. I captained the XI in 1900 and 1901, anyhow for the first time, because there was really no one else! We opposed few teams of any note, or indeed few players of eminence either, though I remember Paish, then about the second best slow bowler in England, being hit all over the place by Charlie Nevile, and several visits by Board, the Gloucestershire wicket-keeper, and Jimmy Cranston, a well known left-hand bat for that county. The latter was fond of a little jumping powder before going into to bat, and used to regale himself heartily from the contents of a silver flask!

George Nicholls, a Somerset player, coached for a period in 1900, and in 1901; being left without a coach, my father enlisted the services of Lord Hawke, who prevailed on the celebrated Tom Emmett to come. Tom had been one of the stalwarts of the Yorkshire XI in previous years, but was really beyond his job in 1901. He was, as he had always been, a great and really amusing wit, but having been afflicted to his detriment with an ever present thirst he was more intent on warning the young against the evils of alcohol than on teaching cricket. Constantly did he say 'Mr Radcliffe beware 'drink for it was fair ruin o' me!' Poor old Emmett became a great responsibility of mine, and one day it was reported to me he had not seen for 24 hours. In due course he was found wandering on a railway line and taken to Leicester Asylum where he died.

During the summer holidays I spent the whole time either playing or watching cricket and I recollect the Australians at Cheltenham in, I think, 1895 and 1896, Blackham, who wore a beard, keeping wicket, Ferris with his curious semi-circular run up to the wicket when bowling, Murdoch, Trumble, George Giffen, the incomparable 'W.G.' and others. When at Rudding I was frequently at Bradford or Headingley with my Uncle Henry, who rarely missed a Yorkshire match, and usually Canon Wood. I have recollections of seeing Bobby Peel, who was the best left-hand bowler in England, Wainwright, John Tunnicliffe and others of the then Yorkshire side, and of Stoddart, and McGregor of Middlesex and Lionel Palairet and Hewett of Somerset. I think Palairet and Spooner were the two most graceful batsmen, with perhaps Stan Jackson and Frank Woolley very close seconds, whom I ever saw.

Fred Corballis, a great friend of the family, invited me to stay with him at Manchester for a Roses Match, and there I watched the great ones of the day, Monkey Hornby, Albert Ward, Mold, etc competing against the Tykes. Mold was a very fast right-arm bowler, but he and Tyler were 'warned off' around 1900 owing to suspected deliveries.

It was in 1900 I think that I was lucky enough to see a hundred made in the then record time of 40 minutes for a first class match. It was at Harrogate where Yorkshire was playing Gloucestershire and the century, 101 to be exact, was made of course by the incomparable G.L. Jessop, with whom W.G. Grace was in for a time and Frank Bateman-Champain for the remainder. I think Champain later entered the Established Church and eventually became Bishop of Knaresborough.

In 1902 I played little cricket until the end of July, and then only a few village matches. The following two years I played for Christ Church and intermittently in 1905, but I had no time for anything except work until after the end of term in 1906. It is sad to recollect that out of three teams some 70 per cent were killed in the 1914 War.

I was very gratified, owing to the kindness of C.E. de Trafford, at being made a member of I Zingari in 1903. Ned de Trafford was Captain of Leicestershire, a very hard hitting batsman, a splendid man to hounds and a connoisseur of port! He rarely spoke at all and enjoyed the name of 'Noisy' amongst his inmates! I think he and Tim O'Brien, both Uncles of Charles Moore, were the only Catholic members of I Zingari in those days.

In 1907 I played for Yorkshire 2nd XI at The Oval, scoring I think either 19 or 29, and it was through taking part in this Match I became associated, as related elsewhere, with Galloway.

At Skaife, by Blubberhouses, Galloway had a little cricket ground whence he gathered many of the elite, Stan Jackson, Bosanquet, Hewett, Gilbert, Joe Hornsby, Charles Wright with his glass eye which, not pleasant to relate, he used to pop in and out! And others of past England & Gents v Players fame taking part. I have vivid recollections of a Match in which one Moss was an opponent. This Moss played for one of the Yorkshire Council teams as a professional, and very fast bowler. He took but two or three steps to the wicket and hurled the ball down at a terrific speed to break back sharply, and he completely defeated Jacker and most of the Internationals. Of course, he undoubtedly threw, as did one Knutton who used to play for Bradford. This Knutton was never no-balled in Council cricket, neither I think was Moss, and I believe it was mutually agreed that he should not be no-balled when playing against the Australians around 1900, with the result that he captured nine wickets.

It was in 1908 – or perhaps 1907, that I was fortunate to see Jessop play one of the 'immortal' innings against the South Africans at Lord's. Daisy was with me, and she being a great friend of Ben Lacey's [Sir

Francis Lacey, Secretary of Lord's], he let us sit in his private box in the new stand then just opened, I shall never forget Jessop's treatment of Kotze the South African fast bowler, and the way he almost knelt down on his right knee and hit balls of great pace to square leg. When Jessop really got going it must indeed have been a problem for the opposing Captain to set his field. Together with us in the box were the future Kings, Edward and George, and one couldn't but be sorry for their tutor, Mr Hansell, who was bombarded with questions 'non-stop'.

I shall always feel I was far too rash to have embarked on first class cricket in 1909, especially such an onerous position as Captain of renowned Yorkshire. In the first place the Yorkshire team were on the downgrade, several leading players having lately given up, several others passing their zenith, and the prestige of Lord Hawke in addition! Hawke was not a great cricketer, but he was certainly in the first class, though what was

far more important he had undoubtedly 'made' the Yorkshire CC XI. When he originally took over, although there were some good players, they were on the whole a rough uneducated lot, and there was much drinking. Peate, Ulyett, Emmett and Freeman were some of the best players. It is related that Freeman on receiving a telegram from the Secretary, Mr Perkins, of MCC asking him to play in a representative Match at Lord's replied: 'Right, meet me at Station, Freeman.'

In the second place, being invited to Captain Yorkshire at a moment's notice did not give me the necessary time to think out the implications, that I was certainly not a good enough player, but that over all other considerations I had most assuredly, owing to ever increasing bouts of ear trouble and consequent giddiness, neither the fitness nor the health for the task. However, I accepted and really completely failed, and I cannot say I enjoyed the experience! Though looking

T.L. Taylor Crown Prince

Thomas Launcelot Taylor was the man designated by Hawke to be his successor as Yorkshire's captain, a position in fact denied him by business claims. He did, however, in time succeed Hawke and Jackson as the club's President, and also presided for many years at the Scarborough Festival so that Hawke's wish that Taylor's considerable capabilities be harnessed for the club were in one way fulfilled.

Born in Headingley, Taylor died in Chapel Allerton. He attended Uppingham, where rugby was his sport, but an early injury turned his attention to cricket and hockey and on arrival at Cambridge he won a Blue at both sports, captaining the hockey team in his third year. He played three times for England at hockey and in 1902 was chosen to play for England against Australia at Lord's, but had to stand down.

According to Hawke he was '…a lion-hearted bat; his style was essentially that of a strong defence but he possessed great pun-

ishing powers'. He batted so well in 1901-02 that in addition to being selected for England he was named, in 1902, as one of *Wisden's* Cricketers of the Year (along with Haigh, Tunnicliffe and Hirst!) and there seems little doubt that he would have had a distinguished Test career had time allowed.

Taylor was also a high-class wicket-keeper but was given few opportunities to prove himself. When he arrived in the Yorkshire team David Hunter had worn the gauntlets for 11 years and was clearly irremovable, although the view of one contemporary critic (E.H.D. Sewell) was that Taylor might have been even better than Hunter 'had he played regularly – Taylor was lighter and nimbler on his pins'.

Amateurs were always under the cosh at Sheffield – Frank Mitchell once had a ginger-beer bottle thrown at him after missing a catch – and it was there that Taylor, letting slip a ball that went for four, was execrated as 'tha ugly little black devil, tha'll hev to do better'n that'.

Irving Washington Wombwell Beauty

William Arthur Irving Washington, from Wombwell, was a left-handed batsman of near genius who, although his county career was contained within the years 1900-02 and he died at the age of 48, is still remembered with almost misty-eyed affection in South Yorkshire.

He was unable to force his way into Hawke's team until 1902 when *Wisden* declared him to be one 'who promised to be very brilliant'. A contemporary publication predicted that 'he bids fair to develop into the finest left-handed batsman in England', all this following a superb display against the Australians at Leeds where, with Yorkshire needing 48 to win on a treacher-ous pitch, the county had lost Brown, Tunnicliffe, Denton, T.L. Taylor and Jackson, the ball jumping around like a firecracker. Washington then joined Hirst who, remark-ably, played the passive role while the 23-year-old in his first full season hit off the runs, finishing nine not out to give Yorkshire a famous victory.

By 1903 illness had overtaken Washington and although he went to South Africa (Griqualand West) in the hope of effecting a cure, his Yorkshire career was limited to just 43 matches. He did have the consola-tion of seeing his nephews Roy and Norman Kilner rise to prominence, and it says much for his personality and play that his memo-ry is kept shining bright by the Wombwell Cricket Lovers' Society.

---

back it is something to have known fairly intimately such immortals of the game as dear old George Hirst and Schofield Haigh, the latter one of the cheeriest nicest souls ever, Wilfred Rhodes and David Denton, one of the greatest 'out' fielders ever, and to have been associated in a lesser way with Archie MacLaren, Walter Brearley, Plum Warner, A.O. Jones, a great athlete, K.L. Hutchings, a magnificent batsman and field-er, Blythe and Woolley , the latter a charm-ing modest man, a great left-hand batsman and wonderful left-hand slow bowler on a sticky wicket who would or should probably attain a place in a world XI.

Of the matches in which I took part the few outstanding in my memory are the third Match in which I played on the lovely Worcester ground on which I had played as a boy. We were beaten by 12 runs, but I played a good innings of 30 not out, as I did against Lancaster on a nasty soft turning wicket the following year, making around 25 not out, out of a total of I think, under 100. In another Roses Match we were in a very bad way and had I think eight down for about 40 at 1.10 p.m., but I managed to remain with George Hirst till 2 o'clock lunch, and after in spite of the crowd roaring every time I received a ball. I remember being hit all over on a beastly sort of wick-et.

My efforts were brought to a close at Sheffield in 1911, Johnny Douglas hitting a ball very hard to me at mid off and splitting my hand twixt thumb and finger. Georgie Hirst said it was entirely my fault as I snapped at the ball! The Professionals were kindness itself to me and no one could have given greater and more loyal help than Hirst who was a man of real commonsense with a deep knowledge of cricket. He kept all the young Professionals in order, taught them how to 'turn out', how to behave on and off the field.

Two Professionals of great ability made the debut under me, either or both of whom would probably have been internationals. Booth and Drake were the two, and entirely unlike in every way. Booth, a charming well educated quiet man, a fine bowler and very useful batsman. Drake, very good natured, but rough and no brain, a splendid left-hand bat and bowler. It is related of him that on making his first big score his wife sent him a telegram of congratulation. Alonzo Drake, being none too sure of his ability to read, turned to Denton, saying 'Open and read it to me' which Denton did saying it was from his (Drake's) wife congratulating him. Whereupon Drake replied 'Give it to me' and when he'd had a good look remarked, 'Garn, you're kidding me, this ain't me wife's writin''!

I believe Drake died shortly after the 1914 War, and poor Booth was killed in the same action on the Somme in France, in which Dolphin, our wicket-keeper, was wounded.

The Booth mentioned was Major Booth who, with Drake, might have become one of the great names. The 1909 season was a Summer of poor weather, an Australian visit helping county finances, and Yorkshire's share of runs and wickets was maintained, as ever, by those imperishables Hirst, Haigh, Rhodes and Denton and, in his last season, the great David Hunter.

This season also brought the death, at the age of 73, of a man whose service to Yorkshire cricket outspanned even Lord Hawke's: that of Joseph Wostinholm, Honorary Secretary from 1864 to 1902. For 40 years Wostinholm was also Secretary of Sheffield United and is given the credit for that club's advance to the First Division of the Football League. 'Shrewd' and 'autocratic' are two regular descriptions of a man who, with Hawke, ruled Yorkshire cricket through the formative years. He was, according to Peter Thomas, 'less a servant of the members, more of a dictator', but the members nevertheless felt sufficiently of his service to vote him a testimonial of £200 and several 'silver articles' on his retirement in 1902. In fact, so highly were his services regarded that the Club had to advertise the post at a salary of £350.

Wostinholm was succeeded by F.C., later Sir Frederick, Toone, who had been Secretary of Leicestershire from 1897 to 1902. A short-list of three from 140 applicants had been drawn up: Toone, E.H.D. Sewell and the Sheffield journalist J.H. Stainton. The final interviews were conducted at the Station Hotel on, according to Sewell:

...a bleak morning. Directly I saw the third [Toone] I knew my number was up but was determined to die as game as possible.

So when Lord Hawke who did the question-ing of the victims before surely the mightiest committee in the world (those who've only seen the United Nations ought to have taken a dekko at the full committee of YCCC when the war drums are throbbing) put the vital question 'Do you go in for betting' I replied at once: 'Well, sir, I had a bet yesterday that I shouldn't get this job.'

Toone saw his first task as that of bringing county cricket's most successful club into the 20th century. He revised the Club's rules, put the organisation of benefits on a more professional basis, and marketed the club so successfully that he doubled the membership of 3,000. He and Hawke ensured the advance and progress of Yorkshire's professionals: up to the outbreak of the Great War the players were paid £5 per home match, £6 for an away match with a £1 winning bonus, plus talent money of five shillings each for special performances, awarded by the captain and distributed at the end of each season. Capped players had to join the Cricketers' Friendly Society and were given Winter pay (32 weeks) of £2 per week. The whole or part of the Winter pay was retained by the club and invested on the players' behalf at a rate of 4%, for their retirement from cricket.

The 1914-18 War accelerated life enormously, and in 1921 the club announced new pay scales: £11 per home match, £15 per away match, £1 winning bonus and £1.50 set aside for talent money. When injured a player received half pay, when out of the team through loss of form, £8 a week up to 31 August. The Committee could, and did, increase bonuses, as for instance when they doubled the talent money available in 1922 and raised it to £450 in 1923.

The club was also concerned about the effect of adverse weather upon benefit matches, and set aside a sum of £200 a year to augment those benefits that the Committee felt failed to raise the sum expected. This system applied from 1905 to 1921 when the Committee decided to guarantee all capped players of ten years' service a benefit of at least £1,000. Capped players of five years' service were guaranteed £250 with an increment of £50 per year up to ten.

The Summer of 1909 was Haigh's benefit year and was remembered for two mighty Roses matches, the second being Haigh's choice. At Old Trafford on Whit Monday, in poor light and with the threat of rain, Brearley came bounding in for 35 overs to take nine Yorkshire wickets for 80 in a paltry first-innings score of 133. The sun broke through on Tuesday for Lancashire to bat on a drying surface, Haigh first taking two wickets with successive balls and then surpassing himself with a hat-trick: Lancashire 89 all out, Haigh 7-25.

Yorkshire, batting again, then lost their first four wickets for 44 and began the last day 88 ahead, Huddleston then carving through the remainder of the innings and finishing with 8-24. So Lancashire needed 123 to win, but Hirst's valiant left arm shook the Red Rose to such an extent that five batsmen were dismissed for six runs; Albert Hornby added 31 with Heap, but three brilliant catches helped to send Lancashire crashing to 57 all out (Hirst six for 23).

The weather was poor again for the return at Bradford on August Bank Holiday, Yorkshire hitting out in the hour's play allowed on the first day to reach 111-4. Next morning, in 14 deliveries, Heap took four wickets for five runs and Yorkshire were out for 159. Then it was Rhodes' turn: his 7-68 meant that Lancashire fell 39 behind. Heap got at Yorkshire again (7-49), and with Lancashire needing 186 to win Rhodes applied the *coup de grace* for Yorkshire to win by 100, leaving spectators in need of stiff refreshment.

The shadows lengthened in 1910. The latter part of the Summer was spoiled by poor weather, and an age ended with the demise of Edward the Peacemaker, who died as the season began. Cricket had lost a friend, for this was a monarch who had played the game, who had an eye for a good stroke as well as a pretty shape. The University of Cambridge had owed money on their sadly now demolished pavilion at Fenner's; the King contributed to the building fund and offered to make up the balance required at the end of term. He was the largest contributor when MCC were struggling to buy the freehold at Lord's; as Prince of Wales (and Duke of Cornwall) it was said he was a very good friend to Surrey.

Bleriot had flown the Channel, the Liberal Party

was in office, the Old Age Pension and the Labour Exchange had arrived, and such was the onrush of change that Yorkshire fell to eighth place, Lord Hawke formally ending his long reign as captain in that November.

The Committee publicly expressed regret at the disappointment of a Summer in which ten matches were won and seven lost. There were high moments, notably against Lancashire at Leeds where Hirst took 9-23, hitting the stumps eight times. At Lord's against the other regular rivals Middlesex, Yorkshire needed 331 to win and accomplished victory by two wickets, the winning run coming from the penultimate delivery, Hirst scoring 137.

Rhodes had a superb match against Surrey on a difficult pitch at Bradford. With the ball he captured 11 wickets for 72, and when Yorkshire needed 157 to win on a surface described as treacherous, Rhodes, in his regular role as opener, hit a fierce 88 not out to bring victory. Another exciting win, by six runs over Hampshire at Portsmouth, featured two of the new players: Booth, and the wicket-keeper on trial to succeed David Hunter, Arthur Dolphin.

Hampshire needed another 32 runs to win when last man John Newman joined Horace Bowell who, coolly and carefully, led his county towards the summit. Hirst, Booth, Rhodes, Haigh, Myers and the Etonian Alfred Legard had all bowled and bowled, and the Portsmouth crowd sensed they were all bowled out. Richard Binns tells the rest of the story:

> Schofield Haigh, a comfortable looking man of medium height, not of little more than corresponding build, and of a most likeable smiling countenance, might have been seen plucking at his thick short moustache and thoughtfully bending his head as he was put on once more to bowl. Some scheme as dark as his skin was simmering in his brain, surely.

> Bowell played him very gingerly. His extreme caution was manifest in the way he increasingly stepped back to deal with balls well pitched up to him.

> Six short of a time, seven wanted for victo-

Alonzo Drake Lonza

Although Hawke believed that Drake's temperament would prevent his becoming a player 'of the highest rank', his sudden death in 1919, from heart disease, at the age of 35, was a major blow to Yorkshire for he and Major Booth, who had been killed in the Great War, were the bowling partnership expected to carry the county into the middle of the 1920s.

Like many families in the mid-19th century, the Drakes moved from the land, near Huddersfield, towards the great new industrial cities and Alonzo was born at Parkgate, near Rotherham, his father seeking a better living in the coal and steel industries of South Yorkshire. The boy had an obvious leaning to sport and his early promise at football took him from Rotherham Town Reserves to Doncaster Rovers, then in the Second Division, scoring as a 17-year-old debutant. He went on to play for Sheffield United (24 goals in the First Division), Birmingham City, Queen's Park Rangers and Huddersfield Town before his cricketing form with Honley, in the Huddersfield League, attracted Yorkshire's attention.

He played for the Colts, a left-arm medium pace bowler and punishing left-handed batsman, in 1908, and Yorkshire felt there was sufficient promise to move him to Harrogate for the following Summer; his record there persuaded the Committee that August that he should be tried in the first team as deputy to Hirst, who needed a rest. Drake took 4-34 against Derbyshire and was returned for the following match, against Middlesex, in which he took 6-34 in nine overs, four wickets falling in one over.

Like many players he failed to justify himself in his second season, but by 1911 he swept into the side, scoring 1,500 runs and taking 84 wickets at 21 each; in 1913 he did the 'double', topping the Yorkshire bowling averages with 115 wickets (7-7 against Somerset at Bath) and in that sad Summer of 1914 rode the fields of England like another Hirst, finishing with 158 wickets.

Against Derbyshire he took 5-6, their innings collapsing from 67-4 to 68 all out; he and Booth bowled unchanged in an innings victory at Bristol and then, at Weston-super-Mare, Somerset were dismissed by the pair for 44 and in the second innings Drake entered history with an analysis of 8.5-0-35-10.

He twice volunteered for war service and was rejected as unfit, continuing his cricket for Honley and playing the occasional charity game, but even then it was clear his health was failing. Snooker was another love and in February 1919, after having been advised by his doctor to stay indoors, he insisted on attending the local Liberal Club to play a match. Three mornings later he suffered a heart attack and died.

He was remembered affectionately by the team as a man of droll humour and for his spells of what Peter Thomas described as 'swift destruction'. On damaged pitches his swing and break either way made him a deadly proposition, but he was known to become downcast on his less successful days, hence Hawke's view of his temperament. 'Lonza' deserves to be better remembered, for he was, as Mick Pope pointed out in his excellent essay, the bowler who beat Verity to all ten.

---

ry. How the crowd cheered. Haigh started his next over…the ball was noticeably well pitched up and Bowell once more went back to it. The bails were seen to fall, Bowell was out, the match was over.

Haigh explained afterwards that he had noted how Bowell had gone back to full-length balls and played on that caution, inch by inch forcing the batsman back until he played on.

Against these successes had to be recorded some dismal batting performances, particularly against Kent's Blythe and Woolley. At Sheffield in June, Northamptonshire achieved an historic victory, their first against Yorkshire. Essex won

Major Booth A light gone out

Major William were his Christian names; he died a 2nd Lieutenant in the West Yorkshire Regiment in the Somme battles of 1916 in the same action in which Roy Kilner was injured. He was 30 years old and but for the Great War might be remembered as one of the game's great all-rounders.

Sutcliffe described him as 'a great batsman and a great bowler', Hawke said: 'England lost one of the most promising and charming young cricketers it was ever my lot to meet. Having gained a commission he was killed "going over the top" gallantly leading his men.' Another captain, Archibald White, added 'A magnificent cricketer and a splendid fellow in every way'.

Booth was a powerful right-hand batsman – he scored 210 at 50 an hour at Worcester in 1911, mostly off drives and square-cuts – and a right arm medium-fast bowler with a very high action. *Wisden* described his bowling: 'he makes the ball swerve away at the very last moment. There is, too, something puzzling about his flight and if the wicket is dong anything he can make the ball pop up nastily.' A comparison was made with S.F. Barnes.

Booth was not a strong man and was used mostly in short spells, but he could be devastating; two hat-tricks, bowling unchanged with Drake in 1914 in two matches, taking more than 100 wickets in 1912-14; three wickets in four balls three times; against Middlesex in 1912 he had match figures of 8-136 and scored 107 not out. His Test appearances (two) were limited only by the conflict.

His was an unusual if brief career: in 1913 he was one of *Wisden's* 'Five' and by the following year the only right-handed member of Yorkshire's attack. In the intervening Winter, on the Sunday of the First Test, Booth, along with Hobbs and Strudwick, was thrown out of a car as it hit a bank approaching a level crossing in Umbito, South Africa, Booth and the driver lay below the overturned car, the cricketer

Major Booth
Mick Pope

escaping with a minor back strain although he did need, according to Clive Porter, a runner when batting in the Test.

Just over three years later he was killed near La Cigny and buried in Serre Military Cemetery Number 1. His death brought sad poems to his local newspaper in Pudsey. His sister, unable to accept that he had been killed, always kept a light burning in the window of their cottage in the hope that he would return. Nor was his room disturbed until after his sister's death in 1950 when, Paul Dyson reported, the cottage, close by the Pudsey Britannia ground, was sold.

His surname is commemorated in a Pudsey side-street, Booth's Yard. In September 1920 a memorial service was held in St Lawrence's Church, Pudsey and a tablet unveiled. He was also remembered by Roy Kilner, who named his younger son Major.

by ten wickets at Leyton, Leicestershire by 259 runs at Headingley, while at Old Trafford, shame of shame, Yorkshire went down by an innings and 111. Brearley took nine wickets in the match, while the elegant Spooner recorded a 200 not out, being missed twice in his first 14 runs.

A wrenched ankle put the doughty Denton out for a month from 15 July. Wilson again scored three centuries but his aggregate dropped to 757, while of the younger players the major hopes were now Drake and Booth. After a trial of skill between Haworth Watson, from Skipton, and Dolphin, the latter finally won the wicket-keeping place vacated by 'Old Ironsides', David Hunter, and was to keep it for the next 22 years.

At Wighill Park that Summer, Hawke arranged a farewell photograph seating himself, cross-legged and flat-capped in the middle of the front row, on the carpet between a downcast Watson and a straw-hatted Wilkinson. Behind him Hirst, between two ladies, exudes good cheer, while Rhodes, standing on a chair at the back alongside Booth, might have been assessing the cameraman's stance. Everard Radcliffe, Hawke's successor, is a tall, fair-haired young man at outside right, obviously of the family but not the inner circle.

Hawke's career epitomised the zenith of the Edwardian amateur cricketer. He scored 16,794 runs in his 29 years of first-class cricket, at an average of 20.15, captained his county and England, toured the then cricketing world, and was respected and admired everywhere. Modern comparisons, or accusations of paternalism, are pointless for he simply would not have understood contemporary attitudes – although he would certainly have been pleased to see the county cricketer well cared for in a respected niche in society.

In 1914 Hawke was elected President of MCC, adding to his life presidency of Yorkshire, and MCC had the good sense to retain him in that position all through the Great War. One imagines that even if Ludendorff's armies had reached London, the Kaiser would have received short shrift at Lord's!

It followed that 1911, a year of glorious Summer – 'how the sun shone' wrote 'Country Vicar' –

had to be a season of considerable change. Radcliffe took the captaincy, although he had deputised for Hawke so often in the two preceding Summers that the Committee was in effect officially sanctioning a change that had already evolved gradually. But Hawke's influence was undiminished, even if emanating only from the Committee room.

Rothery and Myers were each granted £250 and left the county, Booth and Drake were given regular places, and another left-hander of promise, Roy Kilner, was unearthed. For £600 a Winter shed was built at Headingley, enabling coaching and practice to continue throughout the year. However, there was little immediate improvement on the field, the final Championship placing being a gain of one, from eighth to seventh. Eight matches were lost, bringing the number of defeats over two Summers to 15, as many as in the previous six years together, but there were indications that the team was recovering strength and in Booth and Drake the club had two cricketers of the highest promise. Their bowling enabled Hirst and Rhodes to concentrate on batting, thus lengthening both careers.

Yorkshire began by beating MCC at Lord's before being caught on a drying pitch at Leyton, but after that, apart from a surprising defeat by the University of Cambridge, the team recorded eight consecutive victories. Worcester provided a memorable match on a beautiful pitch. Hirst, at 40, was bowling as fast as at any time in his career, taking 9-41 in 15.2 overs, again hitting the stumps eight times. Hirst's performance can be judged by the fact that the next three innings of the match raised 994 runs, Yorkshire winning by ten wickets after Booth, in his second season, scored 210 in four hours, his off-driving and square-cutting being long remembered. Hirst, not to be out-done, then added a furious hundred.

Middlesex ended Yorkshire's triumphal progress at Lord's in June, where the team's catching was so sloppy that a written rebuke was received from Hawke. Not that matters improved the following week at Dewsbury, where three more batsmen were given lives as Northamptonshire reached 401, a record that was even excelled in the return match at Northampton in July in which four batsmen were missed and, despite Rhodes' 14 wickets, the match was lost.

Drake hinted of emerging power by taking six Lancashire wickets for 57 at Old Trafford, following Hirst's 156, performances that ensured a substantial Yorkshire win. The 1911 season was also that of Warwickshire's advance to the front rank in which Frank Foster was so prominent: in Yorkshire's visit to Edgbaston he scored his maiden hundred and then took 12 wickets, but even that wasn't enough to overthrow the old aristos, Yorkshire still winning by four wickets.

However, by late July, when Warwickshire played the return fixture at Harrogate, the balance had swung. Foster continued in tremendous form, scorings 60 in the first innings and 101 in the second (in a total time of only 135 minutes for both innings), and Yorkshire were left eventually to score 247 on a worn pitch. It was a difficult task, but there could have been few excuses for the debacle that followed: Yorkshire dismissed for 58, Benny Wilson being top scorer with 11, Field taking 7-20 and the new champions deservedly taking the crown.

An even worse collapse followed at Aylestone Road where Leicestershire, in their only victory in a programme of 22 matches, dismissed Yorkshire's second innings for 47 (from 27-2), King finishing with 8-17. Radcliffe's team concluded a sorry season with a southern tour that did nothing for their reputation. They were saved from defeat at The Oval, where Surrey had run up 540 in their first innings, by a heavy storm on the third day; they lost by six wickets at Southampton on a pitch on which they had first use; Blythe and Woolley, again, dismissed them for 75 at Canterbury, Kent winning by ten wickets. So the spirit of the side must have been sagging by the time the team reached Hastings, especially after Sussex raised 522-7 declared.

But here was a good, fast pitch and Yorkshire for once took full advantage, Hirst's 218 being followed by Drake's 115, the pair putting on 259 for the fourth wicket in 150 minutes. A second victory that season over Sussex was accomplished by an innings and 32 on the third afternoon. Nottinghamshire, too, had gone down twice, at Trent Bridge and Hull.

Wilfred Rhodes took the Lancashire match at Sheffield as his benefit, a disappointment in that

Yorkshire appeared to have the game won comfortably by the evening of the second day, the public contributing only £83 at the turnstiles on the third. But the Red Rose, only 45 ahead with half their second-innings wickets gone, managed a remarkable recovery through McLeod (121) Makepeace and Hornby, leaving Yorkshire to score 251 in three hours. Three wickets went for 45 before Denton, 101 not out, forced an honourable draw.

It was, in fact, Denton's year, hitting six centuries and scoring 2,223 runs in Yorkshire's matches. Rhodes, Hirst, Wilson, Drake and Booth also passed 1,000, while the untouchable trio of Hirst, Rhodes and Haigh all passed 100 wickets and were well supported by Drake (84) and Booth (79). Worth noting, too, is the fact that All India, as India and Pakistan were then known in cricket, were routed by an innings and 43 at Hull. Denton was to pass 2,000 runs again in 1912.

On paper Yorkshire had the strength to reassert their old supremacy, even if short of at least one more batsman of the highest class, but the 1911 results were below expectations and at the end of the season Radcliffe resigned to be succeeded by Sir Archibald White, who led the side up until the outbreak of the Great War in 1914.

Radcliffe, although nominally captain for only one Summer, had in effect led the side for almost three, so often had he been deputy for Hawke in 1909-10, and he had been in charge of a major reconstruction as Drake, Booth and Dolphin came into the team, a process that was to continue into 1912 when Roy Kilner and Edgar Oldroyd made their presence felt. Indeed, the team photograph of 1912 had a settled, assured, commanding look about it, showing ten capped players and the Colts Kilner and Oldroyd cross-legged on the grass at the front.

White had been in the Wellington School XI in 1894-96 and had played once for Yorkshire, in 1908, before his appointment. He led Yorkshire to the Championship in his first season (a feat emulated by Geoffrey Wilson, Barber, Burton, Vic Wilson and Close), but was able to attain no better than second in 1913 and fourth the following Summer.

Arthur Dolphin Quickhands

Dolphin began with the almost impossible task of replacing David Hunter in the esteem of the team and the affection of the Yorkshire public, and that he was able to lay the ghost of 'Old Ironsides' is tribute enough to his ability and courage.

He spent 22 years as Yorkshire's first choice wicket-keeper, and played just once for England. His contemporary was Surrey's Strudwick, still regarded by some as the finest of all keepers, and Strudwick's view of Dolphin gives some indication of the Yorkshireman's reputation: 'He stood with his right leg a little further back. This helped him take the ball that is going away from the leg to the off which Rhodes and Kilner served up on sticky wickets, so giving him a quicker sweep to the wicket. In my opinion Dolphin moves the balls more quickly than any other keeper.'

John Callaghan, in *Yorkshire's Pride*, points out the high proportion of stumpings in Dolphin's victims: 231 to 488 catches. But, of course, he did keep to an unparalleled variety of bowlers: the left-arm seam, swing and cut of Hirst, Drake and Waddington, the medium-pace off-breaks of Haigh and Macaulay, the left-arm spin of Rhodes and Kilner, the late swing of Booth and Robinson. Sutcliffe wrote of him: 'His quick brain and exceptionally keen eyesight were responsible for disposing of large numbers of batsmen from chances which many keepers would have missed without even affecting their reputations.' George Duckworth, the Lancashire and England keeper said of Dolphin: 'He was the quickest in taking the ball to the stumps'.

Dolphin was also a tenacious batsman, a renowned last-ditcher who once scored 93 against Middlesex. A quiet man who deplored ostentation, he once, according to Callaghan, silenced a raucous and ugly crowd in a public house by merely putting his scarred and bruised hands before him on a table. The ruffians assumed him to be a professional bare-knuckle fighter.

In later years Dolphin became a respected umpire, renowned for never wearing a hat at a time when everyone covered his head.

White's years were also those of Yorkshire's unwanted but growing reputation for stolid, dour batting, a criticism that seems a little unfair of a side that included Denton, Hirst and Booth. Much of the disapproval was directed at Benny Wilson who, after displaying his strokes and hitting well, would inexplicably relapse into implacable defence, patting back half-volleys. Oldroyd, too, soon developed a reputation as a sticker, and the whole team was often accused of 'sitting on the splice'. White admitted to 'Old Ebor':

Benny Wilson and Edgar Oldroyd were apt on occasions to be a little deliberate in their methods. I will say, however, that in nearly every case in which this happened we had made a bad start and their caution was justified, although it may not have been to the liking of the spectators…

At times I own I have had to issue the order to 'sit on the splice'. This I only did when I realised was impossible to win a match but that it might be saved. 'If you can't win a match, why should you be beaten?' was Lord Hawke's great question. I think that a good deal of the criticism of slow play on Yorkshire's part was due to the ignorance of the plan of campaign that the team were endeavouring to carry out.

The other point that should be made about the White era, before a detailed consideration of the last three Summers of the Golden Age, was that both Hirst and Kilner were absent for much of the 1914 Summer, two players who would always contribute much to the enterprise of any cricket team. Another factor in Yorkshire's inability to continue their domination of the Hawke years was a general levelling up among the other counties, as exemplified by the rise of one of the 'newcomers', Warwickshire.

By 1914, before shrapnel and the machine gun mowed down the flower of a European generation, cricket had become a great and much-loved national institution, and for boys in all grades of society it represented a wonderful portal to achievement and glory, if not exactly riches – a magic door. For this was a time of the craftsman, when 'hand-made' was a tautology, when the tradesmen, carpenters, joiners and blacksmiths took great pride in their skills and the rigorous training, from early boyhood, that was needed. And that sense of genuine professionalism, very hard but scrupulously fair, at a time of stern religious instruction, overflowed into cricket, to the game of English willow against English leather.

White's Championship victory of 1912 was Yorkshire's ninth in 20 seasons, and with Rhodes missing six and Haigh one of the matches, called up for the Triangular Test series against Australia

Roy Kilner A delight

Roy Kilner, from Wombwell, could claim to be the most popular Yorkshire cricketer. He never lacked friends at home or abroad at a time when Yorkshire, in their grim, winning mood of the 1920s, were less than welcome on many grounds.

He was a nephew of Irving Washington and inherited some of his uncle's stylish left-handed batting; as a left-arm slow-medium bowler he was skilful enough to play in nine Tests and to undertake two MCC tours; he was also considered by Yorkshire good enough, and of sufficient contrast, to bowl at the other end to Wilfred Rhodes.

Like Rhodes, too, he was adaptable. He first won his place, before the Great War, as a batsman and his play was highly regarded, if considered a little eccentric by orthodox Yorkshiremen. After the war he developed his bowling, just as Rhodes returned to it, to help cover the loss of Booth and Drake. He scored 15 centuries, including a 206 against Derbyshire in 1920, and between 1922 and 1925 his bowling, especially on drying pitches, was feared. He passed 100 wickets in each of those four Summers and his career aggregate of 858 wickets was taken at an average of 17.33.

Yet it is as a personality that he is best remembered and he was a great favourite of Cardus who, fortunately, passed on a little of this delightful man's philosophy. It was Kilner who summed up the dour Roses matches of those days with two remarks: 'What we want is no umpires and fair cheating all round,' and 'We say good morning and after that all we say is

Roy Kilner
Ron Deaton collection

"Howzat?"'
Cricket, then as now, was under self-analysis and when Cardus asked Kilner the essential question, 'What is wrong with the game?' he replied: 'Nowt. Game's all right, it's t'crowd that wants educating up to it.'

In the Winter of 1927-28 he took a coaching engagement in India, hit 283 in a local match (including six sixes and 40 fours) but contracted enteric fever and died in Barnsley on his return. It was reported that 100,000 lined the funeral route to Wombwell Parish Church. Roy was the brother of Norman Kilner of Warwickshire.

and South Africa, to finish first again with a debutant captain was an achievement regarded with both relief and surprise. No wonder then that the XI contributed to buy their new captain a sliver salver.

That same year also shattered the legend that the sun never ceased to shine during the Summers of the Golden Age. It was miserable, only one of Yorkshire's 19 home matches escaping with no interruption. In June at Sheffield and Huddersfield, rain washed out play for four successive days, as it was to do again in successive fixtures at Bradford and Hull.

Nevertheless Yorkshire lost only one match all Summer, that against Middlesex at Lord's. White won the toss and had no wish to bat first on a pitch made soft by preceding rain, but in those days of deteriorating surfaces to send in the opposition was regarded as reckless if not foolhardy. AcCordingley Yorkshire went in and lost the first seven wickets for 76, Booth, Haigh and White rallying the tail to take the innings to 157. Middlesex won a lead of 28 and needed only 139 in the fourth innings; at the close on the second day they needed only 15 with five wickets standing, but elected to wait until the morrow and were lucky that the rain stayed away until later in the day, winning by four wickets.

Difficult pitches meant, of course, that Yorkshire's extraordinarily versatile attack could operate in favourable conditions match after match. Lancashire were routed by ten wickets at Bradford; Hirst, Drake and Haigh doing the damage. In these circumstances it is the side that possesses the batsman who can master the turn

---

Edgar Oldroyd Little Ack

Oldroyd came from Louis Hall's home town of Batley, and much of the Giant's durability and steadfastness ran in his genes. His record, as Peter Thomas pointed out, puts him among the best number-three batsmen in county cricket, scoring 38 centuries for Yorkshire and sharing in ten partnerships of 200 or more, including a 333 with Percy Holmes against Warwickshire in 1922.

He forced his way into the Yorkshire side before the Great War through his tenacious defensive batting, and he developed, in the 1920s, into a hard-hitting middle-order player who could always hold one end in whatever circumstances. In 1931, when he went to play for Pudsey St Lawrence, he won this admiring memory from the boy Hutton: 'One of the best I ever saw on a turning pitch.'

He was one of the characters of the Yorkshire side of his era who won admiring tributes from Cardus and Robertson-Glasgow, the latter addressing him with style and affection in one of his 'Cricket Prints':

His name might have been Jess Oakroyd. He was one of those small, tough, humorous militant men who make the comedy and greatness of a country. They are to be found answering back something or someone which may or may not have existence: fate, a tax collector, Monday morning, a bus conductor, thirst or a Hyde Park orator. They bounce and argue down time's corridors. And they generally win the battle.

Oldroyd could not be one of those who, when bowled by an amateur, accept the unwelcome visitation with a resigned calm; he was very angry indeed; he looked it and he said it. For you had not only wrecked Oldroyd for some hours, you had ended an integral section of Yorkshire. You had wrecked a parish and interfered with the workings of the only county that mattered. There lies the secret of the Yorkshire cricketer. He comes second in his own estimation.

According to John Callaghan, Oldroyd was not too happy when Yorkshire released him in 1931, but he became a professional with Pudsey St Lawrence and he died in Truro, just before New Year of 1965, at the age of 76.

and lift that usually wins; on this occasion it was Yorkshire and Rhodes, who made a masterly 107.

At Nottingham in June, Hirst was nursing an injured knee and with Rhodes out for eight, Yorkshire needed 248 to win. Wilson shored up one end, 150 minutes for 48, while Kilner, who had taken four wickets, added 84 not out aided by another young man, amateur James Tasker, who promising batting career was cut short by the demands of business.

Northamptonshire had a narrow escape at Bradford, at 24-8 in their second innings and needing 143 to escape an innings defeat when time ran out. The sun did shine, brilliantly, at Tunbridge Wells in mid-July where Yorkshire won some revenge for several earlier humiliations. Batting first they scored 543 (Denton 221), Kent eventually going down by an innings and 45, two of their batsmen being run out, according to 'Old Ebor', 'chiefly through the impetuosity of Woolley'. The great left hander did, however, raise 42 and 75 in his two innings.

At Southampton in that same month Fry contributed 186 to a Hampshire first-innings total of 378-4, Yorkshire replying with 429, Denton's 191 reportedly outshining even Fry's grand display. On the second night the Solent saw heavy rain and Hampshire were caught on another drying surface, Hirst and Haigh gleefully inflicting the usual damage to dismiss them for 95, the preliminary to another Yorkshire victory by nine wickets.

In a wet Summer Denton totalled 2,127 in all matches, only Hobbs approaching him with an aggregate of 2,042. If England's selectors regarded him, at 38, as too old, opposing bowlers recognised a master, a batsman who added to the prolific stroke-making of his youth the steadiness and additional defensive technique of maturity and experience. Haigh, at 41, took 125 wickets, Booth and Hirst both following him to the hundred, Drake failing by 13.

Haigh brought red ruin to the Australians at Bradford, returning match figures of 11-36. 'I wish we could take him back with us to Australia,' wrote the touring manager. Hawke was sufficiently confident to tell the annual gen-

eral meeting: 'Yorkshire will have a very excellent team for many years to come.'

Yorkshire won 16 matches in 1913, to 13 in the previous Championship season, yet finished second to Kent and could not complain, for strong as Yorkshire were and excellent as was the effort and teamwork, Kent were accepted everywhere as outstanding and deserving champions.

The pressing questions of the time were Home Rule for Ireland and the intentions of Imperial Germany, both sides of the North Sea frantically building dreadnoughts. Conrad, Lawrence, Yeats and Joyce will be remembered as great writers of the time, while Yorkshire was more concerned by the infernal motor car that had had the effrontery to strike Schofield Haigh on the foot and put him out for most of July. As Hirst was also missing, injured, in that month there remained a suspicion that, good as Kent were, with these interventions Yorkshire might have held on to the crown.

The weather bucked up to bring a fine Summer and, because George V was visiting Merseyside and a special holiday had been proclaimed, three Roses matches were played that Summer, Yorkshire visiting Aigburth for the first time. Lancashire got away to a good start, shooting out Yorkshire for 74 and 53 in the season's opening match at Old Trafford. Heap taking 11-39, Lancashire winning by an innings and 39. Lancashire also won at Liverpool, on another drying pitch, Dean taking 17-91.

By August Bank Holiday, however, Yorkshire were well into their stride and were left to get 217, on a fast, good pitch, in 150 minutes. After half an hour the score was 32-2 with Rhodes and Kilner gone, but after 82 minutes the score had reached 141, Haigh and Benny Wilson driving furiously. With five wickets down, Yorkshire needed 71 in 45 minutes, then 26 in 18. White made a spirited 27 not out and brought out the scores level for Drake, who had been kept back, as a left-hander, to avoid the loss of time on changing the field, to drive Dean for four with six minutes to spare.

After the opening defeat in Manchester, Yorkshire won ten matches and could have won three more had time and the weather allowed.

Rockley Wilson Humorist

Evelyn Rockley Wilson had an extraordinary career even by the standards of the Golden Age, into which he was born in 1879, near Sheffield. Only Rhodes' career spanned a greater number of years, for Wilson first appeared for Yorkshire in 1899 and said his final farewell in 1923.

He was the brother of two excellent cricketers, C.E.M. Wilson, who captained Cambridge and, an all-rounder, appeared intermittently for Yorkshire during 1896-99 before becoming vicar of Sand Hutton, and C.R. Wilson who, while never playing first-class, served the Committee for 32 years. Rockley was described as a 'joyous' batsman of sound defence who appalled the professors with his delight in the hook; he was also an extremely skilful and accurate right-arm spin bowler of low action who moved the ball a little both ways, accompanying all this with a delightful sense of humour: 'My best ball is the one which broke from the off when I meant to break from the leg.'

At Cambridge, on his first-class debut, he appeared as a last-minute substitute for A.J. Webbe's XI and scored 117 not out and 70; he made 108 against Oxford in 1901 and was thus able to claim a century against both Universities 'whilst in residence'. He played only nine games for Yorkshire between 1899 and 1902, partly because of the strength of the side and partly, as noted elsewhere, because the Committee was reluctant to leave out top-class professionals who would do as they were told in favour of amateurs who came and went as they pleased. He began teaching French and coaching cricket at Winchester in 1903, and was then available only in the holidays, not reappearing until 1913.

After the Great War Yorkshire had need of him. Drake and Booth had been lost, the team had to be rebuilt and the 40-year-old schoolmaster was a valuable reinforcement from July. In 1919 Rockley Wilson finished seventh in the national averages and second the following year, being chosen as vice-captain to J.W.H.T. Douglas for the 1920-21 tour of Australia. Although England had a desperate time, losing all five Tests, Wilson finished with 51 wickets at 11.19 each.

Described by R.L. Arrowsmith as 'a brilliant scholar as a boy', he had an astonishing memory for facts and figures and became renowned as a coach, a raconteur and a character. It was ironical, noted Arrowsmith, that articles written by Wilson while on tour in Australia, and published in the *Daily Express*, led to players being banned from writing for the press while on tour.

Such a character appealed, of course, to R.C. Robertson-Glasgow, and it was he who told the most famous 'Rockley' story: 'a noble lord, whose awful majesty hid a kindly heart', according to 'Crusoe', was holding court in the pavilion and, seeing Wilson, shook his hand in passing. 'Lucky to get a touch,' whispered Wilson to his companion. In more recent times Martin Howe has summarised an unusual and colourful career in an admirable booklet.

Haigh was absent when Gloucestershire won at Sheffield by two runs, and at Leeds when Northamptonshire won by 20. Hirst missed Surrey's victory at Hull, but a valuable recruit, Rockley Wilson, reappeared in August, scoring 104 not out against Essex at Bradford and re-established the link between the University of Cambridge and the county. A master at Winchester, Wilson also had a qualification for Hampshire, by residence, and 'Old Ebor' avers that the Committee did not recall the all-rounder who had first appeared in the county team in 1899 until they feared losing him.

Seven members of the 1913 team scored more than 1,000 runs and eight of the side scored centuries – a formidable demonstration of the team's batting power. Booth, 167 wickets at 18 apiece, had confirmed himself as the pace bowler needed and he, Drake and Hirst all managed the 'double'. Indeed, a fourth 'double' was missed by only 14 wickets, and that by the team's number one batsman and former premier left-arm spinner, Rhodes. After 19 years Schofield Haigh retired honourably to the position of coach at Winchester.

Hawke was MCC President for the celebration of the centenary of the opening of Lord's Ground, the other significant event of 1913. Yorkshire in that year, as they were to be in 1939, were experienced, confident, puissant and capable of dominating the Championship for several years. They began with three successive victories by an innings, against Northamptonshire, MCC and Essex.

Mead, with an innings of 213 at Southampton, put a stop to this rampage. Denton (168 not out) and Hirst (146) made the now customary response, raising 312 for the fourth wicket, but as might be expected the match was drawn. The first match at home, against Surrey at Bradford, was a surprise to the faithful, for Hobbs and Hayes both made centuries in the Surrey first innings, Hobbs adding 74 for good measure in the second. Hirst was leading the charge to victory in Yorkshire's second innings when he played on to Fender, and Surrey were winners by 28 runs.

Tom Birtles, who had made his debut the previous Summer, seemed to be a batsman of some promise, following his 40 against Surrey with a much praised 104 against Lancashire at Sheffield. These performances encouraged the Committee to play him regularly, and but for the war years he might have won a place. Birtles did play again in 1919, but was never able to realise his early potential.

Lancashire too, had to settle for a draw, but Rhodes was in masterly form on a soft pitch at Leeds, and Derbyshire went down by an innings. But Yorkshire then struck a lean spell, losing twice to Kent while Hirst was injured and Kilner, still recovering from a Winter illness, was clearly not fully fit. Modern cricketers will recognise some of the factors in the Tonbridge defeat; play against Warwickshire at Dewsbury had not finished until 6.40 pm and that meant, in those days, an all-night journey. The same discomfort and privations, of course, applied to teams facing long journeys to play Yorskhire.

Blythe, 8-55, was the principal reason for Kent's win at Sheffield, but after that Yorkshire, from the first week in July, won 11 of their remaining 12 matches, Lancashire going down by an innings at Old Trafford. But the June wobble was enough to prevent another Championship victory, Yorkshire finishing fourth after winning exactly half their 28 games and drawing ten.

War against Germany was declared on 4 August and the latter part of the Summer was confused. Surrey, declared champions by MCC, cancelled their last two matches but had done enough, as second-placed Middlesex admitted by raising no objection. Middlesex's visit to Sheffield was at first declared off at Lord's, then reconsidered. By the time Surrey were to be visited in mid-August, the army had taken over The Oval and the match was switched to Lord's, where Hobbs reached 202, he and Hayward raising 290 for the first for the first wicket and the Surrey first innings reaching 549-6. 'Old Ebor' felt that the situation was so unreal that the players had great difficulty in concentrating on their play.

Back home Benny Wilson made 208 against Sussex at Bradford before the two final home fixtures – against an England XI at Harrogate and in the Scarborough Festival – were cancelled. Yorkshire then set off on their final tour in the last sunset of the Golden Age, winning at Bristol by an innings and at Weston by 227 runs, and achieving a draw in the very last match with Sussex at Brighton. Two exceptional all-rounders, Major Booth and Alonzo Drake, played in their last match for the county.

Booth and Roy Kilner told 'Old Ebor' at Brighton that both were planning to enlist as soon as they returned home: 'It's our duty, Mr Pullin.' Both joined the Leeds Pals Battalion, along with Dolphin. Booth, commissioned a second lieutenant, was killed on the Western Front on 1 July 1916 in the same attack in which Kilner was wounded in the right wrist, an offensive that brought heavy losses and much grief to the whole of the West Riding. That sorrow stayed with many families right up until the outbreak of the Second World War, and it was a common experience on visiting a house in what is now metropolitan West Yorkshire to see, on the wall, the photograph of father, brother or son, in uniform, and empty shell cases, chromium plated on the mantelpiece.

Drake was rejected for military service on health grounds and died three months after the end of the war, in February 1919. How great was Yorkshire's loss can be seen from some of their last performances. Booth and Drake bowled unchanged against Gloucestershire, Booth taking 12 wickets and Drake eight, the first time this feat had been accomplished since Hirst and Haigh in 1910. Drake then went on to take all ten wickets in Somerset's second innings, finishing with match figures of 15-51, Booth and Drake again bowling unchanged and Booth, on 5-27, deliberately allowing Drake the ball when he saw he had a chance of all ten.

In that fateful year of 1914 Drake took 158 wickets and Booth 155, and each scored more than 800 runs. Almost a century later it is hard to accept that two such splendid all-round cricketers were never to be seen wearing the White Rose again.

Rhodes to Hutton 1919–1939

The Great War was not over by Christmas 1914, as had been the initial optimistic hope, and as the conflict widened and deepened the county cricket clubs had to consider their financial stability and resources. Yorkshire's members, asked to continue their support despite the absence of cricket, responded so well that the club was able to collect £5,560 in subscriptions, a sum that enabled the structure to remain and donations to continue towards the upkeep of playing grounds. Allowances were also given to the professionals who, when duties permitted, were able to appear in charity matches.

The Club office, then in Leeds centre, became the headquarters of the West Riding Volunteers, the County Adjutant being the Major Lord Hawke, a distinguished militiaman of the previous century. When the Major was promoted to Colonel he was followed in the post by Captain Frederick Toone, and should any reader suspect that these jobs were sinecures it should be remembered that the Volunteers comprised 20 battalions of infantry, five motor sections and two ambulance corps.

Yorkshire despatched almost 500 parcels of cricketing materials to military camps at home and abroad, and it was estimated that more than £20,000 was raised for war charities by the playing of matches. Yorkshire cricket's contributions were worthy of her.

After the cessation of hostilities, 1919 brought a colder, harder world. The day of the great amateur had passed and although amateurs would continue to make substantial efforts in first-class cricket for another 30 years, much of the wealth and blood of their families had been spent on the Western Front. Rich patrons were to linger on for another 20 years or so, the Duke of Devonshire's family still supporting Derbyshire, but they became fewer as the World rolled on into the Jazz Age, the hedonism of living for the moment, engendered by the war, continuing into the 1920s.

Cash was much tighter. Clubs had to double admission charges partly to provide for the new Amusement Tax, and MCC, as if fearful that leisure hours and a love of cricket were also in shorter supply, agreed to a programme of two-day Championship matches in 1919, the hours of play being 11.30 am to 7.30 pm. The experiment was regarded as a disaster all round, not least the late closures, there being few spectators left by that hour of the evening – an experience that was to be visited upon the Test and County Cricket Board almost 70 years later when they attempted to continue play until 8 pm or later in order to complete a mandatory number of overs in the day. Essex, never afraid of innovation, did try to keep their public at the ground in 1919 by advertising that 'supper will be provided at the close of play', but by 7.30 pm of an evening, no matter how fine, even the most ardent cricket-lover is anxious for dinner, the odd glass of refreshment and convivial company.

This same year also brought a 'new' method of deciding the Championship. From 1895 to 1909 it had been decided on the basis of one point per win, one point deducted for each defeat, the order being determined by the proportion of points won to games played. An increasing number of drawn games had brought about the next change, in 1910, when the order became dependent upon the percentage of wins to games played. The following year brought the introduction of first-innings points in drawn matches – a system that stayed, despite the anomalies, until 1919 when, with truncated two-day games, it was felt that the 1910 method was best suited to the circumstances.

Roy Webber, who made as detailed a study of the Championship as a professional cricket historian, always insisted that dividing the number of games played by the number of victories promoted the most aggressive county cricket up until the time when all counties played the same number of Championship matches. 'Old Ebor' was one who would not have agreed with Mr

Webber, even though Yorkshire won the first post-war Championship at a time when they were not expected to make a serious challenge. He pointed out that 'every unfinished match meant a lowering of the clubs concerned'.

Yorkshire, in fact, learned of the winning of their tenth Championship at Victoria Station, London at 9 pm in the evening of their last day of the season, on their return from Brighton. Rain had washed out the first day, Yorkshire had declared on the second with a lead of 87, and Sussex were 38-2 in their second innings when, with an hour's play left, the rain returned. Kent needed

Lancashire, Middlesex, Kent, Hampshire and Sussex, but they would also, by the same reckoning, have lost to Surrey at The Oval.

For Yorkshire to have succeeded, after a break of four Summers and with a much-changed team, was a pleasant surprise in the Ridings. Booth, Drake, Benny Wilson and Sir Archibald White had gone, Hirst was 48, Rhodes 42, and Kilner had been wounded. Rhodes and Kilner, both principal batsmen in 1914, had to start bowling again. The new captain was D.C.F. (David) Burton, who had first batted for Yorkshire while a Cambridge undergraduate in 1907. An excel-

Yorkshire CCC 1932, Captain Frank Greenwood, third from right
Ron Deaton collection

to defeat Middlesex at Lord's over the same two days to retain the Championship, and it was only after 'Old Ebor' had telephoned the Yorkshire Post office that the news spread that Middlesex had forced a draw.

Yorkshire, as well as 'Old Ebor', would have had good reason to complain about the scoring method had Kent succeeded, for they had played only 14 matches to Yorkshire's 26, of which 11 were drawn, an increasingly probable result in two-day matches. Yorkshire felt that but for time and weather they would have defeated

lent sprinter at Rugby School, he had won his Blue at Rugby for three successive years and was, not surprisingly, regarded as a brilliant cover-point. He served with the Northumberland Fusiliers before succeeding White, and he developed, always listening to Hirst and Rhodes, into a shrewd captain and useful middle-order batsman. He must also be given much of the credit for rebuilding the side in a difficult period.

With hindsight, Yorkshire might have retained Benny Wilson for another season or so for, at 39, he had a record of 15 centuries. The Committee

Percy Holmes A gloss

It was his great misfortune to be born a contemporary of Sutcliffe and Hobbs: had neither existed it is likely that Holmes, from Oakes near Huddersfield, would have been remembered as an outstanding, possibly great Test-match batsman. He had all the attributes, including a gloss to his batting that meant many of his innings were more enjoyable than those of his partner Sutcliffe. As a pair they were worthy openers to follow Ulyett and Hall and then Tunnicliffe and Brown, and for figures they were unapproachable.

They raised 69 century opening partnerships for Yorkshire, 74 in all matches, and in 1932 they surpassed the 554 of Tunnicliffe and Brown against Derbyshire by one run to set a new world record, the occasion being the match at Leyton against Essex. Sutcliffe played on when 313; thereupon Sellers declared, only to see the scoreboard move back to 554!

The scorers, on checking, could find only 554 runs and while arguments raged in the scorebox, press box and pavilion, 'a reverend gentleman in the crowd', according to Holmes, suggested that a no-ball might have been missed. This apparently convenient solution was met with considerable scepticism, not least by *Wisden*, which commented: 'Some of the circumstances surrounding this Leyton achievement were not quite desirable owing to the scorers being unable to see what was exhibited on the board.' At least one contemporary county captain felt that the Essex captain in that match should have protested at the later alteration.

However, Leslie Duckworth tracked down the two umpires, Frank Field and 'Tiger' Smith, and the later insisted that a no-ball had been missed, the first ball of the opening over of the day which Holmes played to mid-on, not taking a run. 'Tiger' insisted that he had had a signal from the Yorkshire scorer Billy Ringrose who, at that moment, was attending to both scorebooks, the Essex scorer answering a call of nature

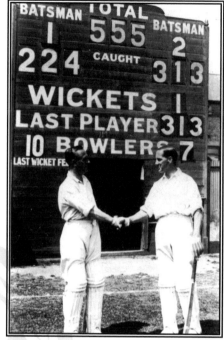

Percy Holmes (left) and Herbert Sutcliffe break the Yorkshire first wicket partnership record at Leyton, Essex in 1932'
Ron Deaton collection

(according to Ringrose).

If the umpire's call was acknowledged that no-ball was not debited until later in the day, after Ringrose had been convinced that he had failed to record it. An unsatisfactory means of breaking a record, perhaps, but as *Wisden* added a little more gracefully: 'Had they [the batsmen] not felt assured they had beaten the record, they could have put on heaps more runs.'

Since 1932 Holmes has been remembered as much for that one day at Leyton as for any of his long list of honours. Yet in his time he was accepted, by all but the selectors, as one of the shining stars in the firmament. A right-hander, he was compared by Peter Thomas to Denton for his attacking approach to the opening bowling, although 'Denton had the conscience to bat further down the list than number one.'

Holmes reached Yorkshire in 1913 via

Lindley Zion Sunday School, Golcar Paddock and then Spen Victoria, batting as low as number ten, but a 61 scored against Middlesex in the following year confirmed the promise his admirers had been reporting to the county club. He first met Sutcliffe when both boys were travelling on the top deck of a Leeds tram between City Square and the Headingley nets. A famous partnership was formed which was to flower in 1919, at Sheffield against Nottinghamshire, after Holmes had made 99 in the opening fixture against MCC at Lord's.

Holmes' aggregate that season was 1,877 and included a partnership with Sutcliffe of 253 against Lancashire. A year later he had moved from 17th to fourth in the national averages with an aggregate of 2,254 at 50.08. Astonishingly he was not selected for Douglas' team for Australia that following Winter (in which, of course, England lost all five Tests) but in the following years he was past 2,000 runs on another six occasions and included a 315 not out against Middlesex at Lord's in 1925.

He played only seven times for England, including once against Australia, Gregory and McDonald, at Trent Bridge in 1921, but was not selected again in that series as one of the selectors decided that he was unsettled by pace. As Holmes was England's top scorer, with 38, it was a harsh judgement. He then toured South Africa under Stanyforth, four times topping 50 in the five Tests, and after his Leyton effort opened with Sutcliffe against All India in 1932, but his great days were past and he retired the following year. He was often taxed as to why he thought he had been given so few opportunities by England, but would turn away such queries with a smile; he once told Norman Kilner: 'I'm not saying, lad. I'm happy playing with my own team.'

He was a very cheerful and popular cricketer, a master, according to Pelham Warner, of the square-cut and hook, and his expertise with the latter stroke hardly suggests he lacked courage; indeed, that same expertise is supposed to have been developed, as a boy, by a school coach who ensured that his charges stayed in line by tethering the back foot to the leg stump.

It is a fact that through much of his 224 not out at Leyton, an innings that lasted seven hours 25 minutes, he was troubled by lumbago.

Holmes' fame may shed a lesser light than that of his formidable partner but it is always a pleasant glow, affectionally remembered. He died in 1971, aged 84, a few miles from where he was born.

---

may have felt that his ultra-cautious batting was unsuitable for two-day matches and taken the decision to draft in new blood – and who can say now, as the names appeared one by one, that they were wrong?

Percy Holmes and Tommy Birtles had appeared in 1913 to be followed the next year by Ernest Smith of Ossett who was thought, all too briefly, to be a possible successor to Wilfred Rhodes or Roy Kilner as the slow left-arm bowler. The season of 1919 was a fruitful one, for among the ten debutants were Herbert Sutcliffe, Norman Kilner, Emmott Robinson, Abe Waddington and a future captain, Geoffrey Wilson.

Burton had since revealed how he began the season with Rhodes and Holmes as his opening batsman with that young man from Pudsey, Sutcliffe, at number seven, and it was only after several discussions with Hirst that, later in the season, he moved Sutcliffe up to number two to create one of the great partnerships. Burton could take less credit for Waddington's introduction, having been hit under the eye by Jack Gregory during a match at Sheffield against the Australian Imperial Forces, and missing several matches. While Hirst stepped in as captain Waddington entered the side in June, and almost immediately Yorkshire sensed they had the bowler they needed to turn them into a team of traditional prowess.

Burton also worked hard on polishing up the fielding, winning praise from Charlie Macartney: 'You have the best fielding side in

Herbert Sutcliffe Man of Style

Sutcliffe is now remembered as the junior partner to Hobbs in the greatest English opening partnership; a right-hand batsman of iron resolve who could seemingly play any bowler on any surface and one who batted the better as the odds against him increased, no matter what the condition. On figures alone he stands among the immortals (50,135 runs at an average of 52, 1,000 runs or more in 21 Summers), but there was much more to the man than that.

Sutcliffe could have become, had he chosen, the first great professional to turn amateur for he cloaked his hard professionalism in an amateur's lifestyle. When in 1939 half the Yorkshire team joined HM Forces, the amateurs became officers as a matter of course while the professionals, Sutcliffe, Verity and later Smailes excepted, were among the ranks. Even the War Office must have accepted that Herbert Sutcliffe would be a disconcerting subordinate for any young subaltern. Sutcliffe played his lifetime's innings with the aplomb of a brigadier.

Sutcliffe was born at Summerbridge, near Harrogate. His father was a medium-pace bowler of such accuracy that he was called for Yorkshire trials at the same time as George Hirst. While Herbert was a baby the family moved to Pudsey where his father played for St Lawrence, while the son played for the other Pudsey club, Britannia, making his first-team debut at 14. He lost both his parents while a small child and was brought up by his three aunts who must have accepted early on that they were nurturing a cricketer.

As a boy he was remembered for his assiduous practice, particularly at the nets, where even as a child he would continue as long as someone would partner him. At 16, on the first day he wore long trousers, he played his first match for Yorkshire Colts, finishing his first season with an average of 35.

He later recalled how, as a Colt facing

Herbert Sutcliffe
Yorkshire Post

George Hirst, a mighty in-swinger came at him 'like a cow's horn' to bowl him. He broke a Bradford League batting record in 1914, when 20, with an aggregate of 715 at an average of 47. In the Great War he served with the Ordnance Corps and then the Sherwood Foresters. While stationed at York he would take French leave to cycle to Pudsey to play for St Lawrence under an assumed name, a common practice at the time that the officers commanding must have winked at.

Before the war ended, Sutcliffe was commissioned into the Green Howards and was playing for West of Scotland. In May 1919 he scored 51 for the Colts against Yorkshire at Headingley, a signal that he was ready for a greater arena.

The Great War, of course, took four years from all cricket careers and when Holmes and Sutcliffe came together to form their mighty partnership, Percy was already 32, Herbert 24, the pairing first being made by Burton, against Kent, at Leeds at the end of June. Both went on to score five centuries that season: they raised five century partnerships, each scored more than 1,800 runs, both averaged over 44 and both were named among *Wisden's* Five Cricketers of the Year, Sutcliffe's first Summer being described as 'without parallel. This being so, the highest honours of the cricket field should fall to him in the near future. By reason of his fine driving he is perhaps a more attractive bat to watch than Holmes but he may not be so strong in defence.'

As Leslie Duckworth observed, 'in the light of their subsequent development these assessments read a little strangely for in later years Holmes seemed the more impatient of the two – and it was Sutcliffe who developed a defence without parallel among modern batsmen'.

Sutcliffe was always a fierce driver on the off side and developed a splendid, dismissive hook. 'Sooty', the veteran Bradford journalist Dick Williamson would assert on rainy afternoons at Park Avenue, 'could hook 'em off his eyebrows'.

Contemporary critics asserted that the hook was Sutcliffe's weakness, a notion possibly based on the fact that this was one stroke with which he lived a little dangerously. He profited from it often enough to ensure that opposing bowlers were most careful in their use of bouncers.

That he could hit is confirmed by his position as the leading six-hitter in Yorkshire's history, including ten in an innings against Northamptonshire in 1933 and eight against Gloucestershire in 1932. When this power was added to his vast patience and enormous defensive technique his scoring feats are understandable: between 1922 and 1935 he never failed to score less than 2,000 runs; in 1931 and '32 he topped 3,000. He scored 112 centuries for Yorkshire and 149 in his career; on the 1924-25 tour of Australia he raised a Test aggregate of 734 runs at an average of 81.55 against Gregory and Mailey.

He was shrewd enough to turn down, tactfully, Yorkshire's offer of the captaincy knowing that an acceptance could only upset players senior to himself, notably Rhodes. He was probably the first professional to use, on hot days, what would now be called a deodorant – Cardus referred to it as 'eau de cologne' and there seems little doubt that some fellow professionals regarded his sleek, black hair and crisp, spotless white shirts and general air of superiority as a bit 'uppity'. But if crowds, particularly at Old Trafford, barracked him, Sutcliffe ignored them utterly and his general good nature, good manners and total competence brought him many friends and admirers and few, if any, enemies.

Cardus, who saw more of him than possibly any other cricket writer except Kilburn, wrote: 'He made a strong contrast to the grim conquering Yorkshire XI of his heyday. He was almost decorative among a company out to kill. No "foony" stuff. Yet beneath the outward show of the debonair Sutcliffe was the true toughness. In his bones' marrow Sutcliffe was Yorkshire enough.' Wrote Kilburn: 'He gave to professional cricketers the same sort of credit-card status that Henry Cotton gave to professional golfers.'

Kilburn also recorded how Sutcliffe used every spare minute to attend to whatever professional or social engagement was occupying him: 'Benefits accruing from personal distinction were interpreted by Sutcliffe (when senior professional) as applying to Yorkshire cricket teams. "Thank you for your invitation to (golf or theatre). There will be (eight or fifteen) in the party."'

Herbert Sutcliffe played 54 times for England and died at the age of 84 in Keighley, living long enough to see both Hutton and Boycott join him as scorers of more than 100 centuries.

England.' Emmott Robinson, patrolling the off side with Burton, was one reason for the improvement, soon joining Waddington in opening the attack with his swing bowling before turning to spin.

The opening weeks of the season were hardly propitious, Yorkshire being dismissed by MCC for 120 before being cracked around Lord's for a massive 488. The reply at least demonstrated that Yorkshire remained obdurate: Hirst 180 not out, Roy Kilner 120, Holmes 99, Burton declaring at 528-8.

A thumb injury to David Denton, which put him out of the team for a fortnight, was a factor in a heavy defeat at Old Trafford, where Makepeace and Parkin helped to contrive a Lancashire victory by 140 runs. Parkin's match figures of 14-140 must have made felicitous reading for him over breakfast.

Nottinghamshire then won at Sheffield by six wickets, Yorkshire making a poor showing against slow bowling in their first innings, but after that the only defeat came, rather surprisingly, from Sussex at Harrogate. The return Roses match was to be remembered particularly, with a fanfare of trumpets announcing to the world the arrival of Holmes and Sutcliffe, for their opening stand of 253.

Parkin had a somewhat painful Bank Holiday, finishing with none for 97. At Dewsbury against Hampshire came one of those meteoric performances that occasionally flash across the skies, when a fast right-arm bowler known to the records only as A.C. (Bill) Williams shattered Hampshire with a return of 9-29 in 77 deliveries, hitting the stumps eight times. He also took 5-67 against Lancashire at Sheffield, but then failed to get a single wicket against Middlesex before drifting off into league cricket.

Yet Bradford had provided Waddington and Emmott Robinson for Burton's new Yorkshire team, and Rhodes had taken up his spinners again, still fiendishly accurate if not turning the ball quite so much (155 wickets). Waddington had an extraordinary start. Entering first-class cricket at the beginning of July, he ended with 100 wickets at a cost of 18.74 each. Rockley Wilson, too, made some invaluable contributions

to the bowling, not least against Middlesex at Leeds when, after an opening stand of 100 in 70 minutes, he dismissed Jack Hearne and Bosanquet in successive overs.

The batting, meanwhile, had taken on a new sheen with the establishment of the county's best opening partnership since Tunnicliffe and Brown. There were seven years between Holmes and Sutcliffe when they came together, the latter having made his debut for the Yorkshire Second XI on the day, he recalled, he went into 'long trousers'. They first came together against Kent at Headingley on 30 June, Holmes collecting a duck, but by the Summer's end they had raised five century opening stands and each had scored 500s. The first major partnership was 279 against Northamptonshire at Northampton, Sutcliffe reaching his century with a straight six. The pair were famous, Holmes in cap, Sutcliffe usually bare-headed, his hair glossed.

Hirst, Denton, Rhodes and Roy Kilner also passed 1,000 runs, seven players in all scoring centuries. The Club had completed a long and arduous climb, and the 1920s, a sunlit upland, lay before them. Frederick Delius, who had fond memories of watching cricket at Scarborough and who was about to be asked to write the incidental music for Hassan, would have caught the mood.

The public greatly welcomed the return of three-day 'proper' Championship cricket in 1920, gate receipts increasing by £5,000 and attendances rising by almost 90,000, but the strains told upon the team, which finished fourth. Burton maintained 'we were every bit as good a side as in 1919', yet the records suggest that by the second half of the Summer the bowling was simply not good enough.

Rhodes and Waddington, sharing 296 wickets, all but carried the attack: Hirst, now coach at Eton, was available, along with Rockley Wilson, in the school holidays; Roy Kilner, absent through illness, took only 27 wickets, Robinson only 53.

No criticism could be applied to Rockley Wilson, who bowled, at the age of 41, his right-arm slow-medium spinners so accurately throughout August that he was chosen as vice-

Emmott Robinson Tactician

Emmott was the first of Yorkshire's Robinsons from Keighley, an all-rounder called up, at the age of 36, to patch up the side in 1919, who stayed to become one of the great characters in the post-Great War side. It was Cardus who spotted that Emmott was the epitome of the ultra-professionalism of Yorkshire of the 1920s, when the environment and upbringing of thrift and hard graft permeated their cricket.

He was a useful right-arm swing bowler (9-36 against Lancashire in 1920) but managed 100 wickets in a season only once and reached 1,000 runs only twice. He was a bits and pieces contributor, lean, wiry, an excellent fielder whose service was not to be measured by the figures in the scorebook but by the time and circumstance of his efforts. Emmott had a keen tactical brain and was given credit second only to Rhodes for the running and supervision of the supremely efficient team.

Cardus was so taken by the man that he wrote of him countless times – to such an extent that Emmott, when a veteran, is once supposed to have protested to the writer that he had in fact been reinvented. If some of Cardus' Emmott stories were tarted up a little they did no one harm, least of all Emmott who, after the Second World War, was engaged to write a newspaper column mostly on the strength of the fame he had accrued through Cardus' writings.

His passion, and uncompromising pursuit of Yorkshire's victories, earned him a place in the affection and memory of his contemporaries. In the season after he retired (in 1931, when 48) he had to be called upon to field as substitute in a Roses match and almost instantly appealed for lbw, from short leg. The umpire, Arthur Morton, upbraided him, adding: 'Anyroad, Emmott, it's got nowt to do wi'three. Tha's not really playing.' He was once asked why he did not pursue his useful off-spin occasionally. 'If I did, and one turned then I'd be off, and Wilfred would be on.'

Robinson went on to become an umpire himself, and coached Yorkshire (1944-46) and Leicestershire the following year. He died in Hinckley in 1969 but his spirit lives on, not least around the ringside at Headingley and Scarborough.

---

captain for the Winter tour of Australia, jokingly describing himself as 'the discovery of the season'.

A great deal of cricket was played in 1920. Kent, for instance, increased their programme from 14 two-day matches to 26 three-day games. Yorkshire's Championship cricket was increased from 52 days to 84. This was 'Lucky' Denton's last season (1229 runs with a top score of 209 not out – some farewell!), and Hirst was playing his penultimate Summer in the ranks.

Middlesex were 1920's eventual champions, but only after two extraordinary escapes against Yorkshire. At Bradford, where Rockley Wilson had match figures of 6-62 (from 44 overs!), Yorkshire, due to a splendid Middlesex second-innings revival, had to score 198 and lost eight wickets for 140 which meant that, with Roy Kilner ill, Waddington and Wilson represented the last hope. With four runs needed Waddington drove Stevens straight back, and with no one in the outfield Yorkshire would have won the match and, as it happened, the Championship. The ball hit the opposite wicket, and in the same over Waddington was bowled.

At Lord's earlier in the Summer, after Holmes and Sutcliffe had raised 191, Middlesex had forced a draw after escaping follow-on by one run.

Headingley's growing reputation as a fine batting pitch was glorified on a sunny weekend in June when Hampshire began by scoring 456-2 on the Saturday (Brown 232), a day's play in which Dolphin conceded no byes. Sunday evening brought heavy rain and Yorkshire, batting in returning sunshine on Monday morning, were caught on a 'sticky', being bowled out for 159 and 228.

Two months later, in similar conditions at Portsmouth, Yorkshire batted first. Holmes and Sutcliffe started with 347, Denton then joining Holmes to take the score to 456-2, with Holmes reaching 302 before Burton declared at 585-3. Holmes' innings occupied seven and a half hours, and he was mildly reprimanded for offering two faint chances between 200 and 271. Faced with the enormity of this total, Hampshire collapsed twice to Rhodes (11-129) and Rockley Wilson (5-20 in 25.1 overs in the first innings). Rhodes also scored 63 not out and completed the 'double' for the 11th time, his only characteristic comment being: 'Fancy scratching for it until this time of year.'

There are various references to the frequency of wearing and dusty pitches during this Summer. At Leicester, Yorkshire brought criticism upon themselves by refusing to gamble on winning a first-innings lead in a match curtailed by the weather. In a Championship decided by percentages of matches played, a 'no result' was a more profitable option than a draw on first innings. Yorkshire claimed that they had sought a first innings lead right up until their last partnership (Dolphin and Wilson) and could have played for a 'no result' an hour earlier, but Burton declined when Leicestershire proposed taking the extra half-hour in order to ensure a decision.

Holmes had a magnificent Summer, averaging 54.97 and scoring seven centuries, including two in the Roses match at Manchester, the first time this feat had been accomplished in a Roses match.

The following year, 1921, a much wetter Summer in the North, saw the post-war reorganisation of the team completed, enabling David Burton to stand down from the captaincy that September conscious of a job well done and with the gratitude of the Club and the Yorkshire public. Burton recalled that through his three years he had received regular messages (as did his predecessor White) from an elderly clergyman who, clearly, was as partisan and hawk-eyed as that 1980s observer Tommy Naylor of Mixenden:

I remember he always finished his letters 'Be strong and play a forward game, your fielding crisp and clean and no mistake in catching clean.' Very often too I would receive a telegram from him before a big game which ran 'Yorkshire expects every man this day to do his duty – Watchman.'

Changing customs are recorded:

It is rather curious that in all his great career Wilfred Rhodes did not perform the hat-trick until we played Derbyshire at Derby [1920] …the following game at Northampton produced the hat trick for Waddington in his first season. I had the ball in each case mounted and presented to the performer instead of giving them new hats.

Burton also regretted the loss, that season, of Humphrey Ward, the son of a Malton Vicar who emerged at Shrewsbury as an outstanding football player (an England amateur cap) and cricketer who won his cricket Blue at Oxford in 1919-20 but played only once for Yorkshire before joining the Indian Civil Service. Denton, due to ill health, was replaced by Oldroyd. Rhodes and Kilner bowled in tandem, Kilner over the wicket.

Burton was obviously a popular and successful captain. He even thanked the press on his retirement from first-class cricket.

The team still lacked a high-class fast bowler, but the arrival of George Macaulay, who was advised by Hirst to reduce his pace to medium and to concentrate on medium pace and off-spin, gave the attack versatility and range in English conditions: Waddington and Robinson with the new ball, swing, seam and cut, Rhodes' classical left arm spin, Kilner a little quicker than Rhodes and often bowling over the wicket, when in tandem, to provide a different line, and now the always belligerent Macaulay, seeking a wicket with every ball.

Hirst and Denton had gone, but Edgar Oldroyd appeared as the supporting cast drop-anchor at number three for the next 20 years, the confidence born of a regular place enabling him to expand a game based upon stubborn defence into an instrument of punishment for Yorkshire's

Abraham Waddington Man of Temper

Waddington appeared in July 1919 from Wakefield cricket, although born in Clayton, Bradford, and had an immediate impact, appearing as he did to many followers as another George Hirst. Both bowled left-arm medium to fast but in very different styles: Hirst was powerful, vigorous, Waddington rhythmical, running in on a curve with a classical delivery. There was much difference in temperament too, for Waddington was a volatile personality, quick-tempered and quick-tongued.

In that first half-season of two-day Championship matches, Waddington's line of attack and versatility brought him 100 wickets at 18.74. In 1920 his return was 140 wickets and as the discovery of the first post-war period he went on Douglas' disastrous 1920-21 tour of Australia in which all five Tests were lost. Waddington, used as a stock bowler, was written off as a failure but he returned to England where Yorkshire used him much more profitably and in the following two Summers he added another 237 wickets. He loved bowling to left-handers.

Running up to bowl on a wet outfield at Huddersfield in 1923, Waddington fell and damaged his arm ligaments and was unable to play again until the following Summer when, after a bad-tempered match against Middlesex at Sheffield, the umpires reported him, writing, 'Waddington's attitude towards decisions incited barracking.' Middlesex cancelled the following season's fixtures against Yorkshire but after MCC, at Yorkshire's invitation, had investigated the matter and Waddington had made a written apology, no break in meetings between the two counties occurred. In August of that same Summer there was one report of bad blood between Yorkshire and Surrey, although no formal protests were made.

Abe Waddington
Ron Deaton collection

Waddington came back for one more fiery Summer, in 1925, when he took 105 wickets, but two years later, his powers seemingly in decline at 34 and troubled by the old shoulder injury, he refused Yorkshire's terms, a disappointing end to a comet-like career.

He was a more than useful batsman, although given to an occasional impetuosity that was the despair of Robinson and Rhodes, and he also played football for Bradford City and Halifax Town. In his sixties he joined Hutton and other cricketers to visit Verity's grave at the Military Cemetery at Caserta and left his white rose cap on the gravestone. Abe Waddington died in Scarborough at the age of 66 and Peter Thomas suggested that a phrase of Leslie Duckworth's might have been inscribed on his tombstone: 'Yes a man of temper, Waddington, but a fine cricketer.'

---

enemies. No less a judge than Leonard Hutton thought Oldroyd the best 'bad wicket' batsman he ever saw play.

The season of 1921 was one of great frustration for Yorkshire, Middlesex keeping the Championship after Yorkshire had been deprived of victory by bad weather in four matches that they firmly believed they would have won. Yet in the match that mattered, against Middlesex at Lord's, Middlesex won by an innings and 72, Sutcliffe having to retire with a pulled muscle after two balls in the second innings. 'Old Ebor' insisted that the injury was no excuse for a deserved defeat.

Another blow occurred immediately at the end of the match when the indomitable Dolphin, standing on a chair in the dressing room to reach his locker, fell to the floor and fractured his wrist as the chair collapsed under him. Yorkshire with-out Dolphin, keeper since 1905, seemed inconceivable, especially as, at the age of 35, his return was uncertain. His deputy, the giant 27-year-old Reg Allen from Wakefield, was highly capable (taking six wickets in an innings that Summer), and Dolphin was in fact to return, as vigorous as ever, the following Spring.

Lancashire, with three second-innings wickets down, needed 192 to avoid an innings defeat at Headingley, with little play being possible on the third day. Leicestershire, with four wickets standing, needed 260 to avoid an innings defeat at Leicester, where there was no play at all on the

George Macaulay Mac

George Gibson Macaulay was related to the fast round-arm bowler Charles Macaulay, also from Thirsk, and uncle to Joe Lister. He, too, wished to be a fast bowler when he first appeared at the Headingley nets, a late starter at 23, part of the new wave in 1919-20, and it was Hirst who spotted that the 'Country Boy's' talents were elsewhere than in speed. He had served in the Royal Field Artillery in 1914-18 and was to join the RAF in the Second World War at the age of 43. Between the two wars, up until 1935, he served Yorkshire with zest and unremitting spirit.

Hirst converted him into a medium-pacer of high delivery who could swing the new ball and spin the old from the off; Yorkshire has never possessed another bowler of such sustained hostility. Macaulay, in Yorkshire's cause, was never satisfied: Leyland recorded that in 1933, after Yorkshire had won by an innings at Old Trafford and Macaulay had match figures of 12-49 including the hat-trick and four wickets in five balls, he was lamenting: 'If only they had to go in again.'

In that same year Macaulay took 7-9 against Northamptonshire; four times he did the hat-trick, he shattered Derbyshire in his second season with 6-3 and his 1,773 wickets for the county cost an average of only 17.08. He took a long but short-stepped, aggressive run that made his shoulders sway, often bowling round the

George Macaulay
Yorkshire Post

wicket to use his huge off-break; almost as much feared was his tongue, and that was among his own team-mates. Madam Tussaud's, it was said, needed new wax-works to replace some destroyed by fire: 'They can have my three slips,' snapped George.

A nimble fielder, especially to his own bowl-ing, and good close catcher (six against

Leicestershire in 1933), he, along with Emmott Robinson and Waddington formed a dangerous squad on Yorkshire's lower batting order, often turning an innings when more illustrious names had failed – Macaulay has, in fact, three centuries to his name. His most famous batting performance was for England against Australia at Leeds in 1926, when he scored 76 in a ninth-wicket partnership of 108 to save the match.

Macaulay played for England eight times in all, including the 1922-23 tour of South Africa, but it was on English pitches he was most remembered and feared. 'Antagonism personified' according to Kilburn; 'the passion in his bowling supplied fuel for his most dramatic performances and gave him a strength to endure when a rather frail physique was obviously hard-pressed.'

Bowes saw Macaulay on entering the side in 1929:

> Fiery, hostile, yes, sometimes even wicked, Macaulay was renowned as one of the most magnificent fielders to his own bowling there has ever been. He knew all the dodges. He glared at batsmen, thought nothing of bowling a fast 'un straight at the head and, pouncing on the ball, as lithe as a panther, could hurl it back at the wicket, fast and true.

Sutcliffe claimed that Macaulay was a charming companion off the field but admitted his wit could be sharp.

He was, nevertheless, a much-admired figure at his Barnard Castle school, where he took a side every year after his retirement, which was hastened by rheumatic attacks. He died while in the RAF, at Lerwick in 1940, aged only 43.

third day. Middlesex were dismissed for 82 at Sheffield – there was no play on the second and third days. Surrey were 210-8, needing 49 to escape an innings defeat on the third day at The Oval where it rained continuously from 3.30 pm onwards.

Yet Yorkshire could make little of 'Tich' Freeman at Bradford, Kent winning by nine wickets. The arrival of Rockley Wilson, after term, gave them an additional match-winning bowler (and occasional batsman) for the last two months, but during this time they did not win a game. There was, however, a highly satisfying reprisal against Kent at Tunbridge Wells: the latter needed 265 to win and had reached 216-5 when Waddington and Macaulay swept out the last five men for 17 runs.

Rhodes, at 44, had another astonishing year: 1,329 runs (including 267 not out against Leicestershire at Leeds) and 128 wickets. Macaulay and Waddington also passed 100 wickets, followed by Roy Kilner (61) Robinson (55) and a late burst by Rockley Wilson (51 at 11.19). Oldroyd, Holmes, Sutcliffe, Robinson and Roy Kilner also passed 1,000 runs, and although Yorkshire could not celebrate F.S.

Jackson's election to the presidency of MCC with the Championship, the team was sound and the future looked bright.

Geoffrey Wilson followed White and Burton in winning the Championship in his first season of 1922, although an operation for the removal of his appendix meant that he missed the closing weeks and the final triumph during an August of variable weather. This was a year when social and environmental changes, precipitated and accelerated partly by the Great War, began to invade the national consciousness. Radio broadcasts ("the wireless") began, women had begun attending the University of Oxford, the United States had introduced prohibition of the sale of alcohol, Ireland was free (although the 'Irish Free State' was engulfed in civil war). The writers of the year were T.S. Eliot (*The Waste Land*) and James Joyce (*Ulysses*), while in Italy members of a new political creed, costumed in black shirts, were proclaiming 'fascism'.

Although Yorkshire's 11th Championship win became, in the end, a cliff-hanger, the start was propitious with six successive victories, including two over Northamptonshire. But by the end of May they were meeting stronger resistance,

Leicestershire, for instance, defending for seven hours and 298 runs. As Yorkshire finished 15 behind on the first innings, this was equivalent, under the scoring method, to a defeat and therefore a serious matter. Lancashire and Warwickshire were then added to the victories before Surrey inflicted another first-innings defeat at Bradford, a match Yorkshire would probably have lost completely but for rain on the third day.

Macaulay (5-31) and Roy Kilner helped Yorkshire to an impressive victory over Middlesex at Lord's, by an innings and 21. But delight was soon dispelled by an inexplicable crash against Nottinghamshire at Sheffield where first Richmond (three wickets in four balls) and then Staples (four wickets in three overs for two runs) caused two batting collapses, the margin of defeat being an innings and 75. Yorkshire did, however, beat Nottinghamshire, their great rivals that Summer, at Trent Bridge, recorded two victories over Kent for the first time in 20 years and demonstrated, almost publicly, the player power in the team.

Against Essex, at Harrogate, an arrangement had been made for the team to catch an evening train to Maidstone for the following fixture against Kent. At the agreed closure time Essex, with their last pair at the wicket, needed 60 to avoid an innings defeat. The Yorkshire professionals, no doubt conscious of the winning bonus, thought the extra half-hour should have been taken and made no attempt to catch the early train, thus necessitating an all-night journey that got the team to their Maidstone hotel just before breakfast.

'Old Ebor' refers to the players' 'momentary petulance'. The difference in the attitude of the professional and amateur is neatly if unconsciously summed up by Geoffrey Wilson: 'I feel personally that any match, however serious it might be, and however much may depend upon the result, should be played in the most friendly spirit. The result should be second in importance.'

Wilson also agreed that Yorkshire had come under increasing criticism in the South for slow batting, 'and I feel bound to agree that at times such criticisms have been merited. A score of 450 or so against the weaker counties may have no more practical value than 250 or 300 yet some batsmen are content to plod along at a slow rate of scoring until they pile up huge individual scores.'

The Sussex match at Hull in 1922 brought an electrifying bowling performance from Waddington of seven wickets for six runs in 42 balls; he took his first four wickets without conceding a run. Sussex were dismissed in their second innings for 20, and although they had some revenge in the return fixture at Brighton, dismissing Yorkshire for 42, Wilson's team was able to achieve victory both home and away.

The power of Yorkshire's bowling can be assessed by the record of having had only two centuries scored against them that Summer. The first came from Ernest Tyldesley of Lancashire, whose 178 enabled his side to take a first-innings lead, but in their second innings they lost their last six wickets to Rhodes and Roy Kilner for only 35, Yorkshire making the 146 needed for the loss of four wickets.

The return match, at Bank Holiday in Manchester, had a finish so memorable that the contest entered the list of great Roses matches. A crowd of 20,000 saw the first day's play when Lancashire made 118 and Yorkshire 108-6. Cardus described the action thus: 'Yorkshire batted moderately well against a capital attack, as Lancashire batted with weakness against an attack of not uncommon quality.' Lancashire toiled over their innings but were forgiven by Manchester when Yorkshire sank to 13-3 (Holmes, Oldroyd, Kilner). Rhodes, carpeted by Cardus for his 'ugly two-eyed stance', had two narrow escapes but stayed with Sutcliffe to add 60, but with the score at 79 Yorkshire had lost Sutcliffe, Rhodes and the captain, leaving Robinson and Macaulay to defy an avid Red Rose attack, adding 29 runs until the close.

Why, Cardus demanded to know, was not Sutcliffe an England batsman? The crowd had opportunity to argue the point at length on Monday, for after morning rain play was abandoned. The third day began with Yorkshire scraping that all-important first-innings lead (by four runs) and then taking five Lancashire wickets, in fragile sunshine and heavy atmosphere,

Maurice Leyland

Registered as Morris (a fact winkled out by Dick Williamson) after his birth in Harrogate, Leyland rightly aspired to the more noble spelling for he is properly remembered as a prince of left-handers. Whether batting first or at number six, bowling his left-arm 'foony stuff' or fielding, Leyland was always a principal contributor to Yorkshire and England (41 Tests). He was born to the game for his father had once been a groundsman at Headingley and the boy was appearing in Moorside's team at 12, batting in the Lancashire League at 14 and was Harrogate's professional from his 18th to 20th years.

It was then that Yorkshire, rebuilding after the Great War, called upon him but his progress was slow, averaging 19 in 1921 and only 13 the following seasons. But the club felt there was potential and he gradually blossomed into one of the peers of what Kilburn called the Silver Age, the 1930s. Leyland possessed a magnificent temperament – he scored 137 on his debut against Australia in Melbourne in 1928 – and a hawk's eye, becoming a devastating player against the great right-hand spinners of his day, particularly O'Reilly and Grimmett.

Of medium height, broad-shouldered and thick chested, he was admirably balanced, always suiting his innings to the needs of the team. Leyland was a superb cutter at a time when many of Yorkshire's old professionals thought the shot too risky. He made a thousand runs a season from 1923 to 1939, scored, in all, 80 centuries including three in the 1934 series against Australia and, as a final reminder to Australia, also scored 187 on his final appearance against them, at The Oval in 1938, for a second-wicket partnership of 382 with Hutton.

Had Yorkshire needed his bowling more often he would have been remembered as an accomplished all-rounder. Even as an occasional performer he took 411 wickets at 26 each, including a hat-trick against Surrey and a seven for 52 against

Maurice Leyland
Yorkshire Post

Lancashire.

A courageous, modest, good-natured man, he distilled his experience for the good of cricket and of Yorkshire, for whom he briefly served as a coach on retirement in 1946. He once corrected Cardus: 'Wickets can't be too good: they can be too slow.' On another occasion when the acerbic Arthur Mitchell told Cardus bluntly that his writing was 'too flowery' Leyland interjected: 'Well nobody can say that about thy batting, Arthur.'

Robertson-Glasgow, as usual, captured much of the flavour of this well-loved cricketer:

When runs come easily on a perfect pitch in the sun and life flows gaily as the sparkling Thames, you might not particularly notice him. His element was foul weather. He would disappear into the haze of Bramall Lane, where a sterner sort of game was being played under the name of cricket and entrench himself among the sawdust and the smoke and off breaks and appeals and do his raw, tough work in silence.

Leyland's attitude to bowlers, suggested Robertson-Glasgow, could, with slight change, be taken from a letter by Dr Johnson: 'Any violence offered me I shall do my best to repel. I shall not be deterred by the menaces of a ruffian. Your rages I defy. Your abilities are not so formidable. I pay regard not to what you say but to what you shall prove.'

For most of two decades Leyland represented all that was best in the cricket of Yorkshire and England, and it was his pride to wear Yorkshire's cap when he batted for his country. He died in Knaresborough, aged 66, and his career is commemorated by a set of gates at the Harrogate ground.

---

for 42, before a mid-innings rally left Yorkshire needing 132 to win in about 160 minutes on a pitch that was damp and slow, but which had sowed suspicion in every batsman's mind.

Sutcliffe was caught on the boundary from Parkin's first ball. Oldroyd was run out brilliantly by Makepeace at 30, and before tea Kilner had gone, hitting wildly at 36. In the third over after the interval Holmes was caught behind, and at 52 Robinson went leg before. Rhodes and Macaulay then added 20 and at 6 pm, after Rhodes had taken two boundaries off Parkin in one over, Yorkshire needed another 44 in the remaining hour (including the extra half-hour) with five wickets standing, and Mancunians were thinking of early buses.

Perhaps Yorkshire were too eager to crush their old rivals. At 89 Macaulay tried to clear long on and was caught, Dolphin was caught at 106 and with Geoffrey Wilson off to hospital (with appendicitis) what had appeared to be a Yorkshire victory was being stood upon its head.

Rhodes, 'a Gibraltar of certitude' in Cardus' words, was firm at one end, and with Waddington and Rockley Wilson to come the odds must have still have favoured Yorkshire, but at 6.30 pm, with 25 needed, Makepeace swooped again. Waddington was run out and was so overcome that he stood unbelieving at the wicket for some seconds before running back to the pavilion. Lancashire thus had 25 minutes, or just under, to break the last pair, while Yorkshire had to get as many runs. Rockley Wilson decided that while he might lose the match, Rhodes was the only one capable of winning it, and he stonewalled through seven overs for two runs while Rhodes inched Yorkshire nearer the target.

So came the last over, Yorkshire needing five, Parkin to bowl at Rhodes. 'The crowd,' wrote Cardus, 'sat in dumb futility, all aching eyes but helpless. The tension seemed to have a low throbbing sound.' Four balls Parkin bowled, and four were patted back to him; and Rhodes said afterwards that had he heard the call earlier he would have driven a four through the off side to at least tie the game. But the chance was missed, the fifth ball had been blocked, and Rhodes scored only a single off the last ball. Death or glory? Perhaps only a Roses match could have ended in such a fashion but, with a first-innings lead in their possession, Yorkshire knew that not losing was more important than victory.

So Yorkshire came to the finale. Nottinghamshire needed to beat Hampshire to have a chance of taking the Championship, while Yorkshire failed to win on first innings against Essex. Nottinghamshire did win, and Yorkshire were frustrated by the weather at Leyton. No play, in fact, was possible until the third afternoon when Essex, batting for 15 minutes, lost a wicket for five runs. The match was recorded as a 'no result' which meant that Yorkshire were champions, and although Trent Bridge no doubt felt aggrieved, Yorkshire had won 19 matches (of 30) and lost two, while Nottinghamshire had won 17 (of 28) and lost five.

Five batsmen scored more than a thousand runs, four bowlers took more than a hundred wickets, and Rhodes and Kilner did the 'double', a quality of individual performance that made invalid any suggestion that Yorkshire were unworthy champions. This they confirmed in the most striking manner in 1923 when such was the weight of their talents and the confidence and authority of their play that they won 25 of their

32 Championship matches.

Yorkshire had won 20 matches in 1901; a figure equalled by Kent in 1913; to win 25 in one season meant virtual annihilation of the opposition. Ten counties were beaten both home and away. They led on first innings against Lancashire, Kent, Nottinghamshire and Sussex and were hopeful of victory at the close. Thirteen matches were won by an innings, and the Yorkshire innings topped 300 12 times and failed to reach 100 only once (against Glamorgan). The opposition were dismissed for less than 100 on 22 occasions.

Yorkshire averaged a fraction under 30 runs per wicket, the opposition a fraction under 15. Only one match was lost, to Nottinghamshire at Leeds in early June, and that defeat still needs explanation for with five wickets standing only 36 were needed for victory. Staples, returning over the wicket, then produced a startling upset, and Yorkshire lost by 25.

That one blemish apart, Yorkshire enjoyed triumph after triumph. At Bradford, for the return Roses match, 26,000 saw play on Bank Holiday Monday. The gates were closed hours before the start, and it was estimated that another 50,000 were turned away. Pictures of Park Avenue on that day show the multitude, mostly middle-aged men and women all wearing hats, and what could be one policeman.

Rhodes, Kilner and Macaulay each passed 100 wickets, Robinson (96) and Waddington (65) following, and what was regarded as a poor season for Waddington is explained by an injury in July, when he slipped on wet grass at Huddersfield and pulled ligaments in his left shoulder. Waddington's virtual absence for the rest of the season meant increased opportunities for Kilner, Macaulay and, returning, Robinson.

Rhodes completed yet another 'double' and his 100 wickets for the 14th time brought him level with Hirst's achievement. Kilner and Oldroyd joined Holmes and Sutcliffe in passing 1,000 runs, and this was the first full season for a left-hand batsman of high promise, Maurice Leyland of Harrogate. Leyland, according to that assiduous journalist and statistician C.R. 'Dick' Williamson of Bradford, was registered as

'Morris' on his birth certificate, but cricket has preferred to remember him by the more princely spelling of his first name, for no one would argue that Leyland did not rank among the nobility of batsmen.

The presence of two high-class left-handers (with Kilner) in the Yorkshire order was another example of burgeoning strength. Kilner, too, in Waddington's absence, spent many an hour in tandem with Rhodes. As 'Old Ebor' recorded:

It was nothing uncommon for Rhodes and Kilner to bowl 40 overs or so in the course of an innings and how securely they could keep batsmen 'pegged down' is shown in their proportion of maiden overs.

On the whole season more than a third of the overs bowled by each of these two left-handers were scoreless while not infrequently half was the registered number…though left arm they are bowlers of distinct characteristics.

Rhodes has less of the finger spin than formerly, nor can he get the same bodywork into his deliveries that he could in his younger days but besides being a master of length he has an almost uncanny method of blocking a batsman's scoring avenues.

Kilner spins the ball probably better than any slow bowler in England and it must have been noted that he bowls over the wicket with a frequency very unusual in the case of left-arm bowlers. The effect is to make a contrast with Rhodes which unsettles the batsman, also it enables Kilner occasionally to slip in his fast 'going away' ball by which many batsmen have been taken unawares, or get them leg before with an illusive straight one.

'Old Ebor' pointed out that Yorkshire had perhaps been slow to assess Kilner's possibilities as a bowler, explaining that when he first appeared in the side there were three left-arm bowlers ahead in Hirst, Rhodes and Drake and that he had to wait for a retirement and a death to be given the chance of fulfilment. Leyland was given his cap before he had played 50 innings.

Arthur Mitchell Ticker

The nickname should be more properly spelt 'Tikka', it being applied first by Yorkshiremen returning from a coaching engagement in India and, as Mitchell put it: 'It stuck.' A Baildon man, dour, hard and patient, he batted right-handed and served Yorkshire mostly at number three in succession to Oldroyd, although he was often pressed as an opener, and this after waiting six years in the Colts for an opening to appear.

He was a wonderful catcher at slip and more notably at gully, especially to Verity, whose ability to make the ball bounce and whip away needed specialist close attention in the field which Mitchell always provided. His batting, he admitted, was based on a solid defence and his obduracy was known to incite opposing crowds, especially Lancashire's, whom he delighted in riling. But he could also score quickly when necessary and was as powerful a driver as any in Seller's team although it was a stroke he would normally use sparingly.

In 1933, the one season when he passed 2,000 runs, he and Sutcliffe scored 105 in 55 minutes against Surrey at Bradford, after Hutton had been dismissed when Yorkshire needed 199 to win against the clock. He passed 1,000 runs ten times in his 17 seasons, scored 39 centuries for Yorkshire (44 in all) and played six times for England.

His call-up is a legend. England were playing South Africa at Leeds and Leyland had to withdraw, through illness, on the morning of the match. Yorkshire were not playing and Sellers was deputed to drive to Baildon, ten miles away, to pick up Mitchell, who was in his garden. 'Let me tidy me-sen up a bit,' he told Sellers, who then drove him at such speed back to Headingley that forever afterwards Mitchell gave the impression that playing in his first Test match came as a relief. He scored 72 of an opening partnership of 128 made in 110 minutes, but although he toured India under Jardine in 1933-34 he could not consolidate a place in the face of the stern

Arthur Mitchell
Ron Deaton collection

competition at that time.

Mitchell was a dry, straight man who was much respected as the county coach after the Second World War and yet it will be for his close fielding that he will be best remembered, making slips to gully as much his kingdom as it had been Long John Tunnicliffe's. 'What's tha doing here?' he queried of the young Hutton when he was first moved into the slips; but the remark 'Ticker' Mitchell's memory will be treasured for came when he was joined in that department by another brilliant young fielder, Ellis Robinson. Ellis made a diving catch followed by a somersault, throwing the ball in the air and catching it again as it dropped. The Headingley crowd were on their feet cheering a magnificent piece of athleticism and co-ordination. 'Gerrup,' growled Mitchell, standing alongside. 'Tha's makkin' an exhibition o' thisen.' Gully, reported Kilburn, became a key position because of Verity's turn and lift and there Mitchell excelled. Mitchell was always ready to pounce, creeping forwards, to make incredible catches from sometimes a defensive bat.

Mitchell was Yorkshire's coach from 1945 to 1970 and he died, aged 74, in a Bradford hospital on Christmas Day 1976. He was, said *Wisden*, 'a wonderful man in a crisis. No match was ever lost until the opposition had got him out.'

Mitchell's austerity, according to Gerald Howat, lay in his total reluctance to award praise or encouragement (he relented a little in his coaching days): 'After one particular burst of sarcasm, Hutton "gave him a wide berth. He was too hard for me." Sutcliffe described him as "grim as a piece of stone from Baildon Moor".'

The fielding in 1923 was said to compare with that of any previous Yorkshire XI, with Macaulay, Kilner, Rhodes and Robinson close in and Holmes, Sutcliffe, Oldroyd and Leyland in the deep. Geoffrey Wilson was an outstanding cover-point, while Dolphin recovered from his wrist injury of the previous year to return better than ever.

The shadow over Yorkshire's cricket – a growing conviction among some spectators and some players that success was an inherent right and failure a blasphemy against God and nature – grew longer in 1924, culminating in a stormy return match against Middlesex that all but brought about a suspension of fixtures between the two county clubs.

The team's first tour was another easy conquest, Glamorgan, Gloucestershire and the University of Cambridge all succumbing, the match at Cardiff ending by 3.30 pm on the second day, with Kilner and Macaulay sharing 16 wickets. Yorkshire were now, to use the modern term, the superstars of county cricket, and Headingley attracted 25,000 spectators for the first day of the first home match, against Surrey. Rain prevented a finish, after Oldroyd's century, but the triumphal procession continued with wins against Northamptonshire and Nottinghamshire, the first indication that all was not well with the temper of a highly successful team coming with the visit to Lord's to play Middlesex. A Test trial claimed Holmes, Sutcliffe, Kilner, Macaulay, Hearne and Hendren.

Middlesex stiffened their side with amateurs who proved to be more consistent than Yorkshire's young professionals. Yorkshire were dismissed for 192, to which Middlesex replied with 456-8, Frank Mann hitting Rhodes for four sixes in his 79, two of them successive hits on to the pavilion roof. The shock to the nervous system was such that Yorkshire's second innings collapsed, the margin of defeat being an innings and 152.

Clearly Yorkshire were seeking revenge when Middlesex visited Bramall Lane in July, but the pitch played more easily than expected and Middlesex, sent in, raised 358, a foundation that ensured a drawn match. A highly unpleasant first day led to the umpires reporting to MCC that Waddington's attitude had incited barracking. Yorkshire asked MCC to set up an inquiry, but this was pre-empted by a letter from Middlesex cancelling fixtures for 1925. They must have been mollified by MCC's report, which substantiated both their complaints and the umpire's report; Waddington's conduct was criticised and the inference was that Yorkshire's general behaviour, and the captaincy of Geoffrey Wilson, were not beyond reproach.

Communications between the two county clubs were not published, but Waddington did write a letter of apology to MCC and fixtures were not interrupted. However, while letters were flying between Leeds and Lord's, Yorkshire came under attack again, in a London newspaper, for alleged incidents in a match against Surrey at The Oval. Whatever the basis for the story there were no complaints from Surrey to Yorkshire, but in a stormy season Yorkshire were left in no doubt about their unpopularity, especially in London. They were in danger, wrote J.M. Kilburn, of becoming 'social outcasts'.

The Oval match brought Yorkshire's third defeat of the season. Left to score 300 on the final afternoon on a wearing pitch Yorkshire, with Holmes, set out to avoid defeat and were roundly accused of wasting time. The loss of four wickets quickly, to Sadler, encouraged Surrey to take the extra half-hour, in which they completed a win by 109.

Earlier in that 1924 season Yorkshire engaged in a Roses match at Headingley that fully deserves the description 'sensational'. The Whitsun weather was uncertain and Lancashire, batting first, spent four hours in compiling 113.

On the Monday, Yorkshire reached 130 before Kilner and Macaulay routed Lancashire for 74, leaving Yorkshire the formality of scoring 57 to win on the Tuesday morning, a vast 30,000 crowd catching their trams or trudging off in some jubilation at such an exhibition of Yorkshire's prowess.

According to Cardus, a good and affable crowd turned up under blue sky on that final morning as Holmes and Sutcliffe, with 25 opening partnerships of 100 or more behind them, walked out to knock off the runs, a small dog raising laughter as he trotted at their heels.

The pitch was still not to be trusted but was, if anything, a little slower than on the previous day, and Lancashire began with their slower bowlers Parkin and Richard Tyldesley. Sutcliffe had scored three of the 57 when he was leg before to the third ball of Parkin's second over, bowled round the wicket and breaking back. Tyldesley, in the next over, gave Holmes four orthodox leg-breaks and then hit his pads with the top-spinner: 2-3. In Tyldesley's next over he caught and bowled Leyland: 3-3. The crowd was silenced, Lancashire suddenly inspired, and Yorkshire aware that a simple stroll had turned into a hard climb.

The score remained at three when Oldroyd was surprised by a vicious off-break from Parkin that he turned into the leg-trap where the diving Iddon missed the catch. Rhodes, at the other end, tried to break the bowler's grip by hitting out and ten were added before Rhodes was hopelessly confounded by another leg-break: 4-13. Before another run could be added Oldroyd was bowled utterly by Parkin; a spasm of rain threatened to end the agony for both teams, Kilner continuing where Rhodes had left off, while Robinson played with caution. Another three runs and Robinson was run out: 5-16. The left-handed Kilner seemed to have the measure of Tyldesley,

actually reaching the boundary, so Lancashire countered his pugnacity by trying to keep him from the bowling.

Turner was bowled by Tyldesley – 7-23 – which brought Macaulay, a batsman given to quick solutions, to join Kilner, and the eighth-wicket pair actually added nine before he, too, was bowled by Parkin: 8-32. Tyldesley then bowled Waddington and had Dolphin stumped, both for nought, and Yorkshire, amazingly, were all out for 33. 'Old Trafford will talk about this famous day till the end of cricket's history,' wrote Cardus.

Again according to Cardus, the conductor of the Leeds tram that was carrying him back to the City station was so overcome by the news that he completely forgot to signal any stops all the way from Headingley to City Square, standing on his platform and shaking his head, saying 'Who'd a tho't it? Who'd a tho't it?'

The Leeds crowd did have the manners to give Lancashire's surprised and happy players, almost dancing for joy in the sunshine, a proper reception as they returned to the pavilion after bowling out Yorkshire for their lowest score in the series. It was a fitting way to crown Lancashire's jubilee year.

All the above suggests that Yorkshire had an unhappy and unsuccessful season, when in fact they celebrated a third successive Championship, winning 16 of their 30 matches in a damp Summer in which five fixtures involving other counties were lost without a ball being bowled. Middlesex had good reason to claim that they were the strongest county and finished second, winning 11 of their 22 games, while Surrey, third, were beaten only once in 24 matches. Middlesex slipped up twice, against Kent, where they failed to take first-innings lead, and against Gloucestershire at Bristol, while Yorkshire rarely gave opponents a second chance.

Five batsmen passed 1,000 runs, Macaulay and Kilner headed the national averages and while Rhodes, Robinson and Waddington were all perhaps a little behind their form of previous years, the five together were unmatched in county cricket.

Arthur Wood Rhubarb

'A rare and vigorous character' was G.D. Martineau's summary of Wood, a short, stocky man from Bradford who succeeded Arthur Dolphin as Yorkshire's wicket-keeper and went on to create two records, since overtaken: he kept wicket in 225 consecutive matches (J.G. Binks) and was the first keeper to pass 1,000 runs in a season (D.L. Bairstow). A witty, cheerful humorist, 'Rhubarb' or 'Sawdust' joined the Bradford club from Eccleshill Parish Church team and was given his chance when Dolphin became an umpire. His ability to take Macaulay, Bowes and Verity, all difficult bowlers, won him his place immediately.

He was especially capable down the leg side and throughout his career, 1927-46, he averaged 60 victims and 700 runs a season, a consistency that might have won him more than four Test appearances. His most famous call came in 1938 for the Oval Test against Australia when he arrived by taxi from Scarborough: 'It's my first Test; I'll do it in style.' He was then 40 and the oldest player to make his debut for England; he went in to bat with the score at 770-6, made 53 in a stand of 100 in 90 minutes, was caught and bowled off a full toss and returned to the dressing room to throw his bat across in mock disgust: 'Just like me to lose my head in a crisis.'

It was Wood who first coined one of cricket's most famous remarks. Verity was being given some fearful hammer by the South African Jock Cameron at Bramall Lane when Wood remarked: 'You've got him in two minds, Hedley. He doesn't know whether to hit you for four or six.' One ball was eventually found in the pavilion roof and presented in time to Cameron's widow, a story confirmed by a witness on the day, John Wood of Rotherham.

Arthur's companions, wrote Kilburn, 'appreciated him as a competent technician who filled a difficult part in a bowling scheme that relied so much on catches from the edge of the bat and they also gave him licence to wear cap and bells in the light relief desirable to balance the intense concentration applied to business on the field'. Asked to stand down for the Cambridge Blue Paul Gibb, towards the end of his career, he did so without complaint.

He died at Ilkley, aged 75, in 1973.

Geoffrey Wilson resigned in the Autumn of 1924, at the age of 29, after winning three Championships in his three years of office. He never revealed his reasons publicly, but probably felt he had to assume responsibility for the clouded Summer and that his departure might help to heal the breach with Middlesex. The Committee, in turn, felt that a firmer hand was needed with some of the more temperamental professionals, and while Hawke used his influence at Lord's to keep the peace he may also have engineered a change of captain. At the same time Hawke, as ever, was defending his 'boys': 'You never meet a "rotter" in these post-war days. They are men, good straight fellows, some of the very flower of the land.'

Wilson took with him the gratitude of the membership and public, for Yorkshire's following was rarely greater than in his years. The players certainly admired him, especially for his fielding, and his farewell gesture to the team was to arrange a coaching appointment at his old school, Harrow, for the man who had been at his right hand through those three Summers, Wilfred Rhodes.

The new man, Arthur William Lupton, was a soldier, an army major who took over the captaincy at the age of 46, although he had made his debut as early as 1908. Born in Bradford, he had attended Sedbergh and was a hard-hitting left-hander and fast-medium bowler who was never quite a first-class player although very successful at club level, notably for Yorkshire Gentlemen. His task was to restore discipline and dignity to the Yorkshire team and this he did admirably, leaving the cricket to a joint dictatorship of Rhodes and Emmott Robinson. In effect the structure was virtually unchanged, but a new and respectable façade was added.

Lupton led the side into 1925, the last English Summer free of Test matches, when the County Championship was the sole competition. Much as many cricket-lovers see 1925 as the end of halcyon days, 'we must not make a fetish of Test matches' was Hawke's warning.

Without Test-match calls, Yorkshire could field their full handsome power to go through the Summer of 1925 undefeated in 32 matches and winning 21. Holmes had a magnificent Summer, scoring six centuries and 2,543 runs; Sutcliffe also passed 2,000 while Rhodes, Leyland, Oldroyd and Kilner all passed 1,000, no mean achievement for the middle-order men who, in a side of such dominance, were rarely given the chance to bat twice in one match. Twelve victories were won by an innings.

Macaulay passed 200 wickets and was at his peak – antagonistic, hostile, demanding a victim with every delivery. Yorkshire's five principal bowlers shared 546 wickets, and as all could use the bat, one can imagine Lupton's team, so well equipped were they for all conditions, winning all four competitions today – the Championship, knockout competitions and the League, and

Twenty-20. True, their fielding might have been shown up, but there was enough tactical intuition and invention in the team to match speed and throwing with intelligence and placing.

The 1925 team photograph exudes confidence: of the 12 players pictured only John Bell, the Batley-born opening batsman who was later to play for Glamorgan, lacks his county cap. Major Lupton looks every inch a man who expects to be addressed as 'sir'. Waddington wears a slight scowl, Rhodes clasps his hands that have wrought miracles in Yorkshire's service, Robinson looks quizzical. There could have been no doubt in the photographer's mind that he was recording champions for posterity.

The matches against Middlesex were, for once, regarded as of even more concern and importance than the Roses encounters. At Lord's Yorkshire recorded a major triumph, winning by an innings and 149 runs; Middlesex were dismissed for 118, Holmes and Sutcliffe replied with a stand of 140, and the declaration came at 538-6 (Holmes 315 in 410 minutes, 38 fours) before Middlesex, despite some resistance from Stevens and Hearne, were bowled out again.

Sussex gave Yorkshire a fright at Bradford in

Wilf Barber Old Tiddly-push

Barber, from Cleckheaton, was in Gerald Howat's words the 'fourth pillar' (after Sutcliffe, Leyland and Mitchell) of Yorkshire's batting in the mid-1930s. A right-hand bat and fast-medium bowler, an excellent fielder, he, like his contemporary Cyril Turner, was an invaluable member of the side who took what few opportunities came his way.

His true value to Yorkshire was to be seen when England demanded three or four players from the side; it was then that players such as Barber and Turner were able to demonstrate their own right to wear the White Rose.

Again like Turner, he had to wait for his place, making his debut in 1926 after joining the Warwickshire ground staff. He went

to Scarborough in 1929 and rejoined Yorkshire in 1932, missing 1,000 runs only once in the next nine seasons and, with Hutton, managing 1,000 again in 1946. Barber twice scored double hundreds, scored 27 centuries for Yorkshire and compiled 346 with Leyland for the second wicket against Middlesex at Sheffield in 1932. He played well enough in 1935 to win a place in two Tests against South Africa.

Kilburn described Barber as 'a handsome batsman, small in stature but upright in style with a liking for the off-drive. He was happier in the routine situation than crisis and he preferred the trustworthy pitch to the turning ball but in his own unassertive way he fitted neatly into Yorkshire's pattern.'

He played on for one match in 1947 and died in Bradford, aged 67, in 1968.

Cyril Turner

Cyril Turner, from Wombwell, batted left-handed, bowled medium pace right, fielded superbly anywhere, yet was a quiet man who, in Kilburn's eyes, was 'self-effacing and made of modesty'. Nevertheless, Turner served Yorkshire over a span of 31 years and was the first to spot, while coaching at Sheffield United, the enormous potential of Freddie Trueman.

His patience can be assessed by his record: he first played in 1925 but did not break into the side until eight years later and did not win his cap until 1934. If substantial contributions from him were rarely needed, he could perform when necessary: 51 out of 101 on a drying pitch against Warwickshire, who raised 45; 7-54 on a bitterly cold day against Gloucestershire; in 1937, against a then strong Derbyshire side, he scored 81 not out and then took 5-45 and 3-63.

Cyril Turner was an ideal reserve, a player who could do a little of everything and accepted his role with good grace and gave it great endeavour. As a fielder he was ranked with Mitchell and Sellers. 'They stopped the breath with their catching,' wrote Kilburn. It was Turner's task, when the boy prodigy Hutton came into the dressing room, to look after him.

He played one season after the war and then became senior professional and coach to the Colts before continuing his service as scorer. He died, still talking and watching cricket, aged 66 in Wath on Dearne in November 1968.

August when, by lunch on the third day, they needed 40 to win with six wickets in hand. The legend is that Macaulay drank champagne for lunch, but this cannot be true for if it were Yorkshire would surely have bought the vineyard and stocked every cellar in the county with the conquering vintage of such penetration and accuracy. Macaulay returned from lunch to bowl 33 balls for five wickets and eight runs, while Kilner, at the other end, took 1-8. It was such an astonishing performance that the crowd, ever ready to cheer a Yorkshire success, were all but struck dumb by such a wonder.

Such was the crowd for Middlesex's visit to Headingley (Roy Kilner's benefit) that Holmes was unable to get to the ground for the start and Yorkshire had to open their innings with Sutcliffe and Leyland who, no doubt to Percy's outrage, began with a stand of 218, the declaration this time coming at 528-6 (Sutcliffe 235). Middlesex were then dismissed for 184, but a gallant rearguard led by Stevens batted out time in the follow-on.

Yorkshire's visit to The Oval in 1925 brought in a crowd of 25,000 on the first day, but the contest, ruined by rain, was left drawn. In the four years 1921-25 Yorkshire lost only six of 122 matches.

The next year, 1926, was that of the General Strike, itself an indication of the strong current for social change in the country. An important rising young novelist was Aldous Huxley, 'Rhapsody in Blue' by Gershwin and Respighi's 'Pines of Rome' could be heard on the wireless, Duke Ellington had formed his first orchestra, and one of the most beautiful sounds in popular music was the golden cornet of Bix Beiderbecke. Of far greater moment in the Broad Acres, however, was the fact that, after four successive Championships, the title was stolen away, and by Lancashire!

Yorkshire lost on a fraction of a percentage – 75.71 to 74.28 – after leading the table for most of the Summer, the difference coming in August when Lancashire won their last three matches while Yorkshire won two but lost on first innings to Surrey at The Oval. As Yorkshire did not lose a match and inflicted upon the new champions one of their two defeats, there was some criticism of the system; in fact Lancashire won 17 of 32 matches played, to Yorkshire's 14 of 31.

As the Summer lengthened, Yorkshire's power waned while Lancashire grew in strength.

Bill Bowes Lofty

His nickname was obvious for a man of well over 6ft and more than a little apposite since William Eric Bowes, from Elland, saw the game from a more distant and objective viewpoint than most of his contemporary professionals, a critical detachment that served him well when he later became a much respected cricket correspondent of the *Yorkshire Evening News* and then the *Evening Post*.

As a fast bowler he was one of the great performers of the 1930s, the spearhead of Sellers' attack, capable of genuine pace, an ability to see the ball both ways and, not least, to use his height (6ft 5in) to win an awkward bounce. So effective were Bowes and his great friend and partner Verity that Sellers, supported by electric fielding, was usually able to disguise, to a generally apprehensive opposition, that the support-ing cast of bowlers were not quite as dead-ly as they appeared. Bowes and Verity, man-aged by Sellers, dominated English county cricket so forcibly in the years up to the Second World War that it seemed that their lingering presence could still win matches for Yorkshire even when they were away playing for England.

Bowes was the son of a goods superintend-ent on the Lancashire and Yorkshire Railway who, no player himself, had the country-man's love of the game and took his small son, on Summer evenings, to watch the local club, Armley, in play: 'My earliest memories are of warm Summer evenings – the sun sinking slowly into a red smoke haze beyond the trees, my father, glass in hand, sitting on the form behind me, enjoy-ing the peace of it all.'

The young Bowes performed the hat-trick for West Leeds High School but his mother wanted him to become a teacher, a career for which he was ideally suited. However, when he left school he started in an estate agent's office and became joint secretary and bowler of the Armley Wesleyan Sunday School Club. One Easter Monday he was invited to play in an impromptu match in a

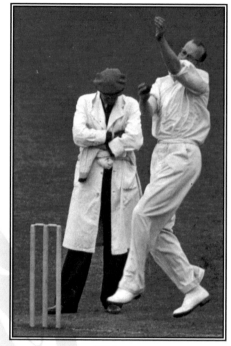

Bill Bowes
Yorkshire Post

Leeds park and his performance led to a further invitation to play for Kirkstall Educational Second XI against Leeds City Gas Works.

By the age of 18 he had learned to type, use shorthand and had a smattering of legal knowledge, all useful skills that would help him later in life. He had to work on Saturdays until 1.15 pm, and on that day managed only a bar of chocolate for lunch but once took six wickets for five runs, including the hat-trick, and won enough from the only collection of his career to buy a pie and treat the team to some 'pop' and to take a proud 'shilling or so' home to show his mother. A career was launched.

Bowes was offered up to £5 a week to turn professional in league cricket (his wages were then £1.22 a week) but a friend per-suaded him to write to Warwickshire for a trial. A neighbour pointed out that MCC, planning fixtures against all the first-class counties, were also seeking to enlarge their ground staff; he was invited for a trial at

Lord's in January 1928, spending the previous Autumn bowling in Armley Park until it was too dark and working in the basement of the estate agent's. He bowled stones at telegraph poles, snowballs at lamp-posts.

At Lord's he bowled for an hour, full out, against, among others, Pelham Warner and the then Assistant Secretary Ronnie Aird, and was offered a season's trial at £5 a week; by this time Yorkshire had been alerted and the Secretary Frederick Toone steered Bowes towards Lord's rather than Edgbaston – 'Yorkshire will be able to play you if you turn out right.' He went immediately to Hirst at the Headingley nets and, characteristically, won another £1 a week on his MCC agreement.

In his first season he performed another hat-trick, against the University of Cambridge at Lord's – the right time, the right team, the right place – won another year's engagement and a rise and on his return to Leeds in September was summoned by Lord Hawke who then concluded a formal agreement with MCC that the 20-year-old should be made available to the county when not required by that club.

In the next two years Bowes, who hitherto had relied on his pace, bounce and a big in-swing, learned diligently, listening to his peers, especially to the then Yorkshire scorer Billy Ringrose, a renowned out-swinger of his day. But it was not until he read an instructional booklet by Sutcliffe, advising a close study of the placing of the feet in delivery stride, that the penny dropped. Once he had included the away swinger in his armoury, Bowes moved from county to Test-class fast bowler.

He took 100 wickets or more in eight of the next nine seasons in an era of batsman's pitches; under a burning sun at Scarborough in 1932 he bowled 40 overs in three and a half hours and took 9-120 against Essex. When pitches did help him he was deadly: in four successive matches in 1935 he took 40 wickets for 321 runs and in August of that same season took 34 wickets in four successive games. His 1,351 wickets for Yorkshire cost 15.16 runs apiece

and it always amused him that his career record also listed 1,251 runs. As a batsman and a fielder he rarely won the approbation of Macaulay and Mitchell.

Bowes was a late selection, behind Larwood, Allen and Tate, for Jardine's Bodyline tour of 1932-33, and although he played in only one Test and took only one wicket, that wicket was Bradman's. In English conditions he made the Australians remember: in 1934 at Lord's he and Verity shared 19 wickets, the pair taking 43 wickets in that series. Bowes did not play until the last two Tests of the 1938 series but finished top of the averages with ten wickets at 18.

Bowes spent two and a half years in prisoner of war camps and returned to England four and a half stone lighter than in 1939; he was never again able to bowl more than medium pace but served Yorkshire for two more years, helping them to a Championship in 1946. He suffered pulled muscles when playing, ironically, in Verity's testimonial match, and although the Club hoped he would continue into 1948 even bowling off-spinners, he retired at the end of that golden Summer: 'Much of the pleasure had gone out of bowling. I had accuracy without pace, there was no nip in my deliveries, the fast yorker was a memory; cricket had become a toil.'

Bowes enjoyed mathematics and conjuring tricks, becoming a member of the Magic Circle, and was a highly respected member of the press from his entry. To many a young reporter he was a friend and genial guide on technical matters, brushing aside thanks by saying: 'I'm only returning a little of the help I received when I first came into the box.' In his retirement years he liked walking his dog on the moors near his Menston home and usually turned up at Headingley for a chat at least once a season.

He died in September 1987. J.M. Kilburn penned an affectionate obituary to his old friend in *The Cricketer* that included the sentence: 'The out swinger had a magnetic quality and Bowes must have bruised more edges than any bowler of his time – in both his careers Billy Bowes was a proud professional and the best of companions.' Asked by *The Observer* to compare Bowes with bowlers a half-century later, Hutton replied: 'He had a little of Willis and a lot of Hadlee.'

Yorkshire won ten of their first 14 matches and drew nine of the last 13 when the weather deteriorated, no less than 11 days of home cricket being washed out. Another influencing factor was the return of a full Test-match programme, Sutcliffe, Kilner, Macaulay and Rhodes all being called upon by the selectors.

The batting remained a bristling fortress to opposing bowlers. Six players passed 1,000 runs and 22 individual centuries were scored despite the loss of Oldroyd after the August Bank Holiday, when he had been struck on the head by the Australian fast bowler McDonald, who had joined Lancashire. The bowling lost a little from August and only Rhodes and Macaulay passed 100 wickets, although Kilner, in all matches, bowled 1,200 overs and of the 890 he bowled in the Championship 340 were maidens – figures a modern bowler may have to read twice to assure himself of their not being misprints.

At Bradford, Lancashire were routed at Whitsun by an innings and 94, their last seven wickets going down in 75 minutes after play had been delayed, on the third day, until 3 pm. Rhodes did not get to bowl. Hendren saved Middlesex at Lord's in the first of the blood matches of that year, but Yorkshire were comprehensive winners at Park Avenue, Kilner taking 6-15 in an hour's bowling on the third afternoon. Glamorgan were beaten by teatime on the second day at Hull, Robinson and Macaulay bowling unchanged in Glamorgan's first innings of 52.

Both Yorkshire and Surrey were sadly under strength at Bramall Lane where Yorkshire's makeshift openers, Leyland and Arthur Mitchell, made a first-wicket stand of 192. Surrey had to follow on, and the Hull fast bowler George Crawford took 5-59. Crawford had first appeared for Yorkshire in 1914 and it is a tribute to his professionalism that he should have returned to have his best, if fleeting, Summer at the age of 36.

The return match at The Oval was the moment when Lancashire overtook Yorkshire in the Championship table, a momentous event in the mid-1920s. Yorkshire struggled to 274, Surrey batted dourly (Hobbs spent almost five hours over 102) but took first-innings lead at 355-9, and although Holmes and Sutcliffe relieved some Yorkist frustrations by hitting 256 in 150 minutes, the match was drawn and, had Yorkshire known it, the Championship gone.

Cardus, the previous season, had echoed national irritation at continuing White Rose supremacy by suggesting, in the *Manchester Guardian*, that Yorkshire be awarded the permanent title of Honorary Champions 'so that the rest of us can get on with enjoying the game'. In fact five years passed before Yorkshire were champions again although they were second twice, third twice, fourth once and lost only seven matches of 142 played.

Cardus would have been in a better humour at the Bank Holiday Roses encounter, for Lancashire batted through the Saturday for 297-2 and went on for nine hours, finally to declare at 509-9. Rhodes, then aged 48, bowled 42 overs to take 7-116. Yorkshire replied with 352 despite Oldroyd's departure for hospital and the match was a stalemate as was, in the end, Yorkshire's Summer. Not since August 1924 had the team been beaten and the preservation of that record had begun to affect the team's cricket, an avoidance of defeat taking priority. When other teams playing Yorkshire adopted a similar attitude, the game became moribund.

At Hull in May 1927, the great run ended with a victory that brought Warwickshire headlines for a week. Yorkshire began with a competent 272, Oldroyd returning with a 67. Warwickshire then built a lead of 121 by the third morning and a draw seemed inevitable after Yorkshire had cleared the arrears without too much trouble. But Yorkshire's last four wickets raised only 22 and Warwickshire, by claiming the extra half-hour, knocked off the 42 needed for a reverberating victory with the loss of just two wickets to Waddington.

There had been no hint of impending disaster. Holmes and Sutcliffe had been as prolific as usual, Macaulay was proving himself a first-class all-rounder and the bowlers were rampant. After Hull, Yorkshire did not run into further trouble until they visited Lancashire at Old Trafford at Whitsun, the champions being unbeaten. Lancashire also had the most-feared fast bowler of his time, Ted McDonald, and he gave Leyland and Sutcliffe a fearful opening barrage, bowling bouncers at batsmen who, in those days, wore protection only on the lower half of the body.

Holmes had been injured in the previous match. Sutcliffe was lbw for a duck, to a ball that did not lift, and Leyland was caught at slip in the first 15 minutes: 10-2. Oldroyd, said to have been never truly happy against real fast bowling since his previous meeting with McDonald, and Mitchell took the score to 38 before the latter was also taken at slip. Oldroyd, relieved to be at the other end, swung at Sibbles and was well caught at sqaure leg, and the first five wickets had gone for 57. George Kennie, a 23-year-old Bradford batsman, brought into this furnace in the absence of Holmes and Lupton, was lbw to Tyldesley in this his only first-class match, for nought, and at 12.50 pm Rhodes, by then 49, marched out to join Kilner with Yorkshire deep in crisis.

Doggedly they pushed Yorkshire along to 93 before Kilner was taken at slip; Rhodes, top scorer with 44, was caught behind off the returning McDonald, but the total of 166 represented a formidable recovery. Lancashire then built upon McDonald's 5-68 by spending 390 minutes in raising 234 before McDonald struck again: 6-67. Lancashire knocked off the 86 runs in two hours for the loss of two wickets.

Middlesex retrieved prestige at Lord's where Haig, 7-33, helped to dismiss Yorkshire for 81. Kilner (53) rallied Yorkshire's second innings but Middlesex managed to win, dashing through the third-day showers. The return match at Sheffield was drawn and distinguished by Leyland's 204 not out.

Eight successive matches in August were interrupted by rain but Yorkshire were able to finish happily, defeating Sussex at Hove by nine wickets, Kilner scoring 91 not out and taking eight wickets. MCC were then beaten by eight wickets at Scarborough in what was in effect a finale to one of the most successful Yorkshire teams and a match that could be considered, certainly within the context of county cricket, as one of the great ones.

The Autumn and Winter of 1927-28 brought great changes to Yorkshire. Major Lupton, his task well completed, retired to the club cricket he loved so much at the age of 49; Arthur Dolphin, after 22 years of magnificent service as a wicket-keeper, retired at the age of 41. Abe Waddington, volatile, temperamental and occasionally brilliant, refused terms. He was 34 and still troubled by the left shoulder ligament he had strained in 1923, taking only 45 wickets at 30.62 in his final Summer, but his departure was a sad loss.

Rhodes was then 50 and Emmott Robinson 35; and an even greater blow was to befall the team. Kilner, then the leading all-rounder, contracted typhoid fever while coaching in India that Winter and was taken from the ship to Barnsley Fever Hospital, but he died on a Spring day, 5 April, a date when Yorkshire and England had been looking forward to seeing him play again. Of the five bowlers who had done so much for Yorkshire in the decade, only one, George Macaulay, could be said to remain at his peak.

Tom Jacques, a fast right-hander from York, had done well enough in his first season to win selection as an amateur for The Rest in the Test trial, taking four England wickets for 53, but while he showed promise he was clearly not ready to fill one of several huge gaps in the side.

Dolphin's successor was to hand – Arthur Wood from Eccleshill, Bradford, who at 29 was experienced both behind the stumps and with the bat, hardened by his long apprenticeship. Wood fitted the gauntlets as comfortably as when Dolphin had replaced David Hunter. That succession, at least, was secure.

But what of the captaincy? Word soon spread that Yorkshire were thinking of reverting to a professional, the first since Tom Emmett the previous century. Neither Hawke nor Toone would comment, but on 2 November 1927 a letter was despatched to Sutcliffe, then touring South

Hedley Verity

Verity died from wounds after leading a company of the Green Howards in night action silhouetted against a blazing Sicilian cornfield under machine-gun fire from the Hermann Goering Division in July 1943. A few years earlier an unthinking Yorkshireman had observed to Bowes and Verity, unaware that they had already volunteered: 'I would have thought anyone good enough to play for England would be good enough to fight for England.' Bowes wrote, 15 years later: 'As it happened Hedley was good enough to die for England.' His batman, Private Renalson, stayed with him until dawn, when he was found by a German officer who arranged for transport to an Italian hospital. After surgery he was thought able to recover, but following three haemorrhages he died the next day.

Verity's manner of dying epitomised his career; he brought style and dignity to professional cricket, to his regiment, to Yorkshire and England. One of the great left-arm bowlers, perhaps nearer medium pace than slow, he had to wait until he was 25 before Yorkshire called him from the Central Lancashire League club Middleton to succeed Rhodes, although they had known of his ability from his days at Yeadon Secondary School and his debut in the Yorkshire Council at 15. Playing as a professional in the Lancashire leagues meant that he reached Yorkshire, for one more Summer under the guidance of Rhodes and Hirst, a hardened and experienced performer, yet Verity was always keen to listen and learn.

When he did succeed Rhodes in his first full season, 1932, he made such an impact that only Rhodes stood as a comparison; Verity took 188 wickets at 13.13 apiece and became the third bowler in Yorkshire's history to take all ten against Warwickshire, including four in one over, all on his 26th birthday. The second season is always crucial for the high-flier but Verity did it again in 1933, 162 wickets at 13.88.

What is more, he repeated his feat of taking

Hedley Verity
Yorkshire Post

all ten, this time creating a world record: against Nottinghamshire at Headingley his analysis read 19.4-16-10-10. Larwood and Voce had shattered the Yorkshire first innings, a thunderstorm intervened and Sellers declared at 71 behind; play did not start until 12.30 pm and by lunch Nottinghamshire had extended their lead by another 35 runs without loss. Verity's first two overs after lunch were maidens, and only another 29 were added as Verity did the hat-trick and twice took two wickets in two balls. He bowled 113 balls without conceding a run and seven wickets came in 15 deliveries for three runs.

All but one of the Nottinghamshire batsmen had made a first-class century, and bowling at the other end was Macaulay who, characteristically, gave not an inch: 'If he's good enough to get nine let him earn the tenth,' he said, 'I'll get it if I can.'

Verity's biographer Alan Hill noted that in neither of his ten-wicket matches did the bowler hit the stumps. In both of these famous performances eight batsmen were caught, one was stumped and one was leg before. His method was the same, pitching on leg stump or middle and spinning the ball away from the right-hander on a varying bounce and speed; he used his height, length, flight and pace in an irresistible number of variations.

The postscript to this remarkable performance came from Holmes and Sutcliffe. Yorkshire needed 139 to win on a pitch that had left Nottinghamshire paralysed and the opening pair knocked them off in 90 minutes. Souvenir scorecards were printed on the ground and hundreds queued afterwards for Verity's signature upon them; he signed until darkness fell and pleaded then to be left off until another day.

Verity had been capped in June the previous (first) season and first played for England a month later; all the bold predictions that 'another Rhodes' had appeared were borne out and after another Summer of sensational success he had to be taken, with Bowes, on Jardine's tour of Australia, the Bodyline episode of 1932-33. Comparisons with Rhodes were, as Home Gordon wrote, 'illogical – their respective methods are entirely different'. When, years later, A.A. Thomson asked Rhodes if Verity had bowled any delivery not used by the old master, he got a reply of mordant wit: 'Yes. The one they cut for four.'

Although Verity had only one good Test in Australia, the Fifth, when he returned match figures of 9-95, he, like Bowes, returned to England and took ample revenge on Woodfull's and Bradman's teams of 1934 and 1938. Verity's batting – he was a quick learner – also showed signs of development in Australia; his style was to be described by Robertson-Glasgow as 'like Sutcliffe gone stale; that is, pretty good.'

At Lord's in 1934, on a drying pitch, Verity took 7-61 and 8-43 against Australia, 14 of those wickets falling to him in one day, a record until Laker's 19 wickets at Old Trafford in 1953. In 1935, '36 and '37 Verity topped 200 wickets per Summer so that 1938, the year of England's crushing of Australia at The Oval, was a setback for Verity, only 158 wickets. He also toured Australia in 1936-37 where, although less successful as a bowler, he did emulate Rhodes once again; after batting number ten for England he opened the innings, with Charlie Barnett, in the Fourth Test in Adelaide.

In his last season, 1939, Verity took 191 wickets. The final fixture was against Sussex at Hove and on the last morning Sellers received a telegram from Leeds advising him to complete the fixture as quickly as possible as war was imminent; Verity took 7-9 in six overs and Sussex were dismissed for 33. For years slip fielders tried to identify the signal that Verity's faster ball was coming when Wood motioned them to stand back. The keeper eventually confessed: 'There was no signal, I just sensed when it was coming.'

After training Verity was commissioned in the Green Howards, which was also Yardley's regiment, passed some time in further training in Northern Ireland and spent his last days before embarkation with his wife Kathleen in London. His sister, Grace Verity, told Alan Hill: 'Kathleen knew it wouldn't be long. He had been issued with his tropical kit but he didn't say anything about his impending departure. One night he said "Kathleen, I'm going now." He put his arms around her and repeated, "This is it. I'm going. I must go tonight." It was a frosty night and she could hear his footsteps right away down the garden path until they died away in the distance.'

Africa with MCC, appointing him captain 'without your status being altered'. Sutcliffe, according to Leslie Duckworth, knew what was in the wind before he left for the tour. Being a shrewd man he may also have guessed that Lord Hawke,

despite protestations of loyalty to the Committee's decision, was not entirely in favour.

Sutcliffe would also have known that a majority

of members, sounded unofficially, were in favour of Rhodes if there were to be a professional captain. According to Kilburn, Sutcliffe replied to Lord Hawke by cable, saying 'Official invitation received yesterday. Many thanks you and committee great honour. Question carefully considered. Regret to decline. Willing to play under any captain elected.'

According to Duckworth, this cable had been preceded by another to Sutcliffe from the Committee, following their letter of invitation, asking him if he would withdraw his letter of acceptance. Sutcliffe was a wise man, and much as he may have been attracted by the thought of becoming Yorkshire's first professional captain for 44 years he must also have realised the rifts that might have opened within the Club between those who insisted upon amateur leadership (a section of the Committee would have preferred Sutcliffe to turn amateur) and those who favoured a professional, the majority of whom wanted the 50-year-old Rhodes as captain. Sutcliffe put the Club first.

Duckworth, no doubt recalling many conversations with Sutcliffe, was to write later (1970): 'I believe he now regrets that he withdrew his acceptance and thinks he would have stuck to his original decision.' That was written 42 years later when professional captains were common if not universal and the amateur had disappeared from first-class cricket; in the climate of the late 1920s his decision was the right one, saving him, one suspects, from a great deal of heartbreak and the Club from strife.

The Committee, casting around, lit upon Captain William Worsley of Hovingham Hall, a right-hand batsman of good club standard who liked to crack the ball. His family's links with Yorkshire cricket went back at least to 1858 when 'Sir William Worsley and the Earl of Carlisle were both in attendance during the All England match at Hovingham.' Captain Worsley's father was a renowned patron of the game, entertaining many famous players at the Hall, as did the new Sir William when he succeeded to the title. His daughter Katherine grew up within sight and sound of Yorkshire cricket, and on becoming Duchess of Kent gave the Club a gracious and royal patronage.

Worsley, an Old Etonian, the third captain in five years, led the side for two years when the loss of Kilner and Waddington might have undermined the whole structure. Much weight was thrown upon Macaulay and the 50-year-old Rhodes, supported by Robinson and occasionally Leyland, slow left-arm. Jacques remained the most promising of the new fast bowlers, but soon realised that his legs would not stand up to bowling every day, and he eventually retired into league cricket and farming.

Other fast bowlers to be tried were Frank Dennis, from Leeds, Charles (Henry) Hall, a tall quick bowler from York, and Arthur Rhodes, a fast-medium all-rounder from Headingley who Yorkshire hoped would prove to be the natural successor to Robinson. An unusual trialist was Harry Bedford, a leg-break bowler from Morley, whose eight wickets did, at least, take him to second in the averages in 1928.

Rhodes, who never ceased to astonish, finished top once again, taking 112 wickets at an average of 19.21 with Macaulay, who missed much of May with a foot injury, taking 117 at 23.75. Rhodes, Macaulay and Robinson delivered 3,660 overs. With the new wicket-keeper, Wood, settling in, all under a new captain, Yorkshire could be more than satisfied with their fourth place, won mostly through the enormous power of their batting; five players passed 1,000 runs to average more than 50, and the team recorded 32 centuries.

Sutcliffe averaged 83.38 for his 2,400 runs and shared with Holmes 11 century opening partnerships. Leyland emerged as a Test-match batsman and tourist, while Mitchell, having faithfully served a long apprenticeship as 12th man, established himself at number three. Another batsman of promise, Wilfred Barber, appeared when England required the senior batsmen.

Robinson took 8-13 when the University of Cambridge were dismissed for 30, but Yorkshire had to wait until June for their first victory, despite passing 500 against Worcestershire (Leyland 247) and Essex (Holmes and Sutcliffe 268). By 1928 the object of a Roses match, with both counties potential champions, was to prevent the other team from taking points; at Bramall Lane Lancashire spent 450 minutes in

Frank Greenwood

Frank Greenwood, born in Huddersfield and educated at Oundle, was a right-hand bat and medium-pace bowler who succeeded Alan Barber as captain in 1931 after making his debut two years earlier. From Barber he inherited the nucleus of the team that was to dominate the Championship for the next decade, a team that greeted the new leadership by losing only one match in taking the title that Summer. That one defeat brought about a change of regulations.

There had been growing concern at the number of drawn matches, bringing an outcry in 1930 when Gloucestershire, who won 15 matches, finished second to Lancashire, who won only ten but who profited from the complicated points system on drawn matches. From 1931, 15 points were awarded for victory instead of eight (and five for first-innings lead in a draw), an incitement for freak declarations.

When Yorkshire met Gloucestershire at Sheffield, the first two days were lost to rain whereupon Beverly Lyon won the agreement of Greenwood for each team to bowl four wides in the first innings before declaring, the match becoming, in essence, a one-innings contest. Yorkshire lost by 47 runs, but Greenwood learned from the experience and proved himself a keen tactician afterwards: he was also a useful batsman, scoring one century and missing another by three runs.

He was also the official captain for the 1932 season but managed only seven matches, his deputy being his successor in 1932, Brian Sellers.

A postscript to the Gloucestershire match, worth recording, is that after Emmott Robinson had bowled the one ball in the Gloucestershire first innings the players tripped off and the Press Association reporter, according to Kilburn, exasperated after the long wait, declared wrongly that it was raining yet again.

---

scoring 385, to which Yorkshire replied with 473 (Sutcliffe 140). Victory at last arrived at Lord's where Yorkshire scored 479 (centuries by Holmes, Oldroyd and Mitchell) and Middlesex were forced to follow on despite five missed catches in Hendren's 67, to be beaten by an innings and 88.

The weather prevented play on the first two days of the match against Glamorgan at Huddersfield, Sutcliffe (147) and Leyland (189) using the third day to break the county's third wicket record.

Yorkshire ran into a fearsome force in cricket in the Nottinghamshire match at Sheffield. Nottinghamshire were dismissed for 134 and when Leyland and Oldroyd appeared to be on their way to establishing a lead, Larwood shattered Yorkshire with what Kilburn described as one of the 'finest spells of fast bowling in history'. Larwood in a few overs bowled, Mitchell, Robinson, Wood and Worsley and had Rhodes lbw, all for seven runs. The batting of both teams recovered in the second innings to ensure a draw.

Yorkshire had to follow on in Holmes' benefit match at Leeds after Middlesex had raised 488, Holmes and Sutcliffe replying in the second innings with a partnership of 290 in 180 minutes. Holmes followed his 179 not out in this match with a score of 275 against Warwickshire at Bradford, scored in 310 minutes and containing 49 fours. Macaulay, bowling on a rain-affected surface at Headingley, took 6-30 against the touring West Indians.

Worsley's second year of captaincy, 1929, brought Yorkshire to a shared second place in the Championship with Lancashire, but it will be remembered chiefly as the threshold for another great era in the county's history. After only one Summer of an under-strength attack the first reinforcement arrived in the form of the tall, bespectacled, shock-haired Bill Bowes from the Lord's ground staff, but born in Elland. Although he was allowed sufficient leave from the MCC to bowl in only 13 innings, he took 40 wickets at 17.77 apiece and finished second to Rhodes.

Brian Sellers Crackerjack

Arthur Brian Sellers won the Championship six times in his nine years of captaincy, from 1933 to 1948, a record challenged only by Hawke and Stuart Surridge. Keighley-born and the son of Arthur Sellers, he led a formidable team with dash and what Peter Thomas described as 'a lust for victory'. When suddenly on the scent of half-expected success, Hutton was reminded of 'a house set on fire, set alight by the sudden flaring truth of the old maxim – a game is never lost until it is won.'

A tall, strong, right-hand batsman he compensated for limited ability with outstanding courage when facing the fast bowlers and sustained, punishing hitting against the spinners. A brilliant fielder in suicidal position, Sellers intimidated dozens of batsmen by his presence and field settings; playing against Yorkshire under Sellers was as much a test of temperament and character as it was of technique.

He scored the first of his four centuries in 1934, against the Australians, and then two years later raised the record score by a Yorkshire amateur, 204 at Fenner's. In 1937 his two centuries were hit against two of the strongest county attacks, those of Kent and Nottinghamshire. The following year he passed 1,000 runs.

He may have owed his original election to the captaincy to the advocacy of his father, chairman of the Cricket sub-committee at that time, but never has nepotism been more justified. While all contemporaries speak of Yorkshire in that period as a team of dedicated professionals inhabiting a happy dressing room, there was always the possibility, under less inspired leadership, of a fall into disarray through lack of success for half the side were regular candidates for England selection. No matter how the team might be weakened by Test calls, Sellers was usually able to whip Yorkshire into match-winning combination, as his record proves.

Sellers read the opposition thoroughly,

Brian Sellers
Yorkshire Post

always used the conditions to advantage, was alert to every tactical nuance and was an extraordinary motivator. He never allowed personal failures – he once began a season with four successive ducks – to affect his leadership as, for example, in 1935 when he lost the toss 13 times, lost Leyland, Sutcliffe, Verity, Bowes, Mitchell and Barber to England at various stages of the five match series against South Africa and yet still won the Championship. Only one defeat was suffered, and six consecutive matches were won in July and another six in August, during which months four Tests were played.

He must have won the heart of that craggy character Alec Coxon when he awarded him his county cap in mid-wicket. Sellers took off his own cap and asked Coxon to try it on. 'It fits OK,' said Sellers. 'You keep it. You've earned it.'

Bowes believed that Sellers was at his greatest in 1946: 'For a side weakened by the war years he set a magnificent example, finishing third in the averages with 33.24. Frequently during the post-war period he would say, "We must keep at it Bill, until Yorkshire have a side again."'

In 1948 he shared the captaincy with Yardley and then retired to the committee room until 1972, the most powerful influence in the county's cricket. To the new recruits of 1946-47 he was often referred to, out of hearing, as the 'Sergeant-Major', in itself an indication of changing attitudes towards authority. Wardle remembers a pre-match lecture by Sellers: 'You've got to concentrate on every single ball in the match and still have enough concentration left to keep an eye on me.'

Sellers' retirement from playing, at 40, was, it can now be seen, a mistake. The Team's newcomers, as Wardle admitted, would have greatly benefited from another two or three seasons of Sellers' leadership and inculcation into the ethos and traditions of Yorkshire cricket.

Not only was his successor, Yardley, very much an officer and a gentleman, he was also captain of England, which meant he missed up to 12 Championship matches a Summer at a time when it was imperative that his dressing-room presence was regular and commanding. The seeds of Yorkshire's discontent may have been sown in the years 1948-50 through Yardley's circumstances and Sellers' good intentions in making way for a younger and, in playing ability, better captain.

Sellers then diverted his tremendous energy and zest of the cause into the committee room, becoming Cricket chairman in 1959 and directing, from his chair, Close and his team of the Silver Sixties, but in 1968 came the first confrontation between a disciplinarian chairman and a very independently minded player.

Illingworth, then 37, was under challenge from a younger off-spinner, Cope. Anxious to prolong his career he asked John Nash, the then Secretary, if the Committee would either release him or give him a contract – 'Please don't mess me about for a year and then sack me when I've missed the chance of getting a three- or four-year contract somewhere else.' Nash, in Illingworth's account, replied that the Club's policy (unlike the other 16 county clubs) was not to give contracts but that he (Nash) had no reason to think that Illingworth would be sacked.

Illingworth was not convinced and decided to seek a contract elsewhere, writing a letter of resignation. According to Illingworth he was then approached by Bill Bowes in the Park Avenue dressing room, in his role as cricket correspondent of the *Yorkshire Evening Post*. Illingworth, upset at learning that the contents of his letter had been already leaked to the press, wanted to know how Bowes had been told. The reply was: 'Mr Nash has rung Sellers and Sellers says that you can go and any bugger else that wants to can go with you.'

There seems little doubt that, in retrospect, there would have been a breach between Illingworth and Sellers at some point, for Sellers probably saw the astute all-rounder in the guise of a barrack-room lawyer, while the player viewed Sellers as an outdated autocrat. The pair had rowed violently on at least one occasion.

The Committee's statement contained the phrase 'a pistol at the head', which in itself suggests a vast distance between the committee room and the dressing room, for other senior players (Close, Trueman) also believed that it was time that Yorkshire got into step and offered the security of contracts instead of an annual verbal agreement. Contracts were available the following year but a legacy of mistrust, an atmosphere of 'them and us', remained in the dressing room.

Sellers was again at the centre of the uproar that followed the dismissal of Brian Close from the captaincy in 1970. Close had won four Championships and two Gillette Cups in his seven years as captain, a record compatible with that of Sellers, but in November of that year he was called to Headingley to be confronted by Sellers and John Nash and told that he had the choice of resignation or the sack. He was 39.

According to Close, Sellers gave him ten minutes to make up his mind. Badly shaken, Close resigned and was told that a statement to that effect would be issued at 2 pm. Close wrote: 'I drove away with my mind in a whirl. I wanted to cry – my vision misted up so much I had to stop and there, by the side of the road [Kirkstall Road], I was sick.'

His wife, Vivienne, persuaded him he should not resign and at noon he rang back to say that he had changed his mind, only to find that the resignation announcement had already been published. Close was asked to appear on television; the Reform Group was formed in his defence. This was the first time members had organised themselves as a body in opposition to the elected committee.

Close later elicited three reasons for his ruthless dismissal: he did not encourage the youngsters; he was not fit; he was too critical of one-day cricket. If all three accusations had been proved beyond all doubt, he deserved better treatment. His departure could be likened only to the treatment of a professional captain by an amateur committee of the previous century, and as such marked the end of an era both in the government of the Club and in its success on the field.

Sellers must therefore be remembered with both gratitude and regret for just as he as a captain enlarged and stabilised the empire founded by Hawke, he was also at least partly responsible for its dismantling. There is no doubt that Yorkshire's history would have been very different if Close had relinquished the captaincy to Illingworth in 1972 and Illingworth to Boycott in 1975.

Sellers served as a major in the Royal Artillery during the Second World War, winning the MBE, and died in Bingley, aged 73. Among his other distinctions were the chairmanship of England's selectors and a tour of Australia as a newspaper correspondent. He never wavered in his belief that what he did was best for Yorkshire.

With Dennis, too, having a better season, Yorkshire were sharper in their seam bowling than for some seasons, and although the number of centuries scored dropped from 32 to 23, it was a damp Summer, almost every home match being affected. Yorkshire's first win, over Essex at Leyton, owed much to Leyland (134) but more especially to Rhodes who, in the second innings, took the first seven wickets for 14 and finished with 9-39.

Rhodes and Dennis helped to defeat Kent at Sheffield but the return match, at Tonbridge in June, brought the first defeat for two years. Sutcliffe and Leyland were absent and Kent started by scoring 421-4 on the first day, Hardinge and Woolley raising 239 in 180 minutes for the second wicket. The weather intervened and on the Monday morning, after Rhodes had taken another four wickets, Kent declared at 471-9.

Yorkshire were dismissed for 108 (Freeman 6-53), and although they resisted more firmly in the second innings the match was over by teatime. With Nottinghamshire, eventual champions, equally determined to give Yorkshire no points, the match at Trent Bridge became a grim affair: Holmes batted for more than nine hours, first in last out, to score 289 in a total of 498, to which Nottinghamshire replied with 190-4 in seven and a quarter hours, George Gunn batting for 320 minutes, Carr 150 minutes for 23. The normally diplomatic Kilburn was moved to write: 'The fantastic and deplorable performances in this match left an unhappy legacy; there have been many occasions since when Yorkshire v Nottinghamshire at Trent Bridge has been neither worth playing in nor worth watching.'

The Roses matches attracted great crowds but little happiness. Both teams by then firmly believed that in order to win the Championship the other side had to be prevented, at all costs, even from taking first-innings points. Lancashire's excellent attack, spearheaded by the great McDonald, was supported by solid but far from adventurous batting; Yorkshire had batsmen to spare but bowlers, without assistance from the conditions, were rarely capable of enforcing their will on good pitches. Neither team had the confidence born of strength and success to seek out victory, nor could they afford defeat.

So bored was Cardus, on the Saturday of the Whitsuntide Roses match at Old Trafford, with Lancashire's batting, that he found more enjoyment from watching another match on the adjoining field where the umpire, he remembered, 'wore a bowler hat'. He did enjoy Leyland's experiments with left-arm spinners, telling *Manchester Guardian* readers that the late Roy Kilner had once predicted that the next development in cricket would be the advent of a left-arm googly bowler. Sixteen years later, Johnny Wardle would appear.

Lancashire took eight hours over their 305 in that match, McDonald soon shooting out Holmes and Mitchell, whereupon Sutcliffe and Leyland, proper to the occasion, set their sights firmly on a first-innings lead. This was achieved, Rhodes bringing his usual stability to the mid-innings, after seven hours, past 3 pm on the third day.

The Bradford return, too, was drawn, although little criticism could be addressed to the players, playing being delayed on the first two days and the match being abandoned before 2 pm on the Tuesday.

The 1929 Summer, rainy weeks before the Wall Street crash in November, did provide an open Championship. Gloucestershire won the most matches but could only finish fourth (and in fact unsuccessfully sought, in the Autumn, to have the points for wins increased and the first-innings award reduced), while Nottinghamshire ended ten points ahead of both Lancashire and Yorkshire – although any one of the three might have been successful up to the end.

William Worsley ended a not unsuccessful captaincy that September and in 1930 was succeeded by Alan Barber who, at 25, had captained the University of Oxford the previous Summer, winning a Blue in each of his three years. Born in Eccleshall, Sheffield, his leadership of Yorkshire in that one Summer left an excellent impression

and an accolade from the recently disappointed Sutcliffe: 'a great captain'.

Appointing a young man with little first-class experience was a gamble, but a highly successful one for Barber was able to give the side inspired leadership in a momentous Summer, the last for Wilfred Rhodes. In his 53rd year the grand old man took 73 wickets and scored 478 runs before taking his legendary prowess and unparalleled knowledge into the service of Harrow. Kilburn's valedictory read: 'He had bowled at a Grace and he bowled at Bradman. At 20, at 30, at 40 and at 50 he had shown himself master of his world, and his kingdom was never usurped.'

Yorkshire without Rhodes was unthinkable as Yorkshire without Peel, or Peate. Horace Fisher, from Pontefract, who was to make his mark in cricket in an unexpected fashion, had deputised for Rhodes occasionally in the two previous Summers, bowling economically without taking wickets. It was to be the great good fortune of both Yorkshire and their new captain that Rhodes' successor appeared, by that same magic that produced Peel for Peate and Rhodes for Peel, in the shape of Hedley Verity.

Bowes had been an imposing newcomer in 1929, but Verity was sensational. Tall, he bowled at nearer medium pace than slow and was enough of a contrast to Rhodes for them to bowl occasionally in tandem for that one Summer. By August it was clear that an old king had been succeeded by a young prince: Verity took 64 wickets, from 406 overs, to top the national averages in his very first season, collecting 26 wickets in the final fortnight.

Yorkshire were fortunate in that Verity, from Headingley, was devoted to the cause. At 21 he had gone into league cricket in Lancashire, leaving Accrington when he discovered that they had once refused to release their professional to Old Trafford and insisting, on his move to Central Lancashire League Middleton, that his contract should include a release clause, in case the call ever came from Yorkshire.

Arthur Booth, a shrewd little bowler from Featherstone whose time would come, and Stanley Douglas from Bradford, were, with

Fisher, also competing for Rhodes' place, but of all the young bowlers who had been through George Hirst's nets it was Verity who had the old man's confidence and, after he had appeared in a friendly match with Sussex, seemingly also that of Rhodes. Any Yorkshire Colt who received the approbation of both the old titans could be fairly confident of playing for England.

Bowes was able to play in twice as many matches as in 1929, and the arrival of two bowlers of such performance transformed Yorkshire. However, although they won two more matches than the eventual champions Lancashire, they could rise no further than third. The inequity of the system (eight points for a win, five points for first-innings lead) told against frustrated Gloucestershire, who won no less than five more matches than the champions.

Macaulay began the season superbly, taking 7-22 in MCC's second innings at Lord's (12-95 in the match), but a nagging foot injury reduced his effectiveness for much of the season. Robinson remained a fine bowler in support (80 wickets at 23.93) but could not be considered a regular match-winner, and the bowling, overall, offered much more promise for the future than it delivered in present fulfilment, neither Dennis nor Hall showing the consistency expected of a county opening bowler.

William Harbord, an Old Etonian who had played for Oxford without gaining a Blue, referred to as an amateur batsman from Tadcaster, was actually born in Rutland but somehow managed to play 16 matches over six seasons for Yorkshire without being found out. He made a century at Oxford and later served the club with distinction as a committee member for York and Vice-President.

Both Yorkshire's defeats occurred at home, Kent, mainly through Woolley, winning at Headingley while Surrey must have upset Robinson, in his benefit match, by winning at Bramall Lane. In a wet Summer with Rhodes, (52) bowling second or third change almost retired, and Macaulay handicapped, the newcomer Verity found pitch after pitch to his liking, much to the frustration of Bowes, who was to become his closest friend. Bowes once burst out at him, while they were sheltering under a tree:

'Ever since you came in to the side it's done nothing but rain.'

Verity had some hard taskmasters. After he had taken 9-60 against Glamorgan he was told, firmly, by Emmot Robinson: 'You should have 'ad 'em for 20. You are pitching about the same place' – Emmott making the point that Verity had to learn to vary his length with his speed without losing direction.

Robinson and Rhodes remained the supreme court, and Bowes recorded how the two veterans would wait until he and Verity returned to the team's hotel whereupon they would be taken up to a bedroom, toilet articles would be arrayed on the bed to represent fielding positions, and the lectures would begin. Verity, having taken 7-26, was on one evening severely castigated by Robinson for conceding a four.

By September 1930, however, Rhodes had already told a disappointed Arthur Booth that Verity had the job, and he is supposed to have told Hawke, as the pair watched the 25-year-old man bowl: 'He'll do.'

Alan Barber handed over a team of Championship potential in 1931 to Frank Greenwood, a 26-year-old former Oundle pupil whose cricket had been learned in the Huddersfield League. A useful batsman, he was an innovative captain, receptive to ideas, a seeker of victories, and in his first Summer he took Yorkshire to an impressive Championship in which they lost only one match and finished, under the latest system, almost 70 points ahead of their nearest rivals, Gloucestershire. The pursuit of victory had been made more attractive by the award of 15 points for a win, and that season is now remembered as one of freak declarations, made with the object of averting a draw at all costs, earning the disapproval of many in high places, including Hawke.

Yorkshire's home match against Gloucestershire, a crucial contest, aroused a worldwide controversy. Yorkshire had been cooped up by the rain in Bradford for two days, and on arrival at Bramall Lane on 3 June spent two more days in shelter. Both teams were eager to play and even more eager to get a result, the two captains, Greenwood and Beverley Lyon,

Frank Smailes

Thomas Frank Smailes was a high-class all-rounder who lost his best years to the Second World War. Born in Ripley, he first appeared in 1932 as a left-handed bat who could adapt his game to circumstances and as a dual-purpose bowler; it was with the ball that he advanced his career.

In the middle to late 1930s Frank Smailes became a vital member of Sellers' Championship teams, being able to use the new ball at fast-medium pace, taking full advantage of English conditions, and then switching to off-spin when the pitch offered turn. He was thus able to fill the gap in the side when Macaulay departed and to cover for Ellis Robinson as the specialist off-spinner. His batting was good enough to qualify him as Yorkshire's principal all-rounder in the years just before and immediately after the war. If Yorkshire had specifically asked for a strong reliable, capable all-rounder who could maintain momentum in the regular absences of Hutton, Leyland, Bowes and Verity then they could not have been granted a better one than Smailes.

Even when the selectors looked at Smailes, fortune favoured his retention by Yorkshire; his form in 1938 was such that he was in the 12 for the Old Trafford Test against Australia when rain prevented a final selection. He did play for England once, after the war, against India but at 34, after an arduous war in the Mediterranean, he was past his best.

He scored almost 6,000 runs, including three centuries, passing 1,000 once (1938), and took 823 wickets at 20.77 apiece. At Bramall Lane in 1938 he took 6-29 and 4-45 against the Australians and the following year reached his zenith, against Derbyshire, also at Bramall Lane, when he followed Verity, Wainwright and Drake in taking all ten wickets (and 4-1 in the second innings). In 1938 Smailes also completed the first 'double' by a Yorshireman since 1926, the ultimate qualification to be an all-rounder.

A Pocklington School pupil, Smailes was commissioned into the infantry during the war and was the first to erect a monument on Verity's grave at Caserta.

---

coming to an agreement.

Greenwood won the toss and sent in Gloucestershire; Robinson's first ball went for four, whereupon Gloucester declared. The local press agency man, according to Kilburn, believed that the rain had resumed. When Yorkshire batted, Hammond's first ball also went for four byes, there came another declaration and the match proper started, Gloucestershire winning by 47. In the course of that Summer similar methods were used in four other matches, the authorities being rightly concerned at what was happening to the first-class game.

All counties suffered much frustration through May and early June when, because of the weather, Yorkshire had to accept a draw in seven of the first 12 matches. But the tremendous potential strength of the side was apparent, with Macaulay and Verity always among the wickets. After the first home match, against Warwickshire, Verity had become an international figure; Warwickshire had struggled to 201 in their first innings at Headingley, Yorkshire won a lead of 97 by tea on the Monday, and at 3.45 pm, the sun just starting to break through on a cold, dull day, Verity had begun a spell of 18.4 overs, six of which were maidens, to take all ten wickets for 36.

It was Verity's 26th birthday, his 14th first-class match, and he was still uncapped. Verity, wrote Alan Hill, saw the whole event in his usual modest fashion, praising Macaulay's effort (18 overs for 20 runs) at the other end, saying: 'It was one of those rare days when everything was set right for the bowler at one end.' That chill evening of 18 May 1931 left a small crowd of no less than 4,000 in raptures, forgetting their means of getting home. One Yorkshireman, according to Hill, declared: 'I've now got two hours to wait for my train, but it's worth it to have seen this.'

Warwickshire felt the weight of Yorkshire's batting in the return match, Holmes and Sutcliffe rattling on 309 runs in 220 minutes, Holmes continuing to score to 250. At Bradford, in another abbreviated encounter, that regular scourge Woolley hit 188 of Kent's 296-4 at a run a minute, the innings including seven sixes, five of them off Verity!

Once the weather broke Yorkshire got into their stride, winning five successive matches by an innings (Bowes, batting 11, played in 25 matches that Summer, being still under contract to MCC, and managed to get to the wicket only 11 times). The big man was in especial form at Lord's, with match figures of 11-99 against Middlesex.

There would have been some muttering at Folkestone during the return fixture with Kent, for Sutcliffe, who had declared himself unfit for a Test match, scored 230 while Woolley was playing for England at Lord's, scoring 80 against New Zealand.

Only Lancashire escaped defeat in that triumphant Summer, Yorkshire taking some fearful stick from Cardus in the *Manchester Guardian* for, after failing to make Lancashire follow on at Old Trafford, they batted out time on the third afternoon. After Sutcliffe had spent 75 minutes, over 11 runs, Cardus mused indignantly: 'If cricket were under the jurisdiction of a body similar to the Football Association I wonder what would happen.'

Cricket's greatest writer also gave his first considered view of Verity:

[He] has a beautiful action – supple, upright and economic. He brings the ball from a height and is quicker through the air than Rhodes (with whom he ought not to be compared; his style is different and his own). He can spin the ball well enough and he has something of that 'extra' pace which made the incomparable Blythe more difficult to 'get at' than most slow bowlers.

At Bramall Lane in August, on a flat pitch, Yorkshire retaliated vigorously to Cardus' criti-

cism, Holmes and Sutcliffe assembling 323 for the first wicket, a stand that was broken only by a masterly diving catch by Paynter on the long-on boundary after 265 minutes. 'A scalding day' was Cardus' verdict, Yorkshire eventually declaring 70 minutes into the second day at 484-7. They did force a follow-on, but were unable to break Lancashire again, Paynter defying them for 87.

Yorkshire had the Championship won by mid-August, a task made easier by a car accident that robbed Nottinghamshire of Larwood, Staples and G.V. Gunn for several weeks.

The individual figures made glorious reading: Sutcliffe scored more than 3,000 runs in all matches at an average of just under 100; Verity took 169 wickets at an average of 12.76, Bowes 117 at 15.08, Macaulay took 97 wickets, Robinson 51, while both Leyland and Holmes passed 1,000 runs. Three other batsmen, including Greenwood, passed 700.

In the Winter of 1931 Leicestershire proposed a further change in the Championship system, points to be awarded only for victories, but then withdrew the motion. Northern counties who, by and large, suffered more from the weather than those in the South-East, are always liable to be suspicious of proposals to remove points from matches that, curtailed by the elements, are doomed to be drawn. Under the Leicestershire system, as Roy Webber pointed out, Kent would have lost one Championship between 1896 and 1950, but would have gained six!

The Summer of 1932 also began badly, Yorkshire winning only one of their first five Championship fixtures, but play was wiped out entirely in two games and confined to one day in a third. Indeed, in May Yorkshire had dropped to 16th in the table, tremor enough to shake the Ridings. What's more, Lancashire had been to Bradford and won by an innings and 50, the first time in five years the Roses fixture had brought a result.

The match was Eddie Paynter's. The great left-hander held the Lancashire first innings together for 210 minutes on a far from easy surface, scoring 152 (including five sixes off Verity) in a total of 263. More rain over the weekend prevented a

Sir Len Hutton

Technically and aesthetically the best batsman to play for Yorkshire, Leonard Hutton
was born in Fulneck near Pudsey, of Scottish
descent, and his promise was such that
even in his early teens he was spoken of as
a future England batsman. In a town that
had already given Tunnicliffe, Major Booth
and Sutcliffe to Yorkshire, the environment
was conducive to cricketers and the young
Hutton was appearing for Pudsey St
Lawrence's second XI when 12 years old.

Sutcliffe spoke of him as a future England
opener and such was his reputation among
the Yorkshire cognoscenti that when he first
appeared at the Headingley nets he had an
audience that included Bowes and Verity,
forewarned by George Hirst. At 16 Hutton
was opening for the St Lawrence first team,
in the Bradford League, with Oldroyd, of
whose technique on turning pitches he
always spoke highly. He was also opening
the innings for Yorkshire II and began his
county career with a duck against Cheshire
followed by another against Lancashire II,
for whom one C. Washbrook made 202 not
out.

The Denbighshire bowlers proved to be
more to his liking and scores of 86 not out
and 128 reassured his admirers; a 69 not
out against a Staffordshire that included the
veteran S.F. Barnes convinced the club that
he was not being advanced too rapidly and
he interspersed his Colts outings with 12th-
man duties for the first team.

Speaking at the pre-season lunch, before
the 1934 season, Brian Sellers indicated
that Test-match calls upon Yorkshire would
provide more opportunities than usual for
young players, names mentioned being
Hutton, Yardley, Kenneth Davidson, an
audacious batsman from Bingley who
promised a fine career but became a professional badminton player, Cyril Turner and
William Harbord.

Hirst, who knew he had a good young batsman in Hutton, was also impressed with the
young man's leg-break bowling and his

Sir Len Hutton
Yorkshire Post

inclusion in the Yorkshire side for the opening Southern tour was greeted with
acclaim, although he followed a similar
course to that in the Colts: playing against

the University of Cambridge, batting at number five, he was run out for a duck. Hutton was nevertheless pushed up the order to open with Sutcliffe against the other University where he made an impressive half-century – 'three hours without a mistake', reported *Wisden*.

His Championship debut, against Warwickshire at Edgbaston, brought another half-century and the wickets of both openers, the first with his second ball in Championship cricket, the *Birmingham Post* hailing him as an all-rounder. He was also reproached, in *The Times*, for being over-cautious.

Hutton was placed under Turner's wing in the dressing room, was seen as Sutcliffe's protégé and was befriended by Bowes and Verity, an introduction that reads in considerable contrast to the greeting given young players entering that same room 20 years later. In July Hutton made his maiden century, almost a double hundred (196) against Worcestershire, the youngest Yorkshireman to score a century, three sixes and 21 fours, and carried his bat.

An operation on his nose, damaged in a Colts match two years earlier, delayed his start to the 1935 season and in June of that year he was ordered to rest. Returning towards the end of July he made three consecutive noughts, but a century against Middlesex and 92 against MCC at Scarborough revived his confidence and before the 1936 season he toured Jamaica with Yorkshire, scoring one century at Montego Bay. However, it was not until July of 1936 that Hutton emerged from under the cloud to score 163 against Surrey at Headingley and the Committee, perhaps anxious to confirm their faith in his future, made him, at 20, the youngest capped player. Ironically his bowling, 4-49 against Lancashire and 8-77 against MCC at Scarborough, won almost as much attention as his batting that season and he was chided for a 'negative attitude'.

By 1937 all doubts were resolved. He began with 161 against MCC, following with a century for The North against The South

(part of MCC's 150th birthday celebrations) and centuries against Worcestershire and Kent, and celebrated his selection to play for England against New Zealand with a massive 271 not out against Derbyshire, then the reigning champions, at Bramall Lane. A third successive century (153) followed against Leicestershire at Hull on his 21st birthday, only for this glut of runs to end abysmally with a duck in his first Test match, at Lord's bowled by John Cowie.

Hutton soon exacted retribution, taking a century off the New Zealanders for Yorkshire and then scoring his first century for England in the Second Test at Old Trafford, and he finished the season in a blaze, becoming the seventh Yorkshireman to score more than 2,000 runs for the club in one season. The apprenticeship, at 21, was over and his aggregate, in all matches, was 2,880.

The following Summer, 1938, was historical both for Hutton and for English cricket. The seemingly invincible Bradman brought his Australians to tour and the young Hutton was second only to Hammond in public attention with all England anticipating that the 22-year-old Yorkshireman would challenge the most prolific batsman in Test-match history. He did not fail.

Hutton scored 100 in the First Test, disappointed in the Second, sat in the pavilion through the washed-out Third and missed the Fourth because of a finger injury (Australia won at Headingley), but returned for the Fifth at The Oval for the greatest individual triumph by an English player, batting for 13 hours and 20 minutes to score 364 and overtake Bradman's world record 334. Hutton's name rang around the world.

Five Yorkshire players (Hutton, Bowes, Verity, Leyland and Wood) shared in England's greatest victory over Australia (an innings and 579); with Leyland, Hutton added 382 for England's second wicket. That Winter he toured South Africa, forming another all-Yorkshire opening partnership with the emerging Paul Gibb, and in the ultimate season before the Second

World War hit 12 centuries including 196 and 165 not out against the West Indies and a 280 not out against Hampshire.

Hutton, at 23, was at a dazzling peak when the war took five years from his career. He also suffered a severe injury to his left elbow that threatened his figure and he made a quiet return, burdened by a giant reputation in Yorkshire's patched-up Championship side of 1946.

The following year, when the sun shone, he confirmed that he was still a great batsman, scoring 11 centuries and passing 2,000 runs, including a 270 not out against Hampshire and a century against South Africa.

Abroad he first saw Australia in Hammond's team of 1946-47, facing Bradman's potent new fast attack of Lindwall and Miller and, after a poor start, scoring 94, 76 and 122 in the Fourth and Fifth Tests and establishing a famous partnership with Cyril Washbrook. He was hurriedly called out, as a late reinforcement, to Gubby Allen's team in the West Indies in 1947-48 and the following Summer, with the Australians touring England again, he recovered his pre-war majesty.

He and Compton gave England hope through a tense, dramatic Test Series in which Bradman commanded the best all-purpose bowling ever seen, while in county cricket Hutton scored ten centuries and passed 2,500 runs. June 1949 was a glorious month and in two Tests he amassed 1,294 runs at an average of 92; 16 innings highest score 201, seven centuries and amazingly, continuing what Tom Naylor called Hutton's 'affinity for ducks', three successive noughts. In all matches that season Hutton achieved the fourth-highest aggregate in history, 3,429 runs at 68, a total surpassed only by Compton, Edrich and Hayward.

Hutton's highest score in that phenomenal Summer was 269 not out against Northamptonshire; his 201 was made against Lancashire (91 runs not out in the second innings and a match return of 5-

75!), he hit 165 and 100 against Sussex at Hove and 206 for England against New Zealand.

In 1950, the year of Ramadhin and Valentine, Hutton carried his bat for 202 not out at The Oval and in Brisbane the following Winter he managed to score 62 in an England total of 122, 156 in Adelaide and 79 and 60 not out in Melbourne in a series won 4-1 by Australia.

In 1952 Hutton became England's first professional captain, an inevitable step by the selectors although the appointment did not win universal approval, with Lord Hawke's famous dictum being much quoted. He scored two centuries in his first series, against India, and with the rampant young Trueman to call upon had a highly successful start, winning three of the four Tests.

The following year, to great acclamation, Hutton led England to victory, after four draws, at The Oval to regain the Ashes, held by Australia for almost 19 years (Hutton lost the toss five times). In the West Indies he squared the rubber, after the West Indies had taken a 2-0 lead, contributing 205 in a total of 414 at Sabina Park during a controversial tour when off-the-field stories began appearing in the media and when the Georgetown Test erupted into a bottle-throwing riot. According to Gerald Howzat, Hutton's biographer, the governor of British Guiana offered the England captain a battalion of the Argylls.

At a time when amateurs were still prominent in English cricket (May, Sheppard, Bailey), the rumbles from the West Indies brought a fresh wave of criticism directed at professional leadership. There was speculation before the next home series against Pakistan that Hutton might be replaced by David Sheppard who, indeed, led in two of the drawn series when Hutton, then 38, rested on medical advice.

In the end the selectors made the right decision and appointed Hutton to defend the Ashes in Australia where, with Tyson and Statham as his spearhead (he wanted Trueman too, but was overruled by his fellow selectors), England won 3-1 after losing the First Test by an innings and 154.

That tour was, in effect, Hutton's last hurrah. After such a triumph the selectors, despite a grumble about time-wasting, had no option but to appoint Hutton for the 1955 home series against South Africa, but continuing lumbar pains caused him to withdraw before the selection process began. He struggled on until the start of July, after taking 194 off Nottinghamshire at Trent Bridge, an innings of more than five hours that seemed to have left him finally burned out. After seeing specialists the following Winter Hutton formally retired in the January of 1956; in the Birthday Honours of that year he received a knighthood, the first Yorkshire cricketer to be so honoured for his playing achievements.

Radio broadcasting, then television followed. In 1957, at a dinner in Manchester Town Hall to commemorate the centenary of Old Trafford, one sad fact of Hutton's career was pointed out: that Hutton was still only 40 and that the world had been granted only a dozen years of his play since his apotheosis at The Oval in 1938.

Hutton played the odd game for MCC and an offer of employment by the *Evening News*, London, brought the reluctant but inevitable decision to leave Pudsey for Kingston-on-Thames. Sidney Hainsworth, a Yorkshire Vice-President, Pudsey-born, who became managing director of a Hull firm of transmission engineers, Fenner Ltd, and a generous benefactor of Yorkshire cricket, found a role for him that lasted 25 years until he retired in 1984. He served briefly as an England selector in 1974-75, but found the office clashed with his business commitment and withdrew. In later years he has contributed fairly regularly to *The Observer*, pieces of great wisdom and no little wit, that are always perceptive.

A man who never enjoyed controversy, he was critical of Boycott's supporters during Yorkshire's traumas of the 1975-85 decade while showing some sympathy for Boycott himself.

The esteem in which he is held nationally was very evident in 1988, the 50th anniversary of his 364, one of the most treasured tributes coming from his fellow batting knight, Sir Donald Bradman.

From a purely selfish point of view Yorkshiremen could have regretted his success with England for the loss of the dressing room's two senior members, Yardley and Hutton. Their absence for so much of those Summers between 1946 and 1954 must have been a handicap in the successful rebuilding of the post-war team. Continuity of leadership is essential for a successful team and neither of these excellent captains was able to give his total attention to Yorkshire's cause at times when experienced direction was a priority.

That Hutton never captained Yorkshire as more than senior professional was simply a quirk of history. He was a contemporary of Yardley's and the pair retired together in 1955. If Hutton's health had been better he might have been tempted to become Yorkshire's first professional captain this century, but the situation never arose. He was tired, too. As his close friend Kilburn observed: 'The playing routine was losing its attraction; he had completed an exhausting journey.' Moreover the Yorkshire dressing room at that time no longer had the appeal for him that it had for some of the fresh-faced young men who were entering the doorway for the first time.

Some players believed, Ted Lester among them, that Hutton might have been persuaded to play on had he been offered the Yorkshire captaincy, but all the evidence suggests that his declining health, the move south and increasing media opportunities would all have severely limited his remaining playing career. The author had the privilege of working with him on his weekly column in *The Observer* and found Hutton enjoying his role as a revered elderly statesman. He was always especially welcome at The Oval, the scene of his great triumph in 1938, where Surrey made him virtually one of their own, and Yorkshire made recompense for any previous or unintended slights by electing him Club President. It is probable, had he lived beyond his years, that he would have become the first ex-professional to become President of MCC.

A right-hand batsman of peerless skill on difficult pitches, Hutton was as good a player against all opposition in all conditions as cricket has ever seen: his off-drive is remembered as one of the great glories of the game.

restart until after lunch on Whit Monday, when Yorkshire were dismissed for 46 ('a dear old lady threatened hysterics' according to Cardus), and although Sutcliffe (61) and Leyland (43) batted defiantly in the follow-on, they could only delay the inevitable.

The team was changing, but losing very little of its power, as the latter half of the 1932 Summer was to prove. Macaulay was now a specialist off-break bowler, Bowes sharing the new ball mostly with Arthur Rhodes, the hoped-for successor to Robinson. Horace Fisher, then left-arm medium, deputised for Verity and won a measure of immortality by taking the first lbw hat-trick, against Somerset, at Bramall Lane. Fisher, the subject of many a legend in league cricket, had figures of 5-12 in that match, and Kilburn reported that when the umpire, Billy Reeves, put up his finger for the hat-trick lbw ball he felt obliged to explain, to no one in particular but the world at large: 'As God is my witness, he's out.'

The most significant difference was in the leadership where, because of Greenwood's increasing unavailability, Brian Sellers, son of Arthur Sellers, a distinguished amateur of the previous generation and long-serving committee member, took the major responsibility. Sellers, by his own example as much as anything, brought to an already successful and confident team, brimming with ability, an extra aggression. Under Sellers it was accepted that Yorkshire fielders (without any protection other than a box) always posted themselves a yard nearer the bat than other county players. It was Sellers who introduced the masseur to cricket, the forerunner of today's support staff.

This extra intimidation of the batsmen, struggling to overcome bowlers of the class of Bowes and Verity (who shared 352 wickets that Summer), explains the great surge that occurred from June – five wins in nine matches and another five wins in July. From August, Yorkshire were supreme.

What became Sellers' team were renowned for their unremitting belligerence, whether expressed in the tilt of Mitchell's cap, the fast, sudden bounce or zip away of Bowes, the hostility of Macaulay, Verity's turn and lift, all whips and scorpions above the shining batting edifice of Sutcliffe, Holmes and Leyland.

But all this was to come after the gloom and disappointments of May, for after Lancashire's salutary lesson, Hampshire won by 49 runs at Headingley – although that was the last taste of defeat. The first southern tour of the Summer brought victories at Bristol, Tonbridge, Leyton and Lord's.

The Essex match, at Leyton, was an historic landmark. Holmes and Sutcliffe broke the 34-year-old record by Brown and Tunnicliffe for an opening stand, 554 at Chesterfield. At 555 Sutcliffe gave his wicket away, not realising that there was confusion over the actual score, an hour passing, so the official version went, before a missing no-ball was discovered. Later Percy Fender, the Surrey captain of that era, was to blame the Essex Captain Charlie Bray for 'allowing' that no-ball to be discovered.

Not that anyone could really jib at the performance, Sutcliffe scoring 313 (one six and 33 fours) and Holmes 224 (19 fours). The match was over early on the third morning, Yorkshire winning by an innings and 313.

Sutcliffe followed this triumph with a 270 against Sussex, his aggregate in three consecutive matches reaching 789. At Bradford, Sutcliffe reached his hundredth 100, 132 in under two hours (eight sixes and eight fours) against Gloucestershire in a match of furious scoring: Yorkshire 472-7, Gloucester 404 (Hammond 147 out of 190 in 130 minutes), Yorkshire 240-6. Bowes won the match as

Paul Gibb*

Gibb's career was a unique one, ranging from success with Yorkshire and England, the University of Cambridge and the Gentlemen to a professional with Essex and finally to first-class umpire. His decision to leave Yorkshire and become a professional with Essex was historic; no other Cambridge Blue (Gibb played from 1935-38) had ever turned professional; nor had one ever become a professional umpire. But Gibb had a penchant for historic 'firsts'.

In his first match for Yorkshire he scored a century – 157 not out against Nottinghamshire at Sheffield (he had, however, scored a century earlier for Cambridge).

In his first Test – at Johannesburg against South Africa during the 1938-39 tour – he scored nine and 106, a record Test debut. Twice in the match he shared century partnerships – with Eddie Paynter of Lancashire – 184 and 168. He scored 58 in his third Test innings of the same tour, a start in representative cricket equalled only by Yorkshire's Herbert Sutcliffe (64, 122, 83). And in the tedious, timeless final Test at Durban his 120 took 451 minutes, the slowest century on record for England in any Test match until P.E. Richardson's 100 in 490 minutes at Johannesburg in 1956-57.

During Gibb's innings at Durban he added 280 for the second wicket with W.J. Edrich, a record for the Anglo-Saxon African series.

Gibb's touring experience was wide. He toured Canada, America and Bermuda with Sir Julian Cahn's team in 1933; he captained a Yorkshire team that toured Jamaica in 1937-38; and after a distinguished war record with the RAF, he toured Australia in 1946-47. He went on this tour as first-choice wicket-keeper, but after only one Test he was replaced by Godfrey Evans.

In 1953-54 Gibb again visited India, this time with a Commonwealth side. Gibb also played two Tests against the Nawab of Pataudi's Indian side in 1946 and at Lord's set up a fifth record for the series of 182 with Joe Hardstaff.

His complete Test figures are impressive; in eight Tests he scored 581 runs averaging 44.59

and he scored two centuries. His University career was a distinguished one. His wicket-keeping ability was so highly thought of that he kept out, in 1935, S.C. Griffith, a future Test keeper.

As well as scoring 122 against Oxford in 1938 he carried his bat through Cambridge's innings of 163 (Gibb 83 not out) against the 1938 Australians under Bradman and his patient batsmanship won him an invitation to meet Bradman's men in the Leeds and Old Trafford Tests. But Gibb, always prone to injury early in his career, missed both. The Old Trafford match was washed out without a ball being bowled, and Gibb was unfit for Leeds.

Gibb's greatest performances were reserved for Essex in the field of county cricket. He scored only two centuries for Yorkshire, his 157 not out against Nottinghamshire and 104 against Warwickshire in 1946. The war must take the blame for his slight returns for the county (1,545 runs at 32.87). He was a dour batsman with the perfect temperament for the big occasion.

Though he wore spectacles he was a fearless wicket-keeper, taking knocks with typical nonchalance and always ready to come back for more. He was a dependable keeper with moments of brilliance. In a Minor Counties against the University of Cambridge match he dismissed seven batsmen, three being stumped in the course of seven balls bowled by H.R.W. Butterworth; he claimed six victims in an innings against an Indian XI at Bombay in 1937-38.

Blessed with an enormous capacity for food in general and ice-cream in particular, Gibb stamped his character on the game and as an umpire he was as imperturbable and as dryly humorous as he was when a player. He died in 1977 in Guildford Bus Station, where he was employed as a driver.

Peter Thomas

The above profile was written by the late Peter Thomas for inclusion in a projected but never published second edition of his Yorkshire Cricketers and is reproduced by permission of Mrs Margaret Thomas.

Gloucester, led by Hammond, raced for victory, by bowling last man Tom Goddard with the first ball of the final over.

More history was recorded in the following match, against Nottinghamshire at Headingley. When a thunderstorm intervened on the second afternoon, Yorkshire were 163-9 in reply to a Nottinghamshire total of 234. Play was delayed on the Tuesday morning before Yorkshire declared, Nottinghamshire being 38-0 at lunch. Verity bowled nine overs without conceding a run and then, as the pitch began drying, the ball started to bite; he did the hat-trick, twice taking two wickets in two balls, and finished with figures of 19.4-16-10-10. Twice in his career, twice in two Summers he had taken all ten wickets. Again Macaulay was the bowler at the other end, declaring this time that he continued to bowl at the stumps: 'I'll do my best to get one.' In one spell of 15 deliveries Verity took seven wickets for three runs. In both his ten-wicket feats the manner and number of dismissals were the same: eight batsmen caught, one stumped, one leg before.

The team had an equal satisfaction at Old Trafford, after the humiliation of Whitsuntide, where Lancashire were beaten by an innings and five runs, Cardus complaining that the 'hordes from Laisterdyke and Kirkheaton and other barbarous habitations' revealed themselves only when Yorkshire was winning. The climax to a glorious Summer came in blazing weather at Scarborough where Essex made 325, Bowes bowling 40 overs for his 9-120 and suffering dropped catches, before Yorkshire's reply was made in a thunder of guns: Sutcliffe reached 100 in 120 minutes and then added 94 in the next 40 minutes; with Leyland he added 102 in six overs, the stand being worth in all 149 in 55 minutes. Hardly surprisingly, a somewhat shattered Essex succumbed by the early afternoon of the third day, the margin an innings and nine runs.

Sutcliffe had another magnificent Summer, 2,883 runs at an average of 80, and Leyland, Holmes, Mitchell and Barber all passed 1,000. Macaulay was third behind the two titans with 84 wickets, the averages actually being topped by a useful all-rounder from Ripley, 23-year-old Frank Smailes, a cricketer of sufficient versatility to be thought of as a successor to Macaulay.

The world turned a little fast in 1933. In Germany a somewhat comical demagogue named Adolph Hitler became Chancellor of that country, and the British Empire, whose status then was analogous to that of the United States today, recognised another dictator alongside Stalin and Mussolini. George Orwell wrote *Down and Out in Paris and London*, and with the US economy in deep recession, unemployment stalked the Western world; the search for quick, sharp solutions was more apparent.

In what might have been regarded in Bradford as an attempt to rob Yorkshire of a third successive Championship, the scoring system was changed again, back to percentages, each county having to play a minimum of 24 matches to qualify. If such a plot existed then it failed miserably, for Yorkshire had a run of 12 successive victories in June, winning 19 games overall. By 18 August the Championship was won again, after which their last six matches bringing three draws and three defeats.

This was partially explained by an injury to Bowes, and it was as well for Yorkshire that Macaulay, at 36 and two years from retirement, had an Indian Summer. Bowling off-breaks around the wicket Macaulay collected 141 wickets at an average of 15, bowling more overs even than Verity. Kilburn makes the point that, as well as Macaulay bowled – he was recalled by England – both he and Verity owed much to the close fielding of Arthur Wood and Mitchell, the latter 'among the leading fieldsmen in the world'.

There were strains showing elsewhere. The great opening partnership of Holmes and Sutcliffe, as famous in their day as Marks and Spencer, managed only one century opening stand. When Percy Holmes took until 17 August to reach his first 50, it was accepted, reluctantly, that an illustrious career was ending.

One of the great victories occurred at Old Trafford at Whitsun when loudspeakers were used for the first time in a Roses match. 'What next,' demanded Cardus, 'side shows for dancing and a bearded lady?' The batsmen were less amused by a pitch that was soon broken and dusty. Sutcliffe went for seven, Holmes for 22, Leyland for three, and when Percy reached the dressing room he predicted the match would not last a day. Mitchell, in a dour, grinding innings of 360 minutes, proved it was possible to stay, and his century enabled Yorkshire to reach 341, an extraordinary achievement in all the circumstances but 'the worst day's cricket I've ever seen' according to the *Manchester Guardian* correspondent.

On the Monday before a crowd of 25,000, the loudspeakers playing Lehár, a fresh sunny morning alive with anticipation of excitement, Yorkshire's last five wickets went down for 54 runs in 75 minutes. Bowes was given only three overs, despite winning movement and bounce before Verity appeared. Macaulay immediately set a leg-trap of four and Lancashire were dismissed for 92 and 93 (Macaulay 12-49), Cardus concluding (on 5 June) with a resigned 'they [Yorkshire] are so obviously the champions of this season'.

At Edgbaston, Yorkshire were defied by Norman Kilner, younger brother of Roy and nephew of Irving Washington, who had left Yorkshire ten years earlier to forge a new career with Warwickshire. In a gritty six hours worthy of his native Wombwell, Kilner scored 197 when no other batsman in his side could exceed 30, all done with a split finger injured while fielding on the first day.

At Kettering, Northamptonshire were beaten before lunch on the second day, Macaulay taking 11-34. When England called on Sutcliffe, Verity, Leyland and Macaulay, two defeats followed at Trent Bridge and Hull, Sussex being the one side to complete a double over Yorkshire that year, finishing second in successive years. At Brighton, with the crown already locked away again in Headingley, Sussex dismissed Yorkshire for 114 and 115. Leyland scored 210 not out at Dover, but Yorkshire, dismissed for 88 in their second innings, were beaten by Kent.

Sussex, not unexpectedly, made a bold assault in 1934 and by later July were favourites to win their first Championship, but only one win in their last ten matches (one more would have been enough) let in Lancashire. Yorkshire dropped to sixth but, in an Australian year, they had more than adequate explanation. Leyland and Verity played in five Tests, Sutcliffe in four,

Bowes in three; no county could have withstood such a diminution of strength. Yorkshire had to treat that Summer as one of experiment, an opportunity to test younger players at first-class level.

Holmes had retired (30,000 runs at an average of 42) and Macaulay, increasingly bothered by rheumatism, injured a finger in 1934 which hastened his retirement. In that Summer he took only 55 wickets, but Yorkshire's consolation, if there could be one at the impending loss of one of the elite, was that Smailes was eager and ready for the first team. Even the magnificent Sutcliffe had to accept that he was on the far and downward slope, although Herbert was already satisfied and content that his successor, a 16-year-old right-hander from Pudsey, was waiting in the wings.

Sutcliffe nevertheless topped 2,000 runs in 1934 while Leyland, six years younger, had his best year. Wilf Barber, from Cleckheaton, who could bat anywhere in the order and field expertly, was now established and made invaluable contributions when the team was weakened by Test calls. Cyril Turner, a patient left-hander from Wombwell, a superb fielder and occasional right-arm bowler, was another who might have achieved far greater fame elsewhere, but who was content in the company of greatness. The jewel, of course, was the boy from Pudsey, Leonard Hutton, for whom Sutcliffe had predicted an England place almost on first sight.

So advanced was the boy in his technique, and so sound in his application and concentration, that when he first appeared at the Winter shed Bowes and Verity, no less, were there to greet him and to bowl to him. Bill Bowes, Sir Leonard recalled in 1987, wanted to know how he had come by his bat (a gift that was an old and trusted favourite) and then advised him, in the kindliest manner, that he needed an instrument of better quality. Had the boy played the violin, Yorkshire would have found him a Stradivarius.

It was firmly impressed upon the 17-year-old that his sole duty in 1934 was the gathering of experience, that runs were far less important than priceless minutes at the crease. He began his first-class career with a duck, the professors pointing out to him that he had begun, as was

Ellis Robinson

Ellis Pembroke Robinson, from Denaby Main, became Macaulay's successor as the team's off-spinner but did not confirm his place in the side until 1937, when he took 78 wickets. He arrived as a leg-break bowler, blessed with long, strong fingers and was advised by Hirst that he had a better chance of reaching the first team by spinning the ball the other way and thus competing for a forthcoming vacancy. He developed such a power of spin that he was often forced to bowl around the wicket and could not always command the length and direction demanded of one of Sellers' spinners.

Robinson was nevertheless a key member, as a lusty, left-handed batsman, of the Championship teams immediately pre-war. He formed, with Mitchell, Turner, Yardley and Sellers, the brilliant close-wicket cordon that captured so many wickets in those years by catching of anticipation and audacity.

Robinson continued for four more seasons after the Second World War but in 1949, at the age of 38, he was allowed to move on to Somerset where he managed one last splendid Summer, 1951, when he bowled 200 more overs at the age of 41 than any other bowler in the team and took 107 wickets.

In retirement Ellis Robinson never lost his enthusiasm for cricket and was elected an honorary life member of the Club.

proper, at the bottom and could not get any worse. In his second match he spent 180 minutes over 57 against the University of Oxford, but before July was out he had scored 196 against Worcestershire.

The new opening partnership of Sutcliffe and Mitchell began with a promising start of 143 against Lancashire on a cold Saturday at Bramall Lane. By Monday the pitch had turned awkward and Verity was soon plucking the Red Rose, with match figures of 8-53 as Lancashire followed on to defeat.

Yorkshire then managed to subdue the new power in county cricket, Derbyshire, at Chesterfield, winning by 102 after losing on the first innings, with Ken Davidson, a stylist right-hander from Calverley, scoring 61. Davidson scored 1,034 runs for Yorkshire that Summer and turned professional, but was later to desert cricket for professional badminton.

Middlesex took advantage of the Test-match absentees at Lord's, winning by two wickets, as did Sussex at Sheffield, Gloucester at Bristol, Warwickshire at Scarborough and Essex at Southend, but there could be no such excuses for the stirring victory by Leicestershire at Leicester, their first over Yorkshire for 23 years.

Leicestershire were dismissed for 94 in the first innings, Sellers then declaring, perhaps over-confidently, at 196-5. But Leicester refused to collapse again and when Yorkshire were left to score 149 on a wearing pitch they were, to their own surprise, bundled out for 93. Leyland's benefit, against Nottinghamshire, brought receipts of almost £2,500, and once a draw was seen to be inevitable, Larwood enlivened a final hour by bowling, at the beneficiary's request, controversial leg theory at Leyland.

It was ironic that Macaulay's last season, 1935, should have seen the introduction of the off-side lbw law, making a batsman liable to dismissal to a ball pitched outside his off stump. The value of every bowler who brought the ball in from the off was enhanced, and some authorities to this day claim that the restrictions thus placed on batsmen reduced much of the handsome stroke-play of the Golden Age.

If Sutcliffe had been displaced in the England side, playing in two Tests that year, he brought all his class and resolution back to the Yorkshire innings, scoring eight centuries, and his achievements cast such a gloss upon all Yorkshire's batsmen that both Mitchell and Barber won England caps, while Wood, whose batting had advanced steadily, became the first Yorkshire wicket-keeper to pass 1,000 runs.

With the bowling heavily reliant upon Verity and Bowes it was surprising that Yorkshire should win the Championship with such authority – 'by this time their successes were beginning to appear rather monotonous' wrote Roy Webber. Certainly no one could argue with a team that could win six successive victories in July and another six in succession in August.

Macaulay's health was such that he bowled in only 14 innings, and although Smailes, now a recognised opening bowler, Bowes and Fisher, still bowling left-arm medium, played their part, there was no obvious successor to the off-spinner. Turner's in-swing brought him 7-45 at Gloucester.

May was a desperate month, a full fortnight swept by bitter winds, the match at Chesterfield being abandoned in a snowstorm. June was not a great deal better, but Yorkshire's stumbling start turned into a steady gallop in July, interrupted only by a sensational fall at Huddersfield.

Essex had been thrashed at Colchester and no one anticipated the electrifying news of the first hour's play in the return match: Yorkshire all out in less than an hour for 31, Read 6-11, Nicholls 4-17. By the close of play that day Essex were 303 ahead, Nicholls having scored 146. The match was all over before lunch on the second day, Yorkshire going down a second time for 99, Nichols 7-37. The Fartown crowd were so stunned that one member even turned on that perennial favourite Leyland, telling him as he returned in the second innings: 'Tha's brok thi bat, tha's brok thi wicket [he had been bowled] and tha's brok thi reputation.' Maurice's reply, if there was one, went unrecorded; he probably returned a sad smile. Kilburn's verdict on one of the most unexpected reverses in Yorkshire's history was simple: 'Everything went right for Essex and wrong for Yorkshire.'

Lancashire, in the next match, caught the full force of Yorkshire's anger and wounded pride. Bowes took 6-16 in a Lancashire first innings of 53 and another six in the follow-on, Yorkshire winning by seven wickets. As England did not think highly enough of Bowes' services, he was also able to play for Yorkshire in the following match at Kettering where Northamptonshire provided him with match figures of 16-35, 18 of his 29.3 overs being maidens.

As a final flourish of prowess Yorkshire ended the 1935 Summer with a handsome beating of the Rest of England by 149 runs, the first victory by the Champions over The Rest for 30 years (the previous winners having been Yorkshire), although Wyatt was unable to bat in either innings for The Rest.

Two new names appeared in the Yorkshire averages for the first time: Paul Gibb, batsman wicket-keeper from Brandsby, who had won a Blue at Cambridge in the years 1935-39, and Ellis Robinson, from Denaby, a right-arm slow bowler who had originally appeared at the Winter shed bowling leg-breaks but was persuaded by George Hirst to convert, with Macaulay's retirement impending, to off-spin.

Gibb, in fact, captained Yorkshire on their first overseas tour, to Jamaica in the Winter of 1935-36. An invitation also went to another Cambridge undergraduate, Norman Yardley, but he was unable to get leave, and with Barber in New Zealand with MCC, 13 players were chosen, including the second-team captain J. Raper, Sutcliffe and Hirst acting as joint managers. The ship, from Avonmouth, took a week to reach the Caribbean, Hirst writing home to say he dreaded the return trip (which was, in fact, much smoother).

Yorkshire won the first match against Jamaica by five wickets, Verity 10-96, Robinson becoming an instant success by big hitting that brought him scores of 68 and 63. Two more five-day matches against Jamaica were drawn, the batsmen enjoying themselves far more than the bowlers. Fisher, renowned for this tight bowling, delivered 46 overs for 33 runs (and 33 maidens), while Verity bowled 59 overs for his 2-91 but did have the satisfaction, in the last match, of scoring 101.

The season of 1936, the year of the Abdication and the beginning of the Spanish Civil War, and of Prokofiev's 'Peter and the Wolf,' was also Derbyshire's Championship, won by the fiery pace of Copson and the artful leg-spin of Mitchell. Eighteen of Yorkshire's matches were

Norman Yardley

Norman Walter Dransfield Yardley, born in Barnsley, was Yorkshire's unluckiest captain. He succeeded Brian Sellers, supervised the rebuilding of the side after the Second World War, presided over some special talents in the 1950s, was popular and able, and yet passed into retirement without winning the Championship; a mystery.

He was an outright player of distinction at cricket (a Blue in all four years at Cambridge), hockey (a Blue) and squash (six times North of England champion). Of all Yorkshire's captains perhaps only Close surpassed him in all-round ability. He led England in 14 Test matches, took huge delight in dismissing Bradman with his thoughtful seam bowling, was a good tactician and excellent close field. Peter Thomas compared him with Lord Peter Wimsey, another cultured man of many parts with a patrician disdain for the ordinary.

Norman Yardley
Yorkshire Post

Yardley succeeded Sellers as captain at St. Peter's, York, won his Blue as a freshman and then inherited the Cambridge captaincy. He first appeared for Yorkshire in 1936, already the unspoken heir apparent to Sellers, was twice in the England XII against Australia in 1938 and was Hammond's vice-captain in Australia in 1946-47.

Yardley scored 17 centuries in his 11,632 runs for Yorkshire and was always a reliable change bowler or fielder. He was in the county's great tradition of being able to turn his hand, successfully, to any part of the game. The single exception was winning the one prize that eluded him in a highly distinguished career which concluded with the chairmanship of England's selectors and the presidency of Yorkshire.

Kilburn, who saw all of Yardley's reign and who might be described as a friendly critic, gave this verdict:

Yardley could do no more than weave a logical, orthodox pattern from the material at his disposal. When the material was inadequate he could not devise success and he did not expect it to fall to him through a disproportionate share of good fortune. Yardley recognised merit as the ground-work of achievement and all his character, all his training, led him to accept failure or success with equal grace and equanimity.

Don Mosey's explanation:

Yardley had been introduced to Yorkshire cricket in the mid-thirties when the side, individually and collectively, would have died for the cause. He had picked up the pieces after the war and it must have come as a total shock to someone with his background to find players in his side who rocked the boat. He had been schooled in that one-for-all and all-for-one tradition and any attitude in the side that showed itself as less than that was alien to him – I cannot see that it diminished him as a human being that this was so; rather, one feels, it diminishes those who rocked the boat.

Illingworth, who entered the Yorkshire side towards the end of Yardley's era, was openly critical in print of Yardley's captaincy and his failure to control two of the big temperaments in the team, Wardle and Appleyard. That Yorkshire team had a captain and senior professional (Hutton) both of whom were relaxed and detached individuals, when it seems that what Yardley needed was a top-class sergeant-major.

It should be emphasised that for most of the Summer both Yardley and Hutton were concerned as much with England's problems as Yorkshire's and it must have been difficult to switch, in hours, from consideration of the difficulties of facing Lindwall and

Miller at Lord's to a decision upon whether Appleyard or Wardle or young Illingworth should have which end at Bath. Neither captain nor senior professional had a regular occupancy of the dressing room in those years, losing an essential continuity that is always vital to a successful team.

Yorkshire tempers, too, were strained by the frustrations, year after year, of chasing home Surrey when, man for man, Yorkshire believed they were the superior cricketers but were never able to prove it. Just one breakthrough, one Championship amid Surrey's magnificent seven, would surely have totally changed the ambience of Yardley's captaincy. Nevertheless Yardley is remembered with great respect and affection by all those who played and worked with him.

affected by the weather, a partial explanation of their fall to third place, but they were also over-reliant upon the bowling of Bowes and Verity, and although Smailes took 130 wickets there was no Macaulay. Yorkshire's ability to contrive victory from impossible situations was no longer assumed.

Sutcliffe, by his own measure, had a poor season with 1,500 runs. Bowes was not in the best of health and is thought to have played when he would have been better resting muscle strains. Verity took 216 wickets in his 1,000 overs, and Smailes proved he was able to fill part of the gap left by Macaulay by turning to off-spin once the shine had gone. Most welcome was the advance of Hutton, now Sutcliffe's partner, to his first 1,000 runs, and Yardley who, on vacation, averaged 30 in his ten innings.

The two matches against the eventual champions Derbyshire were both drawn, as were the two Roses matches, both holiday fixtures suffering from the weather. Leyland scored seven centuries this Summer, overtaking Sutcliffe as the team's premier batsman, including a 263 against Essex at Hull, some retribution for the 'broken bat' jibe.

Yorkshire lost to Worcestershire for the first time since 1909, while at Sheffield, after Barber had

scored an excellent 158, Kent were dismissed for 39, Verity having another of his omnipotent days, finishing with 9-12 in 39 deliveries.

The next year, 1937, saw a resumption of the old Yorkshire-Middlesex rivalry that led, in mid-Summer, to a challenge from London to an extra match, no matter who were champions, to be played over four days. Hawke was reluctant but the Committee sanctioned the match, the players were enthusiastic and it was eventually agreed that all proceeds should go to charity.

Yorkshire lost their opening fixtures, MCC beating them for the first time in 33 years by 25 runs with 20 minutes remaining. Yorkshire were set to make 406 to win, MCC being without Bowes in the second innings because of a knee strain; Hutton stayed five hours for 161, Leyland made a forceful 69, and Smailes was left at 57 not out.

Yorkshire also lost on their second visit to Lord's to Middlesex by an innings and 22, Jim Smith taking 5-36 in the second. After such a result the Middlesex confidence mounted, hence the challenge. The two counties competed fiercely through a Summer in which the 20-year-old Hutton blossomed, scoring ten centuries and reaching 3,000 runs, but if Middlesex could have won their last two matches they would have been champions. They beat Kent, but were then held by their local rivals Surrey.

Yorkshire, despite their bowling limitations, ensured their pre-eminence by winning their last two fixtures against Sussex and Hampshire. Robinson won a regular place, showing his ability to spin the ball without always being in control of his length and direction, while Yardley, again on vacation, hit 600 runs and increased his average to 44. Lancashire won back a little self-esteem when, for once, Verity was outshone by another left-arm bowler, Iddon, Yorkshire taking five wickets before Lancashire scored the 91 they needed.

So to the Challenge Match, scheduled for The Oval from 11 to 15 September. Sellers, who had an outstanding season, being invited to captain the Gentlemen, virtually put Yorkshire beyond danger when he won the toss and batted first, leaving Middlesex to struggle on a damp pitch. Hutton, Sutcliffe and Mitchell, raising 256, gave the champions a grip they never relaxed. Monday's skies were even darker and when Middlesex batted, replying to Yorkshire's 401, they were in immediate trouble before Bowes and Smailes, sinking to 46-6 and then 63-6 before a storm ended play for the day.

Play could not restart until 2.30 pm on the third day, when Yorkshire allowed Middlesex to recover to 185 but were still able to enforce a follow-on. By then the pitch was drying and Verity was in his element, taking 8-43, and by 6 pm, in warm sunshine, Yorkshire were winners by an innings and 115, and the crowd had contributed to £1,329, giving Patsy Hendren an affectionate farewell to the first-class game.

There was one 'might have been' about 1937: Sutcliffe and Hutton had raised 315 in 280 minutes against Leicestershire at Hull when the junior partner was bowled. Sutcliffe was said to have been disappointed, having a target of 556 in mind, but on his 21st birthday, he never mentioned his ambition.

Yorkshire had every reason to feel delighted about the Championship of 1938, for not since 1912 had the feat been accomplished in an Australian Summer. England's demands were heavy, five players being called upon for the Oval Test, and of the two Championship match-

es lost, to Middlesex at Lord's and to Surrey at The Oval, the latter occurred while Tests were being played. Of the other nine matches that clashed with Tests, five were won.

Faced with such a drain on strength Yorkshire had to rely on the lesser-known players to bring results, especially in bowling. Ellis Robinson did well enough to win his cap, 104 wickets at 21 apiece. Leyland contributed 61 wickets at 18, while Frank Wilkinson, an in-swing bowler from Hull, added 24 wickets at 20. In addition to the batting stars, Gibb, Barber and Sellers all made more than 1,000 runs, while Smailes became the first Yorkshireman since Rhodes and Kilner to complete the 'double'.

The team took its share of knocks, too, with Turner, Mitchell, Smailes and Bowes all having to drop out at some point with injury. There was, not surprisingly, some feeling after the defeat by Middlesex at Lord's when, on a very lively first day's pitch, Hutton suffered a broken finger, Leyland a broken thumb and Gibb a split head when he ducked into an expected bouncer that didn't. Middlesex's frustrations can be partially explained by the fact that they finished second in each of the years from 1936 to 1939.

Lancashire were beaten twice, an experience they had not suffered for 28 years. Cardus pleaded with the selectors to pick the entire Yorkshire team, 'with or without Hammond or Paynter', for the last Test. They all but took him at his word.

Middlesex were beaten at Headingley in another important match (England claiming Edrich, Compton, Hutton and Verity) in which Leyland's left-arm spin brought him 4-15.

The Championship apart, the other two great events of the year were Hutton's world record 364 for England against Australia at The Oval and Yorkshire's match with Bradman's Australians at Bramall Lane, the first day's play drawing a crowd of 35,000. To a modern generation, accustomed to watching overseas visitors on television to the point of ennui, it is difficult to convey the excitement spread by the touring team of whom one could only read, glimpse briefly on the cinema newsreels, or watch live.

The whole nation hunched around their radios, waiting for Hutton to break the record. The author, a small boy, was brought in expressly from an Ampthill garden, in Bedfordshire, and ordered to stand silently by the loudspeaker until the magic moment passed, whereupon grandparents, parents and assorted relatives stood up, clapped and cheered and delightedly opened bottles.

Ten years later that same boy queued at Lord's to see Bradman, a long wait from early morning, only to be near heartbroken when the gates were closed with only 20 more yards to go. Today's small boys, fed pictures of the world on television, cannot know either the exaltation or the anguish, and they are the poorer for it.

That is why such a huge crowd gathered in Sheffield, for Bradman's Australians were as fiercely proud of their record as Yorkshiremen, and aimed not merely to stay unbeaten on tour but for annihilation of the opposition. Bradman's 1938 team may not have had the firepower of the side he brought in 1948, but they were not one whit less resolute.

Overnight rain meant play had to start 15 minutes late, and the crowd buzzed when it was learnt that Sellers had won the toss and sent in the Australians. In alien conditions the tourists struggled to 232, Bradman 59, the chief contributor being Hassett who, on his first tour of England, demonstrated both an excellent defensive technique and attacking stroke-play when, with the tail in support, he added 44 in 25 minutes.

Yorkshire in turn had their difficulties and finished 20 behind. Monday's pitch was awkward to negotiate and Bowes, it was said, produced his finest ever spell of 18 overs for only 2-28, although both Badcock and Bradman were missed off him in the slips. However, the last six Australian wickets were swept aside for 32 and Yorkshire needed 150 to win, rain intervening before the second innings could start.

The following morning, Yorkshire soon lost their night watchmen Wood and Verity, for 18, but by lunch Yorkshire needed another 67 for an historic victory with seven wickets standing, Sutcliffe's among them. Sadly, rain showers through the afternoon prevented a restart, and at 4 pm a disappointed Sellers out on the pitch signalled the abandonment.

The last season before the Second World War, 1939, saw Yorkshire as champions again but also brought, in Kilburn's words 'the last triumph of one of the greatest county teams of all time'. Again Yorkshire and Middlesex dominated the table through the Summer when cricket competed with ever more glaring and ominous headlines. Everyone accepted that war was coming; the only question was when.

Yorkshire was actually beaten four times that Summer, but as they also won 20 of their 28 matches there was no argument as to their supremacy. Two world-class bowlers, one world-class batsman and two, Sutcliffe and Leyland, who still had claims; most of the rest of the team were Test class, they were led by a shrewd and fearless captain, and they contained a close-field cordon that has never been surpassed. Six batsmen, in all matches, passed 1,000 runs, Verity took 191 wickets, Bowes 122, and although four players were taken for Test matches such was the supporting cast that Yorkshire only lost one match while weakened.

Gloucestershire defeated the champions twice, once by virtue of a fierce attacking innings by Barnett at Bradford, 90 in an hour, after Sellers had made an ultra sporting declaration: 189 in 100 minutes, time for Gloucestershire to win but not long enough for Yorkshire to bowl them out. At Bristol, Goddard's subtle spin was decisive.

Against these defeats could be balanced the successive victories against Hampshire, Leicestershire and Middlesex, achieved with the loss of only 13 wickets in all. The Derbyshire match at Bramall Lane is still remembered: Yorkshire were bowled out by the Popes for 83, Derbyshire replied with 20, Smailes 4-11, and Jim Smurthwaite, a 22-year-old fast-medium bowler from North Ormsby, who was deputising for Bowes, taking 5-7. Yorkshire batted again, Barber scoring 100 in a total of 310 before Derbyshire were shattered again, Smailes joining Verity, Drake and Wainwright in taking all ten wickets, his analysis reading 17.1-5-47-10.

Much criticism was attracted by a 'batting out' at

Jack Appleyard

Jack Appleyard was one of the finest organisers and innovators that Yorkshire has produced. His foresight brought the thrill of Sunday cricket, featuring big-name players, to Yorkshire during the war years; a delight that was welcomed by often as many as 70,000 people at that natural and splendid arena at Roundhay Park, Leeds. He also kept representative cricket alive in the county during the war years, and over a longer period raised over £20,000 for charity.

The greatest of the matches Appleyard organised was the moving Hedley Verity Memorial Match at Roundhay Park, in 1944 – a match that anticipated the county's official memorial match against Lancashire by a year. With the exception of Test matches the county has rarely seen such a gathering of great contemporary names as Appleyard invited to remember Verity, who had been killed in the war.

Herbert Sutcliffe's XII (repeat XII) was: Sutcliffe, Len Hutton, Arthur Mitchell, Maurice Leyland, Arthur Wood, Wilf Barber, Horace Fisher, Cyril Turner, Frank Dennis, Willie Watson, Ken Fiddling and Ellis Robinson.

Walter Hammond's XII consisted of Hammond, Eddie Paynter and George Duckworth (Lancashire), L.F. Townsend and Tommy Mitchell (Derbyshire), Jim Smith (Middlesex), C.S. Dempster (Leicestershire and New Zealand), Ross Stanford (Australian Imperial Services), G.V. Gunn (Nottinghamshire), J. Bailey (Hampshire),

Les Berry (Leicestershire) and Jack Crapp (Gloucestershire).

Appleyard's sense of occasion persuaded Wilfred Rhodes and Emmott Robinson to stand as umpires; the players wore black armbands, and a two-minute silence was observed by the 10,000 people who ignored the hostile weather that curtailed play. Collections alone brought in £650; £1,000 was donated for a memorial bed at Leeds General Infirmary. That year, 1944, over 100,000 attended Appleyard's August Bank Holiday Festival, paying a record £2,500.

The matches had originated in 1940 when £500 was raised; in 1941 that sum was doubled, with crowds of over 5,000 commonplace. In 1942 over 50 county cricketers appeared for Appleyard, including that charming little Lancastrian, Eddie Paynter, who always played with a brilliance and sense of responsibility to entertain the war-weary Yorkshire crowds.

In all Appleyard's zeal benefited such Yorkshire players as Wilf Barber, Bill Bowes, Frank Smailes, Len Hutton, Johnny Wardle, Bob Appleyard and Frank Lowson. Nor did such involvement dim Appleyard's enthusiasm and zest as secretary of the Leeds and District League. His private life was as colourful as his cricket life was zealous. He began work as a boy of 13 putting price tickets on garments; it ended with his ownership of a thriving business.

Peter Thomas

Bramall Lane against Nottinghamshire, although the points system at the time must take most of the blame. With no chance of a result Yorkshire's average would have suffered by a decision on the first innings, so the object of ensuring a 'no decision' was attained.

The final southern tour, bringing victories at Dover, Bournemouth and Brighton was accomplished in the feverish atmosphere of impending

war. At Dover, Kilburn reported, telegraph boys came to the ground in a constant steam calling up reservists, while communications were so interrupted and delayed that the evening newspaper correspondents found it almost impossible to file their reports.

The Scarborough Festival, Yorkshire heard, had been cancelled. Sutcliffe was the first player to hear from the War Office and did not travel on to

Brighton. On 1 September, with only one match remaining on the fixture list, Verity (7-9) bowled out Sussex for 33 as German troops invaded Poland.

Rail traffic to the North was dislocated; neither seats on trains, nor the trains themselves, could be guaranteed, so Yorkshire set off one sunny mid-afternoon to return by coach. A blackout had been ordered, roads out of London were crowded, and Yorkshire's coach stayed overnight in Leicester where improvised sleeping arrangements were made. By dawn the journey was resumed, players being dropped off one by one until this bizarre return ended in City Square, Leeds. The goodbyes, reported Kilburn, were perfunctory, because no one could antici-

pate the next meeting: 'It was a sad and silent party…and thence departed their several ways one of the finest county teams in the whole history of cricket. It never assembled again.'

Yorkshire's supremacy between the wars can be measured by a glance at the national bowling averages. In 1938 Bowes, Verity, Smailes and Robinson each passed 100 wickets (a feat previously achieved by Rhodes, Macaulay, Kilner and Waddington in 1922). From 1919 to 1947 Yorkshire always had one or more bowlers in the top five of the averages except in 1929 when Rhodes was tenth. In 1922, '23 and '46 Yorkshire bowlers occupied four of the five top places.

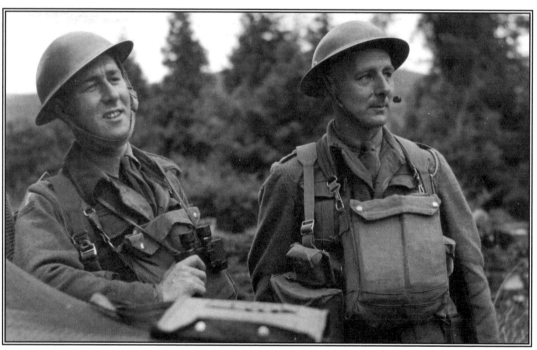

Norman Yardley and Hedley Verity training in Northern Ireland in 1941
YCCC

Yardley to Close 1945–1970

The World War again dealt Yorkshire some hard blows: Verity was killed leading Green Howards across a Sicilian cornfield; Bowes debilitated by years as a prisoner of war; an operation on Hutton's left elbow that shortened his arm; six years from the careers of the other champions of 1939. Sellers, Leyland, Smailes, Bowes, Verity, Hutton, Turner, Robinson, Gibb and Yardley all served in H.M. Forces as did the club Secretary John Nash, a proud record.

Sellers, Leyland and Smailes went into the Royal Artillery. Sellers eventually took charge of a stretch of coastal defence in Sussex and Kent, while Smailes served in North Africa, Italy and Greece. Bowes returned after three years, lighter by 63 pounds; Yardley was commissioned into the Green Howards and saw Northern Ireland, India, Iran, Egypt and Sicily and was wounded by a mortar bomb in Italy. Nash served the Signals in the Middle East. Gibb was an RAF flying-boat pilot over the Bay of Biscay, the North Atlantic, ferried aircraft from Scotland and Northern Ireland to East and South Africa,

and as the war ended in Europe he flew to Ceylon and Burma. Turner and Robinson were also in the RAF; Sutcliffe was commissioned in the Royal Ordnance Corps, while Hutton damaged his arm on a Commando course while an instructor in the Physical Training Corps. So serious was Hutton's injury that his career was threatened, but so successful was the subsequent operation on his arm that a grateful Yorkshire elected the surgeon, Reginald Broomhead of Leeds, to honorary life membership.

The Club was prudent enough to point out to members that heavy expenditure would be needed as soon as the war was over, and many members continued to pay their subscriptions while the authorities used the cricket grounds. One ground, dear old dirty Bramall Lane, was smashed by German bombs in December 1940.

By the Summer of 1945 it was clear that the European conflict, at least, was drawing to a close and although no competitive cricket could be organised, the game stirred again, spurred by

Alex Coxon

Alexander Coxon, a wiry, fast-medium right-arm bowler from Huddersfield, took his opportunity well in Yorkshire's rebuilding after the Second World War. Persistent and hostile, he lacked the pace to reach the highest level but served Yorkshire well for five years up to 1950, taking 483 wickets at an average of 20.91.

He was also a man of temperament and there was for years a rumour of a clash with Compton in the Lord's dressing room during Coxon's only Test appearance, against Australia at Lord's in 1948 when he was one of several seam bowlers to appear as aspiring partners to Alec Bedser. To his dying day he insisted he had Bradman leg before he had scored but the umpire dis-

agreed. Certainly when he left Yorkshire, at the age of 34, he had many years of cricket left which he took with him to the Durham Senior League where he is fondly remembered as Sunderland's most successful professional. He also played for Durham.

John Arlott, in his biography of Trueman, quotes an unnamed Yorkshire player as saying that Coxon's 'face didn't fit'. Close, in biography, referred to Coxon's 'harsh and grating manner'. Bob Appleyard remembered a lion-heart but added: 'Alex took no prisoners'.

Martin Howe, speaking to Coxon's relatives after his death, explained something of his controversial character in a cameo portrait (2008).

Arthur Booth Latecomer

A left-arm slow bowler of small stature but great guile, Arthur Booth, born in Featherstone, gave one magnificent Summer to Yorkshire. At the age of 43 he headed the first-class averages, taking 111 wickets at 11.61, and was thus highly instrumental in the winning of the 1946 Championship.

Booth first appeared for Yorkshire in 1931 when he was among several candidates for the place to be vacated by Wilfred Rhodes, and it was Wilfred who broke the news to him that Hedley Verity had won the race. The little man went off into league cricket and Northumberland, as did another rival Horace Fisher, not to appear again until 1945 when Yorkshire were casting around for a successor to Verity. It was clear that he was a long way ahead of the younger school of Wardle, Mason and Wood.

Booth fought off rheumatic attacks in a damp Summer to help bowl Yorkshire to another title before retiring. He once bowled in tandem with Wardle so that the Committee could assess the merits of the younger man and Wardle gave Booth much credit for his own advance. He was respected as a coach and earned another distinction in that he became the only former Yorkshire professional to become a member of the Lancashire Committee.

Booth played his cricket at a time when a place in the Yorkshire side could be won only by either genius or professionalism of the highest order. He would tell the tale of a Colts match in which he bowled a no-ball and was told, by the captain, to take his sweater at the end of the over. Yorkshire slow left-arm bowlers, he was reminded, were not permitted to bowl no-balls.

---

the deeds of the Royal Australian Air Force's superb young team, a warning of what Bradman had in store for England. Yorkshire organised two-day matches against Derbyshire and the Australian Services and played a third, against Lancashire at Bradford, for Verity's family. Although Sutcliffe had announced his retirement he did make a final appearance captaining a Yorkshire XI against the RAF at Scarborough.

Comparisons between the two post-war eras when on each occasion the team had to be rebuilt are interesting. Yorkshire had given ten players a debut in 1919, which does smack slightly of panic, although Sutcliffe, Wadington and Emmott Robinson were among them. In the seasons 1945-47 Yorkshire blooded 14, which suggests the later team had fewer vacancies – although another explanation might be that in the intervening 25 years professional cricketers had begun to learn to take better care of themselves, preserving their health and fitness.

There were nevertheless, some awkward gaps. Sutcliffe had gone, as had Verity, while Sellers, Wood, Bowes, Leyland, Barber and Turner were in their final years. Mitchell had become county

coach. Gibb, a batsman/wicket-keeper of high class, filled in for Wood successfully enough to be chosen to tour Australia in 1946-47. Bowes was not much more than medium pace but was able, by husbanding his strength and using all his abilities except speed and bounce, to remain highly effective; Smailes turned more and more to off-spin and a new-ball bowler was discovered in Alec Coxon of Huddersfield, an old-fashioned English seamer whose volatile personality fuelled endurance and endeavour.

The batting revolved almost entirely around Hutton, a dependency upon one man that Yorkshire had perhaps not undergone since the days of Ephraim Lockwood. Only Hutton and Barber passed 1,000 runs in Yorkshire matches and of the seven centuries scored Hutton took four, the others coming from Barber, Gibb and Yardley. Yet the middle and tail failed only rarely and no less than eight players passed five hundred runs and, surprisingly, Yorkshire won the Championship yet again. It was, perhaps, a psychological triumph, for with other countries in a similar state of reorganisation it was, wrote one cricket writer, 'quite enough to see the white rose on the caps to put the thought of a follow-on into the opposition'.

It was also a wet Summer and on uncovered pitches Yorkshire found two practitioners of the old skills, slow left-arm and right-hand off-spin, to run through most sides. Ellis Robinson emerged as the senior off-spinner, being selected for a Test trial and appearing for the Players, taking 129 wickets at 14 apiece, including such returns as 7-22 against Glamorgan and 7-24

against Hampshire.

The surprise, mystery and romance of the season all came from the 43-year-old almost creaking figure of Arthur Booth whose slow left-arm bowling headed the national averages at 111 wickets for 11 each, an astonishing performance from a player hardly heard of outside his county. Booth, from Featherstone, had first played for Yorkshire in 1931 but, like Horace Fisher among

Vic Wilson

John Victor Wilson, born near Malton, was a huge, strong left-hander of intense courage and application who anchored the Yorkshire innings at number three from 1948 to 1962, took 521 catches, mostly around short leg, in his 477 matches, scored 29 centuries, passed 1,000 runs 14 times and 2,000 once, hit double-centuries and in all reached almost 22,000 runs at an average of 31.33.

A farmer, Wilson could bat according to the needs of the side and was a formidable driver when on the attack; as a fielder he was so respected he was chosen for all five Tests against Australia in 1954-55 as 12th man without actually appearing for England.

Yet Wilson is honoured and remembered mostly for his three years as Yorkshire's captain, 1960-62, in which he twice led the side to the Championship and to a second place in 1961 when it could so easily have been a hat-trick before retirement. After the furore of Wardle's departure to Leicestershire, Wilson suddenly found himself as senior professional to the 39-year-old Ronnie Burnet, an amateur appointed to the captaincy in highly controversial circumstances. Wilson's steadfast insistence on standing aloof from all factions and in putting the welfare of the team first, made him a loyal and ideal lieutenant to Burnet at a difficult time.

It was natural then that he should succeed Burnet as captain, becoming the first professional to be elected since Tom Emmett

Vic Wilson
YCCC

70 years early. Wilson revealed a natural ability to lead and to motivate a talented team without too often upsetting some of the strong temperaments it contained. In 1961, irritated by constant comparisons, he snapped: 'We know we are not as good as other Yorkshire teams. Judge us by what we do, not by what we should be doing.' He could be firm, too, as when he sent home Trueman, for being late, from Taunton in 1962. A phlegmatic man of great strength, Wilson's authority was rarely challenged; he ruled firmly, fairly and very successfully, laying the foundation for Close and the Silver Sixties.

others, had had little opportunity in Verity's time. Almost 15 years of professional service in the leagues meant, however, that Booth had little to learn in first-class cricket, and if the weather got into his bones occasionally (rheumatism forced him to retire early in 1947) this little man bowled with a superb consistency. It was as if Sellers had walked into a dusty little room, marked 'SLA', opened a locker, taken Booth off a hook, dusted him down and sent him out to confound Yorkshire's foes.

Much of the Summer was cold and wet, poor weather for bowlers approaching middle age, yet fuelled by some distant warmth – perhaps the legacy of those glorious wartime Summers. Yorkshire swept past the University of Cambridge, Glamorgan, Kent and the University of Oxford, this run being brought to a draw by who else but Lancashire in a rain-affected clash at Bramall Lane. Only Somerset hindered progress in June and July, the Yorkshire bowling taking a hammering at Taunton. Booth and Leyland bowled Warwickshire out twice for less than a hundred each innings at Edgbaston, Leyland also contributing 52 runs and Lord's provided another turning pitch for an absorbing struggle against Middlesex. Yardley scored 53 of Yorkshire's 140; Jack Robertson replied with 38 of Middlesex's 74. Jack Young then took 8-31 in a Yorkshire second innings of 108, far too many for the Metropolitans, victory coming by 73 before lunch on the third day.

Despite contributing Hutton, Gibb, Smailes and Bowes to England, Yorkshire defeated Nottinghamshire by an innings at Bradford (Turner 68 and 5-39 in the follow-on). Glamorgan put out Yorkshire for 83 at Sheffield but were still beaten by six wickets, Smailes and Coxon sharing ten wickets; Hutton gave a magnificent demonstration of playing the turning ball in a tense second innings, victory coming when the maestro was on 99.

Hutton was hawk-eyed, too, at Chesterfield, Derbyshire batting for two overs on a pitch that was later confirmed as being 24 yards long before Hutton spotted the discrepancy. The match had to be restarted, Sellers conceding the runs already scored. Yorkshire seemed likely to be beaten, for the first time, by Worcestershire at Headingley; although only 89 runs were needed

neither Hutton nor Sellers was playing, but Willie Watson held one end while Robinson and then Smailes steered Yorkshire to a victory attained only with the last pair at the wicket.

Lancashire made a determined attempt to crack Yorkshire's record at Old Trafford, Leyland and Sellers playing out time. Hampshire were beaten at Scarborough in a festival for off-spinners, only the first of four innings passing 100. The Championship was finally won at Eastbourne: Sussex were all out for 91, Yorkshire for 82. John Langridge was stumped at 34 as Sussex rallied to 115 while Yorkshire, needing 105, lost four wickets for 26 before Leyland defended while Smailes attacked and Yorkshire had won the match and the title before tea on the second day.

The return to cricket had been a happy one. The veterans had reasserted their supremacy, Hutton was the world's premier batsman on a difficult surface and several young players had been introduced who would play a major part in the future: Vic Wilson, a left-hander, built like a rock with a temperament to match; Ted Lester, like Wilson from the North Riding but an unorthodox right-hander with a vast appetite for runs; Gerald Smithson, a left-hander form Spofforth who was to be the first of Yorkshire's post-war players to attract the selectors; two potential left-arm successors to Arthur Booth, Ron Wood from Ossett and Johnny Wardle from Ardsley; a fast bowler from Uppermill who promised genuine speed, John Whitehead; and another left-hand batsman, a gritty character from Holmfirth, Freddie Jakeman, whose fielding made an immediate impact. But there would be a gap, obviously, between the retirement of Sellers' generation and the growing to full maturity of these young players, and in 1946 Yorkshire were resigned to a spell of more accomplishments away from the glare of the Championship.

Perhaps 1947 was more truly the first post-war Summer. The South Africans toured and, seemingly, always in those days brought sunshine with them. It was the Summer of Compton and Edrich, when Middlesex not so much won but stormed the Championship; no score was beyond them. India became independent, the school-leaving age was raised to 15, England's March floods were the worst on record and in

Ted Lester Hawkeye

Edward Ibson Lester, from Scarborough, was among the most unorthodox batsmen ever to play for Yorkshire. A powerful, forcing right-hander, he forced himself to the Committee's attention by his prolific scoring on the excellent batting pitches of North Marine Road and, when the side was being revitalised after the Second World War, whatever doubts Yorkshire may have had about his methods were dispelled by his scoring rate and he became the established number four in what was one of Yorkshire's most powerful orders: Hutton, Lowson, J.V. Wilson, Lester, Watson, Yardley.

The young Lester, along with the young Wardle, was photographed with George Hirst at the Headingley nets in 1939; he played in a Colts trial at York later that Summer. His achievements for Scarborough kept him in the public eye and in 1945 he played in several two-day friendly matches for Yorkshire under the captaincy of Leyland.

In the hot Summer of 1947 Lester grew to full power, hitting three centuries in succession, two of them against Northamptonshire, and finishing even ahead of Hutton in the averages with an extraordinary figure of 73. If he was less prolific in 1948, a wet Summer, he still achieved a century in each innings of a Roses match. John Callaghan recorded an instance of Sellers' attention to detail after the Northampton episode; in a hurry to board the team coach after the match, Lester forgot to put on a tie. Sellers spotted his omission and Lester was obliged to open a suitcase and dress according to the captain's instructions before the coach was allowed to move off.

Lester's highest aggregate came in 1959 (1801) but he passed 1,000 runs six times in his 11 seasons and 228 matches. Especially strong on the leg side, Lester's fast scoring, based on an extremely quick eye and fine co-ordination, could turn a three-day match inside a couple of hours and he was always a dangerous batsman once set.

Ted Lester (wearing cap)and Harry Halliday walking out at Scarborough
YCCC

His last good season was in 1954 (four centuries) when he was having increasing difficulty, because of a foot problem, in playing three-day cricket. Lester then became the Colts' senior professional and captain before launching into a second career as Yorkshire's scorer, a position he held for more than 25 years when he was also guide, counsellor and friend to a line of captains all of whom rarely made a major decision without consulting him. He was able to introduce his own scoring system, and it was no surprise when the county scorers formed their own Association that he should be elected their first president.

Despite the travelling involved, Lester always refused to leave his beloved Scarborough and not until 1988, at the age of 65, did he cease to attend all Yorkshire's away matches. Ted Lester was a qualified MCC coach for more than 30 years.

Gerald Smithson Bevin Boy

Gerald Arthur Smithson, born in Spofforth, was an attractive left-hander of high promise who will be chiefly remembered as the only Yorkshire cricketer to have served as a 'Bevin Boy', a National Serviceman who worked as a coal miner rather than as a member of HM forces.

He played in 39 matches for Yorkshire between 1946 and 1950, and a 98 against Lancashire brought him to the attention of the selectors. Along with Wardle he was chosen for the 1947-48 tour of the West Indies, a selection that brought a debate in the House of Commons and the special government dispensation that was needed before he could be released from the mines to tour the Caribbean.

Norman Yardley (1950) described Smithson's 98 as 'one of the most polished displays of batting I have seen given by so young a player. He began with extreme confidence, making some delighted shots and he was soon cover driving, hooking and cutting with great skill, reminiscent of some of the young Australians.'

Sadly Smithson suffered an arm injury on that tour and missed the whole of 1948 season. On his return he could not establish a place in the side and played for Leicestershire in 154 matches between 1951 and 1956. If his career was brief, he did play twice for England and scored eight centuries for his two counties.

Along with Wardle and Brennan he was one of the three players capped by Yorkshire in 1947, the first time there had been such a wholesale distribution of caps since 1934 (Smailes, Turner, Davidson). Smithson played for Hertfordshire from 1957 to 1962 and died in Abingdon at the early age of 43.

November the Princess Elizabeth married. Yorkshire knew that Leyland, Barber and Turner had retired, with Booth shortly to follow, and that Sellers and Bowes were in their last season, while Gibb, on turning professional, had migrated to Essex. The gaps were many, and it is hardly surprising that in such a time of experiment 25 names were listed in the averages. Nor could there be such surprise at the team's fall to eighth place in the table, the lowest position in 37 years.

Hard pitches suited Lester, for one, and his aggregate of 657 from 11 innings brought him an average of 73 and a professional contract. Smithson won much praise; Watson progressed. Bowes led the averages for the last time, his benefit year bringing a new record for the county of £8,000, while a new fast-medium bowler was uncovered – Ron Aspinall from Almondbury, strong and eager. Wardle won the race for Booth's place perhaps a Summer too soon, yet took enough wickets to win a place, along with Smithson, on the Winter tour of the West Indies. Robinson and Coxon bore the brunt of the bowling and in the conditions more helpful to batsmen spent many a hot and weary day in the field.

A new wicket-keeper from Downside and born in Eccleshill, Don Brennan, became Yorkshire's second amateur in succession.

So many changes inevitably meant that the settling-in process had to be repeated match after match, with the consequent decline in Yorkshire's expected and intended fielding standards. MCC, in the opening match, were allowed to recover to 343-9 in their second innings, sufficient margin to impose a defeat by 164 runs despite Wilson's defiant 74.

Centuries by Hutton at Oxford and Swansea (197 against Glamorgan) brought the more usual victories, Smailes flourishing that strong right arm. Hutton made another century at Cambridge but not until after the University had once enjoyed the county's bowling, Guy Willant and Trevor Bailey scoring hundreds in total of 402. Sussex, aided by some fierce hitting by Hugh Bartlett, won by three wickets at Bradford, although Hutton managed yet another century before missing the next match with throat ailment.

Ron Aspinall

Between 1946 and 1950 Ron Aspinall, from Almondbury, was a candidate to open the bowling for England. Coming into the Yorkshire side upon Bowes' retirement he had two excellent seasons in 1947 and 1949 and was expected, by the England captain of that period, Norman Yardley, to reach Test match status. Yardley first saw him playing in Service teams in the Middle East during the war.

A strongly built, right-arm fast-medium bowler, he formed a good partnership with Coxon that might have carried Yorkshire through to the advent of Trueman had not a strained Achilles tendon in 1950 limited Aspinall's career to 36 matches.

He played seven seasons for Durham before becoming a first class-umpire, where he was always a highly popular figure in the county circuit.

The other senior batsman, Yardley, filled the gap with 137, Yorkshire beating Glamorgan by nine wickets at Sheffield, and although Lancashire managed to stop Hutton's extraordinary sequence at Old Trafford (they confined him to 95 and 86) Yorkshire had by far the better of the draw. Bowes and Coxon, bowling unchanged, saw off Warwickshire at Edgbaston before Gloucestershire managed to reduce Charlie Barnett's benefit match by defeating Yorkshire in two days, Sam Cook taking nine wickets for 42 runs and winning an England cap.

Going home, Yorkshire were able to beat Somerset at Headingley, but the next two matches were drawn and their new humbler circumstances brought to national attention by four successive defeats in mid-Summer. Without Sellers, Yardley and Hutton, Yorkshire lost to Nottinghamshire at Sheffield before engaging Middlesex at Leeds for Bowes' benefit, 41,000 attending over two days. Middlesex were sent in and out for 124 (Edrich 70), Yorkshire were then dismissed for 85 (Yardley 41), and by the close of an eventful day Middlesex extended their lead to 119 with seven wickets standing. Edrich went on to make 102 out of 165, a magnificent innings on a difficult pitch that included two sixes and 11 fours, before Yorkshire fell on the second afternoon for 186, some desperate late hitting atoning for a miserable start of 52-6.

Yorkshire again failed in the fourth innings at Tunbridge Wells; Surrey were the next comfortable victors, despite a 107 from Smithson, in four and a half hours; Gloucestershire achieved a double with a win at Bradford by eight runs. This was a defeat that would have enraged the old professors. With ten runs wanted, Wardle, Brennan and Robinson allowed themselves to be caught off Goddard. Warwickshire, at long last, provided some relief at Headingley, just failing to score the 261 needed for victory, Yorkshire winning by six with less than two minutes' play remaining.

The final tour lifted hearts, two of the younger players emerged: Lester scored a century in each innings at Northampton (126 and 142), while Aspinell had match figures of 14-65. Hutton made 197 and 104 against Essex at Southend and then capped his season with 270 not out at Bournemouth. Bowes bowed out in majestic manner: 30 overs, 5-52. Hutton topped 2,000 runs in all Yorkshire matches, but only two others, Yardley and Robinson took 100 wickets. There was undoubted promise among the younger players – but how much of it was flawed?

If 1947 emphasised how much Hutton and Yardley meant to Yorkshire's experimental teams, then the damper following year proved the point painfully. Yardley inherited the captaincy, as expected, but was also chosen to lead England against Bradman's Australians in all five Tests. He also missed several early matches and, later, in his position as England's captain, was called to other events.

Nor was Hutton in the best health that Summer yet, despite facing Lindwall and Miller and emerging, with Compton, in glory, he still managed to score nine out of Yorkshire's 22 centuries and his batting average was more than double that of the second-placed Watson, 92 to 44. Halliday, Lester and Wilson also passed

1,000 runs suggesting that the batting was gaining depth and assurance, yet the order was still prone to inexplicable collapses, especially when Hutton and/or Yardley were absent. As Kilburn put it: 'In the great years, with the toss won at Brighton, numbers ten and 11 could safely spend a morning on the beach; nobody dare go far from the dressing room in 1948.'

However, it was in Yorkshire's bowling and fielding that the fall from grace was more often apparent. Coxon bowled steadily enough to be chosen to play in the Second Test, while Wardle averaged 18 for his 148 wickets, a formidable

record scarred only by occasional lapses in concentration and accuracy that mystified elder members of the side. Aspinall was less forceful in his second season; Smailes was in his last Summer, while Robinson was dropped for a spell, recovering his more usual form in August. Bill Ford, a schoolmaster from Scarbourgh, was useful reinforcement for the seam attack, while Ken Smales, an off-spinner from Horsforth who was later to gain greater distinction as secretary of Nottingham Forest, was promoted to fill the gap left by Robinson.

By the standards of 40 years later 1948 was a

Don Brennan

Donald Vincent Brennan, born in Eccleshill, Bradford and educated at Downside, was a wicket-keeper of sufficient class to displace Godfrey Evans for two Tests against South Africa in 1951. He was another product of the Bradford League whose career was delayed by the Second World War and who owed his opportunity, after retirement of Arthur Wood, to Gibb's turning professional and removing to Essex.

Tall, slim, Brennan was commissioned during the war and continued to play for Yorkshire, as an amateur, from the age of 27, often acting as vice-captain to Yardley. After his brief Test appearances he toured India and Ceylon the following Winter, but thereafter the genius of Evans prevented a permanent claim to an England place.

Brennan was nevertheless highly regarded by the professionals, especially for his work standing up, keeping as he did such 'difficult' bowlers as Appleyard, Wardle and Leadbeater. He was especially remembered for his leg-side work, regularly described by contemporaries as 'brilliant'.

In his 204 matches for Yorkshire he caught 280 batsmen and stumped 100, his white gloves and dark-blue cap making him a distinguished figure in Yorkshire's team from 1947 to 1953. As a right-hand batsman he was remembered for his defiance rather than his strokes, although he did once add

Don Brennan
Mick Pope

106 with Brian Sellers for the tenth wicket against Worcestershire.

His retirement was brought about by a need to attend to the family textile business, but he represented Bradford on the General Committee from 1971 until illness prevented his standing for re-election in 1984. Brennan was a fierce and outspoken critic of the Boycott group. He died in Ilkley in January 1985, aged 65.

successful year, for Yorkshire won 11 of their 26 Championship matches and lost only four, another indication of the strength in batting. A fourth place in the Championship persuaded many supporters and members that, in fact, the corner had been turned and that the county were about to reclaim their pre-war supremacy. More knowledgeable persons inside the Committee were not happy with the long-term trends, and what was less than obvious to all was that, in the post-war world, attitudes and ambitions were fast changing: the whole concept of gentleman and player was being put into question and all authority was coming under challenge.

MCC again won the opening match at Lord's, Yorkshire falling twice to the left-arm spin of Jack Young – the biter bit. The Australians made a memorable visit to Bradford, Sellers leading the county as Yardley was indisposed while Hassett captained the tourists. Yorkshire batted first on a surface that soon turned, and Miller, as always supremely confident, bowled experimental slow off-spin to dismiss a disappointing Yorkshire for 71. Bill Johnston, too, reduced his pace, demonstrating the enormous cricketing versatility of a team that is still regarded as the greatest ever to tour England.

However, the Australians, too, would have been in trouble had not the irresistible Miller appeared at 38-4 to hit 34, including two sixes, the tourists eventually leading by 30, Smailes 6-51. Yorkshire's second innings was a disaster, Sellers being top scorer with 21, Johnston taking 6-18 in 15 overs. That left the Australian to score 60 for victory but they, too, were 20-5 and 31-6, with Sam Loxton unable to bat; Yorkshire then allowed the fresh-faced young Harvey to escape at short leg, their bowling fell away and Harvey finished the match with a straight six. It was an enthralling match, but one that sharply exposed all Yorkshire's then current frailties. Coxon and Aspinall both had their moment in Yorkshire's later drawn match against the Australians at Sheffield.

In the domestic programme Oxford had the better of a drawn match despite Lester's sparkling 149, defeats coming at Bristol and Birmingham, and Lancashire romping away with first-innings points at Headingley; only a ten-wicket defeat of Northamptonshire at Huddersfield lifted the gloom.

Hutton's 176 not out laid the basis for a defeat at Sussex on another turning pitch at Sheffield. Hutton followed this with 133 against Middlesex at Lord's, and this time Wardle and Robinson were so in command that Middlesex followed on to bring another innings victory. Even a break-in of Hutton's car in London, another indication of changing times, in which he lost his cricket bag and even the petrol from the tank, hardly affected his continuing golden seam.

Another win, against Kent at Bradford, raised hopes that a genuine challenge was developing until George Pope, at Chesterfield, put matters into perspective: Yorkshire were dismissed for 44. Derbyshire made 277 before rain wiped out play on the Monday and permitted only 90 minutes on the last day, Yorkshire thus escaping certain defeat at 37-6. Pope had match figures of 10-25 and he also scored 73.

Surrey's visit to Sheffield was played for Smailes' benefit and Yorkshire won in two days, Coxon taking 6-17 in Surrey's first innings of 42, following on to Yorkshire's 355-5. When Northamptonshire and Surrey (again) were defeated in July, Yorkshire's return to premier place seemed more than a possibility, but another dip in form brought the final disappointment. Lancashire again took first-innings points, this time at Old Trafford, although Lester had the personal distinction scoring centuries in each innings of a Roses match.

Dropped catches enabled Leicestershire to reach 300 on the first day at Sheffield and a match that had begun in high expectation ended in defeat by 66 runs, Yorkshire making a hash of trying to score 267 in 180 minutes. Yorkshire rallied to defeat Worcestershire at Bradford, but then lost on first innings at Worcester.

Victory was vital at Taunton if the challenge was to be sustained in the closing weeks, but the leg-spin of Johnny Lawrence brought another collapse, Yorkshire following on and being saved, in all probability, only by a back injury that prevented Lawrence from bowling again. The bowlers found better form at Bournemouth where Hutton and a new partner Geoffrey Keighley, born in Nice of a Yorkshire family and

Johnny Wardle Chinaman

John Henry Wardle, from Ardsley, was a unique slow left-arm bowler, a genius who could deliver the orthodox ball, turning away from the bat, the chinaman, turning into the bat, and the googly from the back of the hand, apparently an off-break, in fact a leg-break often turning prodigiously. Many left-handed bowlers have been able to produce all three deliveries, but none but Wardle was able to bowl them consistently and successfully at the highest level. It is a modern cricket tragedy that Wardle is not acknowledged and remembered as one of the greatest spin bowlers.

That he is only now being given full recognition for his abilities is due partly to his own nature and a conspiracy of circumstances; even in his Autumn, reconciled with Yorkshire and appointed bowling consultant, he was frustrated in an attempt to tell his side of the story, in an autobiography to be written with the author of this history, by his early death, aged 62, in July 1985.

Johnny Wardle
Yorkshire Post

He did have time to tell me, in preliminary discussions about the book, that his famous chinaman in fact appeared before he became a slow left-arm bowler: 'As a kid I tried to bowl quick but soon realised that I was never going to be big enough or fast enough to trouble good batsmen so I started giving the ball a flip as I delivered and had learned to bowl that delivery before I ever took up slow left-arm.'

Wardle was built like a welterweight, a pugnacious, a quick-tempered and a fierce competitor determined to win his way out of a mining area in the depression years of the 1930s. He shared this environment with another Yorkshire player of intense determination, the comparison being first made by Wardle's friend in the dressing room, Ted Lester: 'In his dedication to the game, his attitude and discipline he most resembled Geoff Boycott.' Boycott, for all his rumbles with authority, achieved most of his ambitions, while Wardle carried a sense of frustration, of touching but not capturing the prizes, almost to his grave.

Alan Hill brought a posthumous compensation to Wardle in his 1988 biography *Cricket Conjurer*, a scrupulous balancing of the facts for and against someone who, even as a boy, was known to be moody. Wardle first demonstrated outstanding ability at Wath Grammar School (a scholarship boy) when he took eight wickets for four runs.

It was at this school, according to Hill, that Wardle suffered the first of a long series of setbacks that were to dog his career: he topped the batting and bowling averages for the school first XI yet was not awarded his school cap. 'He was halfway out of his seat when he realised that the...cap was to be presented to someone else.' It was not until 1956 that Old Wathonians remedied the injustice.

Perhaps this led him to scorn further education and to take a job as an apprentice fitter at Hickleton Main where he could fit his sporting engagements into a colliery life. He had manifold skills as a rugby full-back and a left wing footballer, in which role he joined Wolves' nursery team Wath Wanderers. Playing for Wanderers (he had trials with Wolves) he responded to a heavy foul by a defender by getting up, punching the aggressor and being sent off.

In four of five wartime seasons Wardle won the Yorkshire Council junior bowling prize, sometimes opening the bowling with what Charlie Lee recalled as 'little in-duckers'; he took all ten wickets for Brampton against Rockingham (for 36 runs) in 1940.

George Hirst called him to a net in Barnsley in 1942 and reported good progress by 'Wardle, the Brampton all-rounder'. By 1944 he had taken 113 wickets at 7.85 for Denaby and when the county cricket resumed he was clearly a candidate, along with Arthur Booth and Alan Mason from Addingham. Booth, at 43, headed the national averages in 1946 but had to retire with a rheumatic affliction, leaving the race to Mason and Wardle in 1947, a dry Summer.

Both spinners were given a six-match trial. Mason bowled intelligently but on the good batting pitches of early Summer he managed only two wickets in 77 overs. When Wardle took over he had the advantage of a few damper, dryer pitches and took his chances. He finished with 70 wickets in the Championship at an average of 23, and in August, along with Smithson and Brennan, was given his cap. The question of Verity's successor, a tormenting one for all Yorkshiremen in those early post-war seasons, had been settled. Or had it?

The retirement in quick succession of Bowes, Booth, Smailes and the decline of Robinson meant that more and more work fell on Wardle who, his new captain in 1948, Yardley admitted, 'was first change in any conditions'. Wardle even had to use the new ball on occasions and in those circumstances, experiment, even variation from the stock slow left-hander's ball, was frowned upon. Lester recalled: 'Johnny was crucified by the Yorkshire press who couldn't accept that he was different from his predecessors. Rhodes and Verity didn't

need to bowl chinaman so why should he? Did he think he was a cut above them? And when things went wrong, as they will with any spinner, and he got some tap, they were twice as hard on him.'

In addition, waiting in the wings were Mason and two more slow left-arm challengers, Johnny Ashman and Ronnie Wood. Wardle, as he would reveal privately from time to time, never felt sure despite his county cap and prodigious service to the club (1,247 overs in 1948). Bradman, who batted against Wardle that season, commented: 'There was the usual immaculate length, direction perhaps astray at times, good spin and a deceptiveness of flight more reminiscent of Rhodes than Verity.'

Despite Bradman's approbation, Wardle was chopped in 1949 while his rivals were given trial. Yorkshire wanted Wardle to remodel his action, to present a more classic, cartwheel, sideways-on pose when delivering the ball. Wardle tried to adapt, failed, was dropped and reverted to his old approach which, according to Trevor Bailey, was good for his wrist spin. No further attempts were made to turn Wardle into another Rhodes.

Bowling orthodox, Wardle swept back into favour in 1950, the peak performance being an 8-26 against Middlesex, and in 1953 Bowes, who was also the club's bowling coach, wrote, in commenting on *Wisden's* choice of Cricketers of the Year: 'There is no doubt...that Wardle has been overbowled. With much truth the players named him "perpetual motion Wardle". Originality and experience in his bowling had, of necessity, to be replaced by negative attack.'

In 1952 Wardle bowled 1,847 overs for 177 wickets at an average of 19.54, an almost single-handed attempt to win better than second place for Yorkshire. By then a new generation of bowlers had appeared to offer assistance – Close, Appleyard and Trueman. By 1955 Wardle was able to use his irregular attack more often, taking 195 wickets at 16.14, but by then his place as England's premier slow left-arm bowler had been usurped by Tony Lock who was to admit, years afterwards, that his faster ball was illegal, a fact that Wardle and many other bowlers knew but to which the umpires made almost no objection.

Lock's preference by England's selectors was a thorn in Wardle's side for a decade. According to Hill, 'He could not dismiss the iniquity of his exclusion'. Hill quoted a contemporary Yorkshire player: 'If Johnny had an Achilles heel it was Lock. He shouldn't have shown it. "Come on lads," he would call out. "Just watch that bastard throwing it out there."'

Wardle was not the only Yorkshireman to feel needled by the Lock affair and the memories of that controversy were revived 20 years later when Surrey were one of the counties to complain about Cope's action at a time when authority was much quicker to clamp down on any suspicion of throwing. Cope, of course, was eventually forced into minor counties cricket.

Wardle had been dumbfounded when Bob Berry of Lancashire had been preferred to himself on the 1950-51 tour of Australia – 'an appalling decision' according to one dissenting selector – and then found his pre-eminence challenged by a 'chucker'. The bitterness ran deep. One England player believes that Surrey's other spinner of that era, the Yorkshireman Jim Laker, would not have achieved his historic 19 wickets against Australia at Old Trafford in 1956 if Wardle and not Lock had been at the other end: 'Johnny would have had five or six wickets.'

In fairness to Lock, after watching himself on film he tried, at the age of 30, to remodel his action and won praise from his captain, Dexter, on the 1961-62 tour of India. Many good judges, including Peter May, believe England should have played both Lock and Wardle, but there is no doubt that had Lock not emerged, Wardle would have been as much an England fixture as had been Verity.

Perhaps the greatest humiliation the selectors heaped upon Wardle came in 1953

when, after he had taken four Australian wickets for seven runs in five overs, the selectors replaced him with Lock for the two remaining Tests, a choice vindicated by the recapture of the Ashes but no balm to Wardle's wounded temperament.

He was to have great days at England, on Hutton's tour of Australia and more especially in South Africa where, in 1956-57, he took 26 Test wickets at an average of 13 and headed the tour averages with 90 at 12. His 12-89 at Cape Town, in the Second Test was regarded by Hammond, an onlooker, and Insole, a playing colleague, as the best spin bowling they had ever seen.

From the full glory of that tour Wardle had returned home to Yorkshire as the newly installed senior professional to a newly elected captain, Ronnie Burnet, called up from the Bradford League to impose some discipline and leadership on the dressing room. Wardle, at the height of his fame and in peak form, was expected to take orders from a 39-year-old with no experience of first-class cricket and a confrontation was inevitable. Sadly for the club it meant Wardle's departure into Lancashire League cricket and to Cambridgeshire. The circumstances of the rift are dealt with in Burnet's details.

Hill records that Wardle, speaking to a meeting of miners in South Elmsall after leaving Yorkshire, was asked pointedly: 'Doesn't tha think tha's been a foo-il, Johnny?' Wardle looked at the questioner and replied: 'Aye, I have.'

The loss of such a talented bowler, hard-hitting batsman, consummate entertainer and humorist, the man who Appleyard said knew 'more about bowling than the rest of us put together', was as great a blow as the county had ever suffered. Peel replaced Peate, Rhodes replaced Peel, Verity replaced Rhodes and Wardle replaced Verity, but there the line ended.

Wardle was a devoted family man, 100% professional, who kept himself fit and always ensured he had a good night's sleep; a joker with a keen sense of humour on or off the field. In short he would have made, in his later years, the ideal senior professional and it is not too much of an exaggeration to say that much of Yorkshire's post-war troubles stemmed initially from the decision to sack Wardle. His loss was a grievous self-inflicted wound to the club.

As to his prowess, Hill quotes E.W. Swanton, who saw all of the careers of both Verity and Wardle:

You would want Hedley on your side because you could always be sure of a minimum performance from him. If he had anything to help him he could be very dangerous. In all circumstances he would be steady. Johnny on a bad day could be expensive, but if matters went well for him – if he had wickets that took wrist spin – he could be a good deal the more dangerous of the two bowlers. He also spun it more as an orthodox slow left-hander than Hedley.

---

educated at Eton and Oxford, hit off the 113 runs needed in the second innings.

Hutton raised 166 against Sussex in the final match; Yorkshire declared at 315-9 and after Foord had taken the first four wickets with the score at 75, another success seemed imminent. Sussex, however, managed to reach 192, and the Yorkshire second innings, with Hutton batting down the order because of lumbago, was undervalued and Sussex, set to score 243 in the fourth innings, managed their task for the loss of only five wickets as once again Yorkshire in the field failed to reach moderate standards.

Not for the first time in their history Yorkshire surprised themselves and their critics in 1949 by sharing Championship with Middlesex, an extraordinary performance in many ways, for the team, still being rebuilt, was not considered either settled or able enough for such distinction.

Surrey and Middlesex, who had finished second and third in 1948 were, as expected, the chief contenders, and with a little more consistency earlier in the Summer might have each taken the title. Middlesex, however, did win their last five matches, which meant that Yorkshire had to win their last match against the reigning champions Glamorgan at Newport, a task they accomplished in two days. Nor could Yorkshire be accused of inconsistencies as they themselves reeled off six victories in succession, a brief return to the heady days of Hirst, Haigh and Rhodes.

It was a fine Summer, week upon week of sunshine, captains feeling that their best hope for winning on so many splendid batting surfaces

was to send in the opposition in the hope that the pitch on the first morning might be faintly green and damp. At Fenner's the undergraduate Hubert Doggart and John Dewes piled up the massive scores, while Hutton had another glittering Summer, scoring 2,640 runs for Yorkshire at an average of 69. Wilson, Lester, Yardley and the newcomer from Bradford, Frank Lowson, all passed 1,000 runs and 18-year-old all-rounder from Rawdon, Brian Close, who batted left and bowled right, completed an astonishing 'double' of 1,000 runs and 100 wickets in all matches. Also appearing for the first time that season were the seam bowlers Eric Barraclough (Bradford), Frank McHugh (Leeds), and Freddie Trueman (Maltby), wicket-keeper Jack Firth (Cottingley) and a leg-spinner from Huddersfield, Eddie Leadbeater.

The writer was serving at RAF Hospital, Ely in 1949 when the station adjutant, a very kindly man and cricket-lover, offered seats on a coach to those interested in seeing someone the Flight Lieutenant described as the 'new Lindwall from Yorkshire. His name is Truman, like the President's.'

Fenner's was at its best that day, shafts of sunlight through the trees (were there really so many more in those days?) mellowing the old pavilion, now sadly demolished and replaced by a building that looks rather like a slightly superior supermarket. To be honest neither Trueman nor Close, both of whom bowled, made much of an impression on this observer; nor did Hutton's new partner Lowson, a pale, thin lad who was dismissed very perfunctorily in the first innings. But in fact neither Lowson nor Close looked back again in the Summer, while Trueman, hos-

Brian Close

Dennis Brian Close came from a cricketing family embedded in the Bradford League. That he should appear as an accomplished all-rounder was not surprising itself, but to accomplish the 'double' in his first season and to win an England cap in that same season, at the age of 18, was the stuff of boyhood comic papers. Close went on to enlarge the fantasy of becoming the third most successful captain in the club's history, a captain of England and Somerset, a close fielder of superhuman courage, a batsman of massive power and a bowler of unquenchable optimism. Nor is that sufficient summary of a career that included controversial spells as the Club's chairman of cricket, an England selector and an insurance executive. He had an ability to drive motor cars in such a fashion as to reduce steel-nerved opening batsmen to jelly. He was also a prodigious player of golf, snooker and squash, and good enough at football to play professionally for Arsenal.

Close was playing for Rawdon's first team at 11, developed both his cricket and soccer at Aireborough Grammar, Verity's old school, went on to play for Guiseley and Yeadon and on his appearance at the Yorkshire nets, pre-seasons 1949, Bowes described him as a natural successor to Frank Smailes. Close himself was impressed, but never overawed, by the names in that year's call-up: Smales (Yorkshire and Nottinghamshire), Foord, Lowson, Trueman, Leadbeater, Illingworth, McHugh (Gloucestershire), Horner (Warwickshire), Firth (Leicestershire), and Booth (Warwickshire). Even by Yorkshire's pre-war standards it was a vintage crop.

Close's school results were impressive enough to win him a university place, which he delayed until after National Service. He had signed professional forms (a striker) with Leeds United and cricket was possibly more a pastime than a career when he was invited into Yorkshire's squad for the first Southern tour of 1949; a six-footer, he was shy compared with the other debutants Lowson, who was five years older, and the

Brian Close
Yorkshire Post

even then extrovert Trueman.

Close scored 28 runs and had match figures of 4-102, opening the bowling with Trueman in the starting victory against the University of Cambridge at Fenner's. By mid-season the young prodigy had scored 579 runs and had taken 67 wickets. Selected for the Test trial, then for the Players against the Gentlemen (top scoring with 65), Close was finally selected for the Third Test against New Zealand at Old Trafford.

He was 18 years and 149 days old when he first played Test cricket in a somewhat dampening debut, match figures of 1-85 and a duck, but Close was under orders to chase runs and he was caught on the long-on boundary. In September, Close began the Scarborough Festival with 100 wickets and needing 63 more runs for the 'double' duly accomplished with 44 and 46 not out against MCC. He and Lowson were capped in their first season and Close then went off to serve in the Royal Signals.

He had played only one first-class match for Yorkshire when he was chosen, the following Summer, for Freddie Brown's tour, the actual selection being announced while he was confined to barracks for seven days, the result of a misunderstanding over leave granted to play cricket!

He had a miserable first tour, being injured twice and finding little sympathy from the senior members of Brown's party. Transferred to Arsenal he found that cricket and football were becoming almost incompatible, and although he completed a second 'double' in his second full season (1952) another football injury, this time playing for Bradford City, put him out of all sport for 18 months. He began the 1954 Summer purely as a batsman, but when Appleyard dropped out, he tested his knee, found he was able to bowl again and finished with 66 wickets. By 1955 he was fully restored to all-round glory and, six years after his extraordinary start, his career was fully under way.

Close became one of the most formidable figures, to the opposition, in the English game, whether bowling right-arm seam or off-breaks, batting left-handed stubbornly or spectacularly, or fielding at suicidal short positions. In all his first-class career with Yorkshire, Somerset and England he scored almost 35,000 runs at an average of 33, including 52 centuries and took 1,171 wickets at 26 apiece. He also made 814 dismissals, including one stumping!

Witnesses will affirm they have seen catches taken at second slip off Close's forehead, at short leg; he once stood at silly point, with blood pouring over his boot from a gashed shin, blasting the bowler for the delay in getting back to his mark, with amazed team-mates waiting for him to keel over. Against Hall and Griffith at Lord's in 1963 he saved and almost won a Test match by taking hostile fast bowling on his body. The next day, before he appeared for Yorkshire against Glamorgan at Bramall Lane, a famous picture showed his body to be a mass of ugly purple bruises. Against Glamorgan he bowled 25 overs and took 6-55, then scored 61, then bowled another

16 overs to take 4-19, Yorkshire winning by ten wickets.

Iron player though he was, Close was of most value to the Club for his captaincy; for in his seven years he won four Championships and two Gillette Cups, a record that must have impressed Hawke although not, or so it seemed, Sellers. Mosey described his leadership:

> His side of the sixties, though occasionally exasperated when he went off on one of his mental walkabouts, sometimes moved to laughter at his fixations, nevertheless regarded him in affectionate wonderment and professional respect. As a captain in the field, he had above all, flair. He would bring about a bowling change or switch a fielding position where there was absolutely no reason in the world for doing so and nine times out of ten it came off. He was an implicit believer in his ability to make something happen in the field when nothing seemed likely.

This intuition was a gift he passed on to another great captain, and son of a Yorkshireman, Mike Brearley, of whom David Gower once wrote, 'As a player under JMB I always felt confident that the right thing was being done at the right time and that if Australia were 150 for two then it was probably their fault not his.'

Brearley, in his book on captaincy, had high praise for Close's charisma and embellished the story of the catch at second slip:

> He of all the captains I have known led from the front, his courage was notorious. Fielding incredibly close in at short square leg, the great dome of his head thrust belligerently forward, he was regularly struck by the ball. The story goes that it once rebounded from his forehead to second slip. 'Catch it,' Close shouted...he assured [the Yorkshire players] he was all right. 'But what if it had hit you an inch lower?' one asked. 'He'd have been caught in t'gully.'

Close himself had much praise for Yardley's warmth and understanding of his players and was not too sympathetic to those who saw kindness to young players as weakness, although in later years Close himself took criticism for his reluctance to blood youngsters. Close, typically, would have seen it merely as a defence of his old tried and trusted servants.

Close was an inspiration to his bowlers and it was he, as leader and tactician, who transformed Don Wilson from the somewhat hesitant successor to Johnny Wardle into an international bowler.

Close was an enormous influence upon his bowlers, particularly the spinners and especially Don Wilson. When Wilson was injured and Keith Gillhouley, from Huddersfield, deputised, the latter took 73 wickets at 21 each and Wilson, for that season, could not regain his place. But once Gillhouley moved on to Trent Bridge he was a disappointment to both Nottinghamshire and himself; without Close's inspiration and Yorkshire's aggressive fielding and catching, Gillhouley became an ordinary bowler.

Close's translation to the England captaincy was inevitable. The West Indies, under Sobers were leading England 3-0 with one draw when Close replaced Cowdrey for the last Test at The Oval in August 1966. He immediately insisted upon Illingworth's inclusion and won the Test by an innings and 34, a performance that won him charge against India and Pakistan the following Summer. He led in all three victories against India and although the Pakistanis managed a draw at Lord's, England won at Trent Bridge and The Oval.

Whatever misgivings the selectors might have had about Close's diplomatic skills as captain of England's Winter tour to the increasingly touchy Caribbean, they could not have displaced him after a record of six wins and a draw. But once again, Close was to be disappointed.

Close wrote in his memoirs that he had been warned that Summer that, 'they are just waiting at Lord's for a chance to pre-vent you leading the side in the West Indies. Keep your nose clean.' Yorkshire went to Edgbaston needing to beat Warwickshire to displace Kent as leaders, but Yorkshire trailed by four runs on the first innings and were bowled out for 145 on the third morning, leaving Warwickshire to score 142 to win in 102 minutes.

The innings began in a light drizzle and was interrupted by rain at the beginning of the last hour when Warwickshire needed another 72 runs. Trueman, Nicholson and Hutton needed to dry the ball and Close claimed that in the hubbub from the crowd his instructions on field placings were not always heard and had to be repeated. Yorkshire bowled 16 overs in the first 42 minutes but only 24 in the last 105, six in the final 30, and there is no doubt the Edgbaston crowd was convinced that Yorkshire were deliberately wasting time. Trueman was reported to have been struck by an umbrella, and Yorkshire cars were damaged.

Close was called to appear before a panel of county captains at Lord's and formally censured for 'delaying tactics', an incident that brought about a change in the law and the introduction of the mandatory 20 overs at the start of the last hour's play. Close then found himself criticised in a Sunday newspaper for an alleged attack on a man in the crowd. Close's version was that the incident happened at lunchtime on the second day when he heard an unpleasant remark addressed to him as he came off the field.

He walked into the members' enclosure, put his hand on the shoulder of a spectator and asked the man if he had made that remark. The man said no, Close apologised and also apologised to the Warwickshire club. This version of events was confirmed by the Warwickshire member involved, but the ensuing publicity did Close's cause no good and he knew his chances of leading in the West Indies were fading, even when he won the Oval Test match of that year. More than a decade later another England captain, David Gower, was verbally assailed in that same area of Edgbaston.

Close returned to lead Yorkshire as successfully as before and began the process of rebuilding a team that had lost Trueman, Illingworth and Taylor by 1968-69, to win the Gillette Cup in 1969. The relationship between the Committee and the dressing room was not perfect: Close had one or two clashes and claimed that the resignation of Binks, at the end of the 1969 Summer, stemmed from a critical conversation that brilliant wicket-keeper had with two members of the Committee during an early Gillette Cup tie.

1970 saw Yorkshire recover to fourth in the Championship and Close considered that the side was taking shape again when, in late November, he was invited to 'resign or be sacked'. He fired a parting shot at two Committee members at a dinner later that Winter: 'In the next ten years you will realise your mistake.'

He went off to play for both Somerset and England, retiring in 1977 when he was awarded a CBE for his services to cricket. Returning to Yorkshire he joined the General Committee as a member for Bradford, was Cricket chairman when the pro-Boycott committee took over Boycott's dual role as player and committee man, resuming office during the next series of elections. He was always a strong supporter of retaining first-class cricket at Park Avenue, and was one of the prime movers behind the planned establishment of the Cricket Academy on that site. Indestructible, he was playing golf days after being fitted with an artificial hip and was, too, emotional when elected President of the Club in 2008.

---

tility and raw speed contained by a magnificent action, was shrewdly and carefully nursed by Yardley.

In that dusty Summer Wardle bowled more than 1,000 overs for his 100 wickets, despite being dropped to allow the Committee to assess another left-arm spinner, Alan Mason from Addingham, who took 37 wickets at 28. Close also bowled 920 overs for his 101 wickets at 25, an extraordinary performance for a bowler of 18, for he also batted 42 times to score 958 runs for the county at an average of 28. Ellis Robinson, sadly, slipped down in order and was to move on to Somerset at the end of the season.

Fourteen of the 26 matches were won and only two lost, Surrey hinting of the power to come in their win at The Oval and Worcestershire, leaders for much of the season, winning at Sheffield, another leg-spinner, Roly Jenkins, taking 5-39. The major clashes were with Middlesex, both matches being drawn but attracting huge crowds for what had become the premier fixture in the competition. A good pitch at Lord's meant that both teams reached 300 plus in the first innings, Yorkshire taking first-innings points after Robertson and Brown had raised 198 for the first Middlesex wicket.

In the return fixture at Bramall Lane a crowd of 27,000 sat enthralled through hot sunshine after Yorkshire, sent in, assembled 296-6, Lowson scoring his first century and Yardley 81 as the total reached 336 on the Monday, attended by a mere 18,000. Five Middlesex wickets went for 143, but Denis Compton's was among those remaining who went on to score a century, with brother Leslie contributing 44, and although Compton played on at 287 the Middlesex tail, finding pitch and the wearying bowling much to their liking, took the total to 400 on the third afternoon, Warr and Young adding 98 for the last wicket and Young being last out for 62.

Nothing, however, could diminish the last six matches of the campaign when, on each occasion, the victory had to be won to maintain a viable challenge. Hampshire were beaten by 106 at Hull, and Derbyshire by six wickets at Bradford (Hutton was away scoring 200 for England at The Oval), Yorkshire having to make 185 in 90 minutes in the fourth innings. Warwickshire went down by an innings at Scarborough, Kent by 122 at Dover, and Gloucestershire, after an awkward struggle, by eight wickets at Huddersfield.

Middlesex had then completed their programme and Yorkshire had to extract the maximum 12 points from Glamorgan at Newport. Hutton and Lowson began with 78 before Hever's five wickets in the afternoon brought the innings to a disappointing 224. Nevertheless Glamorgan were left on 32-4 on Saturday evening and although the follow-on was saved Yorkshire were batting again on Monday afternoon with a lead of 108, the declaration coming at 5.30 pm with Glamorgan needing 347. The pitch was wearing, the light deteriorating and Coxon's first ball, 'one of the finest he ever bowled' according to Kilburn, beat Emrys Davies, Glamorgan collapsing for 69.

Lester had another fine season, averaging 38, Brennan won himself a Test trial and the advent of so many promising young players meant that Wilson, Watson and Wardle were all dropped at some time during the Summer. The 1949 season was the high Summer of Yardley's captaincy, Hutton had remained at the summit, the White

Rose bloomed again and not a Yorkshireman alive would have believed that another nine years would pass again before the Championship was won again.

As joint champions Yorkshire were confidently expected in 1950 to improve sufficiently to resume their traditional place at the head of affairs. Instead, a poor start, three matches being lost before the Championship began, brought hesitation. Yet the team settled well and after two small defeats went 23 matches without another reverse, the Committee being able to congratulate Norman Yardley 'upon the spirit of adventure which permeated his captaincy and gave so much pleasure to the spectators'.

Hutton was absent, through injury and representative calls, for half of the matches, but Lowson passed 2,000 runs, Wilson improved and Watson, entering the side in August after soccer

Frank Lowson Shadow

Frank Anderson Lowson's career was summed up in one sentence by J.M. Kilburn: 'He had all the attributes of a Test cricketer except perhaps the driving force of ambition.' A slim, dark right-hander from Bradford, he made his debut, with Close and Trueman, at Fenner's in 1949 at a time when Yorkshire were searching everywhere for a regular opening partner for Hutton. Lowson scored 78 in the second innings against the University of Cambridge and never looked back.

He scored 15,000 runs in his nine years and spent so much time at the other end from Hutton that his cutting and driving could be seen to be based upon the maestro's. Fortunately, said the *Yorkshire Yearbook* of 1985, the selectors saw in him more than just a shadow of Hutton and he was selected for seven Tests, scoring 245 runs, a record, almost all his contemporaries stressed, that would have been much more impressive had he sustained better health.

Alan Ross, describing Lowson's batting against South Africa at Lord's, referred to 'an air of waifish, Sinatra-like melancholy', a

fair description of Lowson's play as seen from the ring, and yet he was a highly effective batsman of sound defensive technique, well organised in his stroke play, who never failed to pass 1,000 runs (1,700 in 1949, 2,100 in 1950) and Yorkshire were sorry to see him go, at the age of 33, when county cricket became too much of a burden for a limited physique.

He died at the age of 59 and for a quiet, unassuming cricketer, won some handsome tributes: 'After Hutton he was, at the time, the most effective batsman in the country and he should have played for England many more times,' said Brian Close. Trueman made the point that when Hutton-Lowson partnership was in full flow it sometimes was difficult, from a distance, to distinguish them apart. 'A good companion, a fine batsman and a good friend' was Hutton's comment. His health may not have been the only reason for his retirement. The Yorkshire dressing room was not a happy one in the 1950s and when Lowson was approached by Michael Stevenson about a particular cricket project, he said: 'I'd like to help but honestly I just don't want to think about those days.'

Fred Trueman Fiery

If Frederick Sewards Trueman was not, in his own words, 't'finest bloody fast bowler that ever drew breath', he does have an excellent claim to the title. He was undoubtedly Yorkshire's greatest fast bowler – only Freeman, from all accounts, could be compared in pace – and most critics would put him among England's first ten, if not first five. He had all the attributes: strength, speed, stamina, determination, hostility, a hatred for defeat, and all the fast bowler's weapons – yorker, bouncer, in-swing and a lethal out-swinger. In his later years he could bowl a highly respectable off-break, and he was a punishing lower-order batsman with a reputable defensive technique and dazzling catcher, especially at short leg.

He was born near Stainton, the fourth child of a miner who encouraged all his children to play cricket, being a useful all-rounder himself. When the boy was 12 the family moved to Maltby where, at the local modern school, young Trueman was richly encouraged in his ambition to become a fast bowler. He advanced sufficiently to be included in the Schools' Federation team's Southern tour (along with Close) and at 17 he was taken by his father to Bramall Lane.

Charlie Lee, a Yorkshire Colt who was later to captain Derbyshire, tells the story in Keith Farnsworth's *Before and After Bramall Lane*:

> We were ready to shut up shop when Cyril [Turner] asked me to put my pads on again. We had two long batting sessions but Cyril explained, 'There's a bloke here brought this lad from Maltby. Reckon he's a bit quick. Let's have a look at him.' Having been at it all day and facing a journey home to Wath, Cyril could have been forgiven for telling them to come back again. But that wasn't Cyril's way and this was one occasion when his patience paid a dividend.

> Old 'Dick' Trueman was a typical miner of the period – dark suit, cloth cap, heavy boots; Fred was in ordinary

Fred Trueman
YCCC

clothes – he had no whites – and a pair of plimsolls. You couldn't imagine the scene was set for a significant moment in cricket history.

There wasn't room for much of a run-up in the nets at the Lane but nevertheless Fred got some pace into his first ball which pitched and shot right over the top of the net and the wall behind me and just missed a tram going down Shoreham Street! Those first few deliveries were all over the place.

Then Fred suddenly got one on line. I played at it, was a bit surprised not to connect and when I turned around there were two stumps sticking out of the net like herrings on a Grimsby trawler.

Lee sat on a tramcar with Turner that evening. 'We sat quiet for some time and then suddenly Cyril began to chuckle and I knew what he was going to say: "He'll play for Yorkshire, this lad, tha' knows. He just needs a bit of control. There's nowt needs doing to that action."'

Trueman made his debut for Sheffield United's third team and by late July had reached the first team, taking 4-47 against Wakefield on his debut although, Lee recalled, when the young man was wayward he would take 'some awful hammer'.

In five matches for United in the late Summer for 1948, Trueman took 15 wickets and his pace brought a recommendation that he should attend the Winter school at Headingley for scrutiny by Mitchell and Bowes, the latter later reporting him to be 'an ideal pupil'. The first report was 'superb action, fairly fast'.

Control, and an impulse to hurl in the bouncer whenever the batsman proved aggressive, was where the young bowler needed attention, but he had made sufficient impression to be chosen to play at the University of Cambridge the following May without an appearance for the Colts, and he accordingly made his debut, along with Close and Lowson. It was a trial, as Trueman was a long way down the pecking order for seam bowlers, led by Coxon, Aspinall, Yardley, Foord and Whitehead.

Trueman took three wickets on the usual placid Fenner's pitch, including that of the University's then outstanding batsman, Hubert Doggart (bowled), and then, on a friendlier surface in the Parks, he had match figures of 6-72, his victims this time including Clive van Ryneveld (bowled).

Trueman was then due to stand down to allow the regulars to return for the more testing Championship matches but an injury to Aspinall late in May, when neither Foord nor Whitehead was available as a replacement, brought him opportunities that were unexpected and unplanned. He made little impact until playing against the Minor Counties at Lord's he produced the first spell of his career that brought him attention, and not just in Yorkshire. In a nine-over morning spell he took five wickets for 30; Yardley kept him on after lunch

for him to return final figures of 8-70, and a great career was launched.

Foord, a schoolmaster, and Whitehead, an undergraduate, were both available later in the Summer and Trueman accordingly went off to make a debut at Yorkshire II, already known as a fast but somewhat wild young bowler. Trueman returned for the match against the New Zealanders at Bramall Lane, a happy family occasion, and in trying to prove himself wrenched a thigh muscle that effectively ended the 1949 Summer for him.

According to his biographer John Arlott, Trueman was among several young players who found the Yorkshire dressing room of the 1950s a far from comfortable place, and Stott traces much of Trueman's mistrust of authority to his early experiences there. But Trueman was never critical, unlike others, of his captain, Yardley, and always spoke of him in the highest terms. It was Yardley who first nicknamed the young man 'Fiery', a description so apt that it became synonymous with Trueman.

Trueman was still working at Maltby Main, often taking night shifts in order to play cricket. It was to some surprise that he was chosen for a Test Trial at Bradford in 1950, the prevailing theory being that the selectors wanted their chosen batsmen, soon to face Lindwall and Miller, to be given practice against pace, however wayward. This, of course, was Laker's match (8-2) and Trueman had little opportunity, although he did recall with great pride that he had bowled his hero, Hutton.

Coxon's departure might have given Trueman an opportunity in 1951, but that was Appleyard's year. The young man had to compete with Whitehead and Foord until a return of 11-94 against Nottinghamshire at Bramall Lane pushed him to the head of the queue, and in the return match at Trent Bridge he performed the first Yorkshire hat-trick for five years, an indication of fast improving control, in an analysis of 8-53. Another good performance, at Harrogate on a flat pitch, convinced the Committee he was the real thing, and in August, at Park

Avenue, he and Appleyard were presented with their county caps by Yardley.

He was summoned by the RAF for National Service at the end of 1951 and the Air Marshals proved to be liberal employers as far as their cricketing prodigy was concerned. For this the Club was grateful as Trueman, 20 at the start of 1951, a year later became virtually the senior pace bowler: Coxon gone, Aspinall retired through injury, Appleyard ill and Foord and Whitehead discarded. Unknowingly, Yorkshire began a near 20-year quest to find an opening partner for Trueman.

Trueman responded magnificently to his opportunity and told Arlott later in the Summer of 1952 he was probably at his fastest. He was 21, stood 5ft 10in, had a 46-inch chest and weighed 13_ stone when fully fit. He took 32 wickets at 14 apiece in four Championship matches, and there was no question that England had to select him for the first of his 67 Test matches. The public, depressed by years of aggression from Australian fast bowlers, were demanding an Englishman of genuine pace.

Hutton was his first (and England's first professional) captain and Trueman began with that now famous spell from the Kirkstall Lane End, before 30,000 at Headingley, which reduced India's second innings to 0 for 4, three wickets to Trueman, in the first 14 deliveries. He finished that series with a record 29 wickets, and the legend was made.

He became the first bowler to reach 300 Test wickets (307 at 21.57). He took ten or more wickets three times in a Test match, and his 20-year first-class career brought him 2,304 wickets at an average of 18.29, figures that qualify for immortality. He was a rumbustious character, falling foul of several captains (including Hutton and Vic Wilson), a raconteur good enough to speak professionally, a journalist, broadcaster and commentator, and it is a scandal that no Prime Minister, not even Harold Wilson who described Trueman as 'the greatest living Yorkshireman', thought fit to propose him an honour until his OBE in 1989.

He served the Yorkshire Committee until swept away in the Boycott tide and thereafter refused to stand again, disclaiming all connections with the Club although he remained an honorary life member. His severance from Yorkshire and the team was never such that he could not be induced to talk, at great length and with little encouragement, about the team. His place in cricket, and in the heart of Yorkshire, will remain unchallenged for ever.

There came a rapprochment with Yorkshire, and with Boycott after the news of the latter's throat cancer was known. When the new Board of Management took office in 2002, it was planned that he would be proposed as the next Club President. A headline-winner to the last, he died in July 2006 on the Saturday morning of an England match.

---

duties, had a magnificent spell, scoring 600 runs, including three centuries, in eight matches. Lester in a damper Summer was 700 runs less successful, but with Halliday, who also passed 1,000 runs, Yardley, Keighley, Sutcliffe and Smithson all available, the batting was rarely inadequate.

Too much of the bowling was borne by Coxon and Wardle, who sent down 2,300 overs between them, Wardle taking 144 wickets and Coxon 113, yet Yorkshire's attack that year may be best remembered for the presence of Leadbeater, the

leg-break bowler who was given 700 overs to take 73 wickets. Yorkshire needed an extra seam bowler to support Coxon, and a regular off-spinner; there were some interesting names on the Colts, including Trueman, Whitehead, Foord, Barraclough and Bob Appleyard, a tall 25-year-old from Wibsey. Hutton's benefit raised £9,000 and he and 1949's prodigy Brian Close were selected for England's Winter tour of Australasia.

The 1951 Championship could have been Yorkshire's but for their contribution to England.

They finished 28 points behind Warwickshire and although the eventual champions beat Yorkshire twice, the defeat at Edgbaston was against a team lacking Hutton, Lowson, Watson, Yardley and Brennan.

Hutton and Watson played in all five Test matches, Lowson, Brennan and Wardle in two, while Yardley's duties as chairman of the Test selectors kept him from some of the county matches; even the Gentlemen v Players reduced Yorkshire's strength. Nevertheless, Hutton and Wilson still had time to score five Championship centuries each; Lowson scored two and Yardley, Lester, Watson, Keighley and Halliday contributed one each. But there remained unevenness in the batting, made more apparent in Hutton's frequent absences, and only three batsmen, Hutton, Wilson and Lowson, passed 1,000 runs in the Championship.

The season will be best remembered for Appleyard's astonishing performance: 200 wickets in all, 169 in the Championship, a seasonal debut that seems unlikely ever to be surpassed. Wardle, with 99 wickets, was his chief supporter. The young Trueman, chided by *Wisden* for sacrificing accuracy and direction by not bowling within himself, managed 75, and in the Summer of generally soft turf Leadbeater had 66 victims with his leg-breaks.

Members and supporters were optimistic. In 1951 the bowling was equipped for any type of wicket pace from Trueman and Whitehead, swing and off-spin from Appleyard, slow left-arm from Wardle, leg-breaks from Leadbeater, and such useful performers as Yardley, Close and Halliday in reserve. Waiting in the Colts were Billy Sutcliffe (son of Herbert), Keighley, Charlie Lee (Rotherham), Doug Padgett (Bradford), Ken Taylor (Huddersfield), Bryan Stott (Yeadon), Ray Illingworth (Pudsey), and Roy Booth (Marsden).

Domestically the year saw the retirement of masseur Bright Heyhirst, after 20 years' service. Maurice Leyland joined Arthur Mitchell as a Club coach, and John Nash was presented with £2,000 of savings bonds to mark his 21 years' service as Secretary. The Club was left with a legacy of £1,000 by Mrs William Wilson of Horsely Gate, near Sheffield, to set up a fund to benefit young cricketers. But damper weather and, perhaps, failed expectations in 1951 caused a drop of £8,000 in gate receipts.

The following year, 1952, brought a glorious failure: Yorkshire excelled themselves in the Championship by finishing second to Surrey, a disappointment remembering the hopes of 1951 yet a splendid performance considering all the handicaps. Trueman's call-up for National Service meant, in the end, that he was available for only four Championship matches. His growing power was clear in his record in those four games – 32 wickets at 14.21 apiece. The grievous loss was Appleyard. After his *annus mirabilis* of 1951 all Yorkshire expected another brilliant year from this wonderful bowler, but a breakdown in health meant he played in only one match.

Yorkshire still managed to win 17 of their 28 Championship matches despite again contributing Hutton, Watson and Trueman to England and Yardley to his duties as a selector. Hutton, with all the cares of captaining England, scored seven Championship centuries. Watson, Lowson, Lester, Wilson and Halliday also passed 1,000 runs, while Sutcliffe and Close reached 950, Close doing the 'double' in all matches. Wardle bore a tremendous burden, as the leading bowler, with magnificent panache. He sent down 1,500 overs for his 158 wickets (at 17.14). Close filled one of the bowling positions (98 Championship wickets), with Halliday (44) and Ron Wood, slow left-arm from Ossett (18), giving good support. Seam bowling was the weakness. Coxon had gone into league cricket, Whitehead had moved on to Worcestershire, Trueman's leave was spent in England service devastating the Indians, and of the six Colts tries only Eric Burgin, from Sheffield United, showed promise with 24 wickets. The fielding and catching, *Wisden* was pleased to note, approached the high standard of pre-war years.

Attendances improved with the weather, the loss of £2,900 in 1951 turning into profit of £690, and after mentioning improvements at Park Avenue, Bradford, the Committee cheerfully claimed: 'The Park Avenue ground will be one of the finest equipped grounds in the country.' But the Committee report of 1953 made no bones about the cricket: 'from the playing point

Bob Appleyard

Robert Appleyard, born in Wibsey, near Bradford, was possibly the best bowler ever to play for Yorkshire; had he first appeared at 21, instead of 27, and kept his health he might now be remembered ahead of Trueman or Verity or Rhodes.

Appleyard was so good because he possessed, in addition to the basic requirements of line and length, such a formidable armoury of deliveries and a keen intelligence that ensured the weapon to hand matched the conditions. Batsmen facing him, even on good pitches, were in a constant state of indecision and it is not surprising that Bowes placed Appleyard in the class of S.F. Barnes and O'Reilly.

His bowling was perhaps made all the more lethal by the apparently innocuous approach. There was nothing especially threatening about his 16-yard run-up and the delivery, while smooth and controlled, contained none of Trueman's sometimes demonic fury or Wardle's mischievous cunning. To many batsmen, facing Appleyard for the first time, he must have seemed ingenuous.

When Appleyard first appeared, from the Bradford League, in the Headingley nets, Bowes, as bowling coach, reported to Arthur Mitchell: 'I can't teach this lad anything. His action and control are good and he spins the ball.' The 'lad' in fact was a late developer, passed over, in Trevor Bailey's opinion, because he did look ordinary in his approach and because he did not fit into any one category of bowler.

After Bowes' report, however, Appleyard played regularly for the Colts and, in 1950, at the age of 26, he was given three first-team matches and managed one impressive spell against Surrey; but, wondered Bailey, would he have been given even that opportunity had not Coxon gone into the leagues and Close been required for National Service?

In 1951, after MCC's batsmen had ham-

Bob Appleyard
YCCC

mered the Yorkshire bowling at Lord's in the opening match, Appleyard was recalled to the first team and in an astonishing first Summer he took 200 wickets at 14 apiece, a debut that in all history can be compared only with that of Rhodes. In that first season he was basically a fast-medium in-swing bowler, using his near 6ft 2in to win bounce, a method of attack supplemented by a deadly yorker and, always, extraordinary accuracy.

Later he worked on his bowling. He had quickly sensed, in the 1950 match at The Oval, when his victims included Peter May, that he had limited future as a medium-pace in-swinger. In that game he had experimented with a slow off-spinner and was delighted to see the batsman swing at what appeared to be an easy picking only to have his middle stump knocked out.

Appleyard worked for hours, often on his own, perfecting an out-swinger. Yardley encouraged him to develop the off-break through the Winter of 1950-51, and

Appleyard soon found that bowling off his first finger, in the orthodox manner, removed the skin and made work painful. He tried bowling off the middle finger and discovered, to his delight, that he could bowl an off-break at almost full pace with no lack of power or control. By mid-Summer of 1951, as Wardle commented, Appleyard was bowling 'sometimes like Alec Bedser, sometimes like Jim Laker'. No wonder batsmen fell like ninepins.

But the tremendous effort of that Summer bit deeply into Appleyard's health. He contracted tuberculosis and missed the next two seasons, the Club sending him to a Swiss sanatorium, and he did not appear again until 1954. But he had, apparently, lost none of the magic, for he took another 127 wickets at 14 each and emerged as an England bowler with seven wickets against Pakistan in his first Test.

He was a natural choice, before Laker, for Hutton's tour of Australia where he proved that his style and success could be extended beyond England's damp climate, Bailey mentioning that his late dip in flight was just as disconcerting. The following Summer a shoulder injury reduced his appearances to three matches from June,

although he still ended with 73 wickets at 11.54. Thereafter, from the age of 31, the wear and tear of professional cricket took an increasing toll on a far from robust frame, and he eventually retired in 1958 when it was clear his extraordinary power had been reduced by physical decline.

Twenty years later, Appleyard reappeared in Yorkshire cricket as a committee representative for Bradford and a vociferous opponent of Boycott's group. He worked hard for the establishment and was one of the principals behind the setting up of the Cricket Academy at Park Avenue, the first step, he hoped, towards a full restoration of the historic Bradford ground.

In his later years he played a principal part in the setting up of the Hutton Foundation, a charity to encourage young cricketers, and it was only fitting that the Club should, in 2006, elect the lad from Wibsey to be the Club President, only the second professional after Hutton to be so honoured. A widely praised biography, *No Coward Soul*, appeared in 2003 and the joint author, Stephen Chalke, chose Appleyard to be the first of a series of interviewees in an historical series on DVD for Leeds Metropolitan University.

of view the worst since 1892, the team finishing 13th in the Championship table compared with the second position in 1952', adding (no doubt after swallowing hard), 'Congratulations are extended to Surrey on winning the County Championship for the second year in succession.'

Yorkshire were not, in fact, as poor a team as their record suggests. In any normal decade they would have won several Championships, but in the 1950s they were a good side, sometimes even a very good side, yet destined to meet, for another five galling years, a great side in Surrey.

There were significant contributory factors to Yorkshire's decline in 1953. Hutton, Watson, Wardle and Trueman were all required by England and Yardley missed some matches through his selector's duties. Trueman, in the

RAF, played in only ten matches, Close, having a cartilage removed, in only two. Appleyard was still recuperating, Lowson missed all of May because of injury, and in a generally damp Summer the free-scoring Lester was curtailed.

Watson, making his famous stand with T.E Bailey against the Australians at Lord's, and Wardle, who took 146 wickets, were deservedly named among *Wisden's* Five Cricketers of the Year. The young player of the year was Raymond Illingworth, who took 69 wickets with his off-breaks and scored 747 runs. Michael Cowan's brisk left arm contributed by 31 wickets at 23.9 each.

Yet all the facts proclaimed that Yorkshire were an indifferent and inconsistent team that Summer, drawing 16 Championship matches and causing *Wisden* to censure: 'A general

Willie Watson

Willie (the name on his birth certificate) Watson was so called to differentiate him from his father, the famous Billy Watson of Huddersfield Town. None the less, his dressing-room name was Billy, even though he remained Willie to the world and left a memory of grace, ease and style of movement, whether playing wing-half for Huddersfield and England, batting left-handed for Yorkshire and England or fielding at the boundary. Willie Watson, tall, fair-haired, brought lustre to any playing field.

He first appeared in 1939, a batsman of fluent style and calm temperament who was even then considered as the possible eventual replacement for Leyland, and played 15 innings in the Championship side of 1946; after Leyland's retirement he confirmed his promise by scoring 1,331 runs in the golden Summer of 1947, an aggregate he exceeded in the much damper climate of 1948. By the following year the Committee's impatience with seeming inconsistencies in the form of younger players brought relegation to Watson, along with Vic Wilson and Wardle, to the Colts.

By then Watson had also advanced in his other chosen career and had reached international status as a footballer, missing most of the 1950 Summer to play football for England in the World Cup, but on his return in August he showed great zest for cricket by hitting three centuries and finishing with an average of more than 70. He went on to score 26 centuries for Yorkshire and to pass 1,000 runs eight times between 1947 and 1955.

By 1951 he had become that rarity, a double international, starting a career of 23 Test matches including two tours, and he reached the zenith of his career at Lord's in 1953 when, making his debut against Australia and with England facing defeat, he batted five and three quarter hours for 109, adding 163 with Trevor Bailey for the fifth wicket to save the match. The *Daily Sketch* led the front page with the story, hailing 'Wonderful Willie Watson', and Watson achieved that rare accolade for a cricketer, a mention in *Time* magazine. Much of England spent that tense day within hearing of the radio commentary.

After that epic Watson might have been expected to occupy one of the highest places in English cricket history, yet he played throughout a distinguished career as if suspicious of fame and publicity, reluctant to take the final step towards being described as a 'great' cricketer.

He left Yorkshire for Leicestershire in 1957 where his form implied that this had effected a release, for he was an outstanding success, heading his adopted county's averages each year, passing 2,000 runs in 1959 at an average of 55. He became Assistant Secretary and captain of his new county before emigrating to South Africa in 1968 to become coach to the Wanderers club in Johannesburg. His full first-class career brought him 25,670 runs at an average of 39, including 55 centuries.

He was elected an honorary life member of Yorkshire and was a welcome guest at the Headingley Test Match.

---

depression seemed to overtake the side, for besides their disappointing bowling, the fielding fell a long way below the high standard which used to make them such a powerful force, and even the batting was unreliable.' Brennan, Yorkshire's wicket-keeper for seven seasons, announced his retirement.

Yorkshire were strong again in 1954, but not strong enough, second yet again to all conquering Surrey. In yet another damp Summer Surrey's all-round bowling strength was decisive, mightily as Yorkshire tried to close the gap. While Surrey had four Test bowlers Yorkshire had three, and though Trueman, Appleyard and Wardle shared 392 wickets, the absence of one or more of the three meant a gap that could not be closed. Close was called up for National

Service in mid-season and none of the Colts was yet ready for sustained front line service.

The batting, with Hutton missing matches on England duty, also appeared strong enough for the task in prospect yet there were often unaccountable failures. Again Lowson, Close, Wilson, Lester and Watson all passed 1,000 runs and all played splendidly on occasion, their difficulty being, it seemed, finding form together.

There was a rare tied match with Leicestershire at Huddersfield and a crushing victory, by 96 runs, by Middlesex at Leeds, a defeat which signalled that the way was open for Surrey to take their third successive Championship.

The next year, 1955, saw a fine Summer in which Yorkshire began with every reason to believe they would break Surrey's monopoly. Yardley's team was in full flower; the captain contributed astute and experienced leadership

Jimmy Binks

James Graham Binks, born in Hull, was another wicket-keeper of the highest class who won little recognition from the selectors, appearing in only two Test matches. He has fair claim to be regarded alongside David Hunter, who kept to Hirst, Haigh and Rhodes, and Brennan (Trueman, Appleyard and Wardle), among the county's best in terms of variety and difficulty posed by the bowlers of their time. Other candidates such as Dolphin, Wood and Bairstow have a

claim to be contenders on their records but had, through most of their careers, more predictable bowling to judge.

Binks won a battle with Roy Booth of Marsden, who was later to serve Worcestershire on and off the field, to succeed Brennan, although the capabilities of the 'lad from Hull' had been known of and extolled for some time previously. He made his reputation in the last two seasons of Wardle and Appleyard and then developed into a vital performer in Close's

Jimmy Binks attempts to stump Middlesex's Peter Parfitt
YCCC

Championship sides of the 1960s, missing not a single Championship fixture between his debut, against Nottinghamshire in June 1955, to his retirement in 1969, 412 consecutive appearances.

This is, of course, a county record, as is his haul of 107 victims in 1960, including 96 catches, another record. Taller than the norm for a keeper, he was a quiet and undramatic performer who won the admiration of the cognoscenti for his ability to stand up to Yorkshire's string of in-swing bowlers of that period such as Platt and Nicholson, the ball coming in to the right-hander being the most difficult for the keeper to measure.

He also became a useful batsman, scoring almost 7,000 runs in his 14-year career, including a 95 against Middlesex at Lord's. Binks was so quick of movement and adept in his timing that he suffered only one injury, a broken finger in 1966, which was not allowed to interfere with his play. Unlike almost all wicket-keepers, his hands were unmarked when he retired from the game to take up a business appointment at the age of 34. As Ted Lester once said of him: 'He could have come straight off the field and played the piano.'

His business career took him to the United States where he and his family settled in California, but he never lost his interest in Yorkshire cricket and returned to be honoured as the first President of the Former Players' Association.

and was still a useful performer with a bat and ball. He had a galaxy of batsmen – Hutton, Lowson, Wilson, and Watson – three Test-class bowlers in Appleyard, Wardle and Trueman, and a highly consistent and sometimes brilliant wicket-keeper in Binks. Behind these nine were a dozen young players striving hard for a place: Close, Illingworth, Platt, van Geloven, Bird, Stott, Oates and Roy Booth. Even when Yardley stepped down at the end of the season, he had an automatic successor in W.H.H. Sutcliffe, an assured and popular young batsman. Helping the second team, and in reserve, was the free-scoring Lester.

The first six matches were won at a canter. Northamptonshire fell by teatime on the second day at Bradford, with Appleyard and Wardle sharing 18 wickets in a match in which Yorkshire, in their second innings, reached 104, the highest total. Gloucestershire went down by an inning at Bristol, Yardley scoring a century and Appleyard striking again (10-110), and it was Appleyard once more, with Yardley contributing 7-60, who caused Somerset's downfall at Headingley. This triumphal procession continued right through May, with Lancashire being beaten by five wickets at Old Trafford. It was the merriest of months for Bob Appleyard who reigned supreme throughout England, taking 49 wickets at eight runs apiece.

After such a start Yorkshire were entitled to feel they had the measure of their deadly rivals from The Oval, Surrey were still level with them and showed no signs of strain. It was Yorkshire who stumbled. A low-scoring match dominated by the spinners was lost by 21 runs at Hove, the last five Yorkshire wickets falling for only 31 runs on the third afternoon. Defeat by Surrey, by only 41, in the next match at The Oval, was no disgrace although more must have been expected after the Champions had been put out for 85 in their first innings (Appleyard 7-29).

What was totally unexpected was a third successive defeat, this time at Bradford, by Hampshire and by an innings. The Hampshire tail retrieved a mediocre start of 93-5 to total 224. Hutton, not a hundred per cent, batted down the order and Yorkshire were routed twice by the spinners in one of their own fortresses, Sainsbury returning match figures of 9-62. Wardle and Appleyard, with England, would also most certainly have reversed the result, although Surrey could have argued that they had to surrender May and Barrington to Test matches and, later in the season, Bedser, Lock, Laker and Loader in turn.

Although those three defeats were soon forgotten in a glorious run of victories interrupted only by the inevitable Roses draw and a defeat by Middlesex, Yorkshire, leading at the end of July, were always conscious of Surrey's two games in

Billy Sutcliffe

William Herbert Hobbs Sutcliffe, son of Herbert, born in Pudsey, was destined to be elected to the office his father had declined in 1928, the captaincy of Yorkshire, in 1956. He succeeded Yardley at the age of 29, with ten seasons of senior cricket and six centuries behind him, and was, at a time when amateurs still took preference, the logical successor. He was both capable and popular.

He did, however, take over at a difficult time. Hutton had retired along with Yardley; Watson and Lester were soon to depart, while the careers of Lowson and Appleyard were in their closing stages. That feature of the dressing room so often mentioned at that time, factionalism, was at its most rampant and it was to Sutcliffe's disadvantage, as Kilburn has pointed out, that he was so well known and so much a part of that talented but unruly team.

After Sutcliffe's first season the Committee report was unequivocal: 'More matches would have been won had the players played in a more determined manner on all occasions.' Sutcliffe had little luck; Trueman had one of his lean years in 1956, while his most promising partner, the left-arm Cowan, broke down. Yorkshire finished seventh and although Sutcliffe was able to take them back to respectability and third place in 1957, he had already informed the Committee, in August, that he would be resigning 'very definitely for business reasons'.

Billy Sutcliffe
Mick Pope

Sutcliffe's experience over two seasons almost certainly led the Committee into seeking a captain who was both detached and a disciplinarian, a path that was to lead them eventually to the choice of Ronnie Burnet.

Sutcliffe later served the Club on the General Committee until losing his seat when opposing the Boycott group. He was always a popular figure with former teammates and members. 'A grand lad, perhaps too nice to be a captain of that team', was one verdict.

hand and despite a prestigious effort, 21 Championship victories including one against Surrey at Leeds, won in appalling light – the Championship remained at The Oval.

Kilburn, in the 1956 *Wisden*, reflected upon the Yardley era:

Yorkshire made mistakes in selectorial judgment as in playing technique and they had therefore to extend the period of experiment beyond the term expected (from 1946). Yardley found himself with as difficult a task as any county captain for he had played long enough to appreciate the needs and desires but could find no illustrations of intentions for the newcomers.

Young Yorkshire did not know what was expected of them and were short of a yardstick for comparison. Social circumstances were a handicap to every county and a particular trial to Yorkshire who have long expected their young players to fit into a given pattern, of proven worth. Yardley's success in captaincy has been limited by the lack of understanding and ambition in some of his players but he has done invaluable work in keeping the good name of Yorkshire cricket at the highest level.

Indeed, in retrospect it can be seen that Yardley was an outstanding captain, his record in Championship placings reading: 4, joint 1, 3, 2, 2, 12, 2, 2. There is much evidence that his players expected a firmer hand but, as we have seen, for many of his years of office Yorkshire were in a peculiar position in that either the captain or the senior professional, or both, were as much concerned with England's fortunes as with Yorkshire's.

Had the Club been less successful in Yardley's time it is possible that more time and thought would have been extended upon the spirit and morale of the dressing room. But as each Spring rolled around the hope was there that the following Summer would be Yorkshire's and that Surrey would be overtaken; yet by each Autumn it could be seen clearly that Surrey always had that extra top-class player, usually a bowler, to tip the balance in their favour. If Yardley was too much of a gentleman, the most common charge levelled at him, then he was also unlucky to have captained the Club at a time when another county could field a side that, certainly at The Oval, was as powerful and ruthless as any team led by Hawke or Sellers.

Surrey won the Championship for a fifth successive year in 1956 – a record – while Yorkshire, in a wet Summer and under a new captain, Billy Sutcliffe, dropped five places to seventh. Equally alarming was a drop in attendances by 92,000, a reflection on both the wet weather and what the Yorkshire public clearly regarded as declining standards.

Seven matches were lost against eight won, and the Committee considered that 'more matches would have been won had the players played in a more determined manner'. In retrospect that may seem a hard judgement, for Yorkshire did have to contend with injuries and a wet spell that contributed to eight of the last 12 matches being drawn, the team being in third position in mid-July.

Hutton became Sir Leonard but was, alas, no longer opening the Yorkshire innings, and although the county had two excellent young batting prospects in Taylor and Padgett neither could yet give an innings of Hutton's confidence and assurance, nor match his appeal at the gate. Only three batsmen passed 1,000 runs, only Watson averaged more than 40, and he, Taylor and Lowson were the only batsmen to contribute centuries.

Pitches were rarely suitable for fast bowling, Trueman taking only 33 wickets this season. Cowan had been sent home from Pakistan with back trouble, throwing more weight on the less-experienced seam bowlers Ryan, Platt, Peter Broughton and Close. The successes were the spinners: Wardle took 105 wickets, Appleyard 94 and Illingworth 85, the last-named passing the hundred in all matches for the first time.

Binks was acclaimed by *Wisden* for his wicket-keeping, but 1956 was remembered mainly for the rain: 11 full playing days were lost from the home programme and play was restricted on many others. The county's experiment in taking a Championship match to Middlesbrough for the first time was reported a success: 'The gate money of £1,467 on a cloudy day showed there is a demand for First-Class cricket in the area.' Ted Lester, who had been unable to play first-team cricket because of foot trouble, was retained as a senior professional with the Colts.

Yorkshire were in better heart in the slightly warmer weather of 1957, although the rain was again blamed for its effect on finances and the team fortunes. The side did finish third, a return to respectability, but the Summer ended in an atmosphere of uncertainty. Sutcliffe, after two seasons, announced he would not be able to captain the team in 1958. Close, a rising influence in the dressing room saw Sutcliffe in light of a friend rather than a captain:

... a super lad. He made himself into a county cricketer because it was expected of him and because he believed in Yorkshire cricket and its divine right to pre-eminence. He was happier having a pint and a natter when

Ray Illingworth Illy

'Raymond', as he is usually addressed, was not a great off-spinner, nor a great batsman, nor a great fielder, but he was sufficiently expert, in his employment of experience, knowledge, tactical insight and psychology as a captain, to be remembered without qualification as a great cricketer. David Gower, who served under him at Leicester, accords him the highest praise.

He was, it should be added quickly, of sufficient class as a spinner to be often named as first choice for England and, in fact, played 61 Test matches. But it was Illingworth's ancillary talents that usually gave him the edge over worthy competitors; he was always involved in the game, at whatever level, and if by some chance the ball ignored him, he would be scheming to seek it out.

'Illy' was the thinking man's cricketer. When he arrived at Grace Road in 1969 to assume the captaincy of Leicestershire he took a look at the ground and ordered the boundary to be increased, the outfield shaved so that the ball did not keep its shine for long, and the pitches made harder. Pace bowlers had to work hard to get wickets, the spinners thrived, the batsmen enjoyed the ball coming on to the bat and the bowling rate went up to ten overs in an hour.

Yorkshire were hoping for similar results when, ten years later, he was recalled as cricket manager and, eventually, captain, but politics prevented his aims being accomplished and he retired at 51 years of age, after his bowling had played a major part in the winning of the John Player Sunday League. He became a highly respected commentator in the media, and Yorkshire lost the services of one of the keenest brains in the game's history.

He was born in Pudsey, the son of a cabinet-maker and joiner from whom he no doubt inherited his delight in seeing a task completed properly and well. At the age of three he and his family moved to nearby

Ray Illingworth
Yorkshire Post

Farsley where, at school, the eight-year-old Illingworth began demonstrating an obvious aptitude for cricket. The school played on the Farsley club ground and the story is familiar of that generation: every spare moment given to practice and nets.

At 15 he was playing for Farsley's first team in the Bradford League and an innings of 148 not out, spread over several evenings and attracting a record attendance, brought him more than local attention. He joined the Yorkshire Federation team's annual tour, along with Close and Trueman, and still recalls, according to his biographer Michael Stevenson, a slender Trueman bowling slow left-arm before the match and very fast right-arm during it, to the great discomfiture of the Sussex schoolboys.

Illingworth spent his National Service at RAF Dishforth where a sympathetic CO ensured that he was given time to further his cricket for Farsley, Yorkshire Colts, and RAF and Combined Services. He made his debut for Yorkshire in August 1951, against Hampshire at Headingley, scoring 56 in a stand with Yardley after Yorkshire had lost four wickets cheaply. By then he had all but forsaken the medium-pace seamers of his boyhood for off-spin and the occasional delivery that 'went with the arm', which 'Illy' was always a master at concealing.

He had yet another year at RAF duty to complete so his appearances in 1952 were restricted to four Championship matches, but the following year, with Appleyard ill, Trueman on National Service and Close injured, he was suddenly a valuable member of the team bearing, with Wardle, the brunt of the bowling. At Hull Yorkshire were 104-5 against Essex when Illingworth joined Yardley to add 146, another 115 being added with Brennan, the 21-year-old Illingworth scoring 146 not out.

Illingworth, according to his biographer, was far from happy in the dressing room of the 1950s, the junior spinner to Appleyard and Wardle and therefore usually bowling when conditions were most inimical to his type of bowling. Even so, the lessons he learned in restricting batsmen when all was in their favour were invaluable later.

He particularly resented, after being put on to bowl by Yardley, being told to 'bugger off' by either Appleyard or Wardle. When 'Illy' did get on to bowl it was always at the wrong end. Neither Wardle nor Appleyard was lenient with dropped catches, and Cowan, Roy Booth and Illingworth all testified to being humiliated on the field to such an extent that they felt their confidence was being eroded. It was a very hard upbringing for a young cricketer, but it must be said that those that did survive also prospered to an extraordinary degree – Close, Trueman and Illingworth in particular.

Illingworth discovered, after a shouting match with Wardle, that relations improved to such an extent that he became the favourite out-fielder, taking 33 catches in the deep of Wardle in one Summer. It was not, however, until the arrival of Burnet and the departure of the two great spinners that Illingworth came into his own as the fulcrum of the Yorkshire attack, able to deliver with nagging accuracy or, in helpful conditions, a sharper spin than almost all his contemporaries. When Yorkshire found a slow left-arm replacement for Wardle in Don Wilson, it was Illingworth's consistency that provided a foil for the likeable Wilson's excesses and experiments. Together, supported by Close's field settings and Yorkshire's tight fielding, they became a formidable combination in the Silver Sixties.

Illingworth's Test career was initially delayed for the same reason he had to wait for full establishment in the Yorkshire side: the ability of those in competition for places. England was awash with good off-spinners in the 1950s, including two of the immortals, Laker and Appleyard, and it was not until 1958 that the 26-year-old Yorkshire all-rounder was selected for the Fourth Test match against New Zealand, at Old Trafford.

He bowled 45 overs, 18 which were maidens, to return with match figures of 3-59, but won congratulations from his captain Peter May. It was during May's term as captain that Illingworth's Test career flourished for there was an obvious empathy between the pair. Once May had gone, and although Illingworth had a valid claim to be England's best off-spinner after Laker's retirement, he was less favoured by England, possibly the result of making his views known on certain aspects of the Duke of Norfolk's management of Illingworth's Australian tour and Dexter's captaincy.

Close's first move on being appointed England captain in 1966 was to recall Illingworth, and he had emerged as Close's second in command and heir apparent to the Yorkshire captaincy without challenge, when in 1968 came the argument over a contract, a situation exacerbated undoubtedly by Seller's autocratic attitude, that led to the resignation of the 37-year-old Illingworth and his move to Leicestershire.

At Grace Road he takes second place only to the architect of the modern county administration, Mike Turner, in the lustre brought to the Running Fox over 20 years: in Illingworth's time as captain of Leicestershire they won their first Championship (1975), the Benson and Hedges Cup twice and the Sunday League twice. Such success restored Illingworth to the England captaincy and when that international career ended he had much to look back upon: regaining the Ashes and leading England in 36 Tests.

A man of such distinction would have been attractive to any county seeking leadership; to Yorkshire Ray Illingworth represented perhaps the only way out of their maze of troubles, beset by factions seeking the deposing of Boycott as captain on the one hand and the Boycott loyalists on the other. Accordingly he was invited back in 1979 as manager and recorded, at the end of that Summer: 'Shirley and I wished we had not moved back.'

Illingworth did take Yorkshire to a Benson and Hedges semi-final against Essex, a match marred by a public dispute between manager and senior professional over Boycott's fitness; without Boycott, Yorkshire lost the match and with it the chance of a final at Lord's that Illingworth believed, in retrospect, would have re-established him in Yorkshire.

In 1980 Yorkshire finished sixth in the Championship when, with a little luck with the weather in the last match, the final placing would have been fourth, but Illingworth's hopes of rebuilding the side were set back when Hampshire resigned from the captaincy and moved to Derbyshire. The following year, under Old, the team suffered eight separate fractures and slipped from sixth to tenth with the agitation against Illingworth reflected almost daily in the Yorkshire press. The Summer ended with Illingworth's controversial preference of the uncapped Neil Hartley as captain in Old's absence and the suspension of Boycott.

Fifteen days after Illingworth's 50th birthday, in 1982, the club dismissed Old from captaincy and handed it to Illingworth to become the first manager-captain in the Club's history. He himself would have preferred Neil Hartley to take over but no doubt sensed that the Committee, under intense pressure from the Boycott group, would have been unwilling to re-open the war on another front.

Illingworth's last 18 months in cricket brought a stabilisation to the team and the winning of a trophy for the first time in 14 years, the John Player Sunday League Championship, an honour that might have been disregarded a quarter-century before, but in the context of the civil war represented as heartfelt and warming prize as any won by Hawke and Sellers. This triumph did not save Illingworth when the new Committee took office after the annual general meeting, but it did restore some spirit to the dressing room as Bairstow succeeded to the captaincy.

Illingworth then departed to become a radio and TV commentator and newspaper correspondent and was offered the job of England team manager in 1986, rejecting it when it became clear to him that he would have at best only partial control of the team matters. 'Illy' would accept himself that he could be a difficult character, but it was Yorkshire's misfortune that England and Leicestershire managed to harness his considerable talents so much more successfully.

England did offer him the management, on his own terms, in 1996, but while the new generation of players acknowledged his expertise and tactical nous it seemed that he and they were at least a generation apart in language and attitude. He remained a fountain of knowledge on the game and was happy enough to go back to his beloved Farsley, in the Bradford League, where he was proud to tell you that he cared for the square and still enjoyed marking out the pitch, a privilege he felt not extended to too many former England captains.

a day's work was over than he was cracking a whip on the field. His problem as a captain was that he had fixed, preconceived ideas about the way a day's play would go. You cannot be rigid in ideas as Billy was and lead successfully because circumstances can change completely with one ball in a long cricketing day …. Billy did not have as much knowledge as his players but he had a good pleasant personality. His trouble was really in handling the bowling and the field placing.

Watson, the senior professional, left to join Leicestershire. Lowson the regular opening batsman was so afflicted by leg trouble that he did not play after mid-June. In compensation the Colts won the Minor Counties Championship under J.R. Burnet, and the changes in the first team did afford some of those Colts early promotion. Bryan Stott, a left-handed batsman from Yeadon, made his debut against Scotland in the last match in May and by the end of the season scored 1,248 runs, hit three centuries and, in late July, established a new opening partnership with Taylor. In the second innings against Nottinghamshire at Trent Bridge their stand of 230 was the best for any Yorkshire wicket for five years.

Finding Trueman a partner was the perennial problem, with Cowan still handicapped. In the early part of the season Appleyard was often called upon to use the new ball, while later in the year David Pickles, a tall right-arm bowler from Halifax, made an extremely promising beginning taking 31 wickets at 19.06 in 12 games. Trueman took 76 wickets, while the invaluable Illingworth did the 'double' for the first time.

For perhaps a decade 1958 was remembered as the unhappy year in Yorkshire's history, a time of dissension and upset on and off the field. The Committee's report concentrated on the weather ('appalling') and the playing record ('disappointing'). Of the real drama of the season, the sacking of three Test players, the reference is remarkable for its omissions:

Doug Padgett

Next to Hutton, Douglas Ernest Vernon Padgett was the most technically correct batsman to appear for Yorkshire in the years after the Second World War, a credential that led to his appointment as Yorkshire's chief coach in succession to Arthur Mitchell.

A right-hander of medium height, neat and stylish, always a pleasure to watch whatever the batting circumstances, Padgett was born in Bradford and developed through the Bradford League and was such an outstanding prospect as a boy that he made his first-class debut in 1951, when Hutton and Watson were playing for England. At the age of 16 years and 321 days, he was the youngest to appear for Yorkshire until Jarvis.

In his 20 seasons Padgett scored 21,124 polished runs at an average of 28.58, exceeding 1,000 runs 12 times and twice playing for England; in addition he toured New Zealand. Padgett scored 29 centuries and all judges agree that he had the ability to have been a regular member of the England team, lacking perhaps, like fellow Bradfordian Lowson, the final spur of ambition.

Padgett was a genial character, a stalwart of Close's team in the 1960s, a splendid and safe deep field and always popular figure on Yorkshire grounds. He also gave lifelong devotion to Bradford City Football Club.

His style was summed up by Kilburn when Yorkshire defeated Sussex at Hove in 1959 to win the Championship. The final target was 215 in 105 minutes and Scott and Padgett got the runs, in a stand of 141, with seven minutes to spare – 'Padgett plundered 79 with the serenity of A.J. Raffles abstracting diamonds from a duchess.'

He retired to a house and paddock on the moors above Bingley but he was always ready to talk cricket, over a pint, long into the night.

After very careful consideration your Committee decided that the services of F.A. Lowson, R. Appleyard and J.H. Wardle would not be called upon after the 1958 season. Your Committee places on record its appreciation of the loyal services of Lowson and Appleyard and has awarded them a joint testimonial in 1959.

Wardle had received a benefit of £8,000 in 1957, but the real bitterness arose from the circumstance surrounding, and the sequel to, his sacking. The new captain, Ronnie Burnet, a 39-year-old amateur, had been appointed on the strength of his leadership and rebuilding of the Colts' team. The notion, true or false depending on one's view of the Yorkshire dressing room, had got abroad that the senior members of the team, after the departure of Yardley and Hutton, had not given Sutcliffe their full backing and support. Burnet was reportedly briefed to 'sort things out', and whether or not he was responsible the fact is that by 1959 only Vic Wilson remained of what might be regarded as Norman Yardley's regulars – Hutton, Lowson, Sutcliffe, Lester, Watson and Wardle.

Lowson and Appleyard had not been in the best health and although their departure (Lowson was 32, Apleyard 33) was surprising it could have been argued that Yorkshire did have a younger opening batsman and a first-class spinner in Illingworth. But the shock came at Bramall Lane on 30 July during Yorkshire's match against Somerset when the club's Secretary, J.H. Nash, announced that the Committee would not be calling on Wardle, 35, who was at his peak: the best slow left-arm bowler of his type in the world, a hard-hitting batsman and an immensely popular figure with the crowd.

He was chosen for the next match, against Lancashire at Old Trafford, but stood down after announcing that he intended to contribute some articles to the Daily Mail. Following the publication of those articles the MCC withdrew their invitation to him to tour Australia. The Yorkshire Committee then stated on 11 August:

> The Committee regret the unpleasant publicity given to their decision to dispense with the services of J.H. Wardle after the present season. In past years Wardle has been warned on several occasions that his general behaviour on the field and in the dressing rooms left much to be desired.
> As no improvement was shown this year the decision to dispense with his services was made as it was unanimously considered that it was essential to have discipline and a

Bryan Stott

William Bryan Stott, from Yeadon, was a stocky left-hander who, with Ken Taylor, formed what was perhaps the most fleet-footed of Yorkshire opening partnerships between 1957 and 1963. In those seven seasons Stott passed 1,000 runs five times (2,034 in 1959) and the pair raised three double-century opening partnerships, often giving Close's team that near essential basis to a Championship win, a large first-innings total raised in quick time.

Stott scored 9,000 runs at an average of 31 in a career curtailed by business commitments. The running between wickets of himself and Taylor was an exhibition of anticipation and understanding; the pair once astonished a Roses match audience by talking five singles off the first over.

Stott and Taylor, with Padgett at three, were almost always capable of a fast and successful start to the innings and had not Stott been obliged to attend to the family business at 29, his playing career might have been distinguished; a longer career would certainly have delayed the establishment of Boycott.

When time became available to him, Stott was able to return to the Club as a member of the General Committee, serving on the cricket sub-committee and paying special attention to the county's schooling and coaching facilities.

When the Board succeeded the Committee, Stott redoubled his efforts on behalf of club and schools' cricket and was one of the leading lights in the foundation of the Former Players' Association.

Ken Taylor

Ken Taylor was a superb athlete from Huddersfield, following Willie Watson as both a gifted cricketer and footballer (Huddersfield Town and Bradford Park Avenue). A right-hander opener who could play with dash, he scored 16 centuries in his 12 seasons (four in 1961, including 203 not out against Warwickshire) and passed 1,000 runs six times; he was also one of the great cover-points in the Club's history.

With Stott he formed a fast-scoring opening partnership for Yorkshire that was able to give Close's team the kind of start enjoyed by Middlesex in the days of Robertson and Brown or by Hampshire with Greenidge and Richards. The pair were famous for their understating between the wickets and Taylor was considered good enough technically to play for England three times, against India and Australia.

He had a fair claim, too, to be considered an all-rounder for he could also bowl medium, naggingly accurate seamers that brought him 131 wickets at an average of 28.

Taylor was also an artist who had studied at the Slade, and after his playing career had taken him to Auckland and Norfolk, he taught at Gresham's School. His son, Nick, showed promise as a fast bowler with Yorkshire, Surrey and Somerset.

His artistic range was demonstrated in a series of sketches of great Yorkshire players in which his ability to recreate their style of batting and bowling was memorable. His career in both sports was celebrated in an excellent book, *Drawn to Sport*, with Stephen *Chalke* in 2006.

happy and loyal team before any lasting improvement could be expected in the play of the Yorkshire XI.

It is felt that recent articles published in the Daily Mail fully justify the Committee's decision. Wardle broke his contract when he wrote those articles without first obtaining permission and the Committee are therefore terminating his contract forthwith.

Wardle then said he would join Nottinghamshire, a move upon which *Wisden* commented: 'Consent of Yorkshire and MCC would have been necessary.' He did, in fact, entertain Lancashire League audiences for several seasons.

Yorkshire had scarcely a happier time on the field. In all, 24 playing days were lost to rain, 17 in Yorkshire, receipts dropped by £5,000 and not one bowler passed the 100 wickets; Wardle, with 76, being the most successful. The three seam bowlers vying to be Trueman's partner – Cowan, Pickles and Ryan – managed only 57 wickets between them. However, Stott hit two more centuries, Close passed 1,000 runs and Philip Sharpe, from Worksop College, made an auspicious start, scoring 141 against Somerset in his third match and finishing with 433 runs in 19 innings.

Before the 1959 season started Brian Sellers, newly appointed Cricket Committee chairman, believed that Yorkshire would need another three years to become Championship contenders. In 1958 they had finished 11th and after a season of turmoil it was expected that a comparatively young team would need time to settle. But to the astonishment of members and to the amazement of the Committee, Ronnie Burnet's team won the Championship.

It was won in style, too, on the afternoon of 1 September at Hove where Sussex set Yorkshire the apparently impossible target of scoring 215 runs in 105 minutes. Stott scored 13 of the 15 hit off the first over; the 50 came up in 20 minutes, 77 in half an hour and the first 100 in 43 minutes. In three minutes over the first hour the score had reached 150, the 200 was reached in 85 minutes and Bolus hit the winning boundary, a deflection to fine leg, at 4.23 – victory by five wickets with seven minutes to spare. Stott scored his 96 in 86 minutes and he and Padgett added 141 in just over an hour for the third wicket. The *Daily Express* exclaimed: 'The White Hot Rose'.

Ronnie Burnet

John Ronald Burnet, from Saltaire, entered county cricket from the Bradford League at the age of 39, won the Championship in his second and last season, thus ending seven years of Surrey supremacy, and won the eternal gratitude of the Club for restoring spirit and harmony to the dressing room. Burnet was also the captain responsible for the sacking of Wardle, in Burnet's first season, 1958.

Burnet had been a useful middle-order batsman for Baildon, then the Bradford League's most successful club, and, more important, a popular captain of the Yorkshire Second XI, developing through the ranks such players as Stott, Taylor, Birkenshaw, Cowan, Ryan, Platt and Don Wilson, the bulk of the team for the next decade. The Committee, wishing to end the factionalism that had arisen in the first-team dressing room, decided to go to the leagues for an amateur captain, rather than a professional, already immersed.

Ronnie Burnet
Ron Deaton collection

In the Winter of 1957, according to Close, Burnet met Wardle at a league dinner and told him that he had been offered the captaincy, adding that if he did not take the offer another amateur, Derek Blackburn of Bradford, was next in line. Wardle, said Close, was deeply disappointed but consoled himself with the thought that, with Watson departed for Leicestershire, he would be the new senior professional, an appointment greeted with delight by Close: 'I had learned more about cricket from Johnny than from all the senior players put together.'

According to Burnet, however, he had to fight for Wardle's seniority as the Committee wanted to leapfrog Wardle and name Vic Wilson. Burnet told Alan Hill: 'I told the Committee that Wardle had to be given his chance and if he performed his duties correctly we should have no trouble.'

That there would be a clash was so obvious that the suspicion remains that it was deliberately engineered. For six weeks all was

peaceful, for Burnet was injured and Wardle led the side, but then he no doubt found life even more galling when the captain returned.

The first clash, according to Burnet, came during a match against Derbyshire at Chesterfield when Wardle reacted with violent language to a suggestion from the captain that he might bowl a fuller length. Burnet then switched him to the less responsive end of a drying pitch, whereupon Wardle bowled 'an over of long hops' and was promptly ordered to take his sweater.

Close dismissed this as one of the 'several brushes' between the pair, and he pinpoints the Sussex match at Worthing as the first real flare-up. Overnight rain had got under the covers at one end and Wardle, much the senior bowler in a very inexperienced attack, expected to bowl to the drying end. But Burnet insisted that Wardle should bowl to the other end and give the advantage to the young off-spinners, Birkenshaw and

Close himself (Trueman and Illingworth were with England). 'We gave away too many runs,' reported Close, and Sussex won a low scoring match that had been Yorkshire's for the taking.

The climax came against Somerset at Sheffield. Burnet was already angry at having to read in the newspaper of the imminent departure of Lowson and Appleyard and complained to the then Cricket chairman Clifford Hesketh: 'My opinion should have been sought. Had I been consulted I would have included a third party – Johnny Wardle. As long as we have him in the side we shall never have any team spirit.'

Hereabouts accounts differ. Alan Hill, from Burnet, reports that a lunchtime meeting took place after Burnet handed Wardle a note in the dressing room informing him that he had been sacked. Close wrote that there had been a further row between the pair that morning when Wardle, taken off after a fruitless spell on a good batting pitch, had been recalled, taken wickets but had been accused by the captain of 'not try-

ing'. Burnet went off, according to Close, to attend a Committee meeting called, it was thought, to pick a side for the next match, against Lancashire at Old Trafford. Wardle, in charge on the field, was resting on figures of 6-46 at tea when Burnet returned to tell Wardle that the Committee wanted to see him. Wardle put on a blazer, to return later with all the colour gone from his usually ruddy cheeks. He had been told he had been sacked.

There is little dispute about what happened afterwards. As soon as the news broke, the *Daily Mail* signed Wardle for an exclusive series of articles (for £400 according to the man who wrote them, Alex Bannister) in which the player attacked the Club, the captain and the conduct of some of the younger players. Wardle warned Yorkshire of the impending publication and stood down voluntarily from the match at Old Trafford. Yorkshire announced a breach of contract and in effect instant dismissal, and MCC, after getting confirmation from Wardle personally that he had seen the articles before publication, withdrew their invi-

Yorkshire CCC at Lords 1959. Captain Ronnie Burnet, centre front row
Ron Deaton collection

tation to him to tour Australia in 1958-59, to the intense chagrin of their captain Peter May.

Could it all have been avoided? Yardley believed that the then Yorkshire engagement system, which meant players had to be notified of an offer for the following year by the end of July, was partly responsible. Had the present contract method been operating, there would have been time for reconsideration.

Billy Sutcliffe thought the decision both unwise and unnecessary. Wardle, we know from many accounts, regretted the *Daily Mail* adventure almost immediately; without that public attack on his captain and club he would have gone on to tour and probably joined Nottinghamshire, who were prepared to make him a handsome offer, the following Summer.

The younger players were split on his presence in the dressing room, but agreed on his value to the side. Long afterwards, Burnet told Alan Hill:

I had the highest possible regard for

Johnny as a cricketer. What happened was an absolute tragedy. He should have been in the side for another 10 years. I would have loved to have captained him when he was a younger cricketer. He would not have become a sour man. But in 1958 his character, and the way he approached the game, were, as far as Yorkshire were concerned, luxuries we could not afford.

Burnet then took over a team that had lost four Test players – Watson, Lowson, Appleyard and Wardle – in a little over a year and promptly won the Championship. He did it, too, with the young Colts he had brought up himself, in a blaze of batsmanship from such as Stott, Taylor and Padgett, even leading Yorkshire to a memorable victory over the Rest of England, scoring 425 after a follow-on to win by 66 runs!

Burnet then returned to his Bradford League, served Yorkshire as a Committee man for many years and, as might be expected, was a very firm and outspoken opponent of Boycott's admirers some quarter-century after his own great battle.

This was sensational scoring in that era.

So Yorkshire returned to Scarborough as Champions, and when challenged by MCC to display their scoring prowess did just that by hitting 260 in 150 minutes to win by seven wickets with no less than 25 minutes to spare.

Yorkshire's cricket had not been so assured and dominant for the entire season. In mid-June they had been only half-way up the table, but a sudden surge of three victories took them to the top and having gained that impetus they thereafter were never out of the first three and always played like contenders. Their only setback came on the western tour with defeats by Somerset and Gloucestershire, being dismissed for 35 at Bristol, lowest total for 24 years.

Burnet's team had great spirit and once success had given them confidence their talents flowed, and this despite a pervading feeling that their

luck was out. Burnet lost the toss on 20 occasions and only once was there a three-figure opening stand. Yet Yorkshire in 1959 did have great faith in their own individual ability and more often than not someone succeeded.

Illingworth did the 'double' and became one of *Wisden's* famous 'Five'. Padgett added 1,787 runs thanks to his highly polished technique, while Stott, starting indifferently, finished gloriously. Close may have been inconsistent but he was also explosive, and Bolus and Bird finished with strong challenges to the places held by Sharpe and Taylor. Platt, with 82 wickets, gave a splendid support to the indefatigable Trueman, while Ryan, Taylor, and Close could all contribute useful spells of seam bowling. Wardle's departure was partly compensated by Don Wilson's advance and a varied off-spin attack of Illingworth, Close and Birkenshaw.

A fine Summer also brought a farewell to the

captain, Burnet, who at 50 decided to make way for a younger man. Having been given the onerous task, in 1958, of restoring authority to the dressing room, and having seen the departure of the nucleus of the fine start of the early 1950s, he cannot have imagined so great a reward as Yorkshire's first outright Championship since 1946.

Ironically Burnet departed knowing that several of his senior players, delighted as they were to be champions, still believed that Wardle should have been retained. Close went further:

> My own choice for the captaincy, being a professional myself, would have been Wardle…He knew his cricket inside and out; he knew the opposition; he knew about field placing and he knew about bowling; he had a shrewd calculating cricketing brain and he was interested in winning matches. He hated losing and most of all he hated losing games which could be won.

Significantly when Vic Wilson, the senior professional, was dropped for a short spell in 1959 and Close won a temporary promotion, he lost no time in telling his captain: 'I don't want the same thing to happen to me as Johnny. If I offer you advice it will be something that has been reasoned out as the best thing for the side, if you disregard my advice I shall stop offering it.'

Nevertheless, according to Close, Burnet had spells during which he paid little attention to his professionals when three matches were lost and one drawn. So Close tried a different tack and told the senior bowlers, especially Trueman and Illingworth, to insist on their field placings. Close, too, maintains that it was he who persuaded Burnet to restore Vic Wilson to the team for the Champions against the Rest match at The Oval and rumours that Wilson was not to be offered a new contract were confounded when the batsman, who had twice been dropped that season, was appointed the captain for 1960.

Wilson thus became Yorkshire's first professional captain of the century. He did not have the good weather of 1959, and there were times when Yorkshire's play slipped below the standard expected of champions, yet by the end of the season Wilson had led the team to a succes-

sive Championship.

Returning to Hove, scene of that great triumph the previous September, Yorkshire lost to Sussex by 32 runs, but the next six matches were won. By 24 May Yorkshire were top again, and although they were disposed by Lancashire in July, their final margin over the oldest rivals was 32 points, a highly satisfactory conclusion after two defeats by the Red Rose.

Trueman, with 132 Championship wickets, had a great season. Platt and Ryan were both handicapped by injuries but the left-arm Cowan returned in hostile fashion, taking 66 wickets, and with Trueman in such sharp form the seam attack was rarely quelled. Illingworth did the 'double' again but the spin attack overall was less impressive, the covering of wickets a handicap. The batting, as in 1959, was rarely reliable yet rarely failed. Stott lost his place for a while but returned in tremendous form, while Bolus replaced Taylor, who moved down the order, as Stott's opening partner Padgett, who hit five centuries, played for England without looking the player all Yorkshire knew him to be.

Binks had a splendid season, becoming the first Yorkshire wicket-keeper to record 100 victims in a Summer. Bolus, Cowan, Sharpe and Don Wilson were all awarded their caps and such was the strength of the side that Bird and the fast-medium bowler Peter Broughton were allowed to leave for Leicestershire. Birkenshaw, too, restive at being denied a place, applied for his release, but the Committee felt he was too valuable a player to lose, a judgement that was to be vindicated in later years.

After successive Championships, Yorkshire began the following season as unchallenged favourites, and had 1961's weather been a little kinder Wilson's ambitions may have been realised. The captain deserved some sympathy, for it was hard to understand a team that could play so well, and then so badly, in a matter of days. Yorkshire's batting in 1961 defied explanation. The batsmen had hit 13 centuries in 1959, a good Summer. The following season, in much damper weather, they had raised the total to 15, a promising advance. In 1961, a year similar in climate to its predecessors, 18 centuries were scored yet five matches were lost (two to

195

Don Wilson

Don Wilson was an unusual Yorkshire cricketer. He was born in Settle, not a natural nursery, and as a left-arm spinner he was the opposite of almost all his great predecessors in that Peate, Peel, Rhodes, Verity and Wardle all considered their basic task to be that of restricting the batsman's strokes and attacking when conditions were totally in their favour, while Wilson was an adventurer who saw his priority as the early downfall of his opponent.

His career greatly advanced by his arrival during Close's captaincy, for Close also believed in unlimited aggression, and it was the field settings and brilliant close catching engineered by the captain that brought Wilson much of his success. When defensive bowling was required Close could normally call upon Illingworth, operating his seam bowlers from the other end.

Don Mosey records that it was Close, early in Wilson's career, who convinced the bowler that he needed a leg-slip on the grounds that although Wilson did not include the chinaman in his armoury, the presence of a fielder in that position would cast doubt in the batsman's mind.

Wilson had the serious disadvantage of having to follow into a team that public hero Wardle. Another misfortune was that Wilson's appearance, tall, lean, angular, almost gauche, suggested he was a beginner long after he had established his place and won England recognition. But eventually his terrific enthusiasm, his unquenchable optimism and belief in always thinking that something was about to happen, inspired no doubt by his captain, won over the suspicious crowd.

He passed 100 wickets three times, in 1966, '68 and '69, and is one of the only 13 bowlers to have taken 1,000 wickets for the Club. In 1966 he twice performed the hattrick, against Nottinghamshire and Kent, and six times in his career took seven wickets in an innings. Although not a fierce spinner of the ball, his height enabled him to win bounce and, with his tail up, Wilson became a valuable weapon for Close, not least because of his unpredictability.

Wilson was also a useful tail-ender, able to swing the bat in a late chase for runs, camouflaging a less than perfect defence with his aggressive attitude. He was a superb fielder anywhere.

He played in six Tests encompassing tours to Australia, New Zealand, India and Sri Lanka, and expanded his communication skills while coaching in Soweto. According to Boycott he was favoured for the captaincy after Close's dismissal and was eventually named vice-captain to Boycott, always an unlikely partnership.

After leaving Yorkshire, Wilson became coach to the Indoor School at Lord's where, in a second career, he won even more approval from cricket generally. In his fifties he claimed he was bowling better than ever, illustrating his oft-repeated belief that: 'There's always something new to learn in this game.'

He was to take that maxim into retirement in the Dales where he continued part-time coaching to the pupils at Ampleforth and was a regular and welcome speaker at cricket clubs and societies.

Middlesex), and as those defeats came towards the end rather than the beginning of the Summer, Hampshire became the new Champions.

The start was auspicious enough, Yorkshire winning seven of the first eight games. Four games without a win from the middle of June was the first hint of fallibility, and although the side rallied with something of its old style in late July, they fell away again in August. Six batsmen scored 1,000 runs but only Bolus averaged over 35, and a Yorkshire innings left a hit-and-miss impression far too often. Yorkshire's attack did all that was asked of them. Trueman and

Illingworth both took more than a hundred wickets, and although Cowan missed much of the season through injury, Platt and Ryan shared 109 victims. An injury to Don Wilson might have been critical had not his replacement, Keith Gillhouley from Huddersfield, bowled well enough to take 73 wickets in his first season.

Yorkshire's President, Sir William Worsley, was elected President of MCC, while in another important position Ted Lester became Yorkshire's scorer in succession to Cyril Turner. In the Colts a young right-handed batsman from Thurnscoe, John Hampshire, continued to make an excellent impression on good judges. Vic Wilson, like Ronnie Burnet before him, was able

Philip Sharpe

Next to Tunnicliffe, Philip Sharpe will be remembered as the finest slip catcher in Yorkshire's history, a short stocky figure who won such confidence from his captains and bowlers that his prowess won him selection for England. He was also a capable right-hand batsman who scored 22,530 runs in his career at 30.73, including 29 centuries; his Test record, 786 runs at 46.23, suggests he was happier in higher company.

He made his reputation by scoring 1,000 runs for Worksop School, and he was capped by Yorkshire in 1960 before joining Derbyshire for two seasons in 1975. A man who enjoyed his cricket along with music (Gilbert and Sullivan, the Black and White Minstrels), cards and hockey, he and Don Wilson brought much fun and laughter into the often fractious dressing room of Close's champions.

Sharpe was an excellent player of fast bowling and might have had a much more prosperous career, in terms of runs, had he played 20 years later, by which time he had become an England selector faced with the task of finding young Englishmen who were capable of dealing with West Indian pace as he had been in 1963 and 1969.

But it is for his 616 catches that Sharpe will be best remembered; such were his skill and co-ordination that bowlers and fielders would claim, after another dazzler, that the ball had actually passed him before the catch was completed. The truth was probably that the ball seemed to have passed, and would have passed any other fielder of his time. In his own position Sharpe was as

Philip Sharpe
Yorkshire Post

much a vital contributor to the Championships of the 1960s as any specialist batsman or bowler.

After retirement he became the General Committee member for York and was popular and capable enough to keep his seat, despite his known opposition to the Boycott group, in the upheaval of 1983. It may have been the recognition, by dour and aggrieved Yorkshiremen of both persuasions, that in Sharpe they saw a man who always kept his sense of humour.

He remained close to the Club through his travel agency, arranging many Yorkshire tours.

to complete his career with a Championship, Yorkshire's 25th, a happy event upon which Maurice Leyland retired as coach after 42 years

of service to the county's cricket.

The 1962 season was dry but cold and Sharpe,

Brian Bolus

Bolus was a right-hand batsman of various talents ranging from his most sedate style with Yorkshire to a sudden, and effective, aggression with Nottinghamshire that earned him the highest honours in the game. He played one match for the Club in 1956, and his progress was steady rather than spectacular. The true measure of his style and dependability was shown in 1959 in two innings that do not rank among his highest, but in quality were certainly among his best.

Yorkshire were destroyed by Smith and Brown of Gloucestershire at Bristol and only Bolus, with 12, reached double figures in an innings score of 35, the last six batsmen all making ducks. In the follow-on Bolus was promoted to opening batsman and he defied the Gloucester attack for almost four hours, scoring 91 of his county's total of 182. In 1960 Bolus hit two centuries, his 146 not out against Hampshire being the highest of his Yorkshire career, and he was awarded his county cap. He scored four more in 1961, another in 1962, and then, inexplicably, controversy crossed his career for the first, but certainly not the last time.

He was not retained by the county, and joined Nottinghamshire – as captain! Here he adopted a swashbuckling style for a time, and it earned him a Test place in two of the matches against the West Indies of 1963 and a tour of India in 1963-64 where he appeared as opener in all five Tests.

He scored 2,190 runs in 1963 and made his highest score of his career, 202 not out against Glamorgan. After serving under Sobers as vice-captain, and then again as captain in 1972, Bolus suddenly left Trent Bridge and joined Derbyshire, as captain in 1973.

Bolus was introduced, doubtless, to spark a

fire in a Derbyshire side losing credibility with its supporters. Confrontation is the price a captain often pays when he attempts to impress a new style and discipline on a side, and in June of that first year he felt compelled to use a measure employed only twice previously in the history of the game. Alan Ward, the Test fast bowler, was dismissed from the field by Bolus at Chesterfield for refusing to bowl a second spell – ironically against Yorkshire. Only Lord Hawke, of Yorkshire, and Lord Tennyson, of Hampshire, had previously taken such an autocratic step. Ward announced his retirement from the game, but in 1974 was back in the side and playing under Bolus. That all was not well is reflected in *Wisden's* review of the 1974 season. Michael Carey wrote: '…team spirit sagged as the season went on. Bolus' leadership, so inspiring in difficult days the previous year, became questionable.'

In the early part of 1975 Bolus stood down from the captaincy and, relieved of the tension and responsibility, showed support for his successor, Bob Taylor, by topping the county's averages with 968 runs at 33.47.

Bolus' undoubted versatility as a batsman and his willingness to accept responsibility perhaps called for too much diversification of a talent that was high but yet not quite of the highest. He graduated in a Yorkshire side that had produced such captains as Watson (Leicestershire), Illingworth (Leicestershire), Close (Yorkshire and Somerset) and Vic Wilson (Yorkshire). That Bolus achieved less than his contemporaries may well be due to the player himself; it is also true that the counties who employed him often expected miracles, and when they did not materialise, insisted on instant sacrifices.

Bolus settled in the Midlands where he became a prominent member of MCC and continued to serve the game for a spell as an England selector.

Harold Bird Dickie

Bird, a right-handed batsman from Barnsley, had three years with Yorkshire before Leicestershire in 1960. His best score was 181 not out against Glamorgan at Bradford in 1959. Another good performance was at his top score of 62 for Yorkshire against MCC at Scarborough. Bird was appointed a first-class umpire in 1970, and it is in this capacity that 'Dickie' Bird has gained public notice.

His approach to the job was affected by modern influences that liberated showmanship – an approach that would have found little favour in the eyes of earlier and legendary umpires such as Syd Buller, himself an ex-Yorkshire player, and Frank Chester. They favoured judicial dignity and authority in isolation; this, indeed, was the accepted norm in their profession. Times changed sharply, and Bird's approach suddenly moved pace for pace with those times. His flamboyance and extravagance of gesture provoked conflicting reactions. It was a dramatic technique that sometimes teetered and often fell into the melodramatic, but it was also, in many ways, an unconscious display.

The natural wit and integrity that enriched Bird, while endearing off the field, was not easily communicated from the square to the circle. Few umpires have excited (or even invited) such attention in an age when the pressures facing officials are more strenuous and opinions more openly asserted.

Television added to the stress and increased the exposure, thus encouraging the indulgences of the eccentric and the assertive. The cameras doggedly tracked Bird at his best and his most excessive. He was an umpire who, during an unhappy and tense bomb scare at Lord's, preferred to sit on the covers and protect the wicket while the alarm was on.

Bird it was who strictly enforced controversial 'front foot law' in 1974, on one occasion no-balling Peter Lever, of Lancashire, nine times in his first six overs, and it was

Harold 'Dickie' Bird
Mick Pope

Bird who crusaded strongly and bravely on the inflammatory question of intimidation, becoming the first umpire to act against the bowling of persistent short-pitched deliveries in 1975.

Bird was, with veteran Tom Spencer, umpire in the dramatic, historic Prudential World Cup Final of 1975 between Australia and the West Indies at Lord's. The match started at 11 am and ended, in chaos, at 8.43 pm on a burning hot day. The ground was invaded by excited West Indian enthusiasts who thought Australia had lost – and had not heard a no-ball called. During the fracas Bird was knocked unconscious as he tried to repel invaders who were rushing the square. The conditions for umpiring could not have been more exacting, for not only was it the longest day of the year and one of the hottest, it was also one of the longest days in cricket history, played throughout to a tin-can cacophony that made conversation impossible, decisions inaudible.

Bird's performance was, from a cricketing

point of view, impeccable, and full of understatement; he hastened to excuse his 'knockout' – 'I just think a few were over-excited.'

Both captains, Clive Lloyd and Ian Chappell, congratulated the umpires. But Bird's sense of the dramatic did not please many; including Jack Fingleton, that eminently sensible commentator and former Australian cricketer. Indeed, there could have been a flashpoint to the match when Bird was uncertain about an appeal from Marsh, the Australian wicket-keeper, for catch off Lloyd. Bird walked slowly to consult with Tom Spencer, the square-leg umpire, debated the question at length, then walked equally dramatically to the wicket, and flourished his forefinger to denote Lloyd's dismissal.

Many felt it was fortunate that Lloyd was on 102 at the time and not 99, for such hesitation and slow deliberation – although justifiable within the law – were so ponderous and theatrical that it could well have sparked anger in what was an otherwise happy, if over-ebullient, West Indian section of the crowd. Against the unhappy Australians of 1977 it seemed that there was no detail too small to occupy Bird's personal attention; the merest trifles occasioned excessive gesticulations, and no opportunity of walking to boundaries to ascertain facts or still spectators was neglected.

Certain sections of the crowd, both knowledgeable and unruly, and sections of the media expressed warm criticism and disapproval. But such individual eccentricities could not conceal the warmth and integrity of Harold Bird. Not since Buller had there been a more balanced and discriminating judge of fair play, for Bird's creed was one of instinctive justice and understanding and he ranks high in the opinion of many players and judges of the game.

Denis Compton said of him: 'Harold Bird is one of those level-headed, strictly no-nonsense types so valuable in cricket. Having played as batsman for Yorkshire and Leicestershire he knows what it is all about.

Now he talks to players firmly, but in a friendly manner, and he obtains results. Most players respect him for it.'

There were mixed problems with the 1976 West Indians. Bird and Spencer, in the First Test, showed early patience and understanding with Wayne Daniel, a raw young fast bowler, obviously striving for length and direction and struggling with his run-up. It was Bird who finally warned him for running on to the pitch in his follow-through. As early as June 1976 Bird warned Daniel for this offence, and also for intimidation after he sent down several short-pitched balls to Arnold Long, the Sussex wicket-keeper and number eight batsman.

The Second Test – in which Bird stood – passed without comment, but the wisdom of his reaction in the First Test bore witness to the steps that were necessary when, at Old Trafford in a match that produced bowling described as 'unsavoury as well as being bad cricket', umpire Bill Alley publicly warned Holding for intimidation.

An unprejudiced verdict on Bird is difficult; it is not what he did, which was always within the law – more the way he did it. As one writer reminded him: 'The owl is considered a wise bird, but it carries out its duties in secret and silence; the peacock is flamboyant and spectacular, but it has no real purpose in life; it is only fine to look upon.'

Bird was approached by Kerry Packer to join his 'World Series', which showed how little the Australian entrepreneur understood about Bird the man, rather than Bird the umpire. Bird wanted no role as ringmaster to Packer's circus. The puzzling thing is that perhaps Bird did not know why he was ever approached in the first place.

Peter Thomas

It is not an exaggeration to describe Bird as a national institution on his retirement. He became everybody's umpire, appearing regularly on television and in print, an extremely funny after-dinner speaker who was rarely away from Yorkshire's major occasions and home matches. Behind the façade of the public figure, the 'professional' Yorkie was a shrewd mind and a brilliant judge in the assessment of players and their capabilities, both physical and mental. Dickie loved to play the somewhat gormless lad from Barnsley, but he was no fool.

He became a regular guest at Lord's and Headingley, set up a Foundation to help young sportspeople and even had a statue commissioned in his native Barnsley. His books were best-sellers.

Derek Hodgson

---

for one, relished the change. His talents, as batsman and fielder, blossomed in the keen winds for he scored 1,800 runs and, just as important, held 71 catches, beating the 1901 record (70) of the renowned Long John Tunnicliffe. Sharpe's batting was crucial in the first half of the season. After a good start (three victories) had won them the leadership, they had a rocky spell of three defeats in six matches without a win.

The fighting spirit which had seemed to fade in 1961 was all too evident this season as Yorkshire regained their competitive edge and re-established themselves, clearly, as the team the others had to beat. There were disappointments. The opening partnership of Bolus and Stott failed so signally that Stott was dropped and Bolus released, and a new pair, the experienced Taylor and the Colt Hampshire, made the eighth partnership tried that season.

Wilson scored two centuries in his last year and was always a solid and heartening figure in a crisis. In his three years of leadership Yorkshire had finished 1-2-1 so that any criticisms of his captaincy – too orthodox, too cautious – were really academic.

Trueman (106 wickets) retained his fire admirably, Illingworth did the 'double' again (including almost 1,500 runs); while Platt faded somewhat, Ryan advanced to 74 wickets. Wilson returned triumphantly to claim the slow left-arm place, 83 wickets at 22, and new, interesting names were those of the right-arm medium-pace seam bowler Tony Nicholson, the Cambridge Blue and all-rounder Richard Hutton, son of Sir Leonard, and Geoffrey Boycott, a bespectacled middle-order right-handed batsman from Fitzwilliam.

A win over Lancashire at Leeds, the first Lancastrian defeat in Yorkshire since 1939, was rightly regarded as a good omen, and from the end of June Yorkshire were unbeaten, winning nine and drawing 11 of their last 20 games. However, the season ended in some tension for, with a match to go, Worcestershire edged in front, leaving Yorkshire having to beat Glamorgan at Harrogate for the Championship.

This deciding match was a thriller. Glamorgan, sent in on a drying wicket, were routed by Wilson for 65, his analysis of 6-24 including two magnificent return catches. Only Taylor, apparently, could deal with the Glamorgan bowlers when Yorkshire batted. First in and eighth out at 100, Taylor batted 140 minutes for 67 in his most vital innings for the county.

Yorkshire's slender lead of 31 was reduced to 18 without loss by Glamorgan when rain washed out play on the second day with 5,000 spectators waiting patiently. The weather relented on the last day, and the ground was filled to a capacity of 10,000 as Illingworth and Wilson got to work on the Glamorgan second innings. They managed just 101, leaving Yorkshire needing 66 to win. Jones completed a hat-trick by bowling Taylor with the first ball of the innings, but that was Yorkshire's last setback. Hampshire, with a mature 24, put the Championship in safe keeping with the loss of only two more wickets.

The Summer of 1963 was one of which Yorkshire could be proud. Despite injuries, heavy Test calls and the advent of a new captain, the county still managed to retain the Championship. At various times, Illingworth, Padgett, Stott and Taylor all missed several matches through injury; England made regular calls on Trueman and Close, and Sharpe, too, was needed by his country.

The weather was far from kind, a definite result being impossible in 12 Championship matches, but when Yorkshire could play they played to some purpose: 13 of the other 16 matches were

Tony Nicholson Teapot

The nickname came from a famous Nicholson pose, standing hands on hips and glaring at some hapless batsman who, in the considered Nicholson judgement, was palpably leg before. In any poll conducted among Yorkshire players and members over the last 40 years, Tony Nicholson would be very close to being elected the most popular cricketer.

Anthony George Nicholson, from Dewsbury, appeared late in Trueman's career after a roundabout route into professional cricket that included a spell as a policeman in what is now Zimbabwe. But he was the great man's best partner; had the pair been of the same generation (Trueman was seven years older, a long span for a pace bowler) they might have formed one of the great pairings.

Nicholson, a man totally without malice and with joyous humour, was a strong right-arm fast-medium bowler who learned how to extract the maximum help from all English conditions and his intelligent mixture of speed, seam and cut brought him an impressive total of victims, many of whom were off guard and relaxing at the thought of escaping Trueman at the other end.

He twice reached 100 wickets and took 879 wickets in his 282 matches at 19.76 apiece. He was selected for the tour of South Africa in 1964-65 but had to withdraw through

Tony Nicholson
Mick Pope

injury, and he did much to encourage the career of the next generation of seam bowlers, including Old and Sidebottom. He retired, in declining health, at the age of 37 and was much mourned when he died in Harrogate ten years later.

A fit and forceful Nicholson, loyal to the Club's cause, could have been a greatly beneficial influence in the dressing room of the late 1970s.

won by an innings, and 57 runs to Worcestershire could be described as overwhelming. Even without Trueman for 12 matches, the attack was powerful. With Platt playing in only one match and retiring, seam support was needed for Ryan, and Tony Nicholson emerged to take 65 wickets at 16.24 apiece. Wilson was leading wicket-taker with 82, and Trueman, despite his absences, recorded the impressive figures of 76 wickets at 12.84 each.

Close had assumed the captaincy in succession to Vic Wilson, an appointment that was as natu-

ral as it was successful. Close's leadership, tactical appreciation and accurate knowledge of each individual's capabilities were soon reflected in the team performances. He averaged 35 with the bat, was a fearless near fielder, and won back his place in the England team. He also had much to do with the startling advances made by the promoted Colts. Of these Boycott had an impressive first season as a regular player, scoring almost 1,500 runs at an average of 46. He began as a middle-order batsman and moved to opener at the captain's suggestion, a position in which he was clearly born to play. Boycott's advance was

Geoffrey Boycott

Geoffrey Boycott, from Fitzwilliam, the son of a miner who died early from an industrial disease, was the most controversial figure in the Club's history, the most prolifically scoring batsman in the records and the captain for eight turbulent Summers. As a right-handed opening batsman he was without peer in the world as a defensive player for a span of over 20 years, and he was usually the premier target for opposing bowlers in the great majority of his 108 Test matches.

He was a capable in-swing bowler of considerable accuracy who became a valuable member, for two or three years, of the Sunday League attack. A poor fielder when he first arrived, he turned himself into an excellent deep field, a safe catcher with a good, accurate throw, and he also served his county and country occasionally at slip. A keen student of the game, his deep knowledge and assessments of players, pitches and conditions were respected around the world. In short, he was qualified as few of his predecessors had been to lead both his county and his country with distinction for many years.

That he failed to do so was due to the many contradictions within his own character. Lester's comparison of Boycott and Wardle is justified: both were South Yorkshire men from mining backgrounds, ambitious, fiercely competitive, ultra-careful in offering friendship, disdainful if not derisive of enemies and with an in-born mistrust of all authority. As all Yorkshiremen knew, Robin Hood was born in Locksley, near Sheffield, probably spent more time in Barnsdale Forest than Sherwood and almost certainly had a Boycott and a Wardle in his band – although not necessarily among the Merry Men.

Both were rebels but emerged at different times into vastly dissimilar circumstances. Wardle was one of several great players in the Yorkshire team of his time; Boycott, from his election to the captaincy, was the only truly great cricketer in the side. Wardle

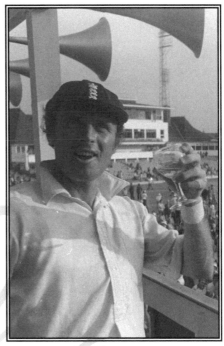

Geoffrey Boycott
Yorkshire Post

was a member of a team that may have had only limited success but could never have been described as unsuccessful; in Boycott's time as captain, Yorkshire had the most disastrous Championship record in their history.

Wardle also made the tactical error of attacking Yorkshire in public print; Boycott was shrewd enough to restrict his criticisms to specific areas on specific points, and although there is evidence to suggest he might have moved to another county had the proper terms been offered, he always professed to his supporters his devotion to Yorkshire.

His early interest in the game persuaded his family to send the ten-year-old Geoffrey to Johnny Lawrence's Cricket School at Rothwell, 14 miles away, a journey that the youngster dutifully undertook, with three changes of buses, through Winter sleet, snow and rain. He joined Ackworth Cricket Club at about the same time (1950) and was on the first team (Yorkshire Council) at

13. Upset at being told he had to wear spectacles, he treasured a letter from Mike (M.J.K.) Smith, captain of Warwickshire and England who, of course, had a highly successful batting career wearing glasses.

At 15 the young Boycott started to play for Barnsley in the Yorkshire League, deepening and extending his roots in the South Yorkshire area. Don Mosey quotes a local cricketer, Alan Kilvington, who saw Boycott grow up: 'He's very open when he's with people he knows and trusts, almost the opposite of the public view of him.' Another view of the 15-year-old batsman: 'He was inclined to be a bit abusive as a lad. He were a slow starter, never a prolific scorer – at fifteen or sixteen I'd think that Martyn Moxon looked far better player than Geoff.'

At 20 Boycott had moved to Leeds, then captained by Billy Sutcliffe, where his defensive play was admired and his scoring rate, in league cricket, heavily criticised. Robin Feather, later to become captain of the Yorkshire Second XI, recalled a Colts match at Durham when Yorkshire needed 46 to win in 45 minutes with Boycott spending eight overs in scoring in five runs.

By 1962 Boycott appeared for Yorkshire's first team in a season of transition, Vic Wilson retiring for Close to assume the captaincy. His 688 runs for Colts had forced attention upon him although he was very much at the back of the field in intense competition places, with such as Hampshire, Sharpe and Richard Hutton much more highly regarded. Boycott was dismissed for four, opening against the Pakistanis at Bradford, in each innings, scored six and 21 not out in his first Championship match, at Northampton, and was considered to have run out Ken Taylor in his third, at Chesterfield.

He spent the rest of the 1962 season in the Colts, with little success, and returned to his applied practice through the following Winter, showing remarkable confidence in surrendering a secure if dull job with the Ministry of Pensions in Barnsley.

He was returned to Yorkshire's first team at Northampton early in May 1963, batting at six and scoring eight. Dropped for four matches, he played only a small part, batting at seven, in a win over Kent, but then, with Yorkshire 56-3 against Lancashire at Bramall Lane on an awkward pitch, Boycott helped Stott to raise 249 for the fourth wicket, completing his own maiden century, 145, a major achievement by a 22-year-old who could no longer be disregarded.

He had, however, not convinced Close that he was an opening batsman and had to wait his turn for injuries and Test calls to move up the order. Boycott hit another Roses century at Old Trafford, scored 90 out of 144 on a difficult surface at Lord's and had three fine innings against Leicestershire; at the end of the season the Committee realised that he had raised 1,628 runs at an average of 45.22, and in October he was presented with his cap.

Boycott began 1964 with three centuries and a 77 in the opening six matches; Test selection was inescapable and a great career was under way, his place at the top of Yorkshire's averages, and near the top of the national averages, became a routine; he became such a fixture at number one for Yorkshire and England as Hutton had been before him. His 146 in the 1965 Gillette Cup Final, including three sixes and fifteen fours, is remembered as one of the finest of all one-day innings and yet, inevitably, was accompanied by controversy.

According to Close the opening pair of Taylor and Boycott had become so bogged down by the Surrey seam attack that he, the captain, went in at three to move things along and told Boycott first to start looking for singles, then to put some force into his shots and finally to 'hit everything'. According to Boycott, his mid-wicket conversation with Close, on the captain's arrival, concerned details as to who was bowling well and who was to be attacked. The extreme version of the story, unconfirmed but part of the legend, is that Close threatened to run out Boycott unless he accelerated.

With Illingworth departed to Leicester, Close had already decided that Boycott was his long-term replacement as captain but had, of course, no say in the decision in 1970 when he was given his 'resign or be sacked' ultimatum. It was certainly too soon for Boycott at that time, in Close's opinion, but the die was cast and at 29, the man from Fitzwilliam, his spectacles having given way to contact lenses, his turn-out immaculate on or off the field, became Yorkshire's 22nd captain in 107 years.

A score of 246 not out against India at Headingley in 1967 brought censure from the selectors and he was dropped for slow scoring. To many of his growing band of admirers this was merely proof of the establishment's attitude towards 'Our Geoff', and few captains entered into their kingdom with as much prestige and general public goodwill.

Close's attitude to captaincy was that it was an act of giving, the total subordination of the individual's ambitions and desires to the welfare and successes of the team, and under that philosophy Yorkshire had flourished achieving their most resplendent spell since Sellers' time. Boycott assumed charge of a team accustomed to this style of leadership, although it was changing fast with the departure, in recent times, of Trueman, Illingworth, Taylor and Binks.

As might have been expected, Boycott began his reign with a blaze of runs, 2,503 in the season at the astonishing average of 102; equally astonishingly, considering the sheer weight of the captain's contribution, Yorkshire finished in their lowest ever position in the table – 13th, the fourth time (all since the Second World War) they had finished outside the leading ten. An indication of a change in public perceptions, even in Yorkshire, came with the sense that such a disaster made no impact on the captain's personal reputation; his light shone all the brighter.

One reason for this failure, according to memoirs since published, was a divided dressing room, and although the Committee has been criticised in some

quarters for allowing Sharpe, Wilson and Hutton to disappear while still capable of considerable contribution to the cause, it must also have been argued that one decision had to be made: either the captain had to go or the captain had to be confirmed in charge.

In the next three years of captaincy by Boycott, Yorkshire finished tenth, 14th and 11th; Andrew Dalton, a very talented but independently minded young batsman from Leeds, refused to play after 1972; Peter Squires, another promising player and brilliant fielder (a rugby union international), was rarely happy, both players preceding an even bigger loss in Bill Athey in 1983.

In 1974, Yorkshire did not win a Championship match until mid-July and in the ensuing discontent over the leadership, five capped players (a sixth, Sharpe, refused) intended to send the Committee a signed motion of no confidence in the captain. The Committee was well aware of the anger in the dressing room, but that motion never reached them because rebels were led to believe that Boycott, who had already stood down from Test cricket, intended to retire.

When, at the end of the season, it was discovered that Boycott was carrying on, the rebels went into exile and by the end of 1975 only Hampshire was left of the team Boycott had taken over in 1971. The first impressions were favourable, for the influx of younger players under Boycott's unchallenged command brought a vast improvement to second place in the table; the title going to Illingworth's Leicestershire, their first.

When it became clear that the advance was no return to full prosperity, the team sliding to eighth in 1976 and 12th following year, when Boycott returned to Test-match cricket, all the old wounds were re-opened, culminating in the return of Illingworth as team manager in 1979 with Hampshire displacing Boycott as captain.

The 'Battles and Leaders of the Civil War' (to quote a famous history of greater conflict in America) are dealt with in the general narrative. Even when forced to choose between a new contract and a place on the General Committee, Boycott proved to be an ambivalent man, highly respected and supported by a majority of his Wakefield constituents and yet to be seen only sporadically at Yorkshire matches or Annual General Meetings. His erratic attendances at General Committee and sub-committee meetings kept him under fire, but rarely was he criticised from his own heartland. Despite sporadic attacks on his personal life from the tabloid newspapers, his popularity with the masses diminished little. His ability to talk fluently and wisely about the game took him inevitably into the media where he flourished again as a people's champion. Reluctant to be officially engaged in coaching he nevertheless helped many players, very quietly. From first to last, Geoffrey Boycott was an enigma.

His career took sudden turns, as when involved in a controversial court case in France or when he contracted throat cancer, but his resilience was undiminished and he entered the new century as an increasingly influential critic in the media.

Marriage, and the entry into his life of a wife and a daughter, seemed to smooth away some of the knife edges. He became less confrontational, and throat cancer brought him first sympathy and then real friendships from some old foes, notably Fred Trueman. He moved home to South Africa after his TV and newspaper commitments turned him into a world traveller, and he returned to the old cause in 2006 when the Board appointed him a director of the Club. His wide knowledge of the game, and many contacts, enabled him to make an invaluable contribution to the rebuilding of the team in the latter half of that decade.

such that he overshadowed the progress of Hampshire, who finished his first regular season only five short of a thousand runs.

Hampshire travelled Boycott's path in reverse; beginning as an opening batsman he was to become the county's regular number four. With Stott joining Platt in retirement at the end of the season, Yorkshire were able to give all three deserving Colts – Nicholson, Hampshire and Boycott – their county caps. Yorkshire went into the lead in the Championship table early in June, faltered towards the end of that month, but from 26 July onwards they stayed ahead, finishing 20 points clear of Glamorgan.

Rebuilding meant that Yorkshire had to vacate their head offices in Leeds, and a Centenary Fund raised £15,610 towards the cost of the new offices and dressing rooms in Headingley, estimated at £21,000. Sir Stuart Goodwin gave £5,000, and another £2,000 came from John Smith's Tadcaster Brewery. Lancashire marked the centenary by presenting Yorkshire with a clock for the new offices.

Yorkshire failed to take a third successive Championship in 1964 and the reason was not hard to find: after 15 splendid seasons, some of

them magnificent, Fred Trueman's career was approaching its end. He finished fourth in the county averages with 67 wickets at 20 each, other counties soon appreciating that the great fire was fading. Yorkshire faltered to fifth place, the first time they had been out of the top two places since 1958.

Nicholson, with 70 wickets, finished well enough to be selected for the Winter tour of South Africa, but had then to withdraw because of back trouble. Illingworth, with 104 wickets and 1,055 runs, was clearly Yorkshire's player of the year. Boycott established himself as England's opening batsman and was joined in the Test side by Trueman, Sharpe and Taylor, a contribution that must have affected Yorkshire's domestic progress.

Close, as captain, attracted criticism on this point, for Yorkshire's champions had become a highly select band. To the regular XI the only additions this season were the Huddersfield Colt Chris Balderstone and, when down from Cambridge, Richard Hutton. The captain's argument might have been that Barrie Leadbeater, Barry Wood and the 16-year-old Chris Old apart, there were no Colts playing well enough to command his attention.

Yorkshire only lost three matches in what became, after cold winds of May and early June, an exceptionally fine Summer. As the pitches improved Yorkshire's deficiencies in attack were revealed and the spell of seven matches without a definite result, in early Summer, set a pattern for the remainder of the year. Binks improved his batting average from 14 to 31 without affecting his consistently high standard of keeping wicket.

The first XI had a happy, unofficial tour of North America and Bermuda in September, and at home the Development Association was formed. The overall loss on matches in a fine and not totally successful season was £10,000. Yorkshire had another fleeting appearance in the Gillette Cup, losing to Middlesex in the second round at Lord's after having a bye in the first.

If the 1965 season was a sad one for traditionalists – Yorkshire were soon out of the running for the Championship – there was a great blaze of glory in September when Yorkshire won the Gillette Cup Final at Lord's for the first time and in brilliant fashion. The Championship record, a rise from fifth to fourth, would undoubtedly have been bettered but for the weather, Yorkshire being robbed of victory on several occasions. Batting, on difficult and varying pitches, was usually hazardous, Hampshire rightly winning praise for being the only batsman to pass 1,000 runs in Championship matches. Boycott, absent from 11 matches through Test duty and injury, scored only one century (in the Gillette Final) and was the only batsman to average more than 50.

The bowling, too, was mostly inconsistent. Trueman had days of devastation and his 115 wickets at 11 runs each was a notable performance, yet he was less effective for England and was disciplined by the Committee for a breach of contract connected with newspaper contributions. Richard Hutton took 58 wickets, nine more than Nicholson, and with Ryan announcing his retirement it was clear that Yorkshire would again have to seek out a young seam bowler. Binks continued his astonishing consistent form behind the stumps and his 308 consecutive matches was easily a Yorkshire record. Less happily remembered was the dismissal for 23 (another record) by Hampshire at Middlesbrough, Yorkshire being defeated by ten wickets before lunch on the second day.

So for once Yorkshire were happy to be involved in the instant euphoria of one-day cricket. Leicestershire were beaten comfortably by six wickets at Leicester, Boycott contributing 56. Somerset were dismissed for 63 at Taunton (Trueman 6-15) for a seven-wicket win, while Warwickshire were a much tougher proposition and five batsmen had to be run out for Yorkshire to get home by 20 runs.

Boycott's 146 against Surrey in the Final was possibly the finest innings of his career. Losing Taylor at 22, he and Close then added 192, of which Close contributed 79, for the second wicket, a foundation that enabled Yorkshire to total 317-4 in the 60 overs. Surrey, faced with such a massive total, were always struggling, their later batsmen paying the penalty for trying to hit Illingworth (5-29). Yorkshire, it seemed, had at long last accepted one-day cricket.

Mrs F. Frazer gave the club £10,000 in memory of her late husband Hector Frazer, the money to be used for an indoor shed at Headingley. Gate receipts dropped by £8,000, so a contribution of £3,000 from the Development Association was gratefully acknowledged.

Yorkshire's 27th Championship in 1966 was won with more than a few tremors. Early in August they dominated the table with a lead of 40 points before taking a slide that brought them only one victory in the next seven matches. At the start of the last match Worcestershire, also with one match to play, were only six points behind.

In a Summer of indifferent weather and poor pitches the introduction of a 65-over rule for the first innings brought further distortion to the game and extra pressure on the batsmen seeking form. Although five Yorkshire players passed 1,000 runs, only Boycott and Close averaged more than 30, and the team were often indebted to Trueman and Wilson for late, quick runs. Nicholson overtook Trueman in overs and wickets (105 to 101) despite having his action scrutinised – and passed; but neither Illingworth nor Wilson was as effective as expected. Binks was as immaculate as ever and Yorkshire's fielding

John Hampshire Jake

John Harry Hampshire, born in Thurnscoe, was a powerful right-hand batsman and occasional and underemployed leg-spinner. The son of the former Yorkshire Colt, he was always regarded as the pick of his class and yet could not establish himself beyond the ranks of the best county batsmen. Eight appearances for England, including a century on debut, against the West Indies, are a poor reflection of his true ability.

As a boy he was outstanding and anticipated success as the elder son of a man who had bowled for Yorkshire in 1937 and played football for Manchester City. He emerged, like Trueman, from the Cyril Turner-Charlie Lee school at Bramall Lane, as a leg-spinner who could bat. He later recalled the time when, as a trialist, he gave 'Ticker' Mitchell an opportunity to display his black humour: Tony Clarkson, who was later to play for Somerset, hammered the young spinner, bringing from umpire Mitchell the remark: 'There's one thing about it, lad. Tha's giving it plenty of air.'

From Rotherham Town and School he graduated to the same Federation that included Boycott, Jack Birkenshaw and Duncan Fearnley, later the Chairman of Worcestershire. At 15 the young Hampshire was playing for Town's first team and a year later was receiving offers from Northamptonshire and Warwickshire; not until 1959 was he asked to play for Yorkshire Colts at Chesterfield and was then made 12th man, while a batsman who made 181 for the first team the day before, Dickie Bird, returned to his regular place with the Colts. At the end of that season H.D. Bird was released by Yorkshire to join Leicestershire and another unforeseen career. This, at least, left a Colts place for Hampshire, now less a spinner, much more a batsman.

Hampshire's future was assured next season when, for the Colts, he scored 120 in a stand of 256 with Stott against Northumberland and shared an opening partnership of 145 with Sharpe at Old

John Hampshire
YCCC

Trafford against a Lancashire team including Tattersall, Malcolm Hilton, Pilling and Bond. By 1961 he was an occasional first-team member, scoring 129 and 54 for Minor Counties against the Australians, and admits to being surprised the following season, when the first senior batting vacancy occurred, that it should have gone to Boycott and not himself. The rivalry between the pair, seen much more acutely by the less extrovert player, then began and dogged Hampshire for the rest of his career.

Hampshire, usually tolerant, went on to make his career in his own style, that of a fierce driver with a good defence when necessary, a safe catcher and a number four called by England in 1969. In his 23 years of first-class cricket, including two for Derbyshire after he had resigned the Yorkshire captaincy, he scored 28,059 runs at 34, including 43 centuries, almost all of which were good to watch.

In 1978 he overtook Boycott in the county averages for the first time and was then appointed captain for two seasons before resigning after personal attacks on his wife and children from extreme Boycott support-

ers. He later became a first-class umpire and manager of a cricket school, qualifications that opened further career opportunities.

remained almost beyond reproach, while Close crowned a Championship year with his appointment as England captain for the final Test against the West Indies.

So to the last match: Worcestershire lost to Sussex, leaving Yorkshire as Champions even without a 24-run victory over Kent at Harrogate, where the young Underwood took 11 wickets in the match. It was in this match that Don Wilson recorded a second hat-trick of the season, his first coming against Nottinghamshire at Worksop. The Gillette Cup was held the minimal length of time for, after a bye in the first round, Yorkshire lost the first tie of the new season, falling by 40 runs to Somerset at Taunton.

Notable Colts that season were the Leeds pair Barrie Leadbeater and Geoffrey Cope, John Waring from Ripon, Chris Balderstone from Huddersfield and Chris Old from Middlesbrough.

Although 1967 was the year of Yorkshire's 28th Championship, the most potent memory of the Summer dates from 16, 17 and 18 August at Edgbaston and a drawn game with Warwickshire. After gaining a lead of four runs on the first innings, Warwickshire were eventually set to score 142 to win in an hour and 40 minutes. In the event Yorkshire bowled only 24 overs in that time, only two in the last 15 minutes, during which time, reported *Wisden*, they left the field to the umpires and batsmen during a shower. Warwickshire failed to win by nine runs and the acrimony aroused had many repercussions. The 'Laws' were changed, first-class matches ending in a mandatory 20 overs from the start of the last hour. Close, as captain, was censured publicly for his tactics, and a minor incident with a spectator during the game, which was heavily sensationalised, led eventually to his sacking as England's captain.

Curiously, the official Yorkshire report for the season makes no mention of this match or its aftermath, an indication, perhaps, of the Committee's feelings on that matter at that time.

Considering Close, as England's captain, missed 11 Championship matches and that Boycott played in five Tests and Illingworth in four, Yorkshire did well to retain the Championship.

May was cold and wet, only one of six Championship matches were finished. Yorkshire were defeated twice in June and not until mid-July did they reassert themselves, in much better weather conditions. By August the team, often with Trueman in command, were in full flight and the defeat of Kent at Canterbury was ominous for the opposition. With two matches remaining Yorkshire needed 14 points from a possible 24 to keep their title. At Middlesbrough, Warwickshire were crushed by 229 runs, Wilson taking 13 wickets, and the final fixture was against Gloucestershire on a ground of happy omen, Harrogate.

Yorkshire were sent in on a soft wicket, but masterly batting by Boycott and Sharpe raised 127 for the first wicket in between showers. By the second day the drying had begun and Gloucestershire were dismissed twice for 134 and 99, 20 wickets falling in the day, 14 of them to Illingworth, whose second-innings analysis read 13-9-6-7.

Such a triumphant ending to the season masked the difficulties ahead. Only Boycott averaged more than 40 among the batsmen and the all-conquering seam attack of Trueman and Nicholson was showing signs of wear and tear. Two younger quick bowlers, Old and Peter Stringer, showed promise, but both broke down, and Richard Hutton's arrival from Cambridge had less impact than was hoped. Cope appeared as an off-spinner of definite potential, and in one department Yorkshire could claim unchallenged pre-eminence: fielding.

Yorkshire had an adventurous if unsuccessful time in the Gillette Cup. In the first round, in the last week of May, the weather prevented play on three successive days at Leeds. Play eventually began, in a match reduced to ten overs a side, at Castleford where Cambridgeshire, who included

Richard Hutton Archie

Richard Anthony Hutton, eldest son of Sir Leonard, was a tall, strong, right-handed all-rounder capable enough to have played in five Test matches. His nickname derived from a sharp sense of humour and a radio programme from his youth, but his sometimes savage wit was not always appreciated in a Yorkshire dressing room that tended to look askance at public school graduates.

His father sent him to Repton because of its reputation as a cricket school, which Sir Leonard thought, shrewdly and correctly, would bring him less pressure on the boy because of his name. In 1959 he scored more than 700 runs for the school, became captain in 1961 and had his father lbw for three when MCC visited Repton.

He scored more than a thousand runs that season, topping both the batting and bowling averages, fast-medium. He was turned down by an Oxford College but once installed at Christ's, Cambridge, he joined Tony Lewis and Mike Brearley in the 1962 University team.

Yorkshire gave him a debut in a Roses match at Old Trafford that year and he went on to become a highly capable all-rounder, scoring 5,000 runs and taking almost 500 wickets at an average of 21. He was also a fine slip catcher and an eminent candidate as an alternative captain to Boycott, either in 1970, when Close was dismissed, or later when there were several meetings between groups of players and members of the Committee to discuss the captaincy.

Hutton, who later qualified as an accountant, was never shy in making known his opposition to Boycott's style and methods and as a tall, well-spoken, well-educated person he was an obvious standard-bearer for the rebels. There is evidence, too, that several members of the Committee were in favour of a change of leadership in Hutton's favour.

Don Mosey, who as a reporter was close to Yorkshire in the 1960s, believes Hutton should have displaced Boycott:

> As events turned out he certainly could not have brought a more melancholy state of affairs than the regime of Boycott produced. He was certainly worth his place in the team simply as a player; he got on well with other members of the side and yet his background and own personality equipped him to stand, at times when it was necessary, aloof from personal friendships within the team and to take a long objective view at the progress of the game. Above all in his favour was his attitude to captaincy – 'An essential part is the ability to make other people play to the best of their ability and beyond it. I think all the successful captains of sides which have not been outstanding have had that ability.'

There is a good case for Hutton, but was such a change possible given all the circumstances of the time? Hutton would almost certainly have had the support of most senior members of the dressing room but there were some players who would have objected (Bairstow, Sidebottom, Stevenson). Could the Committee have carried out such a change, deposing the hero Boycott for a Cambridge Blue and public-school product and the son of a very famous father?

One of the first lessons of democracy is the realisation and acceptance that the best man for the job is rarely the one who gets elected, and all the Club's history from 1980 suggests that any attempt by the Committee to replace Boycott by Hutton would have brought the overthrow of the Committee that much sooner.

Hutton was a man of several talents and was able to combine a career in the City with the editorship of *The Cricketer* magazine until he moved back to Yorkshire in the late 1990s. He had much to offer cricket, and the Club, and both the outgoing Committee and the incoming Board might have sought to harness his ability.

Johnny Wardle, scored 43-8, their opening batsman, David Fairey, hitting Trueman for six. The minor county then fielded in drenching rain while Yorkshire made 46-4, Wardle taking two wickets.

Old, the Middlesbrough Colt, took four for 32 at Old Trafford, but Lancashire totalled 194, and Yorkshire, despite a steady start, were dismissed for 190, four runs being needed from the last five deliveries.

For the first time both Yorkshire's first and second XIs won their respective Championships and the Australian were beaten at Sheffield: so 1968 was, on record, one of the great years. There were, however, many sad overtones to a jubilant Summer. Trueman retired (and when would Yorkshire see his like again?) as did Ken Taylor, while Illingworth moved to Leicestershire after a contractual dispute with the county.

Illingworth's departure proved to be a total catastrophe, a move that cost Yorkshire more dearly than almost any other in the Club's history. *Wisden* touched on Illingworth's value, unaware of the storm to come:

> [His] off-spin was the foundation of the Yorkshire bowling. He could be relied upon for economy and for decisive attack when conditions gave him opportunity, and as his batting and fielding reflected his long experience and high competence he was clearly the outstanding all-rounder. He was also a respected counsellor on the field to Close, the appointed captain, and to Trueman who acted during the period of Close's absence through injury.

Illingworth's skill and sagacity tilted the balance against Yorkshire for a whole decade. With him they would have struggled to maintain their high place in county cricket; without him they went into deep decline.

For a few short months Yorkshire basked, metaphorically at least, in an Indian Summer, the weather itself being wretched. Boycott, fortunately, was in tremendous form until he injured his back in July; Sharpe, Padgett and Hampshire all made their contributions and Yorkshire's middle and tail, led by Illingworth, rarely had a cumulative failure. Nicholson enjoyed the latter part of the season when Richard Hutton also showed encouraging form as an all-rounder, and Old made further progress.

Bonus points, awarded for performance in a first innings limited to 85 overs, were happily embraced by Yorkshire, 160 of the 270 raised for the Championship coming this way. Kent, finishing second, won one more match, but Yorkshire, defeating Surrey by 60 runs at Hull just before 5 pm on the third day, ensured that they could not be overtaken.

A fall from grace was expected after the departures of 1968, but a drop from first to 13th, then the lowest position in Yorkshire's history, surprised even the pessimists. The winning of the Gillette Cup, for the second time, was little consolation. Trueman and Taylor retired and Illingworth moved to Leicestershire; Close missed most of the latter half of the season due to injury, Nicholson broke a finger and lost form, while Boycott, Sharpe and Hampshire were required for representative games.

Not surprisingly, Yorkshire played ten Colts during the season and while the team at full strength was still capable of doing honour to the title champions, a weak and inexperienced side was rarely able to represent Yorkshire in the manner expected by supporters and public. The Championship season was made all the more depressing by the success of Yorkshire batsmen in other spheres. Boycott, Sharpe and Hampshire all scored centuries in Test matches, Close scored 146 against the New Zealanders and Sharpe hit another century against MCC. The Championship century was Boycott's 105 not out against Somerset at Headingley.

In the first seven Championship matches Yorkshire managed six draws and one defeat, a start only mildly excused by the wet weather. Gloucestershire were beaten at Middlesbrough, but only two more victories – and only 30 batting bonus points – were obtained all season. Hampshire scored a splendid maiden century for England at Lord's, but his county form was unconvincing until August, while neither Boycott nor Padgett passed 1,000 runs.

Among the Colts, Leadbeater played a determined innings of 76 in the Gillette Final and Woodford showed distinct promise. Old, who with Leadbeater was awarded a cap, took 55 wickets at 17, but Wilson was the mainstay of the attack taking 85 wickets. Hutton, with 500 runs and 50 wickets, made a useful contribution, while Cope, the off-spinner, did not advance as well as expected. In short, the team lacked the presence and personality of Trueman, whose powers may have waned but was still capable of intimidating the opposition; Taylor's experience and steadiness at the start of an innings; and most of all, the all-round ability and tactical expertise of Illingworth.

That all was not well in the dressing room was confirmed during the Winter when Jimmy Binks, the most consistent top-class wicket-keeper in cricket and Close's deputy as captain, announced his retirement. The Committee took cheer from one-day competitions, the second of which, the John Player Sunday League, was launched in 1969. Yorkshire finished eighth in this new League without showing any great enthusiasm for the novelty. Indeed, senior players were openly hostile to the 40-over competition, compelling, as it did, the abandonment of much of the training and disciplines they had learned.

Yorkshire's happy days in 1969 were mostly in the Gillette Cup. The bowling and catching overwhelmed Norfolk at Lakenham and the batting, Boycott and Sharpe opening with 137, was too good for Lancashire at Old Trafford. Boycott (92) and Close (96) helped Yorkshire to raise 272 at The Oval, Surrey failing by 137, and the Final was reached before a packed Scarborough ground where Nottinghamshire, including Sobers, were beaten by 68.

With Boycott injured, Yorkshire opened with Leadbeater and Woodford against Derbyshire in the Final at Lord's, scoring 219 in the 60 overs and then dismissing Derbyshire for 150, Close and Wilson taking three wickets each.

The Yorkshire public had become accustomed to shocks in the seasons since the war, but few events startled them as much as the Committee's

Chris Old Chilly

In Mike Brearley's time-honoured phrase, Christopher Middleton Old was 'a displaced gene away from greatness'. A very high-class all-rounder he was unfortunate to spend the bulk of his career in the troubled 1970s and '80s; had he been able to play in a settled and successful side he could have emerged as one of the most successful players of the post-war period.

He was nevertheless a powerful presence in his 16 years with Yorkshire, two with Warwickshire and 46 Test matches, scoring almost 8,000 runs and taking more than 1,000 wickets. Two outstanding performances stick in the mind: Old Trafford where, taking over the captaincy from an injured Hampshire, he scored a century twice to win a Roses match almost single-handed; another at Headingley where, returning as a Warwickshire player, he bowled his new county to an outstanding and emphatic victory.

Chris Old
Yorkshire Post

The brother of the rugby international Alan Old, 'Chilly', a nickname dispensed by Hampshire that gave the opposite impression of Old's amiable, gregarious nature, appeared from Middlesbrough at an opportune moment to replace Trueman as Nicholson's opening partner – although as a boy his talents were such that it was difficult to predict whether he would become known as a bowler or a batsman. His height, increasing pace and ability to use seam and swing turned Old into a right-arm quick bowler who could bat left-handed.

Coming in to bat down the order meant that his natural hitting powers were developed, and with the growth of one-day cricket he adapted very successfully. His century in 37 minutes against Warwickshire in 1977, on a third afternoon when no result was possible, is among the fastest in history.

At the best Old was highly admired and respected by his captains. Hampshire wrote of him (1983):

> …as good a practitioner with the new ball as we saw in his time. When he was past his pomp, so to speak, he traded all-out speed for his accuracy and guile and became a supreme player in that field. I was lucky enough to go into the 1977 Centenary Test in Melbourne and saw him bowl quite superbly there. I am told of his

immensely long spell into the wind at Wellington of the following year – 30-11-54-6 – into a real snorter of a gale coming down the Hutt Valley.

What Old lacked was the essential streak of ruthlessness in his character and toughness in his frame to reach the very front rank. He was remarkably fallible to injury, so much so that when a new bowling machine was installed at Headingley, that broke down regularly, it was immediately dubbed 'Chilly'.

So although he was the natural choice to succeed Hampshire as captain in 1982, he was unable, at 34, greatly to affect the course of events upon the field and found leading side containing a General Committee member and ex-England captain in Boycott, managed by another ex-England captain in Illingworth, altogether too much for his essentially good-natured personality.

After being replaced as captain by Illingworth in 1983 he moved on to Warwickshire and later played for Northumberland. He was then able to impart his experience to children when he became a cricket consultant to the Humberside Education Authority. He retired to a business in the South-West but never lost his interest in cricket and was believed to have been one of the candidates for Director of Coaching in 2007.

---

decision at the end of this season to dispense of Brian Close. Their Statement read: 'After long and careful consideration your Committee decided not to re-appoint D.B. Close as first team captain for 1971 and in view of this decision it was also decided that he should no longer be a playing member of the team.' The Committee then went on to pay tribute to Close's 22 years' service that encompassed almost 23,000 runs and nearly 1,000 wickets, while in his eight years as captain he had won the Championship four times and the Gillette Cup twice.

The uproar that followed was not confined to the

public at large. Yorkshire's members, as loyal to their own cause as the Brigade of Guards, also revolted, forming an Action Group from within their own ranks that brought such pressure on the Committee that changes were forced.

Yet the furore did not reinstate Close, and the wave of sympathy for a great cricketer obviously broken-hearted by the decision was transferred in time to his successor, Geoffrey Boycott. Boycott heard the news while touring Australia with MCC, and as he was expected to continue as a regular member of the England team the Club appointed a vice-captain, Don Wilson. That the Committee should take such a

David Bairstow Bluey

David Leslie Bairstow, a stocky Bradfordian with red hair and blue eyes, an Australian characteristic that won him his nickname (another inspiration of Hampshire's) was one of the great wicket-keepers whose full ability was never measured. He played during a time of covered pitches and was thus rarely offered the opportunity to demonstrate what he could do while standing up to the stumps or keeping to high-class spin bowling. Ted Lester, who saw all the great post-war wicket-keepers, rated Bairstow as good as Binks when standing back.

His record puts his ability beyond question: there are ten instances in the Club's history of a wicket-keeper claiming six or more victims in an innings, Bairstow performing the feat five times, including a seven against Derbyshire at Scarborough in 1982; he is one of six wicket-keepers in the game to have 11 or more dismissals in a match (11 caught in the same match); and is the only Yorkshire wicket-keeper to have passed 1,000 runs in a season three times (1981, 1983, 1985).

After Binks' unexpected retirement Neil Smith, from Ossett, who was later to play with distinction for Essex and Cheshire, was the original replacement, but by 1970 it was clear that an early opportunity had to be given to the 17-year-old Hanson Grammar schoolboy Bairstow, who was showing more promise of outstanding ability. He was, in fact, due to take his A-level examinations that day and actually sat them at 6 am in order to make his debut against Gloucestershire at Park Avenue later.

Bairstow spent the rest of that season under Close and in May 1971, under Boycott, he took six catches (equalling David Hunter's record) in the Whitsuntide Roses match and another three in the second innings. Yet it was 1973 before Bairstow was capped, a delay brought about not so much by any lack of faith in his future but more probably by a feeling that so much natural ebullience needed a little restraint.

David Bairstow
YCCC

Bairstow also faced competition to follow Alan Knott and Bob Taylor as England's wicket-keeper and although he played in four Test matches he only once began a tour, to the West Indies in 1981, as senior keeper, the selectors seemingly preferring the more reliable defensive technique of Paul Downton at a time when every run was invaluable.

But he was recognised as the one player who could, as new Yorkshire captain, unite warring spectators and members in the aftermath of the 1983-84 Committee upheaval, and in the three years he did so. By leading from the front and by the exhibition of ferocious loyalty to the Club, he settled a dressing room that could have been split again and again. In retrospect, from the Club's view, it was a setback that he did not accept Close's suggestion that he should captain the side as a batsman, this allowing Steven Rhodes to stay with the county, but after the recent frequent departures of Yorkshire captains he did have good reason to be highly suspicious of the offer.

In the end his captaincy lived and died in the Benson and Hedges semi-final in June 1984 when they lost to Warwickshire by three runs, Bairstow being caught at full stretch on the boundary by the tall Paul Smith when the former was going for a six. A Lord's final at that stage in his career would have sealed his term of office, as it did for his successor.

Although he lost his place briefly in 1988, at the age of 37, he returned in September to claim his 1,000th first-class victim, and indicated then that he would not go gently, becoming second only to David Hunter in the aggregate number of victims.

After retirement Bairstow developed several business interests including radio commentary, and followed the cricketing career of his son Andrew with great paternal interest. It was a major shock, in January 1998, when he committed suicide, the sequel, it was thought, to financial worry. Although Andrew's first-class career was limited, David would have been delighted with the progress of his second son, Jonathan, regarded in 2007 as one of England's most promising young batsmen.

---

decision at the end of the 1970 season was even more surprising in that Close had apparently rebuilt the side after the upheavals of 1968-69.

Yorkshire climbed from 13th to fourth place in the Championship and at one time in mid-season were seriously considered as contenders again. Despite Close's return to form after an uncharacteristic lean start (353 runs in his first 15 first-class innings), Yorkshire were too inconsistent to aspire to trophies. Of the regular batsmen only Hampshire advanced sufficiently to gain a tour place. Wilson and Leadbeater both missed several matches through injury. Cope increased his wickets from 37 to 75, despite the unsettling news of another investigation into his action.

Two interesting newcomers appeared. Yorkshire were expected to have difficulty in replacing the immaculate Jimmy Binks as wicket-keeper and their first choice, Neil Smith, was displaced in early July by another Bradfordian, 18-year-old David Bairstow. This young man's natural enthusiasm behind the stumps or when batting soon won him a regular place and high praise. Smith, meanwhile, proved that Yorkshire's original judgement had not been unfounded by departing for a distinguished career with Essex. The other new name was that of Phillip Carrick, a left-arm slow bowler from Leeds, who took 6-85 in the second innings of MCC's match in the Scarborough Festival.

A clue to the Committee's disquiet at the Summer's end came in the financial report – 'the most disastrous in the history of the Club' – recording a loss of more than £8,000. Half of this loss could be attributed almost directly to Yorkshire's elimination from the Gillette Cup, in wintry weather, in the first round, a stark contrast to the Final triumph of 1969. As the team won only five of their 16 John Player League matches, Yorkshire's record in the lucrative one-day games was extremely disappointing and the captain's clearly expressed dislike of some features of limited-overs cricket did not further his cause in the committee room.

As a player and a personality Close had always found 100% acceptance rare. Kilburn noted his disappointment: '...he was 32 years old, saddled with a public reputation for irresponsibility, seen as a gifted batsman and a bowler of modest but uncrystalised talent and recognised within the Yorkshire team as a tactician whose views had sometimes received less than due appreciation in the period of Wilson's captaincy.'

For Mosey, his captaincy was: '...brilliant at getting the best out of others, at pointing out faults in technique and ways of improvement. That is why he was an inspirational captain. He had an encyclopaedic knowledge of the strengths and weaknesses of opposition players and of his own team. Rarely, one is forced to conclude, did he look at his own fallibility. If only he had been...able to adopt an attitude of do-as-you-would-be-done-by there is no telling what heights he might have achieved.'

As captain of Somerset, Close won golden opinions from young players, who were none the less more than a little afraid of his reputation (there is a tale of one young batsman, dismissed through making an error for which he had been previously castigated by his captain, crawling back into pavilion by a back window rather than face Close's wrath by returning up the steps). Ian Botham once said of him: 'He gave me the killer instinct.' Yet he was also a protective leader, and Richard Hutton's memory of him was that: '…he protected the players under his command…his approach earned him the support and the loyalty of his team and made his verbal ear-bashings the more tolerable.'

Kilburn sensed that major changes were coming and warned: 'Extension of television and a redirection of much cricket writing towards the cult of the personality helped shift the focus of loyalties from the corporate to the individual.'

Boycott to Bairstow 1970–1986

If the first rift between the government of the Club and the members was the dismissal of Wardle in 1958, the sacking of Close 12 years later brought full dissent into the open in a manner unknown for almost a century; the following 12 years were to bring bitter controversy, unending argument and eventually a revolt that would topple the Committee. Only success on the field could have averted tragedy that had the crashing inexorability that accompanies the downfall of a regime. No blood was shed in the Ridings – at least none was recorded as having been lost – but much bitterness ensued, legal fees abounded, the Club won enormous media attention and the membership, whether for or against the Committee, flaunted their emotions so strongly and publicly that observers and reporters reacted first in sorrow, then in anger and, finally, in derision, a mood that matched that of much of the rest of the cricketing world.

If the catalyst was the captaincy and personality of Geoffrey Boycott, the cause was the deep dissatisfaction with the team's performances, finishing as they did 13th, tenth, 14th and 11th in the seasons of 1972-75. Boycott, as captain, had to take a major share of the responsibility, but there were many other factors in the worst decade in the Club's history: the invasion of the domestic game by world-class overseas players that almost overnight transformed Yorkshire from one of the stronger to one of the weaker teams; the covering of pitches, reducing efficiency of the county's traditional cutting edge, spin bowling; the growing emphasis on one-day cricket, reducing the need for the traditional arts, especially wicket-taking; the swing to limited-overs cricket in the leagues, cutting the harvest of potential Test-class, if not first-class cricketers, in a competition in which the accurate medium-pace all-rounder was the most valuable player.

To blame Boycott for all this is to contribute to that school of history that ascribes the fall of the Romanovs to Rasputin; yet just as a Richelieu

might have at least delayed, if not averted the revolution, so a captain of different temperament might have been able to bring to the Club an adhesive rather than divisive influence.

That Close would so soon follow Illingworth meant that the Club had lost its two major tactical influences inside two years. That Brian Sellers should step down from his perhaps too autocratic chairmanship of the Cricket sub-committee, a direct result of members' criticism of the Close sacking, meant that the powerful voices that had dominated the field and the committee room through the Silver Sixties had all gone. And while it would have been unfair to say that a vacuum of leadership existed, the new control, both on and off the field, was uncertain and lacked experience.

Even the decision to appoint Boycott before Phil Sharpe may be challenged. In retrospect, Boycott was certainly the more forceful personality and on those grounds the Committee sought to recruit the driving force that had turned the shy boy from Fitzwilliam into a world-class batsman. However, they also overlooked Sharpe as vice-captain, to take charge while Boycott was playing for England, preferring Don Wilson and thus removing the experienced and amiable Sharpe from authority inside the dressing room. According to Boycott it was Wilson, not Sharpe who almost became captain before Boycott.

Without Boycott, who had broken his arm in Australia, Yorkshire's poor start in 1971 turned into catastrophe. When Boycott did return to the side, his own form contrasted so strongly with that of his colleagues that the first argument began: was Boycott, who became the first Englishman to average 100 in a season (a figure three times better than that of Sharpe), playing for himself or for Yorkshire? Years later Boycott was to maintain that Yorkshire did not win a match in which he did not make a big score. He also produced statistics to prove that almost all the batting and bowling points were gained

Richard Lumb

Richard Graham Lumb, from Doncaster, was the most successful of Boycott's opening partners, a tall right-hand batsman of courage, even temperament and good defensive technique. He scored 221 centuries in his 13 seasons starting with 114 in difficult circumstances in a Roses match at Old Trafford, when 23.

In all, Lumb scored 11,000 runs at an average of 30 and passed 1,000 five times. With Boycott, Lumb shared five opening partnerships of more than 200 and their total number of opening century partnerships is surpassed only by Sutcliffe and Holmes, 29 to 69. Against Sussex at Leeds in 1974 Boycott and Lumb shared century opening stands in each innings, the eighth pair to do so.

Lumb, a generous and easy-going man, played twice in Test trials and was close to selection for England on a number of occasions. With his height and reach he might have also been a first-class slip, but he was not an ambitious man as he proved when he was offered the captaincy after Boycott.

Lumb married the sister of South Africa's then best wicket-keeper and emigrated to that country in 1984. He was a batsman who, in happier circumstances, might have made a much more substantial contribution.

Richard's son Michael, born in South Africa, qualified for Yorkshire by residence in 2000 and won his cap as a hard-hitting left-hander and brilliant outfield. It was a major disappointment to the Club and to many followers when this popular player elected to join Hampshire in 2006.

---

under his leadership. Back in 1971, the debate was under way.

One player who was successful enough that season to be called upon by England was the all-rounder Richard Hutton, elder son of Sir Leonard, whom Boycott was to blame for leading an ill-starred and flickering players' rebellion against him that same year. Boycott called a players' meeting at the house of a friend; the Cricket sub-committee under the new chairman, John Temple from York, called another, and although both events passed almost unnoticed at the time, the civil war had begun. Of the senior players Hutton, Wilson and Sharpe made no bones about their opposition to Boycott's continuing captaincy, while Hampshire, Nicholson and Padgett seemed aghast that the Yorkshire dressing room should come to this.

Boycott himself recorded of that time: 'I wish I had given up the Yorkshire captaincy at the end of the year.' It is fascinating to consider what might have happened had he resigned, but in retrospect there seems to be not the slightest possibility that Yorkshire could have accepted his departure from office and, probably, thence to another county. Both then and for years to come,

Boycott was almost the only star in the sky above the Broad Acres.

So the battle lines were drawn and the new Secretary, Joe Lister, the successor to John Nash, who was a batsman good enough to play twice for the first team before joining Worcestershire, was soon to realise that he had a dressing room as factional as an Italian court of the Renaissance. An outsider would have seen that the bowling had deteriorated alarmingly in that Wilson had lost form and Cope, although promising, was not yet an Illingworth, while if any of the three regular seamers Nicholson, Hutton or Old was unavailable for any reason, there was little reserve strength.

That Winter brought the retirement of Padgett, who became coach in succession to Arthur Mitchell and second-team captain. Boycott would have preferred to keep the commonsensical Bradfordian, a wise and experienced judge, in the first-team dressing room for another season, and Padgett offered to continue for a while as player-coach, but the Club's decision was that he was needed with the Colts. In theory this was probably the correct decision, but in practice it meant that a voice of moderation had gone.

Phillip Carrick Fergie

Carrick, a talented slow left-arm bowler who had to temper his skills to the demands of one-day cricket, and a useful right-hand batsman, was a thinking cricketer who derived great satisfaction in seeing the Club through stormy water into a sunlit calm when he led the team to victory in the Benson and Hedges Cup competition at Lord's in July 1987.

By the standards of the Club's great eras it was only a minor triumph, yet the satisfaction of actually winning a competition again, in the high-profile, televised circumstances of a Lord's final, did much to dissipate the anger, bitterness and frustrations of the previous decade. When Yorkshire were given a standing ovation, before the Sunday match at Scarborough the following day, a Middlesex cricketer accustomed to playing in the echoing emptiness of Lord's on a Championship day, observed: 'It was very moving to see that the game meant so much to so many people.'

Phillip Carrick
YCCC

Carrick, born in Armley but a product of the Bradford League, came from a cricketing family, and at 15 was a member of the Farsley first team and playing for Yorkshire Schools. At 17 he first played for the Colts and made his debut the following year when Wilson was injured. At 21 as Wilson lost form, Carrick was moving towards seniority in 1973, taking 8-33 against Cambridge. But his cap was delayed for another three years, being awarded, to his intense disappointment, when he was coaching and playing in South Africa.

In 1978, batting superbly on a bumpy Headingley pitch against a rampant Lancashire attack, he made a maiden century that qualified him to be termed an allrounder. How good a bowler he might have been in the days of uncovered pitches is hard to assess, but he was shrewd enough to point out, on one occasion, that a spinner's figures, in the 1980s, might well depend upon the fixture list: 'If you happened to play both at Bradford and Swansea, where the ball would turn, you could double your wickets.'

Much of Carrick's career was spent bowling at the leg stump without recourse to spin or flight because containment was the only task allotted to him. When conditions did favour him he could strike, as a 12-89 against Derbyshire in 1983 attests.

In 1985, at the age of 22, when starting his benefit year (£73,020), he told Jane Harrison: 'All I ever wanted to do was to be a Yorkshire cricketer and now I just want to continue playing until they sack me.' He added: 'I'd like to see Yorkshire competing in a Lord's final again. We haven't been there since 1972.'

His election to the captaincy in 1987 was not a complete surprise for he had deputised successfully when Bairstow, with one of his rare injuries, was absent. Nevertheless his initial success surprised even friends for in the first half of the 1987 Summer Yorkshire were almost invincible and, very briefly, younger followers of the Club had a glimpse of county cricket as it had appeared to a Yorkshireman at the turn of the century.

The anti-climax, after the Cup win, demonstrated how difficult it is to sustain a Championship challenge without at least one Test-class bowler. Carrick was able to supervise the advance of Paul Jarvis who, had he not broken down halfway through

1988, might have given Carrick a second successful year as captain.

Indeed Carrick, in different times and circumstances, might have become one of Yorkshire's great captains. He was a thoughtful, innovative leader and could have contributed substantively to the Club's history as a coach and possible manager had he not died suddenly in January 2000 at only 48 years.

Despite the undercurrent of rumour and intrigue, the 1972 Summer began so well that Yorkshire followers were temporarily deluded into thinking the storm had passed, Yorkshire's limited success in one-day cricket, particularly on Sundays, had given the impression that they found adaptation difficult but they swept through the newly-created 55-over Benson and Hedges competition to reach the Final. Another indication of things to come was a match award, early in the zonal series, in which the adjudicator, Bill Voce, gave Barry Wood, then with Lancashire, the prize. In the same match Don Wilson had taken 5-26. When asked, Boycott naturally enough replied that he thought Wilson should have the award; the subsequent headline, 'Boycott Lashes Voce', should have warned him of what he was up against.

By early June Yorkshire had actually climbed to the top of the Championship table when one blow after another fell upon the side: Wilson lost form alarmingly, Cope's action was questioned, and worst of all, Bob Willis broke a finger of Boycott's in a Gillette Cup tie, which meant that his batting for the rest of that Summer was as much a gradual easing back into play of an injured hand as scoring runs. Spirits were low, and when Yorkshire lost the Benson and Hedges Final to Leicestershire, a victory engineered by Ray Illingworth and sealed by a former Yorkshire Colt, Chris Balderstone, acrimony flared again.

Hutton was continually being mentioned as an alternative captain, but as he had taken only a one-year contract and he had hinted of business commitments his longer cricketing future must have been, to some of the Committee, in doubt. Certainly Hutton made it clear that any

Yorkshire team under his leadership would not contain Boycott, so that once again the Committee was brought up against the harsh reality that while they might want to change the captain it was probable that a majority of the members, supported by an irate public and most of the popular press, would seek to sack them if they did. Their attitude can rightly be criticised as being head-in-the-sand, but it is difficult to see what alternative was open to them other than to temporise and hope that the dressing room would settle down of its own accord.

They had some reason for hope: the team had raised itself to tenth place in the Championship (a marginal improvement perhaps, but three places nevertheless), had reached the Benson and Hedges Final and finished joint third in the John Player Sunday League (40 overs). A new generation of bowlers was emerging in the two left-arm spinners Philip Carrick from Leeds and Mike Bore from Hull, who first appeared bowling slow-medium, Underwood-style, and three seamers all of whom were to serve Yorkshire well in differing and difficult circumstances, Christopher Old, Arthur Robinson (Northallerton), a strong left-armer who rejoiced in the nickname 'Rocker' and who compensated in heart for whatever he may have lacked in ability, and the steady Howard Cooper (Great Horton). In addition Hampshire had emerged to join Boycott as a Test batsman, Bairstow was developing into a top-flight wicket-keeper and punishing tail-ender, and a tall new opener with excellent defensive technique had emerged from Doncaster – Richard Lumb.

The Winter of 1973 brought more controversy for at a public forum the question 'What's wrong with Yorkshire cricket?' was put to a panel including Boycott. His reply embraced many suggestions, including a team manger (possibly Ted Lester, the then scorer), and a central ground owned by the club – which would have meant, of course, that several traditional grounds would lose their fixtures. By then the media was well aware that Boycott's sayings sold newspapers, and the Committee had to agree to another meeting in which, according to Boycott, the captain was 'icily ticked off' by the Chairman of the General Committee for pronouncing upon policy. Boycott wrote later that he did not know what the Club policy was, and it was this valid point that may have led to the inclusion of the Club captain and coach in selection meetings. Hampshire recorded in his own memoirs that it was during this period that he went to see Boycott to put some points of dissension to him and 'hoped I had achieved something'.

That Winter was a dramatic one for the Yorkshire Club: the President, Sir William Worsley, father of the Club's patron the Duchess of Kent, died, as did Wilfred Rhodes and Arthur

Wood, and any hopes that followers might have had of a new Spring in 1973 were dashed. Wilson, dropped the previous Summer, was dropped again and Carrick and Bore given a run; Cope, his action remodelled by Johnny Wardle, returned to the side, but seemed reluctant to use his full power of spin and made little impression.

Despite an improvement in the batting, a splendid return after an operation by Tony Nicholson and an impressive advance by Old, the Championship position was 14th, another all time low. Only three Championship matches were won and the nadir was a defeat in the Gillette Cup by Durham, the first victory by a then minor over a first-class county. Yorkshire were bowled out for 135 at Harrogate and lost by five wickets, a result that rang round the world confirming, from Wellington to the Windwards, that there was trouble at t'mill.

For the first time the sense of disquiet in the Club surfaced from within the Committee, the former captain Ronnie Burnet, one of Bradford's

---

Graham Stevenson Moonbeam

Graham Barry Stevenson was one of the great unrealised talents of recent history. A right-arm batsman and bowler from Ackworth, he had the ability to bowl fast at the highest level and as a batsman was a hitter of prodigious power. His great lack was confidence in his own ability; in different circumstances and in a successful side, Stevenson might have matured into an all-rounder with the talent to match Botham at his own game.

His figures of 4,000 runs and 450 wickets in 13 seasons tell almost nothing about his career. Fair, strongly built, he could win bounce on a hard pitch and move the ball in more usual English conditions. His range of strokes was limited but his favourite, a lofted drive between long on and long off, was worth travelling to see. He could also take excellent catches anywhere and his throw-in, from the boundary, was bullet-like, catching many an unwary batsman, among them Brian Close when captain of Somerset.

Stevenson's most glorious moment came in a night match at Sydney when England, needing 35 to win with two wickets standing and 30 balls remaining, relied on the comparatively untried Bairstow and Stevenson to win the game. Stevenson, batting number ten, hit 28 not out against Dymock and Thomson in a fiery demonstration of hitting that left the Hill, normally so noisy and ebullient, strangely hushed.

Stevenson scored one of his two first-class centuries when batting at number 11 against Warwickshire and, partnered by the number one, Boycott, set a new last-wicket record for the country of 149. Stevenson also holds the record for the highest number of sixes in a Sunday League game (John Player/Refuge Assurance) – ten, when he smote Somerset for a tempestuous 81 off 29 balls at Middlesbrough on 4 June 1984.

His nickname was bestowed upon him by Don Wilson when Stevenson first appeared, as a round-faced smiling 18-year-old in the dressing room.

representatives, saying publicly that Hutton should be captain. The Boycott camp quickly pointed out that Hutton had been available for only ten first-class games in the Summer of 1973, an absence that had brought forward the career of two young seamers from South Yorkshire, Arnie Sidebottom, also a Manchester United footballer, and Graham Stevenson.

Nevertheless a team was taking shape, the principal weakness being in the spin bowling for unless Cope or Wilson could recover their form, Yorkshire, for so long the academy of arts and sciences in spin bowling, would be without a seasoned spinner. Not that such mundane matters as team-building were allowed to interfere with the increasingly uncivil war.

To traditionalists the saddest moment of the Summer of 1973, even more depressing than the defeat by Durham, was the closing of the famous old ground at Bramall Lane, the Club's birthplace. Sheffield United, the host club, had been in effect taken over by the football section of the Committee, who decreed that there was no place in this modern world for cricket at Bramall Lane. A grandstand was built across the pitch and the old Victorian pavilion knocked down to provide a car park. J.M. Kilburn had no regrets, believing that cricket had run its course at the Lane, but United Cricket Club, a famous local institution, was left homeless and there remained an element of doubt about the future of the first-class game in one of its founding cities.

The dinner to mark the end of Bramall Lane fired fresh argument when Fred Trueman, later to become the Committee member for Craven, attacked Boycott's captaincy; one by one, it seemed, the main protagonists were taking position and showing their colours. Another Committee member from Bradford, Don

---

Bill Athey Bumpah

The nickname was given to the schoolboy as praise for his skill in hooking attempted bumpers. Charles William Jeffrey Athey, a neat, stylish right-hand batsman, fine close field and occasional medium-pace bowler, was the best batsman to emerge from Middlesbrough, from a cricketing family.

His talent and technique were outstanding enough to mark him from his first appearance, in 1976, as the long-term successor to Boycott as number one for Yorkshire and England. Even as a pale, shy young Colt his ability to play on a difficult pitch, as on one celebrated occasion at Northampton, marked him as a coming international. In seven Summers with Yorkshire he scored more than 6,000 runs, including ten centuries, four in 1982, twice passing a thousand runs.

Although he never expressed discontent publicly, Athey was said to be unhappy with the atmosphere in the dressing room and in 1984, after marrying the sister of a Middlesex cricketer, he moved to Gloucestershire in whose service he regained his place in the England side and

Bill Athey
Mick Pope

succeeded to the county captaincy in 1989. Athey's departure, along with that of Steven Rhodes, was a serious setback to the club.

Brennan, joined in the attack on Boycott's leadership in 1974, a year allotted to the captain's benefit, which inadvertently proved to be a rallying point for the growing pro-Boycott anti-Committee faction. To the outsider it seemed incongruous that the county captain, the only world-class player in the side, should come under constant criticism from the names that belonged to previous generations. Those members of the Committee, including Joe Lister, trying to keep the Club on course and on an even keel were not helped by waves from either side – for Boycott was never averse to expounding his own views as to how the Club should be directed, once notably in an article in the *Sunday Mirror* co-written with Ted Dexter.

Yorkshire's Sheffield fixtures had by then moved to the home of the Collegiate Club at Abbeydale Park and it was there, amid the sponsor's tents, that the captain, already being assailed in the press for his alleged weakness against left-arm seamers, particularly the Indian Solkar, revealed that his benefit plans were in disarray after a disagreement with his organiser. Once again a Boycott story seized the headlines, the team's performance became an irrelevance and the Club was made to appear merely a stage upon which one dramatic act after another was unfolded.

There was a row about the Roses match at Headingley, in which the Cricket chairman and the captain were made to look either absent-minded or foolish, or both. Boycott withdrew from selection for the Second Test against India and had another finger broken, Yorkshire then losing to Worcestershire by an innings at Hull. By this time all the popular newspapers had a man permanently stationed in the Yorkshire press box, less concerned with the cricket than with the next Boycott story, which was never long in coming.

Speculation that the Committee would sack Boycott at the end of that Summer was freely aired in the press, and although officially denied by the Club, the rumours continued. A petition, signed by Hutton (playing his last full season), Nicholson and Wilson and calling for Boycott's removal, was supposed to have been drawn up to be presented to the Committee, but the other two senior members of the team, Sharpe and

Hampshire, were not, according to Boycott, in full support, so it was torn up.

No one could doubt that 1974 was a low point for the captain. A string of injuries, concern about his form for England, the Club, dissent in the dressing room, a suspicion that he was being deliberately downgraded in the list of possible Test captains, all caused him to contemplate an early retirement. Fortunately for both him and the club, Yorkshire, with injured players returning, had a reasonably successful and happy August, winning four matches in the Championship and three in the Sunday League.

The team moved up three places in the Championship, to 11th. Lumb won his county cap, and enough promising Colts in the clever seamer Steve Oldham (Sheffield) and the batsmen Colin Johnson (Pocklington) and Peter Squires (Ripon), the latter an England rugby union three-quarter who certainly enlivened the fielding, emerged to suggest that a new wave of talent might be forthcoming. What was essential, in the Committee's view, was that the bickering of 1974 had to cease, and in September of that year Boycott was re-elected captain (although by a margin of only one vote, according to Boycott) and Wilson, Sharpe and Hutton all ended their careers with the county.

Wilson was able to take his gift of communication and love of the game into a greater career as head coach at MCC; Sharpe moved on temporarily to Derbyshire before returning to Yorkshire as a Committee member for York; while Hutton went off to a career in the city and publishing. Not one of the three has happy memories of his later years with Yorkshire.

Thus 1975 began with, at the very least, the feeling that the air had been cleared. Boycott was unchallenged in the dressing room although records that he had been asked, the previous Autumn, by one Committee member: 'What do you think of Hampshire as captain?' – an indication, perhaps, that the leadership issue was at best only in suspense.

Despite worries about his mother's declining health, his principal but unannounced reason for declining the England Winter tour of Australia (a decision that rebounded upon him when he sought TCCB permission to make a short tour of South Africa in the February), Boycott did approach the Committee Chairman Arthur Connell, and the new President, Sir Kenneth Parkinson, for a pre-season meeting in which he put several points to them upon the future of the Club, finishing by saying that he was contemplating giving up Test cricket to concentrate on Yorkshire. The fact that the Cricket chairman, John Temple, was bypassed did not help his cause with the less sympathetic members of the Committee.

There was certainly a massive improvement in Yorkshire's Summer: the team rose to second in the Championship, without ever looking likely to finish on top, were fifth in the Sunday League and enjoyed their Benson and Hedges campaign. A new team had taken shape, based on a sound opening partnership of Boycott and Lumb, averaging 64, that briefly hinted at former great combination. Leadbeater and Hampshire, the latter named vice-captain, gave the middle a touch of class and an array of strokes; Bairstow was fast becoming an England contender, Old was a Test all-rounder, Nicholson, although in his last season, still a formidable force, especially in one-day matches, Sidebottom and Stevenson gave full support, while Cope seemed to have mastered his new action and Carrick was developing well. What was especially pleasing, in view of the increasing emphasis on one-day cricket, was that a new generation could all bat and there would be many occasions in the next few years when Yorkshire would field a team all of whom had completed at least one first-class century.

The reserves, too, were strong, with such players as Andrew Dalton, John Woodford, Robinson, Cooper, Bore, Johnson and Squires all awaiting their chance, and for a short while many Yorkshiremen felt that the corner had been turned and the Club could look forward to a rise to and a camp upon the summit. In that hot, old-fashioned Summer Boycott passed 2,000 runs, Lumb 1,500 and Hampshire 1,000, while the two spinners blossomed, Cope with 69 wickets and Carrick 79, both at an average of 21.

What Hampshire called the 'honeymoon period' did not last too long. Boycott was re-elected captain unanimously but quickly spotted that two of his regular critics, Don Brennan and the former

Colts captain Robin Feather, had missed the crucial meeting. Boycott, with first broken finger and then a strained back, was missing from 16 May until 14 July; Old also broke down and the team, without the leading batsman and bowler, inevitably suffered. Nicholson had retired, his vast experience, genial good humour and ability to remove the best opposition in his day was sorely missed, and the lack of success brought rumblings about the leadership of the vice-captain, Hampshire.

The team dropped to eighth in the Championship, third from bottom in the Player League and suffered a second-round exit in the Gillette Cup, but the greatest humiliation was a knock-out in the Benson and Hedges Cup at Barnsley by the Universities of Oxford and Cambridge. Yorkshire's seamers, particularly Old who strained his shoulder, bowled badly on a hard pitch with short boundaries, and so stunned was the dressing room afterwards that the door stayed locked until after a prolonged inquest. In retrospect it will be seen that the Universities had an exceptional side, for it contained Roebuck, Tavare, Marks, Parker, Coverdale and Gurr, all of whom were to play first-class, three of them for England.

That fact, however, was lost upon the Yorkshire membership and public at the time, and although Boycott could not be blamed the dissatisfaction grew, as the hopes that had blossomed in 1975 withered away, to the point that Committee debates grew fierce again. Boycott later wrote that the Cricket sub-committee wanted to sack five uncapped players and that the one who did leave, Squires, departed against the captain's recommendations. He sought caps for Robinson, Carrick and Cooper, and won two of those battles.

Unexpectedly and probably against the wishes and hopes of all connected with Yorkshire cricket, 1977 was another turning point. With injuries cleared, the team restored to strength and the younger players recognised in their approaching maturity, there was some expectation that the revival begun two years earlier might have picked up steam again. This time, however, the disruption came from another source – the England selectors.

Kevin Sharp

Kevin Sharp, from Leeds, was a fair-haired good-looking left-hander whose early career, like his appearance, resembled David Gower's. Indeed, in their school days he was thought to have the more potential.

He made his debut as a 17-year-old but did not score his first century until four years later, although his opportunities, in an unsettled side, were irregular. He went onto score 11 centuries, passing 1,000 runs in 1984. Sharp's potential had been underlined in 1977 when he scored 260 not out for Young England against the Young West Indies, and he became part of the England Under-19 team the following season.

His occasional off-spin bowling brought the sobriquet 'Freddie Laker' and he took some notable catches both close to the wicket and in the field. He rested during part of the 1980 season on medical advice and often gave the impression that as a player he would have been much happier on the old three-day, one-competition schedule.

After his benefit season in 1991 he captained the Second XI, played Minor Counties cricket with Shropshire and returned to the club as coach, eventually becoming batting coach. An engaging personality, he was able to impart successfully his experience of a long career and served Yorkshire with distinction into the new century.

Approaches had been made to Boycott in 1976, seeking his assistance against the growing power of the West Indies, but his broken finger and possible bribe (according to Boycott) of the vice-captaincy under Greig of the Winter tour of India, Sri Lanka and Australia were deterrents to his return. There is evidence from several quarters that he was genuinely reluctant to leave his young players and they, in turn, were anxious not to lose the one player in the side whose mere presence, very often, was guarantee against defeat.

Despite the loss of Old, through injury, Yorkshire were unbeaten in their first 12 matches and when Old returned after missing 12 fixtures he thrashed Warwickshire's occasional bowlers for century in 37 minutes, then the second-fastest in history. Warwickshire managed to bowl 42 overs in 90 minutes in a match that was an avoidable draw, as Old hit six sixes and 13 fours in 107 made in 41 minutes, his second 50 coming off only 21 deliveries.

Boycott was then lured back into the England side against Australia at Trent Bridge, rewarding the selectors with a slow but invaluable century, adding an 80 not out in the second innings and then, to scenes of great euphoria, completing his hundredth century against Australia in the Fourth Test at Headingley. It was a highly charged occasion and all honour was due the man, returning to cricket at the highest level to

demonstrate his then unmatched quality as an opening batsman. A lesser, but no less significant point was the amount of money and number of runs Boycott had passed up by his self-imposed exile from Test cricket.

However, the captain's absence from the Yorkshire team was felt immediately. Five of the next nine matches were lost and it was clear, according to Hampshire, that Boycott's attention was now fixed firmly on his resuscitated international career and that Yorkshire's cause was secondary. Boycott maintains that while Yorkshire officials publicly supported his returning to play for England, they were privately insisting that his prime duty lay with Yorkshire; nor was he prepared to take the blame for the county's defeats while he was away with England.

The situation became political and commanded front-page attention when the news broke that England captain, Tony Greig, had been an agent in organising a private tournament, Kerry Packer's 'World Series'. That meant a new captain for the Winter tour of Pakistan and New Zealand, and although the primary position went to Mike Brearley of Middlesex, the tour vice-captain was Boycott; the implication being that his long-term ambition to lead England might still be realised.

In a radio broadcast that Winter Don Brennan made a case for a change of captain on the

Jim Love

James Derek Love, a tall, fair right-hander who could drive with immense power, was born in Headingley and made his debut in 1975, emerging as a highly influential player in one-day matches who was rarely able to translate his undoubted ability into first-class game.

His ability to accelerate the scoring rate brought him England recognition in one-day matches and there were times in his career when the Club hoped that he would prove to be the successor at number four to Hampshire. He passed 1,000 runs twice and scored 13 centuries, but it was as a forcing batsman in limited overs that his full value was to be seen, and he was rightly declared the Gold Award winner for his outstanding batting in the Benson and Hedges victory at Lord's in 1987.

Northamptonshire, having scored 244-7 in their 55 overs, reduced Yorkshire to 103 for 3-29 overs when Love, supported in turn by Sharp, Bairstow and Carrick, led a furious counter-attack that resulted in Yorkshire's needing four runs off the last over with Sidebottom, at number eight, Love's new partner.

Three singles were scrambled off the first four balls; Sidebottom should have been run out off the fifth and although Love only blocked the final ball, with the scores level, Yorkshire were winners on the loss of one less wicket, Love finishing 75 not out and, for a man who rarely showed his emotions, punching the sky.

Following his benefit year he played three seasons with Lincolnshire and then won new attention by coaching Scotland to the World Cup Finals of 1992. After retirement he combined business interests with coaching and management and took several MCC teams abroad.

grounds that Boycott did not inspire his teammates and that he would not, in the foreseeable future, be available often enough to retain the leadership. Whatever validity there was in Brennan's argument was drowned in an uproar from members and followers to whom Boycott had become England's, and perhaps the world's, number one batsman, a leading member of the Test hierarchy and the heir apparent; a knight errant trailing clouds of glory.

Brennan was rebuked by the Club Chairman Arthur Connell, and the Reform Group, originally formed to protest against Close's dismissal, took on a new life with a fast-expanding membership. Brennan's head was called for and although the Committee then had no power to expel a properly elected member, the former wicket-keeper did step down from the Cricket sub-committee in an effort to calm the furore.

Then, for the first time, came appearance of two distinct factions: the Reform Group, who gave unwavering support to Boycott whether he wanted it or not – and sometimes, it seemed, to his embarrassment – and the Committee and their supporters. War had broken out. The media were divided, the popular press and the mass of the public on the whole supporting the rebels and Boycott, the quality newspapers and a majority of the members, at that time, standing by the Committee. Local radio, by and large, was pro-Boycott, reflecting the views of their listeners, and the BBC stations pro-Committee, while television, sensing a great story but often unsure of both facts and background, thrashed around like a huge safari party caught in dense jungle. Views were sought in voice and print, meetings called, letters written, lawyers consulted, jokes cracked, barbs exchanged; it was a tale altogether so rich in character, humour, intrigue and plot that perhaps only Dickens or Trollope could have done it full justice.

It was, of course, much less funny to the entangled principals, especially to those embattled on the Committee trying to see both sides of the argument and to the harassed Secretary Joe Lister, who was to bear the brunt of a tempestuous decade. Yorkshire's playing record since 1977 will preclude Lister from being named alongside such as Ellison, Toone and Nash, but he can take credit for being the executive officer who steered Yorkshire through even stormier waters than the great Sheffield controversies of a century before.

Amid all the shot and shell a new batsman had emerged in Boycott's absence: an accomplished right-hander from Middlesbrough, Bill Athey, who hinted from an early age that he had the ability to reach international level, and in whom the Club had high hopes of his one day succeeding Boycott as Lumb's partner; some saw Athey as a possible county captain.

The Committee members, who had spent a Winter under fire from the Reform Group, then loosed their own thunderbolt: from 1979, they announced, Ray Illingworth would be returning from Leicestershire to become Yorkshire's team manager on a three-year basis. The negotiations to bring in Illingworth, Leicestershire's highly successful captain, had been conducted mostly by telephone by no more than three or four members of the Committee, so careful was the Club to ensure that there were no leaks. The reaction of one reporter at the press conference announcing Illingworth's appointment was this: 'It's very clever. They've sacked Boycott without sacking him.'

Two days later Illingworth told the Yorkshire Post: 'I will be in charge and I will have the final say on all cricket matters, including team selection.' This, of course, was a direct infringement of Boycott's authority as captain, and the Reform Group, on one side, girded themselves for the vital battles of 1979. In the meantime Yorkshire had another season to play under the old regime and, obviously, much hinged upon their record.

Boycott, meanwhile, had returned from the Winter tour less pleased with his international prospects. An injury to Brearley had left him in charge of England in New Zealand where, for the first time, a Test match was lost. Objective opinion on that defeat was that there was little Boycott could have done about it, signalling as it did the rise in New Zealand cricket and the advent of Richard Hadlee, but in all the circumstances, Boycott's personality being as it was, it did not enlarge his circle of friends.

That there was also considerable potential in the side was proved in 1978 when the Championship position improved to fourth from 12th – and perhaps only in Yorkshire could this have been seized upon by both factions as ammunition. Boycott captained the side in 12 matches, Hampshire in ten, both winning five, so the argument flared over whether Hampshire might make the better captain and, with success, restore peace. As Hampshire displaced Boycott at the top of the county's batting averages (the first time Boycott had lost the premier position since 1963) there was the faintest hint, also, that he might be overtaken as the principal batsman.

The rivalry between Boycott and Hampshire was fuelled by an incident during the Yorkshire visit to Grace Road in June. Illingworth and Hampshire had dinner together, in the course of which, according to both separate accounts of the conversation, the new team manager told the vice-captain that Boycott did not trust Hampshire. Wrote Hampshire: 'I went straight up the wall. For seven years I had refused to take sides against him…Now I learned that he had obviously told other people he did not trust me for it to get back to Illy.'

Boycott, in his memoirs, flatly denied ever having made such a remark but added: 'I regarded Hampshire as something of a fence-sitter, a man who would rarely stand up and be counted. I regarded him as a basically weak individual but I certainly did not consider him untrustworthy.' Boycott goes on to say that he then wrote to the Committee supporting Hampshire's position as vice-captain.

Whatever the absolute truth (is there such a thing?) of the incident, the division between the pair flared up a month later at Northampton. The facts are simple enough. On 17 July on a good pitch and against a standard county attack, the Colt Athey scored 114 in 210 minutes with 15 fours; Boycott, reported *Wisden*, took 367 minutes over 113 with ten boundaries, not one of which came in his half-century. When Hampshire joined Colin Johnson Yorkshire needed 33 off the last ten overs to win a fourth batting bonus point, but the fourth-wicket pair added only 11. At the wicket Hampshire told Johnson he was taking full responsibility for the famous 'go-slow', writing later: 'Call it a brainstorm if you like but towards the end of that innings I decided I was going to play the way we had seen Boycott play so many times.'

Hampshire recorded that the Northants team soon sensed what was going on and began laughing. From the Northampton press box, one of the best views in county cricket, it was also clear to this observer and the then cricket correspondent of the *Yorkshire Post*, Terry Brindle, that something extraordinary was happening. Standing by the boundary boards was a member of the Cricket sub-committee, former captain Billy Sutcliffe, who soon confirmed to a now agitated media contingent that the incident had been noted and it would be referred to the Committee. Boycott wrote that his innings took four and a half hours: '…pretty grim stuff, I admit, but my thumb injury was still giving me a bit of bother and I wasn't playing well at the time'. Boycott needed 86 overs to reach his century, 90 to reach 113.

At this point the two accounts diverge, Hampshire says he returned to the inner Northampton dressing room, empty of all but Boycott who said nothing to him, sitting with his head in his hands. Boycott says that Hampshire was challenged on his return by a furious David Bairstow, who wrote: 'I was angry at what was happening and refused to pad up.'

By the following morning the media representation had all but doubled and the Club was again under fire from all directions. The inquest took place at Bradford during the following match, a rain-affected Gillette Cup tie, both players being called before the selection committee (Temple, Sutcliffe, Burnet), the Club then making the grave error of issuing a non-committal statement on the grounds that the whole affair was an internal matter. Hampshire left without comment; Boycott, as was his right as captain, staying to answer questions.

Hampshire was then further angered to read the following day that he had been reprimanded, and he warned: 'What they did say, which made sense, was that if I had wanted to make a protest I should have gone for the one remaining point available and made my views known afterwards, off the field.'

Boycott's recollection is of the sort of bland non-statement that was bound to excite the curiosity of the press. 'Reporters buttonholed me (they had been waiting around until 8 pm) and frankly I saw no reason to protect Hampshire or the Committee. The whole hearing was rigged to put me in unfavourable light and I wasn't having it.'

The captain made it clear to the inquiry that he had expected disciplinary action against Hampshire, citing suspensions imposed upon Trueman, by Brian Sellers, for minor infractions. In retrospect a firm statement, if not action was demanded, and the only conclusion the historian can reach over this curious episode is that with major changes on the way, including the known arrival of a team manager and the (then unknown) displacement of Boycott as captain, the Committee must have felt its first duty was towards the team, and rocking the boat in midstream was at best unhelpful.

The rivalry between the Boycott and Hampshire camps grew more intense when the Daily Express revealed that Derbyshire would offer Hampshire the captaincy if Yorkshire were to release him. As Hampshire had already been sounded out about the Yorkshire captaincy, he was frank enough to tell Derbyshire that he would be happy to join them – but only if he was passed over.

The decision was taken at the end of September to replace Boycott with Hampshire, the news reaching Boycott as he flew back from a short break in Bermuda, carrying in his pocket a telegram announcing that his mother had died of cancer. To lose a beloved parent and a prime position all within a few hours was a double blow enough to rock any man, and it is hardly surprising that Boycott left England, for the England tour of Australia under Brearley, in an emotional state. The Club, inevitably, attracted some bitter criticism from the Reform Group's allies and no doubt wished heartily themselves that their timing had been a little better. Eight of the General Committee had, in fact, voted against the change.

Whatever the chronology, the deed had been done – in effect a declaration of war for by then the county was hopelessly divided between pro- and anti-Boycott factions and the man himself

Martyn Moxon

Martyn Douglas Moxon was another product of that prolific South Yorkshire nursery between Barnsley and Wakefield. His father, again, was an excellent league cricketer and coach to Wombwell Cricket Lovers, so the young Moxon was given an early love for the game.

A strong, forcing right-hander, Moxon captained Yorkshire Schools at Under-15 and Senior Schools, and captained the North of England Under-19 tour of Canada in 1979. On his debut in 1981 he became the first Yorkshireman to score centuries in his first two home Championship matches, and his 116 was the highest debut until it was overtaken by Ashley Metcalfe.

Despite his early success he had to wait until 1984 for a regular place, after scoring 153 against Lancashire in his first Roses match the previous year, and would have made his debut for England against the West Indies at Lord's, but for a rib injury in that season.

On the following tour of India, he missed a chance of establishing his place as England's regular opener by having to return to attend the funeral of his father, and he had to wait until 1986 to make his Test debut. A quiet, studious man with university qualifications and a business degree, he became an excellent first slip and occasionally useful medium-pace swing bowler. He was appointed the Club's vice-captain in 1989.

The captaincy followed a year later after a Test career of ten matches dogged by injury and ill luck was ended. The team he led, despite the introduction of an overseas player per season, was never stronger than mid-table, but he did accumulate sufficient experience of leadership, and of coaching, to be appointed the Club's first Director of Coaching when a back injury forced early retirement in 1997. He had been a prolific scorer in those later years, including a 274 not out against Worcestershire in 1994, the year after he had been named among *Wisden's* famous 'Five'.

England too began taking notice. Moxon coached an 'A' team to Bangladesh and New Zealand in 1999-2000 and became assistant coach to the England team on the following Winter tour. His advance in that direction, an abrupt departure from Yorkshire in January 2001, was a shock. The cause was a dispute over payment while he was with England, and was the first public indication of an attempt to slash costs before the impending financial crisis became known.

He then spent six seasons with Durham where his methods and leadership turned the county team into a Championship force and produced a string of young players for England. It was no surprise when, in the Winter of 2006-07, when Yorkshire needed a successor of David Byas, they turned to Martyn Moxon. One member put it, as Moxon made his first appearance at the annual general meeting in March: 'It didn't feel as if Martyn had ever been away.'

---

must have flown later out of Heathrow, with the England team, a little grateful to be putting it all behind him.

It would have been unlike Boycott not to react, and before departure he duly appeared, in his county blazer, on the *Michael Parkinson Show*, the prime British television chat show of that time, to make some characteristically trenchant comments about the Committee. Calls for him to be disciplined brought another appearance

before the Committee, on 23 October, when he was accompanied by his solicitor, Duncan Mutch of Barnsley, who presented a dossier aimed at proving that Boycott had had poor support during his captaincy.

Arthur Connell, the General Committee Chairman who, with Michael Crawford, the Treasurer, had been generally regarded as a moderate and bridge-builder during the controversy, then poured fuel on the fire when, in answering the questions afterwards on the Committee's statement, he replied: 'It is nothing to do with what Boycott has done or has not done. It is to do with what he is.'

While the former captain and the new captain spent the Winter in Australia (Hampshire for Tasmania), the pair having a frosty meeting in Hobart, the storms blew in full force in Yorkshire. The Reform Group, re-formed in Huddersfield in October 1977, collected signatures to call for a special general meeting that would ask to reinstate Boycott as captain and express their lack of confidence in the Cricket sub-committee. The Group opened a membership account, engaged lawyers and solicited all the Club's members.

The Committee countered by challenging the Group's list of signatures, pointing out that some of the names listed belonged to members who were not up to date with their subscription and therefore technically unable to vote. The Committee also called for a special general meeting to seek a vote of confidence in themselves. The Group responded with a High Court hearing in Liverpool (13 November), the judge agreeing with the Group and calling on the Committee to 'pay heed to the requirements of the petitioning members'.

The meeting eventually took place in Harrogate on 9 December and the Committee won comfortably, the move to reinstate Boycott being defeated by 2,224, the confidence vote by 1,355, the Cricket sub-committee vote by 870. However, many Reformers left that meeting angry at what they had regarded as an intrusion by the incoming team manager Ray Illingworth. A letter from Illingworth to the Committee, written before the September sacking of Boycott, was read out to the special general meeting, the team manager affirming that the great majority of the players wanted a change of captain.

Boycott later claimed that the players' poll organised by Geoff Cope, upon which the finding was based, was fraudulent in that Old had refused to give an opinion and Bairstow and five of the junior players had not been asked. There is no doubt that Illingworth's letter rallied support for the Committee in the hall, but the consequence was that many of the Reformers felt they

had been cheated and that Illingworth, in their eyes, was then firmly in the camp of Hampshire and the Committee.

This, then, was the background to the 1979 season, Hampshire's first as captain, with Boycott, despite rumours of his moving elsewhere (even Lancashire was mentioned), still a Yorkshire player with a new two-year contract. The Committee had avoided a direct clash of wills between Illingworth and Boycott, but in order to win their argument with many recalcitrant members and supporters, and with the public at large, a successful season was crucial.

A good run to the semi-final in the Benson and Hedges Cup was promising, but the overall position declined to seventh and the conclusion was that Yorkshire were a fairly ordinary mid-table team. The younger players such as Stevenson, Sidebottom, Athey, Kevin Sharp and Jim Lowe were inconsistent and although two useful Colts appeared, the all-rounder Neil Hartley (Shipley) and the fast bowler Alan Ramage (Middlesbrough), the end product was disappointing. Hampshire was criticised for being too defensive, Old struggled with injuries, Cope returned for a third time without being able to bowl, under scrutiny, with his old venom, while the new young off-spinner Peter Whiteley (Otley) obviously needed time.

Carrick advanced as an all-rounder, but the need for him to bowl negatively at the leg-stump in the one-day games affected his first-class form. The one player to shine, inevitably, was Boycott, averaging 100 for a second time in his career (the only batsman to do so) and even topping the bowling averages, a feat not achieved since the glory of George Hirst in 1910. Hampshire later wrote that he felt sometimes as if 98% of the crowd were against him, willing him to fail: 'A sort of anarchy was reigning throughout the county's cricket. The manager, the captain, the Committee were being reviled by people professing to have the Club's best interests at heart and the players, especially the younger and less mature ones, cannot have helped feeling that there was a lowering of standards all around them.'

If Hampshire's assessment of the mood of the dressing room was correct then it was not surprising that 1980 was yet another disappointment, only five Championship matches being won. Cope finally retired to bowl happily and unchallenged in minor cricket for several years, a talent discouraged by officialdom. If there was a flaw in Cope's action it was all but indiscernible unless seen on a slowed film. He could never have done physical harm to a batsman and yet there were fast bowlers in the first-class game who were known by everyone to throw the odd delivery but who had been clever enough never to be caught on film.

Carrick, too, was less effective, while the seam attack had to be chosen from the fittest in a continuing list of causalities. Love, Athey and Sidebottom were all capped and it was clear that all had outstanding ability yet without the application to produce it consistently. Athey was a batsman of high promise and performed particularly well in the John Player League, but only after the first six matches had been lost and the team had been eliminated from the Benson and Hedges Cup. However, a late rally took the side to sixth place in the Championship and in Simon

Paul Jarvis

Paul William Jarvis was the youngest player on debut for Yorkshire (16 years two months in the Player League, 13 days later in the Championship), displacing Padgett, the only other player to start at 16. His father played for Marske for 30 years and a brother appeared for both England Schools, and Paul was chosen for Marske Under-14s at the age of eight.

A right-arm, fast medium bowler and hard-hitting tail-ender, he was bowling second change for Marske first team at 15 and would have played for Colts that same year had he not been sitting school examinations. After five Colts matches in 1982 he made his debut in the John Player League against Lancashire, his first-team debut coming in the next match, against Barbados, to be followed by a Championship debut at Hove against Sussex, all in a fortnight.

Winter cricket in Australia, a shortened run, added control and the ability to deliver the occasional genuinely fast ball brought him seven wickets in one innings in each of 1985, '86 and '87, including a hat-trick against Derbyshire in 1985. He was chosen as reserve seam bowler for the England Reliance Cup party in 1987-88 and was expected to be a firm challenger for an England place when he broke down at Hove in mid-1988 and spent the rest of the Summer attempting to shed a back strain. He nevertheless finished fourth in the national averages with 37 wickets at an

PAUL JARVIS
YCCC

average of 17 and, fitness permitting, was on the verge of a successful career for Yorkshire and England at the age of 23.

He did make nine Test match appearances but a history of intermittent injuries meant that his early promise was never fully fulfilled, and in 1994 he was allowed to move to Sussex and then to Somerset, leaving a memory of a pleasant and popular personality upon whom perhaps too much expectation was placed too soon.

Dennis, from Scarborough, a nephew of Sir Leonard Hutton, the Club seemed to have discovered the most potentially hostile left-arm quick bowler since Cowan.

The fighting was by no means over, but for a spell the shooting was sporadic. In an effort to stall speculation the Club offered new contracts to the three senior players, Boycott, Hampshire and Old, in mid-July, a well-meaning effort that only brought further criticism, both factions seeing the gesture as appeasement. Hampshire meanwhile had had enough. His wife was insulted in a supermarket, his children at school, and, as he wrote: 'I could not for the life of me understand the personal bitterness with which they seemed to hold me responsible for the fact that their man was not captain.'

Illingworth's next choice was Richard Lumb, but he made it clear that he had no wish to lead a team containing two ex-captains, Boycott and Hampshire. So on 3 September, at Scarborough, Chris Old was offered the captaincy, and he went off the following January to tour the West Indies with England (and Boycott) under Ian Botham's captaincy. Always a cheerful, gregarious character, Old firmly believed that he could improve the atmosphere in the dressing room and returned from that tour to tell the manager and Hampshire: 'Boycott is my senior professional and vice-captain and all the help I want I'll get from him.'

According to Illingworth the harmony lasted until 27 May in the 1981 season when, at Dartford, the team manager castigated Boycott and Bairstow for leaving the ground under the impression that there would be no play before lunch. Both returned in time to take the field for a start earlier than expected, but when Old, according to Illingworth's memoirs, later that day asked Boycott for some advice the reported reply was: 'It's nothing to do with me. You get on with it, you're the captain.'

Old had wretched luck. In a wet Summer the side suffered eight fractures, and nine players in all were injured at one point or another; only once in the entire season were all ten capped players available, and even then Old played when less than 100%. A drop to tenth, in all the circumstances, was a not unreasonable perform-

ance, but one decision by the manager and one incident sparked further controversies.

Looking ahead, too far in the view of many, Illingworth indicated his future Yorkshire captain by naming the 25-year-old Neil Hartley to head the side against Warwickshire on 29 July. Amid all the injuries and in Old's absence both Hampshire and Bairstow had led the team, but Hartley's appointment was a major shock – not least to Bairstow, who felt very strongly as the professional next senior in line that he should be given an opportunity of leadership. A furious argument in a cocktail bar in the Royal Hotel in Scarborough, where the team were staying, between Illingworth and Bairstow spread, in many colourful versions, like wildfire around the county.

Hartley, according to gossip, had been favoured because he was then courting Illingworth's elder daughter Vicki. In fact the relationship had ended the previous year, but a good tale was not to be spoilt. Illingworth always maintained that Hartley would have made a highly successful captain, a claim that the Club recognised partially in 1987 when he was appointed Colts captain. Impartial judges accept that with Old injured, Boycott on Test duty and both Hampshire and Lumb disinclined, Hartley did a good job with limited resources and little opportunity.

Illingworth believes that Hartley might have succeeded to the job in 1983 had not the Committee been overthrown by the Reformers; certainly Bairstow, whether he welcomed it or not, found himself the Reformers' alternative candidate for office and yet another fracas was under way. Illingworth had provided his opponents with further ammunition and they made good use of it, a further stock falling into their hands in September when Boycott, in an unexpected television interview in York, said he was seeking a 'clear-the-air' meeting with Illingworth, wanting an explanation for his omission from the team for the Fenner Trophy Festival matches.

Illingworth's stated intention was that Boycott should rest after the Test match and return for the final Championship match against Northamptonshire, also at Scarborough. The following morning the manager, after consulting the captain (Old) and two members of the Cricket sub-committee (Brennan and Trueman), formally suspended Boycott for the rest of the season for making unauthorised public statements in breach of the disciplinary clause in his contract. What Illingworth did not know was that Boycott had excised the disciplinary clause before signing his last contract, a fact known to himself, his solicitor, the Club Secretary (Lister) and Arthur Connell's successor as Chairman, Michael Crawford.

There has possibly never been more uproar before the start of a county cricket match. Boycott changed, but did not leave the ground as he had promised to sign some bats for Bairstow's forthcoming benefit. Mysteriously television crews appeared at the ground, and the Reform Group members were busy collecting signatures calling for another special general meeting – this time with the intention of dismissing Illingworth. The furore was such that members and supporters spilled into the out-field, through which the Northants fielders had to make their way, dodging arguing groups of Yorkshiremen.

The situation had its humorous moments. When Tim Lamb, later the TCCB's Secretary, offered a mild passing comment he was told to 'bugger off back to South Africa', the intended target, of course, being Allan Lamb, some yards away. A press colleague, Richard Streeton, left the press box for closer investigation and introduced himself to one angry dialogue by saying: 'Excuse me, I'm from *The Times* of London,' and then got no further. He was told, very firmly: 'Tha can sod off! It's nowt to do with thee.'

Illingworth believes to this day that he was deliberately ambushed; that he was set up to suspend Boycott and provoke an end-of-season crisis, the Reform Group being aware that he was overstepping his authority. Boycott insisted that he had been given permission by the Club Secretary to make the television interview. With almost whoops of joy the media fell upon what they saw as the inevitable outcome; Boycott or Illingworth? One, they decided, would have to go.

Whatever the view from the press box, or the committee room, the dressing room saw the whole episode as especially depressing. Lumb and Martyn Moxon (Barnsley) walked out to bat to a little perfunctory clapping, as if the start of the match was a minor and inconsequential sub-plot; rarely can a Yorkshire opening pair have been greeted with so little enthusiasm on a home ground. One watching player, Hampshire, finally decided that morning to sever his links and join Derbyshire; similar thought must have crossed younger minds.

Moxon was a tall, powerful right-hander, and Paul Jarvis, from Redcar, a promising quick bowler who at 16 was the youngest ever player to appear for Yorkshire, an indication of both his ability and the dire weakness of the attack. Moxon became the first Yorkshireman since Cecil Tyson to score a century on debut, with 116 off a strong Essex bowling; he then underlined his entry into the records by becoming the first Yorkshireman to score centuries in his first two home matches.

Alas, there was far too much happening off the field for either of these young men to receive more than fleeting attention. On 17 September the General Committee met for what the media saw as the shoot-out between Illingworth and Boycott, solicitors being present. In the event the hullabaloo at Scarborough was glossed over, much to Illingworth's indignation, although it was clear that Boycott could not be charged with breach of conduct.

A Committee of Inquiry consisting of seven members of the General Committee was set up under an independent chairman; the Committee was instructed to look into all aspects of Yorkshire cricket and make recommendations. Thirty-two witnesses were called, beginning with Illingworth, but Boycott, to the anger of a body he already believed biased against him, had gone on holiday before joining England's tour of India and his evidence would not be heard for months.

Meanwhile the media, thwarted of a dénouement, kept the pot boiling by conducting a poll of players, which provided a substantial majority for Illingworth and against Boycott. The Committee of Inquiry's report mentioned this, one member of the General Committee resigning in protest at its publication, and also came out

Neil Lloyd Rosebud

Neil Lloyd is the only cricketer to appear in this history who did not play for the Club's first team. He is included because he made such an impression in his 17 years of life before his death in September 1982 that a commemorative booklet was published and a trophy to be awarded to young cricketers after him.

Born in Ackworth, and of a physique that had to be strengthened by Winter training, known to his colleagues as 'torture sessions', he was a left-handed batsman whose stroke play and technique brought him a fast-growing reputation from the age of 13. The son of Doug Lloyd, a left-hand batsman and wicket-keeper good enough to attract offers from Nottinghamshire and Northamptonshire, the boy went to the same school, at Hemsworth, as Boycott. He first fielded for his club, Ackworth, as a nine-year-old and played for the second XI the following year. At 13 he was playing for Yorkshire Schools, scoring a record aggregate of 1,240 runs in the next three Summers, including three centuries. At 16 he joined the Yorkshire staff, the season after making his debut for the Colts.

At 17, in 1982, he was chosen to play for the England Under-19 team against the West Indies at Hove, after which he joined his father and several Ackworth members for a holiday at the Scarborough Festival. There he developed the first symptoms of a neurological disease and a week later he died in a Wakefield hospital.

Keith Andrew, the National Cricket Association's chief executive and former England wicket-keeper, said of him, after watching him on an Under-13 course: 'Probably for the first and only time in my life I am forecasting that a 12 year-old boy will play cricket for Yorkshire and England before he is 21 years old.'

Steven Coverdale, then Northamptonshire Secretary and once Yorkshire Colts' wicket-keeper, wrote of him:

The loss the game suffered by his death can never be measured though surely he would have proved to be a magnificent cricketer. But life is more than cricket and in life Neil was a magnificent individual. When he died the game and the county lost a young man of immense talent. But we all lost a very dear friend.

strongly for the disbandment of the Reform Group: 'We believe that the presence of this body has done untold harm…it has addressed itself to many matters to which it was not fully informed; it has made statements…which have been detrimental to the club.' The team, the Inquiry concluded, would be better off without Boycott.

In order to move more quickly the General Committee set up a sub-committee of three (Burnet, Trueman and Sutcliffe) with the power to make quick decisions in cricketing matters, in effect to give Illingworth immediate support. The trio were soon named the 'Peacemakers' by the media, which must have given them an occasional chuckle in troubled times. Illingworth, desperate to reinforce the attack, recalled Oldham, who had been allowed to move to

Derbyshire, and publicly regretted the loss of prospects such as Tim Boon and Neal Mallender, who moved on to other counties. Hampshire had already gone, and there were rumours that Athey was unsettled.

Even the unthinkable, the holy writ of Yorkshire cricket, was publicly aired: should Yorkshire abandon the birth qualification and sign an overseas professional? When the members were polled they gave a decisive rejection and Illingworth returned to team planning for 1982. Whatever he had in mind was swept aside in a desperately poor start, culminating in a disastrous weekend at Middlesbrough when, on successive days, Northamptonshire began the Championship match with an opening stand of 278 and followed with a Sunday League score of 282. Illingworth wrote: 'It was terrible, and something had to be done. And the next week, as soon as the county game was over, Chilly [Old] was relieved of the captaincy and the Committee asked me to take over at Ilford, fifteen days after my 50th birthday.'

Old had, in fact, been contemplating resignation and Illingworth's reappearance on the field did remove the dichotomy from the direction of the team. The new captain also managed to establish a kind of armed truce with Boycott and results did improve, particularly in the one-day competitions where Illingworth was able to bring his experience and ability to bear. Sidebottom took 62 Championship wickets, with patched-up support as Old, Stevenson and Ramage were all again afflicted by injuries. A NatWest semi-final against Warwickshire was lost at Edgbaston, Yorkshire having to bat first on a pitch that improved during the day, confirming that the team had recovered a sense of purpose and were no longer a chopping block. Even the sniping off the field fell away, although any Yorkshireman attending a match would soon realise that he was in the presence of two heavily armed camps, highly suspicious of any movement.

A tenth position in the Championship represented an honourable recovery, and there was a slight swelling of optimism for 1983. Old departed for Warwickshire (and was to inflict a terrible hiding on Yorkshire, with bat and ball, at Headingley) and the actual play that Summer could hardly have gone worse for a Club celebrating its 150th anniversary: Yorkshire finished bottom of the Championship table (no reason to celebrate for the Reform Group, but plentiful opportunity to hammer the Committee and Illingworth). The side did, however, win the John Player Sunday League, their first trophy since 1969 (an achievement for Illingworth and the Committee). Yorkshire managed only one Championship victory, at Southampton, lost four successive matches in one spell and failed to win a home match for the first time. The Sunday League was won by the ability of Illingworth and Carrick, two spinners, to put the brake on the middle part of the opposing innings, and Yorkshire's ability, especially in the tail, to flail away at almost any target.

The euphoria of the winning of the League at Chelmsford, a delight to the younger element of the team who had never known success, was shadowed by growing storm clouds. On the previous 13 August, against Gloucestershire at Cheltenham, another incident had occurred involving Boycott that had received as much prominence as the Northampton 'go-slow'.

According to Illingworth the day had begun badly when he had to reprimand Boycott for his rudeness in dealing with several small boys seeking autographs (and apologise to some Gloucestershire members). On what all agree was a good pitch, with a short boundary, Boycott scored 140 not out in 375 minutes, facing 347 balls. Illingworth, seeing that a fourth batting bonus point might be missed, claims that he tried to signal Boycott to speed up progress, even sending out a message with an incoming batsman, Sharp. Called for a quick run, Sharp was run out and when Stevenson was also dismissed quickly the bonus point was lost. With 35 minutes to go, Illingworth recorded that he sent another message to Boycott and Love, the 12th man, asking for quick runs in the hope of declaration; Boycott scored another six runs.

Boycott's version '…accepting that there may have been misunderstandings I totally reject that I wilfully refused any instructions from Illingworth.'

Bairstow's view of the incident: 'I do believe there was some kind of breakdown in communications and that Boycott was in some confusion – it also has to be said that with his [Boycott's] vast experience he should have had a good idea of what was needed without having to be told.'

David Warner, of the *Telegraph and Argus*, Bradford, asked Illingworth if he intended to report Boycott for slow scoring. The reply: 'I can't say. You had better draw your own conclusions', which Warner promptly did.

Boycott wrote that Illingworth said nothing to him on his return to the pavilion that evening. The press that weekend was full of speculation about another confrontation and the following week both captain and senior professional were called in to appear before the three Peacemakers at Headingley. The statement afterwards read: 'We are satisfied that in this instance his [Boycott's] batting was not in the best interests of the side and again he had been told that he must play the sort of innings the side needs irrespective of his own ambitions.'

It was, the Peacemakers hoped, an announcement carefully attuned to the mood of the moment, saying what had to be said in a moderate manner. 'Does this mean', asked Don Mosey of the BBC, of Ronnie Burnet, 'that Boycott has been reprimanded?' He had, said the sub-committee chairman. Boycott denied that he had been reprimanded as such, claiming he had a letter from Burnet saying just that. The Reform Group was up in arms and when Boycott, in the next match at Bradford, scored a century in each innings against Nottinghamshire; the old Park Avenue pavilion almost shook with the pent-up emotion inside. Both factions realised that there could now be no bridging of the issue this time: a definite decision had to be made.

At the tempest's very height, in August 1983, *The Guardian*, scarcely bothering to hide its Lancastrian connections, could not resist linking Yorkshire's difficulties with another current cricketing concern in a deliciously risible leader:

Of the 38 paintings on show in the Lord's Memorial Gallery 16 are fake according to a report. Fourteen of the suspect works come from the collection of the late Sir Jeremiah Colman, described as a 'mustard magnate', and could well be of a single hand…

Assuming that the Mail on Sunday's report is correct there seems a reasonable chance that more such pictures will have found their way into other collections and that these two may see the light before long.

There were, for instance, unconfirmed reports yesterday that a work said to be entitled 'Sir Geoffrey Accepts the Repentance of his Detractors' had been found in a disused fish store in east London. Attributed to Andrea Mantegna (1431-1506) it depicts a scene on Lord's Cricket Ground some time in the closing years of this century. Illuminated in a sublime shaft of sunlight, Geoffrey Boycott stands at the wicket, his bat raised above his head in modest acknowledgement of the ovation raging around him. By scoring 238 not out in 95

minutes he has just ensured that Yorkshire have at last regained the County Championship. In the foreground, a gnarled figure all in white, dimly recognisable as Mr Raymond Illingworth, lies full length in abject supplication.

Beside him, on bended knee, one hand outstretched, the tears of penitence coursing freely down his face, is Mr Ronnie Burnet, chairman of the county's peace-keeping committee. In the top left-hand corner of the painting a host of cherubic figures, possibly angels, possibly members of the MCC ground staff, hymn the apotheosis of the hero. A flurry of activity at the pavilion gate announces the imminent arrival of Her Majesty the Queen, who has come hotfoot from the Palace on hearing the news to confer upon Mr Boycott that knighthood which has so long eluded him. The jovial bearded figure at the bottom right-hand corner of the canvas is Mr Bill Frindall, who had just calculated that this is the first occasion in the history of the game in which a batsman who has made 238 runs in 95 minutes has been knighted on the field of play in the presence of Signor Mantegna.

The police last night were said to regard the painting, masterpiece though it unquestionably is, as yet another forgery. A statement by the chairman of the Art Treasures subcommittee of the Yorkshire County Cricket Club, however, said that this was not necessarily the case. It might equally well prove, Mr Trueman said, to be an authentic piece of work of the great Paduan master, painted in a moment when he had been vouchsafed an uncannily prophetic vision of what the County eleven would achieve either next season or the season after that.

The Reformers began collecting signatures for the calling of another special general meeting, but before the procedural machinery clanked into action again Illingworth pre-empted one issue by announcing that he was resigning and retiring at the end of the season. He had become increasingly concerned about his wife and family, about the obscene phone calls and barrage of letters; on one occasion, he records, two players left the dressing room to ensure that his two

Ashley Metcalfe Panache

Ashley Anthony Metcalfe had the most auspicious start of any Yorkshire batman. A stylish, adventurous right-hand batsman from Horsforth, he had broken Bradford League records when he first appeared, as Boycott's partner, against Nottinghamshire at Bradford in 1983, scoring 122. He had been accepted by the University of London when he took up a professional contract, but could not command a first-team place until Boycott's retirement when, apart from a spell in 1988, he became Moxon's regular opening partner.

With Moxon he scored 282 for the first wicket against Lancashire at Old Trafford in 1986. Metcalfe had a poor start to 1988 but recovered splendidly to pass a thousand runs for a third time, including a 216 not out against Middlesex. He had a natural flair for attack, which prompted some judges to suggest he should bat at number three or four, but he made it clear that he liked to attack the new ball in the manner of the player he most admired, Barry Richards.

In April 1986 he married Diane, the younger daughter of Ray Illingworth. He left Yorkshire in 1995 before spending two years with Nottinghamshire. He later played for Cumberland while expanding his business interests returning to manage the Indoor School in 2009.

---

daughters passed safely through the car park.

It was then Illingworth's turn to receive a flood of support, publicly and privately, from Yorkshire members and public alike. When, three weeks later, Yorkshire had won the Sunday League, he softened and said he would be happy to continue, but only on a part-time playing basis. He still had a year of his contract remaining.

Amid all the rumbling of the Nottinghamshire match at Bradford a remarkable debut had taken place: Ashley Metcalfe, a slim, confident 19-year-old right-hander from Farsley, had opened with Boycott and emulated Moxon of two years before with a century on his first appearance, an impressive 122 containing some auspicious stroke-play from Yorkshire's youngest centurion on debut.

At the next meeting of the Cricket sub-committee, on the morning of 3 October, it was decided by a unanimous vote to release Boycott, to appoint Bairstow as the new captain and to confirm Illingworth as team manager. At the General Committee meeting that afternoon those decisions were endorsed by a majority of two to one; it was as if beacons blazed from a high point in Yorkshire.

The following Sunday the Reform Group met at Ossett, 400 strong according to one report, and called for the Cricket sub-committee to reconsider. They did this, on 17 October, and voted unanimously to reaffirm their decision. The same afternoon the General Committee again voted: 18-8 in support. This time the Chairman, Michael Crawford, issued a statement in which the reasons for the decision were reviewed: room had to be made, it was pointed out, for younger players such as Moxon and Metcalfe and in order to help retain promising talents (Athey was joining Gloucestershire). The Committee felt that 'the necessity to build team spirit for the good of Yorkshire cricket must override the interests of any one individual'.

Crawford also appealed to the members to consider the cost to the Club of another special general meeting (£10,000 was the estimate) – 'but if 2.5 per cent of its [the Club's] members think that money spent convening a special general meeting is better spent on printing, postal and hire charges and professional fees then the General Committee, whilst strongly disagreeing, will have to incur such expenditure.'

What followed was all-out propaganda war in which the Reform Group had the advantage of having their three members on the General Committee – Reg Kirk, Peter Charles and Sid Fielden – join colleagues outside the Club while the Committee, bound by procedure, was left in

Richard Blakey

Richard John Blakey, born in Huddersfield and graduate of the Elland Club, was a correct right-hand batsman of excellent temperament who first made his name for his ability to make big scores: at 18 he scored a record 273 not out for the Colts and at age 20 scored 204 not out against Gloucestershire for the first team. In 1987, his first full season, he scored 1,387 runs, including four centuries, a performance that evoked comparisons with the young Hutton and led to his being elected Young Cricketer of the Year.

Blakey was also a useful and improving wicket-keeper and in 1988, when he, and most Yorkshire batsmen, had a difficult time and lost form, was used more often as a keeper, at one point that Summer displacing Bairstow.

So with England actively seeking a wicket-keeper who could bat up the order, Blakey's succession to Bairstow brought him the attention of the selectors. He toured India with England in 1993 but failed to establish himself in two Tests before being replaced by Alec Stewart. Blakey went on to serve Yorkshire in his dual role for 18 seasons, often acting as vice-captain and, on his retirement, as a coach. He left behind a memory of possibly great talent unfulfilled, a career not unlike those of Lowson and Padgett before him.

---

a position where it could usually react only through the one person empowered to pronounce upon policy, Chairman Michael Crawford. In this situation, with one tabloid newspaper (the *Daily Star*) actually issuing 'I Back Boycott' stickers, and given the Yorkshireman's natural propensity to defy authority, the odds were soon mounting against the establishment.

One last attempt was made to be seen to be fair to both sides:

> During the course of the year surroundings were taken as to the possibility of Geoffrey Boycott's retiring at the end of the season for which he had already been granted a testimonial. Geoffrey indicated that it was at that time his wish to continue playing after next season and it had been his hope that he would regain his place as an opening batsman for England. The General Committee had taken the decision to award Geoffrey Boycott a testimonial independently of any decision in regard to his contract because it was felt that members of the club and the cricket-loving public should have the opportunity of showing their appreciation of Geoff Boycott's years of service to the county since his benefit in 1974.

The incongruity of sacking Boycott and simultaneously offering him a testimonial could not have occurred to the Committee in what was a laudable, if misconceived effort to treat the Club's most famous player with absolute impartiality. The media soon left the Committee in no doubt as to how the public would view that statement. The reference to a future Test career for Boycott was also puzzling to the cricket public at large: Boycott had returned early from the tour of India under a cloud after an argument with the management over his fitness, and then played a leading part in an unauthorised tour of South Africa, for which he was to receive a three-year suspension from international cricket.

The special general meeting was called for 3 December 1983 at Harrogate, but an immediate complication arose as to the eligibility of those members who were in arrears with their subscriptions. The club tried to impose a date, 24 October, when all those who had not paid their subscriptions for 1983 would be ineligible. Two members, supported by the Reform Group (soon to change their name to Yorkshire Members 1984), took legal opinion and although it was clear that both the Committee and the dissident members were acting correctly, under two different rules, counsel warned the Club that with up to 800 members in dispute over the rights, any decision from the meeting on 3 December could be ruled invalid in another court.

Bob Appleyard, not then a member of the

General Committee, proposed a compromise whereby Yorkshire would give Boycott a new one-year contract on the understanding that he would be prepared to bat down the order. By then attitudes had hardened and both sides needed confrontation if only to clear the air, although the then chairman of the Public Relations sub-committee of the club, Julian Vallance, warned that the costs of the SGM, including the legal charges, had risen to £25,000.

The new date set was 21 January 1984, an unfortunate delay which saw what amounted to a general election campaign stretching over almost two months, during which considerable bitterness was engendered with both sides holding meetings and conducting publicity campaigns in an effort to win an argument that divided the Ridings as nothing had since perhaps the General Strike of 1926.

'Members '84' sought votes of no confidence in the General Committee and the Cricket sub-committee, and the reinstatement of Boycott as a player. Before the meeting, the Cricket chairman Ronnie Burnet, expanding on a suggestion that the Committee was not bound by the SGM's decision but only advised, added: 'If we find we are duty-bound to reinstate Boycott we might all resign and seek re-election on the Boycott issue.'

After a four-hour debate Members '84 were victorious on all three issues. The call for Boycott was won by 4,115 votes to 3,109; the votes of confidence in the General Committee (3,609 to 3,578) and the Cricket sub-committee (3,997 to 3,209) were both lost, but the margin in all three contests was sufficiently narrow to give the General Committee the confidence to seek re-election en masse.

Doug Ibbotson reported in the *Daily Telegraph*:

On balance the '84 Group provided the more forceful and persuasive oratory and it became apparent from the enthusiastic response to the opening speech by Sid Fielden, a South Yorkshire detective sergeant, that the vast majority of the 1400 members present were on their side.

But if Fielden, who is also a Methodist lay preacher, fired the converted with evangelical

zeal then the masterly summing up of Brian Walsh, a Queen's Counsel finally confirmed that the dissidents had carried the day in terms of preparation and delivery.

Despite the intensive lobbying almost 3,000 members refused to vote for either side, a possible indication of confusion over the issues and an uneasy sense of an injustice having been done to Boycott – the General Committee's belief that in sacking Boycott and giving him a testimonial they were acting with total propriety and in absolute fairness being a very difficult case to present to members on the periphery of the argument, who were more than a little dismayed at the stark division within the Club.

Accordingly the General Committee resigned en bloc and not all offered themselves for re-election, three of the principals, President Norman Yardley, Chairman Michael Crawford and Robin Feather intimating they would not be seeking office again. Most members agreed that the loss of the trio was a heavy price to pay on top of the new meeting cost estimate of £30,000. (This sum almost halved the profit for 1983, announced as £48,000 on 17 February.)

To ensure that the poll and the counting of votes were beyond criticism, the Club engaged a firm of Leeds accountants to conduct the operation and the results were known the evening before the Harrogate AGM: Members '84 swept the board and some of the most famous names in Yorkshire cricket – Trueman, Burnet, Platt, Sutcliffe, Burgin – lost office. Of the old Committee the only survivors were Raymond Clegg (Bradford), Bryan Stott (Wharfedale) and Phil Sharpe (York), although Close, of the new-comers, was expected to be very much in their camp. Burnet lost Harrogate by 21 and Sharpe's majority was only 12. Boycott defeated Dr Turner by 56, and he and his supporters were expected to have a substantial majority on the new General Committee.

Peter Briggs, secretary of Members '84 but who was ineligible to stand because of his residence in Manchester, said the group would be disbanded but would 'keep the promises made to Members'. These included the reinstatement of Boycott, who would thus become the first committee member who was also a paid professional of the Club, and a promise of more open government, such as the release of committee minutes to members on request. The first meeting of the new General Committee, on 8 March, elected Reg Kirk, a chartered secretary from Hull, as the new Chairman and, a little surprisingly, Close as Cricket chairman.

The full impact of the redistribution of power was not felt until a month later when Illingworth's contract was paid up after the second meeting of the new General Committee. After a six-and-a-half-hour meeting there was obvious dissent, for the newly elected Treasurer, David Welch, resigned and the Club dispensed with the tradition of exchanging committee members with the Headingley landlords, the Leeds club, which meant the departure of Norman Shuttleworth. Both Welch and Shuttleworth were regarded as supporters of the old establishment. Welch, who was later to return to the Committee as a member for Rotherham, left saying: 'The Club is being run by a caucus and I fear to forecast the future.' Close, too, was upset by Illingworth's departure and was reported as saying: 'It's a terrible waste of ability and money.'

Nor did Close receive the Cricket sub-committee he was seeking, the only other ex-cricketer joining him being Sharpe, which meant that Close would always be outvoted by three laymen on the sub-committee and by the Chairman, who had a casting vote, a point of procedure that became very important in the ensuing months. The new Committee's view was that the manager-captain relationship had not worked and that a partnership between Close and Bairstow was the best formula for success on the field.

6

Bairstow to Carrick 1987 – 1988

No Yorkshireman truly belived that all the troubles and disaffection of the two previous years had been put aside when the players reported for training, amid snow showers, on 25 April 1984, but almost everyone was prepared to give the new regime a trial, while the partnership of Close and Bairstow was granted almost honeymoon status. The difficulty that might arise from having a senior professional in the dressing room who was also the leader of the majority on the General Committee was not overlooked, merely shelved in a sense of common purpose.

Bairstow began his reign by winning from Close an assurance that the captain would pick the team, the Cricket chairman having a supervisory role. Peter Townend, a chartered accountant from Halifax, was elected Honorary Treasurer to replace David Welch, while three Colts (Stuart Fletcher, 19, a seamer from Lascelles Hall, Ian Swallow, 21, an off-spinner all-rounder from Sheffield United, and Paul Booth, 21, a left-arm spinner and batsman from Huddersfield) were given second XI caps at the pre-season lunch, always an indication that they were on the fringe of first-team selection.

Boycott and Moxon were the new opening partnership, Lumb was nominated to fill the departed Athey's place at number three, and, on paper and provided the seam bowlers stayed fit, Yorkshire had good reason to expect a reasonably successful Summer. The bowling did not look strong enough to win three-day matches but, as John Player League Champions, the side had proved their capability in one-day cricket.

The first match at Taunton, against Somerset led for the first time by Ian Botham, brought an unexpected victory by three wickets, after two declarations by Botham. Stevenson's bowling broke down but Yorkshire gave an ample declaration of their power in a run chase. It gave Bairstow a fine start, perked up the dressing room and then sent the team back to Headingley for a handsome seven-wicket win in the opening

Benson and Hedges match against a weakened Leicestershire. Even a defeat in the opening John Player fixture did not dampen spirits, although Bairstow recorded having words with Boycott. Two more victories (one Championship) followed before Sidebottom pulled a hamstring at Edgbaston which meant, halfway through May, that both Bairstow's principal seam bowlers were injured.

Sidebottom was only just fit enough to return for the Whitsun Roses match, a draw, before Bairstow was selected for the three one-day internationals against the West Indies and to some surprise, Yorkshire settled down apparently amicably under Boycott's captaincy. Two Championship matches were drawn but an astonishing innings by Stevenson, hitting 81 off 29 balls, brought a delayed John Player victory against Somerset at Middlesbrough. In Bairstow's absence the Bradford wicket-keeper Steven Rhodes also won high praise.

Yorkshire entered the Benson and Hedges semi-finals after an encouraging victory at Hove where the young Fletcher, having to bowl the final spell, gave a highly encouraging performance. A draw at Basingstoke in mid-June, a match Yorkshire should have won as Hampshire were without both Gordon Greenidge and Malcolm Marshall, dimmed Championship ambitions; but in the next Sunday match an encouraging debut came from a right-hander from Keighley, Phil Robinson, whose sheer weight of runs in the Colts had forced his selection. Metcalfe too, was making it plain that he could not be contained in second-team cricket.

Bairstow's career as a Yorkshire captain hinged, in the end, on the Benson and Hedges semi-final against Warwickshire at Headingley – which he lost, by three runs. Had he taken Yorkshire to their first Lord's final since 1969 the one certain panacea for all Yorkshire's ills – success on the field – would have come in 1984 instead of 1987 and would have satisfied both dressing room and the membership.

Headingley sold out; Bairstow won the toss and sent in Warwickshire, who scored 276 off the 55 overs. Stevenson, who may not have been a hundred per cent, conceded 70 runs in his 11 overs and the current common fault of all the Yorkshire bowlers, wides and no-balls, helped raise the extras to 19. Boycott fell to Old in Warwickshire's attack, Moxon raised 50 off 81 balls, Sharp rallied the middle and when Bairstow and Stevenson added 71 in ten overs Yorkshire seemed likely to pull off an astonishing victory. But Stevenson was brilliantly caught on the boundary while Bairstow, aiming for six, was also caught on the ropes by the tall Paul Smith.

Good bowling by two left-hand spinners, Carrick and Booth, brought Yorkshire a Championship victory at Northampton, where Moxon suffered a cracked rib that delayed his England debut. By the time Yorkshire met Essex at Leeds at the end of June, four senior players and the promising Fletcher were absent through injury; by Monday the captain, who had been struggling with an Achilles tendon injury and cracked knuckles, had developed an alarming rash that took him out of the match for the day. Essex totalled 547, their highest against Yorkshire, winning by an innings and 153, the heaviest defeat at Headingley since the opening of the ground in 1891.

A patched-up Yorkshire went down to another ignominious defeat, by 37 runs to minor county Shropshire at Telford, and although weakness through injuries (Moxon, Hartley, Stevenson and Bairstow all played below par) played a major part in Yorkshire's third humiliation in 11 years, there was no excuse to be offered afterwards. Gloucestershire were beaten in a run chase at Bradford. To soothe the hurt (Athey scoring a century for Gloucestershire), Boycott passed 45,000 runs in completing his 142nd century (100 in 148 minutes). Yorkshire then had to apologise to Gloucestershire after the Sunday match at Scarborough for the loutish, and probably drunken, barracking of the English-born black fast bowler David Lawrence.

As the season fell away and success once more became a stranger, the inevitable reaction came off the field. The captain was called to a special meeting of the Cricket sub-committee convened to discuss the team's apparent inability to field a fully fit side. Rumours also floated of a Boycott return to captaincy, but the man himself killed those instantly by saying that eight years in that job was long enough. He was also honest enough to admit that he would not refuse the job of team manager, were it to be offered.

At the end of August the media seized upon what looked like another flare-up at The Oval when Yorkshire had to take the field without Boycott and Moxon, both declared unfit on the morning of the Championship match against Surrey, a match Yorkshire went on to lose by an innings and 195. According to the tabloid newspapers the Cricket chairman was hurrying south to investigate; according to the captain, Close had a business appointment in London and his presence at The Oval was planned. Yorkshire's opening batsmen in that match were Metcalfe and Sidebottom.

An innings victory over Derbyshire at Chesterfield lifted morale, Sharp, Robinson and Metcalfe all contributing useful performances, yet perhaps the true barometer of Yorkshire's fortunes lay in the fact that there were as many reporters at Barnsley, where Boycott was playing in the second team to prove his fitness, as at Queen's Park.

By then the so-called 'dual role' controversy had taken wings and Close, as Cricket chairman, was known to be opposed to giving Boycott another contract as a player while he remained a member of the General Committee. On 12 September the General Committee met and later announced that all the first-team players would be given new two-year contracts and that Boycott and Colin Johnson, the latter becoming a successful Colts captain, would be awarded one-year contracts. A decision on reappointing Bairstow as captain was deferred.

It was obvious that Close was on a collision course with the majority of the General Committee, and the significant decisions came at the end of October when the Cricket chairman's proposal, echoing a newspaper opinion of Illingworth's that if Boycott was to remain a Committee man he should also be captain, was dismissed.

A new President emerged, no one having been found to fill the vacancy since Yardley's resignation (although approaches were reportedly made to Lord Hanson, Sir Harold Wilson and Sir James Hill) in Viscount Mountgarret. Yorkshire-born and formerly of Eton and the Irish Guards, Lord Mountgarret was known to be a keen cricket-lover who managed his own estate near Ripon and who would have time for the Club's affairs. Of much more immediate interest to Yorkshire at large was the appearance of a sudden rift in the dominant majority on the General Committee, with Sid Fielden and Brian Walsh, architects of the 1983 revolution, both publicly attacking Boycott's dual role.

On the vexed question of captaincy a proposal was passed, by 11 votes to ten, asking Bairstow to continue to lead the side as a batsman, thus making room for Steven Rhodes who, it was clear, would not be content to stay much longer in the Colts. The meeting was interrupted while Close consulted Bairstow, and when the latter refused to give up the gauntlets, the Committee voted 16-5 to reappoint him captain without qualification.

On 30 October Close resigned from the Cricket sub-committee with England selector Phil Sharpe following suit a day later. On the same day another group of members, opposed to the General Committee and led by the former Committee members Desmond Bailey and Bob Platt, later to be known as 'Yorkshire Cricket Devotees', was launched; a year's uneasy peace was over. One of the newer committee men, allegedly a Boycott supporter, burst out: 'I'd rather breed pigeons than to speak to newspapers, to be truthful.'

By 9 November Close had also resigned his General Committee seat, using his freedom to attack Chairman Reg Kirk and the majority of the General Committee, saying that he had been 'used by a Boycott-dominated committee'. He accused Bairstow of 'hitching his wagon to Boycott's star', but then softened the blow by telling the *Yorkshire Post*: 'I felt that David had a rough ride for the simple reason that he did not know who his boss was. He owed his allegiance to Geoff because if he did not protect him his

power could guarantee Bairstow's days as captain were numbered.' Kirk reacted by saying that 'we have never had the slightest difficulty in controlling Boycott. If Brian Close thinks he cannot control him then he should get off the Committee.'

The rise of 'Yorkshire Devotees' kept in being Yorkshire Members '84, and both sides were soon issuing statements to rally support. Sid Fielden's criticism of the dual role brought him a letter from Boycott's solicitor asking him to stay away from a meeting of Boycott's supporters in Ripon, while by the end of November Rhodes was given formal permission to join Worcestershire, a decision that was to be attacked bitterly and frequently over the next few years.

Close joined Devotees, and Sharpe attacked Members '84 for allegedly leaking Committee information. Another blow for the Committee was a TCCB decision, announced on 12 December, that Headingley would no longer occupy a permanent place on the Test-match rota, a sharp slap to Yorkshire pride that brought further criticism upon the head of Chairman Kirk, the Club's chief delegate at the meeting. The year ended with the Devotees (at that time known, to the huge delight of the media, as the 'Lovers') proposing another vote of no confidence in the Committee for the AGM on 2 March, adding further resolutions designed to strengthen the central government of the Club and making it more difficult to call general meetings.

The season of goodwill was barely over in January 1985 when, in the first week, slates of candidates were announced for Committee elections and the first hint of a pendulum swing in the news that five Committee members generally regarded as either anti-Boycott or moderate had been returned unopposed.

The publication of a letter to Chairman Kirk, from an elderly lady member, alleging financial payments to Sidney Fielden, brought a further escalation of the war of words. Fielden, after an unhappy 48 hours, emerged with one of the memorable statements of the whole war: 'He [Boycott] is a very great cricketer. I wish I had never met him.'

Amid the threats of further legal action, with the piquant possibility of Brian Walsh QC acting on Fielden's behalf against Boycott's lawyers, the news that David Byas, a 21-year-old strong left-hander with a prolific record for Scarborough, had been given a contract was almost unnoticed. By the end of January no fewer than 31 resolutions, mostly dealing with rule changes, had been tabled for the AGM and the Committee then set up a rules revision sub-committee charged with the task of sifting wheat from chaff and drawing up acceptable changes for the AGM, a move that was predictably denounced as an attempt to 'prolong Boycott's tenure on the Committee for another year'.

In fact the rules sub-committee, composed of the President, Chairman, the Club's new solicitor Duncan Mutch and three members of the General Committee, was an attempt to balance views of both factions. Lord Mountgarret was at that time very much an unknown quantity on the Boycott issue, although it was very plain to those who had interviewed him that he had absolutely no intention of being an ornamental figurehead. The Viscount had the military man's direct, even abrupt, approach to problems and was not averse, as he confided, 'to knocking a few heads together if necessary'. It was obvious from the start that whatever power he gained, or was granted, would be used forcefully.

Boycott meanwhile went back to his constituency to receive the endorsement of the Wakefield members, reiterating that even if the Devotees did enforce a change of rule that prevented a player from serving on the Committee he would resign his seat, a stance that was loudly applauded in the hall.

Yorkshire Television tried to get Kirk and Close to debate the issue in a studio, Kirk declaring 'I'm determined to avoid any unnecessary contention,' Close refusing to meet the designated substitute Peter Briggs. In Northampton a group of touring Yorkshire rugby players were refused an extra round of drinks, the landlord's excuse being: 'Any more and you'll be fighting among yourselves.' The Committee, opening the election campaign, pointed out that the membership figure had risen; the Daily Telegraph suggested that recruits might not be joining for the cricket.

By that time the *Yorkshire Post* could have awarded the cricket letters from readers a half-page every day, so heavy was the flow and urge to contribute to the debate. Ten days before the AGM cricket recovered a little ground when the Club announced that Johnny Wardle, then aged 62, would be appointed a bowling coach from 1 March and would accompany the team on away matches as a guide and counsellor to the captain, an appointment that implied that the future of the senior professional might be in doubt. Blakey and Booth returned from a Young England tour of the West Indies as considerably more experienced players, while former captain John Hampshire reappeared as the manager of a new indoor cricket school in Sheffield.

On 26 February the new President entered the lists for the first time with a typically forthright denunciation of Committee members who criticised the club: 'What I deprecate is that certain members have resorted to actions that undermine the running of the Club. Eventually it might be necessary to suspend members from the Committee.'

Another row flared up on the evening of the AGM after the Committee had refused to include an amendment from the Devotees on the agenda, but threats of legal action did not materialise. The election results, announced before the meeting, were pronounced a 2-2 draw: the Devotees won seats in Bradford (Close being re-elected) and in Sheffield, but failed to win Hull (where Kirk was re-elected) or Craven (Trueman's former seat).

The 1985 AGM took up most of Saturday in Leeds. The Committee survived the confidence vote (545 to 297) in the hall, more narrowly outside, but were attacked so fiercely over their proposal to refer all the rule changes to the sub-committee (three lawyers warning them of legal pitfalls) that they agreed to hold another special meeting in Harrogate on 30 March purely to discuss rule changes and, in effect, the drawing up of a new constitution. The one clear winner was the new President who, swinging a bat declared: 'This is not for hitting each other but for knocking other counties for six' – an act that might have come from Churchill, Montgomery or Hailsham, but one that went down magnificently with the membership who, it was clear, saw in

Mountgarret the long-sought unifying figure.

The Committee did take advantage of their restored power by reappointing Kirk as Chairman, defeating Brian Walsh's challenge by 11 votes to eight, removing Fielden from the chair of the Public Relations sub-committee, Peter Quinn (North Riding) taking over and blocking Close's path back to the Cricket sub-committee, Tony Vann (Leeds), a regular club cricketer but without first-class experience, replacing him. The Committee also changed solicitors after the debacle over the rules revision.

By then a majority of the General Committee were highly sensitive to attack on two points: the cost of yet another special meeting, estimated between £5,000 and £8,000, and uncertainty over the propriety of the 'dual role'. Could an employer be also an employee without accepting full responsibility and power of becoming managing director (if the constitution of the Club were to provide such a position)?

At that point, towards the end of March 1985, Mountgarret intervened again, held talks with both camps and persuaded them both to cancel the SGM, to instruct the rules sub-committee to continue with their task and then, when a new constitution had been drawn up, submit it to legal opinion. The President warned that his compromise was vulnerable to legal challenge from any member, but by then it seemed that both sides were seeking a way out of the impasse.

No attempt was made to force the SGM and a month later a referendum of members, in which only a third bothered to vote, gave a clear majority to a change of rule that would end the 'dual role' controversy. As Yorkshire returned to practice in April – Bairstow having taken the contracted players for a fitness training course with the army at Catterick – a change in the selection procedure was announced, the final word going to a selection sub-committee of Cricket chairman Tony Vann, captain David Bairstow and senior professional Boycott.

A new rules revision sub-committee was set up under the President, consisting of the Chairman (Kirk), the Treasurer (Peter Charles) and General Committee members Peter Quinn, Brian Walsh QC, Tony Cawdry (Halifax) and Tim Reed (Sheffield), the last-named a solicitor – a reasonable representation of both sides. At the annual pre-season lunch Bairstow was delivered a strong speech on behalf of the dressing room: 'We are not pawns in a chess game with the prize an end to our credibility. This Club was formed to play cricket, not to become a debating society...there is no doubt that the differences of opinion off the field have, and will continue to have, an adverse effect on the players.' Cricket chairman Vann also struck a controversial note when he declared: 'We shall be more impressed with a rapid, match-winning 70 under pressure than with a five-hour century on a shirt-front.'

Bairstow began the 1985 Summer with, once again on paper, a reasonable strong side: in fitness and in form he had six first-class seamers, Sidebottom, Stevenson (both of whom played for England), Dennis, Jarvis (who would play for England), Fletcher and Chris Shaw, a right-arm fast-medium bowler from Hemsworth who, at 20, had made an impressive debut in 1984, his forte being accuracy. Those players represented the best all-English attack in county cricket, but Bairstow's difficulty was keeping them fit and he was bedevilled by a succession of serious breakdowns during the Summer. A sprained wrist caused Boycott to miss early matches, giving an unexpected opportunity to Richard Blakey, aged 18, from Elland, a right-handed batsman whose obvious class had already been demonstrated for Young England. Blakey was also rumoured to be a useful wicket-keeper, a valuable talent after Rhodes' departure for Worcestershire.

Boycott's testimonial, it was revealed in May, raised almost £150,000, a testimony of the esteem in which he was held by the public at large. Blakey shone in a drawn Roses match at Old Trafford; by the beginning of June the Yorkshire attack (against Viv Richards and Somerset) had been stricken again, the responsibility being carried by Fletcher, Jarvis, Booth and Carrick, only the last-named being capped. Shaw and a 19-year-old all-rounder from Cleckheaton, Chris Pickles, were drafted in to score a notable Sunday victory over Hampshire at Middlesbrough, Boycott returning and, in characteristic fashion, scoring centuries in successive Championship matches. A century against the touring Australians at Headingley was a gilt-edged certainty, but a reasonably serene if inconsistent Summer flared into argument at Harrogate.

Asked to score 271 in what became 59 overs by Worcestershire, who dangled the carrot, Yorkshire meandered to 124-3, Boycott finishing on 64 not out. Bairstow made an attempt to score runs quickly but he was isolated and was reported to be 'shaking with anger afterwards', but the Committee took no action and what could have become another Northampton, or Cheltenham, was this time filed away for possible use as ammunition. Cricket chairman Vann said that 'in view of the senior players the target was high by 20 or 30 runs'.

Bairstow unleashed some of his frustrations with a century before lunch against Leicestershire at Bradford, his fourth first-class; Sidebottom went off to play for England and collected another injury, and three successive defeats in July sent Yorkshire to the bottom of the Championship table. The team's last hope of recognition in 1985, the NatWest competition, ended with a contentious defeat by Somerset at Headingley after which Somerset captain Ian Botham provoked a diplomatic incident by accusing a section of the Leeds crowd of making racist remarks about Viv Richards. Richards had affected to walk after an appeal for a catch behind, but had returned to end premature Yorkshire celebrations and effectively win the tie. The umpire said afterwards that he had neither seen nor heard a snick, which would have ended the matter, but Botham's radio statement and Yorkshire's reactions blew up another media storm.

By the end of July Yorkshire were settled into bottom place in the Championship, 105 points behind the leaders Middlesex but with, the optimists pointed out, two games in hand. Boycott, Moxon and Phil Robinson batted well enough at Worksop to avert what would have been four defeats in five Championship matches, while the captain hit his third undefeated century of the Summer against Derbyshire at Bradford, the spinners Carrick and Swallow then completing a victory that lifted the team six places.

Early in August the Daily Telegraph reported that Derbyshire were proposing that each county be allowed to play two overseas professionals, a move that immediately brought rumours that Yorkshire were considering abandoning their 120-year tradition of fielding only native-born players. Bairstow, Boycott and most of the players were said to be in favour and although the last referendum of members had voted 90% against, the notion that all other counties would be allowed two world-class players put pressure upon Yorkshire to compete by fielding, at the very least, one outsider. The suggestion floated in the Yorkshire media was that Yorkshire should insist on all players being born within the county with the one exception.

On the eve of the Headingley Roses match the first fruit of the rules revision sub-committee's work was revealed, to be decided upon at the next AGM in February 1986: the Club would be governed on a daily basis by a Management Committee under the President, who would have a much more executive role; no player would be able to serve as a committee member once existing contracts expired (i.e. Boycott could continue in the dual role until 1987); and 400 members at least, not 2.5% of the membership, would be required to sign a requisition for a special general meeting.

So serious was Yorkshire's casualty list that another seam bowler had to be drafted in from leagues – Peter Hartley, a strong right-hander from Keighley who was 25 and who had served Warwickshire for a spell. The fact that Yorkshire, once the nursery for a quarter of English domestic cricketers, were having to take up players rejected by other counties did not pass without comment, but in fairness to Hartley he did learn quickly, made excellent contributions with bat and ball and not undeservedly won a county cap. Hartley was a diligent cricketer even if the lack of consistency was one of his hallmarks, bringing as it did the nickname 'Somedays', originating, according to his captain, in the phrase 'Some days he does, some days he don't.'

The pressure on Bairstow, knowing his position was under threat, caused him to respond with the best batting of his career; but he also kept wicket when, by his own later admission, he was far from fully fit. Due to the battle against injury, both personal and of the team, seeking to take the side up the table, and his own individual effort – the Daily Telegraph described Bairstow's three-year captaincy as 'a series of uphill cavalry charges' – he became short-tempered over moments of sheer bad luck, clashed with umpires and was officially reprimanded. The TCB sub-committee followed this with a suspension from four John Player League matches, but Bairstow's bristling endeavour and unflagging effort in the end took Yorkshire to 11th in the table, an improvement of three positions on 1984 and a far better finish than the public would have expected after the nadir of July. Hartley finished with 5-75 against Nottinghamshire at Scarborough, he and Fletcher carrying a burden in the closing weeks that was far beyond their experience.

The Winter of 1985-86 was the quietest for years, possibly an indication of the President's success in keeping continuing arguments under cover. The first move towards setting up a new indoor cricket school was made with a brisk debate, which did not reach the media, on the relative merits of siting the school at either Headingley or Park Avenue. If Leeds won the contest, it was predicted, Bradford might lose first-class cricket.

Bairstow's disciplinary appeal resulted in what amounted to a deferred sentence: his suspension from four John Player League games was to take effect only if he was involved in further disciplinary action before the end of 1987. Strains surfaced between President Mountgarret and Chairman Kirk, especially over the Club's reaction to the Somerset Botham-Richards furore – Kirk wanted the matter referred to the TCCB – and the Chairman only just survived a confidence vote (11-11) in September, the President refusing to use a casting vote on what he considered to be a 'personal matter'.

Bairstow was relieved to be given another season as captain; Boycott was given another one-year contract; contracts were also awarded to Shaw, Hartley and Pickles while Oldham replaced Colin Johnson as second-team captain, and the Club and the Committee reiterated their commitment to fielding only Yorkshire-born players.

November brought the sad news that Park Avenue, with the Bradford club £50,000 in debt and little hope of further aid from local authorities, was in danger of closure. By 1 December a further 12 months' reprieve had been won, but only through the generosity of a hard-pressed Bradford City Council. The Yorkshire Club were offered the ground but were chary of taking on such a huge commitment, especially when it was clear that all the support that was required for the new indoor school was available at a site across the road from the Headingley Ground in Leeds.

Almost immediately it became clear that President Mountgarret and Chairman Kirk were on diametrically opposite paths. Kirk, referring to the new constitution, told the *Yorkshire Post*: 'The only reason the package of rules is being bludgeoned through is to get rid of a 45 year-old cricketer.' Mountgarret retorted on 20 December by saying that if 'Mr Kirk cannot accept majority decisions then he has no course but to resign'. Mountgarret also accepted that if the new constitution were rejected at the AGM then he, too, would have to leave the office.

Two days into 1986 Kirk resigned the Chairmanship of the General Committee (although keeping his Hull seat), saying: 'I have been disgusted with the personal attacks directed against me.' He added that he wanted freedom to campaign against the new constitution. A day later the Club announced that four Committee members – Jack Sokell (Barnsley), Sid Fielden (Doncaster), Phillip Akroyd (Dewsbury) and David Drabble (Sheffield) – had been returned unopposed. In a critical situation when every vote was vital, what had once been parochial elections were scrutinised with almost parliamentary attention.

At snow-covered Headingley on 9 January the President was confirmed as caretaker Chairman, but news was received that an alternative set of rules, put forward by Kirk's group, would be proposed at the AGM, then set for 22 February, a move that had both sides consulting lawyers once more. At an emergency meeting on 19 February, three of the dissidents, Peter Quinn, Peter Charles and Roy Ickringill, were effectively barred from a General Committee that voted 11 to four with two abstentions to turn itself into a sub-committee of those supporting the new constitution. There was an angry response from those barred, Ickringill complaining: 'We are faced with a naked dictatorship.'

Quinn resigned as Public Relations chairman, adding: 'We've seen nothing like this since Lord Hawke's time.' January ended on a knife-edge: the Club was threatened by legal action both by those who wanted the alternative constitution on the AGM agenda and also by their opponents who intended to claim that they were being prevented from putting amendments to the alternative constitution. *The Daily Telegraph* commented, a little wearily: 'It is a case worthy of King Solomon whose adjudication might be, from precedent, the setting up of two Yorkshire clubs, Boycottshire and Othershire.' The Committee, with little option, elected to go ahead with their own agenda and risk court action again.

The General Committee member for Huddersfield, Tony Ramsden, a popular and respected man who had defeated Bob Platt in 1983, died unexpectedly in the month of the AGM, while more distress calls were heard from Park Avenue where, it became clear, Bradford City Council's offer of £15,000 would not be enough to save the ground. News of the closure came on the eve of the AGM; acting perhaps as a sharp reminder to the 11,000 Club members that civil war inevitably brings some form of devastation in its wake. A united Club might have been able to devote more attention, and resources, to keeping Park Avenue alive, although heroic efforts were made by two of the Committee's Bradford representatives, Raymond Clegg and Appleyard.

Boycott was in Jamaica when the 1986 AGM took place in the City Hall, Sheffield – an absence that brought derisive comments from his opponents in the hall. The meeting was a landslide for Mountgarret, 92% of the 35% of members voting backing the President and the new constitution. By the following Tuesday, Close was restored to the job of the Cricket chairman, Fielden to Public Relations, Tony Cawdry became the new Finance Chairman, while the new General Committee chairman was the Queen's Counsel Brian Walsh, whose witty and forceful speaking made him the outstanding candidate. Almost as an aside, Park Avenue's three Championship matches were transferred to Headingley.

Boycott then had a Summer in which to decide whether to seek to continue his playing career, at 45, with another contract, or resign his seat on the General Committee. The new Cricket chairman, Close, promised that captain Bairstow would be able to command the team in 1986 'without interference or favours – he will certainly be tested this year without someone more powerful than him in his own team'.

Almost the first move of the new government was to designate 1987 as a benefit year for the Club, the immediate target being to raise £200,000 towards the £500,000 needed to build the new indoor school at Leeds. The City Council offered £115,000 in exchange for partial use during school hours, and the departing metropolitan West Yorkshire Council deserve to be fondly remembered for their gift of £100,000.

An indication of future planning, before the season began, came with the appointment of Phil Carrick, as vice-captain to Bairstow. A studious player, Carrick was a skilful left-arm bowler whose career had been restrained by covered pitches and one-day matches, but who had developed into a very useful late-order batsman of excellent defensive technique. On the Committee two vacancies were filled by men who could be described as Mountgarret supporters, Bob Platt recovering his old seat in Huddersfield while Reg Kirk's unexpected resignation in Hull opened the way for Geoffrey Denton; for good or ill the Club was being steered in one direction.

Despite's Boycott's absence the Championship began, as it had in Bairstow's first year of captaincy, with an exciting victory at Taunton, Somerset just failing to score 324 in what became 75 overs, Peter Hartley's diving boundary catch bringing a win by five runs off the last delivery. One-day victories over Somerset (John Player League) and Lancashire (Benson and Hedges), the second by eight wickets (Moxon 106, Boycott 55), brought a stirring first ten days to the Summer, the shadow of continual crisis fleeing in a sunburst of success that sent a sense of well-being flooding through the Club, members and supporters.

By 10 May, after another nerve tingling victory over Sussex by one wicket with five balls to spare, Yorkshire actually led the Championship table; a fifth successive victory was a John Player win at The Oval, the run coming to an end in a Benson and Hedges zonal defeat, by eight runs, at Trent Bridge. The Nottinghamshire victory also cost Boycott a pulled hamstring and the end of what had been a valuable opening partnership with Moxon. Uncertainty was the root cause of a vital defeat by Worcestershire, four batsmen being run out, in another Benson and Hedges competition at Headingley, costing a place in the quarter-finals, and Yorkshire lost their Championship lead at Chelmsford in late May when Essex won another exciting contest by 26 runs with 38 balls remaining.

Headingley, for the Roses match, had a touch of old times about it, for Lancashire and Yorkshire were first and second in the table. Jarvis emphasised his growing power, at 20, with a return of 5-60 (following his 6-78 against Essex), but the match became a ninth successive draw in the series, the final day being remembered for a 55 mph gale that took caps, bails and (according to the *Yorkshire Evening Post*) even a chair, under grey cloud. Ireland were well chastised at Malahide, 'maintaining Yorkshire's unbeaten sequence in this fixture' the Yorkshire Post noted wryly.

Jarvis went on to record match figures of 11-92 against Middlesex at Lord's, the best performance by a bowler there since Wardle's 12-90 in 1950, and with Sharp and Metcalfe, the latter blossoming even beyond his admirers' expectations, Yorkshire remained second throughout June.

Five successive draws were punctuated by Boycott's 150th century at Middlesbrough (passing Sutcliffe) and Sidebottom returning a career-best for 72, but injuries to Stevenson and Sidebottom again weakened the bowling, and although both Metcalfe and Jarvis had excellent Summers the momentum could not be maintained, the final position of tenth being a disappointment after so many high hopes in May.

In all ten successive matches were drawn, but the batting remained solid – never more so than when Moxon and Metcalfe raised 282, the second highest in Roses history, at Old Trafford. Metcalfe scored six centuries in his 1,803 runs,

and he and Jarvis were both capped.

The Autumn of 1986 was one of speculation. The Club's new constitution meant that Boycott had to choose between remaining a member of the General Committee or continuing as a player, and there would be considerable interest in a notion that he would remain as the representative for Wakefield but appear for Derbyshire. In the event he retired from cricket and ended an era.

Would Bairstow remain as captain? There had been several disagreements over team selection between the captain and the Cricket chairman, Brian Close, culminating in the chairman's overruling the captain over the choice of team for a John Player League match against Warwickshire, in the event Bairstow was forced to surrender Chris Shaw to the Yorkshire XI for the Under-25 Final at Edgbaston, not a happy augury for a future season.

Who would succeed Bairstow if a change was made? Boycott was firmly favoured in one quarter, the next senior professional Carrick in another. A third view was that Bairstow should be given another year without Boycott in the dressing room. Not until 15 November was the decision made when the General Committee endorsed 12-7 a 5-1 decision by the Cricket sub-committee that Carrick, at 35 should replace Bairstow, 35. Close explained: 'We have no doubt that David's wicket-keeping suffered over the last season because of his extra responsibilities.'

Carrick was shrewd enough to realise that he was inheriting the crown of thorns at a more opportune moment than most of his immediate predecessors. Boycott, for good or ill, had departed and, wrote David Hopps in the *Yorkshire Post*, 'the county possesses the best crop of youngsters for a generation in terms of ability but even more strikingly in attitude. They are all ready to learn.'

The year ended with Boycott's announcement that he had rejected the offer of a two-year contract with Derbyshire (a planned autobiography was due to be published that would have been subject to TCCB scrutiny had he remained a player), adding that he believed Lord

Mountgarret and certain Committee members were trying to 'hound me out of the club'. Carrick's captaincy thus began under critical eyes from the boundary.

In February the new Indoor School at Headingley, costing £500,000, 'a shiny green and white palace bigger than the Lord's school' according to *The Independent*, was opened, bringing Yorkshire's players into practice earlier than any previous year. Boycott was re-elected to the Committee and Carrick, the Club's sixth captain in nine years, began with a personal point in his favour: the TCCB, by a narrow majority, agreed to uncover pitches for an experimental season. As the run-ups were left covered and the Summer was mostly cold and dry the trial was inconclusive and the batting lobby reversed the decision for 1988.

By the second week in May Yorkshire had won four matches, including two in the Championship, and by the following week the sequence was stretched to seven straight wins. Not until 23 May, with Somerset hanging on in their second innings at 61-7, was the gallop stopped in the Championship, although Benson and Hedges surge continued, a nine-wicket victory over Hampshire (Metcalfe and Blakey hitting 100 in 22 overs) taking them into the semi-final.

Yorkshire were drawn against Surrey at what had become happy Headingley. Ian Greig, the Surrey captain, followed the accepted one-day pattern by asking Yorkshire to bat first, Moxon responding with a superb 97 from 160 deliveries, while Love, foreshadowing his Final form, went to 40 in 19 balls, hitting three sixes. With form support from Bairstow, Yorkshire raised 238. The Surrey innings, interrupted by the weather, stretched into Friday after the second day was lost to rain, the Yorkshire seam bowlers dismissing them for 162 in the 49th over.

By early June, despite the intervention of rain and gloom, Yorkshire had joined Lancashire as joint Championship leaders, but in the Roses match at Old Trafford there was a rare outburst from Jack Simmons after Yorkshire had held on to draw, the last pair, Blakey and Stuart Fletcher, staying for 18 overs. Simmons claimed that Fletcher had been caught at silly point off his bowling; umpire David Evans turned down the appeal but Lancashiremen continued to claim that Fletcher was out.

A nine-wicket victory in murky Headingley put Yorkshire on top of the Championship table at the end of June but the unfamiliar strain for the team, of seeking two prizes simultaneously, became evident. Northamptonshire, the other Benson and Hedges finalists, gave the Yorkshire bowling a fearful thrashing at Northampton where, asked to score 283 to win in 45 overs, the target was achieved by seven wickets with nine balls to spare (Jarvis 1-85, Sidebottom 1-66). Worse followed at Trent Bridge, where Nottinghamshire won in two days, on this occasion the Yorkshire batting collapsing, but a comfortable nine-wicket victory over Glamorgan at Headingley did much to calm nerves before the fateful sunny morning at Lord's.

Northamptonshire were sent in to bat and lost Cook, Larkins, Bailey and Lamb for 92 runs to the opening burst of Jarvis, but Fletcher and Peter Hartley were punished in a stand of 120 by Capel and Williams; the eventual total of 244 meant Yorkshire's batsmen had to average more than four runs an over to win. An opening stand of 97 by Moxon and Metcalfe gave them the necessary foundation; there was a tremor in the middle when Williams took three wickets while only six runs were scored, but Love's batting was reassuring and confident and although the scores were tied Yorkshire took the handsome Cup, amid great jubilation, by losing fewer wickets.

A senior Northamptonshire official, trailing despondently down the stairs in the Lord's pavilion at the conclusion, was not cheered by a greeting from an equally senior MCC official: 'Hard luck, old man, that you should lose by such a margin, but cricket needed a Yorkshire victory.'

Boycott's absence from the Club's happiest day for almost 20 years was much remarked upon, and Carrick clashed with reporters at the post-match press conference when he assumed that they were trying to make him say that the team improved because of Boycott's absence.

The team took a long and merry coach ride north

to win a John Player League match against Middlesex before a cheering Scarborough crowd, but the following week they knew they were back with the steel and sawdust, Surrey bowling them out for 121 at The Oval as a prelude to what would have been a substantial victory but for rain. The next fixture, against Sussex at Hastings, a contest in which Yorkshire would have been hoping for victory, was washed out entirely and by the time the next Roses match was due, in the remaining days of July, Yorkshire were still the Championship leaders but by only one point from Northamptonshire, who had three games in hand.

The Headingley square, under fire for much of the Summer for its alleged inconsistencies, had been treated to a heavy rolling by a machine of several tons' weight, which must have persuaded any lurking devils to scamper off sharply, for all bowlers had next to no help for the remaining month of the 1987 season and with Yorkshire also due on that other batting pitch, Scarborough, any real hope of the Championship faded rapidly; for them to have won their first Championship since 1968 they needed to sustain a higher performance level than was possible and, more important, for their challengers to falter. Nottinghamshire, with Rice and Hadlee in their ranks for a last Summer, made certain of plucking the rose.

The season ended with Headingley being reassured that Test matches would continue to be played on its controversial surface, although the visit of the TCCB's Inspector of Pitches was an obvious warning.

That Winter, 1987-88, brought the introduction of mixed three- and four-day matches in the Championship, but restored the covering of pitches. The next Summer was a deep disappointment for Carrick and all those who believed a genuine revival had taken place, a fall from eighth to 13th in the Championship table and meagre results in the one-day competitions combining to restore the clouds over the Club and revive muted criticism of the Committee.

The weather was little help, the defence of the Benson and Hedges Cup starting with a match at Headingley, against smarting finalists Northamptonshire, that was washed out.

The start in the Championship was a painful one, three successive matches being lost in what became the worst start in the Club's history. What had been regarded as the strongest department in the team, the batting, collapsed time and again on what were, unarguably, poor surfaces but in circumstances in which previous Yorkshire teams, penetrative in bowling and relishing such conditions, would have thrived at the expense of the opposition.

In an effort to restore confidence Carrick shook up the order, moving Metcalfe down and dropping Blakey altogether, trying various opening combinations including giving a long spell to the Sheffield United all-rounder Ian Swallow. Even when Yorkshire did play themselves into a winning position, as against Hampshire at Middlesbrough at the beginning of June, rain robbed them of both the points and a chance to restore confidence.

An interesting finish at Northampton, that could easily have brought Yorkshire another success, also ended in early rain, and a defeat by Warwickshire at Headingley, their first double over Yorkshire since 1951, took Carrick's team to the foot of the Championship table. At that point, in late June, Carrick had scored the second most runs (273) and topped the batting averages, Moxon the senior batsman was averaging 26, while Blakey, the wonder of 1987, was averaging just 13.

June did not pass, however, without relief and on 29 June, at Hove, the first win of the season was recorded only to be followed by another trouncing, from Middlesex at Lord's. An unexpected victory in a run chase against Leicestershire, third placed, at Headingley was made the more welcome by the fact that it was accomplished without the fast-improving Jarvis whose back, strained again at Hove, cost him both a possible place in the Third Test match and the rest of the Summer for Yorkshire.

Yet from the nadir of Lord's the team, buttressed by the hard-working seam trio of Sidebottom, in his benefit year, Fletcher, who was to win his cap for his efforts, and Shaw, rallied well. The batting settled into recognisable form, Philip Robinson improved sufficiently to win his cap, the strong Scarborough left-hander David Byas, after years apparently beyond the fringe, forced his way into regular contention for a place, and especially pleasing to the traditionalists was the sight of Paul Booth, the Colts' left-arm spinner, winning a place by the strength of both his bowling and batting.

In late July Yorkshire narrowly failed to defeat the next champions, Worcestershire, losing by 21 runs in a late-afternoon chase through a drizzle. Even more satisfying and uplifting was a thorough thrashing of Lancashire, by ten wickets in two days at Headingley, a result that even Hawke would not have sniffed at; injuries had removed both Lancashire's opening bowlers, but Yorkshire's win was achieved by some hard and sensible cricket, a reaffirmation of the principles of attacking play.

At Abbeydale, the then current champions Nottinghamshire avoided a follow-on by seven runs and a Summer that had begun in abject gloom was brightened by the Autumn when, in a welcome gesture, Bairstow was restored to the wicket-keeping and Blakey to his batting, enabling the keeper to take his 1,000th victim for Yorkshire. The gesture might have been sentimental but was justified for few players had better expressed the character of Yorkshire cricket, during their careers, than Bairstow.

As 1988 ended there was a certain familiarity about events: there was an argument continuing over the use of one ground for first-class cricket (a ground staff and 'academy' were planned to help revive Park Avenue), discussion about strengthening the team (even a proposal to recruit Viv Richards was aired) and conversations about improving the government of the club. It was even suggested in one corner that the Duke of York should stand for the presidency, but the House of Windsor had the good sense and discretion not to become involved.

Yorkshire traditions die hard, as a brewery discovered when they tried to remove the portrait of Richard III from an inn sign and replace 'The King's Head' with that of Henry VIII. Such was the uproar in Malton that they soon backed down.

The key question facing the Club in the last decade of the 20th century was that of adaptation. The birthright qualification had served the Club splendidly and remained a source of great pride to players, members and the Yorkshire public, but would a new and perhaps a more cosmopolitan generation continue to accept the self-imposed handicap that prevented recruitment from outside the county?

When, in 1988, Hampshire fielded a cricketer who had been actually born inside the boundary the news was broadcast with some astonishment and delight; even Lancashire, with all their resources were progressing to the point where almost half their staff had been born elsewhere.

By judicious manipulation of the rules it was possible for a county club to engage as many as half a dozen top-class players born overseas; London, with its highly energetic West Indian population, began supplying a steady stream of British-born or qualified cricketers, recruiting areas denied to Yorkshire.

When a player lost form, or heart, became ill or simply too old, 16 county clubs could immediately register another. Yorkshire had to wait until another youngster emerged from the Colts and while the waiting was not too long in more leisured days of purely Championship cricket, when skills and experience could be accumulated steadily, in the more frenetic world of three one-day competitions, one of which began in April, a boy's confidence could be shattered in ten days. All counties found great difficulty in producing young English players of outstanding ability, but only Yorkshire could not help fill the gaps from outside.

English cricket needed Yorkshire to succeed, but when days in the sun were so few and far between, the chill of repeated failure began to gnaw at Yorkshire bones.

Elsewhere the game continued to act as both manual and mirror to the society it served, the South African schism was cricket's struggle for equality; Lancashire tried hard to persuade its male members to allow females into the pavilion while on Easter Sunday in Wombwell, one of the heartlands, Canon David Hawkins was reported to have surprised his parishioners by taking guard in front of the altar and hitting a number of soft-ball deliveries down the aisle. 'I told a parable about cricket,' he explained.

Moxon to Byas 1989–2001

In 1989 Carrick signalled the end of his captaincy with a letter to the Committee urging the abandonment of the birth qualification and the recruitment of an overseas player. This had followed a disastrous string of results that sent Yorkshire from 13th to 16th in the Championship and from eighth to 11th in the Refuge Assurance League. Even the new-found reputation as a one-day team, a notion dismissed derisively by the traditionalists, suffered as the team failed to reach the knock-out stage of the Benson and Hedges Cup and were dismissed from the NatWest Trophy in the second round.

Carrick's team were hit hard before the season began. Hartley returned from South Africa with a back strain and played once; Shaw, of whom much had been hoped, reported persistent neck pain and was unable to play at all, a preliminary to the ending of his career. Moxon missed the first five weeks of the season with a broken arm, Fletcher was handicapped by elbow and back strains while Bairstow broke a thumb on June 28 and thereafter made only three Sunday appearances.

For all these misfortunes it was the general demeanour of the team that depressed Yorkshiremen, causing the Cricket chairman Brian Close to say at one point: 'I have never seen a Yorkshire team so lacking in fight.' They were bowled out for less than 200 12 times in the Championship.

The bowling was carried by Jarvis (548 overs), Arnie Sidebottom, then 35 (576) and Carrick (679). These three took 142 Championship wickets while the supporting bowlers, all 17 of them, managed 149.

Moxon, on his return, was as consistent as ever, Metcalfe survived a lean spell to finish with 1,230 runs, and Blakey returned to form with 1,159 but his successful deputising for Bairstow was a hint of the future. The middle order was never settled, not one of Phil Robinson, Sharp,

Byas and Love advancing his career. Indeed Love was not retained and departed to a successful playing and coaching career in Scotland.

Hope, as ever, rested with the list of emerging players: Simon Kellett, Neil Nicholson, Darren Gough, Ian Houseman, Ian Priestley, Jeremy Batty, Paul Grayson and Matthew Doidge, but Carrick's letter, and the depressing results, caused a furore that brought heated exchanges at a specially called Committee meeting at which Boycott was to the fore.

The Cricket sub-committee, charged with doing something but not anything that would upset the membership, eventually proposed the appointment of Steve Oldham, then 41, a former Yorkshire and Derbyshire seamer and coach, as Cricket Manager on a two-year contract while Padgett was made Club Coach on a three-year agreement.

There was an improvement in 1990, from 16th to tenth in the Championship and from 11th to sixth in the Sunday League, but it was not dramatic enough to appease the critics both in and outside the Committee. Martyn Moxon's captaincy brought a fresh air to the dressing room, now shorn of such strong and controversial characters as Boycott and Bairstow, the latter appearing in only five Championship matches.

Moxon was always prepared for a death-or-glory run chase on a third afternoon, enterprise that partly disguised the essential weakness of the side: only once were Yorkshire able to claim all 20 wickets, but were themselves bowled out twice eight times.

The batting was erratic, the only success being Metcalfe, who became the first since Boycott in 1971 to pass 2,000 runs in a Summer. Blakey inherited Bairstow's gauntlets but his batting fell away so rapidly that he had to be dropped down the order, a sorry decline in a potential England batsman. Robinson was a steadying influence

David Byas Bingo

There was never any doubt about the chief quality David Byas brought to Yorkshire cricket: strength. An East Riding farmer, he was always wind-burned, a man clearly capable of considering fast bowling of much lesser concern than those Winter gales off the North Sea. To his strength of arm and shoulder he added height (6ft 4in) and an application to the job in hand that was positively Victorian.

He had played hockey for England Under-21 after leaving Scarborough College and the local cricket club thought so highly of him that he became Scarborough's captain at 21, the youngest ever. His scoring record at North Marine Road attracted Yorkshire's attention and he first played in 1986, when 23, when the obvious parallel with Vic Wilson, another East Riding farmer and who led Yorkshire to the Championship in 1960, was noted.

Byas initially found county cricket difficult and he did not become a regular contender until 1988, working hard on his technical deficiencies, especially against spin, and it was not until 1999, when he scored 1,500 runs and won his cap, that he could be considered a regular. Once there, however, his potential for leadership was obvious and five years later he succeeded Moxon to captaincy.

He was not the boldest or the most astute of tacticians but his leadership signalled that Yorkshire would again be expecting each and every player to perform to the maximum and that he would not be content with middling success. He did endure some frustrating years, finishing twice second in the Championship and once second in the National League. He was fortunate, he would agree, that his captaincy coincided with a surge of talented young players, especially fast bowlers, from the Second XI and the Academy, but those young men had to be moulded and pointed in the right direction.

Byas' steadfastness under fire brought him

David Byas
Yorkshire Post

close to Test selection in 1995, when he averaged 56. Another asset he brought to any team was his superb catching, normally at second slip, where he came to be regarded as in the same class as his great predecessors 'Long John' Tunnicliffe and Phil Sharpe. Although he would smile with embarrassment at any suggestion that he was a great captain, he did lead his teams with drive and determination and many cricket followers throughout England were pleased when this dedicated and singular man did take his team to the Championship in 2001.

His nickname 'Bingo' was bestowed upon him by the Yorkshire captain on his debut, David Bairstow, the implication that, coming from Scarborough, he would be addicted to slot machines, candyfloss and kiss-me-quick hats, and like most cricket nicknames it was intended to be satirical. 'Bingo's' notion of high life was an interest in motor racing, rugby union, a pint of Guinness at the close of play and back home to his wife, his children and his farm.

He announced his retirement in 2002 but was persuaded to play another season by Lancashire thus becoming the first player to be capped by both counties. Yorkshire's Board of Management brought him back to Headingley as Director of Cricket in 2004. But when he was superseded by Martyn Moxon in 2007 he declined another appointment with Yorkshire. His strict sense of discipline did not endear him to some senior members of the team but he was fondly remembered by members and supporters. Under Byas Yorkshire never finished below sixth.

---

without making a convincing claim on a regular place.

There were two interesting developments. Although Byas lost form with the bat, his move to slip suggested Yorkshire might have their most able practitioner in that vital position since Sharpe. Through the help of Bob Appleyard, a Morley-born all-rounder named Craig White was recruited from the Australian Academy to Yorkshire's new establishment at Bradford. Cricket manager Oldham was so impressed that he gave White immediate promotion to the first team, a middle-order batsman and off-spinner.

Historically, however, the most important event of the year was a Committee vote in November to drop the insistence upon Yorkshire birth for newly-registered players. The media began to speculate about Yorkshire's first overseas player but the true priority was a more domestic matter.

A year previously Padgett had discovered a promising seam bowler in Doncaster schools cricket, Peter Martin. Once his birthplace was revealed as Accrington the Yorkshire coach reluctantly informed Old Trafford and Martin went on to an illustrious career with Lancashire and England. Padgett then realised that Michael Vaughan, an outstanding Sheffield and England schoolboy batsman, might follow the same route, being born in Eccles of a family related to the famous Lancashire Tyldesleys.

Rather than lose Vaughan, the Club accepted that the world had become truly cosmopolitan. Vaughan was so much a Sheffield lad that he supported the Wednesday, and it would clearly be unfair to him to insist that he followed his cricket career elsewhere. The bridge having been crossed, over some angry correspondence and a few resignations, the next step was to find a match winner from abroad.

The 1991 season was a turning point. The much-mourned death of the Club's favourite son, Sir Len Hutton, brought the election of a new President in Sir Lawrence Byford, a former HM Chief Inspector of Constabulary who, while being a dedicated follower, was open to new ideas and a man accustomed to making decisions swiftly and seeing them realised. His dynamic and confrontational style was not universally popular, and when he added the post of Chairman to his portfolio he became the single most powerful figure in the county's cricket since Lord Hawke.

Joe Lister, Secretary since 1972, died suddenly during the Winter, a sad loss to the Club for he, along with the then Chairman Michael Crawford, had striven so hard to maintain the Club's equilibrium and dignity during the severest excesses of the civil war when, as *The Daily Telegraph* suggested, Yorkshire were about to break into two, 'Boycottshire and Othershire'. Lister's other qualities included a deep love and respect for the traditions of the game, often expressed through a very dry sense of humour.

Yorkshire's increasing cosmopolitanism was confirmed in the appointment of his successor, Chris Hassell, who joined from a similar position with Lancashire. Hassell also had wide experience of football, being a former secretary of Everton, and was thus well versed in the growing and complicated world of players' contracts and in dealing with the fast-expanding, overwhelming power of television.

The Byford-Hassell partnership tended to act quickly and decisively, thus treading on more than a few toes and upsetting a few applecarts, but the Club did give the impression of movement. The traditionalists, while accepting that young players such as Vaughan, wherever born, needed to be kept in Yorkshire cricket, resisted any quick changes until July of that Summer

Darren Gough

Charles Dickens would have seen Darren Gough as a character created to bring a ray of light, a chuckle, even a guffaw, into one of his more sombre tales. England's premier fast bowler at the turn of the century was at heart a self-confessed entertainer, a jester and clown who loved his audience and needed to be loved in turn. When his ambitions and inclinations crossed, especially when wearing Yorkshire's cap, Gough could be hurt and confused enough to want to hit back. The Sunday newspaper who employed him hurried to provide the means.

'Goughie', in tabloidspeak, was the Barnsley lad who made it big. Yorkshire crowds gave him an affection probably unmatched in the Club's history. Yorkshire has had many colourful characters who have struck up a career-long empathy with the crowd but none, probably, have had Gough's appeal. Johnny Wardle was a match for him on the field; off the field Wardle could be as withdrawn or introspective as Geoffrey Boycott. Gough exuded warmth wherever he might be.

At his school in Monk Bretton he played cricket, football, rugby and took part in athletics. As a midfielder he had trials with Rotherham and eventually arrived at Yorkshire's Academy in 1987, making his Second XI debut the following year. In his second match, at Old Trafford in July, he finished with 3-39 in Lancashire's first innings, his victims including the Cambridge captain, Mike Atherton. Otherwise he did not have a distinguished year and his first-class debut, against Middlesex at Lord's in 1989 was a surprise and owed something to the prevailing casualty list. He made an impressive start, taking five wickets in the match, including that of Mike Gatting, but made his debut even more memorable by playing an unwitting part in a press-box joke that found him described in a leading broadsheet as 'the son of a Barnsley ratcatcher'. The legend was born.

However, a sequence of injuries limited his

Darren Gough
Ron Deaton collection

appearances for Yorkshire for the next three Summers and he must have been close to being released but for his willingness to learn and the sense, among the coaches, that he possessed considerable potential. Around that time a Yorkshire II's player told the author: 'We miss Goughie when he's with the first team. He makes us laugh.'

Encouraged to bowl fast by the West Indies captain Richie Richardson, then Yorkshire's overseas professional, he sloughed off adolescent weight, discovered an accurate length and line and to the great pleasure of both the Club and supporters, won his county cap in 1993 after taking 57 wickets at an average of 26. He was summoned to serve England's 'A' team in South Africa the following Winter and found an American bride.

In 1994 he made his Test debut against New Zealand, taking a wicket in his first over and scoring 65, a signal that he was then ready for the international stage. He wowed Australia in 1994-95, Sydney and

Melbourne taking to a player in which they could clearly see much of the larrikin. Injury cost him his place the following year, a Summer he devoted to Yorkshire's cause, taking 66 wickets at 22. Recalled by England in 1998 he became, in the words of selectors' chairman David Graveney, 'the pulse of the team'. He was, naturally, one of the first to be offered one of England's new central contracts and became the nation's favourite cricketer.

His international success, however, meant he played in only three championship matches in 2000, and one less the following year when Yorkshire won the Championship in effect without him. His availability for Yorkshire became an issue

with the captain David Byas, and although it was reported that he had been offered the Club captaincy in 2004 he opted to join Essex where he had three successful seasons, recreating the ambiance of his early days at Yorkshire.

While with Essex he won a televised dancing competition that brought him international fame so that when, in the early part of 2007, Yorkshire formally offered the captaincy and a two-year contract, no one at the newly-dubbed Headingley Carnegie needed to introduce him; the number of TV crews indicating the level of interest. In the next six weeks Gough probably attracted more media attention than his 31 predecessors as Yorkshire captain put together.

---

when Sir Lawrence spelled out a few home truths.

The team were in bottom place in the Championship and had been knocked out of the one-day Cup competitions. Yorkshire faced a loss of £100,000 on the season and had lost 3,000 members since 1987. Oldham and the players advertised their demand for an overseas player and on 19 July Yorkshire announced the signing of Australia's premier fast bowler Craig McDermott for the following Summer.

Immediately there were whispers from Australia that their Board had no wish to see McDermott enduring the wear and tear of a full county season and just as the *Yorkshire Yearbook* had gone to print with a full profile of 'Billy the Kid' the news arrived that McDermott needed a groin operation and would not be able to fulfil his contract.

For once the Club acted swiftly and decisively through secretary Hassell who flew out to India to sign the 19-year-old wunderkind Sachin Tendulkar as the replacement. Commercially and publicly the signing was a success for this handsome young man made his runs with great style, he attracted a great deal of Asian interest and he deflected the oft-repeated criticism that Yorkshire were a club tinged with racism.

One elderly lady member of many years' stand-

ing was heard to refer to Tendulkar as 'ower Sachin', which was an acceptance as valid as the freedom of Barnsley, while in Leeds and Bradford it was said that Indian restaurants were serving two new dishes: a Boycott curry and a Tendulkar curry, the difference being that the runs came more quickly with the latter.

Tendulkar, alas, did not score enough runs, making one Championship and one Sunday League century. He had not the experience, in his first Summer of county cricket, to buttress an uneven batting order in which Metcalfe was to lose his place. Kellett played well enough to displace him and to win his own cap while Byas assumed the captaincy when Moxon was unavailable.

Tendulkar went home early, missing the last four Championship matches, amid rumours of severe homesickness. The team slipped to 16th in the Championship and 15th in the Sunday League and made no impact in the knock-out competitions. Jarvis, Carrick and Hartley all gave of their best, Mark Robinson won his cap, but Gough and Pickles, in who much faith had been placed, were both disappointing, the latter being released. The bowlers would say, rightly, that they had little help from the field, especially at slip.

Carrick reached his 1,000 wickets and moves were made to replace him as principal left-arm spinner, first by the all-rounder Grayson, who was later to join Essex and England, and second by the signing of Richard Stemp from Worcestershire. The season ended in some acrimony with the Cricket sub-committee wishing to sign a young fast bowler as Tendulkar's replacement, only to be overruled by the General Committee, who wanted an established world famous name and who plumped for the West Indies captain Richie Richardson.

Alas, like Tendulkar before him, Richardson found English conditions in 1993, so friendly to seam and swing, a severe handicap to his reputation as one of the world's leading batsmen and managed to average only 34 when Yorkshire would have been expecting another ten runs per innings. Once again the overseas player failed to bring the anticipated response from a batting order not short of ability but low in confidence and self-esteem.

The bowling, despite another Summer of dropped catches, was chiefly responsible for the rise to 12th in the Championship and ninth in the Sunday League. John Callaghan commented in the *Yorkshire Evening Post*: 'measured against the yardstick of the county's history, such modest achievement hardly merited applause'.

There were straws in the wind. Jarvis had a good Summer but was released, with two years on his contract outstanding, because of his poor fitness record and because of the advance of Mark Robinson and Hartley and, most of all, of Gough who had managed only 16 wickets, at 35 each, in his first eight matches.

He was dropped but recalled when Jarvis suffered another injury. Thereafter he found both pace and accuracy to take 39 more wickets at 21. With White, too, showing he could bowl with deceptive pace the Club felt that a seam attack was taking shape. Richardson is given most of the credit for Gough's improvement, reportedly taking the young man aside (as no doubt he did with Courtney Walsh and Curtly Ambrose from time to time) to say 'Don't let a batter do that to you. You can bowl quick. Give him one.' Fired up, Gough did just that, realised he could be a genuine fast bowler and immediately blossomed.

The spin bowling was again disappointing,

Stemp fading after a bright start and the off-spinner Jeremy Batty hardly being seen enough to be given a fair assessment. The lack of home victories, in both league competitions, caused Cricket chairman Brian Close and Secretary Hassell to call a meeting with the players in July. The sense of disappointment was acute in both members and public in that the cherished birthright tradition had been discarded with little improvement in fortunes.

1994 could be said, in retrospect, to be the year that first saw the light at the end of the tunnel, although anyone suggesting such a notion at the time would have been derided. Richardson had such a poor second season that he departed early, declared mentally and physically exhausted. The team slipped a place to 13th, but there was an improvement to fifth in the Sunday League.

Ray Illingworth, then England's team manager, was assailed for favouritism for being the first to spot the potential of Gough and White, and although their loss to England undoubtedly interrupted any possible revival, the stalwart Hartley and Mark Robinson were supported by a new wave of seam bowlers, the first fruits of the investment in youth, Chris Silverwood, Gavin Hamilton, Alex Wharf and Stuart Milburn.

The batting, too, showed a hint of the resilience to come, for despite Richardson's disappointing return, five players, Moxon, Vaughan, Byas, Blakey and Grayson, passed 1,000 runs. The crucial weakness was the lack of capable spinners, although Illingworth never lost faith in the left arm Stemp, who was called up twice by England, without playing, and joined an 'A' team tour of India.

A decision to develop Vaughan's off-spin meant that Jeremy Batty asked for his release (he joined Somerset) while Gary Keedy, Stemp's highly regarded deputy, unable to see a first-team future with Yorkshire, also sought a new club and, despite intense efforts by Yorkshire to reassure him, was snapped up by Lancashire.

The Summer ended, not unusually, in confusion. An effort was made to sign a South African all-rounder to replace Richardson – he wasn't interested in playing for Yorkshire – but a West Indian trialist fast bowler, Leroy Weekes, was

Craig White

A telephone call between Bob Appleyard, the former England bowler, then a Yorkshire committeeman and later President, and Jack Potter, director of the Australian Cricket Academy in Adelaide, started the career of a player who was to become England's leading all-rounder in the last decade of the 20th century.

Appleyard was seeking advice on the setting up of a similar cricket academy in Yorkshire, originally based at Bradford Park Avenue, whose continuing existence as a cricket ground owed much to the faith of Appleyard and fellow Bradfordians.

Potter obliged and then added: 'By the way, we've a lad of yours here who would be grateful for a chance in county cricket.' He went on to explain that the 18-year-old White had been born in Morley but had been raised in Victoria. A right-hand batsman, he was also capable of keeping wicket and bowling off-spin and had appeared for Australia at Under-17 and Under-19 levels, but still retained a Yorkshire qualification.

Appleyard quickly arranged sponsorship for White to become a founder member of the Yorkshire Academy, but on his arrival at Headingley the coaches, especially Steve Oldham, were so impressed by his obvious natural ability that he was immediately drafted into the first-team squad and in fact never reached the new Academy. He topped the Second XI batting averages in 1990 as a first-team fringe
player, his record including a 209 and 115 not out against Worcestershire.

By 1993 he had won his cap and had switched to seam, Richard Blakey pointing out that his fast-medium action disguised the menace in his quicker delivery that accelerated off the pitch swiftly enough to force Blakey to stand back as far as he did for the accepted fast bowlers. His potential attracted Raymond Illingworth, then Chairman of England selectors, who chose him against New Zealand in 1994 and for the 1994-95 tour of Australia where, how-

Craig White
YCCC

ever, he failed to establish a place in the national team. A selector said around that time: 'We have no doubts about Chalky's ability. He is the one who has to be convinced.'

In the next four years White developed, for England, from a batsman who could bowl to a bowler who could bat. His accuracy and deceptive pace made him a natural selection to bowl the closing overs in one-day matches. He became adept at attacking left-handers from around the wicket and his value hugely increased, especially abroad, when he found he was able to win reverse swing from an ageing ball. As a batsman he was always happier when attacking and Yorkshire often used him as an opener in one-day matches; he also became the county's regular first slip.

White became one of the first 12 players to be awarded a central contract by England, giving the selectors first call on his services at all times, in 2000, a year in which his performances in a triangular one-day series against the West Indies established him among the world rankings. He did find that bowling long spells put excessive pressure on his back and by 2001 he had to drop out of the home series against Australia, recovering fitness by playing for Yorkshire purely as a batsman. He married a Scarborough girl and settled by the sea without ever losing his Australian accent, a no doubt wel-

coming sound in the following years to Michael Bevan, Darren Lehmann, who became his brother-in-law, Wayne Clark and Yorkshire's other Australian recruits. History might conclude that Yorkshire needed Australians to demonstrate how to win again and that White was the first of those tutors.

added and the 1995 overseas player, it was announced, would be the New South Wales left-hander Michael Bevan.

An unexpected event in the Winter was the resignation of Moxon after six years as captain. His achievement in restoring some unity to the Yorkshire dressing room had been recognised, in addition to his personal contributions to the game, by his nomination by *Wisden* as one of the five cricketers of 1993. He later emerged as team manager, Oldham concentrating on setting up what became, in the next five years, the most admired youth development programme in English cricket.

There were other changes, under the Byford-Hassell regime, that also proved to be significant. Byas became captain, Close was succeeded as Cricket chairman by Bob Platt, a Huddersfield businessman who had bowled in-swing opposite Fred Trueman in Close's Championship years.

Bevan, fierce hitter or stubborn defender and useful change spinner, became the first overseas player to have a substantial effect on the team's performances and he, Moxon, free of leadership problems, and Byas had successful Summers. While neither White nor Gough could continue to enhance the progress made in 1994, Hartley glittered in the sunset of his own career, despite injury, taking 81 wickets. Vaughan persevered with his off-spin but Stemp, the specialist, seemed unable, despite a desire to succeed, to improve. Yorkshire were weak on turning pitches.

Silverwood and Hamilton confirmed that they were both first-class performers, and the emergence of Anthony McGrath and Richard Kettleborough revealed two more candidates for the batting order. The team rose to eighth in the Championship and reached the last eight of both

knock-out competitions. By September the Committee felt that some definite decisions could be made: Kellett, Grayson and Milburn were released, Bevan was re-signed and made vice-captain and the possibility of acquiring a permanent home, away from the Headingley lease, near Wakefield, was announced.

For the first time for almost a quarter-century Yorkshire emerged as contenders again in 1996. The new government, through Sir Lawrence Byford to Hassell to Byas, from Cricket chairman Platt to groundsman Andy Fogarty, who had arrived in 1995 from Old Trafford, gave the Club a sense of purpose and the feeling that all were proceeding down the same path, not always quickly enough and sensibly, but in the right direction.

This was confirmed, later in the Summer, when Gough, Silverwood and White were all chosen for the England Winter tour while Vaughan and McGrath joined the 'A' tour. Until then Byas had charge of a settled side, the runs coming from Bevan, Vaughan, McGrath, and Blakey while the seam attack, Hartley, Gough, Silverwood, White and Hamilton, bristled. Spin was again weak and although Stemp was capped, no doubt as an encouragement, the temptation to turn to Vaughan, when the surface was helpful, meant that the specialist spinner had few opportunities.

Bevan was recalled by Australia in August, opening the way for Kettleborough to return and score a match-winning century against Essex, while the England Under-19 captain Alex Morris, a talented all-rounder, was claiming attention. Such performances caused little excitement outside the county for in statistical terms the team rose only from eighth to sixth in the Championship but in one-day cricket the improvement was marked by a rise of nine places, to finish third, in the Sunday League and in reaching semi-finals of both knockout competitions, the winner on both occasions being Lancashire.

Off the field Yorkshire finally limited their play to Headingley and Scarborough, from 1997, thus losing all their traditional out-grounds but one. In the day of the near universal motor car it was probably a sensible decision, but the retreat from Hull, Huddersfield, Bradford, Sheffield and Middlesbrough did disenfranchise many elderly cricket lovers who were disinclined to travel outside their home areas.

More controversial was the decision in October to move, funding permitting, to a new purpose-built £50 million cricket stadium on the outskirts of Wakefield, near the junction of two motorways. The Leeds Rugby club, Headingley's landlords, quickly signalled their opposition while Leeds City Council, who had not been the most encouraging when presented with previous improvement plans for Headingley, suddenly awoke to the possibility of losing Test cricket.

Some Leeds members formed a 'Save Headingley' group, but the majority of the Club's members – research revealed that the bulk of the membership then resided between Leeds and York – backed the committee on the move. It was a Winter of much smoke and crackling in the undergrowth, reminiscent of the years when every Yorkshire cricket story began with the words 'Geoffrey Boycott'.

One decision that Winter proved to be the wisest for many a year. Bevan, touring with Australia, was unavailable as the overseas professional, and the first choice as his replacement was his adventurous NSW teammate Michael Slater, a right-hander opener. Once again the Yearbook dutifully introduced him to members to learn that Slater, like McDermott, would not be coming. Yorkshire then turned to another left-hander, Darren Lehmann of South Australia, who was also capable of bowling left-arm spin and who entered the dressing room as though he had spent his formative years with Bowling Old Lane in the Bradford League, so much was he at home. A more instant success was impossible.

On the field the bright promise of 1996 faded; the team finished sixth again, the knockout competitions yielded no more than quarter-finals and the Sunday League ranking dropped to tenth. England saw the best of Gough, who also carried injuries; Hartley missed seven Championship matches for a hernia operation while White suffered a sore back.

Much responsibility fell upon Silverwood and Hamilton until the arrival of two young left fast bowlers, Ryan Sidebottom, son of Arnie, and Paul Hutchison. The latter made a sensational start with 11-102 against Pakistan 'A' followed by 23 wickets at 16 runs each in his first four Championship matches.

The batting was also patchy with Moxon and Vaughan injured and McGrath out of form. Of those promoted not one of Kettleborough, Morris and Bradley Parker looked permanent, and Yorkshire were so grateful for Lehmann, for his 1,557 runs and his inspiration of the dressing room that he was re-signed for 1998, a decision not popular with Bevan, who had been given to understand that he was returning. The team's gathering strength was reflected in the unexpected number of departures, Hartley to Hampshire, a move vigorously opposed by Byas, and Kettleborough to Middlesex. Alex Morris and his younger brother Zac, another England Under-19 player, also went to Hampshire while off-spinner Gareth Batty, brother of Jeremy, joined Surrey.

The long wrangle over a new headquarters provoked tensions in the Committee, Sir Lawrence Byford eventually standing down as Chairman but retaining the Presidency, Keith Moss of Pudsey taking the chair, while veteran Committee member Sid Fielden resigned during the row but was then re-elected by his South Yorkshire members. The Leeds Rugby club had made it clear that Yorkshire would not be released from their 99-year agreement at Headingley, doubts arose as to whether the Wakefield proposal was viable financially and the Committee had to swallow their pride and reconsider how to turn Headingley into a modern Test-match ground for the new century. Not far from Middlesbrough was the shiny new Riverside ground of Durham, who were making no bones about their ambition to win Test-match status.

Michael Vaughan

Michael Vaughan's registration for Yorkshire signalled the end of the tradition of employing only cricketers born in the county and in a sense reversed a curious story from almost a century before. In those days the birth qualification was taken very seriously, and not only in Yorkshire. So when the Club received a letter from MCC saying that Cec Parkin, who had made his debut in 1906, playing one match, was in fact born in Durham (the name of the informant never emerged) Parkin was released to Lancashire, for whom he was to take 901 wickets at an average of 16.

Parkin was born in Eaglescliffe, 20 yards over the Yorkshire border. Vaughan was born in Eccles but moved with his family, at the age of nine, to Sheffield where he emerged at the Collegiate club as an outstanding right-hand opening batsman who went on to captain the England Under-17 and Under-19 teams. He was related to the famous cricketing Tydlesleys of Lancashire.

Having lost bowler Peter Martin, from Doncaster Schools but Accrington-born, to Lancashire, the committee this time decided, despite some furious opposition from the diehards, that another outstanding prospect would be retained, and Vaughan, so much a Yorkshireman that he was a devout follower of Sheffield Wednesday, joined the Academy. He made a half-century on debut, against Lancashire, as Martyn Moxon's partner and with three centuries in his first season, passing 1,000 runs, had launched what all hoped would be an outstanding career.

A tall, elegant player who became an outstanding deep field and later gully, Vaughan was also developing as a useful off-break bowler until his opportunities were limited by the arrival of Richard Dawson. His Test career was slower to progress than expected; his batting always carried a sheen of class but he rarely produced the consistent big scores that impress selectors. He did lead the England 'A' team in South Africa and Zimbabwe in 1998-99 with conspicuous success.

Michael Vaughan
Yorkshire Post

He did look the part of an England batsman by 2000-01, impressing international observers with both his temperament in defence and his audacity in attack, and he was one of the first players to be awarded a central contract by England. A one-day century against Somerset at Taunton in 2001 was especially memorable. Recognition as one of the nation's outstanding players, with the attendant financial rewards, must have been pleasing but in Yorkshire terms a central contract meant that Vaughan could not be considered as the natural successor to Byas as captain when the latter retired in 2001. Despite ill luck with injury he stayed on course to lead, eventually, both his county and his country.

He was ranked the world's number one batsman after England's tour of Australia in 2000-01 and emulated previous Yorkshiremen F.S. Jackson, Len Hutton and Ray Illingworth when he led England to an Ashes series victory against Australia in 2005 before a series of knee operations caused him to be an intermittent international captain during the next two years. After a fourth knee operation his determination ensured a return as England's captain in New Zealand in 2007, and he won another place in history by becoming the first Test captain to take an unchanged team into a sixth successive match, against South Africa at Lord's in 2008.

Five successive victories to close the Summer, finishing with a ten-wicket victory at Hove, signalled Yorkshire's return to the front rank in 1998. Third place was the best achieved since coming second in 1975, but what cheered members and supporters most was that the team clearly contained the potential for so much more. Never in the Club's history had there been so many able fast bowlers available: Gough, Silverwood, White, Hamilton, Sidebottom, Hutchison and Hoggard, six of whom were to be eventually capped by England while wearing the white rose. The talented left-arm Hutchison, on his day perhaps the most penetrative of all, would have joined them but for a string of injuries, and the remodelling of his action, that brought his release to Sussex two years later.

Yet this was Hutchison's year for White's recurring difficulties, with his back, reduced him to batting after the first five matches; Gough was almost always away with England and, when available for the last three matches, had to rest a hamstring. Hamilton emerged as a potent all-rounder, 56 wickets and 572 runs. Hoggard's pace and hostility marked him as another coming champion, and his 31 wickets in the last six matches masked Gough's absence.

Equally pleasing was the arrival of the stocky right-handed opener Matthew Wood who just missed 1,000 runs in his first season and included a 200 not out against Warwickshire. Byas contributed four centuries and if Lehmann was less effective, losing part of the Summer by an Australian re-call and to a back strain, Yorkshire still managed to be joint leaders in the total of batting bonus points.

Blakey, with 69 victims, was the country's leading wicket-keeper and although the attack was much less effective on turning pitches, Stemp being released to Nottinghamshire, Ian Fisher, left arm, and James Middlebroook, off-spin, could both bat and bowl well enough to be considered future all-rounders and useful cricketers. Yorkshire reached the semi-finals of the Benson and Hedges Cup, but Lancashire, again, put an end to any hopes in the NatWest Trophy competition.

They led the Sunday League at one point but paid for their run in the Championship with a later slump in the one-day form, finishing ninth. So it was that 1999 was all the more disappointing in that from being at one point in contention for all cricket's four major trophies they finished with nothing and slipped three places in the Championship. Byas said that team played 'to only two-thirds of their ability'.

The major weakness, apart from the lack of class spinners, most of that work being done by Vaughan and Fisher, proved to be the batting. Greg Blewett, another South Australian signed to replace Lehmann, chosen to tour, never came to terms with English pitches, especially Headingley's, and had to wait until Scarborough in late Summer to demonstrate his undoubted class. Wood had a dismal second season and lost his place; Vaughan had style and ability but could average only 27. Richard Harden, signed form Somerset to strengthen the middle order, broke his hand in his first match and was thereafter an intermittent performer.

However, his absences meant that the Club had to recall McGrath, dropped the previous year, and he responded well enough to win his cap. For the first time in the century not one Yorkshire batsman reached 1,000 runs.

The one-day form was a series of crashing disappointments. Having reached a Lord's final (the Benson and Hedges Super Cup) for the first time since 1987, Yorkshire were soundly thrashed by Gloucestershire, who repeated their success in the semi-final of the NatWest Trophy, although Yorkshire's batsmen, led by Byas and Gary Fellows, an all rounder from Halifax, gave them a fright in the closing overs.

The National League, the re-styled one-day league competition, began with five victories

Chris Silverwood Spoons

Chris Silverwood was a natural-born fast bowler. Tall, loose and athletic, he also won a karate black belt and enjoyed a fast motorbike. His passion for action and speed was spotted at school. He was encouraged to attend nets in his home town of Pontefract and from there fast tracked to the Yorkshire Academy.

He was 18 when he began making intermittent appearances for Yorkshire II in 1992 making his first-class debut the following year after several seamers senior to him had been released. As his physique and stamina developed he became an increasingly valuable member of the attack but his breakthrough did not come until the 1996 season when, at 21, he took 47 wickets, won his county cap and was elected Young Cricketer of the Year.

The following December he won a first England cap against Zimbabwe but he had to wait another two years before winning his second cap on England's tour of South Africa when he became a regular member of the England attack, a position he was unable to maintain the following Summer despite some outstanding performances. In 1999 he took 59 wickets at 20 and showed increasing confidence as a batsman, turning several matches by his fierce hitting as a tailender, he was also a fast outfielder with a powerful arm.

On form Silverwood was one of the fastest English bowlers at the turn of the century, capable of bowling out the best with his exceptional pace and movement, but his performances were mercurial and it was his inconsistencies that persuaded England, on several occasions, to choose lesser but more reliable performers ahead of him.

After two seasons of intermittent injury he was released to join Middlesex in 2007 where he again enjoyed success, pleasing many Yorkshire supporters who remembered his bowling with admiration and affection.

---

and ended with seven defeats. That Yorkshire did enough to finish in the First Division of both competitions, both leagues having been split into two classes, was due mostly to the bowlers and this despite Hutchison, Gough and Hoggard missing most of the season through injury. In their absence Silverwood bowled so well he was first chosen for the 'A' tour and then promoted to the full England tour of South Africa. He was well supported by White, Hamilton and the now advancing Sidebottom. Yorkshire needed them all.

Yorkshire's progress was handsomely recognised by the England selectors in 2000 who called on Gough, White and Vaughan regularly, all recipients of the new central contracts that gave England first call at all times on their services, and then added Hoggard before the end of the Summer. Sidebottom, too, might have been a candidate had he not suffered a hip injury after taking 22 wickets in four matches. In all the circumstances Yorkshire did well to finish third or, as many members would contend, second but for the intervention of the Board.

Lehmann returned in full glory, averaging 67 from his 1,447 runs and including a century off 89 balls against Kent at Canterbury, the fastest of the season. A delighted Yorkshire promoted him to vice-captain and contracted him for three more seasons.

Byas, Wood and McGrath would all have been disappointed with their batting, Blakey made only 262 runs and lost his place to Simon Guy but Hamilton returned from a disappointing tour of South Africa to show true quality again with bat and ball. The frequent gaps in the team sheet meant that no less than nine players made a debut, six of them in the Championship.

There was limited joy in one-day cricket. Yorkshire lost a Benson and Hedges quarter-final to Surrey far more decisively than the margin of seven runs suggested. Despite having all their England players available Yorkshire lost a fourth round NatWest tie at Northampton in circumstances that left their captain seething. The National League, despite a crushing opening defeat by those perennial victors

Gloucestershire, promised a trophy until, leading, Yorkshire crashed under the floodlights at Canterbury.

Despite all their handicaps, Yorkshire remained potential champions until the closing weeks. Pitch liaison inspectors, introduced to impose a level standard of pitches in county cricket, had cleared Headingley against Kent with a verdict of not proven but at Scarborough, in the final match of the season against champions Surrey they were docked eight points for what was declared to be an unsatisfactory pitch.

It was undoubtedly green and the new ball seamed but few present would have agreed with the Board's verdict that there was variable bounce. *The Times* suggested that Yorkshire had been fined on a 'totting-up procedure'. *The Sunday Times* named former England captain Mike Denness, the Board's Chief Inspector, the 'Pitchfinder General', and Yorkshire committeemen threatened 'blood on the walls' at the Winter meeting of county clubs. The loss of eight points meant that Yorkshire finished third behind Surrey and Lancashire and lost the £50,000 prize money for coming second.

In the end Yorkshire submitted apparently meekly, the threat of losing the £5,000 that had to be posted for an appeal, at a time of stringent economy, seemingly enough. The Scarborough groundsman, who had battled bravely all Summer against sometimes incessant rain, was retired and the matter subsided to the sound of much grinding of teeth in the Ridings. It was hinted, but never confirmed, that one of the reasons for Moxon's departure later that year, to become coach of Durham, was not unconnected with Yorkshire's lack of fight in this instance.

A very popular figure, Moxon ostensibly left his native county over the economies imposed upon the Club by the need to help raise the £10 million required to redevelop Headingley once the Wakefield project had been abandoned. Yorkshire had to find £4 million from their own resources, an enormous burden for a cricket club with few alternative sources of income, but they had little option; unless Headingley was rebuilt and its facilities greatly improved Test-match status would have been lost.

With Moxon gone the Club made a bold move, reaching out to Perth to sign the Western Australian coach Wayne Clark on a three-year agreement. He had won the championship and one-day trophies for the WACA but admitted to a limited knowledge of English cricket and English conditions. It was, Yorkshire officials agreed, a gamble.

After 33 years of disappointment and frustration Yorkshire became England's champions again on 24 August 2001, just after noon and shortly before the rain, threatening Scarborough all morning, arrived in strength. The catch that won the match against Glamorgan, and the title, was fittingly taken by Byas, running, from slip. Had Simon Jones, Glamorgan's number 11, chosen to block out, rather than hit out (he made 46) the weather might have caused a drawn match, and although Yorkshire, with eight wins in 13 matches, were still probable champions, the conclusion might have been tense rather than celebratory. In their last two matches Yorkshire lost to Surrey and Essex.

In truth the tide had flowed Yorkshire's way all Summer. Surrey, the previous champions and favourites, contributed, at various times over the Summer, eight players to England while their principal bowler was required by Pakistan for seven matches. Byas, with a farmer's instinct, gambled successfully on the weather more than once and the decisive stroke was the discovery of two bowlers: Steve Kirby and Richard Dawson.

Kirby's arrival was sensational. He was signed from Leicestershire Second XI before the Headingley match against Kent in early June as a late replacement for Matthew Hoggard, called on by England. Born in Bury, tall, lean, wiry and red-haired, he took 5-9 in 29 balls and finished with 7-50, a figure that turned out to be the best ever by a Yorkshire bowler on his first-class debut (Wilfred Rhodes took 13-43 against Somerset but had played previously against MCC). Kirby finished the Summer with 47 wickets at an average of 20.85 and one leading umpire thought England should have selected him, such was his sustained pace and hostility.

Indeed that belligerence, which contained a menacing glare and advance down the wicket,

Gavin Hamilton

Scottish cricket has always had strong links with Yorkshire so Gavin Hamilton's eventual arrival at the Academy could have been predicted, notwithstanding a roundabout route. A tall, talented all-rounder, he was born in Broxburn but went to school in Kent, played cricket for Sidcup and would surely have been playing for Kent had he not returned to West Lothian after leaving school. He made his debut for Scotland in 1993 and a return of 5-65 against Ireland attracted the attention of the umpire, Jack van Geloven, formerly of Yorkshire and Leicestershire.

The Scotland coach Jim Love, formerly of Yorkshire, endorsed van Geloven's recommendation and Hamilton was recruited into the Academy where he gradually moved up through the Second XI until his sudden surge in form in 1998 turned him into a Test player. In that Summer he scored five half centuries in the last eight matches and his individual performance against Glamorgan at Cardiff, 149 runs and ten wickets in the match, was the best since the days of Hirst and Rhodes. He went on to become Scotland's outstanding player in the 1999 World Cup before being selected for the following England tour of South Africa.

He had a disastrous experience in the one Test he played, collecting a pair and taking punishment when he bowled, and was virtually ignored after that by the selectors although his capabilities, especially in one-

Gavin Hamilton
Yorkshire Post

day cricket, made him a regular contender for a place in the England squad. A cheerful, engaging personality, Hamilton would be delighted to subscribe to the old Edinburgh definition of a Yorkshireman as someone 'good enough to be a second-class Scot'.

He never recovered his pre-Test confidence and after also finding bowling difficult he tried to sustain his career as a batsman but was released by Yorkshire to Durham and from there he returned to Scottish cricket.

caused considerable comment in the media and forced Byas to reprimand him, on the field. Off field Kirby seemed a totally different character, relaxed and popular and by September he could claim to be the second Yorkshire cricketing hero born in Lancashire, after Vaughan.

Dawson was Yorkshire through and through, a tall, fair-haired off-spinner with whirling action that brought a few tut-tuts from the pundits. He arrived via Doncaster Town and the University

of Exeter with some recommendations from Devon that made him first-choice spinner after making his debut at Headingley three weeks after Kirby. His season's 30 wickets were expensive but his brilliant fielding and hint of batting promise (two sixes on debut) won him a place in England's squad for the Winter tours of India and New Zealand. Yorkshire would have undoubtedly preferred he gained more experience before being exposed to India's juggernaut.

The batting, led by Lehmann's average of 83.29, was usually strong enough. Wood came back to form with 1,000 runs and his cap, Byas hit four centuries and White, once free of England responsibilities, made a formidable return as an opener with reduced bowling duties. Vaughan, when available, made audacious contributions. Lehmann's 252 against Lancashire at Headingley, then highest innings in a Roses match, will be long remembered as will his 191 off 103 balls in a National League game at Scarborough. Elsewhere in limited overs Yorkshire were inconsistent, losing in the Benson and Hedges semi-finals, losing in the quarter-finals of the Cheltenham and Gloucester Trophy and just avoiding relegation from the League.

Byas' triumph had come two days before his 38th birthday so it was no great surprise when the season ended with his announcement that he was retiring, the assumption being that he would return to his family's farm in the East Riding. But there were rumours of strain below the surface of success: Darren Gough, easily Yorkshire's most popular cricketer and an England idol, bowled only 88 overs in the Championship and members and supporters were critical of his limited appearances with the county, on and off the field.

In the match after the Championship had been won, a disastrous innings defeat at the Oval, Byas was able to field only four capped players, the inference being that the selection was made by coach Clark and not the captain. Had the captain been at odds both with his coach and his team's most famous player?

Despite the disappointing end to the season all such misgivings were put aside in a general euphoria across the Broad Acres. One famous Yorkshireman declared that the Club were set to resume a dominance comparable with those of the 1930s and 1960s. Lehmann remembered that time in his autobiography (2005): 'Wayne had somehow managed to unite a side that had always had the potential to win but had never delivered. He and David worked so well together to shape a team that believed in itself. We went to play some of the best cricket in my time there with a new positive attitude we had been missing in previous years.'

Lehmann to Gough 2002–2008

In all Yorkshire's history there have been few years to match 2002 for frustration, disappointment, dismay and finally anger on the part of members. After all the glitter and renewed confidence of the previous Summer there could have been few greater contrasts and the winning of the Cheltenham and Gloucester Trophy, on 31 August, only served to emphasise how ruinous had been the previous weeks.

How much the team's performances were affected by the disaster off the field is difficult to determine. At the annual general meeting in March the honorary treasurer Peter Townend had warned of an impending financial crisis. The Club shop could not account for up to £100,000 – police investigated but no charges were brought – and by mid-August, at the bank's insistence, the Committee were replaced by a four-man Board of Management led by the owner of the Costcutter supermarket chain, Colin Graves of York, and including a financial expert Brian Boutell, the Club president Robin Smith, a lawyer, and a former player as Director of Cricket, Geoffrey Cope. The last-named was the only survivor of the previous Committee.

The chief executive Chris Hassell was replaced by Colin Graves, on temporary leave from his business, while the former Committee were dispersed among the Honorary Life Members and Vice-Presidents. These men represented many years of devoted unpaid service to the Club and hardly deserved so abrupt a dismissal, being overtaken as they were by the enormous financial changes sweeping through county cricket and left vulnerable by the fact that the famous Yorkshire County Cricket Club possessed not a square foot of land, hardly a stick of furniture, to offer as collateral for the debts about to be incurred by rebuilding a ground owned by others.

The Committee of 2002 paid heavily for the lack of foresight by their predecessors in the 1930s when Yorkshire, wealthy and successful, could have bought their half of Headingley without great strain. There had been other opportunities, post-war, to make successful agreements that had also fallen by the wayside, partly because for many years Yorkshire and the landlords Leeds Cricket, Football and Athletic Company, the Rugby League club, had cohabited amicably. When it came to the crunch, with the bank insisting on solid financial guarantees, the government of the Club had to pass on.

The membership, normally feisty and reluctant to change, was so shaken by such revelations that an extraordinary general meeting later that month endorsed the changes rather than see the Club founder into bankruptcy and agreed to allow the Club's borrowing limit to rise to £10 million, the first move towards an extensive re-funding needed to rebuild and renovate Headingley as a Test match venue. The arrival of two more potential Test grounds, in Durham and Hampshire, to challenge Leeds on the rota, was reminder enough that the England and Wales Cricket Board, financially driven as never before, were impatient for improvement. The first step, the new Yorkshire Board indicated, would be to negotiate with Leeds Rhinos' owner Paul Caddick.

After Byas' departure the Committee, in one of their last major decisions, had appointed as the Club's new captain the Australian Darren Lehmann to complement the Australian coach Wayne Clark. Members were a little unsure about the new regime. Players turned out for a pre-season function in disparate track suits and too many were spotted unshaven. The assumption was that an Australian air of casualness and relaxation had been introduced. In fact, compounding the disorder off the field, the new uniforms had not arrived in time. The team's hirsute appearance was a part of a bonding exercise that the players thought amusing and enjoyed.

It was a bad start made worse by sudden weakening of the team. The new England system of central contracts meant that two leading players,

Vaughan and Hoggard, disappeared almost entirely. Gough was injured, White realised that his back would not support long bowling spells while the side's other invaluable all-rounder, Gavin Hamilton, lost his ability to bowl. Silverwood, like Gough, was only intermittently fit, neither Kirby nor Dawson were as successful in their second full season, while Matthew Wood, 1,000 runs in 2001, lost form so badly he had to be dropped.

With the Championship due to be split into two divisions Yorkshire knew they were bound for relegation long before it happened. Five of the first six matches were lost despite the captain's always-consistent form. When Lehmann was recalled to Australia's Test team, the team was led by Blakey and with another Australian Matthew Elliott deputising for Lehmann there was a minor revival, but two victories were unable to prevent a fall to bottom. For the first time since 1983 Yorkshire were unable to win a home match.

Blakey, acting as wicket-keeper captain, managed to pass 1,000 runs batting mostly from number seven, a fine achievement, and was in charge of the season's one highlight, a stirring victory over Somerset in the C&G Final at Lord's to which Elliott contributed a sparkling unbeaten 128 and was signed as the overseas professional for 2003.

Repercussions were inevitable: coach Clark could not agree on a revised contract as bowling coach and left a year early. The Club's losses for the year amounted to £1.3 million. When Lehmann, now a regular Test choice, announced he would not be available for 2003, Yorkshire concluded that the wisest (and cheaper) option was to rely on their own: Anthony McGrath was named the new captain, the youngest appointment, at 27, since that of Brian Sellers 70 years before. To further save cash the Club announced that they would appoint only one overseas professional (Elliott) and not the two then allowed by regulations. Spring, as ever, brought hope of a quick revival, a straight return to the First Division and a financial recovery.

Lehmann recalled:

Wherein the previous year luck had smiled on us this year whatever could go wrong did. We didn't play well. The weather was bad just when we needed it to hold up and we couldn't seem to get us wickets no matter how hard we tried. Many guys just seemed to be on a bad run and couldn't turn it around. I was absent on international duty for Australia for about eight weeks of the season and that didn't help.

The end result saw us being relegated to the second division and you can imagine the flak we got for that – from champions to wooden spoonists in one season. I tried my best but some people saw my captaincy as more lenient than that of David Byas and some felt this was the sole reason we went down. This isn't entirely true...but I do allow players some freedom to play their own game and to learn from their mistakes.

Perhaps bizarre is the right word to describe the 2003 season. Promotion to the First Division was not achieved although had rain and bad light not intervened on the last day of the season, against Gloucestershire, a possible victory would have been conclusive. Anthony McGrath had no sooner been acclaimed as county captain, in a good start, when he was whisked away by England and finished by resigning and being chosen for a one-day series in the West Indies. Michael Vaughan, who in earlier times would have been the natural choice as Yorkshire's captain, became England's.

Neither of the team's Test all-rounders Craig White and Gavin Hamilton, were able to bowl. The overseas player Matthew Elliott, such a success in 2002, returned to Australia with a knee injury and to attend to a terminally ill brother-in-law and never returned. In an effort to fill the gap Yorkshire hired three replacements at short notice, Yuvraj Singh, at 19 one of India's most promising young batsmen but one totally inexperienced in English conditions, the New Zealand captain Stephen Fleming who, for all his medals, seemed rarely consulted on the field, and finally Damien Martyn of Australia who, in one memorable afternoon, left an imperishable memory among those watching.

So much of the season revolved around Matthew Wood, the vice-captain, whose personal

Anthony McGrath

Anthony McGrath and Michael Vaughan were contemporaries at Yorkshire schools and the verdict of coaches at the time was that the boy from Bradford would have the starrier future. 'Anthony's hungrier' was one comment. The ability, and the desire, to score runs never left McGrath but just as Vaughan's career seemed to have been guided, a push to the elbow at every corner, McGrath's tended to skid awkwardly. The 2003 season was a turning point.

He made his debut in 1995 at 19 and his powerful right-hand driving attracted immediate attention. *Wisden* mentioned his 'obvious class'. The following Summer brought him one short of 1,000 runs and selection for England 'A' whereupon he consolidated his position in the first-class game but remained in the background for selection for a full cap. He developed as an exceedingly useful medium pace right arm swing bowler and in fact topped Yorkshire's averages in 2002.

Then came 2003. With Darren Lehmann having a sabbatical year and Vaughan captaining England, McGrath accepted an invitation to captain his county. Almost immediately he was called up by England whose coach, Duncan Fletcher, applied rigidly the rights of call-up embedded in the central contracts. McGrath, consequently, was caught between a first Summer as Yorkshire captain and a first season as an England player. The climax came in a Trophy one-day match at Worcester. McGrath was recovering from injury and fully expected to lead Yorkshire; he was knocking up before the start when a call from Lord's ordered him withdrawn because of an impending England fixture. Officially he was pronounced not fully fit. Yorkshire, the Trophy-holders, lost.

He played four Tests that Summer, against Zimbabwe and South Africa, and finished with a highly respectable average of 50, but was then demoted to being a one-day squad player where, used as a bits-and-pieces performer, his career never took off. He did return to Yorkshire and seemed to have assuaged all disappointments with a blaze of runs for his county under Craig White's leadership.

White's resignation, in 2006, seemed to unsettle McGrath for he then asked Yorkshire for his release, rejecting a return to the captaincy and a three-year contract, but Darren Gough's arrival brought a rapprochement and another successful campaign: 931 runs at 46.55 with another 731 runs, at 44.93. Yorkshire were relieved when this talented and invaluable player indicated, late in 2007, that he would not be using the release clause in his contract, staying to become Gough's vice-captain then succeeding him in 2009.

response was to score 1,339 runs at an average of 53.56, including five centuries, one a double. In the absence of Vaughan and McGrath, the only batsman to come near him was Michael Lumb, who just missed his 1,000. The bowling, with Silverwood, Sidebottom and Kirby all taking wickets freely, should have been incisive enough to guarantee promotion, but the spin support was thin while the batting developed an alarming habit of collapsing in the second innings. With Wayne Clark gone Kevin Sharpe was named first-team coach and his partnership with McGrath looked promising until England intervened.

The defence of the C&G Trophy ended at Worcester where McGrath, recovered from injury and expected to play overnight, was declared unfit after a call from Lord's and when Hoggard broke down with a knee injury another campaign faded out. Relegation in the National League, the other one-day competition, did not improve humour and the end of these campaigns meant more changes. David Byas returned from Lancashire to become the new Director of Cricket, Cope becoming Director of Operations with Kevin Sharp re-emerging as batting coach.

After month of rumours Darren Gough left Yorkshire to move nearer his family in the South

Matthew Hoggard

Until 2000, Brian Close held the great distinction of being the only known England player to have been awarded his country's cap before that of Yorkshire. Matthew Hoggard, 51 years later, matched that distinction against the West Indies only to find himself overtaken two years later by Richard Dawson, selected by England to play in India in December 2001 while still wearing the white rosebud in county matches.

Hoggard emerged from Pudsey schools cricket and developed through the Academy where his strength and exceptional pace marked him out while he was a teenager, provoking rumours of attempts by other counties to poach him with offers of substantial contracts. He followed Paul Hutchison, left arm, into the first team thus giving the Club's then Chairman Keith Moss the opportunity to proclaim proudly that two Pudsey lads were opening the bowling for Yorkshire.

Hoggard played for Yorkshire II at 17, played for England Under-19 and in 1998 served as a net bowler before the Test against South Africa in 1998. Allan Donald was so impressed he arranged for Hoggard to spend two seasons playing first-class cricket for Free State where, he admitted, he learned very quickly, particularly from Donald.

Like most modern fast bowlers he suffered a spell of injury in 1999 but by 2000 he was back among the challengers, taking 50 wickets at 24 and demonstrating that he could also make the ball swing in addition to working up considerable pace. He was reserve behind Gough, Caddick and White in the successful tour of Pakistan and Sri Lanka in 2000-01, but his 20 wickets at 9.25 represented a loud knock on the door. He was a significant performer, despite his England calls, in Yorkshire's Championship winning team of 2001 when his calm temperament, application and willingness to bowl no

Matthew Hoggard
Yorkshire Post

matter what the condition made him captain's favourite.

For most of the first decade of the 21st century he was an automatic choice for England, usually opening the bowling, and played a major part in the reclamation of the Ashes in 2005.

Hoggard became such an integral part of Michael Vaughan's England team that Yorkshire crowds saw little of him at his peak when he was the regular first choice for England to take the new ball. In Spring 2005 he was ranked the fifth best seam bowler in world cricket. What made him a popular favourite, especially in his home county, was his deep loyalty to his roots, his Baildon home and his eagerness to turn out for Yorkshire whenever the chance arose.

and joined Essex. White became the new captain, Lehmann returned as the overseas professional and the second vacancy for such was filled by Ian Harvey, an Australian all-rounder who had done wonders for Gloucestershire, especially in the one-day game. The Board made stringent economies in all fields and took a grip in the critical financial situation, and one ray of light was the winning of the Second XI Championship, darkened only by the departure to Nottinghamshire of the successful coach Arnie Sidebottom.

Arnie's departure was followed by that of his son Ryan, a left-arm seamer who played once for England and who, after joining Nottinghamshire, developed into a highly accurate and penetrative performer of his type, playing a considerable part in his new county's success. His departure, along with that of Gough and Hamilton and the virtual retirement of White meant that Byas had to build virtually a new seam attack from scratch.

The new 20-over competition was launched on a Saturday morning at Headingley and attracted a 5,000 crowd and looked to be an immediate hit with the younger element in the crowd, especially with the children. Yorkshire began the last championship match, at Headingley on 17 September, against Gloucestershire, needing a win to gain promotion.

Yorkshire batted first and those present witnessed an astonishing 238 from Damien Martyn that encompassed the seasons' fastest century – 65 balls to win the Lawrence Trophy – off 159 balls including seven sixes and 38 fours. He had scored 87, and suffered a broken nose in his one previous innings for Yorkshire and then insisted in playing in this vital fixture. Many veterans recall this as the best innings they ever saw and more than one posed the question: 'Could Bradman be better than this?'

The Club suffered other losses; Viscount Mountgarret, the president who played a major role in reuniting the Club in the mid-1980s, died along with the popular and highly respected cricket correspondent of the *Yorkshire Post*, Robert Mills, the latter only 51 years of age. A sequence of county *Yearbooks* belonging to Lord Hawke and embossed with his name fetched

£6,500 at auction.

In the mid-1990s Yorkshire's seasonal progress became something of a joke; it was written that they were the only county to hold their end-of-season dinner in July. When Phil Carrick's team won the Benson and Hedges Cup in 1987 it began a trend that saw Yorkshire in several successive seasons begin in storming form and then almost inevitably fade away in August.

Hopes were so high in April 2004. David Byas' return as Director of Cricket was widely applauded, Craig White's appointment as captain was equally popular and the two targets, promotion in the Championship and in the Totesport (one-day) League seemed certain to be attained, especially after an opening win against Essex and five wins in all competitions in June.

From then onwards nothing went right: England, having already claimed Michael Vaughan and Matthew Hoggard, added Anthony McGrath as a permanent 12th man. Australia called on both the overseas players Darren Lehmann and Ian Harvey at various times. Ryan Sidebottom, in his day a left-arm swing bowler of Test class, was sorely missed after preferring to join Nottinghamshire.

These were predictable weakenings and could be anticipated. What was unexpected was the injury and loss of form of key players. White flourished as captain and all-rounder until a back strain in June all but ended his bowling career and his Summer. The Club's remaining fast bowler Chris Silverwood also broke down to miss the second half of the season while Steve Kirby, who Yorkshire hoped would emerge as a leading strike bowler for many years fell away and shocked the membership by opting, in September, to leave for Gloucestershire.

Harvey, who had been signed from Gloucestershire as one of the world's leading all-rounders, especially in one-day cricket, was a grave disappointment, suffering both injury and loss of form. Michael Lumb, capped in 2003 and expected to reach his full potential, managed only 546 Championship runs in 13 matches, while wicket-keeper Simon Guy, Richard Blakey's expected successor, fell below expectations with both bat and gloves.

Darren Lehmann

Such was Yorkshire's admiration and affection for Darren Scott Lehmann that when he retired from county cricket in 2006, after seven magnificent seasons as the county's overseas professional, the Club immediately presented him with a silver cap and Honorary Life Membership, a distinction accorded previously to only to one other Australian, Sir Donald Bradman. 'Boof', or The Boffer, nicknames picked up in his early days in Gawler, South Australia, when playing Rules football, was more than an honorary Yorkshireman; he was, as they say 'one of our lads', an accolade not awarded lightly in a county still harking back to the days when its cricketers had to be born inside the boundaries of the Ridings.

For a start he wasn't the stereotype Australian cricketer, tall, lean, laconic. Stocky, balding, jocular, gregarious, Lehmann shared with many of his hosts a love of bitter ale and tobacco. Such a lifestyle may have horrified the fitness gurus but never seemed to affect Lehmann, whether playing in England or for his home State, for Victoria, or for Australia. It may have been because of the blokey image that he did not make a first Test appearance until he was 28 and was not considered a regular in the side until a recall at the age of 33.

Lehmann nevertheless finished with a Test average of 44.95 from his 27 matches, hitting five centuries and ten fifties, a consistency that he maintained in the domestic game where his first-class figures read 82 centuries at an average of 57.63. Nor did his build prevent his becoming an outstanding one-day player where his prodigious left-hand batting, his fierce driving and immaculate placing fuelled by a hunger for runs, made him a roaring success for his teams. He is one of the few cricketers to win a place in both *Wisden* and *Wisden Australia's* Cricketers of the Year list (2001 and 2005), and he became the leading scorer in Sheffield Shield/Pura Cup history in 2005. He was a winner of the Sheffield Shield in 1991 and 1996 and of the County

Darren Lehmann
YCCC

Championship in 2001.

He came to Yorkshire as second choice in 1997 after Michael Slater had been forced to withdraw after selection by Australia. Yorkshire's record with overseas professionals was poor; of his predecessors only Sachin Tendulkar, more a boy, could be said to have captured the county's attention and even Tendulkar, by his standards, struggled in a damp Summer. Lehmann changed that perception with four centuries and 1,500 runs in his first Summer, averaging 63. In his seven seasons – he took a break in 2003 – he scored 26 centuries and 43 fifties, took 35 catches, some of them stunners, and added 61 wickets with his nifty slow left-arm. His career average, 68.76, is the best by any Yorkshire player.

He managed another eight centuries and 38 fifties in his 130 one-day matches for the country. In his final innings, against Durham at Headingley Carnegie, he could have overtaken Hirst's record score of 341, made at Leicester in 1905, but endeared himself to Yorkshire forever by getting himself bowled after a tired swish on 339, adding: 'I'm quite happy that the record should stay with George Hirst, who was probably a better player than me' to which David Warner, the *Telegraph and Argus* correspondent, responded: 'Only a better bowler, surely?'

David Byas, Lehmann's captain and then manager for most of his Yorkshire career, added that when Lancashire heard the news of his impending retirement, at the Old Trafford fixture, they lined up five

bowlers to each shake him by the hand and wish him a happy retirement. Warner, in a farewell eulogy in the *Yorkshire Yearbook* of 2006, dubbed him 'The Great Entertainer'.

Darren Lehmann married Craig White's sister and the pair of Yorkshire Australians bought adjoining retirement plots in Adelaide where some lucky visitors will be invited to have a beer, and to listen to the tales and laughter until the early hours.

Scorecard signed by Darren Lehmann after his innings of 339 for Yorkshire vs. Durham.
Ron Deaton collection

There were unexpected breaks in the clouds. Australian Phil Jaques, the son of a Sheffielder, deputised magnificently for both Lehmann and Harvey, scoring 1,118 runs in his 11 Championship matches including a memorable 243 on a difficult pitch at Hampshire's new ground, the Rose Bowl. Ismail Dawood from Dewsbury became Yorkshire's wicket-keeper at the age of 27, after serving other counties, and made steady contributions. Richard Dawson, taking 36 wickets with his off spin and reinforcing that contribution with his batting and superb fielding, finally persuaded the Club to cap him

three years after playing for England. History may conclude that the most significant development of a hugely disappointing season was the arrival of Ajmal Shazad, an 18-year-old seam bowler from Bradford who while at Woodhouse Grove had been, according to *Wisden* 'the most discussed schoolboy cricketer in the country'. Shazad made his debut against Worcestershire in a Totesport match and would have played more but for a back strain. The appearance of Dawood and Shazad signalled the entry of the first products from the county's great nursery of second generation children from Asian immigrant families.

And many Yorkshire followers will remember with gratitude Michael Vaughan's brilliant 116, on one of the rare occasions when England would release him, in the C&G quarter-final against Lancashire. Sadly, one swallow did not make a Summer.

There was no question about the targets for 2005: ranked second class in both the Championship and the League, Yorkshire had to convince a dwindling membership and a sceptical public that they were capable of recuperation without their star overseas player Darren Lehmann, leading batsman Michael Vaughan and leading bowler Matthew Hoggard, both of whom were required almost all Summer, by England. Of the Championship-winning attack of 2001, Gough had moved to Essex, Silverwood contributed only 142 overs because of further injury, Hamilton had joined Durham, Sidebottom had gone to Nottinghamshire and White was unable to bowl because of knee and back strains.

That promotion to the First Division of the Championship was achieved was, in retrospect, an unexpected accomplishment, realised by the strength and depth of the batting and the arrival of a fast bowler previously unknown: Deon Kruis, 30, was a South African who qualified to play in England under European Union laws, a so-called 'Kolpak' player. Tall, whippy, consistent and tenacious, he had been playing league cricket with Blackpool and was recommended to Yorkshire by Allan Donald, the great South African fast bowler, to whom the Club would be eternally grateful. Kruis was a major find, taking 64 wickets at an average of 30.64. He became the spearhead and took much weight off the medium-pacer Ian Harvey and the 20-year-old Tim Bresnan.

Harvey had a much more successful season, scoring 772 runs and taking 30 wickets at 26.26, while Phil Jaques, Australian son of a Sheffield family, ensured that Lehmann, taking a break in his long contract, was not missed in the averages. Jacques averaged 64.71, contributing 1,359 runs. Anthony McGrath also passed 1,000, White made 873, Matthew Wood 803, while Joe Sayers, newly arrived from the University of Oxford, Yorkshire's first Blue from the Parks since Geoffrey Keighley, raised 477 runs in nine

innings.

By the middle of May Yorkshire had won three Championship and three League matches and did not lose a first-class match until the last of the season on what director David Byas described as a 'sub-standard pitch' at Northampton. 2005 might have been the Club's first unbeaten season since 1928.

Elsewhere the story was less happy. Thirteen successive defeats left the League season in ruins: Harvey apart, Yorkshire did not have a bowler experienced and skilled enough to bowl successfully in one-day matches. That said, they did contrive to reach the semi-final of the C&G Trophy only to arrive late at the Southampton ground where they were easy meat for a powerful Hampshire team. The Twenty-20 Cup was, once again, a foreign language.

David Byas, as Director of Cricket, was well aware that Yorkshire's elevation had been won principally by some heroic bowling efforts from Deon Kruis and Tim Bresnan and that bowling reinforcements were crucial to a survival in the upper tier of the Championship. He promised that every effort would be made to sign a top-class fast bowler for 2006 and he certainly succeeded in capturing a name – Jason Gillespie, who with Glenn McGrath had formed the spearhead to Australia's world championship team of the previous five years.

Sceptics were quick to point out that Gillespie was available only because he had been dropped by Australia during the losing Ashes Summer of 2005, but Byas' choice seemed endorsed when Gillespie briefly returned to Australia's squad and, indeed, became the world's most famous nightwatchman with an innings of 206 not out against Bangladesh .

As ever in April, hopes were high but it all began to go wrong when Kruis pulled a calf muscle and missed three Championship matches, not surprisingly taking time to work up to his form of 2005. Gillespie, while never collared, did not take wickets until the latter half of the Summer and Bresnan, pushed up to fill gaps, began well enough, bowling and batting to be chosen for England's one-day squad, but then disappeared with a stress fracture. The three leading seamers

Richard Dawson Billy

Bewildering was the appropriate word for Richard Dawson's rise in 2001. He began the year he graduated in Sport Science from the University of Exeter as Yorkshire's second choice off-spinner. As neither he nor the left arm Ian Fisher was given sufficient opportunities on the prevailing seam-friendly surfaces, with Gough, White, Hoggard, Silverwood, Hamilton and Sidebottom all vying for a place, Dawson's prospects did not look especially promising. His parents, concerned about his future, had sought a meeting with coach Steve Oldham who reassured them that he was part of Yorkshire's future.

He was included in the squad to travel to Yorkshire's opening first-class fixture in Canterbury but injured a finger in fielding as 12th man, which delayed his county debut until 29 June at Headingley, first seeking attention with an innings of 37 against Leicestershire that included two leg-side sixes off Philip DeFreitas. Tall, slim, his fielding caught the eye, followed by his zest for bowling, in which he used the advantage of his height to win bounce and demonstrated an ability to turn his off breaks and experiment with the arm ball. The press box, accustomed to a succession of Yorkshire spinners small to medium in stature and low in confidence, sat up.

Dawson's temperament was equally impressive when he took a battering against Northamptonshire on a flat pitch at Wantage Road, finishing with 3-153 in the match. His figures were not much better in the high scoring defeat of Lancashire but in the next Headingley match, against champions Surrey, which put him in direct competition with their Test spinners Saqlain and Ian Salisbury, Dawson finished with 6-98 and more than journalists were sitting up. *The Independent* asked when it was a Yorkshire spinner had last taken six wickets in an innings at Headingley and the *Yorkshire Post* gave the answer: Phil Carrick against Warwickshire in 1989.

Suddenly the air was alive with the queries.

Who was Richard Dawson? He was Doncaster born and played for Doncaster Town, first attending their nets, with his playing elder brother, when he was seven, and winning his first representative honour with Yorkshire Under-11 team at Batley Grammar school. He was chosen for England at Under-14 and captained the national Under-15 team. He also captained Yorkshire's Under-15 team to championship.

When he first attracted the Club's attention he was regarded as a batman who could bowl a little and he took that description to the University of Exeter, where his degree course included psychology, anatomy, sociology and education. He impressed the captain of Devon (and former Somerset captain) Peter Roebuck, who mentioned him to the author, as an outstanding prospect, in 1999. Said Roebuck: 'He doesn't bowl scared. He likes to win. He has something of the Daniel Vettori about him, a wit that takes him beyond the humdrum, a willingness to flap his wings, a sense that cricket is not merely about figures and rewards.'

Dawson captained the University and was then in turn vice-captain and captain of British Universities. Having been contracted by Yorkshire since 1999 he graduated and awaited Yorkshire's call in Spring of the following year.

After his performance against Surrey he played in another six Championship matches as Yorkshire homed in on the title, finishing with 30 wickets at an average of 33.80, significantly bowling more first-class overs, 315, than any Yorkshire bowler. When the tour party for India was announced Dawson's name was among them; whether he would have made his England debut, his 11th first-class match, had Robert Croft, the senior off-spinner, not declined the tour, in Mohali, is a question. But he followed Brian Close and Matthew Hoggard, among the county's post-war players, to win a England cap before Yorkshire's.

Had England held their catches he might have taken six wickets on debut; he did have the satisfaction, in his second Test in Ahmedabad, to dismiss Sachin Tendulkar, then regarded as the world's premier batsman.

Thereafter his career stalled. While his batting and fielding improved to the point he could be classed as a genuine all-rounder, his off-spin became inconsistent. He was also talked of as a future Yorkshire captain and had been offered a further contract when he left to join Northamptonshire in 2007. He was even less successful at Wantage Road and drifted out of cricket, a sad loss to the game.

managed only 101 wickets together.

Off-spinner Dawson, a thinking cricketer ever trying to improve, had a disastrous time as a bowler, taking only eight wickets and was released, with great regret by many Yorkshiremen, to Northamptonshire. The batting struggled to make a good start and both the original choices, Matthew Wood and Sayers, suffered relegation at one point. When the captain, White, concluded that his bowling days had been ended by the chronic threat of back strain and converted to opening batsman, some stability returned. The middle order, where Lehmann and McGrath both had wonderfully successful Summers, and where Lumb played several valuable innings, kept Yorkshire just about afloat until mid-July when the story of the season really began.

Yorkshire, in their history, had never fielded a leg-spinner regularly. Rockley Wilson played in the school holidays in the 1920s and Eddie Leadbeater deputised for Wardle in the 1950s, but the Club's preference was always for a left-arm spinner, who could be trusted to bowl more accurately and thus less expensively. Leadbeater, despite playing for England, and despite playing 81 matches and taking 201 wickets for Yorkshire, was never awarded a cap, a shameful omission.

In July 2006 all such considerations were swept aside when Byas selected not one but two, Mark Lawson and Adil Rashid. The choice was made easier by the fact that both were more than useful batsmen – Rashid was ranked as an all-rounder – and eager fielders. Rashid, 18, took 6-67 on his first-class debut against Warwickshire at Scarborough. Lawson, three years older, had first appeared in 2004, and played in the next two matches, taking eight wickets.

On August 16, against Kent at Headingley, with relegation still a threat, Byas picked the pair in tandem and they responded, on an unhelpful pitch, with aggregates of 31 runs and three wickets in a match reduced to a single innings contest. Back to Scarborough and the flags flew, the pair sharing 12 wickets and sudden media attention. Lawson, it was reported, bowled like his idol Shane Warne, while Rashid showed similarity of style to the great Pakistan and Sussex spinner Mushtaq Ahmed.

Another six wickets were shared in the final draw against Durham and despite a back strain Rashid was chosen for an England 'A' tour that Winter. The Durham match was Lehmann's farewell after seven magnificent seasons and, ever the showman, he went out in style, compiling 339, a record individual score for Headingley and only two short of the county record, set by George Hirst in 1905. The great Australian left-hander then endeared himself to Yorkshire hearts by adding: 'I wasn't too bothered about the record. George Hirst was a better player than me,' a remark that was capped by the Bradford *Telegraph and Argus*' correspondent David Warner: 'Well, a better bowler!'

Lehmann was presented with a silver county cap, and honorary life membership (only the second non-Yorkshireman after Bradman) but all this came after the immediate post-season shocks. Within minutes of the close of the Durham match White announced his resignation as captain, feeling that three years was enough and that he could stand down with dignity after seeing the team safe from relegation.

No Lehmann, no captain for 2007. Worse followed: McGrath, the obvious candidate to succeed Lehmann, and Lumb announced that they both wanted to leave. The Club announced that they would be seeking a new Director of Cricket and that Byas would be offered the post of Cricket Development Director. The turmoil lasted all Autumn. When Byas made it clear that he was not prepared to accept what he saw as a demotion – and cleared his desk – Stewart Regan, the Board's choice of a young chief executive with experience in sports administration, business and marketing, faced a situation that was to be a severe test of his diplomatic and executive skills.

Geoffrey Boycott, who had replaced Geoff Cope on the Board, used his connections to bring Younus Khan, the Pakistan vice-captain, to the Club as one of the overseas professionals. Younus' arrival, announced on 27 October, as one of the world's best batsmen (his astute leg-breaks were to be seen and valued later) made Lehmann's departure less painful. Then, on 2 November, Yorkshire announced a real coup: Chris Adams, who had twice led Sussex to their only championships, would be joining as captain and Director of Cricket.

Adams duly arrived at Headingley, was pictured in a Yorkshire shirt, made the right noises and then rang back the following morning to announce that he would, after all, be staying with Sussex. If Yorkshire were privately furious they were publicly polite and dignified. The feeling on the county circuit was that Adams had made the right choice: in Sussex he would always be a hero and by staying he would not have to uproot a young family. In Yorkshire the expectations would be so high he would be under constant pressure and, being an outsider, could expect twice the flak.

Meanwhile another batting place was filled when Yorkshire announced on 26 January 2007 a three-year contract for the South African Test batsman Jacques Rudolph, again a signing through Boycott's good offices. Rudolph arrived as a 'Kolpak' player, not an overseas professional, who was allowed to make his living within the European Union under trade agreements. Under an informal agreement between the counties Kolpak players were not supposed to be recruited if they had played for their native countries within the previous 12 months.

On those grounds the 25-year-old Rudolph, who

surrendered his Test career for the duration of the contract, was ineligible but the agreement had no basis in law and Yorkshire, despite disapproving noises from several directions, including the ECB, got away with it. Rudolph hinted that he might, like Kevin Pietersen of Hampshire and England, settle in this country. Stewart Regan deflected criticism neatly by pointing out, discreetly, that Yorkshire hardly deserved lectures from other counties on the value of developing home-grown talent.

Another stroke of luck was Pakistan's early elimination from the World Cup tournament being played in the West Indies, allowing Younus to join Yorkshire three weeks earlier than expected. Gradually the pieces dropped into place: the second overseas professional's place had been filled in December 2006 by the returning Jason Gillespie, and the final coup came the following late February when, in the space of nine days, it was revealed that Darren Gough would be returning (from Essex) as captain and Martyn Moxon (from Durham) as Director of Cricket.

Members cool to Gough were delighted with Moxon's return. Gough, winner of a television dancing competition while with Essex, attracted media attention like no Yorkshire captain before him and many Yorkshiremen with a sense of history had a quiet chuckle thinking of how Hawke or Sellers might have reacted to the ensuing hullaballoo. Gough, as a child of the television age, was never fazed by either camera, microphone or tape recorder, and the consequent publicity and exposure brought instant dividends in increased membership and Test match bookings. Yorkshire were news again.

The first benefit of Gough's return was a change of mind by Anthony McGrath, on 2 March, who not only agreed to the new contract but became vice-captain, saying: 'I have been very impressed by the progress Yorkshire have been making and, most importantly by the appointment of a captain whom I fully support.' Sadly, Michael Lumb could not be dissuaded from departing and duly joined Hampshire.

When the 2007 season got under way, in the warmest April for 300 years, the momentum given to the team by the reinforcements, Gough's leadership and Moxon's direction brought

Ryan Sidebottom

Ryan Sidebottom's debut for England, against Australia at Lord's in 2001, seemed almost inevitable. The son of Arnie, who also bowled seamers for Yorkshire and England and by then the coach in charge of Yorkshire, Ryan had the additional virtue of being one of those rare cricketers who can bowl fast left-arm.

He emerged, along with Silverwood and Hoggard, from the Academy in the mid-1990s, and although entry to the first team was delayed for a while by his fellow left-arm seamer Paul Hutchison, a series of injuries to the latter brought Sidebottom his first-team debut in 1997. He had an out-standing Summer in 2000 and was on course to win awards and be chosen for an England Winter tour when he was badly injured in his run-up at Scarborough in July and did not play again.

He regained his place in the England pecking order with a successful 'A' tour of the West Indies the following Winter and did win promotion to a full England cap, as a reward, the next Summer. He was an improving deep fielder and a stubborn tail-ender and must have been disappointed,

Ryan Sidebottom
Yorkshire Post

like Silverwood, not to have been chosen for the Winter tour of India in 2001-02 when both Darren Gough and Andrew Caddick elected not to tour.

---

resounding victories over Surrey and Durham and the better of a draw against the Championship favourites Hampshire. It was not until nearly mid-May that the team lost, and then in a one-day match against Leicestershire.

The first victory, at The Oval, was of such dimensions, 348 runs, as to leave many members in disbelief. It was Yorkshire's first Championship win in Kennington for 29 years (a statistic slightly distorted by the seasons in which the two clubs had played in different divisions), it was Yorkshire's second heaviest defeat of Surrey in history and several county batting records were swept away. Four batsmen, Rudolph, on debut, Bresnan, Gillespie and White, the last-named in the second innings, hit centuries; Bresnan and Gillespie's 246 was a ninth-wicket record, Gillespie's 123 not out set a

new highest score for a number ten, while Rudolph and Rashid, with 190 for the sixth wicket, forged a new record against Surrey.

A Yorkshire start of 127-5 hardly suggested the splendours to come, but when Surrey did get to bat they faced a total of 594-9. Their response, with Newman and Ramprakash adding 196 for the second wicket, hinted at another high-scoring Oval draw but once Rashid had tempted Newman into giving a catch into the deep the breach was made. The leg-spinner took another three wickets in the next 14 balls. Gough chose not to enforce a follow-on, White and Sayers raised 163 for the first wicket in a race to boost the lead; a second declaration left Surrey to make 517 to win but they were blown away by Hoggard and Gough on the last day.

The following week brought a one-day win against Nottinghamshire followed by a nine-wicket trouncing of Durham, and for a few days Yorkshire's ebullient captain could swagger in the company of Hawke, Sellers and Close. Hampshire, at Headingley Carnegie, proved a more durable opposition, raising 665 runs and forcing a draw and although Worcestershire were hammered, by an innings and 260, to confirm the leadership of the Championship table, the team's season had in fact already reached its peak by the second week of May.

There followed the wettest Summer since records began. Hours, then days, without play followed, practices were driven indoors and then the Twenty-20 competition arrived to bring further disruption to form. The south-eastern counties had marginally better weather, and thus more play, and Sussex, in the end, deservedly retained the pennant, Yorkshire losing disastrously to Lancashire, in Leeds, and Sussex, at Hove. The one-day competitions were a familiar tale, forcing wins followed by inexplicable collapses. As Martyn Moxon said, in summing up a Summer when, despite the setbacks, Yorkshire were still in contention until the final week: 'We must be more consistent.' Rudolph proved to be a great success, reaching 1,078 runs, taking some high-class slip catches and the occasional wicket and was awarded a longer contract. Younus, undoubtedly a batsman of high class, was sporadic and less successful in the damp, McGrath averaged 46 and just missed 1,000 runs, indicating in the Autumn that he would be staying with Yorkshire. If Rashid's 40 wickets were expensive (39.45) he made a spectacular advance as a batsman, with 790 runs at an aver-

age of 46 and was, at 19, acclaimed by both the Cricket Writers' Club and his fellow professionals of the PCA as the Young Cricketer of the Year.

Gough kept going splendidly at age 36 to take 37 wickets at 23.67, contributing useful batting and, as always, proving a redoubtable competitor with bat and ball in the one-day competitions. Some of his captaincy decisions were less rewarding, notably a decision to bat first (after a day-night match the previous evening) against Lancashire at Headingley, the scoreboard at one point reading 22-5. Two of the Colts, the slow left-arm David Wainwright and the vigorous all-rounder Richard Pyrah made an impact in limited overs and many members felt that both, and the high-scoring left-hander Adam Lyth, might have been given a longer run in the Championship.

Certainly the last fortnight of the Summer brought fierce argument among members and supporters when the Club, using vacancies caused by national recalls, enlisted two Pakistani Test players, the former captain Inzaman and the off-spinner Tahir, to reinforce the side. Their performances brought some not unexpected derision directed at a county that was once so insistent on playing only its native sons.

Rain and injury followed Yorkshire into 2008 when both the contracted overseas professionals (only one was permitted to play at a time) were injured in May. The Club were able to shed their meaningless one-day name Phoenix and re-emerge, courtesy of their partner, as Yorkshire Carnegie.

A Quiet Word from the Bank

Perhaps Yorkshire's greatest concern as the Club entered the 21st century was the retention of Test match status for Headingley in the face of declining income. All those Test match grounds outside of Lord's, where MCC's 18,000 members provided a cushion against any hard fall, faced a similar situation. Yorkshire, Lancashire, Surrey, Nottinghamshire and Warwickshire, the traditional Test match counties, had to update their facilities and improve their capacities if they wished to remain on the Test circuit before the growing challenge from Durham, and, in the distance, Hampshire and Glamorgan.

With attendances and membership subscriptions reducing, alternative income had to be found beyond the annual distribution by the England and Wales Cricket Board of the money received from Test matches and the televising rights. Only Yorkshire, of the Test match counties, were without the collateral provided by income accruing from ownership of the ground. Yorkshire had nothing to offer in going to a bank for a loan beyond 150 years of history and tradition, assets impossible to evaluate by even the most sympathetic and supportive of bankers. Lord Hawke's cosy arrangement of 1890, whereby Yorkshire would rent a ground from the Leeds Cricket, Football and Athletic Company (aka Leeds Rhinos from 1995), the two Clubs exchanging board members, gentlemen to gentlemen, over brandy and cigars, became a source of bitter argument in the closing years of the century, with lawyers on call.

Yorkshire had long been aware of the approaching crisis and in 1997 the Committee, under Byford's leadership, offered an alternative route with a bold plan to build a brand new stadium close by the confluence of the M62 and M1 motorways, near Wakefield. Yorkshire's decision to leave Leeds alerted the city, council and citizens, to the possible departure of a major medium of international publicity. Leeds, at the turn of the century, prided itself on being the UK's fastest growing city, but in Trinidad and Tasmania, Leeds was a place where England played Test matches.

The Rhinos, in turn, made it plain that they would not forgo a profitable rental arrangement and, in particular, the loss of income from food, drinks and advertising ensuing from the lease, without substantial compensation. At one point, in the months of hectic negotiations that followed, they issued writs against both Yorkshire CCC and Wakefield Council. Some Yorkshire members based in Leeds and in the so-called 'golden triangle' between York and Harrogate, an area that formed, after the retreat from Sheffield, Hull and Middlesbrough, the Club's heartland, were equally vociferous against the prospect of moving eastwards.

All had seemed in place when the 1997 AGM, held in Leeds Town Hall, approved, by a 3-1 majority of members, a move to the new £50 million stadium at Durkar by the River Calder. The winding down at Leeds was due to start at the end of that Summer with the final departure coming in 1999. Championship matches, possibly even Test matches, in 2000, would be played at Durkar. A debate began over what to call Durkar with 'New Headingley' the favourite proposal. 'At least it would be one up on Old Trafford' commented the 1998 Yearbook.

The planned move also confirmed the advance, in many eyes, that the Club had made under the joint management of Sir Lawrence Byford as President and then Chairman of the General Committee and Chris Hassell, as Chief Executive. Byford, who had risen from beat constable to HM Chief Inspector of Constabulary, had been elected President in 1991, the same year that Hassell succeeded the late Joe Lister. Byford also became Chairman of the General Committee that year to emerge as the most powerful individual in Yorkshire cricket since Lord Hawke had combined both presidency and captaincy in the early years of that century.

Byford, as his service record suggested, was accustomed to making decisions quickly and acting decisively and must have found Yorkshire's form of government, a labyrinth of sub-committees – 'democracy gone mad' was one description – a tortuous experience. Hassell, with a footballing background that included the secretaryship of Everton when that football club was the fiefdom of multi-millionaire John Moores, was well suited to act as bridge between the General Committee and the President. When, in 1993, Keith Moss, elected to the Committee with an outstanding record as an administrator and money-raiser in the Bradford League, became Yorkshire's Finance Chairman, the Club seemed all set to advance into the 21st century with flags flying and trumpets blowing. What appealed to many members was that all three men arrived in office without baggage, without being regarded as pro- or anti-Boycott, in the argument that had riven the Club for the better part of 20 years.

Yorkshire even made use of new technology, signalling their ambition to be thought cool and up-to-date, with a video tape 'Gathering Pace', and it was at Byford's initiative that the Club set up its first marketing department. He also, after much debate among members, won acceptance for the recruitment of an overseas player, the Club's first being Sachin Tendulkar, secured after winning a substantial sponsorship from Yorkshire Television.

With the Club's accounts moving into the black, the major obstacle remained: the Rhinos' ownership of Headingley. When Byford became a member of the small ECB Executive Committee it was made plain to him that the ECB was very unhappy at the amount of cash accruing to the Rhinos from Leeds' Test match receipts. Yorkshire's offers to buy the ground were declined so the decision was taken to try to find a new ground. Chris Hassell circulated Yorkshire cities. Leeds offered a site at Bramham but no financial support. Wakefield offered the Durkar enclave with no building costs, those to be carried mostly by regeneration grants from the EEC.

As negotiations dragged on, with Leeds Rhinos, Leeds and Wakefield Councils and the various sports funding bodies, including the National Lottery, the Club became increasingly reliant upon Robin Smith, a 56-year-old lawyer, senior partner with the Club's solicitors in Leeds. By 1998 it was clear that links with Leeds and Headingley were all but unbreakable and that the funding for the move to Durkar, dependent upon several sources, was uncertain. The Club had to recognise that there was no alternative than to concentrate all resources upon major developments at the headquarters ground. Money had to be raised, quickly, to ensure that Headingley remained a Test match venue and that the food, drinking and advertising income be absorbed and expanded. The final blow for Wakefield came when the Government ordered a public inquiry into the planning application, the suspicion arising that Deputy Prime Minister John Prescott had been pressurised by Leeds' Labour MPs.

Two major structures were put in hand, the complete rebuilding of the old Western Terrace to produce a new West Stand of 21st century proportions and the erection, on what was once the bowling green, of a new East Stand that combined offices, an indoor school, a Long Room for members and a hotel, the rooms of which could be converted into hospitality boxes for major occasions. In addition an old disused warehouse across St Michael's Lane from the ground was converted, initially through the initiative of Committee member Tony Vann and a sympathetic and generous Leeds businessman Arnold Ziff, into a palatial new indoor school and cricket centre, attractive enough eventually to win sponsorship from the Bradford and Bingley Building Society. The total cost was estimated at £9 million and the money had to be borrowed.

Keith Moss and the Committee were able to win a grant of £2.5 million from Sport England, £1.5 million from Leeds City Council (relieved that Test cricket was staying in the city), £1 million from investments, £2 million from the Bank and then finally a further £1 million loan from Leeds City Council phased over ten years. Sir Lawrence Byford accepted the new reality but stepped down from the presidency after nine years and the Committee, no doubt aware of tricky times ahead, nominated Robin Smith as his successor in 2000, Keith Moss becoming Club Chairman. Byford, and Smith had seen the role of president changing from being mostly ambassadorial to direct leadership in difficult circumstances.

Smith was expected to behave in Committee and in public as an impartial and supportive President and as someone who would be beyond personal criticism when problems occurred and became public. How this was to be achieved while he was a participant in the decision-making process by his presence at Committee meetings was, he thought, a mystery and very worrying when things began to go awry. Although the Championship was won, amid great jubilation in 2001 after a gap of 33 years, the 2001 balance sheet made alarming reading: a loss of £231,523 while the income from the shop fell from £32,522 to £460, flashing red lights everywhere. The crash came the following Spring: a loss of more than £1 million was reported while the shop showed a deficit of £174,290.

Both figures staggered the membership and although there were many separate causes – players' salaries topped £1 million for the first time, an expensive computer system had to be replaced, administration and marketing costs ballooned while ground expenses rose by £140,000 because of the new arrangements at Headingley – there were angry calls for heads to roll. Police inquired into the shop fiasco but no charges were laid, although it seemed impossible for such a disaster to happen without some dishonesty.

The appointment of a marketing manager had been controversial, the Committee being split, angrily, as to the level of his qualifications. Other factors contributing to the overspend were the demands of the new Health and Safety regulations, Leeds city's rules on access, the Rhinos' priority on parking and access in fixture overlaps or clashes – this a result of the switch to Summer Rugby League in 1995 – and revised details from consulting engineers. Nevertheless, as Moss pointed out, both the new West and East Stands were completed on time despite having to change the contractor for the East Stand after the original builder had sought an extra £1 million in the price with no guarantee of meeting the original date. That both projects were on schedule put Yorkshire in credit with the ECB in the protracted talks over future Test match programming.

Twice Smith surprised the Committee by intervening at meetings to warn of the peril of increasing debt. Yorkshire had existed for 140 years without being obligated to anyone for cash – 'Why do we need extra money?' Secretary Joe Lister had asked on one famous occasion in a debate over subscriptions. For the first time Yorkshire, a members' club, had to keep creditors happy and, when the builders' demands for payment increased prematurely, the Bank had a quiet word. Smith feared outside pressures would force the Committee to call an extraordinary general meeting to sanction increased borrowing at a time when the team were heading for the Second Division, only a year after winning the Championship. Members and supporters were restive and if the Committee was forced into an EGM, a row, unholy even by Yorkshire's standards, was certain.

Smith left in mid-Summer for a short holiday in Portugal before being summoned to an emergency Committee meeting at which Chairman Moss revealed that the surveyor had warned that the contractors' bills were likely to exceed expectations by £2 million. The Bank had another quiet word: how was the gap to be bridged? All departments had been asked to make savings, but it was clear there would still be an unfundable debit.

As both President and legal adviser Smith then had to explain to the Committee that members were exposed to a risk of personal liability if the Club tried to soldier on without adequate financial resources. Another approach had to be made to the Bank, this time with a convincing argument, and Smith prepared a recovery plan.

It was clear to Smith that the banker – Wayne Bowser of HSBC in Leeds – would have to be confident that Yorkshire could fulfil any fresh pledges and for that the Club needed a new system of governance plus outside reinforcements of stature and substance and new funding. At the crucial meeting Smith took with him one member of the current Committee, the former England spinner Geoff Cope, to represent the cricket element and a man not without business experience. He also invited along Colin Graves, head of the Costcutter supermarket chain and a cricket devotee, a player and pillar of the Dunnington club in the York Senior League, and Brian Boutell, an accountant of great experience, head of KPMG in Leeds, and of considerable standing in the banking community in West Yorkshire; a man with 'an unrivalled reputation for probity and common sense' was one description. Boutell had no need to present credentials as to his tenacity and staying power: at the age of 54 he had completed the New York Marathon.

Smith's proposals, endorsed enthusiastically by the quartet, were drastic: Yorkshire's governance would change, from rule by committee elected by members, to a Board of Management whose authority would be a mandate from the AGM. For the first time succession planning would be possible. Costs would be slashed drastically, income increased (Costcutter seconded a top-rated marketing professional Ian Bishop to Yorkshire at no expense), Colin Graves would act as Chief Executive for at least two years, replacing the retiring Hassell, and negotiations would start to buy the Headingley ground, and its income streams, from Leeds CF&AC.

Wayne Bowser agreed to the rescue plan and also to support Smith in explaining the Bank's position to the Committee which, in turn, had to be persuaded to transfer all its powers to the Board and to accept the new constitution to be put to members. At the crucial meeting Moss, as Chairman, quoted Macbeth: 'If it were done when 'tis done, then 'twere well it were done quickly.' Graves and Boutell waited outside the door while Smith and Cope strongly advocated the new plan. This was, suggested one commentator afterwards, perhaps the only occasion in history when turkeys actually voted for Christmas. But, in truth, there was no alternative and the Committee, for all the criticism hurled at them for two years, had the good sense to see that without the Bank's support there would be no Club. Wayne Bowser's realistic appraisal of the Bank's requirements was the crucial argument.

The credit for resolving the crisis at that meeting, with no spillover, went to Chairman Keith Moss, who assessed what had to be done and then withdrew. Years afterwards Smith paid this tribute: 'Keith resigned immediately after that meeting and earned my admiration. It was a self-

less act in support of the Club. His legacy will remain in the new East and West Stands and the Cricket Centre.'

The Club's total liability was either £12,682,000, or £6,900,000, both very serious figures depending upon different starting calculations, when the new Board, endorsed by 96% of the membership at an EGM in December 2001, took office with Smith as President and Chairman, Graves as Chief Executive, Boutell as Director of Finance and Cope in charge of Cricket. The hospitality budget, costing £30,000 in 2001, was cut to the bone, leaving most of the Club's elder statesmen aggrieved. The cricket budget, the core business, was maintained and protected.

The Board had to advance on three fronts: to maintain credibility with the Bank, to negotiate successfully with the Rhinos and the club's owner Paul Caddick and to convince the ECB that Headingley was the right and proper place for Test matches. The crunch came in 2005 when the ECB, as a condition of continued Test matches in Leeds, laid down a 31 December deadline for confirmation that Headingley, and the vital income streams, were Yorkshire's.

By then the Rhinos had drawn a third partner into the Headingley complex, Leeds Metropolitan University, and with their support a triangular arrangement was arrived at whereby the University would have, in effect, another campus on the ground, using part of a planned new stand on the Rugby Ground. Smith had previously approached the Vice-Chancellor with the idea that a new pavilion, to be built on the Kirkstall Lane side of the Cricket Ground, could also house a university department; the plans were complementary. The terms of the deal to buy the ground, though not ideal, satisfied the central ECB requirement for a negotiated 15-year Test match staging agreement. The purchase of the ground and its income streams was completed, just, by the 31 December 2005 deadline with a further £9 million loan from Leeds City Council. The financial surge was instant with the 2006 balance sheet showing a profit of £276,000 and the new income streams bringing in £1 million a year.

The rescue plan complete, Smith stood down as President and Chairman but remained a member of the Board while Graves, without whose support and bank guarantees through the crisis the Club could not have survived, became Chairman. Geoff Cope retired and his vital cricketing input was replaced by the election of former Captain and Committee member Geoffrey Boycott, the benefit of whose world-wide contacts was felt immediately. The Board went outside cricket to find a new Chief Executive in Stewart Regan, a 41-year-old with an outstanding record in the Football League Championship. The most tumultuous five years in the Club's history, to much of which Yorkshire's following was oblivious, their attention being riveted on the roller-coaster progress of the team, settled into the exceedingly warm Spring of 2007.

It had been, as one Board member put it, 'a hairy ride'. Without the financial crisis there would have been no constitutional reform. Without a new governance there would have been no bank support. Without bank support there would have been no purchase of the lease and the retail streams. Without ownership of the ground and the income ensuing there would have been no staging agreement with the ECB and probably no more Test matches in Leeds. Without Test matches ... ? Sometimes there is a rhythm to events, or what Bismarck called 'the iron dice of destiny'.

Weather Fine, Wicket Good: Yorkshire Grounds

Before the start of each day's play in every first-class match played in England for most of the last century, the representative of the Exchange Telegraph Agency in the press box had to telephone to London the state of the weather and the pitch; he needed to be conservative in his assessments. The ExTel's copytakers and sub-editors did not take kindly to judgements outside the norm: ''Ere mate, wot's all this abaht then? Wicket dangerous? You can't say that. Wicket wearing? Will that do? Thanks mate. 'Ear from you at 11.30, then?'

Each partner having had a little joke, the day's business started as it had done in Yorkshire from around the middle of the 19th century as the county side had turned out at Darnall, Hyde Park, Bramall Lane, Holbeck, Wakefield, Bradford, Dewsbury, Hunslet, Headingley, York, Halifax, Huddersfield, Hull, Harrogate, Scarborough, Barnsley, Middlesbrough and Abbeydale. We have read much of some of the exploits on those early grounds, and we owe the following account of the smartly named Savile Town, Dewsbury, to Peter Snape.

Yorkshire played county cricket there, usually during Dewsbury Feast week, from 1867 to 1933 and of the first-class counties only Middlesex and Glamorgan were never visitors. In 1921 a crowd of 11,000 saw the first Saturday start to a Championship match, against Sussex, and a total of 29,000 watched Warwickshire four years later. Even the Roses match was scheduled at Savile Town in 1886 but Lancashire never got on the field, all three days being washed out.

According to Snape, Dewsbury was favoured because the Club President Ellison, enjoyed grouse shooting with Lord Savile's agent and once the President had satisfied himself that the ground was large enough (the playing area is bigger than Park Avenue's), county cricket continued there until 1933 when complaints about the lack of covered accommodation ended that era. Grace, Jessop, Spofforth all appeared at Savile

Town, although there were grumbles late last century when it was said that the local hotel accommodation was 'hardly suitable for gentlemen cricketers'. Cambridgeshire were Yorkshire's first opponents there, Luke Greenwood and Tom Emmett sharing 14 wickets in a four-wicket victory. Ted Wainwright performed the hat-trick, Hirst took three wickets in seven balls against Nottinghamshire, Oldroyd hit three centuries in five years, Sutcliffe topped 200 in successive seasons. Greenflies stopped play when Jessop was batting in 1904 and seven years later the Northamptonshire visit coincided with the coronation of George V. At lunch interval a baritone led the singing of the national anthem, accompanied by the orchestra of the Dewsbury Empire. In 1899 Derbyshire took the field in their normal clothing, their kit being sodden after the dressing room had been flooded by a tap left on overnight, as Yorkshire scored the 32 needed to win. In 1890 a manufacturer living nearby offered to buy supper for the players if one could put a ball through his conservatory window, and giant Australian Bonnor duly obliged.

Yorkshire's headquarters are now at Headingley Carnegie but that ground did not enter the schedule until 1890, Lord Hawke being Chairman of the Leeds Cricket, Football and Athletic Co Ltd (now better known as Leeds Rhinos, the Rugby League Club). Nine years later Headingley joined Trent Bridge on the Test match rota, giving the ground premier position in the county, a status Bramall Lane did not relinquish without a struggle, promoting a Test match in Sheffield in 1902.

David Thornton, in his booklet *A Century at Headingley*, hints at Saxon origins – 'The Forest Clearing that belongs to Hedde' – and by early last century the land was owned by Lord Cardigan, presumably of the Balaclava family. A club named Leeds St John's played rugby there, in blue and amber, and when the new Leeds club set about erecting a stadium, at the then sensational expense of £20,000, there were only a few protestors.

A resident of Cardigan Road wrote to the *Yorkshire Post* in July 1890, complaining that 'great quantities of ash-pit refuse are being used for raising the level of ground round the cricket field. The smell arising from this garbage is disgusting.' Critics of the Headingley pitches from other parts of the kingdom should note carefully that no part of this 'disgusting garbage' is reported as being on the cricket field.

On 27 May 1890, a crowd of 5,000 attended the opening of the new ground to watch Leeds play Scarborough and a famous ground's history began. In 1893 it was favoured by rugby union, the Yorkshire Cup Final being played there as was a Scotland-England international attracting a record 30,000. Eight years later came the split, with Leeds joining the newly formed Northern Union that became in time Rugby League. In June 1891 Yorkshire played their first match, a friendly, at Headingley, and lost to Derbyshire by 45 runs. Two months later the first Championship game was played there, a draw against Kent.

Jackson scored Headingley's first first-class century, 145 against Nottinghamshire in July 1894, and in June 1902 Yorkshire bowled out the Australians there for 23 (Jackson 5-12, Hirst 5-9). Sutcliffe scored 270 there, Verity took all ten against Nottinghamshire in May 1931, but the ground will perhaps be best remembered for Bradman. The great Australian scored 334 there in 1930, 304 in 1934, 106 and 16 in 1938 and 33 and 173 in 1948. His 309 in a day in 1930 (105 before lunch, 115 between lunch and tea, 89 to close) is an innings that appears unsurpassable.

Headingley had long held a reputation for helping swing bowling when under cloud cover, so it is not surprising that Trueman who could swing the ball in addition to using the seam, all at considerable pace, should find it a highly successful home. It has been a good ground for England, despite the many complaints over the years; the defeat of Australia in 1956 was the start of six successive victories at Leeds.

Boycott scored his 100th century at Leeds in August 1977, and in July 1981 Headingley laid claim to promoting the greatest ever Test match;

England followed on to Australia in the Third Test and on the Monday morning resumed 92 behind with three wickets standing. With nothing to lose Dilley and then Botham began hitting out, Botham picking up the tempo to score a magnificent 149 not out. Australia needed only 130 to win with most of two days remaining, but an inspired Willis, shrewdly captained by Brearley, took 8-43 and to the exhilaration of most of the United Kingdom, England won an astonishing victory by 18 runs.

Hawke's vision, and that of Sir Edwain Airey, Chairman for 32 years, was enlarged after the Second World War although, in the view of many, the ground was not improved by the building of a new small pavilion, square to the pitch, to house Yorkshire's offices and the dressing rooms after the move from Park Row in the city centre. In early 1989 the two clubs, Yorkshire and Leeds CF&AC, unveiled a planned new development of the Grandstand and West Terrace costing £2.7 million, stopped by local objections.

Bramall Lane was part of the Duke of Norfolk's estate, not inappropriate because that most 'Yorkshire' of England kings, Richard III, revived the dukedom. 'Lord's is upper class, Worcester New Road is middle class, Bramall Lane is working class and proud of it' is an old saying about this grimy but much loved old stadium, focus of many of the hopes and dreams of the Sheffield grinders and cutlers, hosting as it did the Sheffield United Cricket and Football Club as well as Yorkshire. Near the city centre, it cost little to reach and until just after the Second World War the crowd was renowned for its appreciation of the finer points; an ovation for a performance at Sheffield, it was reckoned, was worth a gold watch elsewhere.

Such was the industrial haze surrounding the ground – although in 1855 it was chosen as a site because, the Duke stated, 'it was free from smoke' – that it became a visitors' joke that when they went in to bat every chimney for miles around was immediately stoked up. Yet both Bradman and Sutcliffe held it in affection, Sutcliffe declaring it to be 'fitting Yorkshire cricket better than any other ground'.

Visitors were also targets for verbal volleys, sometimes witty, sometimes crude, usually caustic. Denis Compton, batting on yet another pitch drying after rain, spent much time battering at offending pieces of turf and was assailed by 'Dosta want roof t'cave in?', the implication being that there were miners beneath the square.

In 1968 Bramall Lane gave Trueman, on his home first-class ground, his greatest moment. Deputising for Close as captain, he allowed Yorkshire to pile up 335-9 and then helped dismiss the Australians for 148 and, following on, 138 (Trueman's match figures were 6-83, Ilingworth's 8-67).

In 1972 the Football Club foreclosed on cricket, Yorkshire and United's cricket section being exiled to find new homes. Yorkshire became guests of the Collegiate Cricket Club in leafy Abbeydale, as contrasting an environment to Bramall Lane as could have been found in Sheffield. Boycott certainly took to Abbeydale, scoring five centuries there including two superbly defiant innings against Derbyshire on very difficult pitches. In 1983 Derbyshire recorded their first win over Yorkshire for 25 years.

Yorkshire first played at Park Avenue, Bradford in 1881 and continued for 104 years until the burden of ground maintenance and the improvement required by law proved to be too much for both the Bradford club and Yorkshire. Park Avenue's demise as a cricket ground was followed almost immediately by the formation of a society, 'The Friends of Park Avenue', dedicated to winning back first-class status. The temporary establishment of the Cricket Academy there in 1989 was a pledge of help from the county club.

Park Avenue was thought by many members and supporters to be the most 'Yorkshire' of all the county grounds, dominated by a stylish old Victorian pavilion that always seemed on the point of collapse, with two sides of the ground white-walled and fronted by wooden benching. For most of its life the end opposite the pavilion was occupied by the rear of the Bradford Park Avenue Football Club's grandstand, surmounted by a clock, a recognised target for the big hitter. The small playing area, particularly straight, made it hazardous for spinners and both Rhodes and Verity suffered for their art before Bradford's shrewd and perceptive crowd.

Scarborough is best known for the Festival, the traditional end of the English cricket season during the early days of September. Yorkshire first played there in 1896 and since then it has become renowned for its ability to combine good cricket with a vacationing air, indeed, Kilburn described the town as 'first-class cricket on holiday'. Sadly much of the Victorian elegance of the resort has disappeared under a multitude of slot-machines and fast-food takeaways and one cannot now imagine why Delius chose to spend time there at the end of the last century.

Yet North Marine Road retains its charm: the pavilion is unspoilt, despite alterations, the marquees and the flags and the band bring an authentic touch to the Festival and the press box remains one of the best-sited in the world. Scarborough's resplendent years were during the Edwardian Golden Age when all the great names expected to end their Summer in that town in the great traditional fixtures Yorkshire v MCC, Gentlemen v Players and an invitation (Levenson-Gower's, Pearce's) against the touring team.

Lord Londesborough was the first great patron and it was his grandson, Osbert Sitwell, whose autobiography was quoted in George Plumptre's *Homes of Cricket*: 'there was feasting in the hot tents of the rich at the ground's edge. My grandfather, the founder and the president, delighted to entertain…the tents blazed with ties of the cricketing clubs and the port-wine coloured faces of the aficionados, and between the rounds of cold salmon and cold chicken we would have to sit and watch…'

C.I. 'Buns' Thornton first raised the invitation XIs and was also renowned for hitting the ball over the high Victorian lodging houses at the Town End and into adjoining Trafalgar Square. In more recent times the Australian Pepper reached the Square over the buildings.

The pitch has a reputation for helping free-scoring batsmen. Lester and Byas being graduates, but the early morning sea air, somewhere between a mist and a drizzle, known locally as a 'fret', can give considerable help to seam bowlers and there have been a few startling collapses in Scarborough's history. In the 1980s the Festival was given over almost entirely too one-day cricket, which attracted the holidaying public and swelled the Club's funds but won little favour with the traditionalist Yorkshire members. England played New Zealand in a Prudential Trophy one-day international in 1978 and in 1989, for the first time, the Roses Championship match was allocated to North Marine Road.

Another festival took place at Harrogate in mid-season, giving a welcome opportunity to cricket-

Hull had become so neglected that it was no real surprise when Anlaby Circle was first struck off the Championship list and then, off the one-day schedule.

Acklam Park, meanwhile, developed into a splendid playing area, supplying other parts of England with chief groundsmen of impeccable credentials. First-class cricket arrived in 1956 and in the early years the pitch had a poor repu-

A packed Headingley for the July 1948 Ashes test match
Yorkshire Post

lovers to visit that handsome town that seems to have captured much of the North Yorkshire charm once held by Scarborough. In the Silver Sixties Harrogate became Yorkshire's favourite ground, for four of the six Championships in that decade were won at St George's Road.

It was also at Harrogate, during the Tilcon Trophy one-day competition, that umpire Don Oslear first formulated the solution to finding a result when the weather had washed out a chance of a full match by devising a competition of skill that involved bowling at a single stump.

Yorkshire played at Hull until superseded in the fixture list by Middlesbrough, where the club committee at Acklam Park always seemed the more aware of just what was required to attract and to keep a first-class fixture. The facilities at

tation with batsmen – Yorkshire were dismissed for 23 by Hampshire in 1965 – but since then all teams have enjoyed their visit to the most northerly ground where, given good weather, the crowds were large, enthusiastic and warm-hearted.

The decision to play all Yorkshire matches in just Leeds and Scarborough made commercial sense, was popular with the players, but was a mistake. Roads crowded with traffic and a decline in public transport meant that many members and supporters in such major centres as Sheffield, Hull and Middlesbrough were lost to cricket. Sky television's persuasion of the Rugby League to move their fixture list to the Summer months was another factor in diminishing support for first-class cricket in the county.

Finale: Come April

So, partly by accident but mostly by design the Yorkshire Club entered the 21st century with a home, albeit a Victorian mansion, rooms of which had to be leased to two other landlords in order to raise the funds necessary for modernisation and refurbishment. The partnership with one of those landlords, Leeds Metropolitan University, may indicate the way ahead for other struggling county clubs. Joint ventures with schools, colleges, libraries or universities may provide them with the extra subsistence they need to progress without being totally dependent upon those sources, sponsors, advertisers, television companies, whose main objective is always a growing number of subscribers/customers.

Education is an area that no British government dare deprive of funds and if cricket clubs can put up a convincing case, as they surely can, for the sport to be part of that learning programme then a guaranteed income may ensue. It is a fond thought.

What does seem clear is that the audience for cricket worldwide is changing and that county clubs will have to adapt to survive. In the Spring of 2009, there were two distinct areas of appeal to the public: there is still a huge attachment to the first-class game, whether Championship or Test matches, an interest not accurately reflected in attendances at county matches. And there is an enormous following for the limited-overs version, especially in its most simplified form, Twenty-20. Cricket, like music, will, it seems, have to accept that it must cater for those who want Rachmaninov and those who want rock-'n'roll.

Cricket became more cosmopolitan as the world grew smaller and restrictions on movement and employment withered away. So many Polish plumbers were working in England in 2008 that Poland has had to recruit plumbers from the Ukraine who, in turn, had to seek out plumbers in Kazakhstan.

And what of climate change? If that takes place as quickly as some scientists are predicting then the playing seasons may have to be readjusted. Were the drenched Summers of 2007 and 2008 a sign of things to come? Will cricket be driven under roofs, played under lights?

Whatever happens, all who love cricket must guard the game's foundation, a garden nurtured over centuries. J.M. Kilburn, in 1937, in a moment of sentiment, wrote: 'When we are told that Larwood has bowled down seven wickets we do not think of flying stumps so much as pounding feet and a whirling arm circling and circling in a magical curve. As cricketers we are all artists and as artists we are all more nearly god-like in our mortality. All this is done for us by a game, a dear lovely game, that will be ours until green fields and sweet sunshine have passed from the earth.'

Kilburn was mortified by the commercial advance of limited-overs cricket, warning, in 1975: 'The soft options of bread and circuses marked the fall of Rome.' The game's relations with the media also troubled him and he related (in 1972) how disturbed he had been at the conclusion of a Roses match when one captain, speaking afterwards, had disparaged the match and the opposition, remarks seized upon by the newspapers. Afternoon rain cleared and he took a walk down a country lane on a clear evening and came upon the resumption of a village match: 'Time stood still in a distillation of delight. Cricket was itself again and all was well with my world.'

The North's other great cricket writer, Neville Cardus of the then *Manchester Guardian*, was also convinced that whatever happened in the professional game, cricket itself was safe while it remained true to its basic principles. He had a lovely memory of the last match of the 1930 season at Dover:

I said goodbye to a season on a field which

lay silent in the evening sunshine; the match was over, the players gone. I stayed for a while in the falling light and saw birds run over the grass. While Woolley batted the crowd sat in white tents, banners all round, a blessed scene, wisps of cloud in the sky, green grass for our feet, 'laughter of friends under an English heaven'. It was all over now as I stood in the little field alone, in the glow of a declining day. The passing of summer...I thought, there can be no summer in this land, without cricket.

It was Cardus, too, who wished all who loved cricket 'a good winter's sleep and a quick renewal of life next April'. We know the Hambledon men, the gamblers in Dorset Square, the doughty lads of Lascelles Hall, all in their time pondered upon cricket's future. Perhaps all we need to reflect upon is what is surely one of the sweetest phrases in the English lexicon: 'Come April.'

A packed Headingley in 2008
YCCC

Bibliography

A Fourth Innings with Cardus, Neville Cardus (Souvenir, 1981)

A History of Cricket, Altham and Swanton (Allen and Unwin, 1947)

A History of Yorkshire Cricket, J.M. Kilburn (Stanley Paul, 1970)

A Yorkshire Diary, David Bairstow (Sidgwick and Jackson, 1984)

Before and After Bramall Lane, Keith Farnsworth (private publication, 1988)

Boycott, Don Mosey (Methuen, 1985)

Boycott, Geoffrey Boycott (Macmillan, 1987)

Boycott, John Callaghan (Pelham, 1982)

Carr's Illustrated Dictionary of Extra-Ordinary Cricketers, J.L. Carr (Quartet, 1983)

Cricket All the Year, Neville Cardus (Collins, 1952)

Cricket Campaigns, Norman Yardley (Stanley Paul, 1950)

Cricket Choice, Alec Bedser (Pelham, 1981)

Cricket Conjuror, Alan Hill (David and Charles, 1988)

Cricket Heroes, The Cricket Writers' Club (Queen Anne, 1984)

Cricket Hotch-Potch, Tom Naylor (Fretwell and Brian, 1984)

Cricket Memories, 'A Country Vicar' (Methuen, 1930)

Cricket: A History, Roland Bowen (Eyre and Spottiswoode, 1970)

Cricket's Silver Lining, David Rayvern Allen (Collins, 1987)

Cricketer International (The Cricketer Ltd, various editions)

Crusoe on Cricket, R.C. Robertson-Glasgow (Pavilion, 1985)

Days in the Sun, Neville Cardus (Hart-Davis, 1948)

Family Argument, John Hampshire (Allen and Unwin, 1983)

Fred, John Arlott (Eyre and Spottiswoode, 1973)

From Bradman to Boycott, Ted Dexter (Queen Anne, 1981)

Hedley Verity: A Portrait of a Cricketer, Alan Hill (Kingswood, 1986)

Hirst and Rhodes, A.A. Thomson (Epworth, 1959)

History of Yorkshire County Cricket, 1833-1903, Rev R.S. Holmes (Constable and Co, 1904)

History of Yorkshire County Cricket, 1903-1923, A.W. Pullin (Chorley and Pickersgill, 1924)

History of Yorkshire County Cricket, 1923-1949, J.M. Kilburn (Yorkshire CCC, 1950)

Holmes and Sutcliffe, Leslie Duckworth (Hutchinson, 1970)

I Don't Bruise Easily, Brian Close (MacDonald and Jane's, 1978)

Illy, Mike Stevenson (Midas, 1978)

Jackson's Year, Alan Gibson (Cassell, 1965)

John Arlott's Book of Cricketers, John Arlott (Lutterworth, 1979)

Jubilee Book of Cricket, Prince Ranjitsinhji (Blackwood, 1897)

Just My Story, Len Hutton (Hutchinson, 1956)

Laughter at the Wicket, Harry East (Whitehorn, 1980)

Len Hutton, Gerald Howat (Heinemann Kingswood, 1988)

Neil Lloyd: An Appreciation, Tony Woodhouse (Wombwell Cricket Lovers' Society, 1982)

Opening Up, Geoffrey Boycott (Arthur Barker, 1980)

Overthrows, J.M. Kilburn (Stanley Paul, 1975)

Parkin on Cricket, Cecil Parkin (Hodder and Stoughton)

Put to the Test, Geoffrey Boycott (Arthur Barker, 1979)

Recollections and Reminiscences, Lord Hawke (Williams and Norgate, 1924)

'Talks with Old Yorkshire Cricketers' (Old Ebor, *Yorkshire Post,* 1989)

Thanks to Cricket, J.M. Kilburn (Stanley Paul, 1972)

The Book of Cricket, Pelham Warner (Dent, 1922)

The Boundary Book, Leslie Frewin (Pelham, 1986)

The County Cricket Championship, Roy Webber (The Sportsman's Book Club, 1958)

The Essential, E.W. Swanton (Harper Collins, 1990)

The Happy Cricketer, 'A Country Vicar' (Frederick Muller, 1946)

The Roses Matches, 1919-1939, Neville Cardus (Souvenir, 1982)

The Slow Men, David Firth (Allen and Unwin, 1984)

The Spinner's Turn, Patrick Murphy (Dent, 1982)

The Spinners' Web, Bailey and Trueman (Willow, 1988)

The Summer Game, Neville Cardus (Hart-Davis, 1948)

The Tempestuous Years, Ray Illingworth (Sidgewick and Jackson, 1987)

The White Rose (Yorkshire CCC, various editions)

The Yorker (Yorkshire CCC, various editions)

Vintage Cricketers, E.M. Wellings (Allen and Unwin, 1983)

We Don't Play it for Fun, Don Mosey (Methuen, 1988)

Wisden Cricket Monthly (John Wisden & Co, various editions)

Wisden Cricketers' Almanac (John Wisden & Co, various editions)

Yorkshire CCC Yearbook (Yorkshire CCC, various editions)

Yorkshire Cricketers 1863-1985 (The Association of Cricket Statisticians, 1986)

Yorkshire Cricketers, 1839-1939, Peter Thomas (Hodgson, 1973)

Yorkshire Post Benefit Book (Yorkshire CCC, 1987)

Yorkshire, J.M. Kilburn (Convoy, 1950)

Yorkshire's Pride, John Callaghan (Pelham, 1984)

List of Player Portraits

Tom Marsden
Harry Sampson
James Dearman
Andrew Crossland
George Anderson
Isaac Hodgson
Roger Iddison
Billy Slinn
Lascelles Hall
Joe Rowbotham
Edwin Stephenson
George Freeman
John Thewlis
George Atkinson
Luke Greenwood
Tom Emmett
The Halifax Connection
George Pinder
Ephraim Lockwood
Allen Hill
George Ulyett
Louis Hall
Billy Bates
Ted Peate
George Harrison
Martin Bladen Hawke
Joe Preston
Ted Wainwright
Saul Wade
David Hunter
George Hirst

Bobby Peel
David Denton
Frank Mitchell
John Tunicliffe
F.S. Jackson
Ernest Smith
Bobby Moorhouse
Lees Whitehead
J.T. Brown
Frank Milligan
Schofield Haigh
Wilfred Rhodes
T.L. Taylor
Irving Washington
Alonzo Drake
Major Booth
Arthur Dolphin
Roy Kilner
Edgar Oldroyd
Rockley Wilson
Percy Holmes
Herbert Sutcliffe
Emmott Robinson
Abraham Waddington
George Macaulay
Maurice Leyland
Arthur Mitchell
Arthur Wood
Wilf Barber
Cyril Turner
Bill Bowes

Hedley Verity
Frank Greenwood
Brian Sellers
Frank Smailes
Sir Len Hutton
Paul Gibb
Ellis Robinson
Norman Yardley
Jack Appleyard
Alec Coxon
Arthur Booth
Vic Wilson
Ted Lester
Gerald Smithson
Ron Aspinall
Don Brennan
Johnny Wardle
Brian Close
Frank Lowson
Fred Trueman
Bob Appleyard
Willie Watson
Jimmy Banks
Billy Sutcliffe
Ray Illingworth
Doug Padgett
Bryan Stott
Ken Taylor
Ronnie Burnet
Don Wilson
Philip Sharpe

Brian Bolus
Harold Bird
Tony Nicholson
Geoffrey Boycott
John Hampshire
Richard Hutton
Chris Old
David Bairstow
Richard Lumb
Philip Carrick
Graham Stevenson
Bill Athey
Kevin Sharp
Jim Love
Martyn Moxon
Paul Jarvis
Neil Lloyd
Ashley Metcalfe
Richard Blakey
David Byas
Darren Gough
Craig White
Michael Vaughan
Chris Silverwood
Gavin Hamilton
Anthony McGrath
Matthew Hoggard
Darren Lehmann
Richard Dawson
Ryan Sidebottom

Index